T

KHO

LANGUAGES

The Routledge Language Family Series is aimed at undergraduates and postgraduates of linguistics and language, and those with an interest in historical linguistics, linguistic anthropology and language development.

According to a widely accepted hypothesis, the Khoesan languages represent the smallest of the four language phyla in Africa, geographically distributed mainly in Botswana and Namibia. Today, only 30 or so Khoesan languages may still exist, with about 300,000 native speakers. In other words, most Khoesan languages were already extinct before a sound scholarly interest in them could begin to develop.

Drawing together a distinguished group of international experts, with much of the material taken from data collected by the authors' own fieldwork, this volume presents descriptive, typological, historical-comparative and sociolinguistic material on Khoesan. *The Khoesan Languages* contains eight parts: an introduction, an overview of genetic relationships, a typological survey and profile of Khoesan, four chapters covering core linguistic areas of Khoesan phonetics and phonology, tonology, morphology and syntax, and a final chapter tackling major issues in Khoesan sociolinguistics, as well as discussions of language contact.

Comprehensive and scholarly, yet also lucid in its coverage of a broad range of languages, dialects and sub-groups, this unprecedented and original work represents the current state of Khoesan linguistics.

Rainer Vossen is a University Professor and Executive Director of the Institute of African Studies at the University of Frankfurt am Main, Germany.

ROUTLEDGE LANGUAGE FAMILY SERIES

Each volume in this series contains an in-depth account of the members of some of the world's most important language families. Written by experts in each language, these accessible accounts provide detailed linguistic analysis and description. The contents are carefully structured to cover the natural system of classification: phonology, morphology, syntax, lexis, semantics, dialectology, and sociolinguistics.

Every volume contains extensive bibliographies for each language, a detailed index and tables, and maps and examples from the languages to demonstrate the linguistic features being described. The consistent format allows comparative study, not only between the languages in each volume, but also across all the volumes in the series.

The Austronesian Languages of Asia and Madagascar
Edited by Nikolaus Himmelmann & Sander Adelaar

The Bantu Languages
Edited by Derek Nurse & Gérard Philippson

The Celtic Languages 2nd Edition
Edited by Martin J. Ball & Nicole Müller

The Dravidian Languages
Edited by Sanford B. Steever

The Germanic Languages
Edited by Ekkehard Konig & Johan van der Auwera

The Indo-Aryan Languages
Edited by George Cardona & Dhanesh K. Jain

The Indo-European Languages
Edited by Paolo Ramat & Anna Giacalone Ramat

The Iranian Languages
Edited by Gernot Windfuhr

The Languages of Japan and Korea
Edited by Nicolas Tranter

The Khoesan Languages
Edited by Rainer Vossen

The Mongolic Languages
Edited by Juha Janhunan

The Munda Languages
Edited by Gregory D.S. Anderson

The Oceanic Languages
Edited by John Lynch, Malcolm Ross & Terry Crowley

The Romance Languages
Edited by Martin Harris & Nigel Vincent

The Semitic Languages
Edited by Robert Hetzron

The Sino-Tibetan Languages
Edited by Graham Thurgood & Randy J. Lapolla

The Slavonic Languages
Edited by Bernard Comrie & Greville G. Corbett

The Tai-Kadai Languages
Edited by Anthony Diller

The Turkic Languages
Edited by Éva Csató & Lars Johanson

The Uralic Languages
Edited by Daniel Abondolo

THE KHOESAN LANGUAGES

Edited by
Rainer Vossen

LONDON AND NEW YORK

First published 2013
by Routledge
2 Park Square, Milton Park, Abingdon, Oxon OX14 4RN

Simultaneously published in the USA and Canada
by Routledge
52 Vanderbilt Avenue, New York, NY 10017

First issued in paperback 2020

Routledge is an imprint of the Taylor & Francis Group, an informa business

British Library Cataloguing in Publication Data
A catalogue record for this book is available from the British Library

Library of Congress Cataloging in Publication Data
Vossen, Rainer.
The Khoesan languages / Rainer Vossen.
p. cm. – (Routledge language family series)
Includes bibliographical references and index.
1. Khoisan languages. I. Title. II. Series: Routledge language family series.
PL8026.K45V68 2012
496′.1–dc23

2012016016

ISBN 13: 978-0-367-57047-7 (pbk)
ISBN 13: 978-0-7007-1289-2 (hbk)

Typeset in Times New Roman
by Graphicraft Limited, Hong Kong

CONTENTS

EDITOR'S NOTE

The publication of this book has been announced for a long time. The idea to compile a reference work on Khoesan languages emerged in the early 1990s and was given definite shape on the occasion of a multidisciplinary symposium that was organized by the editor and was held in Tutzing at Lake Starnberg in the south of Germany in July 1994. Apart from Africanist linguists, philologists, anthropologists, historians, archaeologists, and folklorists from all over the world attended that conference, but not all the contributors to this volume were present at Tutzing. This explains to a certain extent why a few authors are not happy about the spelling *Khoesan* which, in this book, is preferred to the traditional "Khoisan" because it is more adequate to the pronunciation of the word. There had been an extensive debate about this matter at Tutzing, the result of which was consent to the use of *Khoesan* throughout the book.

In the following years, authors commenced working on their contributions, as 2001 was envisaged as the year of appearance of the book. Ever since, publication was retarded for reasons which are too many to be singled out here. As a consequence, updates of papers were needed from time to time. I wish both to apologize for the considerable delay in making this volume available to the public and to express my sincere gratitude to the publisher, the authors as well as the intended audience for their apparent patience. At the same time, I would like to acknowledge the editorial support that I was given by Dr. Erhard Voeltz at a critical moment of preparing the typescript.

ILLUSTRATIONS

MAPS

FIGURES

TABLES

CONTRIBUTORS

Hans den Besten†, University of Amsterdam, The Netherlands, and University of Stellenbosch, South Africa

Christopher Ehret, University of California, Los Angeles, USA

Edward D. Elderkin, University of Namibia, Windhoek, Namibia

Tom Güldemann, Humboldt University, Berlin, Germany

Wilfrid H.G. Haacke, University of Namibia, Windhoek, Namibia

Bernd Heine, University of Cologne, Germany

Henry Honken†, Sarona, Wisconsin, USA

Christa Kilian-Hatz, Goethe University, Frankfurt am Main, Germany

Christa König, Goethe University, Frankfurt am Main, Germany

Jacobus Abraham Louw, Pretoria, University of South Africa

Amanda L. Miller, Ohio State University, Columbus, USA

Wilhelm J.G. Möhlig, University of Cologne, Germany

Hirosi Nakagawa, Tokyo University of Foreign Studies, Japan

Bonny Sands, Northern Arizona University, Flagstaff, USA

Mathias Schladt†, Cologne, Germany

Gabriele Sommer, University of Bayreuth, Germany

Hessel Visser, Summer Institute of Linguistics

Rainer Vossen, Goethe University, Frankfurt am Main, Germany

Thomas Widlok, Radboud University, Nijmegen, The Netherlands, and University of Cologne, Germany

ACKNOWLEDGEMENTS

The editor and publishers would like to thank the following copyright holder for permission to reproduce the following material:

Map: The distribution of Khoesan languages († = extinct) © Jonas Vossen, designer. Reproduced with permission of Jonas Vossen.

ABBREVIATIONS

A	aspect
ACC	accusative
ADJ, adj.	adjective
ADV, adv.	adverb(ial)
Af	affricate
affr.	affricated
Afr.	Afrikaans
AGR	agreement
Al	alveolar
AND	andative
AP	adverbial phrase
APPL	applicative
ART	article
As	aspirated, aspiration
asp., Asp.	aspirated
ASS	associative
ASST	assertive
ATTR	attributive
AUX	auxiliary
BCE	Before the Common Era
BEN	benefactive
BG	background
BVC	Back Vowel Constraint
C	consonant
C	common/collective gender
CAUS, caus.	causative
CDP	Cape Dutch Pidgin
Ch.	chapter
CL, cl.	noun class (marker)
COM	comitative
COMP	comparative
COMPL	completive
COMPLT	complement(izer)
CON	connective
CONJ	conjunction
CONN	discourse connective
CONS	consecutive
CONT	continuous; contingent
CONV	converb
COP	copula

CORR	correlative particle
CS	comparative series
DAT	dative
DEC(L)	declarative (particle)
DEF	definite
DEI	deictic
DEM	demonstrative
Dep., DEP	dependent
DIM	diminutive
DIST	distal
DISTR	distributive
DO	direct object
DOM	tonological domain
Dt	dental
dtr.	ditransitive
DU	dual
EG	egressive
egr.	egressive
EH	Eastern ǂHoan
eject.	ejective
ELA	elative
EMPH	emphasis
Engl.	English
esp.	especially
EVID	evidential (particle)
EX, EXCL(.)	exclusive
EXCLAM	exclamatory
EXIST	existential copula
EXP	experience
EXT	extension
F	feminine
fig.	figuratively
FOC	focus
FREQ	frequentative
fric.	fricative
FRU	frustrative
FUT	future
GEN	genitive
gen.	generic
GER	gerund
Gl	glottal
H	high (tone)
HAB	habitual
HF	high falling (tone)
HORT	hortative
HS	hearsay evidential
ID	identification
ideoph.	ideophone
IG	ingressive

IMP	imperative
IMPF	imperfective
IMPS	impersonal
IN, INCL(.)	inclusive
INCL	inclinative
IND	indicative
INDEF	indefinite
INGR, ingr.	ingressive
INSTR	instrumental
INT	interrogative
INTENT	intention
intr.	intransitive
INTS	intensifier
IO	indirect object
IPA	International Phonetic Association
IPFV	imperfective
IPT	imperfect
IRR	irrealis
JUNC(T)	juncture
KhA	Khoekhoe Afrikaans
L	low (tone); local
Lb	labial
Lg.	language
LINK	linker
lit.	literally
LOC	locative
LP	locative phrase
Lt	lateral
L2	second language
M	mid (tone)
M	masculine
MF	mid falling (tone)
MIM	mimesis
MLT	multiple
MPO	multi-purpose oblique
N, n.	noun, nominalized
N1, N2, etc.	noun class 1, 2, etc.
N	nasal consonant
NARR	narrative
NCl	nominal clause
NEG	negation
NEM	new-event marker
NEUT	neuter (gender)
NK	Northern Khoesan
N.Kh.	Namibian Khoekhoe
NOM	nominative; nominalization
nom.	nominal
NOMIN	deverbal noun
NP	noun phrase

nsl.	nasalized
NSt	noun stem
NUM	numeral
O	object
OAGRM	object agreement marker
OBJ	object
OBL	oblique (case); obligation
OCP	ordering in click place
o^m	object marker
o.s.	oneself
OQ	oblique
P	predicate
pal., Pal.	palatalized
PART	participle; particle
PASS	passive
p.c.	personal communication
PERF	perfect; perfective
PERM	permansive
PF	predication focus
PGN, pgn	person–gender–number
phon.	phonetic
physiol.	physiological
PJ	Proto-Ju
PKh	Proto-Khoe
Pl	palatal
PL, pl.	plural
POSS	possessive
POSS:PRO	possessee pronoun
POSS:PRON	pronominal possessee
POSTP	postposition
POT	potential
PP	postpositional particle/phrase
PRES	present
PRET	preterite
PRIV	privative
PRM	Proto-Rift-Mbugu
PRO	pronoun
PROG	progressive
PRON(.)	pronoun
PROX	proximal
PSE	post-subject enclitic
PTCL	(ordinal number) particle
PURP	purpose
Q	question marker
QUOT	quotative
REC	reciprocal
RECT	recent
REDUPL	reduplication
REF	reference

REFL	reflexive
REL	relative (pronoun)
REM	remote
REP	repetitive
RES	resumptive pronoun
REV	reverential
S	subject; sentence
SAK	South(ern) African Khoesan
s.b.	somebody
SC	Southern Cushitic
SEQ	sequential
SG, sg.	singular
SH	super high (tone)
SIL	Summer Institute of Linguistics
SIM	similative
SL	super low (tone)
sp.	species
SPEC	specifier
STAT	stative
s.th.	something
SUBJ, subj	subject; subjunctive
SUFF, suff.	suffix
Sw.	Swahili
SWAPO	South-West Africa People's Organization
T	tense
T	temporal
TA(M)	tense–aspect(–mood)
TBU	tone-bearing unit
TEMP	temporal
TERM	terminative
TF	term focus marker
TL	target language
TOP	topic marker
TP	temporal phrase
TR, tr.	transitive
trad.	traditional
Uv	uvular
v.	verb(al)
V	verb; vowel
ṽ	nasal vowel
VBL	verbal
vcl., Vcl.	voiceless
VCl	verbal clause
vd., Vd.	voiced
VE	verbal extension
vel., Vel.	velarized
VGP, VGp	verbal group
v.i.	intransitive verb
Vl	velar

VOC	vocative
VOT	Voice Onset Time
VP	verb phrase
v.t.	transitive verb
wh	interrogative word
1	first person
2	second person
3	third person
I	juncture I (Khwe)
II	juncture II (Khwe)
{ }	alternative(ly)
#	word boundary
*	reconstructed, ungrammatical or false form
<. . .>	graphemic unit
/. . ./	phonological unit
[. . .]	phonetic unit
-	morpheme boundary
←	developed from
⇒	transformed to
<	derived from
>	changed to

CHAPTER ONE

INTRODUCTION

Rainer Vossen

1 GENERAL BACKGROUND

The Khoesan languages are considered to be the smallest of the four major language phyla on the African continent. For a long time, they were labelled and commonly known as "Bushman" and "Hottentot" languages. Between twenty and thirty languages and dialects are actually being spoken, but in the past their number must be assumed to have been considerably higher. While numerous Khoesan varieties are known to have vanished in the course of the nineteenth and twentieth centuries, others may have disappeared already long before a sound scholarly interest in Khoesan had commenced to take shape. And several of the still existing languages are severely endangered or even moribund.

Socio-historic background

A brief outline of the fateful encounter of the European immigrants with the Khoesan-speaking population of southern Africa might be helpful at this point. In principle, this encounter began in 1652 with the founding of a supply post by Jan van Riebeeck on behalf of the Dutch East India Company. The station was erected in Table Bay (near present-day Cape Town). At the time the Cape region was inhabited by light-skinned people who lived off cattle-keeping and later became known as "Hottentots". The same area, and much more so the adjacent hinterland, were also the habitat of another group of people, of brownish complexion, who were reported by contemporary observers to be ethnically and culturally different from the cattle-keepers. They lived from hunting and gathering, showed in small (hunting) groups and were physically shorter than the cattle-herders. In the literature they were initially referred to as "San-qua", "Sun-qua", or simply "San", but as early as 1654 the name "Bosmanneken" appeared; a term that in the sequel recurred as "Bosjesman", from which the commonly employed label "Bushman" was ultimately derived (cf. Köhler 1975: 305).

The Europeans' momentous lack of judgement towards the languages and cultures of the indigenous inhabitants of the Cape region persisted for more than three hundred years. Contemporary descriptions and pictures bear witness to the prejudices which served for the justification of unparalleled campaigns of persecution and annihilation of Khoesan-speaking societies. In search of pasture for their livestock Dutch frontier farmers from the Cape Colony were forging ahead deep into the interior of the southern African subcontinent. In the savannah areas, where at the time game still occurred in abundance, they soon came into contact with foraging "Bushman" groups. Although their languages were perceived by Europeans as similar to "Hottentot" – mainly because of the clicks –, the "Bushmen", contrary to the Cape "Hottentots", were neither in possession of cattle nor tribally organized. They were therefore regarded as very "primitive", devoid of any culture and religion.

"Bushmen" were seen by the frontier farmers (mostly Trek Boers) as rapacious scoundrels. They were denigrated as "Banditti", often driven and chased like animals; as a result, the majority of these small hunter-gatherer societies had become extinct as early as the mid-nineteenth century. Those who survived the murderous rush were deported to farms where they were forced to carry out convict labour. Alongside the rapid loss of their cultural identity the languages of these Cape "Bushmen" also disappeared at once (cf. Keuthmann and Vossen 1997). (For a detailed essay on South African Khoesan language and social history, see Traill 1995b.)

Demographic figures

Much of what is said in the literature about the number of Khoesan speakers is, and can probably not be more than, guesswork because of the limited availability of reliable statistical data. Most figures must therefore be regarded as approximate, although some estimates appear to be more realistic than others. This may partly be explained by a lack of differentiation between population size and number of actual speakers. While demographic prevision tells us that the Khoesan population is likely to increase considerably in number in the next few decades, the majority of Khoesan languages will in the long run hardly have chances of surviving in view of the socio-economic and political changes that have taken place in southern Africa in recent times. Several communities have already given up their languages in favour of (putatively more prestigious) neighbouring Bantu languages, such as Tswana. Estimating, against this background, the total number of speakers at around 300,000 must happen with reservations. Moreover, it should be noted that the majority are speakers of basically one language, i.e. Khoekhoegowab.

Geographical distribution

Today, most of the Khoesan-speaking peoples live in the southern African republics of Botswana and Namibia; however, some reside in adjacent areas in Angola, Zambia, Zimbabwe and South Africa. The two East African outliers ("isolates") Hadza and Sandawe, whose affiliation with Khoesan has frequently been questioned over the last thirty years (see below and Chapter 2), are located in Tanzania, almost half a continent away from the nucleus of the language phylum (cf. Map).

Nomenclature

Khoesan is used here as a cover term to refer to those African languages which make use of click consonants as regular speech sounds and are not members of the Bantu (especially Southeastern and Kavango) or South Cushitic (Dahalo, Kenya) language families, where clicks are also known to form a systematic part of phonological inventories – mainly as a result of language contact. Although the term would seem to imply genealogical relationship between *all* languages subsumed under this label, its employment in this book (and elsewhere in the more recent literature) is largely due to pragmatic reasons, as the validity of the hypothesis of a common descent (from a hypothetical Proto-Khoesan language) has for a long time and for good reason been questioned and remained controversial to this day (see below and especially Chapter 2).

In historical perspective, the term *Khoesan* ("Khoisan" in its original spelling) was coined in 1928 by the German scholar Leonhard Schultze to establish a physical anthropological connection between "Hottentots" and "Bushmen", which was meant to be reflected by the two components *khoi*, meaning 'person', and *san*, meaning 'foragers', in *Khoekhoe* (alias "Khoikhoi" alias "Hottentot"). Only two years later, Isaac Schapera (1930) took a decisive step by using "Khoisan" to allude to a corresponding social anthropological and linguistic connection between the two divisions. Since 1960, Oswin Köhler adopted "Khoisan" to elaborate on a probable linguistic genetic coherence, even though he avoided speaking of a language family or phylum and, instead, established a "Khoisan area" (*Khoisan-Sprachbereich*). After several revisions of his African language classification of 1949–54, Joseph Greenberg followed Köhler in 1963 and, ultimately, popularized "Khoisan" to become a widely used label for the languages under consideration.

It was Greenberg (1963b) again who with a view of the internal group structure of Khoesan, helped to get the geographic labels *Northern*, *Central* and *Southern* for the three branches of his *South African Khoesan* (SAK) commonly accepted. These labels had previously been used by Dorothea F. Bleek (1929, 1956) to refer to the "Bushman" division of Khoesan languages. Later on, Köhler (1975: 314f.) proposed to replace the geographic labels by terms deriving from the root for 'person' in each of the three branches of SAK: *Zhu* (i.e. *Ju*) for Northern, *Khoe* for Central, and *!Wi* for Southern SAK. As for Northern and Southern SAK, at least, this idea actually goes back to Westphal (1971: 381f.), who within Southern SAK had even distinguished further between *!Wi* and *Taa* languages. Ever since, the two sets of labels, geographic and "indigenous", have been used by Khoesanists side by side. Most recently, two new labels were introduced to the literature: *Tuu*, meaning 'people', to replace former Southern SAK ~ !Wi–Taa (!Ui–Taa) (Güldemann 2005), and *Kx'a*, based on the root for 'ground, soil', to refer to "a new Khoisan genealogy" that links up Ju with the former SAK "isolate" ǂHoan (Heine and Honken 2010).

Members of Central SAK (alias Khoe), most of which became (better) known only years after World War II, were initially allocated to smaller units called "groups". The fact that some of these groups appeared to be more closely related to one another than to others was first taken into consideration by Westphal (1962b), who confronted *Classical Hottentot* with the rest of "Hottentot", for which he proposed the name *Tshu-Khwe Hottentot* (*tshu* and *khwe* meaning 'person' in the languages concerned). A few years later, Köhler (1971b) replaced Westphal's Classical Hottentot by *Khoekhoe*, a term that has since been given preference in the literature. In his historical comparative analysis of Khoe languages, Vossen (1997a) renamed the Tshu-Khwe branch as *Non-Khoekhoe*, but for understandable reasons that label did not please the experts and was hence replaced with *Kalahari Khoe* (Güldemann and Vossen 2000).

Finally, for solely practical reasons and following the notion of a South African cluster of Khoesan units, the two East African "isolates" Hadza and Sandawe were summarized by Sands (1998a) under the geographic designation *Eastern Khoisan*; restrictive use has so far been made of this term, though.

Endonyms and exonyms

An enormous variety of names for both ethnic groups and linguistic entities turn up in the literature on Khoesan. Some are self-names (endonyms), others are externally motivated or have been assigned from outside, more often than not by geographical neighbours (exonyms). Multiple designation is rather the rule than the exception. Research has shown that in a number of cases it is anything but easy to indisputably identify names with a particular group of people, language, dialect or speech community. Köhler

(1971b) offers an interesting survey of names related to the Khoe family. Winter (1981b) contains a very useful cross-linguistic overview of names that show up in sources published before 1980, while Treis (1998) provides an updated account of Khoesan language names and their variants. In this book, however, the aim is to make as much use of endonyms as possible and/or functionally adequate.

Language classification

A few remarks on this important issue have already been made above (see the section on Nomenclature) and, in addition, a whole chapter of this book (Chapter 2) is devoted to the question of classification and the concomitant controversy that was sparked off by Greenberg's concept of Khoesan as a language phylum in 1950 and 1963. His so-called Macro-Khoesan hypothesis, which is largely a result of lexical comparisons based on the criterion of resemblance in shape and meaning, proceeds from the following internal classification: At first, a distinction is made between South African Khoesan (SAK) and the two East African isolates, Hadza and Sandawe. SAK contains three major branches: Northern, Central and Southern. Northern Khoesan presents itself essentially as a dialect cluster consisting of three or four major units, with a considerable degree of mutual intelligibility. The Central branch is made up by approximately fifteen to twenty different languages or dialects, whereas Southern Khoesan today is virtually represented by two living members only, viz. !Xoon (!Xóõ) and N|uu(ki); remnant speakers of the latter language were met as late as around the time of political change in the Republic of South Africa in the early 1990s. Due to lack of data, two languages were disregarded in Greenberg's classification: extinct Angolan Kwadi and highly endangered ǂHoan (ǂHõã) in Botswana.

Greenberg's hypothesis has found both adherents (e.g. Argyle 1994; Ehret 1986; Honken 1977, 1988, 1998; Ruhlen 1994; Starostin 2003, 2008) and opponents (especially Westphal 1962a, 1962b, 1971). Given the serious difficulties of proving a genetic relationship between *all* Khoesan languages, a third group of scholars (e.g. Köhler 1975, 1981; Sands 1998a; Traill 1980, 1986b, 2001) suggested, directly or indirectly, to use the term "Khoesan" as a cover for all non-Bantu/non-Cushitic African click languages irrespective of eventual genealogical implications. (As stated in the section on Nomenclature above, the present book also pursues this trend.) This notion was taken up by Güldemann and Vossen (2000), who proposed a pragmatically oriented classification based on mixed genealogical and typological criteria. A major difference to Greenberg's classification lies in the grouping together of Northern and Southern Khoesan under the label "Non-Khoe" (as opposed to Khoe alias Central Khoesan) on the one hand, and the assignment of ǂHoan to the same division on the other hand. Very recently, Heine and Honken (2010) applied the comparative method to prove a genetic relationship between Northern Khoesan and ǂHoan and established a new Khoesan subfamily called Kx'a (cf. Nomenclature above). Meanwhile, this view seems to have been accepted by a number of Khoesanists; to my knowledge, however, the proposal has not been debated yet in any detail. Whether, after all, the linguistic affinities within Non-Khoe are more likely due to a southern African *sprachbund* than to a genealogical relationship is a question that was raised by Güldemann (1998b) and is currently under debate.

Like Greenberg, Güldemann and Vossen (2000: 102) have listed Sandawe as "isolate". In 2010, however, Güldemann and Elderkin come to the conclusion that a genealogical relationship to Central Khoesan (Khoe) cannot be excluded or may even be likely. Likewise Kwadi, whose position was declared to be "undetermined" in Güldemann and

Vossen (*ibid.*), is presently seen as a member of an extended Khoe-Kwadi family rather than a single unit (Güldemann 2004b).

State of documentation

As compared to other African language families, Khoesan languages are still poorly documented. Güldemann and Vossen (2000: 103f.) contains the latest overview of published and unpublished sources on the better-known languages to which, however, an encouraging number of new contributions were added in recent years, or are awaiting publication in due time. The following brief survey is confined to monographic studies.

With respect to South African Khoesan, two important works on Northwestern (Ekoka) !Xun have been made available: a dictionary (König and Heine 2008) and a grammar (Heine and König 2012). Collins and Namaseb's (2011) sketch grammar of N|uuki is the first in-depth description of this dying Tuu language. A dictionary (2003) as well as a grammar (2008) of the Central Khoesan Khwe language were provided by Kilian-Hatz, while Haacke and Eiseb's (2002) comprehensive Khoekhoegowab dictionary has enormously enriched the literature on Namibian Khoekhoe. Moreover, a trilingual !Xoon–Setswana–English dictionary compiled by Traill, Nakagawa and Chebanne is in its final stages, and a concise grammar of ǂHoan by Collins and Gruber is currently being worked on.

Finally, three new valuable monographs on Sandawe must be mentioned: two grammars by Eaton (online, a revised version of her PhD thesis of 2002) and Steeman (2011), and a dictionary compiled and edited by Ehret and Ehret (2012) on the basis of Eric ten Raa's data collection of the 1960s and 1970s.

Orthographic diversity

From a comparativist point of view, one of the most serious obstacles in Khoesan linguistics is the lack of cross-linguistic writing conventions. Although an attempt was made in this connection in the 1990s, the initiative failed mainly for three reasons. First, for some of the languages (e.g. Namibian Khoekhoe, Khwe, Ju|'hoan) there already existed officially recognized practical orthographies that would not be sacrificed just because of scientific convenience. Second, some Khoesanists tend to be more individualistic than others and, for whatever reason, prefer their own idiosyncratic spelling to concessionary proposals. And third, some Khoesan languages would seem to raise certain difficulties in accommodating a general orthography for Khoesan languages. The experts have largely learnt to cope with this state of affairs (though few of them are comparativists), but for the non-specialist the juxtaposition of several writing systems might be a challenge. This may also be the case in this book. It is hoped, however, that the contributors' descriptions of phonological inventories of the languages under study will help to minimize eventual problems of understanding and interpretation.

2 TYPOLOGICAL CHARACTERISTICS

The structural properties of Khoesan languages are laid out in sizeable detail in separate chapters on phonetics and phonology (Chapter 4), tonology (Chapter 5), morphology (Chapter 6), and syntax (Chapter 7). In addition, a cross-linguistic typology is dealt with in a special chapter (Chapter 3). At this point, it may therefore suffice to draw the reader's attention to some chief characteristics in order to gain a provisional overview and impression of the structural nature of the "phylum" as a whole.

Phonetics and phonology

The largest number of features shared by Khoesan languages are identifiable in their sound inventories. The occurrence of clicks, suctive-ingressive consonants that are seldom, if ever, found outside the Khoesan sphere, appears to be the most prominent phenomenon in this respect and has widely been responsible for the apprehension of Khoesan as a family or phylum. Five basic click types (also called "influxes" after Beach 1938) are to be distinguished: bilabial (symbolized by ʘ), dental (ǀ), alveolar (!), palatal (ǂ), and lateral-alveolar (ǁ). Each type can be released in various ways (e.g. voiceless, voiced, aspirated, glottalized, etc.). This secondary articulation is called click accompaniment ("efflux" after Beach 1938). Click type (influx) and accompaniment (efflux) combine to constitute phonemic click sounds that are essential *inter alia* for lexical distinctions in terms of minimal pairs.

Clicks are a peculiar feature of Khoesan languages, but they stand for only part of the complexity inherent in the phonological inventories. A considerable number of egressive consonants, too, exhibit a complex structure that is largely based on primary and secondary articulation patterns. Vowels may occur in different colourings (commonly oral and nasal and, in addition, pharyngealized, glottalized, breathy in some languages), combinations of which are also possible. Furthermore, Khoesan languages make use of suprasegmental tools such as tone or pitch-accent at the lexical and grammatical level. Syllabic phonological segments such as vowels and nasal consonants serve as tone-bearing units.

The word structure is characterized typically by CVCV, CVV, and CVN sequences. Tri- and other polysyllabic sequences are very rare and can often be shown to be a result of influence from neighbouring Bantu languages.

Morphology

Khoe languages as well as Sandawe and Hadza have a rich inflectional and derivational morphology, whereas Non-Khoe (especially Northern Khoesan) languages tend to be a lot more syntactic-analytically oriented. However, all better-known languages have a noun class system with varying agreement patterns. The Khoe system is overt and primarily sex-oriented; as a rule, person, gender (masculine, feminine, common) and number (singular, dual, plural) combine to constitute the so-called PGN enclitics. Word categories depending on the nominal head agree with the latter grammatically. Sandawe and Hadza work along similar lines. Non-Khoe languages (except !Ui and ǂHoan) have a covert (Ju) or sort of mixed (Taa) system which is semantically nature-oriented (e.g. animacy, shape, certain types of food, body-parts). There are four classes in Ju and five in Taa. While Ju nouns are morphologically unmarked for class membership, Taa nouns are often marked by class-related endings. Class membership in Ju can only be identified through grammatical agreement on certain pronouns.

The verbal systems of Khoe languages are complex throughout. Verbal extensions (derivative suffixes) are very common. In general, they serve to alter or modify the meaning of the verbal base; moreover, they reduce or increase the valence of the verb (e.g. in passive or intransitive constructions) and, hence, impact on syntactic structures. Tenses and/or aspects are numerous and, in most Khoe languages, there are also various strategies to express negation (cf. Vossen 2006). Non-Khoe languages, on the other hand, have a restricted verbal morphology and draw particular attention because of their verb-serializing attitudes.

Syntax

At this level, Khoesan languages pursue different paths. In Khoe and Sandawe, the dominant word order appears to be S(ubject)–O(bject)–V(erb). Nominal modifiers precede the noun and adverbial phrases are most frequently placed at the beginning of a sentence or clause. Non-Khoe languages are predominantly SVO orientated with a nominal head–modifier order (associative constructions excepted). Tanzanian Hadza represents a special case in that here, the verb occurs sentence-initially, hence VSO.

Lexical specifics

One may hold that, in principle, Khoesan languages make a distinction between nouns and verbs. Very often, however, a syntactic context is required in order to exclude misinterpretation. In !Xoon, for instance, *ǂ'án* means 'think, assume' but also 'thought'. A similar observation can be made for Khoe languages. Thus, *kx'ùí* in Naro means both 'speak' and 'speaking, talking'; if, for example, this lexical base is extended by the feminine singular enclitic *-sà* (hence: *kx'ùí-sà*), the semantics changes to 'language; law'. A particularity of Non-Khoe and Sandawe as well consists in the occurrence of number-sensitive suppletive stems, as in ǂHoan *!kù* (SG) and *ǂq'aí* (PL) for 'take, get'.

3 THE INTENDED AUDIENCE

This is a reference book, providing a set of descriptive, analytical, and typological statements about Khoesan. It is intended to be useful to, and to meet the interest of, different populations of readers: undergraduate and graduate students and others wanting an introduction to the Khoesan language sphere; Khoesanists and general linguists as well as non-linguistic scholars specializing in sub-Saharan Africa; language typologists and comparativists; theoretical linguists and, perhaps, language planners. It is also to be hoped that this book will play an important role in the attempt to direct the general public's attention to the overall complex of problems of the Khoesan-speaking population, whose cultures are changing rapidly and whose languages will for the larger part remain seriously endangered. Authors were asked to write as clearly as possible and to provide bibliographical information beyond the references they have made in their contributions – for readers wishing to become engrossed in the topic. Readers should bear in mind, however, that it can sometimes be difficult to write for an audience as diverse as described above.

4 THE CONTENTS

The book consists of eight chapters (including this first, introductory chapter). There are two chapters about comparative aspects. Chapter 2 is on genetic relationships. The preamble indicates the present state in Khoesan language classification with a sketch of previous positions in order to situate the rest. Two chief positions can be identified in current research, roughly "lumpers" vs. "splitters". Whereas "lumpers" believe in deep relationships along the lines of a Khoesan phylum (and even beyond), "splitters" take a more conservative view by demanding cross-linguistically well-attested regular sound correspondences as proof of genetic relationship. Chapter 3 contains a typological survey of Khoesan languages focusing on patterns of shared vs. non-shared structural features. It concludes with an attempt at a typological profile of Khoesan.

Chapters 4 through 7 are descriptive and cover core linguistic areas. Chapter 4 gives an overview of the segmental phonetic-phonological structure, including notes on word and syllable structure, phonotactics, and morphophonological alterations. In Chapter 5, the tonological structure of some better-known languages is dealt with. Chapters 6 on morphology and 7 on syntax comprise nearly two thirds of the book and may, therefore, be interpreted as central components. In the case of two languages, the authors decided in favour of joint morphosyntactic descriptions because separate analyses were conceived as artificial in view of the (largely) analytical nature of the respective languages. Hence, the morphosyntax of Eastern ǂHoan has become part of Chapter 6, while !Xun is found in Chapter 7. In the latter chapter, interlinearized and translated sample texts are included in the description of the Southern Khoesan (Tuu) languages East !Xoon and ǀXam. An example of major patterns of Khoesan lexical structure can be found in Chapter 6 with reference to the Central Khoesan (Khoe) language Khwe; here, the focus is on a highly elaborated semantic field in Khoesan languages, namely plant names.

The last chapter discusses questions of language contact in time-perspective and against the background of specific Southern and East African demographic and social settings; it also tackles some major issues in Khoesan sociolinguistics. The different scenarios of linguistic impact represented here touch upon both Khoesan-internal and external contact situations and, with regard to the latter, demonstrate patterns and strategies of borrowing from a bidirectional viewpoint: Khoesan influence on non-Khoesan languages and *vice versa*.

Irrespective of current debates about Khoesan internal and external relationships, the classificatory scheme underlying the core linguistic chapters 4 through 7 is Greenberg's. Within each chapter the order of languages/language groups is as follows: 1 Hadza – 2 Sandawe (i.e. East African Khoesan) – 3 South African Khoesan – 3.1 Northern Khoesan (Ju) – 3.2 Central Khoesan (Khoe) – 3.3 Southern Khoesan (Tuu) – 3.4 Eastern ǂHoan – 3.5 Kwadi. The sections on Central Khoesan show the following order in each case: Namibian Khoekhoe – !Gora (except Ch. 5) – Haiǁom (i.e. Khoekhoe) – Kxoe subgroup – Naro – ǁGana subgroup (i.e. Kalahari West) – Shua subgroup – Tshwa subgroup (i.e. Kalahari East). As for Southern Khoesan, the subsection on East !Xoon precedes the description of ǀXam. Since in this book only better-known languages and dialects (a very relative denotation in the case of Khoesan) have been taken into account, some (sub)group representations are confined to the description of selected varieties, in particular: Kxoe subgroup (Khwe and ǁAni, Ch. 5; Khwe, Ch. 7); ǁGana subgroup (ǀGui, Ch. 5 and Ch. 7); Shua subgroup (Cara and Deti, Ch. 5); Southern Khoesan (!Xóõ~!Xoon, Ch. 5).

Within given spatial limits, authors have made every effort to illustrate their descriptions and analyses as copiously as possible. Users of the book will find linguistic examples, tables and figures consecutively numbered within each chapter. A map at the end of this introductory chapter shows the approximate distribution of both extinct and modern Khoesan languages.

5 GEOGRAPHICAL COVERAGE

When consulting the map, readers will see that the Khoesan-speaking area is not evenly covered. This is mainly due to, and corresponds largely with, the present-day state of documentation and information. On the whole, the following languages and dialects are taken into consideration to a greater or lesser extent:

East African Khoesan:

Hadza (also known as Hatsa, Kindiga, Tindiga, Kangeju), spoken by some 800 persons at Lake Eyasi (around Yaeda Chini) in north-central Tanzania.

Sandawe (Sandawi), spoken by an estimated 40,000 persons, most of whom are still resident in north-central Tanzania. Speakers in a diaspora outside this area find it difficult to bring up their offspring with a knowledge of Sandawe. Dialectal differences exist, but are minor. Hunziker *et al.* (2005) postulate three areas: East, Central and West; Central and West form a grouping against the Eastern. The same work reveals a popular impression that a respected variety of Sandawe is that used by speakers associated with Mangastaa in the central area. The description in this book is based on work with a language consultant from Mangastaa. (Sources: Elderkin, p.c.; Hunziker *et al.* 2005.)

South African Khoesan:

Northern Khoesan

!Xun, spoken by an estimated 15,000 to 20,000 persons (according to source) in central and southern Angola, north-eastern Namibia and north-western Botswana. The language described in this book has come to be known under a variety of different names. The main reason for referring to both the people speaking this language and the language itself as !Xun, rather than using any of the many other names that have been proposed, is simple. In virtually all varieties of this language, this term is used, in some form or other, as an ethnonym (in addition to denoting 'human being'). There is only one alternative name that needs to be considered: Ju or Zhu, or any of its variant forms. The reason for not adopting this name here is that its use as an ethnonym is confined essentially to two dialects, i.e. the ones that will be referred to in this book as E1 and E3 (see below).

!Xun can be described as an L-complex, that is, as a cluster of speech forms that are linked by a chain of mutual intelligibility, but speakers at the extreme ends of the chain do not understand one another. For example, !Xun speakers of central Angola do not normally understand !Xun speakers of north-eastern Namibia or north-western Botswana. Still, all available evidence suggests that there is no language boundary separating the various !Xun communities. Since there is every reason to believe that all the !Xun varieties that have come to our notice so far are linked by some intelligibility chain, there is a preference towards treating the various speech forms, traditionally subsumed under the label Northern Khoesan, as a single, even if complex, language. A list of the !Xun dialects that have been identified is provided in the chart below. (Sources: Heine and König 2001, 2012.)

Branch	Cluster	Dialect (reference form)
1 North-western (*NW)	1.1 Northern	N1
		N2
	1.2 Western	W1
		W2
		W3
	1.3 Kavango	K
2 Central	2.1 Gaub	C1
	2.2 Neitsas	C2
3 South-eastern (*SE)	3.1 Ju|'hoan	E1
	3.2 Dikundu	E2
	3.3 ǂX'áó-ǁ'àèn	E3

Central Khoesan

Khoekhoe

Namibian Khoekhoe (Nama/Damara, Khoekhoegowab), spoken by over 200,000 persons in Namibia and adjacent parts of Botswana and South Africa. N.Kh. is an official language of Namibia, where it is used at all levels of education and in the media as well.

!Gora (!ora, !Ora, Korana) is said to be spoken by just a handful of persons in South Africa. For a long time it was believed to be extinct.

Haiǁom is spoken by roughly 16,000 to 18,000 persons in north-western Namibia. Haiǁom and ǂĀkhoe are variants of the Khoekhoe language which have been considered separate dialects (cf. Haacke *et al.* 1997) but are also virtual synonyms of one variant (Heikkinen, n.d.). Widlok (1997: 123) considers ǂĀkhoe as "a way in which some Haiǁom speak their language" and the contributions to this volume concerning Haiǁom, which are based on the late Terttu Heikkinen's and Widlok's own research work, strongly reflect that way in which Haiǁom in the northern part of Namibia (north of the Omuramba Owambo) speak their language.

Kxoe subgroup

Khwe (Kxoe, Kxoé), spoken by approximately 8,000 persons mainly in Western Caprivi (northern Namibia) and adjacent areas in north-western Botswana. There are also pockets of relocated Khwe speakers in South Africa.

ǁAni (ǁÀnídàm, Xùúkhóédàm), spoken by probably less than 1,000 persons on both banks of the upper Okavango river in Ngamiland, north-western Botswana.

Buga (Boga, Xúúkhóédam), spoken by an estimated 1,000–2,000 persons along the east bank of the Okavango river in north-western Botswana.

Naro

Naro (Nharo, Nhauru, ǁAi, !Ai, Kà̱bé̱[khòè], Qáβé[khoe]), spoken by approximately 14,000 people in the Ghanzi District of western Botswana and, according to Guenther (1986: 1), "in Namibia to the west, mostly in the vicinity of the town of Gobabis". Naro would seem to present itself as a dialect cluster.

ǁGana subgroup

ǁGana (Gǁanasikxoi), spoken by an estimated 2,000 persons "in a large area centered on the Central Kalahari Game Reserve, reaching north to the southeastern part of the Ghanzi farming region and south to the Kang, Tsetseng and Motokwe areas", Botswana (Tanaka 1978: xvii).

ǀGui (Gǀwi), said to be spoken by circa 2,500 persons in roughly the same area as ǁGana (see above).

ǂHaba (ǂHábásàkx'úí), spoken by an unknown number of persons in the vicinity of the Kgwebe Hills, north-western Botswana.

Shua subgroup

Ts'ixa (Xúúkhòèdam; cf. ǁAni and Buga), spoken by probably less than 300 persons mainly in Mababe, to the east of the Okavango basin. According to Anne-Maria Fehn (p.c.), who is currently conducting fieldwork among the Ts'ixakhoe, the language is highly endangered.

Danisi (Madenass[en]a, Demisane, Danísá), spoken by an unknown number of persons in Central District, Botswana. (Source: Köhler 1971b.)

Deti (Tatí, Tetí, Tsetí, Dètídam), most likely extinct. The Deti people reside mainly in Central District, Botswana, in and around settlements such as Rakops and Gomaxa.

Cara (Tçara, Cáràdàm), spoken by an unknown number of persons in and around Gweta, Nata, and Mopipi (Central District, Botswana).

ǀXaise (Kaisi, ǀHaíse), spoken by an unknown number of persons in and around Gweta, Nata, and Mampswe (Central District, Botswana).

Tshwa subgroup

Cua (Tyua, Tshwa), spoken by an unknown number of persons in Central District, Botswana, in places such as Nata, Dukwe, Motsetse, etc.

Kua (Kúàdàm), spoken by an unknown number of persons in Bae, Metsemonate, Masethlarobega, ǁXoe, Mosolotsane, Nyunitsudi, Lephephe, Ngware, Lake Xau (cf. Traill 1986b: 420), and Malatswae (Central District, Botswana). Kua presents itself as a strongly diversified lectal cluster (Traill, p.c.).

Tsua (Tshòé, Tsúàdàm), spoken by an unknown number of persons in Central District, Botswana; places of residence cannot exactly be determined. The data presented in this book derive from a consultant who lived in Malatswae.

Southern Khoesan

!Xoon (!Xóõ, !xõ), a dialect cluster; spoken by just over 4,000 persons in the southern Kalahari, Botswana, and central-eastern Namibia.

ǀXam (ǀkham), an extinct language whose speakers lived widely scattered over the western part of present-day South Africa.

ǀHaasi (Kiǀhasi), an extinct dialect whose speakers are reported to have resided at the Lower Nossob river.

ǁXegwi (ǁkhegwi), a presumably extinct language that was spoken near the source of the Vaal river in present-day eastern South Africa.

Eastern ǂHoan (ǂHõã, ǂhũã), spoken by an estimated 200 persons in south-eastern Botswana.

Kwadi (Cuepe, Curoca, Cuanhoca), an extinct language that was spoken in coastal areas of south-western Angola.

REFERENCES

Argyle 1994; Beach 1938; D.F. Bleek 1929, 1956; Collins and Namaseb 2011; Eaton 2002; Ehret 1986; Ehret and Ehret 2012; Greenberg 1950, 1963b; Guenther 1986; Güldemann 1998b, 2004b, 2005; Güldemann and Elderkin 2010; Güldemann and Vossen 2000; Haacke and Eiseb 2002; Haacke *et al.* 1997; Heikkinen n.d.; Heine and Honken 2010; Heine and König 2001, 2012; Honken 1977, 1988, 1998; Hunziker *et al.* 2005; Keuthmann and Vossen 1997; Kilian-Hatz 2003, 2008; Köhler 1960, 1971b, 1975, 1981; König and Heine 2008; Ruhlen 1994; Sands 1998a; Schapera 1930; Schultze 1928; Starostin 2003, 2008; Steeman 2011; Tanaka 1978; Traill 1980, 1986b, 1995b, 2001; Treis 1998; Vossen 1997a, 2006; Westphal 1962a, 1962b, 1971; Widlok 1997; Winter 1981b.

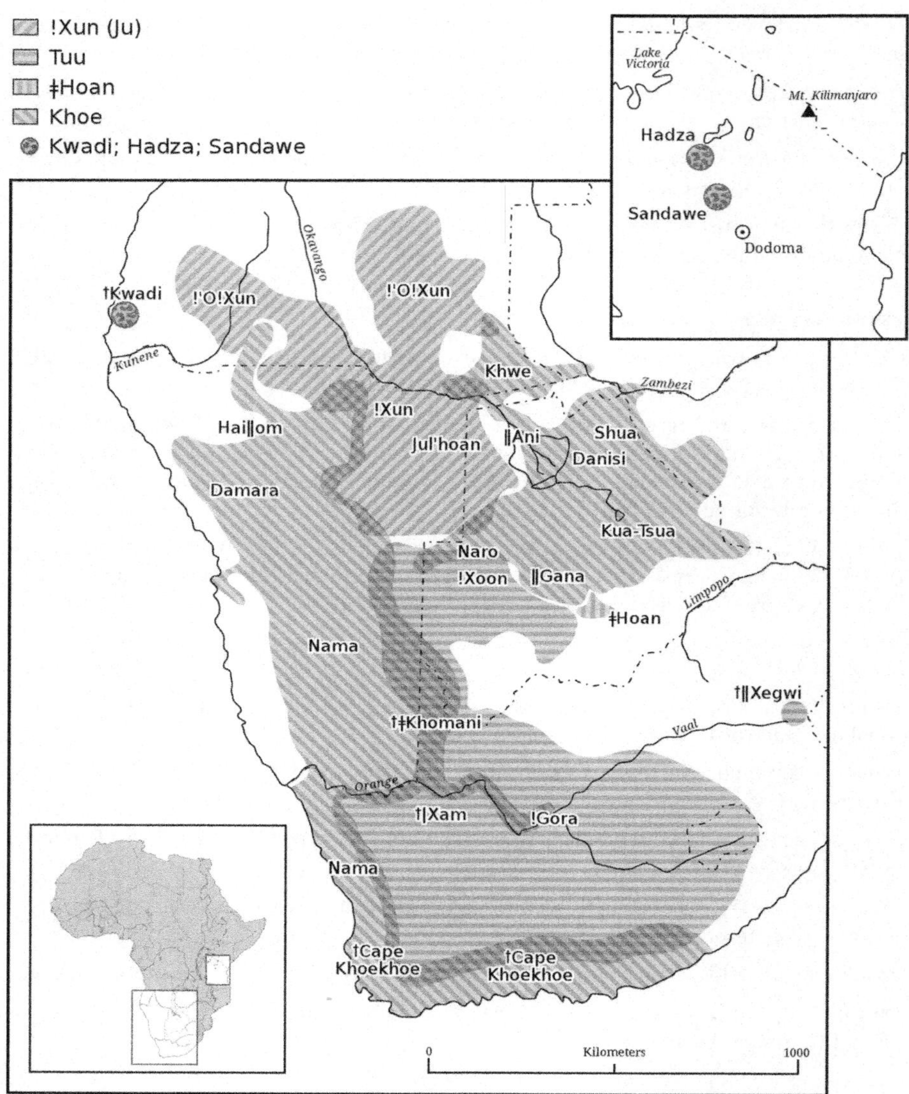

MAP 1.1 THE DISTRIBUTION OF KHOESAN LANGUAGES († = EXTINCT) © JONAS VOSSEN, DESIGNER

CHAPTER TWO

GENETIC RELATIONSHIPS: AN OVERVIEW OF THE EVIDENCE

Henry Honken†

1 INTRODUCTION

The term "Khoesan" embraces some thirty languages in southern Africa and two in Tanzania, which are characterized by spectacular phonetic systems and structures markedly different from their neighbours. These languages are sometimes referred to as the "Click Family" since the most prominent feature of their phonologies is the proliferation of sounds produced by velar suction. Since these are the only languages on earth in which clicks are both part of the native phonology and not marginal,[1] there has been from the very first a natural presumption that they might be related. But as the following quotations suggest, scholars have not been unanimous on this point:

> . . . two languages of East Africa containing clicks, Sandawe and Hatsa, will be shown to be related to the languages of the Bushmen and Hottentot.
>
> (Greenberg 1966: 66)

> In Southern Africa there are four unrelated Bush language types. . . .
>
> (Westphal 1963: 244)

> Although the Nama and !Xũ languages are unrelated. . . .
>
> (Snyman 1970: xiii)

> To my mind, the position of the Khoisan family in the classification of the world's languages is the most important unresolved problem in linguistic taxonomy.
>
> (Ruhlen 1994: 45)

> The correct conclusion is that the lexical overlap between the two languages !Xóõ and ǀGui has nothing to do with descent.
>
> (Traill and Nakagawa 2000)

This wide divergence of views mirrors an ongoing controversy in historical linguistics over the nature and kinds of evidence that are acceptable, reliable and convincing in proposals of more distant relationships. Some such proposals – the relationship of Hittite and Indo-European or Ritwan and Algonkian – have been universally accepted while others, such as the linking of Japanese with the Altaic languages, cause linguists to choose sides and take up arms. Khoesan would seem to belong to the second group.

My purpose in this chapter is to review the two major approaches to Khoesan, the various proposals which have been made, and evaluate the likelihood of each in light of the evidence presently available.

2 PREVIOUS WORK IN THE FIELD

All of the South African Khoesan languages are tonal and several papers have dealt with the problem of reconstructing the tonal systems. Beach (1938) devoted two chapters to the history of Khoekhoegowab tone and root structure. Citing his own data from Nama and Korana, he broached his famous suggestion – still the starting point for work on Khoe tone – that the four lower tones in Nama are the result of phonetic split. Winter (1981a) extended this approach to Khwe, another language in the Khoe family. In an attempt to reconstruct tonal patterns in the verbal system, Vossen (1986a) used his own field data to compare four Khoe languages: ǁAni, Deti, Cara and Kua.

Elderkin's (1988) analysis of statistical patterns in Juǀ'hoan initial consonants accounted for both pharyngealized and laryngealized vowels in terms of changes in the initial consonant and tone. Elderkin also reconstructed the tonal system of Juǀ'hoan in terms of two tonemes selected for twice on each stem. This is the only paper so far to deal with Ju tone from a historical perspective.

More recently, Honken (2008) extended Beach's hypothesis of a split in the lower tones to other Khoe languages and Elderkin (2008) reconstructed the Khoe tonal system.

The only Khoesan family which has been firmly reconstructed is Khoe. Baucom (1974) made an early attempt in a paper somewhat limited by its reliance on poor data. Köhler compared Khoekhoegowab and Khwe vocabulary in selected semantic fields (Köhler 1963) but without attempting a reconstruction. His paper is also notable as the first to describe click replacement.

Traill (1986a) discussed this interesting sound change in more detail as did Vossen, who has provided the first complete formal demonstration of the unity of Khoe. His reconstruction (Vossen 1997a) was based on data from eighteen Khoe languages, most of them not previously studied, and covered phonological, structural and lexical aspects.

Köhler (1973/74) presented a list of similar words in Khwe and Juǀ'hoan. Traill and Vossen (1997) discussed the correspondence of *!* and *ǀ* in many Ju languages. Various papers by Honken and Elderkin discussed the origin of pharyngealized vowels in Khoesan. Ehret (1986) offered etymologies in South African Khoesan, Sandawe and Hadza, with an attempt to reconstruct the proto-sound system. Ruhlen (1994) added further Khoesan etymologies in support of Greenberg's original paper. Sands (1998a) critically analysed previous historical work and used a number of different methodologies to evaluate the probability of a Khoesan family.

The two major classifications, Greenberg and Westphal, will be discussed later. Many more references can be found in Sands (1998a).

3 AGREEMENTS AND DISAGREEMENTS

The traditional division of South African Khoesan into Northern, Central and Southern going back to Bleek (1929) has been widely accepted. But it is clear that these units are not all on the same level of relationship. Southern, in particular, is much more diverse than Northern or Central. At the same time, the generally negative reaction by Khoesanists to Greenberg's classification has led to some changes in terminology that avoid the question-begging term "Khoesan". In the remainder of this chapter, the more current terms Ju (Northern), Khoe (Central) and !Ui-Taa[2] (Southern) will be used instead of the older terms.

The unity of the Khoe group has been acknowledged since the earliest studies and it is worth asking why this group has been so readily accepted while larger relationships such as Khoesan itself have been met with much scepticism by many researchers.

The Khoe languages have a moderately complex agglutinative structure with a nominal gender system and verbs marked for tense, aspect, passive, causative and other categories. In his reconstruction of Proto-Khoe, Vossen (1997a) was able to show that there are numerous correspondences in the morphemes that mark these categories in all the Khoe languages: the pronominal and nominal gender systems, tense and aspect particles, the use of a juncture morpheme in the verb complex, and many others. Moreover, in addition to lexical correspondences in all the major semantic fields, Vossen was able to demonstrate many valid sound shifts, ranging from the shift of *ts' to /' in Khoekhoegowab to complex sound changes like click replacement (cf. Table 2.1). In short, Khoe is a classic example of a genetic family and Vossen's analysis follows classical lines.

TABLE 2.1 EXAMPLES OF CORRESPONDENCES IN THE KHOE FAMILY

Gloss	Khoekhoe	Naro	Khwe	Deti
PRON.1SG	*tìí̋-tà*	*tíí-rá*	*tí*	*tá*
M.SG	*-p*	*-ba, -mi*	*-ma*	*-ma*
F.SG	*-s*	*-si*	*-si*	*-sa*
RECIPROCAL	*-kù*	*-ku*	*-kū*	*-kū*
PERFECTIVE	*hä̏ä*	*hàã*	*-hā*	*-hā*
'smoke'	*/'áǹ*	*ts'ínì*	*ts'ánì*	*ts'ání*
'chin'	*!ä̀ń-s*	*!gànī*	*gyàní*	*gàní*
'hard'	*!ā̋rí*	*!ārī*	*kyérí*	*kárí*
'hippo'	*!xàò-s*	*!xāò*	*xáō*	*xáò*
'ear'	*ǂàē̋-p*	*ǂēē*	*ǂéé*	*céé*
'black'	*ŋǂü̏ù*	*ŋǂùú*	*ŋǂgúú*	*yùú*

But when we turn to proposals of more distant connections, the evidence offered is often disappointingly thin, confined for the most part to lexical resemblances. For example, Greenberg devotes most of the six pages on South African Khoesan to proving that Khoekhoegowab is not a "Hamitic" language. Most of the "Hottentot" (Khoekhoegowab) constructions he considers are not widely paralleled in Ju or !Ui-Taa and, although he states that "analysis shows a number of real points of contact" (1966: 70) between "Hottentot" and "Bushman" (Non-Khoe) pronouns, these points are not discussed in detail.

All researchers in the area agree on the following: that the Cushitic language Dahalo (Elderkin 1976) and Bantu languages such as Xhosa (Louw 1974 and this volume, section 8.1), Yeyi (Sommer and Vossen 1992 and Sommer, this volume, section 8.2) and Manyo (see Möhlig, this volume, section 8.3) have borrowed their clicks, that Khoe and Ju are valid genetic units and that the speakers of South and East African Khoesan languages have probably been in their present locations for thousands of years (Barnard 1992: 29; Ehret, this volume, section 8.9). Beyond these few points, however, opinions diverge sharply.

The two principal approaches are those of Greenberg (1966) and Westphal (1971) and we may say that Khoesan historical linguistics takes place between the positive pole of Greenberg and the negative pole of Westphal. Greenberg accepts the traditional tripartite division of Ju, Khoe and !Ui-Taa as a given and unites them with Sandawe and Hadza in a larger "Click Family". Westphal splits Khoesan into Khoe ("Hottentot" in his terminology), four unrelated "Bush" languages – Ju, !Wi, ǁXegwi and Taa – and for good measure puts Sandawe, Hadza, Kwadi and even |Xam (generally classified as !Ui-Taa) each into its own family. Greenberg's classification is thus maximally lumping; Westphal's is maximally splitting.

One might anticipate that such sharply contrasting alternatives would provoke an interesting and profitable debate. Unfortunately, researchers have shown a tendency to talk past each other. Ruhlen (1994) gives only one reference for Westphal in his bibliography[3] and, even though Westphal's articles on this subject are almost all direct attacks on Greenberg, he frequently seems to misconstrue Greenberg's arguments.

4 SOUTH AFRICAN KHOESAN

4.1 The Khoe family

The genetic unity of Khoe is at this point undisputed. All Khoe languages share numerous words not found elsewhere. There are many characteristic[4] sound changes, especially the well-known series of click replacements in the Kxoe, Shua and Tshwa subgroups and in ǁGana in the Naro-ǁGana subgroup (cf. Table 2.2; see Traill 1986b and Vossen 1997a for details).

TABLE 2.2 EXAMPLES OF CLICK REPLACEMENT IN KHOE

Language	'aardvark'	'giraffe'	'springhare'	'back'
Naro	*!gòò*	*ŋ!ābè*	*ǂgòō*	
|Gui	*!góò*		*ǂgòō*	
ǁGana	*góò*	*ŋábì*	*ǂgòō*	*ŋǂóró*
Khwe	*gōó*	*ŋgyábē*		*ŋǂgóró*
Deti	*góó*	*ŋábè*		*yóró*
Cara	*góò*	*ŋgábè*	*jòò*	
Danisi			*dyóò*	*ndyóró*
Kua	*góò*			*yóró*
Tsua		*gábè*		

Unlike the Non-Khoe languages, with their one and two phoneme pronouns, Khoe languages have elaborate pronouns with distinct elements marking person, number and gender. For instance, in Khoekhoegowab, *k-* marks masculine gender, *s-* marks feminine and *t-* common, while *-e* marks first person plural and *-o* marks second person plural. Similar elements are found in the same order in Danisi (Shua subgroup) (see Vossen 1997a: 246f., Güldemann 2004b; cf. Table 2.3).

TABLE 2.3 PRONOMINAL STEMS IN KHOEKHOEGOWAB AND DANISI

Khoekhoegowab	MASCULINE	FEMININE	COMMON
1ST PLURAL	*-ke*	*-se*	*-ta*
2ND PLURAL	*-ko*	*-so*	*-tu*
Danisi			
1ST PLURAL	*-ke*	*-se*	*-tse*
2ND PLURAL	*-kao*	*-sao*	*-to*

Such repeated elements give a cohesion to the Khoe pronominal systems that makes the relationship obvious on inspection.

The nominal gender system distinguishes masculine and feminine gender and singular, dual and plural number. There is also a gender-indefinite category usually called common gender. Again we find many correspondences, including masculine singular labial (Khoekhoegowab *-p*, Naro *-ba*, Khwe *-ma*, etc.), feminine singular *-s* and common plural *-n*. Widespread verbal elements include the juncture, reciprocal, reflexive and passive endings (Köhler 1962, Vossen 1997a), the perfective and some tense-aspect particles and negative markers.

Kwadi, a now extinct and little-studied language of Angola, which is currently classed as affiliation indeterminate (Güldemann and Vossen 2000: 102) may be a distant outlier of Khoe. Although Kwadi is structurally quite different from Khoe, there are marked similarities in the pronominal systems. Güldemann and Elderkin (2010) propose some thirty well-supported potential cognates and others more tentative. Kwadi appears to have undergone extensive click loss: 'go' Kwadi *kõ*, Proto-Khoe *!ũũ; 'fish' Kwadi *'au-*, Proto-Kalahari Khoe *ǁ'au; 'eat' Kwadi *'ɲũũ*, Proto-Khoe *ǂ'ũũ, but 'blood' Kwadi */'o-*, Proto-Khoe *ǀ'ao; 'one' Kwadi */ui*, Proto-Khoe *ǀui. Another interesting correspondence is occasional loss of final *m*: 'two' Kwadi */a*, Proto-Khoe *ǀam; 'top' Kwadi *'ɲa*, Proto-Khoe *ǂ'am. Even in the absence of a genetic relationship, it is clear that Kwadi has had close contact with Khoe.

4.2 The Ju family

The Ju languages are very close and, according to Heine and König (2001: 1), are best regarded as a dialect chain, a group of speech communities in which neighbouring lects are mutually intelligible but speakers at the ends of the chain do not understand each other.

The only Ju languages studied in detail are Juǀ'hoan and the !Xũũ lects spoken in Ovamboland and Ekoka, although there is an early study of Bleek's (1928) describing ǂX'auǁ'ê. Assuming that these are representative, we can say that Ju languages share the following characteristics: a gender system of four to five classes based on meaning marked by pronominal, deictic and possessive concord, suppletive singular and plural forms for some verbs and a separate set of pronouns for the possessee. The elements *-a* and *kV* (*ko* in Juǀ'hoan, *ke* in !Xũũ) are used to mark verbal extensions with *kV* appearing if there is a second extension.

The most interesting sound change in Ju involves a number of words in Juǀ'hoan with initial *!* which correspond to !Xũũ words with initial *ǁ*, a sound change recently studied by Miller-Ockhuizen and Sands (1999), who propose that the alveolar and lateral clicks in this series are reflexes of a retroflex click, a click type which seems at this point to be found only in Ju (see Snyman 1997). This raises the types of sound changes known to affect clicks to four: click loss, click replacement, click accompaniment shift, and enclicking.

Click loss is a sound shift in which the influx part of the click is lost, leaving the accompaniment, which in turn may undergo other changes. For example, the alveolar click with glottal accompaniment is replaced in Shua languages by a glottal stop but the palatal click in the same series is replaced by a laryngealized palatal glide: Proto-Khoe *!'ãã 'know' > Cara *'áã*; Proto-Khoe *ǂ'ũũ 'eat' > Cara *ˀyúũ* (cf. Vossen 1997a: 433, 507f.).

Traill and Vossen (1997) differentiate click loss from click replacement in which the influx part of the click is replaced by a different influx. The only certain example of this so far are those Ju languages which have a lateral click in some words where Ju|'hoan has an alveolar click. Traill and Vossen suggest on typological grounds that the alveolar click is primary in this series (i.e. Proto-Ju *! > *ǁ*) but do not cite any comparative evidence.

Since some Ju languages have a retroflex click in these words, Miller-Ockhuizen and Sands's (1999) proposal that *!!*, *!* and *ǁ* are all reflexes of Proto-Ju *!! seems far more likely.

4.3 The position of ǂHõã

ǂHõã is remarkable in three ways: it was discovered in relatively recent times, it is the only non-!Ui-Taa Khoesan language to have the labial click and it shares an impressive number of lexical items with Ju languages, spoken at a considerable distance from the ǂHõã area.

While ǂHõã may not be a link between Ju and !Ui-Taa as Traill (1973) at first proposed, it remains the most likely candidate for a relationship between two Non-Khoe language groups. The following points are striking.

A comparison of Gruber's unpublished ǂHõã wordlist with Ju|'hoan reveals some 200–250 good matchings;[5] many of these words are otherwise unique to Ju (see Table 2.4):

TABLE 2.4 ǂHÕÃ–JU|'HOAN LEXICAL MATCHINGS

Gloss	ǂHõã	Ju|'hoan
'eat'	*'ám*	*'ḿ*
'duiker'	*ʘ'ú*	*|'áú*
'wildebeest'	*!gȉ*	*!gai*
'rot'	*!kű̃i*	*!úí*
'sit (sg.)'	*|nã̋*	*n|áng*

Both ǂHõã and !Xũũ have a subclass of nouns that form their plurals by vowel change and a shift in tone, a process rare in Khoesan. Examples are:

TABLE 2.5 PLURAL FORMATION BY VOCALIC AND TONAL SHIFT IN ǂHÕÃ AND !XŨŨ

ǂHõã (Collins 1998: 32)	SINGULAR	PLURAL	!Xũũ (Heikkinen 1987: 106f.)	SINGULAR	PLURAL
'eye'	*ʘkoa*	*ʘkòén*	'owner'	*kxàò*	*kxàó*
'tooth'	*ts'iu*	*ts'èón*	'person'	*zù*	*zùʰú*
			'my child'	*mí-mà*	*mí-mèʰé*

ǂHõã and the Ju languages have a particle in *kV̌* that marks verbal extensions (Collins 2003) and a subclass of verbs with a *kV-* prefix. Particle and prefix have the same vocalism in both ǂHõã and Ju (full data is available for only Ju|'hoan and !Xũũ as spoken in Ekoka and Ovamboland areas). Examples for particle and verb type are:

TABLE 2.6 *KV* PARTICLE AND PREFIX IN ǂHÕÃ, !XŨŨ AND JU

ǂHõã (Gruber 1975)		!Xũũ (Heikkinen 1987)		Ju|'hoan (Snyman 1970)	
kì	generalized preposition	*kè*	transitive particle	*kò*	transitive particle
kì kx'à nǎ̃	'on the ground'	*|'úwá tọ́ kè ǂà*	'put honey in the pot'	*kò tàfèr |hó*	'on the table'
kí-cí ǂ'àmkõe kì !kõa	'show the man the house'	*kè-tsạ̃i*	'hasten'	*gu|'a da'ama ko !'heima*	'caught for the child the rabbit'
kí-tsù'u	'steal'			*kò-ts'àùn*	'jump away'

Finally, there are at least half a dozen matchings among the suppletive singular and plural verb forms such as 'rise (sg.)': ǂHõã *kyú*, Ju|'hoan *tsáú*, !Xũũ *tsáó*; 'stand (pl.)': ǂHõã *||gǎ̃*, Ju|'hoan *||gà*, !Xũũ *||gà*.

Most recently, Heine and Honken (2010) have made an attempt to systematically compare Gruber's ǂHõã data with !Xũũ and Ju|'hoan by applying the comparative method. The results are most striking in that they were able to establish extensive sets of regular sound correspondences for consonants and vowels which have laid the basis for reconstructions at all levels. In conclusion, a new subfamily called "Kx'a" has been proposed to replace the former "Northern Khoesan" and unclassified ǂHõã.

4.4 !Ui and Taa languages

!Ui-Taa languages differ far more among themselves than the various branches of Khoe. Nevertheless, in some cases, there are interesting points of contact. ||Xegwi, for instance, appears to have had complex singular and plural forms like those in !Xóõ (Lanham and Hallowes 1956) and there are even some correspondences, as in 'tree': !Xóõ *ʘnà-je*, pl. *ʘnà-ã*; ||Xegwi *ʘnoo-zi*, pl. *ʘno-ŋ*. Unfortunately, most of the !Ui-Taa languages became extinct before they could be adequately described.

The only surviving !Ui-Taa languages are !Xóõ and N|uu; aside from |Xam, the other languages in this group are poorly documented though there is a fair amount of material on ||Xegwi. As nearly as one can tell from the literature, these languages seem to have been classified together because they share certain key lexical items and have similar pronominal systems. But, although many researchers in Khoesan would be sceptical of a relationship between Ju and !Ui-Taa, Ju|'hoan has some lexical items in common with !Xóõ (for example, 'artery', Ju|'hoan *!oq'ùn*, !Xóõ *!òhõ*) and the two languages also have similar pronominal systems. It is hardly reasonable to rely on a criterion in one case, which in the other is rejected as a basis for classification (but see, e.g., Hastings 2001 for a different view).

The most surprising new development in Khoesan linguistics was the discovery of eight surviving full speakers of N|uu, a language which had been thought to be extinct. This discovery was largely due to the efforts of Nigel Crawhall (2004), who based his PhD thesis on the sociological and historical aspects of N|uu. A number of researchers are now engaged in studying N|uu phonology and structure and the new data will undoubtedly make a re-evaluation of the status of !Ui-Taa possible.

5 EAST AFRICAN KHOESAN

Two languages of East Africa, Sandawe and Hadza, also use clicks as regular speech sounds. Greenberg classified these languages as coordinate branches to South African

Khoesan in a larger "Click Family", but Hadza is currently regarded as an isolate by nearly everyone.

5.1 Sandawe

Sandawe has often been associated with Khoesan, especially the Khoe group, but surprisingly little evidence has been offered to support this view. Moreover, those researchers claiming a relationship have largely ignored three major differences between the sound systems of South African Khoesan and the Tanzanian language which would have to be reconciled in any complete comparison. The first of these is the dramatic difference in the relative proportion of click words. In the South African languages, click words constitute 80 per cent or more of the total vocabulary; in Sandawe and Hadza, the proportion is more like 20 per cent. Next, all South African Khoesan languages[6] have a palatal click which is lacking in Sandawe and Hadza. And third, all South African Khoesan languages[7] have a velar friction click accompaniment which is not found in the Tanzanian case. Researchers have sometimes compared the latter two with the alveolar click and the aspirated click release but for the most part the comparisons have been unconvincing.

Unquestionably, there has been some sort of contact between Sandawe and at least Khoe since some of the lexical resemblances are so striking that they are unlikely to be the result of chance:

TABLE 2.7 SANDAWE–KHOE LEXICAL CORRESPONDENCES

	'four'	'to smell'	'ripen'	'to swallow'
Sandawe	*hàká*	*hìmé*	*ǁ'ìné*	*tîm*
Khoekhoe	*hàká*	*hằm̀*	*ǁ'ǻń*	*tóm̀*

But the number of these is very small (50–60). In addition to the lexical matches, there is the intriguing correspondence between the gender markers: M.SG Sandawe *-e*, *-we*, Khoekhoe *-p* and F.SG Sandawe *-su*, Khoekhoe *-s* (Güldemann and Elderkin 2010). Nevertheless, there is some doubt as to whether these few bits of evidence will support a genetic connection.

Among the eight or nine structural points which Greenberg cites, some, like the resemblance between the Sandawe and Naro masculine and feminine third person singular pronouns, are truly impressive. Others seem more limited. For instance, Greenberg compares Sandawe F.PL *-tsi* with Naro *-dzi* but this suffix is cited for only a single word: 'woman' *thame-tshu*, pl. *thame-tshi*. Similarly, M.PL *-ko*, which Greenberg compares to Khoekhoe *-kù*, seems to be limited to *ŋǀŏ:kó* 'children'.

Güldemann and Elderkin (2010) regard a genetic connection between Sandawe and the Khoe family as promising. Like Greenberg, they base this contention on resemblances in the pronominal systems and other markers and a small amount of lexical evidence.

Sandawe first person singular *tsí* is compared to Proto-Khoe *ti and Proto-Khoe third person singular base *xa- and suffixes M.SG *bV, *mV, F.SG *sV are compared to Sandawe demonstrative base *he* and suffixes *-we*/*-m*, *-su*. To these correspondences, already proposed by Greenberg, they add second person singular Sandawe *hàpú* and Proto-Khoe-Kwadi *sa. The similarities in the gender-number suffixes are truly striking and, as Greenberg says, Naro M.SG *xà-bá* and F.SG *xà-sá* "completely parallel" Sandawe *hè-wé* and *hè-sú* respectively.

At the same time, it is necessary to point out that these similarities must be evaluated in a wider context. What makes the Khoe pronominal system such powerful evidence for Khoe genetic unity is the fact that the individual pronouns have a complex inner structure showing detailed correspondences everywhere in Khoe but this structure has no parallel in Sandawe. The danger of comparing pronouns in terms of overall similarity without regard to their internal structure is clear when we note that the Ju|'hoan pronouns *mi*, *ha*, *e*, *i*, *si* resemble English *me*, *he*, *we*, *ye*, *they* in form and meaning but few linguists would suppose these two languages to be related.

There are also phonetic problems. The initial consonant of *tsí* is said to be palatalized (Güldemann and Elderkin 2010: table 7 and following comment) but this is the only example of palatalization in the data and the only example where Sandawe *ts-* corresponds to Khoe *t-*.

Similar problems surface in the discussion of demonstratives. Greenberg compares the *-a* remote and *-e* near contrast of Sandawe *na* 'there' and *ne* 'here' with Khoekhoe *ǀnaa* 'that' and *nee* 'this' but the same front vowel/near ~ back vowel/far contrast is found in the Papuan language Korafe: *e* 'this/here', *a* 'that/there (near addressee)' and *o* 'that/there (not location of speaker or addressee)' (Foley 1986: 75). Güldemann and Elderkin (2010: section 3.2) suggest that Sandawe *ne* and *na* are derived from Proto-Khoe *nǀéè and *nǁàá by declicking but no convincing evidence has been presented to show that this sort of random click loss ever occurs.

Though the evidence given, especially the similarities in the gender markers and some of the better lexical comparisons, makes some sort of contact between Sandawe and Proto-Khoe quite certain, it falls short of establishing a genetic relationship.

5.2 Hadza

With Hadza, the argument is even weaker. As Sands (1998a) has pointed out, the data from Bleek which serves as Greenberg's basic corpus has a high proportion of transcription errors. As a result, there are several misinterpretations in Greenberg's analysis. For example, Hadza *-ta*, which Greenberg compares to Khoekhoegowab 1SG *-ta*, is actually a present tense marker. According to Sands, there are sufficient errors to seriously weaken a third of the cognates offered by Greenberg.

The most substantial evidence Greenberg offers relies on similarities in the gender markers. He compares Hadza masculine and feminine possessive particles *ma* and *sa* with Naro nominal gender markers masculine *-ba* and feminine *-sa*. Hadza nominal suffixes masculine plural *-bi'i* and feminine plural *-be'e* correspond to verbal suffixes *-mi'i* and *-me'e* and Greenberg compares these to the "same alternation" in Naro masculine singular *-ba*, which shifts to *-m* before prepositions and the possessive particle *di*.

Greenberg (1966: 74) notes that the "third person independent pronouns show the same ha- base as those of Sandawe, the independent ha of the Bushman languages and the xa- third person base of Naro." It is certainly true that many Khoesan languages have both demonstratives and third person pronouns with an initial *h-* or glottal stop:

TABLE 2.8 KHOESAN DEMONSTRATIVES/PRONOUNS WITH INITIAL *H-*

Language	Demonstrative/pronoun	Meaning/function
!Ora	*he*	this
Khwe	*'á-mà*	this one (M.SG)
	'í-mà	that one (M.SG)
Ju|'hoan	*he*	this
	ha	3rd person singular pronoun
!Xóõ	*'VV*	demonstrative (with variable vowel)
	eh	3rd person singular pronoun
ǁXegwi	*'e-la, 'e-na*	demonstrative
	ha-	3rd person singular pronoun
Sandawe	*he*	this
	ha	that
Hadza	*ha-ma*	demonstrative (M.SG)

But demonstrative bases of the form *V*, *'V*, *hV* are found in several unrelated languages: Latin *hic*, *haec*, *hoc* 'this', Japanese *a-re* 'that', Basque *hau* 'this', *hura* 'that', nor do the details in the Khoesan set correspond in a paradigmatic way. The *b* ~ *m* alternation in Naro is found in the masculine singular and correlates with a feminine singular *si*/*s* and common plural *ni*/*n* alternation in the same environments but Hadza *b* ~ *m* is found only in the plural and the gender difference is marked by a vowel alternation. Since in Hadza there are three bases: proximate *ha-*, distal *bV-*, remote *na-* (cf. the feminine singular forms *ha-ko*, *bo-ko*, *na-ko*), *ha-* is not the general demonstrative base that it is in Sandawe and Hadza lacks the *i*/*a* near/remote symbolism.

6 FOR AND AGAINST

The strongest argument which Greenberg advances for Khoesan as a genetic unit is the canonic form. All South African Khoesan languages appear to share an idiosyncratic stem form which must be CVV, CVN or CVCV, clicks can only occur initially, internal consonants are largely restricted to *b*, *m*, *n*, *r*, there are strong restrictions on the occurrence of vowels (the underlying vowel in the first syllable is normally *a* or *o*, only *a*, *i*, *u* can follow a nasal, and so on). It is curious that this argument has been so widely ignored since it is not clear that such a uniform stem structure could have arisen from areal influences.

Greenberg suggests that sceptics convince themselves by examining Bleek's vocabularies, and indeed a number of basic lexical items are widespread (see Traill 1986b, Sands 1998a). In general we find an 8–10 per cent lexical overlap between languages from different Khoesan groups (Greenberg 1966: 68 puts this at 50 per cent between Central and either Northern or Southern and Westphal 1971 at 1–2 per cent). Greenberg also notes that, although the pronominal systems are superficially quite different, they share a number of markers such as 1PL *e*/*i* and 2PL *o*/*u*.

In response to these arguments, critics have pointed out that, while some of the lexical correspondences are striking, they show an unexpectedly low degree of sound change. This is not the case within accepted genetic groups such as Khoe, leading to the paradoxical result that the transition from Proto-Khoe to its branches seems to show much greater change than the shift from Proto-Khoesan to Ju, Khoe and !Ui-Taa would entail. Nor are there any characteristic sound changes linking the Khoesan groups as there are between the branches of Khoe.

But the most serious weakness of the proposed Khoesan family is the almost complete lack of any widespread structural correspondences. The few Macro-Khoesan structural features which have been noted, such as the prevalence of nominalizing suffixes in *-s* (Khoekhoegowab *-si*, Khwe *-ça*, !Xóõ *-sa*, Ju|'hoan *-sí* etc.), could well be the result of chance or borrowing.[8]

The most impressive example of morphological evidence for a possible Khoesan family is what Collins (2003) has called the linker, a particle in *k-* that marks various extensions of the verb including objects, locative and instrumental phrases. Collins has argued that the many parallels between ǂHõã and Ju|'hoan in the use of this particle provide strong evidence for a relationship and the present author would agree. A similar linker is found in !Xóõ, where it shows concord with its satellite, the underlying form being *kâ*.

Even closer parallels can be found here between !Xóõ and ǂHõã since in both languages the passive prefix has the same form as the linker: !Xóõ *ké qáe sà'ã* 'in its mother's face' (Traill 1994: 184), *èh ń bà tá̰ã* 'he hears', *èh ń bà kâ tá̰ã* 'he is heard' (Traill 1994: 310); ǂHõã *ki gyeo na* 'in the road', *ǂ'amkoe ki- ǁgon-'a* 'a person was struck' (Collins 2003).

The tree diagram below is not meant to replace the classifications of Greenberg and Westphal. What it does is summarize the presently available evidence for genetic connections in the Khoesan area. Note that a dotted line indicates that the connection is tentative (as between Kwadi and Khoe) or may be due to borrowing.

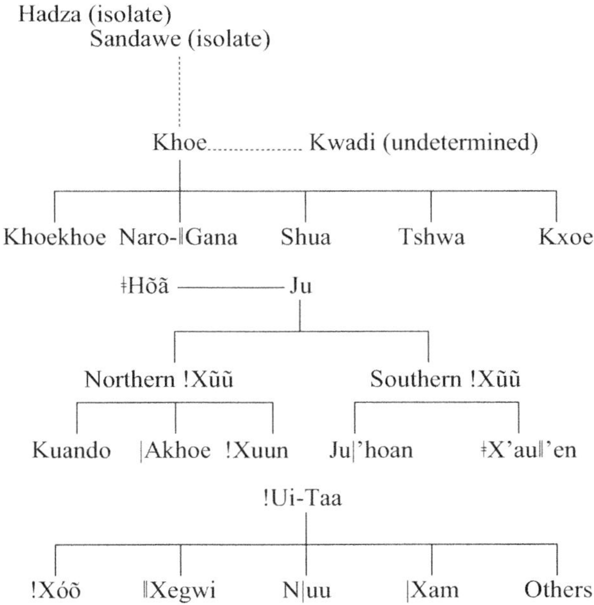

In conclusion, although there are a number of intriguing lexical and structural similarities, which may be the result of some deep and ancient underlying connection, no formal demonstration of the genetic unity of Khoesan has been made which is convincing and satisfying to all Khoesanists.

NOTES

1 In some Southern Bantu languages, as much as 15 per cent of the lexicon may begin with clicks, but this vocabulary is thought to be borrowed from neighbouring Khoesan languages (Louw 1974, for Xhosa borrowing from Khoekhoe; Sommer and Vossen 1992, for Yeyi borrowing from ǁAni). It is in this sense that I am referring to "native phonology".

2 Most recently, Güldemann (2005) has referred to Southern Khoesan as the Tuu family, based on the common !Ui and Taa word for 'people' (!Xóõ *tùu*, ǁXegwi *tu-ŋ*, Nǀuu *cu-ke*).

3 This is a citation of Westphal's response to Traill (1973), included only because Traill's response to Westphal's criticism is cited. Westphal's (1971) most complete statement of his views is not mentioned nor any of his other papers on the subject.

4 Even loanwords may show regular sound correspondences. What I mean by a characteristic sound change is one that defines a group and has the property Nichols (1992: 48) calls individual-identifying, i.e. has a probability of random occurrence of one in a hundred thousand or less. An example from Indo-European is Grimm's Law, which defines Germanic as a separate branch. An example within Khoe would be the loss of voicing in the clicks which defines Khoekhoe as a sub-family.

5 By matching I mean a candidate for cognacy: in an initial comparison, items which have the same gloss and show phonetic correspondences found elsewhere in the data set are said to be matched. Further research may confirm matchings as cognates.

6 The only exception appears to be ǁXegwi. There has been some speculation (Lanham and Hallowes 1956) that the palatal click shifted to a lateral affricate in ǁXegwi (cf. 'moon' ǂKhomani *ǂ'oro*, ǁXegwi *tl'olo*).

7 Ladefoged and Traill (1994) found that their Khoekhoe informants realized this click type as an aspirated click but Beach (1938) described the accompaniment as velar friction and Khoekhoe words with this accompaniment correspond to words in other Khoe languages with velar friction.

8 Cf., for example, Japanese nominalizing suffix in *-s*: Japanese *aka-i* 'red', *aka-sa* 'redness', and the similarities between !Xóõ and Khwe complement structures as in !Xóõ *ñ bà káne ká kákúũ-sa* 'I want quietness' (Traill, from taped examples of !Xóõ sounds) and Khwe *Tí nǂóm̀ -ca yávà-na-hã* 'I would like to build' (Kilian-Hatz 2003: 149).

REFERENCES

Barnard 1992; Baucom 1974; Beach 1938; D.F. Bleek 1928, 1929; Collins 1998, 2003; Crawhall 2004; Ehret 1986; Elderkin 1976, 1988, 2008; Foley 1986; Greenberg 1966 [1963b]; Gruber 1975; Güldemann 2004b, 2005; Güldemann and Elderkin 2010; Güldemann and Vossen 2000; Hastings 2001; Heikkinen 1987; Heine and Honken 2010; Heine and König 2001; Honken 2008; Kilian-Hatz 2003; Köhler 1962, 1963, 1973/74; Ladefoged and Traill 1994; Lanham and Hallowes 1956; Louw 1974; Miller-Ockhuizen and Sands 1999; Nichols 1992; Ruhlen 1994; Sands 1998a; Snyman 1970, 1997; Sommer and Vossen 1992; Traill 1973, 1986a, 1986b, 1994; Traill and Nakagawa 2000; Traill and Vossen 1997; Vossen 1986a, 1997a; Westphal 1963, 1971; Winter 1981a.

CHAPTER THREE

TYPOLOGY

Tom Güldemann[1]

1 INTRODUCTION

Apart from classifying languages genealogically, language groups can be established on the basis of shared linguistic features, independently of their genealogical relations. This is the topic of typological and areal linguistics. For the time being, this is a particularly useful approach in Khoesan studies in order to come to grips with the commonality and diversity in this language group, because genealogical classifications have heretofore been unsatisfactory. It is also called for by the fact that Khoesanists are still sounding out the terrain due to the comparatively late accessibility of sufficient data. Finally, it is relevant because of the claim about an old age of Khoesan in southern and eastern Africa in connection with the hypothesis advanced and empirically substantiated by Nichols (1992) that population and areal typology yield better results in the historical study of languages when great time depths do not (yet) allow the application of historical-comparative methodology.

The idea that common linguistic features, at least of Southern African Khoesan, can be assessed in terms of areal-typological explanations is not new, but has been entertained briefly by Greenberg (1959: 24) and Heine (1975b: 44f.). At that time, however, there were still great gaps in the data. Today the situation has changed considerably and typological comparisons in Khoesan are no longer impossible. A first attempt in this direction was made by Güldemann (1998b). He suggested that certain commonalities of Khoesan languages could be explained if parts of pre-Bantu southern Africa were conceptualized as a linguistic area, called there the "Kalahari Basin".

The following typological survey consists of two major parts: morphosyntax and phonetics/phonology, treating Khoesan as a whole. Table 3.1 gives the sample languages, their classification, and the respective data sources.

2 MORPHOSYNTAX

Güldemann (1998b) is a very preliminary attempt at giving a morphosyntactic profile of the Southern African Khoesan area based on a set of features from Nichols (1992). This is expanded here by using an enlarged language sample (including eastern African Khoesan), taking more features into account, and having recourse to more extensive and reliable information on particular languages and linguistic features. The list of features and the relevant values for non-privative features are as follows (the abbreviations are used in Table 3.2):

1–6 Clause organization
1 Position of subject vis-à-vis verb: Subject–Verb (SV), Verb–Subject (VS), Variable (V)
2 Position of object vis-à-vis verb: Object–Verb (OV), Verb–Object (VO), Variable (V)
3 Unmarked verb position in the clause: Final (F), Medial (M), Initial (I), Variable (V)
4 Dominant alignment type: Neutral (N), Accusative (A)
4a Alignment for pronouns: Neutral (N), Accusative (A)
4b Alignment for nouns: Neutral (N), Accusative (A)

TABLE 3.1 SAMPLE LANGUAGES, CLASSIFICATION, AND PRIMARY SOURCES

Language	Branch	Family	Sources[1]
Hadza	–	Isolate	M: Sands (this volume*, p.c.); P: Sands, Maddieson and Ladefoged (1996)
Sandawe	–	Isolate	Elderkin (1989, field notes, p.c.)
Kwadi[2]	Isolate	Khoe–Kwadi	M: Güldemann (this volume*)
Northern Kua[3]	Kalahari Khoe	Khoe–Kwadi	P: Traill (1980), Vossen (1997a)
Khwe	Kalahari Khoe	Khoe–Kwadi	P: Köhler (1981)
ǁAni	Kalahari Khoe	Khoe–Kwadi	M: Heine (1999)
G|ui	Kalahari Khoe	Khoe–Kwadi	P: Nakagawa (1996a, 1996b)
Standard Khoekhoe[4]	Khoekhoe	Khoe–Kwadi	M: Hagman (1977); P: Beach (1938)
Ju|'hoan	South	Ju	M: Dickens (2005); P: Snyman (1975a)
ǂHoan	–	? Isolate	M: Collins (p.c.); P: Traill (1980), Bell and Collins (2001)
East !Xoon[5]	Taa	Tuu	M: Güldemann (this volume*); P: Traill (1985)
ǂKhomani	!Ui	Tuu	P: Doke (1936), Traill (1997)
|Xam	!Ui	Tuu	M: Güldemann (this volume*)

Notes:
1 M morphosyntax; P phonetics-phonology; * see there for original sources.
2 classified with Khoe according to Güldemann (2004b).
3 tentative synopsis of two possibly diverging varieties; henceforth just Kua.
4 Namibian standard shaped by Nama, Orlam and Damara varieties; henceforth just Khoekhoe.
5 henceforth just !Xoon.

4c Alignment for verb inflection: Neutral (N), Accusative (A)
5 Fixed clause slots and nominal marking according to slot position
6 Serial verb constructions

7–9 Noun phrase organization
7 General position of noun phrase head: Final (F), Initial (I)
8 Head position in genitive construction: Final (F), Initial (I), Variable (V)
8a Juxtaposition type*: {possessor–possessed}
8b Attributor type*: {possessor–attributor–possessed}
8c Possessor-proform type*: {possessor–(possessor pronoun–possessed)}
8d Possessed-proform type*: {possessed–(possessor–possessed proform)}
8e Inalienable possession (if applicable, predominant type of encoding: a, b, c, or d)
9 Position of adposition vis-à-vis object: Variable = preposition or postposition (V); Final = postposition (F); preposition, postposition, and their Combination = circumposition (C)

* exemplified with head-final order

10–12 Morphology in general
10 Phonotactic dichotomy of C(C)VCV in lexemes vs. CV in grams
11 Final position of bound grams vis-à-vis host dominant
12 Derivationally productive use of reduplication

13–16 Verbal morphology
13 Regular verbal cross-reference of subject
14 Regular verbal cross-reference of object (in addition to nominal object)
15 Elaborate system of morphological derivation
16 Compound verbs

17–20 Nominal and pronominal morphology
17 First-person inclusive pronoun
18 Gender system
18a Number of genders
18b Number of agreement classes co-varying with gender
18c Gender–class ratio
18d Gender manipulation for derivational purposes
18e Gender marked overtly on the noun
19 Number system
19a Number of categories: 2 singular–plural, 3 singular–plural–dual
19b One regular marking pattern
19c Double marking (e.g., suffix in addition to reduplication, stem change, etc.)
19d Number-sensitive stem suppletion
19e Indexing of number on other parts of speech (like predicates, adjectives)
20 Grammatically productive use of compound nouns

Many of the features are straightforward or are surveyed according to Nichols's (1992) methodology (e.g., alignment types); some must be explained and exemplified here (the number of a following example is keyed to the number of the relevant property).

Feature 5 refers to a special property found in some Khoesan languages: they mark nominal constituents according to their clause position, which is defined by linear order, and not according to configurational syntactic relation. One consequence is that nominals with the same semantic role but with a variable clause position can be marked differently. This is shown: in (5a) from Nama, all constituents after the pronominal subject enclitic *-gu* have the suffix *-a*, viz. the object *marite* (*-te* < *ti-a*) and the lexically repeated subject *ǀgawipriesterga* (*-ga* < *-gu-a*) (an initial nominal subject would lack *-a*); in (5b) from Juǀ'hoan, the position of postverbal non-subjects can be exchanged, but the occurrence and position of the verb suffix *-a* and the preposition *kò* remain the same.

(5) a. *o-gu* *gye* *ǀgawi-priester-g**a*** *mari-te* *ū*
then-3M.PL:SUBJ DECL high-priest-M.PL:SUBJ money-F:PL:OBJ take
'Da nahmen sie, die Hohepriester, das Geld . . .' [then the high priests took the money] (Dempwolff 1934/35: 90)

b. *ha* *kú* *ǀohm-**a*** *!aìhn* ***kò*** *gǀúí* or
3SG IMPF chop-VE tree MPO forest
ha *kú* *ǀohm-**a*** *gǀúí* ***kò*** *!aìhn*
3SG IMPF chop-VE forest MPO tree
'He was chopping the tree in the forest.' (Dickens 2005: 39)

The four associative (alias "genitive") constructions under (8) are also exemplified. The last three types all display a segmental marker (bold in examples); they differ according to whether the marker is a medial attributor or a generic proform repeating either the possessor or the possessed (hence the labels for the last two construction types).

(8) a. *'àm* *gyè* (ǂHoan)
1SG mother
'my mother' (Gruber 1973: 429)

b. *ja-s* ***a**-b* (!Ora)
cloak-F.SG ATTR:3M.SG
'his cloak' (Beach 1938: 192)

c. *!ù.m* *'ée* *Θàa* (East !Xoon)
eland.3 3.PRON child.3
'Eland's child' [lit.: eland, his child] (Traill, unpubl.)

d. *uto-a* *Foundation* ***ma*** (Ju|'hoan)
car.3-? foundation 3:POSS
'a Foundation car' [lit.: car, one of the foundation] (Dickens 2005)

Example (9) from ǂHoan demonstrates an adpositional structure, regularly encountered in some Khoesan languages under certain syntactic conditions, in which relational markers occur before *and* after the noun.

(9) *kì* *|'óõ-qà* *!qhà'ne*
MPO tree-PL beside
'beside the trees' (Gruber 1975: 38)

My approach to grammaticalized noun categorization alias gender, which is treated under (18), is explained in detail in Güldemann (2000b). The most important point is a consistent distinction between gender and agreement class. As a result, two structural types of gender systems can be identified; their difference is captured by the value of the gender–class ratio, namely a distinction of <1 vs. ≥1. (Note that the number of genders given by Güldemann [1998b: 144] for !Xoon and, for the record, Tswana referred to agreement classes, which has been corrected here.) What is meant by "gender manipulation for derivational purposes" is exemplified in (18d), from Nama: the switch of a noun to another gender for rendering a different semantic feature.

(18d) *pén-i* vs. *pén-s*
pen-M.SG pen-F.SG
'the pen' 'the unusually fat pen' (Hagman 1977: 23)

Number marking is a complex issue in several Khoesan languages. Related to this is a major distinction made here between languages displaying a regular number marking pattern and languages where the devices are often lexicalized and unpredictable. Examples for the second type, including the recurrent occurrence of double marking on one noun, are provided in (19c) from N|huki (!Ui branch of Tuu). Number-sensitive stem suppletion of predicates is demonstrated in (19e) from Sandawe.

(19c)

Meaning	Singular	Plural	Marking device
'white person'	*|hũ-si*	*|hũ-ke*	(suffix)
'man'	*ǂoo*	*tyu-ke*	(stem suppletion + suffix)
'child'	*|oba*	*|oe-ke*	(stem change + suffix) (Westphal, unpubl.)

(19e)

Meaning	Number of	Singular	Plural
'go'	subject	*hik'(i)*	*ni'*
'stand'	subject	*ǁume*	*hlee*
'carry'	object	*siee*	*tlaa* (Kagaya 1993: ix)

Finally, the derivational use of nominal compounds is exemplified in (20) with ǁXegwi (!Ui branch of Tuu).

(20) *kwi-kl'oo* *!kholo-q'iŋ* *noni-Θari*
person-man horse-woman buck-child
'man' 'mare' 'small buck' (Lanham and Hallowes 1956: 112)

The results of the morphosyntactic language survey are given in Table 3.2.

TABLE 3.2 MORPHOSYNTACTIC FEATURES OF KHOESAN LANGUAGES

Language[1]	1	2	3	4	4a	4b	4c	5	6	7	8	8a	8b	8c	8d	8e	9	10	11
Hadza	V	VO	I	A	N	N	A			I	I			♦	♦		V		♦
Sandawe	SV	OV	F	A	A	A	A	♦		F	F	♦					F		♦
Kwadi	SV	OV	F	A	A	A	?	?		F	F	♦	?	?	?		F	(♦)	♦
ǁAni	SV	V	V	A	N	N	A			F	F	♦	♦		♦		F	♦	♦
Khoekhoe	SV	OV	F	A	N	N	A	♦		F	V	♦	♦		♦		F	♦	♦
Ju|'hoan	SV	VO	M	N	N	N	N	♦	♦	I	F	♦		♦	♦	c	C	♦	♦
ǂHoan	SV	VO	M	N	N	N	N	♦	♦	I	F	♦	♦		(♦)	a	C	♦	♦
!Xoon	SV	VO	M	A	N	N	A	♦	♦	I	F	♦	♦	♦		a	C	♦	♦
|Xam	SV	VO	M	N	N	N	N	♦	♦	I	F	♦	♦	♦		a	C	♦	♦

Language	12	13	14	15	16	17	18	18a	18b	18c	18d	18e	19	19a	19b	19c	19d	19e	20
Hadza	♦	♦	♦	(♦)		♦	♦	2	4	0.5	♦	♦	♦	2	♦		(♦)	♦	
Sandawe			♦	♦			♦	2	3	0.7	♦	♦	♦	2	♦		♦	♦	♦
Kwadi	♦		?	?	?	♦	♦	2	5	0.4	?	♦	♦	3	♦		♦	?	♦
ǁAni	♦		♦	♦			♦	3	8	0.4		♦	♦	3	♦				♦
Khoekhoe	♦		♦	♦	♦	♦	♦	3	8	0.4		♦	♦	3	♦				♦
Ju|'hoan					♦	♦	♦	5	4	1.2	♦		♦	2			♦	♦	♦
ǂHoan	(♦)				♦			x	x	x	x	x	♦	2		(♦)	♦	♦	♦
!Xoon			♦		♦		♦	6	5	1.2	♦	(♦)	♦	2		♦	♦	♦	♦
|Xam	♦				♦	♦	♦	2	2	1.0	♦		♦	2		♦	♦	♦	♦

Note: 1 ? no information; preliminary analysis; feature is: x not applicable; blank absent; ♦ present; (♦) present in restricted form.

A number of important conclusions can be drawn from Table 3.2. First, the Khoesan sample as a whole has very few features in common; these are predominantly host-final morphology (11), nominal number marking (19), and, except ǂHoan, a nominal gender system (18). Since all these properties are frequent cross-linguistically, they do not identify a genuine linguistic entity.

The commonalities across Khoesan increase as soon as Hadza is excluded, which deviates in six crucial features (1, 3, 8, 9, 13, 20) from the rest of the sample. Nevertheless, the features shared by the remaining Khoesan languages are still outnumbered by the differences. More homogeneous language types can only be identified when a second split is recognized: Sandawe and Khoe–Kwadi on the one hand vs. Tuu, ǂHoan, and Ju on the other.

The linguistic type constituted by Sandawe and Khoe–Kwadi can be defined by the constituent order in both, the clause domain (1, 2, 3) and the noun phrase (7, 8, 9), the alignment type (4), certain properties of noun categorization (18c, 18e), and the type of number marking (19b).

It is also worth evaluating the profile of the geographically defined group Southern African Khoesan which shares features relating to 1, 8, 11, 13, 19, and 20. Head-final genitive constructions (8) irrespective of the word order in other contexts (cf. general head-*initial* noun phrase order in Ju|'hoan, ǂHoan, !Xoon, and |Xam) and host-final morphology (11) have previously been discussed as an areal feature of pre-Bantu southern Africa (Güldemann 1999). However, even the earliest Khoesan sources from the nineteenth century, focusing on Khoekhoe and !Ui languages, have observed structural heterogeneity rather than homogeneity (cf. Bleek 1869). Parallel to these findings, but now taking all attested Southern African Khoesan lineages into account, it is argued in Güldemann (1998b) and Güldemann and Vossen (2000) that a major typological split separates Khoe–Kwadi from the remaining languages, called "Non-Khoe" for convenience. Although these two groups are also internally diverse, they represent on a more abstract level two language types which differ markedly from each other in constituent order (2, 3, 7, 9), clause and predicate structure (5, 6, 16), verbal derivation (15), noun categorization (18c–e), and number marking (19a–e).

This generalization needs, however, an important qualification: the Khoekhoe branch of Khoe deviates from its genealogical group in some important respects and, then, aligns itself with Non-Khoe in the features 5, 16, and 17 (see below for an explanation).

3 PHONETICS AND PHONOLOGY

In his comparative study of Khoesan sound systems, Traill (1980: 167) has drawn attention to the fact that "these languages differ widely from one another in numerous phonetic details, affecting not only subtle aspects of pronunciation but, more importantly the size and composition of the phonological inventory of clicks, non-clicks and vowel types." The importance of this observation must not be underestimated, given that the presence and functional load of clicks as a phonetic-phonological commonality tend to be viewed as the major genealogical feature of Khoesan. Thus, a thorough comparative typological study of as many sound systems as possible is one of the urgent tasks in Khoesan research. Unfortunately, a full picture of the sound inventories of all languages is still lacking. The following survey can only provide a general idea of the degree of commonality and diversity within Khoesan.

The choice of a number of compared features concerning consonants is motivated by a particular approach to Khoesan sound design for which the reader can consult Güldemann (2001). This deviates in various respects from traditional analyses (accordingly, my analysis of certain segments is not necessarily identical with that in the data sources); however, it can take care of all Khoesan consonant types attested so far, in particular the many click accompaniments, and thus provides a good basis for a comparison across this group (see Table 3.3).

Only some essential points of my approach can be mentioned here. First, I consider the sets of lateral and affricate consonants in most of Khoesan to be parallel in phonological behaviour to sets constituted by places of articulation; they are thus treated on the horizontal feature axis of Table 3.3. Even more important are two other assumptions: (a) clicks and non-clicks make up one integrated system of consonants, and (b) a great number of distinctive stop segments can be analysed as clusters of two simple phonemes. This approach results *inter alia* in a parallel treatment of basic nasal clicks and nasal egressive sonorants as well as of glottalized clicks and egressive ejectives. Related to these assumptions is the view that the phoneme systems are internally structured in terms of consonant subclasses; of particular importance are different types of what I call "consonant elaboration". This notion underlies the distinction between "simple", "complex", and "cluster" segments in Table 3.3.

In general, a particular focus of the present cross-Khoesan comparison is on the size and structure of the phoneme inventory, parallel to Traill (1980). The features are of different diagnostic value: some are generally relevant in Khoesan, while others record a fairly restricted phenomenon which may even be rare in the group as a whole. The properties surveyed in Table 3.4 are as follows (relevant consonant features are keyed to the numbers of columns and lines in Table 3.3):

1–10 Consonants
1 Number of distinctive segments (segment total of entire system)
2a Number of non-stops (segment total of lines 1, 2, 13, 14 except nasal clicks)
2b Number of stops (segment total of lines 3–12 and of nasal clicks in lines 13, 14)
% Proportion of 2b vis-à-vis 1 in per cent
3a Number of non-clicks (segment total of columns 1–4 + 10–12)
3b Number of clicks (segment total of columns 5–9)
% Proportion of 3b vis-à-vis 1 in per cent
4 Number of places of articulation for non-clicks (columns 1–4 + 10–12)
4a Uvular (column 11)
4b Palatal (column 4)
4c Lateral
5 Number of click types alias influxes (columns 5–9)
5a Bilabial click (column 9)
5b Palatal click (column 8)
6 Number of gestures elaborating a plain voiceless stop (voicing, lines 5–12, and possible combinations thereof)
6a "Extensive" voicing alias "voice lead"
6b Prenasalization of plosives
6c Aspiration (line 5)
6d Ejection/glottalization (line 4)
6e Glottalization with nasal click (line 14)
6f Posterior fricative cluster offset (line 6)
6g Posterior plosive cluster offset without aspiration or ejection (line 7)
6h Number of cluster types (lines 6–12)
6i Number of click series in terms of traditional accompaniments alias effluxes

TABLE 3.3 CROSS-KHOESAN CONSONANT CHART IN A PRACTICALLY ORIENTED ORTHOGRAPHY

		1	2	3	4	5	6	7	8	9	10	11	12
		EG[1]	EG	EG	EG	IG	IG	IG	IG	IG	EG	EG	EG
		Lb	Al	Al-Af	Pl	Lt	Dt	Al	Pl	Lb	Vl	Uv	Gl
1. Non-nasal sonorants	Plain	w	l/r		y								
2. Fricatives	Plain	f	s		c						x		h
	Voiced	v	z		j								
3. Simple stops	Plain	p	t	ts	tc	ǁ	ǀ	!	ǂ	Θ	k	q	’
	Voiced	b	d	dz	dj	gǁ	gǀ	g!	gǂ	gΘ	g	gq	
4. Complex stops	Plain + Gl		t’	ts’	tc’	ǁ’	ǀ’	!’	ǂ’	Θ’	k(x)’		
	Voiced + Gl		dz’	dj’							g(x)’	q’	
5.	Plain + As	ph	th	tsh	tch	ǁh	ǀh	!h	ǂh	Θh	kh	qh	
	Voiced + As	bh	dh	dzh	djh	gǁh	gǀh	g!h	gǂh	gΘh	gh	gqh	
6. Stop clusters	Plain + /x/		tx	tsx	tcx	ǁx	ǀx	!x	ǂx	Θx			
	Voiced + /x/		dx	dzx	djx	gǁx	gǀx	g!x	gǂx	gΘx			
7.	Plain + /q/					ǁq	ǀq	!q	ǂq	Θq			
	Voiced + /q/					gǁq	gǀq	g!q	gǂq	gΘq			
8.	Plain + /kh/					ǁkh	ǀkh	!kh	ǂkh	Θkh			
	Voiced + /kh/					gǁkh	gǀkh	g!kh	gǂkh	gΘkh			
9.	Plain + /qh/					ǁqh	ǀqh	!qh	ǂqh	Θqh			
10.	Plain + /k(x)’/	px’	tx’	tsx’		ǁx’	ǀx’	!x’	ǂx’	Θx’			
	Voiced + /k(x)’/		dx’	dzx’		gǁx’	gǀx’	g!x’	gǂx’	gΘx’			
11.	Plain + /k’/					ǁk’	ǀk’	!k’	ǂk’	Θk’			
12.	Plain + /q’/					ǁq’	ǀq’	!q’	ǂq’	Θq’			
13. Simple nasals	Plain	m	n		ny	nǁ	nǀ	n!	nǂ	nΘ	ng		
	Voiceless					nhǁ	nhǀ	nh!	nhǂ	nhΘ			
14. Complex nasals	Plain + Gl	’m	’n			’nǁ	’nǀ	’n!	’nǂ	’nΘ			

Note: 1 Af = affricate, Al = alveolar, As = aspiration, Dt = dental, EG = egressive, Gl = glottal(ization), IG = ingressive = click, Lb = labial, Lt = lateral, Pl = palatal, Uv = uvular, Vl = velar.

7 Number of elaborated stops except simple voiced (segment total of lines 4–12 + 14)
8 Number of elaborated clicks except simple voiced (segment total of the intersection of lines 4–12 + 14 and columns 5–9)
% Proportion of 8 vis-à-vis 7 in per cent
9 Number of consonant cluster segments (segment total of lines 6–12)
10 Number of click cluster segments (segment total of the intersection of lines 6–12 and columns 5–9)
% Proportion of 10 vis-à-vis 9 in per cent

11–12 Vowels
11 Number of monophthongic vowel qualities
12 Number of vowel colourings
12a Nasalization
12b Pharyngealization
12c Glottalization
12d Breathy voice
12e Number of combinations

13 Tone as dominant suprasegmental feature

14 Phonotactic stem pattern (basic C(C)VCV, derived C(C)VV and C(C)VN)

Needless to say, the list of surveyed features does in no way pretend to be exhaustive. For example, Traill (2001) has suggested another fruitful approach, i.e. to compare the distribution of the distinctive segments of languages over their lexicons. He observed a surprising homogeneity of !Xoon and Ju|'hoan regarding the relative frequency of the individual stops as stem-initial segments. What significance the result of this binary comparison has for Khoesan as a whole remains unclear. In any case, Traill's (2001: 448) hypothesis that "underlying the synchronic [East] !Xóõ and Zhu [= Ju|'hoan] lexicons is an ancient identity that has been preserved in the typological details" urges future researchers to undertake a similar study with a cross-Khoesan scope as soon as the required data are available.

The results of the phonetic-phonological survey are summarized in Table 3.4. An analysis of these data leads to the following conclusions. First, parallel to the morphosyntactic comparison Khoesan as a whole is a rather heterogeneous group. Only a few features do not show considerable variation within the sample: 2b/1 per cent, 4, 6c, 6d, 11. Given that these are not very prominent from a cross-linguistic perspective, there is again little substance for identifying an entity "Khoesan". One is essentially left with the role of clicks and the typical phonotactic stem pattern (14). Other features have more diagnostic value for an intra-group assessment, because they are only shared by subsets of Khoesan and pattern differently over the sample languages.

One clear observation is the typological remoteness of Hadza and Sandawe, which somewhat echoes the findings of the morphosyntactic comparison. They deviate from the general Southern African Khoesan trend in more than a third of the features distributed over almost all feature domains: 1, 2b, 3b, 3b/1 per cent, 4c, 5, 5b, 6, 6b, 6f, 6h–9–10, 7, 8. To a large extent this will be a function of their different geographic setting. At the same time, it strengthens the reservation to the assumption that the plain existence of clicks is of any significance for a genealogical classification. This is especially clear in the case of Hadza, which is unique vis-à-vis the rest of Khoesan in three additional and very basic sound features, viz. 12~12a, 13, 14; it is less valid for Sandawe because a closer affinity with Southern African Khoesan in these crucial aspects is discernible.

TABLE 3.4 PHONETIC-PHONOLOGICAL FEATURES OF KHOESAN LANGUAGES

Language[1]	1	2a	2b	%	3a	3b	%	4	4a	4b	4c	5	5a	5b	6	6a	6b	6c	6d	6e
Hadza	50	12	38	76	41	9	18	7			♦	3			5		♦	♦	♦	
Sandawe	44	11	33	75	29	15	34	6			♦	3			3		(♦)	♦	♦	
Khwe	69	12	57	83	33	36	52	6	♦			4		♦	7/8		♦	♦	♦	
Kua	66	9	57	86	36	30	45	7	♦	♦		4		♦	7/8			♦	♦	
G|ui	90	13	77	84	48	52	56	7	♦	♦		4		♦	11			♦	♦	
Khoekhoe	32	6	26	81	12	20	62	4				4		♦	3			♦	♦	
Ju|'hoan	92	13	79	86	44	48	52	6				4		♦	11	♦		♦	♦	
ǂHoan ??	93	?	?	?	34	59	63	7	♦	♦		5	♦	♦	10			♦	♦	♦
!Xoon	126	9	117	85	43	83	66	6	♦			5	♦	♦	14	♦		♦	♦	♦
ǂKhomani	64	10	54	84	23	41	64	5		♦		5	♦	♦	8			♦	♦	♦

Language	6f	6g	6h	6i	7	8	%	9	10	%	11	12	12a	12b	12c	12d	12e	13	14
Hadza			0	3	20	3	15	x	x	x	5	(1)	(♦)				x		
Sandawe			0	5	13	6	46	x	x	x	5	1	♦				x	♦	(♦)
Khwe	♦	♦	3/4	9	31	20	64	14	12	86	5/6	1	♦				x	♦	♦
Kua	♦	♦	4/5	9/10	32	18	56	17	11	65	5	1	♦				x	♦	♦
G|ui	♦	♦	8	13	56	40	71	36	32	89	5	2	♦	♦			0	♦	♦
Khoekhoe	♦		1	5	14	12	86	4	4	100	5	1	♦				x	♦	♦
Ju|'hoan	♦		6	12	58	36	62	31	24	77	5	4	♦	♦	♦	♦	4	♦	♦
ǂHoan ??	♦	♦	7	13	?	35	?	?	27	?	5	4	♦	♦	♦	♦	?	♦	♦
!Xoon	♦	♦	9	17	88	63	72	52	43	83	5	4	♦	♦	♦	♦	8	♦	♦
ǂKhomani	♦		4	11	31	26	84	16	14	88	5/6	3/4	♦	♦	♦	♦	?	♦	♦

Note: 1 ? no information; preliminary analysis; . . ./. . . alternative analyses; feature is: x not applicable; blank absent; ♦ present; (. . .) present in restricted form.

It is well known that Standard Khoekhoe, too, does not follow the Southern African Khoesan trend in some respects. In this survey it turns out to be closer to the eastern African languages in nine features: 1, 2b, 3b, 6, 6h–9–10, 6i, 7. To a large extent, this is due to its more reduced phoneme inventory; in the features 1, 2a–b, 3a, and 4, it is even the language with the lowest sample value. Since this divides the Khoe family, a somewhat trivial conclusion is that also inventory size is not directly diagnostic for genealogical classifications.

Turning to what used to be subsumed under the umbrella term "San" languages, only distantly or non-related G|ui, Ju|'hoan, ǂHoan, and !Xoon stand out in having a particularly large number of segments in the whole system and its subparts: 1, 2b, 3b, 6h, 6i, 7, 8, 9, 10. !Xoon holds the record in terms of inventory size, its enormous distance from all other figures being in itself a problem that deserves some explanation. The phenomenon as such can clearly be related to an extensively employed process of series formation by elaborating stop consonants, and clicks in particular; this correlates with the availability of elaboration gestures (6). Three of the four above-mentioned languages: !Xoon, G|ui, and ǂHoan cluster geographically in south-central Botswana, while Ju|'hoan appears to be isolated in the north-western Kalahari. (Languages in between such as Naro and ǁAni have smaller inventory sizes; speech varieties closer to the southwest, belonging to the Ju and Tuu, groups, are not yet documented.)

Other features pattern somewhat differently, but they usually involve two or more languages from this "complex core" group in addition to languages not belonging there. Thus, ǂKhomani associates with this group in showing at least the vowel colourings pharyngealization and glottalization (12–12b–12c), and only with !Xoon and ǂHoan regarding the existence of bilabial (5–5a) and glottalized nasal clicks (6e). Also Khwe and Kua are linked to the core group with respect to uvular (4a) and palatal plosives (4b), as well as a special type of cluster offset (6g).

In general, it seems that the surveyed features hardly ever coincide with genealogical groups. They also do not correspond to the major morphosyntactic split running through Southern African Khoesan between Khoe–Kwadi and Non-Khoe, which partly follows genealogical lines; an exception are multiple vowel colourings (12a–d), apparently restricted to the Non-Khoe group. Thus, phonetic-phonological isoglosses seem to even less "respect" genealogical boundaries; instead, many of them indicate areal patterns.

It should be noted that there exist systematic implicational relations between certain features due to inherent properties of the relevant sounds. Isoglosses that are not independent from others would have a different status for grouping Khoesan languages. For example, Traill (1980: 187) states that "preglottalized nasals only exist in languages with glottalized vowels"; considering Güldemann's (2001: 12f.) analysis that nasal clicks behave phonologically like egressive nasals, the above correlation could be extended to preglottalized nasal clicks (6e) which also occur in languages with vowel glottalization only (12c). In a parallel fashion, it is hypothesized by Güldemann (2001: 41f.) that a plain posterior plosive exists as a cluster offset (6g) only in languages with a uvular egressive (4a), or that languages having clusters (6h) will always possess the one with a posterior fricative offset (6f). Finally, the predominantly high figures in the columns of 7/8 per cent and 9/10 per cent reveal that clicks have a greater tendency than non-clicks of being elaborated by co-articulations, in particular in the form of clusters (6–6h). This seems to be increased the more a language relies on clicks for the distinction of lexical meaning (3b/1 per cent).

4 TOWARD A TYPOLOGICAL PROFILE OF KHOESAN

The most important conclusion from this typological survey is that the Khoesan group as a whole does not share a large number of significant linguistic features, neither in the morphosyntactic domain nor in phonetics and phonology. Clicks aside, there is no such thing as a "Khoesan language type".

Another significant observation mentioned previously is that sample subgroups established by morphosyntactic and phonetic-phonological properties rarely match. These two domains can, therefore, not be combined when integrating Khoesan or its subgroups into the African context.

Since the phonological function of clicks is such a quirky feature, not much can be said about Khoesan sound design vis-à-vis other African languages. It must be recognized, however, that not only the existence of clicks fails to consistently single out all languages subsumed under Khoesan vis-à-vis other African languages, but also the impact of clicks on the phoneme inventory: a Bantu language like Yeyi (Sommer and Vossen 1992) has a more complex ingressive system than such Khoesan languages as Hadza, Sandawe, Kwadi, or Khoekhoe. Excluding Hadza (and partly Sandawe), the only unique Khoesan feature is its typical phonotactic stem pattern in conjunction with the special role of clicks in the lexicon; the typological or historical significance of this feature remains to be determined.

In morphosyntactic terms, too, Khoesan-internal diversity prevents a comparison of the group as a whole with other language groups on the continent. Meaningful generalizations mostly apply to the Khoesan subgroups established above: (a) Hadza, (b) Sandawe + Khoe–Kwadi, and (c) Non-Khoe (Tuu, ǂHoan, and Ju).

Hadza seems to fit well in the East African context; at the same time, its overall isolation in the present Khoesan survey confirms Sands's (1998b) finding that a genealogical relation to any other language in this group is quite unlikely.

Sandawe, besides its East African affinities, is typologically leaning towards southern Africa in sound design *and* grammar. This relation is reciprocated in grammar by one Southern African Khoesan group: Khoe languages display a typological connection only to East Africa, according to Heine and Vossen's (1981: 429–35) typological classification of African languages based on noun categorization, nominal case marking, verbal derivation, and constituent order. Kwadi shares some of these features and is most likely related genealogically to Khoe so that this language can be added here. In phonetic-phonological terms Khoe is squarely embedded in its southern African context.

Non-Khoe in southern Africa turns out to be another robust structural type. It is overall homogeneous regarding phonological complexity for both consonants and vowels; many of its members beat most other languages in the world in terms of inventory size. Morphosyntactically it shows some interesting parallels with isolating West African languages of the Kwa and Benue-Congo families. At the same time, it displays features which are rare on the African continent; for example, a special noun categorization type (Güldemann 2000b), complex and as yet poorly understood number marking (see *inter alia* Collins 1998), and a special syntactic treatment of postverbal nominal constituents (Güldemann and Vossen 2000: 109f.; cf. feature 5).

As mentioned above, the distribution of some linguistic characteristics across Khoesan shows areal patterns not following genealogical lines. These can best be explained by a partly shared history of certain linguistic populations in a geographic sub-area. While this is especially clear for the Khoesan split of eastern vs. southern African languages, features also demarcate compact zones within Southern African Khoesan (cf., e.g., palatalization as discussed by Traill 1980: 175–82). If such features cluster, it is possible to speak of linguistic areas whose identification is essential for a better synchronic and diachronic understanding of Khoesan in general. Although research on language contact and areal subgroups has only started, some such southern African Khoesan areas as the Cape region (cf. Güldemann 2002, 2006b) and the central Kalahari (cf. Traill and Nakagawa 2000) already emerge from the available data.

NOTE

1 I am grateful to C. Collins, E.D. Elderkin, and B. Sands for making available and explaining their first-hand data to me. It goes without saying that the present analyses are not necessarily theirs.

REFERENCES

Beach 1938; Bell and Collins 2001; Bleek 1869; Collins 1998; Dempwolff 1934/35; Dickens 2005; Doke 1936; Elderkin 1989; Greenberg 1959; Gruber 1973, 1975; Güldemann 1998b, 1999, 2000b, 2001, 2002, 2004b, 2006b; Güldemann and Vossen 2000; Hagman 1977; Heine 1975b, 1999; Heine and Vossen 1981; Kagaya 1993; Köhler 1981; Lanham and Hallowes 1956; Nakagawa 1996a, 1996b; Nichols 1992; Sands 1998b; Sands *et al.* 1996; Snyman 1975a; Sommer and Vossen 1992; Traill 1980, 1985, 1997, 2001; Traill and Nakagawa 2000; Vossen 1997a.

CHAPTER FOUR

PHONETICS AND PHONOLOGY

1 HADZA

Bonny Sands

The sound system of Hadza described here is largely based on Sands *et al.* (1996), and on short periods of fieldwork conducted by the author in 1991 and 1997.

1.1 Vowels

Hadza contrasts only seven vowels: */i e a o u ĩ ũ/*. Vowel length, pharyngealization, glottalization and breathiness are not contrastive, and vowel nasalization is only marginally contrastive. The five vowel qualities are shown in (1).

(1) Hadza vowel qualities

i	*ŋǁi-ʔi*	'put poison on it (F.SG)'
e	*ŋǁe-ʔe*	'put poison on it (M.SG)'
a	*ŋǁa-ʔa*	'scavenge'
o	*ŋǁ'o-ʔo*	'wash, bathe'
u	*ŋǁuʔú-*	'snore'

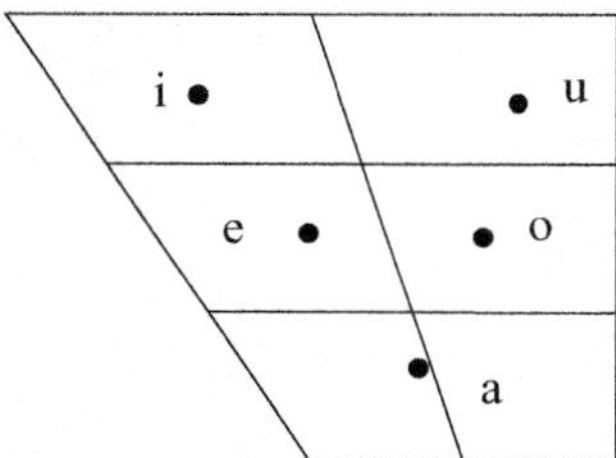

The nasalized vowels */ĩ/* and */ũ/* occur in very few lexical items, e.g. *ɬĩɦe-* 'to blow nose', *saɦũɦe-* 'be quiet!'. Contrastively nasalized vowels may have resulted from the deletion of a voiceless nasalized aspirated click, with the retention of the nasalization and aspiration.

Phonetic vowel length occurs when two vowels of identical vowel quality occur together, either through elision of a consonant, e.g. */kʰaɦa/* ~ [kʰaː] 'to climb', or through the addition of a morpheme, e.g. [ʔukʰwaːkʰo] (*/'ukʰwa-akʰo/*) 'it is an arm'.

1.2 Consonants

1.2.1 Egressive consonants

Oral stops distinguish five places of articulation, while nasal stops distinguish all of these except glottal, and also contrast the palatal-alveolar place (cf. 2).

(2)

	Bilabial	Alveolar	Palatal-(alveolar)	Velar	Labio-velar	Glottal
Plosive	pʰ p b	tʰ t d		kʰ k g	kʰw kw gw	ʔ
Ejective	(p')			k'	k'w	
Nasal	m	n	ɲ	ŋ	ŋw	
Prenasalized stop	mpʰ mb	ntʰ nd		ŋkʰ ŋg		
Central approximant			j		w	ɦ
Lateral approximant		l				

Ejectives (cf. 2), fricatives (cf. 3) and prenasalized stops (cf. 2), each only contrast at three places of articulation, while affricates (cf. 3) contrast at only two places of articulation.

(3)

	Labio-dental	Alveolar	Palato-alveolar
Prenasalized affricate		nts ndz	ndʒ
Central affricate		ts dz	dʒ
Lateral affricate			ƛ
Ejective central affricate		ts'	tʃ'
Ejective lateral affricate			tƛ'
Central fricative	f	s	ʃ
Lateral fricative		ɬ	

Hadza has a three-way Voice Onset Time (VOT) contrast in the plosives, i.e. voiceless unaspirated /*p t k*/, voiceless aspirated /*pʰ tʰ kʰ*/ and voiced /*b d g*/. Prenasalized stops contrast only voiceless aspirated /*mpʰ ntʰ ŋkʰ*/ and voiced /*mb nd ŋg*/, and affricates contrast only voiceless unaspirated /*nts ts ntʃ tʃ*/ and voiced /*ndz dz dʒ*/. Both stops /*p' k' k'w*/ and affricates /*ts' tʃ' tƛ'*/ occur with a glottalic egressive mechanism, but fricatives /*f s ʃ ɬ*/ and lateral affricates /*tƛ*/ are always voiceless. The ejective bilabial /*p'*/ occurs in only a few lexical items.

All of the egressive consonants occur in word-initial position, as in (4), and all but /*ŋw*/ have been documented in intervocalic position (cf. Sands *et al.* 1996). The consonant /*ntʃ*/ is only known from two lexical items, i.e. /*ntʃa*/ 'clitoris', /*ŋ‖'intʃino-bi*/ 'fangs', and has not been previously recognized as a contrastive consonant.

(4) Words containing contrastive egressive consonants

Bilabial:

pʰ	*pʰandʒu-pʰe*	'(is a) plant sp.'
p	*patáku'ʃé*	'palm of hand'
b	*badá*	'hole'
p'	*p'á'ùwé-*	'to split'
m	*mákʰo*	'clay pot'
mpʰ	*mpʰalamaɦo-kʰo*	'slingshot'
mb	*mbalata-kʰo*	'cockroach'

Labiodental:

f	*fá-*	'to drink'

Alveolar:

t^h	t^h*asé*	'long'
t	*titʃ'i-*	'black'
d	*daʕaŋga*	'flour'
n	*nát*^{h}*i*	'donkey'
nt^h	nt^h*uli-bi*	'beer'
nd	*ndag*^{w}*e-ko*	'notch'
s	*sámaka-p*^{h}*i*	'three'
l, ɾ	*lalá-k*^{h}*o*	'gazelle'
ɬ	*ɬanó*	'python'
ts	*tsipití*	'porcupine'
ts'	*ts'áke-*	'to steal'
nts	*ntsá-k*^{h}*o*	'star'
dz	*dzá-*	'come!'
ndz	*ndzop*^{h}*a*	'bottle'

Palato-alveolar/palatal:

ʃ	*ʃamu-ko*	'Swahili'
tʃ	*tʃatʃa*	'galago sp.'
'ʃ'	*tʃ'á-k*^{h}*o*	'guineafowl'
ntʃ	*ntʃa*	'clitoris'
dʒ	*dʒándʒai*	'leopard'
ndʒ	*ndʒa*	'reedbuck'
j	*jámu-a*	'land'
tʎ	*tʎákáte*	'rhinoceros'
tʎ'	*tʎ'áʔa-*	'to sing'

Velar:

k^h	k^h*alimo*	'animal'
k	*káŋga*	'mongoose sp.'
g	*gaʃa-bi*	'honey beer'
k'	*k'apáku-bi*	'jaws'
$ŋk^h$	$ŋk^h$*ólo-'ák*^{h}*o*	'(is a) heart'
ŋg	*ŋgat*^{h}*á*	'head ornament'
ŋ	*ŋaŋa*	'kind of fruit'

Labialized velar:

k^hw	k^h*wala-*	'to vomit'
kw	*kwa'í*	'warthog'
gw	*gwanda-k*^{h}*o*	'shirt'
k'w	*k'wa'u-k*^{h}*o*	'eggshell'
ŋw	*ŋwapo-k*^{h}*o*	'ditch'
w	*watʃ'o*	'mongoose sp.'

Glottal:

ʔ	*ʔá'ɦú*	'skin'
ɦ	*ɦaka*	'to go'

1.2.2 Click consonants

The nine contrastive clicks of Hadza are shown in (5). All occur word-initially and medially, as in (6). Hadza has three types of clicks: dental (central) [ǀ], alveolar (central) [!] and palatal-alveolar (lateral) [ǁ]. These types occur with three click accompaniments: voiceless oral [ǀ, ! and ǁ], voiced nasal [ŋǀ, ŋ!, ŋǁ], and voiceless nasal with glottalization [ŋ̊ǀ', ŋ̊!', ŋ̊ǁ']. Tucker *et al.* (1977) record a bilabial click in a stem used in greeting a long lost sibling, but we were only able to elicit this stem, */pʰaʔa-/*, with a bilabial stop which may be preceded by a kiss on one's hand.

(5)

	Dental	Alveolar	Palatal-(alveolar)
Central oral click	ǀ	!	
Lateral oral click			ǁ
Central nasal click	ŋ̊ǀ' ŋǀ	ŋ̊!' ŋ!	
Lateral nasal click			ŋ̊ǁ' ŋǁ

(6) Words illustrating contrastive consonants of Hadza

Dental:

ǀ	*ǀútʰi-*	'neck'	*ǀaǀa*	'large flat rock'
ŋ̊ǀ'	*ŋ̊ǀ'ats'e*	'to reheat'	*táŋ̊ǀ'e*	'belt'
ŋǀ	*'ŋǀátʰá*	'tongue'	*ǀikílí'ŋǀa*	'pinky (finger)'

Alveolar:

!	*á'!ákú-*	'to jump over'	*!o'!ó-kʰo*	'back of head'
ŋ̊!'	*ŋ̊!'ojé*	'wax'	*ɦaŋ̊!'ákʰo*	'rock'
ŋ!	*ŋ!ána*	'mongoose sp.'	*ŋ!ikiŋ!i-*	'to push a lot'

Palatal-alveolar (lateral):

ǁ	*ǁa'pʰá*	'stump'	*kaǁá-*	'to hunt'
ŋ̊ǁ'	*ŋ̊ǁ'ekʰwá*	'root sp.'	*kʰaŋ̊ǁ'é*	'to jump'
ŋǁ	*'ŋǁáʔa-*	'to scavenge'	*koŋǁaɦete*	'man with two wives'

1.3 Segmental phonology

1.3.1 Consonantal variation

The alveolar click */!/* can be produced with a range of phonetic realizations, from a very quiet, weak click, to a loud pop, or as a noisy "flapped" or "plopped" click in which the tongue tip makes contact with the bottom of the mouth after the release of the front click closure. Denti-alveolar, alveolar, and post-alveolar closures for */!/* are in free variation.

In intervocalic position, the approximant [l] can appear as [ɾ].

Ejective velar */k'/* is pronounced with heavy frication [kx' kʎ̝̊'] by some speakers.

The voiceless nasalized clicks */ŋ̊ǀ' ŋ̊!' ŋ̊ǁ'/* are always produced with voiceless nasal airflow during the click closure.

When a vowel precedes the click, either within a morpheme, e.g. [hãŋ̊!'a-kʰo] 'rock', or across morpheme boundaries, the vowel becomes partially nasalized.

An initial aspirated obstruent or voiceless click will have a shorter VOT (i.e. less aspiration) than the obstruent in a phonologically identical second syllable. Many of these cases derive from a morphologically productive rule of initial syllable reduplication to indicate emphasis or to derive an agentive nominal.

One lexical item has a click/non-click variant: [ʔets'a-k^{h}o] ~ [ŋ̊|'ets'a-k^{h}o] 'house'.

A few lexical items have an alternation between */kw'/* and */p'/* counterpart, e.g. [p'aʔu-] ~ [kw'aʔu-] 'to split'.

1.3.2 Vocalic variation

Vowel height harmony takes place across morpheme boundaries within a phonological word. Mid vowels */e o/* are raised to [ɪ] and [ʊ] before a high vowel */i u/*, e.g. */haŋ| 'akwe + p^{h}i/* [haŋ|'akwɪp^{h}i] 'are gullets', */hik'o + p^{h}i/* [hik'ʊp^{h}i] 'are wooden-tipped arrows'. Vowel harmony can spread to earlier syllables, e.g. */loʔo + p^{h}i/* [lʊʔʊp^{h}i] 'are long horns', but cf. */tɬ'oma + p^{h}i/* [tɬ'omap^{h}i] 'are heads'.

Final vowels often become voiceless [i̥ e̥ ḁ o̥ u̥] in final position, particularly when preceded by a glottal stop or any other voiceless stop.

2 SANDAWE

Edward D. Elderkin

As analysed here, Sandawe syllable structure is made up of:

(7) Consonant
Labiovelarisation
Vowel
Closure
Nasalisation
Voicing
Final nasality
Tonal values

Syllables in word-initial position always have a consonant and a vowel. Word-internally, syllables without initial consonant are heard.

2.1 Consonants

(8)

	Clicks			Non-clicks					
Fricative				f		s	ɬ	x	h
Glottalised/ejective	!'	|'	‖'			ts'	tɬ'	k'	ʔ
Aspirated	!^{h}	|^{h}	‖^{h}	p^{h}	t^{h}	ts^{h}		k^{h}	
Voiceless	!̥	|̥	‖̥	p	t	ts	tl	k	
Voiced	!̬	|̬	‖̬	b	d	dz	dlʒ	g	
Nasalised/nasal	!̃	|̃	‖̃	m	n				
Sonorant				w	r	j	l		

The non-click lateral series shows a gap: there is no aspirated laterally released plosive. Little friction is heard in the lateral release of *tl*. The laterals have a humped tongue, not a flat one.

The friction of /, *s* and *ts'* is alveolar, more forward for the release of /; that of *ts^{h}*, *ts* and *dz* is alveolo-palatal. Following a vowel, the glottalised clicks are preceded by a short nasal segment.

2.2 Labiovelarisation

A syllable which has *i*, *e* or *a* as the vowel quality may have distinctive labiovelarisation at the syllable beginning. This is shown by *w*; note that *w* is a symbol which therefore can represent one of three phonological units – a consonant, labiovelarisation and a closure (see next section): all three uses are present in example (16).

(9) *tʰwĭː* 'bird'
tl'wã̂ː 'rain'

In principle, labial consonants may not appear with labiovelarisation; however, some recent loans show this.

(10) *ʔùbwâbwà* < Sw. *ubwabwa* 'type of porridge'

h and *ʔ* are also not found with labiovelarisation; but see (21).

2.3 Vowels

(11)
i *u*
e *o*
a

Vowels may be long or short, three or two moras respectively. They also occur nasalised. Nasalised vowels are usually long, but short nasalised vowels may be heard in conversation. Vowels are usually voiced.

2.4 Closure

The following are found as closures to a syllable, following the vowel; each has the value of one mora.

(12)
m *n*
w *j*

(13) *ǀ'áːm̀* (3M.SG) 'old, worn out'
ǀ̃íǹ 'to eat (meat)'
ɬáːẁ (3M.SG) 'good'
ǀ̥èẃ 'buffalo'

The closures *w* and *j*, following short vowels, sometimes give pitch patterns identical to those on long vowels.

(14) *tʰâː* 'He runs.'
tʰâj 'You run.'

Occasionally, two closures have to be analysed in the same syllable; this has been noted with *jj* (see 18 below), and with *mm*.

(15) *ǀ'áːm̀m̀sésì̥*
ǀ'áːm̀ m̀sé sì̥
old 3M.SG seem 1SG
'I thought it was an old one.'

Sequences of a closure and a similarly articulated initial consonant are also found.

(16) *k'wăːẃwòː*
k'wăːẃ wà ò
be ill MLT 1PL
'We are ill.'

2.5 Nasalisation

Syllables may be oral or nasalised.

(17) *ĩ* *ũ*
ẽ *õ*
ã

Before a pause, the auditory impression is often that a nasalised segment finishes with velar nasality. Phonetically both the vowel and any ordinarily oral closures following it are nasalised, but here, nasalisation is only transcribed on the vowel.

(18) *hèwéʔ`w̥ã̀jj*
hèwé ʔ`w̥à j̀ ː̃̀
3M.SG MLT PRO SPEC
'those of his'

2.6 Voicing

Sandawe has voiceless vowels. They are oral and short and, following most consonants, only the two qualities *i̥* and *u̥* are found.

(19) *ǀ̥ísì̥* 'I come.'
ǀ̥îsù̥ 'She'll come.'
tʰásḭnóː 'liver'

However, a glottal stop is often released without a voiced vowel following, but the period after the release has the length value of a short syllable; the voiceless vowel which results takes its quality from the adjacent vowels, usually the preceding vowel: this is transcribed by specifying voicelessness and tone, but omitting a vowel symbol.

(20) *bábáʔ`t̥ò* 'cockroach'
dìʔ̥̀sěː 'old man'
wáʔ̥́méː 'his companion'

Occasionally, after *ʔ*, the syllabicity is lost: this often happens in forms of the verb 'give', where an otherwise impermissible co-occurrence of glottal stop and labiovelarisation is then heard:

(21) *ʔíʔwàː* 'Give it to them.'

Syllabicity may also be lost when ʔ`̥ is clause-final in a clause introduced by *hí*, when the glottal stop is often heard without audible release.

(22) ^{1}*hísà* ^{2}*ǀ̥î:ʔ* ‘when she came’

2.7 Syllable-final nasality

A short nasal segment is sometimes found, with no moric value, in syllable-final position.

This may be (i) homorganic to a following consonant, giving phonetically a prenasalised consonant.

(23) *hù*^{m}*bù* ‘cow’
mì^{n}*dà* ‘shamba’

Some donor languages, for example, Bantu languages, have prenasalised consonants as phonological units; in Sandawe I have preferred not to analyse them as such, partly because of the existence of (ii) following. Other reasons include their absence in word-initial positions, the very frequent ^{m}*bo* (for which alternatives exist, *ʔì*^{m}*bô* or *bô*) being the only exception. Loans with initial prenasalised consonants in the donor language lose them in Sandawe; unassimilated loans retain the prenasalisation.

(24) *dêgè* ‘aeroplane’ < Sw. *ndege*

(ii) Non-homorganic to a following consonant; there are two types:

(a) a labial nasal, ^{m}, can be found before a glottal stop (which is initial in the following syllable).

(25) *tl'ȍ*^{m}*ʔ`ş̥é* ‘to speak a lot of nonsense’

(b) a velar nasal, ^{ŋ}, is found only in a couple of instances, where a following velar plosive has been deleted.

(26) *tá:*$^{ŋ'}$*nà* ‘to, in front’ (cf. *tá:*^{ŋ}*gì̥* ‘in front’, *nà* ‘to’)

In some places, I found it difficult to distinguish between a nasalised vowel followed by a consonant and an oral vowel followed by a short nasal homorganic to the following consonant. The interaction and possible overlap between these two needs to be assessed further.

3 SOUTH AFRICAN KHOESAN

3.1 Northern Khoesan

Amanda L. Miller

3.1.1 Introduction

While there are many Northern Khoesan varieties, Juǀ'hoan is the only one which has been described in some detail. There is a 5,000 word (2,000 root) dictionary (Dickens 1994), and I have recorded a database containing six speakers' production of all of these roots, as well as all of the complex words in Dickens, and 300 new words. Ekoka !Xun is the next best described variety with a dictionary (König and Heine 2008) containing about 4,200 !Xun entries and a comprehensive grammar (Heine and König 2012). On

Okongo !Xung there exist a 1,200-wordlist and a basic grammar. Other varieties have been ignored completely, despite differences from Ju|'hoan in their phonologies. In this section, I will focus on Ju|'hoan phonology, but I will attempt to cover known interesting properties of other NK varieties not found in Ju|'hoan in the relevant sections. The sound inventory of Ju|'hoan contains 89 consonants and thirteen oral vowels. There are six monophthongal vowels and seven diphthongs, as well as four contrastive vowel phonation types: modal, breathy, glottalized and epiglottalized.[1] All of the non-modal vowel phonation types have restricted tonal patterns. The consonant inventory contains 47 click consonants, which are organized into four main click types, with twelve different click accompaniments.

3.1.2 *Vowels*

There are five monophthongal oral vowel phonemes in Ju|'hoan, as well as [ə], a raised variant of /*a*/ that occurs before high vowels and [m]. Figure 4.1 shows a scatterplot of the first and second formant frequencies of all six vowels produced by three female and three male speakers in acoustic vowel space. Additionally, there are the diphthongs [əi] and [əe], which are allophones of /*i*/ and /*e*/ that occur only after consonants with secondary dorsal articulations, which includes the back clicks [! ǁ] (Miller-Ockhuizen 1999b, 2003; Miller 2011). Snyman (1975a, 1975b) and Dickens (1994) claim that there are diphthongs [ui oe oa] as well. The initial portion of these rimes is glide-like when there is a monotonal root tone pattern. If the root tone pattern is bitonal (SL–L, L–H or H–L), then the diphthong appears as a glide vowel sequence. The diphthongs [əu, ao] do occur, and appear to be separate phonemes, as I have not yet uncovered any predictable environment where they occur.

Ju|'hoan vowels are produced with one of five voice qualities. Oral vowels are produced with modal phonation, and contrast with comparable nasal vowels, breathy vowels, epiglottalized vowels, glottalized vowels, and diphthongs in voice quality (partially breathy, and partially epiglottalized vowels) (Miller-Ockhuizen 2003; Miller 2007).

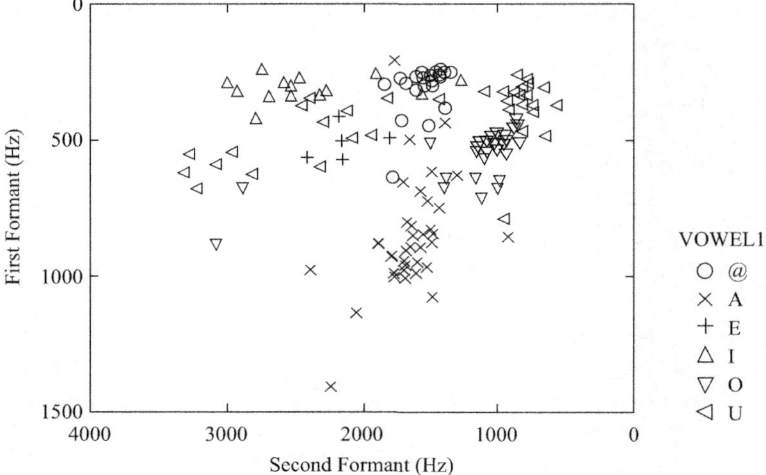

FIGURE 4.1 1ST AND 2ND FORMANT FREQUENCIES OF JU|'HOAN ORAL VOWELS

Nasalized vowels are limited, and only [ũ ĩ ã] monophthongs occur, as well as the nasalized diphthongs [ə̃ĩ ə̃ẽ ə̃ũ ãõ] and [õã õẽ ũĩ]. There are no mid nasalized vowels. Breathy and glottalized vowels of all five vowel qualities occur.

Epiglottalized vowels are always non-high back vowels. There are fully epiglottalized vowels, and partially epiglottalized vowels, which are followed by modal offglides. Fully epiglottalized vowels are always non-high back vowels, resulting in the following phonemes: [o̰o̰ a̰a̰ o̰a̰ a̰o̰]. Partially epiglottalized vowels allow only non-high back vowels in the initial epiglottalized portion, but all vowel types occur in the second modal portion of the rime. The following partially epiglottalized vowels occur: [a̰a a̰e a̰i a̰o a̰u o̰a o̰o o̰i o̰e o̰o o̰u]. Additionally, epiglottalized vowels [a̰] and [o̰] occur in CVm roots. Epiglottalized vowels have vastly different first through third formants from like quality modal vowels.

Glottalized vowels are most commonly monophthongal. Thus, we find [aʔa eʔe iʔi oʔo uʔu]. The diphthongs [əʔe əʔi əʔo əʔu oʔa uʔi] occur as well. The raised non-high back vowels also co-occur with <m> in the following combinations: [ʊʔm əʔm].

Nasalization can occur with any other phonation type. However, the other vowel phonation types never co-occur with each other. That is, we never find breathy epiglottalized vowels, breathy glottalized vowels or glottalized epiglottalized vowels. However, we do find epiglottalized nasal vowels, breathy nasal vowels and glottalized nasal vowels. This seems to be a general OCP constraint against any two guttural features within a root, since non-modal vowel types (besides nasal) never co-occur with aspirated, glottalized or uvularized consonants, and medial consonants never bear guttural features (Miller-Ockhuizen 2003; Miller 2007).

While Snyman (1970, 1975a, 1975b) and Dickens (1994) maintain that there is a vowel length contrast in Ju|'hoan, there is no evidence to support their claim. There are no minimal pairs. Rather, all monosyllabic words contain long vowels due to a minimality constraint in the language, and there is no contrast. This is supported by the fact that single vowels in monosyllabic roots are nearly twice as long as single vowels in either syllable of bisyllabic forms (Miller-Ockhuizen 2000, 2003).

Height harmony in Ju|'hoan governs the co-occurrence of different vowel types within the root. I mentioned above that [ə] is a raised variant of [a] that occurs only before high vowels, while [a] only occurs before [a], whether the following vowel is within the same syllable as part of a diphthong, or in the second syllable of a bisyllabic root. The high vowels only co-occur with other high vowels, and there are a few alternations where root high vowels are realized as lower variants when preceding the diminutive suffix [ma], such as in the pairs *!ú* [!ú] 'name' and *!úmà* [!əúmà] 'grandchild; namesake', *tsú* [tsú] 'uncle' and *tsúmà* [tsəúmà] 'nephew', *|'ùdshù* [|'ùdsʰù] 'mother-in-law', [|'ùdsʰəùmà] 'older sister-in-law'. Interestingly, [i e] also do not occur in the first syllable of bisyllabic roots.

3.1.3 Consonants

Ju|'hoan has one of the largest consonant inventories of the world's languages. The complete inventory is given in Tables 4.2 and 4.3 at the end of this section. Click and non-click consonants occur with all of the same manner and guttural features. There is a four-way VOT contrast between plain voiceless, voiceless aspirated, voiced and voiced aspirated clicks and non-clicks. Similarly, all click and non-click consonants (except labials) occur with uvular fricated releases, and ejected uvular fricated releases. Miller-Ockhuizen (2003) and Miller (2007) refer to consonants with the ejected uvular fricated releases as epiglottalized consonants.

3.1.3.1 Egressive consonants

Ju|'hoan contrasts labial, alveolar, and velar stops and nasal consonants. Stop consonants exhibit a four-way VOT contrast. Nasal consonants are found at three places: [m n ŋ], though only [m n] occur in initial position of roots, and [ŋ] only occurs in root-final position following back consonants, especially [! ǁ]. The aspirated labial nasal [mʰ], only occurs in the diminutive plural morpheme, and never occurs in any recorded Ju|'hoan roots. Voiced and voiceless fricatives occur at the alveolar [s z] and palatal [ʃ ʒ] places of articulation. Additionally, there is a voiceless uvular fricative [χ]. Affricates [ts tʃ tχ kx' tʃx] also occur. The glides [w y] also occur, but are very infrequent. The flap [ɾ], along with [β], a spirantized variant of [b], only occur in medial position. The only two additional consonants which occur in medial position are [m n]. The limited contrasts in medial consonants can be seen as an additional aspect of the guttural OCP constraint mentioned with respect to limitations on vowel phonation type combinations, although the fact that consonants with guttural features never occur in medial position, even when the initial consonant is unmarked, signifies that there is a positional constraint at work as well (Miller-Ockhuizen 2003; Miller 2007). The set of medial consonants [β ɾ m u] can be thought of as unmarked laryngeally, having no laryngeal specifications.

3.1.3.2 Ingressive click consonants

Ju|'hoan has four click types, produced at dental [|], post-alveolar [!], palatal-alveolar [ǂ] and lateral alveolar [ǁ] places of articulation. These types exhibit a four-way VOT contrast, just as found with non-click consonants. Nasalized clicks also occur, and these exhibit a three-way VOT contrast with voiced aspirated nasal clicks, unaspirated nasalized clicks, and voiceless aspirated nasal clicks. Just as with non-clicks, voiceless unaspirated nasal clicks are lacking. All click types also occur with glottal releases, uvular fricated releases, uvular affricated ejected releases, voiced uvular fricated releases and voiced uvular affricated ejected releases.

Grootfontein !Xung has a retroflex click (Miller-Ockhuizen and Sands 1999, 2000; Miller 2011; Sands and Miller-Ockhuizen 1999, 2000; cf. also König and Heine 2008 for Ekoka !Xun). These two sounds have not yet been documented in any of the world's languages. Snyman (1997) argues that the retroflex click type is a variant of the alveolar click-type found in Ju|'hoan, but there is no phonological environment which would allow us to predict where one variant would occur. They meet the classical definition of separate phonemes. Sands and Miller-Ockhuizen (1999) and Sands (2010) argue that Proto-Northern-Khoesan contained five click types: *|, *ǂ, *!, *ǁ and *!!, with *!! merging with ! in Ju|'hoan and with ǁ in Northern Khoesan languages, such as Mangetti Dune !Xung and Ekoka !Xun. The proto-retroflex click type *!! remained a retroflex click type in Central Ju languages, such as Grootfontein !Xung. König and Heine (2008) describe a retroflex click type occurring in Ekoka !Xun. This click corresponds to the palatal click in other Ju languages (Sands 2010). Miller *et al.* (2011) have shown that this click type is not a true retroflex click, but rather a fricated post-alveolar click, which contrasts with the more typical abrupt post-alveolar click type that occurs in the same language.

3.1.3.3 Phonological patterns

Despite the places of articulation reflected in the click names, phonologically the dental and palatal click consonants pattern together with other front consonants in allowing a contrast between front and back vowels following them. The alveolar and lateral alveolar click types pattern with the back consonants in only allowing back vowels, and the cross-place diphthongs [əi, əe] following them (Miller-Ockhuizen 1999b, 2003; Miller 2011). Traill (1985: 89–92) dubbed this constraint, which is found in all Southern and Northern Khoesan varieties at least to some extent, the Back Vowel Constraint (BVC). He claims that all clicks are subject to the BVC and only allow back vowels following them. Front vowels following the dental and palatal [ǀ ǂ] click types arise through assimilation of a back vowel to a preceding front consonant and following front vowel. Miller-Ockhuizen (1999b) argues that there is no evidence in Juǀ'hoan that there are ever back vowels between front vowels and front clicks. That is, there are no [əe] or [əi] diphthongs following coronal consonants or front clicks. The diphthongs [əe əi] occur following secondarily dorsalized consonants: back clicks [ǃ ǁ] and uvularized click and non-click consonants. Miller-Ockhuizen (1999b) analyzes this as spreading of the [dorsal] feature from V-place onto the following front vowel, resulting in diphthongization of that vowel.

The BVC in Mangetti Dune !Xung is only active with high vowels (Miller-Ockhuizen and Sands 1999, Miller-Ockhuizen 1999b). The forward released lateral click [ǀǁ] patterns with the other back clicks [ǃ ǁ] in the language.

As mentioned earlier, there is also a guttural OCP constraint in Juǀ'hoan that rules out any two guttural features within a given root. McCarthy (1991, 1994) argues that pharyngeal and laryngeal features are grouped together under a guttural node, while Halle (1995) argues that they are grouped together under the laryngeal node. Miller-Ockhuizen's (2003) approach is more similar to Halle's approach. Table 4.1 below shows the frequency of occurrence of different consonant release properties with different vowel phonation types:

TABLE 4.1 CO-OCCURRENCE OF CONSONANT AND VOCALIC GUTTURAL FEATURES IN JUǀ'HOAN

Vowel ↓ Consonant→	Plain	Voiced	Aspirated	Ejected	Uvularized
Modal	521	242	243	261	179
Breathy	139	58	**1**	**1**	0
Glottalized	73	22	**1**	**1**	0
Epiglottalized	169	49	**4**	0	0
Total	902	371	249	263	179

All combinations of non-modal phonation types on consonants and vowels within the same root are bold in the table. Note that for most cases, there are no roots exhibiting these combinations. The one aberrant example containing a glottalized consonant and a glottalized vowel is in the word *ds'ò'ó* 'hartebeest'. The single example of a glottalized consonant with a breathy vowel is the word *dsù'ụ́* 'ostrich'. The single example of co-occurring aspiration and a breathy voiced vowel is *ǁʔ*^{h}*äöh* (which is phonetically [ŋ̥ǁ^{h}äöh]) meaning 'panda tree'. As was also found by Elderkin (1988: 132), the four words containing epiglottalized vowels and aspirated consonants all contain initial nasalized clicks. The four words are *!ʔ*^{h}*öäqn* (which is phonetically [ŋ̥!^{h}öäqn]) 'to bend', *nǂ*^{h}*äqnà* 'elephant's trunk', *nǂ*^{h}*äqò* '*Oxygonum alatum*', and *nǁ*^{h}*äqèn* 'carrot'.

TABLE 4.2 CONSONANT INVENTORY OF JUǀ'HOAN – STOPS, FRICATIVES AND APPROXIMATES

I. Simple consonants:	Bilabial	Labio-dental	Dental/ alveolar	Palatal	Dorsal	Glottal	Lateral alveolar
Vcl. pl. egr.	p		t		k	ʔ	
ingr.			ǀ	ǂ	!		ǁ
Vcl. asp. egr.	p^{h}		t^{h}		k^{h}		
pl. ingr.			ǀ^{h}	ǂ^{h}	!^{h}		ǁ^{h}
Pre-vd. asp. egr.	b^{ɦ}		d^{ɦ}		g^{ɦ}		
pl. ingr.			gǀ^{h}	gǂ^{h}	g!^{h}		
Vd. pl. egr.	b		d		g		
ingr.			gǀ	gǂ	g!		gǁ
Vcl. nsl. egr.							
ingr.			ǀ'	ǂ'	!'		ǁ'
Vcl. asp. egr.							
nsl. pl.[2] ingr.			ŋ̊ǀ'^{h}	ŋ̊ǂ'^{h}	ŋ̊!'^{h}		ŋ̊ǁ'^{h}
Vd. nsl. pl. egr.	m		n		ŋ		
ingr.			nǀ	nǂ	n!		nǁ
Vd. nsl. asp. pl.	m^{ɦ}						
ingr.			nǀ^{ɦ}	nǂ^{ɦ}	n!^{ɦ}		nǁ^{ɦ}
Vcl. fric.		f	s	c	x	h	
Vd. fric.		v	z	j			
Approximate	w		r	y			l

TABLE 4.3 THE CONSONANT INVENTORY OF JUǀ'HOAN – AFFRICATES

II. Affricates	Dental/alveolar	Palatal	Dorsal	Lateral alveolar
Vcl. affr. egr.	ts	tʃ		
Vcl. asp. affr. egr.	ts^{h}	tʃ^{h}		
Pre-Vd. asp. egr.				
affr. ingr.	ds^{h}	dʃ^{h}		
Vcl. eject. affr. egr.	ts̬	tj	kx', tkx'	
ingr.	ǀkx'	ǂkx'	!kx'	ǁkx'
Vd. eject. affr. egr.	tz'	tj		
ingr.	gǀkx'	gǂkx'	g!kx'	gǁkx'
Vcl. affr. with egr.	tsx	tʃx	tx	
Velar fric. release ingr.	ǀx	ǂx	!x	ǁx
Vd. affr. with egr.	dzx	dʒx		
Vel. fric. release ingr.	gǀx	gǂx	g!x	gǁx

3.2 Central Khoesan

3.2.1 Namibian Khoekhoe and !Gora

Wilfrid H.G. Haacke

3.2.1.1 Phoneme inventory

The phonetic description by Beach (1938) of the phoneme system of the "Hottentot" language was hailed as a classic and still remains valid in its essence. The present account is descriptive, following the conventional dichotomy between egressive consonants and clicks. (For an attempt to accommodate all kinds of consonants in a single paradigm, cf. Güldemann 2001.) Khoekhoegowab (N.Kh.) (Nama/Damara) in 1970 became the first Khoesan language to receive an officially recognized orthography. This orthography has, with minor amendments, been adhered to for language planning purposes ever since (see Haacke 1989).

3.2.1.1.1 VOWELS

Both N.Kh. and !Gora have a balanced basic system of five oral vowels: */i e a o u/*. (The sixth vowel mentioned by Beach, the central vowel, is a neutralized vowel and hence not phonemic.) Of these, all except the mid-front vowel */e/* have nasalized counterparts in certain phonotactic contexts. Laryngeal phonation is not used distinctively.

It is still customary to distinguish short and long (oral) vowels in N.Kh. (cf. *Nama/Damara Orthography No. 2*). This, however, is unfounded, as so-called "long" vowels are juxtaposed identical vowels, just as so-called "diphthongs" are juxtapositions of non-identical vowels. Each vowel in these combinations represents a separate syllable nucleus and is a distinct tone-bearing unit. Roots are consistently disyllabic, with the exception of (rare) trisyllabic roots that consist of a combination of a disyllabic with a monosyllabic morpheme. Contrary to conventional claims, no monosyllabic radicals occur; only monosyllabic grammatical formatives. Vowel juxtapositions in roots arise through the elision of the intervocalic consonant C_2 in the canonical structure $C_1V_1C_2V_2$. Only four consonants can occur as C_2: *w*, *r*, *m* and *n* (cf. Table 4.4). If the deleted intervocalic consonant was oral, the vowel combination will be oral ("long", if identical vowels; "oral diphthong", if not identical); if the consonant was nasal, the combination will be nasalized because of spreading ("nasal vowel", if identical; "nasal diphthong", if not identical). It follows that so-called "nasal" vowels have the same length as so-called "long" (oral) vowels, both consisting of quasi-geminates. "Nasal" vowels, thus, are a secondary development (through spreading), as originally Proto-Khoekhoe had only oral vowels.

TABLE 4.4 THE FOUR INTERVOCALIC CONSONANTS OF ROOTS IN N.KH.

	Oral	Nasal
Bilabial	*w* = [v/β/b]	*m*
Alveolar	*r*	*n*

Because of certain constraints applicable to vowel combinations, particularly to mid vowels, only the combinations presented in Table 4.5 occur.

TABLE 4.5 COMBINATIONS OF V_1 AND V_2 IN A ROOT (IN N.KH. ORTHOGRAPHY)

	C_2 was oral						C_2 was nasal				
	i_2	e_2	a_2	o_2	u_2		i_2	e_2	a_2	o_2	u_2
i_1	ī	–	–	–	–	i_1	î [ĩĩ]	–	(îa)	–	–
e_1	–	ē	–	–	–	e_1	–	–	–	–	–
a_1	ai	ae	ā	ao	au	a_1	âi	–	â [ãã]	–	âu
o_1	–	oe	oa	ō	–	o_1	–	–	ôa	–	–
u_1	ui	–	–	–	ū	u_1	ûi	–	ua	–	û [ũũ]

The following instances exemplify the historical development of so-called "long" and "nasal" vowels and oral and nasalized "diphthongs" (from Haacke 1999). While in the following cases both the original CVCV root and the truncated (so-called "monosyllabic") CVV or Cṽṽ root still exist next to each other, in most cases the source of the truncated root has been lost (cf. Table 4.6).

TABLE 4.6 HISTORICAL DEVELOPMENT OF VOWEL SEQUENCES IN N.KH.

Oral dissimilar vowels	**CV_1CV_2**	>	**CV_1V_2**	(so-called "oral diphthong")
	ǁgàrè	>	*ǁgàè*	'ape, mime'
Nasalized dissimilar vowels	**CV_1NV_2**	>	**$C\tilde{v}_1\tilde{v}_2$**	("nasal diphthong")
	tòmắ.s	>	[tõãs] = *tȍắ.s*	'wild cucumber'
Oral pseudo-geminates	**CV_1CV_1**	>	**CV_1V_1**	("long" vowel)
	pùrű	>	[pùű] = *pū*	'topple over' (tr.)
Nasalized pseudo-geminates	**CV_1NV_1**	>	**$C\tilde{v}_1\tilde{v}_1$**	("nasal" vowel)
	mùnű	>	[mȕű] = *mû*	'view, admire'

The fact that in rare cases certain words appear with oral vowels in some lects, while with nasal vowels in others – e.g. N.Kh. *ǀoa* against !Gora *ǀôa* ('kiss'), or Central Khoekhoe *ǀgôas* against Haiǁom and ǂĀkhoe *ǀgoas* ('girl') – shows that derivations are not in all cases strictly regular according to the lost C_2, but that mutations do occur. Beach (1938: 203) justifiably regards the !Gora tendency to replace nasal *ã* with oral *a* as an "individual and irregular peculiarity".

Beach (1938: 197) observes that in !Gora a close back vowel *u* as V_1 may be lowered to a "closish" *o*, if V_2 is a close vowel; e.g. *ǀkhuru* > *ǀkhoru* ('sour'), *ǀunib* > *ǀonib*. This co-occurrence of *o* with *i* should, however, not be misconstrued as justification for the erratic spelling of the ethnonyms *Kh**oi**kh**oi**n or *Kh**oi**san, as *Khoe* has its origin in *kh**o**Ce*. Original radicals with the structure ***CoCi** are not attested; hence a vowel combination *oi cannot exist either.

3.2.1.1.2 CONSONANTS

The inventories of consonants are very similar between N.Kh. and !Gora, with the fundamental difference that with egressive consonants voicing was still distinctive with !Gora but is no longer with N.Kh. N.Kh. has twelve authentic egressive consonants, while !Gora has fifteen (because of the voicing distinction). The click system is comparatively modest for Khoesan languages, with a balanced system of four primary articulations and five or six secondary articulations for N.Kh. and !Gora respectively.

3.2.1.1.2.1 EGRESSIVE CONSONANTS

When reading an N.Kh. text, a reader has to be aware of the fact that the plosives [p], [t] and [k] are regularly unvoiced in initial position, irrespective of the actual spelling. While in the older, church literature the use of *p*, *t*, and *k* against *b*, *d* and *g* is inconsistent, the standardized orthography as from 1970 has introduced a systematic distinction. In order to avoid diacritics, the letters *p*, *t* and *k* are used for roots with one of the higher tonal melodies (/`˝/, /´`/ and /˝´/); *b*, *d* and *g* for lower melodies (/˵`/, /˵´/, /``/, /`´/); e.g.

(27) ***tőá*** 'come to an end'
dȍà 'tear' (v.tr.)
dȍá 'tear' (v.intr.)

For the intervocalic bilabial consonant the same orthographic principle may be applied to achieve tonal distinctiveness (i.e. *b* against *p*), or a non-committal *w* may be used. The pronunciation is normally voiced and varies freely between [b~β~v].

In !Gora voicing is distinctive, but Beach (1938: 214) observes that because of the "very weak aspiration" of both voiced and unvoiced plosives, the distinction is very difficult to hear in fluent speech. Minimal pairs with identical tonal melody (here "mid level") do exist in !Gora:

(28)

!Gora	Khoekhoe	
taop [taop]	*táòb* [taop]	'shame'
daop [daop]	*dȁòb* [taop]	'road'

In N.Kh. the voiced plosives, together with some other consonants (particularly *h*, *m*, *kh*, *ts*, the !Gora "glottalic affricate" [kx'] and the delayed voiceless fricative release (X*h*) and the nasal accompaniment (X*n*) of clicks) have acted as depressor consonants that have created an additional, extra low toneme /˵/, and therewith two extra melodies commencing with that toneme: /˵`/ and /˵´/. The following tonogenetic relations exist between !Gora (designations by Beach) and N.Kh. (see also Table 4.7 for the egressive consonants):

(29)

!Gora (Beach)		Khoekhoe
mid-level + vcl.	>	/´`/
mid-level + vd.	>	/˵`/
low-mid falling + vcl.	>	/``/
low-mid falling + vd.	>	/˵´/

Subsequent to the depression the voiced consonants became devoiced in N.Kh., which makes this development a typical case of tonogenesis. (For details, cf. Beach 1938: 214ff.; also Haacke 1999: sections 2.2.3 and 2.3, where it is argued that tonogenesis actually caused a register split underlyingly.)

Certain consonant reflexes differ between !Gora and N.Kh. N.Kh. *ts* has two allophones in !Gora: [ts] and [th]. In !Gora [ts] appears before front vowels *i*, *î* and *e* or a morpheme boundary; [th] before all other vowels. Beach states that the !Gora plosive *kh* is the equivalent of the N.Kh. affricate *kx*. It is my impression, however, that the aspirated plosive is far more common in N.Kh. than the affricate.

!Gora contains a consonant that N.Kh. does not have: a glottalic affricate *kx'*, which Beach (1938: 223) also describes as a "velar 'scrape' plus a glottal plosive". This sound equates to the N.Kh. glottal stop, which is not represented in the orthography. It appears that in !Gora *kx'* is the non-depressor allophonic complement of the ordinary glottal stop, as cognate roots in N.Kh. in *all* recorded cases have a *non*-depressed melody, e.g.

TABLE 4.7 NAMIBIAN KHOEKHOE (N.KH.) AND !GORA EGRESSIVE CONSONANTS

Manner of air-stream release	State of the glottis	Language	Place of articulation						
			Bilabial	Labiodental	Dental	Alveolar	Prepalatal	Velar	Glottal
Plosive	voiceless	N.Kh.	p		t			k	’
		!Gora	p		t			k	’
	voiced	N.Kh.	V[b]V		–			–	
		!Gora	b		d			g	
	aspirated	N.Kh.						kh	
		!Gora			th			kh	
Ejective	voiceless	!Gora			(ts’)				
Affricate	voiceless	N.Kh.			ts			(kx)	
		!Gora			ts			kx’	
Fricative	voiceless	N.Kh.		(f)		s		x	h
		!Gora				s		x	h
	voiced	N.Kh.	V[β]V	V[v]V					
		!Gora							
Affricates	voiceless	N.Kh.						kx’	
	voiced	!Gora					(dʒ)		
Lateral	voiced	N.Kh.				(l)			
		!Gora							
Trill	voiced	N.Kh.				r			
		!Gora				r			
Nasal	voiced	N.Kh.	m		n				
		!Gora	m		n				

(30) !Gora Khoekhoe

kx'a	*ā* [ʔáà]	‘drink’
kx'up	*ūb* [ʔűúp̋]	‘pus’

On the other hand, roots commencing with the more frequent glottal stop in !Gora have both depressed and non-depressed cognates in N.Kh. This loss of distinction in !Gora may have been another symptom of the ongoing language death.

A parallel case exists between !Gora *ts'* and *ts*. However, only four words are on record with *ts'* (Meinhof 1930: 93): *ts'oa-l'ai* (‘a Bushman tribe’), *ts'uni-ts'e-b* (‘an animal in water’), *ts'ururu* (‘mosquito’), *ts'u-ts'u* (‘shut eyes’).

Another historical link between !Gora and the peripheral northern Damara dialects, i.e. excluding the Nama dialects, is revealed in the lateral variant [l] of the alveolar nasal *n*, which appears in the overwhelming majority of cases: Meinhof (1930: 89) lists *lū* (‘swear’) for !Gora, which is *nū* in Nama dialects, but *nū* or *lū* in Damara and Haiǁom dialects of N.Kh.

3.2.1.1.2.2 CLICKS

Both N.Kh. and !Gora have four primary click articulations or influxes (see Table 4.8); but while N.Kh. has five secondary articulations (effluxes), !Gora has a sixth one, a glottalic affricative efflux X*x'*. Like its egressive equivalent, it is a non-depressor much

TABLE 4.8 CLICK CONSONANTS OF N.KH. AND !GORA (SPELLING OF KHOEKHOE)

Release→ Click ↓		Velar			Glottal		
		voiceless					
		plosive	affricate	nasalized	stop	fricative	affricate !Gora only:
		g	kh	n	’	h	[x’]
Dental	ǀ	ǀg [ǀ]	ǀkh [ǀkx]	ǀn [ǀ]	ǀ [ǀ’]	ǀh [ǀ¯h]	[ǀx’]
Alveolar	!	!g [!]	!kh [!kx]	!n [!]	! [!’]	!h [!¯h]	[!x’]
Palatal	ǂ	ǂg [ǂ]	ǂkh [ǂkx]	ǂn [ǂ]	ǂ [ǂ’]	ǂh [ǂ¯h]	[ǂx’]
Lateral	ǁ	ǁg [ǁ]	ǁkh [ǁkx]	ǁn [ǁ]	ǁ [ǁ’]	ǁh [ǁ¯h]	[ǁx’]

more consistently than the glottal stop influx. Beach (1938: 250) also cites evidence of an earlier division of the velar plosive into a voiced and a voiceless version.

3.2.1.2 Phonotactics

To what has already been said above about the structure of radicals, it should be added that all roots commence with a consonant in N.Kh. and !Gora. Roots that in the N.Kh. orthography commence with a vowel, actually commence with a glottal stop, as Meinhof (1930) correctly indicates for !Gora; e.g. N.Kh. *ā+b* [ʔȁá-], !Gora *'a-b* (‘cavity’).

All consonants, including clicks but excluding the allophones [w] and [r], can occur as C_1, while C_2 is confined to the oral/nasal bilabials and alveolars *w*, *r*, *m* and *n*, as mentioned earlier. The alveolar plosive *t*/*d* ([t] in N.Kh.) is realized as alveolar trill [r] intervocalically, while the bilabial plosive can be realized as (voiced) fricative intervocalically: [b] or [β~v].

Apart from the elision of C_2 discussed above, V_2 can be elided alternatively, but only if C_2 is nasal and so it can still act as a tone-bearing unit: N.Kh. *ǀkhȁná* > *ǀkhȁń* ‘crack’ (v.intr.).

For statistical information regarding the distribution of onset and intervocalic consonants, final vowels, and tonal melodies, see Haacke (1999: tables 7–11).

3.2.1.3 Morphophonology

It is a characteristic feature of N.Kh. (and presumably !Gora) that assimilatory or dissimilatory changes are confined to a minimum, both in segmental and suprasegmental phonology. The most conspicuous assimilation in N.Kh. occurs around the bilabial plosive when preceded by a nasal consonant. The PGN marker of the third person masculine singular is realized as *-b* when preceded by a vowel (the most frequent situation); when preceded by a nasal (or, in loanwords, any other) consonant, it assimilates fully to the consonant and a latent vowel *-i* appears:

(31)	*khoe+**b***	‘man’
	*xam+**mi***	‘male lion’
	*ǀgan+**ni***	‘chunk of meat’
	skol+i [skol**li**]	‘school’ < Afrikaans: *skool*

Assimilation also occurs with, *inter alia*, the adjectival/adverbial suffix *-be*, as in (32):

(32) *ǁgam+**be**+b > *ǁgam**me**b* ‘tea-bush’ (also: *ǀgau**be**b*)

Palatalization of the velar plosive before front vowels is a regular occurrence, e.g. N.Kh. *kō* [koo] or *kē* [kʲee] ('see'), or the indicative marker spelt *tje* in !Gora and *gye* in the non-standardized orthography of N.Kh.

The consonant of the passive suffix *-he* (*-e* in some N.Kh. dialects) is reported to assimilate to the preceding consonant in !Gora, e.g. *ǁ'anǁ'an+he > *ǁ'anǁ'an+ne* ('be cooked').

With vowels the most conspicuous changes occur between the PGN markers and the oblique case marker *-a*, by way of either elision or assimilation. Various stages of development are manifested in different languages and dialects, e.g.

(33) *gu+a* > *ga* (N.Kh.), *gua* (!Gora, peripheral Damara) 3M.PL
di+a > *de* (N.Kh., !Gora) 3F.PL
-i+a > *-e* (N.Kh., !Gora) 3NEUT.SG
du+a > *do* (N.Kh., !Gora?) 2C.PL

3.2.2 Haiǁom

Thomas Widlok

Haiǁom and ǂAkhoe are variants of the Khoekhoe language which have been considered separate dialects (Haacke *et al.* 1997) but also virtual synonyms of one variant (Heikkinen, n.d.). Following my previous work (Widlok 1997: 123) I consider ǂAkhoe as "a way in which some Haiǁom speak their language" and the contributions to this volume concerning Haiǁom which are based on the late Terttu Heikkinen's work and my own work strongly reflect the way in which Haiǁom in the northern part of Namibia (north of the Omuramba Owambo) speak their language.

Due to its closeness to Nama/Damara, researchers who dealt with Haiǁom and ǂAkhoe have largely followed the orthographic conventions developed for Khoekhoegowab when describing the phonology of Haiǁom and ǂAkhoe. However, the work of Heikkinen, who carried out extensive linguistic work among ǂAkhoe speakers, is coloured by the fact that she had worked with both Nama speakers and speakers of northern variants of South African Khoesan, especially !Xũũ. Her phonological description of ǂAkhoe therefore reflects influences from both these neighbouring languages.

3.2.2.1 Vowels

Divergences with regard to orthographic conventions do not cause any problem with regard to the representation of the oral vowels /*i e a o u*/ that are shared by Nama and Haiǁom in both their short and long versions. The same applies to the nasal vowels /*ĩ ã ũ*/ and to the non-nasalised and nasalised diphthongs.

(34) Diphthongs of Haiǁom as in Nama:
ae ai ao au
oa oe
ui

(35) Nasalised diphthongs of Haiǁom as in Nama:
ai au
oa
ui
ia

Note that Heikkinen (n.d.: 17) further distinguishes *ia, ua, ui, oe* as phonetically corresponding to *ya, wa, wi, we*, respectively.

3.2.2.2 Consonants

3.2.2.2.1 EGRESSIVE CONSONANTS

As in Nama/Damara, Haiǁom has three plain stops: bilabial */p~b/*, dental */t~d/* and velar */k~g/*. Note that Heikkinen did not follow the standard Nama/Damara orthography to alternate between <*p t k*> and <*b d g*> according to tones. Instead she shifted her own orthography from <*b d g*> in the beginning to <*p t k*> in her later work.

The fricatives */s x h/* are also like those in Nama (see Hagman 1977: 7; Haacke 1988). The same applies to the two nasals */m/* and */n/* and to the alveolar flap [r].

Haiǁom (or at least ǂAkhoe) differs from Nama/Damara in that apart from the velar stop, it possesses two nasalised stops: bilabial *mb* and dental *nd* are common phonological features of ǂAkhoe. Examples for *mb* include lexemes that were definitely or probably borrowed from other languages: *mburu* 'plough', *mbabus* 'pumpkin', *mbisis* 'cat' – but also lexemes where such a connection has not been shown, e.g. *mboko* (nonsense [interjection]), *mbara* 'to have nose-bleeding', *mbi* 'to go mad'. Examples for *nd* seem to be predominantly lexemes that are identical with Nama lexemes but which are realized with a nasalised stop, for instance *ndeba* vs. Nama *neba* 'here', *ndai* vs. Nama *nai* 'to be astonished'.

In concordance with her treatment of the affricate */kh/* as an aspirated sound, Heikkinen classified */kh/*, which is common in both Nama and ǂAkhoe, as an aspirated stop (Heikkinen, n.d.: 8). Interestingly, she adds two further aspirated stops, namely the bilabial *ph* and the dental *th*. For both she provides only one example each: *!omaphu* 'to blow' and *theǂan-am* 'to seal', plus the ideophone *phara* 'imitating sudden arrival'. Apart from */kh/* there are two further, alveolar, affricates in ǂAkhoe: */ts/* (as in Nama) and *ndz*. For the latter one Heikkinen has only two examples: *ndzo* 'to smear scented powder on' and *ndzaiba* 'a species of honey-making insect'.

3.2.2.2.2 CLICKS

When analysing ǂAkhoe or Haiǁom click consonants the assumption that Haiǁom is virtually identical with Nama/Damara slowly gives way to a more complex description. In her early work, Heikkinen presents a list of click consonants that follows closely what had been established for Nama: the four influxes (ǀ dental, *!* palatal, ǂ alveolar, ǁ lateral) are given in combination with five effluxes (see Hagman 1977: 10):

1. with glottal stop (written without apostrophe according to the official Namibian orthography of Nama/Damara);
2. aspirated (written with an *h* following the click symbol, as in Nama);
3. unaspirated, i.e. followed by a vowel without a pause between them (written as in Nama as *ǀg, ǁg, ǂg,* and *!g*);
4. nasalised (written with an *n* following the click symbol, as in Nama);
5. affricated (written with a *kh* following the click symbol, as in Nama).

In her later work Heikkinen not only changed the orthography towards that of !Xũũ, respectively Juǀ'hoan (see Dickens 1994), but also suggested a different notation for the combinations of influxes and effluxes (see Table 4.9):

TABLE 4.9 CLICK CONSONANTS OF HAI‖OM[1]

	Dental	Alveolar	Lateral	Palatal
Without pause (plain)	ǀg (ǀ)	ǂg (ǂ)	ǁg (ǁ)	!g (!)
With fricative efflux (aspirated)	ǀkh (ǀh)	ǂkh (ǂh)	ǁkh (ǁh)	!kh (!h)
With delayed aspirated efflux (pausal, soft)	ǀh (ǀ'h)	ǂh (ǂ'h)	ǁh (ǁ'h)	!h (!'h)
With pause (pausal, hard)	ǀ (ǀ')	ǂ (ǂ')	ǁ (ǁ')	! (!')
With nasalised efflux	ǀn (ŋǀ)	ǂn (ŋǂ)	ǁn (ŋǁ)	!n (ŋ!)

Note: 1 Notation and orthography of Heikkinen (n.d.) added in parentheses.

As Table 4.9 illustrates, Heikkinen has altered the nasalised and "plain" (non-stop) click consonants in terms of orthography. The value of the remaining click consonants has been altered in the following manner: whereas aspirated and pausal effluxes were previously categorically distinguished, they are now represented as two types of pausal click consonants, namely "hard" (with a glottal stop at the beginning) and "soft" (with a delayed *h* at the beginning). Whereas fricative and aspirated effluxes were previously categorically distinguished, "fricative" has now disappeared as a separate category and is effectively treated as a possible value of the "aspirated" category. Although it would probably be unwise to adopt the altered classification of the late Heikkinen for practical language material, my own work with ǂAkhoe speakers has shown that there is fluctuation between aspirated and fricative effluxes which needs to be recognised in language analysis (see also Westphal 1971).

3.2.2.2.3 PHONOLOGICAL ALTERNATIONS

No oppositions are formed by the following variations:

- The voiced denti-labial fricative *w* varies with *b* and *p* as described above. This is not different from Nama (Hagman 1977: 45) but *w* seems particularly frequent in ǂAkhoe in the disyllabic word stems such as *hawe* 'but'.
- The aspirated affricative *tsh* varies with the non-aspirated *ts*, as in *tsa* 'to taste' or *tses* 'day'. The aspirated affricative is typically realized by ǂAkhoe who have been exposed to the Owambo (Bantu) language in school or in another setting dominated by the Owambo language and who find the *ts* difficult to produce.

3.2.3 Kxoe subgroup

Rainer Vossen

3.2.3.1 Vowels

The vocalic phoneme inventories of the three principal members of this subgroup (Khwe, ǁAni, Buga) coincide remarkably: there are six oral (/*i e ɛ a o u*/) and three nasal vowels (/*ĩ ã ũ*/). The latter are confined to CVV lexical and CV grammatical morphemes. Vowel length is not contrastive. In the literature it is claimed that vowels occur as both monophthongs and diphthongs (cf. Köhler 1981: 485f., Vossen 1986b, Kilian-Hatz 2008: 21f.), but comparative evidence suggests that the so-called diphthongs rather represent vowel sequences.

3.2.3.2 Consonants

Although the subgroup as a whole appears to be largely homogeneous, ǁAni differs from both Khwe and Buga especially with respect to the click inventory.

TABLE 4.10 EGRESSIVE CONSONANTS IN KXOE VARIETIES

	Bilabial	Labiodental	Alveolar	Post-alveolar	Palatal	Velar	Uvular	Glottal
PLOSIVE								
Voiceless	p		t	*tc* ts**		k	q	’
Aspirated	ph*		th	tsh**		kh		
Voiced	b		d	*dj* dz**		g		
Pal. vcl.						*ky*		
Pal. vd.						*gy*		
Asp. pal.						*khy*		
Vel. fric. vcl.			tx	*tcx* tsx**				
Vel. fric. vd.			**dx**	**dzx**				
Ejective			t’	*tc’* ts’**		kx’		
FRICATIVE								
Voiceless		*f*		*c* s**		x		h
Voiced		*v*				ɣ		
NASAL								
Plain	m		n		*ɲ*	ŋ		
Prenasalised	*mb*		*nd*			ŋg***		
RESONANT								
Liquid			l*					
Glide	w				y			

Notes: * not in Buga; ** not in Khwe; *** not in ǁAni; *italics* = Khwe only; **bold** = Buga only.

3.2.3.2.1 EGRESSIVE CONSONANTS

All varieties have relatively symmetric systems with between 26 and 36 phonemes (including borrowed segments) that distribute over six to eight places and four major manners of articulation (see Table 4.10). The phonotactic constraints are basically the same as throughout the family: while almost all egressive consonants occur in C_1 position, C_2 is restricted to a handful of sounds such as /*b*/, /*d*/ (in its allophonic realisation form [r]), and some nasals. Word-final C_2 permits only nasals (i.e. CVC = CVN).

3.2.3.2.2 CLICKS

Kxoe click inventories are largely symmetric: four basic click types (influxes) combine more or less systematically with nine (Khwe, Buga) and eleven (ǁAni) accompaniments (effluxes). For Khwe, Köhler (1981: 486ff.) establishes an evenly balanced inventory consisting of 36 click phonemes (four-by-nine influx–efflux combinations), including the “borrowed” voiced alveolar click /*!g*/, while Kilian-Hatz (2008: 24) identifies only 32 phonemic segments because of major gaps in the alveolar click type series (only five instead of nine accompaniments). In ǁAni we observe an anomaly with regard to the voiced velar fricative click accompaniment that seems to be restricted to the lateral click type (thus: /*ǁgx*/). Finally, in Buga no evidence was found for the existence of a voiced nasal alveolar click. Table 4.11 below summarises these findings.

Like in all South African Khoesan languages, clicks occur exclusively in initial position on lexical roots and grammatical morphemes as well.

3.2.3.2.3 PHONOLOGICAL ALTERNATIONS

Phonological variation has been observed in all varieties for both egressive and ingressive (click) consonants and has been described in more detail by Vossen (1997a: 94–104; Vossen 1986b for ǁAni in particular). Just a few major alternations will be highlighted here.

TABLE 4.11 KXOE CLICK PHONEME INVENTORIES

CLICK TYPE / ACCOMPANIMENT	Dental: ǀ	Palatal: ǂ	Alveolar: !	Lateral: ǁ
Voiceless	ǀ	ǂ	!	ǁ
Voiced	ǀg	ǂg	!g	ǁg
Voiced nasal	nǀn	nǂn	n!n	nǁn
Prenasalised voiced	nǀg	nǂg	**n!g**	nǁg
Voiceless uvular	ǀq	ǂq	!q	ǁq
Voiceless velar fricative	ǀx	ǂx	!x	ǁx
Voiced velar fricative				*ǁgx*
Ejective velar	ǀx'	ǂx'	!x'	ǁx'
Prenasalised vd. velar fricative	*nǀgx*	*nǂgx*	*n!gx*	*nǁgx*
Aspirated	ǀh	ǂh	!h	ǁh
Glottal	ǀ'	ǂ'	!'	ǁ'

Notes: *italics* = ǁAni only; **bold** = not in Buga.

As for egressive consonants an allophonic relationship has been noted for the voiced alveolar stop /*d*/ that occurs word-initially (C_1) only, and is replaced by an alveolar trill [r] or flap [ɾ] in intervocalic position (C_2, C_3, etc.) in all varieties. Under the same circumstances, according to Köhler (1981), Khwe speakers replace the voiced bilabial stop /*b*/ by its fricative counterpart [β], whereas Kilian-Hatz (2008: 23) has attached phonemic status to it (as /*v*/ in her spelling, cf. Table 4.10 above). In Buga, on the other hand, palatalisation processes have affected a good number of (mainly) stops; some of these are systematic (/*g k ŋg kh*/) while others may be described in terms of free variation (/*t ts d s y*/ and, again, /*ŋg*/; cf. Vossen 1997a: 102ff.).

Concerning ingressive consonants, mention must be made of ongoing processes of click loss and click replacement which, to this day, appear to have affected the alveolar click phonemes only. In Khwe and Buga such alternations prove to be more advanced than in ǁAni.

3.2.4 Naro

Hessel Visser

3.2.4.1 Vowels

Naro has five oral and three nasal vowels:

(36)

Oral vowels	Front	Central	Back
High	*i*		*u*
Mid	*e*		*o*
Low		*a*	

(37)

Nasal vowels	Front	Central	Back
High			
Mid	*ẽ*		*õ*
Low		*ã*	

There are also two pharyngealised vowels. Pharyngealisation only occurs on the first vowel.

(38)

Pharyngealised vowels	Front	Central	Back
High			
Mid			<u>o</u>
Low		<u>a</u>	

The set of five oral vowels corresponds to the set of three nasal vowels: when the vowels are nasal, there is no contrast between high and mid in front vowels and back vowels.

3.2.4.2 Consonants

The consonants are presented in several tables, according to their occurrence in different positions in the word.

The following three tables show the distinctive consonants in different positions in the root: first of all those which are found in initial position in all three of the above-mentioned structures (Tables 4.12 and 4.13). Table 4.14 contains only those consonants which are found as C_2 in the CVCV root structure.

TABLE 4.12 NARO ROOT-INITIAL EGRESSIVE CONSONANTS

	Labial	Alveolar stop	Alveolar affricate	Velar	Glottal
Nasal	m	n			
Voiceless stop	(p)	t	ts	k	ʼ
Aspirated stop	(ph)	th	tsh	kh	
Velar fricative release		tx	tsx	kx	
Ejective		t'	ts'	kx'	
Voiced stop	b	d	dz	g	
Voiceless fricative		s		x	h

Remarks:

(a) For reason of symmetry, affricates are shown next to their corresponding stop phonemes.
(b) /*kx'*/ is actually a voiceless ejective stop with velar fricative release, but it is not in contrast with the voiceless ejective stop, so it is placed under the stops.
(c) The bilabial stops /*p*/ and /*ph*/ are rare.
(d) Other consonants found exclusively in loanwords are *f* and *l*.
(e) /*dz*/ is phonetically sometimes realised as [dz], sometimes as [z]. For reasons of symmetry, *dz* is written.
(f) [w] is left out here, because there is only one example: *wèé* 'all'. It can be interpreted as the fricative allophone of /*b*/.
(g) The following consonant combinations are occasionally found in loanwords: *br*, *dr*, *ng*, *fl*, *pl*, *sk*.

Naro clicks are pronounced at four points of articulation: dental, alveolar, palatal and lateral. There are seven accompaniments: a voiceless, voiced, and prenasalised series of clicks, and four additional series with a special release: clicks followed by a glottal stop, clicks followed by aspiration, clicks released into a voiceless velar fricative, and clicks released into an ejective velar fricative. Clicks only occur root-initially.

TABLE 4.13 NARO CLICKS (MOUTH AIR)

	Dental	Alveolar	Palatal	Lateral
Voiceless	ǀ	ǂ	!	ǁ
Voiced	ǀg	ǂg	!g	ǁg
Nasal	ǀn	ǂn	!n	ǁn
Ejective	ǀ'	ǂ'	!'	ǁ'
Aspirated	ǀh	ǂh	!h	ǁh
Fricative release	ǀx	ǂx	!x	ǁx
Ejective fricative release	ǀx'	ǂx'	!x'	ǁx'

TABLE 4.14 NARO ROOT-MEDIAL CONSONANTS

	Labial	Alveolar
Nasal	m	n
Voiced stop	b	
Trill		r
Approximant	w	y

Remarks:

(a) In some words, */p t s kx' g x/* show up as root-medial consonants, e.g. *g*: *hagu* 'dog'. It is, however, probable that the words in which these consonants occur are combinations of two or more morphemes.

(b) [d] and [r] are in complementary distribution, so they are allophones: [d] occurs in root-initial and [r] in root-medial position.

(c) The case of */w/* and */y/* is not totally clear, as they may be interpreted as vowels followed by a suffix *-a*. Examples: *ǁgãwa* 'trickster figure', *huwa* 'story', *ǂxãya* 'something flat, paper', *zãwa* 'squint'.

Only the bilabial nasal [m] is found in root-final position. It occurs in roots with the structure CVN.[3]

3.2.4.3 Syllable and root structure

The following syllable structures occur:

(39) Syllable structure Example Gloss

Syllable structure	Example	Gloss
CV	*ǀaba*	'be hungry'
V	*!áò*	'long'
N	*ǀám*	'sun'
NCV	*nǀámá*	'when?'

Syllabic nasals only occur in interrogative words:

(40) *nǀáma* 'when?'
nta 'how?'
nda 'where?'

The latter example can be interpreted as prenasalisation, but as prenasalisation does not occur in Naro further, I interpret [n] here as a syllabic nasal.

The following root structures are found:

(41)

Root structure	Example	Gloss
CVV	*ǀáò*	'buffalo'
CVN	*ǀám*	'sun'
CVCV	*ǁaba*	'be hungry'
CVVCV	*ǀgoaba*	'spider'
NCV	*nda*	'where?'
NCVCV	*nǀámá*	'when?'

The distribution of consonants and vowels is as follows:

(a) The oral vowels */a/* and */o/* can occur after any consonant. */p/* and */ph/* are exceptional cases.
(b_1) Pharyngealised vowels do not occur after ejective and aspirated consonants. In rare cases vowels are pharyngealised after consonants followed by a velar fricative.
(b_2) Consonants before a pharyngealised vowel are generally voiceless, but they tend to get some voicing, varying from speaker to speaker. I have not found conclusive contrasts between voiceless and voiced consonants before pharyngealised vowels yet.
(c) The pharyngealised *a̲* is more frequent than the pharyngealised *o̲*. It also occurs in more different environments.

VV distribution in CVV roots can be described thus: The first vowel in the root structures CVV, CVN and CVCV may be rounded or unrounded, pharyngealised or not, */a/*, */o/*, */a̲/* or */o̲/*. The second vowel may be any of the five oral vowels */a e i o u/*. These (second) vowels may be nasalised. There is no contrast between nasalised [ẽ] and nasalised [ĩ], nor between nasalised [õ] and nasalised [ũ], so there are three distinctive nasalised vowels, */ã/*, */ẽ/* and */õ/*.

We may summarise the possible V_1+V_2 combinations as follows: oral+oral, oral+nasal, pharyngealised+oral, and pharyngealised+nasal.

Summary of possible sequences:

(42)

	V_1	C_2	V_2
	a	b	a ã
	o	r	e ẽ
C_1	a̲	m	i
	o̲	n	o õ
	u		

The unrounded vowel */a/* as first vowel may be realised in different ways, depending on the environment. Generally it is realised as [a]. If the first consonant is either labial or alveolar and the second vowel is a front vowel, */a/* is realised as [e] or [i]. Whether */a/* is realised as [e] or [i] depends on the second vowel: if the second vowel is */e/*, */a/* is realised as [e], if the second vowel is */i/*, */a/* is realised as [i]. Likewise, the rounded vowel */o/* is realised as [u] when the second vowel is */u/*. (There is no apparent influence from the first consonant to be noted here.)

Because there is no contrast between *ai* and *ii*, nor between *ae* and *ee*, the pronunciation of words with [ii] or [ee] or [eẽ] may vary: *ii* → *ai*, e.g. *teẽ* → *taẽ*.

One exception to this rule has been found so far: the words *káí* and *kíí* seem to be used differently: *káí* 'be big' vs. *kíi* '(my) big brother'.

Examples of realisation as [e] or [i] after labial consonants: *bèe* 'be afraid', *bíì* 'milk'.

Realisation as [e] or [i] after alveolar consonants: *ǀ'ee* 'fire', *ǂgèè* 'stiff', *séè* 'take', *ǀii* 'song', *síí* 'go', *ǂii* 'call'.

Realisation as [a] after post-alveolar consonants: *ǀgàe* 'female', *!náé* 'pass', *!áé* 'bind', *ǀae* 'chew', *ǀgàí* 'cheek', *ǀnàì* 'jump', *!áì* 'kick', *!xáí* 'clothes'.

When labial and alveolar consonants are released into velar fricative, it is the fricative that determines the phonetic realisation. As it is post-alveolar, /a/ is realised as [a], e.g. [ǂii] 'call' but [ǂxáí] 'eye', [ǀèè] 'exclamation' but [ǀxáé] 'important'.

A further influence can be attributed to the second vowel. The unrounded vowel /a/ is realised as [e] when it is followed by /i/: /ǂxáí/ → [ǂxéí].

Likewise, the rounded vowel /o/ is realised as [u] if the second vowel is /u/ or /i/, e.g. *túú* 'rain', *ǀúí* 'one'.

If the second consonant is /n/ or /m/, V_2 can be considered as a nasalised vowel so that there is no contrast between *a*/*i* or *o*/*u*.

As for V . . . V co-occurrences in $C_1V_1C_2V_2$ nouns and verbs, the same vowel distribution is possible as in CVV words. Vowels cannot be nasalised in lexical roots that have a $C_1V_1C_2V_2$ structure.

A further influence of the environment on the phonetic realisation of vowels is the anticipation of vowels: the second vowel is anticipated and is inserted between the first vowel and the second consonant: /CV_1CV_2/ → [$CV_1V_2CV_2$]. It seems that this phenomenon occurs especially on names, but it is also found in other words:

(43) Composite words:

/ǁxagu/	→	[ǁxaugu]	–(name)
/!aǀe/	→	[!aeǀe]	–(name)

(44) Simple words:

/!nona/	→	[!noana]	'three'
/Koba/	→	[Koaba]	(name)
/ǀore/	→	[ǀoere]	'pray'
/ǂGoxa/	→	[ǂGoaxa]	(name)

The last case may be an example of vowel anticipation, but it may also be that the root is *Gǂoa*, so that the /a/ is just part of the word. If, however, the root in the word is *Gǂoo*, we have a case of vowel anticipation.

This process seems also to occur in the opposite direction so that the first vowel was repeated after the following consonant: /CV_1CV_2/ → [$CV_1CV_1V_2$]. It does not seem to occur too often, and in perhaps questionable circumstances: /ǀNaoka/ → [ǀNaokoa] (name).

Concerning V in CVN nouns and verbs, only /a/ and /o/, /a̲/ and /o̲/ occur. The distribution parallels, therefore, the situation found for the first vowel in CVV and CVCV structures. This is to be expected, as it is assumed that V_2 was elided from a word with an original CV_1NV_2 structure:

(45)

Canonical form	Example	Gloss
C a m	*ǀám*	'sun'
C o m	*ǀom*	'suck'
C o̲ m	*qo̲m*	'close a hole'
C a̲ m	*ca̲m*	'cut meat'

3.2.5 ǀGana subgroup

Hirosi Nakagawa

This phonological account is based on data from three ǁGana (i.e. Molapo, Thomelo and Xade) and three ǀGui varieties (i.e. Khute, Thomelo and Xade dialects). The labels

"Molapo", "Thomelo" and "Xade" approximately indicate the representative areas in which each dialect is or was spoken, but "Khute" is a label locally given to ǀGui residents in the mid-western part of Kweneng District. I refer to these varieties generically as ǁGana–ǀGui dialects and specifically as ǁGana (ML), ǁGana (TH), ǁGana (XD), ǀGui (KH), ǀGui (TH), and ǀGui (XD).

Important documentations on ǁGana subgroup phonology include Vossen (1997a: 108–13) surveying the core phonological structure of the ǁGana subgroup, Nakagawa (1996a, 1996b) for the synchronic description of ǀGui phonology, Traill and Vossen (1997) and Traill (1986a) dealing with click replacement, and Nakagawa (1998) discussing palatalisation in ǁGana–ǀGui dialects.

3.2.5.1 Root structure

The vast majority (over 90 per cent) of the roots of ǁGana–ǀGui dialects have the segmental structure CVV, CVCV or CVN. In describing the occurrence of segments, I refer to their positions in terms of C_1 (root-initial C), C_2 (root-medial C), V_1 (the first V), V_2 (the second V) and N (the final nasal consonant).

3.2.5.2 Vowels

Below I outline the vowel system of ǀGui (XD), the only variety for which I have investigated the vowel inventory systematically. Because of limited space, I just list the phonemes and summarise their important phonetic realisations. There are five plain (/*i e a o u*/), three nasal (/*ĩ ã ũ*/), and two pharyngealised (/*a̰ ṵ*/) vowels. The rounded vowel /*u*/ is regularly realised as [wə] or [uᵊ] before N. This articulation involves a transitional lip-gesture from rounded to unrounded. Note that this diphthong-like vowel is monomoraic. The two nasal close vowels, /*ĩ ũ*/, are phonetically more open than the plain close vowels /*i u*/, and were transcribed phonetically as [ẽ õ] in Nakagawa (1996b). The pharyngealised vowels, unrounded /*a̰*/ and rounded /*ṵ*/, have the following two constraints: (i) they occur only in V_1; (ii) they do not occur if preceded by a uvular and/or ejective consonant. (Note that they do occur after the glottal plosive and the click with glottal plosive accompaniment.) It should be pointed out that /*ṵ*/ is optionally realised as [wə̰] or [ṵᵊ] which involves a certain transient lip-rounding articulation from rounded to unrounded like /*u*/ followed by N.

3.2.5.3 Consonants

3.2.5.3.1 CLICKS

The click system of ǁGana–ǀGui dialects is characterised by two aspects: (i) it has the most complex set of click accompaniments in the Khoe family; (ii) the alveolar click has undergone so-called click replacement, whereby the extension in the lexicon varies from one dialect to another. As shown in Table 4.15, the four influxes and thirteen click accompaniments are found in ǁGana–ǀGui. Their combinations make 52 contrastive syllable onsets in C_1. Here I will not discuss the controversial issue of whether these syllable onsets are single segments or not, and will simply call these syllable onsets click consonants. The 52 click consonants are exemplified in Table 4.16.

The transcription used for click consonants requires two comments. First, I basically follow a systematic approach suggested by Ladefoged and Traill (1994) and implicitly adopted by the *Handbook of the International Phonetic Association* (HIPA 1999: 20f.): the first symbol before the influx, namely *ŋ*, *ŋ̊*, *g*, *k*, *ɢ* or *q*, stands for the posterior

TABLE 4.15 CLICK CONSONANTS IN ǁGANA–ǀGUI DIALECTS

Accompaniment	Dental	Alveolar	Lateral	Palatal
(1) Nasal	ŋǀ	ŋǃ	ŋǁ	ŋǂ
(2) Voiced velar plosive	gǀ	gǃ	gǁ	gǂ
(3) Voiceless unaspirated velar plosive	kǀ	kǃ	kǁ	kǂ
(4) Voiceless aspirated velar plosive	kǀ^{h}	kǃ^{h}	kǁ^{h}	kǂ^{h}
(5) Unaffricated velar ejective	kǀ’	kǃ’	kǁ’	kǂ’
(6) Voiced uvular plosive	ɢǀ	ɢǃ	ɢǁ	ɢǂ
(7) Voiceless unaspirated uvular plosive	qǀ	qǃ	qǁ	qǂ
(8) Voiceless aspirated uvular plosive	qǀ^{h}	qǃ^{h}	qǁ^{h}	qǂ^{h}
(9) Unaffricated uvular ejective	qǀ’	qǃ’	qǁ’	qǂ’
(10) Affricated uvular ejective	kǀx’	kǃx’	kǁx’	kǂx’
(11) Voiceless uvular fricative	kǀx	kǃx	kǁx	kǂx
(12) Glottal fricative	ŋ̥ǀh	ŋ̥ǃh	ŋ̥ǁh	ŋ̥ǂh
(13) Glottal plosive	ŋ̥ǀ’	ŋ̥ǃ’	ŋ̥ǁ’	ŋ̥ǂ’

TABLE 4.16 WORDS ILLUSTRATING THE CLICK CONSONANTS OF ǁGANA–ǀGUI

	Influx			
	Dental	Alveolar	Lateral	Palatal
(1)	ŋǀàà *stomach*	ŋǃàà *to choose*	ŋǁáè *to sing*	ŋǂáà *to stare*
(2)	gǀáà *to shelter*	gǃáā *to hurt*	gǁáà *to hibernate*	gǂáá *to move smoothly*
(3)	kǀáá *to skin*	kǃàā *to miss*	kǁàà *to visit to inform*	kǂáà *to patch*
(4)	kǀ^{h}áā *to put into grass*	kǃ^{h}àā *piece*	kǁ^{h}áā *to cultivate*	kǂ^{h}áá *pan*
(5)	ɢǀáā *to open*	ɢǃáī *to be wrinkled*	ɢǁáà *to twinkle*	ɢǂàã̄ *spleen*
(6)	qǀāā *fossil river, Okwa*	qǃàē *to hunt*	qǁáā *to be dry*	qǂáà *transparent*
(7)	qǀ^{h}áà *to peep*	qǃ^{h}áā *to cough out*	qǁ^{h}áà *to spread*	qǂ^{h}áà *lying*
(8)	kǀ’áò *to bend down*	kǃ’áá *thigh*	kǁ’áā *flower*	kǂ’áà *to faint*
(9)	qǀ’áā *to carry*	qǃ’áò *a kind of grass*	qǁ’áū *big animal spoor*	qǂ’áē *to spit*
(10)	kǀxáā *meat*	kǃxáà *diarrhoea*	kǁxáà *to be daytime*	kǂxáā *to move s.th.*
(11)	kǀx’áé *to fall*	kǃx’áó *neck*	kǁx’áà *to wash*	kǂx’áī *accessory*
(12)	ŋ̥ǀháá *to find inside*	ŋ̥ǃháá *to lack horns*	ŋ̥ǁháā *to cut anus off*	ŋ̥ǂhâā *to go before*
(13)	ŋ̥ǀ’áò *blood*	ŋ̥ǃ’áēē *to be frightened*	ŋ̥ǁ’áá *bat-eared fox*	ŋ̥ǂ’áā *to hide*

closure involving each click consonant. Second, I use the symbol *x* for the uvular articulation in (10) and (11), following the convention of Vossen's (1997a: 108f.) transcription for the ǁGana subgroup languages.

3.2.5.3.1.1 INFLUX

The four-way distinction of influxes found in the ǁGana subgroup is not uncommon among Khoesan languages, but it is noteworthy that two "abrupt" (Traill and Vossen 1997: 23) influxes, *!* and *ǂ*, tend to have an interesting phonetic detail of "weakening" in ǁGana–ǀGui dialects: speakers of ǁGana–ǀGui dialects frequently pronounce these two influxes with weak intensity. See Traill and Vossen (1997: 44–51) for a full discussion about this "weakening" which reveals the phonetic basis of a historical sound change called "click replacement".

3.2.5.3.1.2 CLICK ACCOMPANIMENTS

An important feature of click accompaniments in ǁGana–ǀGui dialects is a set of eight velar and uvular click accompaniments, i.e. accompaniments (2)–(9) in Table 4.15. The identical eight-way distinction also exists in non-click velar and uvular stops, as will be shown in Table 4.17. This full set of velar and uvular consonants is attested in Khoesan languages only in ǁGana–ǀGui dialects and in !Xóõ (Traill and Nakagawa 2000: 11). As reported by Nakagawa (1996a), clicks with glottal plosive accompaniment (13) involve nasality, which is expressed in transcription by *ŋ* before each influx symbol. The nasality involved in this accompaniment is clearly reflected in its allophonic accompaniment found only in ǀGui (KH), namely the preglottalised nasal accompaniment. In ǀGui (KH), clicks with glottal plosive accompaniment are realised as those with preglottalised nasal accompaniment, *ʔŋǀ*, *ʔŋ!*, *ʔŋǂ* and *ʔŋǁ*, if followed by a pharyngealised vowel. For example, all dialects have *ŋǀʔáḿ* 'heading direction'; *ʔŋǀà̰m̀* 'twig' occurs in ǀGui (KH) while *ŋ̊ǀʔà̰m̀* 'twig' occurs in other dialects. Preglottalised nasal accompaniment is cross-linguistically rare, and has so far been attested only in !Xóõ (Traill 1985: 134f.) and ǂHoan (Collins 2001: 474).

3.2.5.3.1.3 CLICK REPLACEMENT

The click replacement that ǁGana–ǀGui dialects have undergone is illustrated in a simplified form in Table 4.17, which compares ǀGui, which has not undergone click replacement, with ǁGana (ML), which is most advanced in click replacement. As shown in this table, in this sound change click consonants with the alveolar influx change into non-click consonants which are identical to their click accompaniments. A gap in (12) indicates that the replacement for *ŋ̊!h* is not attested.

A closer comparison of relevant words among ǁGana–ǀGui dialects reveals that the click replacement involves variation in lexical extension according to dialects. Table 4.18 illustrates an aspect of the variation. Words with the alveolar click in ǀGui and their cognates in ǁGana fall into one of the four classes. Class 1 has preserved the alveolar click in all ǁGana–ǀGui dialects. Class 2 has undergone click replacement only in ǁGana (ML), class 3 in ǁGana (XD) and ǁGana (ML), and class 4 in all ǁGana dialects.

Another aspect of the variation involved in the click replacement is illustrated in Table 4.19. As exemplified in (1), *k!x* in ǀGui corresponds to *kx* in ǁGana (TH), and to *x* in ǁGana (XD & ML). This correspondence indicates that *kx* is an intermediate stage of the sound change from *k!x* to *x*. In other words, the effect of click replacement is further advanced in ǁGana (XD & ML) than in ǁGana (TH).

TABLE 4.17 CLICK REPLACEMENT IN ǁGANA–ǀGUI DIALECTS (SIMPLIFIED VERSION)

	ǀGui (all dialects)	ǁGana (ML)
(1) Nasal	ŋ!	ŋ
(2) Voiced velar plosive	g!	g
(3) Voiceless unaspirated velar plosive	k!	k
(4) Voiceless aspirated velar plosive	k!^{h}	k^{h}
(5) Unaffricated velar ejective	k!’	k’
(6) Voiced uvular plosive	ɢ!	ɢ
(7) Voiceless unaspirated uvular plosive	q!	q
(8) Voiceless aspirated uvular plosive	q!^{h}	q^{h}
(9) Unaffricated uvular ejective	q!’	q’
(10) Affricated uvular ejective	k!x’	kx’
(11) Voiceless uvular fricative	k!x	x
(12) Glottal fricative	ŋ̊!^{h}	
(13) Glottal plosive	ŋ̊!’	ʔ

TABLE 4.18 LEXICAL EXTENSION OF CLICK REPLACEMENT IN ǁGANA

	ǀGui (all)	ǁGana (TH)	ǁGana (XD)	ǁGana (ML)	Gloss
Class 1	g!uba	g!uba	g!uba	g!uba	‘welt’
Class 2	g!obe	g!obe	g!obe	**gobe**	‘roar remotely’
Class 3	g!uma	g!uma	**guma**	**guma**	‘forearm’
Class 4	g!aa	**gaa**	**gaa**	**gaa**	‘awl’

Note: Words in bold have undergone replacement in the relevant dialects. Tones and omitted.

TABLE 4.19 ǁGANA–ǀGUI VARIATION IN EFFECT OF CLICK REPLACEMENT

	ǀGui (all)	ǁGana (TH)	ǁGana (XD & ML)	Gloss
(1)	k!xaa	kxaa	xaa	‘diarrhoea’
(2)	g!ai	gei	gii	‘red-crested korhaan’
(3)	k!ae	kæe	kee	‘tie’

Examples (2) and (3) in Table 4.19 indicate that the assimilation of V_1 to V_2 is more advanced in ǁGana (XD & ML) than in ǁGana (TH). This assimilation, which was once blocked by the alveolar click, can be regarded as an effect of click replacement. In this case, as well, the effect of click replacement is more advanced in ǁGana (XD & ML) than in ǁGana (TH).

3.2.5.3.2 EGRESSIVE (NON-CLICK) CONSONANTS

The system of non-click consonants of ǁGana–ǀGui dialects is characterised by the largest inventory in the Khoe family. The non-click consonants occurring in C_1 are classified in Table 4.20 and exemplified in Table 4.21. The large inventory is due to the complexity of the stop system, which has four different states of the glottis (i.e. voiced, voiceless, aspirated and ejective) and five oral places of articulation (i.e. labial, alveolar, palatal, velar and uvular), with only one gap of the bilabial ejective. Notice that the four-way distinction extends to the alveolar affricate class */dz ts ts^h ts’/* as well.

The affricated velar ejective */kx’/* requires comments. First, this sound involves a lateral release in all ǁGana–ǀGui dialects and would be transcribed as [k^{L}x’]. Second,

TABLE 4.20 NON-CLICK CONSONANTS OCCURRING IN C_1 IN ǁGANA–ǀGUI DIALECTS

	Bilabial	Alveolar	Palatal	Velar	Uvular	Glottal
Nasal	m	n*		ŋ*		
Voiced plosive	b	d	ɟ	g	ɢ	
Voiceless plosive	p	t	c	k	q	ʔ
Voiceless aspirated plosive	p^{h}	t^{h}**	c^{h}	k^{h}	q^{h}	
Unaffricated ejective		t'	c'	k'	q'	
Voiceless fricative		s			x	h
Voiced affricate		dz				
Voiceless unaspirated affricate		ts				
Voiceless aspirated affricate		ts^{h}				
Affricated ejective		ts'		kx'		
Stop+uvular fricative		tx**	cx**	kx*		
Stop+affricated uvular ejective		tkx'**		ckx'**		
Affricate+uvular fricative		tsx				
Affricate+affricated uvular ejective		tskx'				

Notes:
*/*n*/ and /*ŋ*/ do not occur in ǀGui dialects; /*kx*/ occurs only in ǁGana (TH).
**/t^{h}/, /*tx*/ and /*tkx'*/ do not occur in ǀGui (KH & TH), where these three sounds are realised as /c^{h}/, /*cx*/ and /*ckx'*/.

TABLE 4.21 WORDS ILLUSTRATING NON-CLICK CONSONANTS IN C_1 IN ǁGANA–ǀGUI DIALECTS

bàā *father, daddy*	dḁ̀ī *crowned plover* (*Vanellus coronatus*)	dzáā *frighten*	ɟìā *owner*	gàā̃ *duck*	ɢábā *eat on the palm*	
páá *bite*	tā̰ã *Rhigozum brevispinosum* Kuntze	tsāā *disappear*	cèn̄ *stand*	kàō *promise*	qâã *Acanthosicyos naudi-niana* (Sond.) Jeffrey	ˀāã *wear*
p^{h}àbà *immature seed of melon*	t^{h}a̰rì *dull* (*of edges*)	ts^{h}áā *water*	c^{h}ám̄ *soft, easy*	k^{h}áó *back of thigh*	q^{h}àā *error*	
	t'áá *carve*	ts'āā *squeeze to extract moisture*	c'íbè *cut clearly with a small knife*	k'áè *belch*	q'ám̄ *hot sand of a fire*	
				kx'àà *drink*		
		sáá *miss a shot*			xáé *have sex*	háā̃ *exist*
mâã *give*	núú *what* [ǁGana]			ŋúū *hut* [ǁGana]		
	txām̄ *lace up*	tsxâã *hate*	cxām̄ *lace up* [ǀGui (KH & TH)]			
	tkx'ám̄ *termite sp.*	tskx'āē *blue or green*	ckx'ám̄ *termite sp.* [ǀGui (KH & TH)]	kxáà *diarrhoea* [ǀGui (TH)]		

the symbol *x* used in this sound indicates the velar (not uvular) articulation: static palatograms show that this sound involves the velar closure rather than uvular. Third, *kx'* in the consonants /*tkx' ckx' tskx'*/ involves the uvular articulation. The symbol *x* used in /*x tx cx tsx kx*/ stands for the uvular fricative, as indicated in Table 4.20. The uncommon sound /*kx*/ is attested only in ǁGana (TH). As mentioned before, this sound reflects an intermediate stage of the click replacement process from *k!x* to *x*. In this dialect this intermediate stage is phonologised, and is contrastive with the original non-click consonant /*x*/. Phonetically, /*kx*/ is not an affricate in a conventional sense, but a hetero-organic consonant cluster [kχ], i.e. the voiceless velar stop followed by the voiceless uvular fricative.

TABLE 4.22 PALATALISATION IN ǁGANA–ǀGUI DIALECTS

	Naro	ǁGana	ǀGui (XD)	ǀGui (TH & KH)	Gloss
Class 1	túú	**cúú**	**cúú**	**cúú**	'rain'
Class 2	tãá	táã	**cíã**	**cíã**	'different'
Class 3	tạ̄ū	tạ̄ū	tạ̄ū	**cạ̄ū**	'tired'

Note: For comparison Naro cognates are cited from Visser (2001) in his notation. Words which have undergone the palatalisation are in bold.

ǁGana–ǀGui dialects have undergone a historical palatalisation which has changed *d*, *t*, t^h and *t'* into *ɟ*, *c*, c^h and *c'*, respectively. According to the extent to which this sound shift has spread in the lexicon of each dialect, ǁGana–ǀGui dialects are classified into three groups, i.e. ǁGana (all), ǀGui (XD) and ǀGui (TH & KH). Table 4.22 illustrates the dialect grouping. Words with *d*, *t*, t^h, *t'*, *ɟ*, *c*, c^h or *c'* in ǁGana–ǀGui dialects fall into one of three classes (1–3). Class 1 has been affected by the palatalisation in all ǁGana–ǀGui dialects, class 2 has been affected in three ǀGui dialects, and class 3 has been affected in ǀGui (TH & KH). In other words, the ǁGana dialects are more conservative in preserving *d*, *t*, t^h and *t'* than the ǀGui dialects, among which XD is more conservative than the other two dialects.

3.2.5.3.3 ǁGANA–ǀGUI DIALECT VARIATION IN TERMS OF THREE PARAMETERS

As described above, the six ǁGana–ǀGui dialects show a range of phonological variation that can be summarised in terms of three consonantal parameters, i.e. degrees of (i) click replacement, (ii) palatalisation, and (iii) preglottalised accompaniment, as illustrated in Table 4.23. Degrees of the three parameters are expressed with values 0–3 for each dialect. This table indicates that the six dialects constitute a continuum in the order of ǀGui (KH)–ǀGui (TH)–ǀGui (XD)–ǁGana (TH)–ǁGana (XD)–ǁGana (ML). It should be pointed out that the succession of dialects does not agree with the geographical distribution of these dialects (two THs are discontinuous, and so are the two XDs). Why they do not agree is a question which should be explored from a historical perspective in future research.

3.2.5.3.4 CONSONANTS OCCURRING IN C_2 AND N

Like other South African Khoesan languages, ǁGana subgroup languages show a strong constraint on consonants in C_2. ǀGui allows only /*b r m n j w*/ in C_2. The two glides, /*j*/ and /*w*/, in C_2 are very rare in the lexicon. In N /*m*/ and /*n*/ occur.

TABLE 4.23 ǁGANA–ǀGUI DIALECT CONTINUUM IN TERMS OF THREE PARAMETERS

	ǀGui (KH)	ǀGui (TH)	ǀGui (XD)	ǁGana (TH)	ǁGana (XD)	ǁGana (ML)
Click replacement	0	0	0	1	2	3
Palatalisation	3	3	2	1	1	1
Preglottalised accompaniment	1	0	0	0	0	0

Note: Degrees of the three parameters are indicated with values 0–3 for each dialect. Palatalisation lacks value 0 because all ǁGana–ǀGui dialects have undergone more or less palatalisation.

3.2.6 Shua subgroup

Rainer Vossen

3.2.6.1 Vowels

All languages have five oral (*/i e a o u/*) and three nasal vowels (*/ĩ ã ũ/*). There are also sequences of oral and nasal vowels. Diphthongisation of V_1 in CVCV roots has been observed in all varieties as follows: Ts'ixa and Danisi <*oa*>, Deti <*oe oa ua*>, Cara <*ai oa ui ua*> and ǀXaise <*ai oa*>.

3.2.6.2 Consonants

3.2.6.2.1 EGRESSIVE CONSONANTS

In spite of differences in the inventory sizes, which range from 27 (Ts'ixa) to 37 (Danisi), a majority of egressive consonants occur in all Shua languages. These are specified in Table 4.24. There are four manners of articulation (plosive, fricative, nasal, resonant) in the subgroup as a whole, and seven places of articulation (bilabial, alveolar, post-alveolar, palatal, velar, uvular, gottal) which are shared only by Danisi, Cara and ǀXaise; Ts'ixa and Deti lack palatal and uvular consonants, respectively.

The below table shows that Shua languages share at least 24 egressive consonant phonemes. The two velar ejectives are mutually exclusive: the occurrence of */kx'/* in

TABLE 4.24 EGRESSIVE CONSONANTS COMMON TO ALL SHUA LANGUAGES

	Bilabial	Alveolar	Post-alveolar	Velar	Glottal
PLOSIVE					
Voiceless	p	t	ts	k	'
Aspirated		th	tsh	kh	
Voiced	b	d	dz	g	
Ejective		t'	ts'	*kx'* k'	
FRICATIVE					
Voiceless		s		x	h
NASAL					
Plain	m	n*	ɲ	ŋ	
Prenasalised				ŋg	
RESONANT					
Glide			y		

Notes: * phonemic status in Ts'ixa uncertain; *italics* = Ts'ixa and Danisi only.

Ts'ixa and Danisi is contact-induced (< Kxoe; see Vossen 1991), while */k'/* is a regular East Kalahari Khoe reflex of Proto-Khoe */kx'/ (cf. Vossen 1997a: 305f.).

In addition to these overall shared phonemes, all inventories contain some exclusive or only partly shared segments. Thus */tx/* and */tsx/*, for instance, are exclusive segments in Cara while */dy/* and */nj/* are confined to |Xaise. Moreover, some phonemes were found to occur in only one lexical form, e.g. */dy ɲ ŋ nj/* in |Xaise.

In principle, the phonotactic constraints are the same as in other Central Khoesan languages.

Borrowed segments also form part of Shua consonant inventories. Their occurrence is often positionally conditioned. Hence, in Ts'ixa */f ntx/* only appear word-initially and */nt ŋg ŋk/* word-medially, whereas */mb nd/* may show up as both, C_1 and C_2. Deti exhibits */mb ŋk/* in medial but not in initial position. An interesting case is */ŋg/* because it occurs initially as a genuine phoneme derived from Proto-Khoe, and as a borrowed segment in medial position. The same holds true of Ts'ixa. In Danisi, */l ŋk/* are restricted to C_2 position but */mb/* appears both word-initially and medially. In Cara and |Xaise, */l mb ŋk/* are medial consonants; beyond this, Cara also has */nd w/* word-initially and */ŋg/* word-medially.

3.2.6.2.2 CLICKS

Generally speaking, East Kalahari Khoe languages have suffered enormously from processes of click loss and click replacement. At first sight, however, Ts'ixa appears to be an exception to this rule in two respects: it has the largest number of click phonemes (27 as against 14 in Deti, for instance), and it makes use of both alveolar and palatal clicks which have otherwise disappeared almost completely from the sub-family. Vossen (1991) has argued that Ts'ixa, just like its closest relatives, once lost the two basic click types but later on reintroduced them as a result of intense contact with Kxoe varieties. In other words, the employment of alveolar and palatal clicks in Ts'ixa is contact-induced. Interestingly enough, Ts'ixa speakers tend to use these re-established click sounds (except */ǂh/*) side by side with their egressive substitutes, as exemplified in (46):

(46) *ǂ* varies freely with k^y and t^y
ǂg varies freely with d^y
nǂg varies freely with d^y and nt^y
ǂx varies freely with t^yx
ǂ' varies freely with $t^{y'}$

Obviously, some of these egressive substitutes overlap with one another. Thus, [d^y] may equally replace */ǂg/* and */nǂg/*; and for */ǂ/* and */nǂg/* even twofold replacement has been noted.

The click inventory of Ts'ixa is shown in the following table.

TABLE 4.25 TS'IXA CLICK PHONEME INVENTORY

CLICK TYPE / ACCOMPANIMENT	Dental	Palatal	Alveolar	Lateral
Voiceless	|	ǂ	!	‖
Voiced	|g	ǂg	(!g)	‖g
Voiced nasal	n|n			n‖n
Prenasalised voiced	n|g	nǂg		n‖g
Voiceless velar fricative	|x	ǂx	!x	‖x
Aspirated	|h	ǂh	!h	‖h
Glottal	|'	ǂ'	!'	‖'
Prenasalised vd. velar fricative	n|gx			n‖gx

Shua languages other than Ts'ixa have between two and four basic click types combined with seven to eleven accompaniments (see Table 4.26). However, only dental and lateral clicks are used in a systematic way; i.e., alveolar and palatal clicks only occur sporadically (never in Deti though) with just a few words.

TABLE 4.26 SHUA CLICK PHONEME INVENTORIES (WITHOUT TS'IXA)

CLICK TYPE ACCOMPANIMENT	Dental	Palatal	Alveolar	Lateral
Voiceless	ǀ		![1,2]	ǁ
Voiced	ǀg		!g[2]	ǁg
Voiced nasal	nǀn		n!n[1]	nǁn
Prenasalised voiced	nǀg			nǁg
Voiceless uvular	ǀq[1,2]	ǂq[2]		ǁq[2]
Voiceless velar fricative	ǀx		!x[2]	ǁx
Voiced velar fricative				ǁgx[2]
Ejective velar	ǀx'[2]			ǁx'[2]
Prenasalised vd. velar fricative	nǀgx[2]			nǁgx[2]
Aspirated	ǀh		!h[1,3]	ǁh
Glottal	ǀ'	ǂ'[1]	!'[3]	ǁ'

Notes: 1 Cara; 2 Danisi; 3 ǀXaise.

Like in all South African Khoesan languages, clicks occur exclusively in initial position on lexical roots and grammatical morphemes as well.

3.2.6.2.3 PHONOLOGICAL ALTERNATIONS

Morphophonological change and free variation have been observed in all varieties and especially for egressive consonants; for a more detailed description, see Vossen (1997a: 114–24). The most common alternations are the following:

As for egressive consonants an allophonic relationship has been noted for the voiced alveolar stop /*d*/ that occurs word-initially (C_1) only, and is replaced by an alveolar trill [r] or flap [ɾ] in intervocalic position (C_2, C_3, etc.) in all varieties. Under the same circumstances Shua speakers tend to replace the voiced bilabial stop /*b*/ by its fricative counterpart [β]. Moreover, palatalisation processes have affected a good number of (mainly) stops.

Concerning ingressive consonants, mention must be made of the still ongoing processes of click loss and click replacement which are particularly advanced in Deti.

3.2.7 Tshwa subgroup

Rainer Vossen

3.2.7.1 Vowels

Tshwa languages have five oral (/*i e a o u*/) and three nasal vowels (/*ĩ ã ũ*/). The latter occur in V_1 position only. There are also sequences of oral and nasal vowels. Diphthongisation of V_1 in CVCV roots has been observed in both Kua (<ai oa ua>) and Tsua (<ai oa>).

3.2.7.2 Consonants

The two varieties under consideration have 34/36 (Tsua/Kua) egressive and 23/26 click consonants. In addition, their inventories contain three borrowed non-click consonants each.

3.2.7.2.1 EGRESSIVE CONSONANTS

There are seven places and four major manners of articulation, as shown in Table 4.27 below:

TABLE 4.27 EGRESSIVE CONSONANTS IN TSHWA VARIETIES

	Bilabial	Alveolar	Post-alveolar	Palatal	Velar	Uvular	Glottal
PLOSIVE							
Voiceless	p	t	ts	c ky	k	q	'
Aspirated		th	tsh	*ch*	kh		
Voiced	b	d	dz dy	j	g		
Implosive				'y			
Vl. uvular-fricative		tx	tsx	cx			
Ejective		t'	ts'	c'	k'		
FRICATIVE							
Voiceless		s			x		h
NASAL							
Plain	m	n		ɲ	ŋ		
Prenasalised					*ŋg*		
RESONANT							
Glide	w		y				

Note: *italics* = Kua only.

To some extent the occurrence of egressive consonants is positionally constrained. In both varieties /*n*/ is confined to C_2 position; /*w*/ was found to occur exclusively as C_1 in Tsua and as C_2 in Kua. All other phonemes are largely confined to C_1 position. In intervocalic position /*d*/ is relatively often retained as such, while in Tsua it is replaced as a rule by [r] or [ɾ].

The palatal plosives are largely a result of click loss and click replacement. /*c*/ and /*ky*/ appear in the same vocalic environment, and although their phonemic nature has been proven synchronically they seem to go back in some lexical examples to the same proto-phoneme, viz. */ǂ/. /*ky*/ is fully palatalised as a rule: [ki] ~ [k^yi]. /*dy*/ was found to occur before front vowels only.

Borrowed segments are /*l nd ŋk*/ in Kua and /*l mb nd*/ in Tsua; they are restricted to medial position.

3.2.7.2.2 CLICKS

Both varieties dispose of well-established series for the dental and lateral basic types. In contrast to this, alveolar and palatal clicks strongly testify to relic character, as is the case throughout East Kalahari Khoe languages. The existence of a total of nine such clicks must not obscure the fact that most of them are used in just a small number of lexical items. Tshwa click inventories are summarised in Table 4.28.

Like in all South African Khoesan languages, clicks occur exclusively in initial position on lexical roots and grammatical morphemes as well.

TABLE 4.28 TSHWA CLICK PHONEME INVENTORIES

CLICK TYPE / ACCOMPANIMENT	Dental	Palatal	Alveolar	Lateral
Voiceless	ǀ	ǂ	!	ǁ
Voiced	ǀg	ǂg[1]		ǁg
Voiced nasal	nǀn			nǁn
Prenasalised voiced	nǀg[1]		n!g[1]	nǁg
Voiceless uvular	ǀq[2]			
Voiceless velar fricative	ǀx	ǂx[2]	!x	ǁx
Voiced velar fricative	ǀgx			ǁgx
Prenasalised vd. velar fricative	nǀgx[1]			nǁgx[1]
Aspirated	ǀh	ǂh	!h	ǁh
Glottal	ǀ'		!'	ǁ'

Notes: 1 Kua only; 2 Tsua only.

3.2.7.2.3 PHONOLOGICAL ALTERNATIONS

These seem to be very few and limited to Kua: */dz/* has a free variant [z] and */j/* is realised as [dy] or [dʒ] before back-rounded vowels.

3.3 Southern Khoesan (Tuu)

Tom Güldemann

3.3.1 Taa (East !Xoon dialect)

3.3.1.1 Introductory remark

Anthony Traill's phonetic and phonological research on the East !Xoon variety of Taa (called by him just !Xóõ) and other languages occupies a special place in Khoesan linguistics. It not only resulted in the heretofore most extensive description of a Khoesan sound system (Traill 1985) but is also an indispensable reference for the study of other languages and comparative Khoesan. That the study of a Taa dialect has gained such an importance for Khoesan as a whole is not entirely surprising, though, because it appears to be the language with the greatest complexity of phonological distinctions on earth. The following section attempts to give an overview, rather than a complete outline of this sound system; the reader is referred to Traill's relevant publications for further reading.

3.3.1.2 Vowels

East !Xoon has a typologically unremarkable system of five distinctive vowel qualities. Nevertheless, tone aside, the total of lexically distinctive vocalic contrasts in stems is 44. This apparent discrepancy is caused by the existence of several vowel colourings or phonation types: vowels can be nasalized, breathy, pharyngealized, glottalized, and show combinations thereof. While nasalization is associated with the second or both vowels of a sequence, the locus of the other three features is only the first mora. All attested segments are given in Table 4.29.

TABLE 4.29 THE INVENTORY OF VOWEL COLOURINGS IN EAST !XOON STEMS (AFTER TRAILL 1985: 68)

a o u e i	Breathiness	Pharyngealization	Glottalization	Nasalization
Nasalization	ãh õh ũh ẽh	ã̰ õ̰ ṵ̃ + breathy ã̰h	ã’ õ’ ũ’ ẽ’ + breathy ãh’ õh’	ã õ ũ ẽ
Glottalization	ah’ oh’ uh’	a̰’ ṵ’	a’ o’ u’ e’ i’	
Pharyngealization	a̰h o̰h ṵh	a̰ o̰ ṵ		
Breathiness	ah oh uh eh ih			

3.3.1.3 Consonants

The following presentation of consonants is based on two assumptions, namely that (a) click and non-click segments can be integrated in one consonant system and (b) a variety of complex segments are clusters of two basic ones, more specifically, of a simple stop (= onset) and an egressive obstruent articulated further back (= offset). The whole argument for this analysis cannot be laid out here and the reader is referred to the more extensive discussion by Güldemann (2001) and Nakagawa (2006). Nakagawa’s research and the ongoing documentation of Taa indicate that adjustments will be necessary concerning the structure of the system and the phonological characterization of individual segments. The most important points for the systemic structure of Table 4.30 are the phonological association of ejective egressives and clicks with glottalization as well as of nasal egressives and nasal clicks. Moreover, since affricates pattern phonologically with places of articulation, they are integrated on the horizontal feature axis.

The extraordinary number of 126 lexically distinctive consonant segments is not caused by particularly many places of articulation. The major means for an extensive series formation, particularly with stops as the most important consonant class, are the wide employment of so-called “voice lead” (Traill 1985: 145–49) and the elaboration of basic segments by posterior co-articulations. Stop consonants can be classified according to the existence and the complexity of such an elaboration gesture into (a) those without a posterior elaboration called here “simple”, (b) those with aspiration and glottalization called “complex”, and (c) those with a posterior obstruent called “cluster”.

Under the present analysis, plain voiceless clicks and plain nasal clicks do not have an accompaniment or efflux in the conventional sense, but are basic segments without any elaborating co-articulation. The distinction of simple vs. complex segment is also found with nasals, because the plain nasal not only has a counterpart on the voice dimension but also with glottalization. The variety of clusters is generally a function of the inventory of velar and uvular egressives, which provide the possible cluster offsets. In East !Xoon, these are the velar fricative /*x*/, the plain uvular plosive /*q*/, an aspirated posterior plosive /*kh*/~/*qh*/, the velar ejective /*kx’*/, and the uvular ejective /*q’*/. The cluster analysis brings the inventory size of basic East !Xoon phonemes down to 74. The complex~cluster distinction also takes care of the two types of aspirated clicks: while the so-called “delayed” aspiration represents a complex aspirated segment, “normal” aspiration is analyzed as a cluster simple click+aspirated stop (its voiced counterpart had not yet been identified by Traill 1985).

3.3.1.4 Phonotactics

This multiplicity of sounds is distributed unevenly over meaning-bearing units. The general phonotactic pattern of lexical stems is a bimoraic structure $C(C)_1$-V_1-C_2-V_2.

TABLE 4.30 THE INVENTORY OF INITIAL CONSONANTS IN EAST !XOON STEMS

(43 egressives + 83 ingressives)	EG[1]	EG	EG	IG	IG	IG	IG	IG	EG	EG	EG
	Lb	Al	Al-Af	Lt	Dt	Al	Pl	Lb	Vl	Uv	Gl
Non-nasal sonorants (1)		l									
Fricatives (4)	*f*	s							x		*h*
Simple stops (11+10)											
Plain	p	t	ts	ǁ	ǀ	!	ǂ	ʘ	k	q	’
Voiced	b	d	dz	ǁg	ǀg	!g	ǂg	ʘg	g	G	
Complex stops (14+15)											
Plain + Gl		*t’*	ts’	ǁ’	ǀ’	!’	ǂ’	ʘ’	k(x)’	q’	
Voiced + Gl									gkx’		
Plain + As	ph	th	tsh	ǁh	ǀh	!h	ǂh	ʘh	kh	qh	
Voiced + As		dth	dtsh	gǁqh	gǀqh	g!qh	gǂqh	gʘqh	*gkh*	*Gqh*	
Stop clusters (9+43)											
Plain + /x/		tx	tshx	ǁx	ǀx	!x	ǂx	ʘx			
Voiced + /x/		dtx	dtshx	gǁx	gǀx	g!x	gǂx	gʘx			
Plain + /kx’/	*p’kx’*	t’kx’	ts’kx’	ǁkx’	ǀkx’	!kx’	ǂkx’	ʘkx’			
Voiced + /kx’/		dt’kx’	dts’kx’	gǁkx’	gǀkx’	g!kx’	gǂkx’	gʘkx’			
Plain + /kh/~/qh/				ǁqh	ǀqh	!qh	ǂqh	ʘqh			
Voiced + /kh/~/qh/				*Gǁqh*	*Gǀqh*	*G!qh*					
Plain + /q/				ǁq	ǀq	!q	ǂq	ʘq			
Voiced + /q/				ǁG	ǀG	!G	ǂG	ʘG			
Plain + /q’/				ǁq’	ǀq’	!q’	ǂq’	ʘq’			
Simple nasals (2+10)											
Plain	m	n		ǁn	ǀn	!n	ǂn	ʘn			
Voiceless				ǁn̥	ǀn̥	!n̥	ǂn̥	ʘn̥			
Complex nasals (2+5)											
Plain + Gl	’m	’n		’ǁn	’ǀn	’!n	’ǂn	’ʘn			

Note: 1 Af = affricate, Al = alveolar, As = aspiration, Dt = dental, EG = egressive, Gl = glottal(ization), IG = ingressive, Lb = labial, Lt = lateral, Pl = palatal, Vl = velar, Uv = uvular, *italic* = only in Traill (1994).

Minor patterns are C(C)-V_1-V_2, which result from the loss of C_2, and C(C)-V-N in which V_2 is replaced by the nasals *m*, *n*, and (dialectally) ŋ.

The use of parentheses in the initial C-slot indicates that it can be constituted by a cluster or a non-cluster consonant. In general, this initial position shows by far the most distinctions, in that virtually all segments of Table 4.30 can occur there, and it also favours the strongest consonants like clicks, clusters, plosives, etc.

As discussed by Traill (1985: 164f.), the second consonant position displays only a small fraction of phonemes, which are given in Table 4.31, and these are comparatively weak segments. The two palatals *dʸ* and *ɲ*, not occurring in Table 4.30, only occur in this slot. The first and third rows of Table 4.31 give, respectively, emphatic and weakened allophones of the normal segments in C_2.

TABLE 4.31 THE INVENTORY OF STEM-INTERNAL CONSONANTS IN EAST !XOON

	Labial	Alveolar	Palatal
Emphatic	p:	t:	tʸ:
Normal	b	l	dʸ:
Weakened	ß		j
Nasal	m	n	ɲ

Vowels in the first slot are subject to various restrictions. The most important one is the "back vowel constraint" (Traill 1985: 89–92), which states that vowels must have the feature [+back] when following a back consonant. It is still disputed which segments fall under this characterization: while Traill views all clicks as [+back], Miller-Ockhuizen (1999a) excludes the dental and palatal series. Traill (1985: 92–95) also mentions constraints on the co-occurrence of initial consonants and vowel colourings: glottalized consonants are incompatible with pharyngealized, breathy and glottalized vowels; segments with aspiration and the velar fricative are not found before pharyngealized vowels; and all aspirates and fricatives do not co-occur with breathy vowels.

If the second consonant slot is not occupied by a segment, two vowels appear adjacent to each other. While unlike vowels in sequence have been, and mostly still are, analyzed in Khoesan languages as phonemic vowel diphthongs, Traill (1985: 97) breaks with this approach in his treatment of East !Xoon. Especially prosodic considerations lead him to the conclusion that there are no phonemic glides and diphthongs, but only sequences of two full vowels. The possibilities for both VV and VCV stems are as follows: *aa, ae, ai, au, ao*; *oa, oe, oi, ou, oo*; *ua, ue, ui, uu*; *ee*; *ii*.

3.3.2 Other Tuu languages[4]

3.3.2.1 Introductory remarks

A first general statement to be made about the sound systems of other moderately recorded Tuu languages like ǁXegwi, |Xam, Nǁng (including N|huki and ǂKhomani), |Haasi, and |'Auni is that they are considerably less complex compared to East !Xoon. There are several possible explanations for this. For one thing, given that Taa has by far the most complex phoneme system of Khoesan in general, the difference between it and other Tuu languages may reflect a situation that characterized the family from very early on. This is unlikely to be the only answer, though.

The specific sociolinguistic histories of the different speech communities in their respective linguistic areas also accounts partially for the difference between Taa and the rest of Tuu, from both a diachronic and synchronic perspective. The geographic location and attested history of some languages show that their speakers have been in long and intimate language contact with other Khoesan and/or non-Khoesan languages and it is reasonable to assume that the resulting bilingualism has influenced the dynamics of sound changes occurring in them. This can account for the loss or appearance of certain sounds and explain the existence of features that seem to characterize a particular geographic sub-region rather than the entire Tuu family.

In some cases, there is also the possibility that bilingualism and the continually shrinking size of the speech community at the time of recording may have had a negative impact on the proficiency of remaining speakers. In fact, some informants no longer used their language in daily communication and were apparently in a situation of language shift like, for example, the only person providing data on |Haasi.

Finally, there is evidence for another, quite important factor: the relatively small size of the phoneme inventories is to a considerable extent an artifact of the historical and practical circumstances prevailing at the time of early Khoesan research. The other Tuu languages have not been documented and analyzed with a degree of sophistication comparable to the one applied to !Xoon, because the knowledge in phonetics and phonology was still very limited when they were recorded; nobody could expect such an enormous multiplicity of speech sounds. Consequently, the suspiciously high number of homonyms in |Xam in Bleek (1956) – the only large lexicon published on a Tuu language other than Taa – could partly be due to the non-recognition or misinterpretation of certain phonologically relevant features. Another factor that must have caused deficiencies in the analysis is the extremely short duration of the research on all languages but ǀXam. A look at the !Xoon dictionary shows that some distinctive segments are rare in its lexicon; in a short-term study, such phonemes would easily be missed. This might have happened to comparable cases in the languages at issue. This explains *inter alia* some of the apparent gaps in certain consonant series found in all languages except ǀXam. Based on his analysis of the still available audio recordings, Traill (1997: 7f., 1999: 13–16) indeed reports omissions or misinterpretations of certain sounds in the existing descriptions of ǂKhomani (Doke 1936) and ǀHaasi (Story 1999). The current research with the last speakers of Nǁng also shows that the phoneme inventory is larger.

It will be clear from the above remarks that the analyses below can only be an approximation to the real sound design of these languages. Moreover, they cannot always be stated on exclusively language-internal grounds but must be based to a large extent on typological considerations with a particular bias toward the data of Taa.

3.3.2.2 Vowels and suprasegmental features

Early transcriptions may display a high number of symbols and diacritics for vocalic segments. It is fairly certain that these do not all reflect phonologically distinctive vowel features. Apart from cross-Khoesan evidence we have clear hints to this effect from comparing different transcriptions of varieties of the same dialect cluster or even one and the same variety. Thus, Bleek (2000) has about ten vowel symbols for her ǁŊ variety, while Doke (1936: 64) gives only six phonemes and Westphal (field notes) even a conventional five-vowel system for closely related ǂKhomani and Nǀhuki, respectively; all these data represent closely related varieties of the Nǁng dialect cluster. Traill (1999: 15) argues in a similar fashion for the reduction of ǀHaasi's vowel system as presented by Story (1999).

Another question concerns the status of vowel sequences in stems. As mentioned above, the respective Taa facts do not render themselves to establishing phonemic glides and diphthongs according to Traill, but favour instead an interpretation in terms of sequences of two vowels. Nevertheless, with the exception of Lanham and Hallowes (1956: 100f.) regarding ǁXegwi, all previous treatments list several diphthongs and even triphthongs. It is unclear whether the entire range of arguments from prosody, stem phonotactics, and morphology in Traill's analysis of Taa are also relevant for other Tuu languages. At least the general relevance of the C(C)V(C)V-design of lexical stems would suggest that it could also be applied to these Tuu languages and the available data do not seem to contradict this. Comparative data and inconsistent transcriptions also show that segments with a notation C*w*V are at least historically sequences of a back vowel and a non-back vowel. The transcription of triphthongs and similar orthographic strings also seems to be related to this. Thus, the initial vocalic segment in all ǂKhomani triphthongs described by Doke (1936: 67) and in many ǀXam stems with three vowels involves a gesture of lip rounding. Also, Lanham and Hallowes (1956: 101–105) describe in ǁXegwi a full series of labialized consonants followed by one or two vowels; comparative data suggest for many of these items an earlier initial back-rounded vowel (cf. such ǂKhomani–ǁXegwi pairs as *sõe* vs. *swĩi* 'fat', *ǂnui* vs. *dlwĩi* 'ear', or *ǂoe* vs. *ʃwee* 'wind'). The apparent consonantalization of this first vowel seems to have led to the lengthening of the second vocalic segment, which would have restored the expected V-V sequence. In general, despite the diverging descriptions the rest of Tuu possibly also had originally, like Taa, only sequences of two vowels.

Finally, it is clear from descriptions, and also from later audio recordings, that various vowel colourings were also distinctive in other attested Tuu languages, parallel to Taa. Although early scholars could not yet be aware of the existence and complexity of all possible suprasegmental vowel features, they were already partially recording them in the nineteenth century. What Bleek and Lloyd (1911: viii) call in ǀXam "the nasal pronunciation of a syllable", "a rough deep pronunciation of a syllable", and "an arrest of breath" can be identified with nasalization, pharyngealization, and glottalization, respectively. The same scholars also observed that "the tone is occasionally the only distinguishing feature in words spelt otherwise alike, but having a different meaning." Similar findings, although partially involving different analytical and technical tools, terminology and orthographic representations, were explicitly or implicitly made in all later descriptions of Tuu languages.

Since it is not possible to give a concise treatment of each language separately, the following set of features is a general summary of what can be assumed for vowels in the attested Tuu languages other than Taa: (a) five distinctive vowel qualities; (b) two-vowel sequences in stems (less probable, a set of diphthongs); (c) vowel colourings like nasalization, glottalization, and pharyngealization; and (d) the existence of at least lexically distinctive tone.

3.3.2.3 Consonants

Most information on consonant phonemes will be given in the individual language charts which are organized like Table 4.30 in the section on Taa. Except for ǀXam, the symbols of the original sources are retained as far as the segments are listed there. The following discussion in the subsections can only focus on some remarkable features and problems in the analysis.

One generalization can be made for all languages. As an important difference to Taa, in fact the major reason why they have considerably smaller inventories, they usually possess only one series of voiced consonants. This is not too surprising, because the extensive use of the feature [+voice] in Taa is so far found elsewhere in Khoesan only in Juǀ'hoan.

3.3.2.4 ǀHaasi

The description by Story (1999), Traill's (1999) introduction to this publication, and Traill (1997) provide the only available information on this language from the Lower Nossob area, which is one of the least studied regions where Tuu varieties were spoken. These data allow one to establish the tentative consonant chart in Table 4.32.

The considerable gaps in some stop series suggest that the data do not represent the complete sound inventory of the language. Apparent systematic differences to Taa are (a) the existence of an additional palatal place of articulation and (b) the lack of nasals other than the plain type, and of click clusters with the offsets */kh/~/qh/* and */q'/*.

3.3.2.5 ǀXam

Most research on ǀXam was carried out in the nineteenth century. Important sources are Bleek and Lloyd (1911, field notes), Bleek (1928–30), and Meriggi (1928/29), all treating particularly the ǀXam varieties of Strandberg and Katkop, and Müller (1888), which is based on ǀXam data collected by Th. Hahn. The high level of phonetic detail which these early scholars transcribed in a language confronting the linguist with a number of then unknown speech sounds can only be admired. Owing to W.H.I. Bleek's untimely

TABLE 4.32 THE CONSONANT SYSTEM OF |HAASI

<table>
<tr><td rowspan="2">(25 egressives + 30 ingressives)[1]</td><td>EG</td><td>EG</td><td>EG</td><td>EG</td><td>IG</td><td>IG</td><td>IG</td><td>IG</td><td>IG</td><td>EG</td><td>EG</td><td>EG</td></tr>
<tr><td>Lb</td><td>Al</td><td>Al-Af</td><td>Pl</td><td>Lt</td><td>Dt</td><td>Al</td><td>Pl</td><td>Lb</td><td>Vl</td><td>Uv</td><td>Gl</td></tr>
<tr><td>Non-nasal sonorants (1)</td><td></td><td>r~l</td><td></td><td></td><td></td><td></td><td></td><td></td><td></td><td></td><td></td><td></td></tr>
<tr><td>Fricatives (3)</td><td></td><td>s</td><td></td><td></td><td></td><td></td><td></td><td></td><td></td><td>x</td><td></td><td>h</td></tr>
<tr><td>Simple stops (11+10)</td><td></td><td></td><td></td><td></td><td></td><td></td><td></td><td></td><td></td><td></td><td></td><td></td></tr>
<tr><td>Plain</td><td>p</td><td>t</td><td>ts</td><td>tj~kj</td><td>‖</td><td>|</td><td>!</td><td>ǂ</td><td>ʘp</td><td>k</td><td>q</td><td>ʼ</td></tr>
<tr><td>Voiced</td><td></td><td>d</td><td>dʒ</td><td>gj</td><td>‖g</td><td>|g</td><td>!g</td><td>ǂg</td><td>ʘb</td><td>g</td><td></td><td></td></tr>
<tr><td>Complex stops (5+7)</td><td></td><td></td><td></td><td></td><td></td><td></td><td></td><td></td><td></td><td></td><td></td><td></td></tr>
<tr><td>Plain + Gl</td><td></td><td></td><td>ts’</td><td></td><td>‖’</td><td>|’</td><td></td><td></td><td></td><td>kx’</td><td></td><td></td></tr>
<tr><td>Plain + As</td><td></td><td>th</td><td>tsh</td><td></td><td>(n)‖h</td><td>|h</td><td>!h</td><td>(n)ǂh</td><td>ʘph</td><td>kh</td><td></td><td></td></tr>
<tr><td>Stop clusters (1+9)</td><td></td><td></td><td></td><td></td><td></td><td></td><td></td><td></td><td></td><td></td><td></td><td></td></tr>
<tr><td>Plain + /x/</td><td></td><td></td><td>tsx</td><td></td><td>‖x</td><td>|x</td><td>!x</td><td></td><td>ʘpx</td><td></td><td></td><td></td></tr>
<tr><td>Plain + /kx’/</td><td></td><td></td><td></td><td></td><td>‖kx’</td><td>|kx’</td><td>!kx’</td><td></td><td></td><td></td><td></td><td></td></tr>
<tr><td>Plain + /q/</td><td></td><td></td><td></td><td></td><td>? ‖q</td><td>? |q</td><td></td><td></td><td></td><td></td><td></td><td></td></tr>
<tr><td>Nasals (4+4)</td><td>m</td><td>n</td><td></td><td>nj</td><td>‖n</td><td>|n</td><td>!n</td><td>ǂn</td><td></td><td>ŋ</td><td></td><td></td></tr>
</table>

Note: 1 *Italic* segments only in Traill (1999: 13f.), ? segments uncertain.

death, however, the |Xam data were never subject to a systematic analysis on the part of the two researchers most familiar with the language. Thus, the material necessarily has certain inevitable limitations for a phonological description according to modern standards: the transcriptions do not distinguish between phonological features and systematically irrelevant phonetic details, they display considerable fluctuation in the orthographic representation of a given linguistic item, and the orthography is strongly influenced by the conventions for writing Nama, which perpetuate some misconceptions about certain click accompaniments.

Winter (1981b: 350f.) and Traill (1995a) demonstrate that it is possible to clarify to a certain extent the phonological value of early orthographic symbols in |Xam (and other Khoesan languages) by means of a wider comparison that takes older transcriptions and related synchronic data into account. For example, clicks written as *!k* and *!* are in the majority of cases */!/* and */!'/*, respectively; also, *!k* and *!kh* should sometimes be read rather as */!x/*.

In comparison with other Tuu languages, |Xam has a low number of places of articulation. More remarkable is the lack of aspirated egressive segments, which is typologically unusual, as discussed briefly for ǂKhomani by Traill (1997: 7). However, there is a natural explanation for it in that it is related to a general phenomenon in this geographic area. This gap is also found in Nama and neighbouring Khoekhoe varieties and can be explained there by a regular sound change, namely the lenition of aspirated plosives toward affricates (Beach 1938: 218–21). In fact, this not only applies to aspirates but also to ejectives. For |Xam, too, there is good evidence that aspirated and ejective plosives are phonologically present at least in the form of affricates. Apart from Bleek's (1928–30: 83) remark that the fricatives *s* and *x* occur after homorganic plosives, hence *ts* and *kx*, the range of orthographic symbols for alveolar and velar eggressives with a fricative gesture suggest at least a three-way distinction: presumably between a fricative, a simple affricate, and an ejected affricate.

For the relevant alveolars, one finds the symbols *(t)t'*, *ts'*, *ts*, *ss'*, *(s)sh*, *(s)s*, which are partly interchangeable across different tokens of a given lexeme. Dickens (1996) shows with L. Lloyd's transcriptions of a Ju variety that her symbols *sh* and *s* may sometimes represent affricates like *tsh, ts*. Comparative evidence is also relevant; compare, for example, Bleek's ǀXam transcription *ss'aa* 'come' vs. Hahn's *ts'aa* in Müller (1888) and the pair of cognates for 'thing', ǀXam *tsaa* vs. East !Xoon *thaa*. All this suggests the existence of the following three alveolar phonemes with friction: either /*s*/, /*th*/~[tsʰ], and /*t'*/~[ts'] or /*s*/, /*ts*/, and /*ts'*/.

The orthographic series representing velar egressives with friction is *χ*, *χ̊**, and *y*. Their description in Bleek and Lloyd (1911: 438) and Meriggi (1928/29: 123) as well as comparative and typological considerations justify the assumption that there were at least three phonemes, /*x*/, /*kh*/~[kxʰ], and /*k'*/~[kx'], and possibly also /*kx*/, even though their distinctness was not always transcribed consistently. Such a series of velars has repercussions in click clusters. Since one is confronted with phonetic friction in at least three potential cluster types, /*!x*/, /*!kh*/~[!kx], and /*!k'*/~[!kx'], it is clear that transcriptions in this domain are particularly problematic. Finally, Müller (1888: 3) mentions the sounds *tx* and *tsx*, which qualify as instances of non-homorganic clusters with the velar fricative offset *x*.

TABLE 4.33 THE CONSONANT SYSTEM OF ǀXAM (PRELIMINARY)

(21 egressives + 37 ingressives)	EG	EG	IG	IG	IG	IG	IG	EG	EG
	Lb	Al	Lt	Dt	Al	Pl	Lb	Vl	Gl
Non-nasal sonorants (3)	w	r~l	y						
Fricatives (3)		s						x	h
Simple stops (7+10)									
Plain	(p)	t	ǁ	ǀ	!	ǂ	ʘ	k	'
Voiced	b	d	gǁ	gǀ	g!	gǂ	gʘ	g	
Complex stops (4+10)									
Plain + Gl		t'~ts'	ǁ'	ǀ'	!'	ǂ'	ʘ'	kx'	
Plain + As		tsʰ	ǁh	ǀh	!h	ǂh	ʘh	kx	
Stop clusters (1+12)									
Plain + /x/		tx~tsx	ǁx	ǀx	!x	ǂx			
Plain + /k'/~[kx']			ǁx'	ǀx'	!x'	ǂx'			
Plain + /kh/~[kx]			ǁkh	ǀkh	!kh	ǂkh			
Nasals (3+5)	m	n	nǁ	nǀ	n!	nǂ	nʘ	ng	

The whole consonant system is given in Table 4.33. The fact that it is compact and quite similar to the Taa one in terms of basic principles of series formation bears witness to the depth of analysis that Bleek and Lloyd had reached in their research.

For the record, there is a final feature relevant for the sound inventory of ǀXam: certain characters of its oral literature are identified by their typical way of pronunciation (Bleek 1875: 6; 1936). These speech forms are partly characterized by both egressive and ingressive sounds that are alien to the conventional phoneme system.

3.3.2.6 ǁXegwi

Lanham and Hallowes (1956) is the major source for ǁXegwi. This was cross-checked with the consonant charts given by Westphal (1971: 415) and Traill (1997: 4).

There are several striking differences from the languages discussed previously. Most importantly, the ratio of ingressives vs. the phoneme total of 0.31 is one of the lowest in Southern Africa as a whole; Tuu languages have normally the highest figures in this group. Related to this is the complete absence of the palatal click series, which has already been discussed by Traill and Vossen (1997: 41f.) in connection with the replacement and/or loss of clicks in languages that are in an environment of sociolinguistic domination by non-Khoesan click languages. It is noteworthy in this respect that one possible target of change of palatal clicks are velar lateral egressives; lateral consonants indeed exist in ǁXegwi as well as in the Bantu languages with which it has been in intimate contact, while they are unprecedented in Tuu.

There are other features of sound design which might be due to Bantu influence. ǁXegwi is so far the only attested Tuu language with voiced fricatives and affricates. Furthermore, eggressive stops with friction are far more numerous and have an apparently different phonological status: while the feature [+affricate] behaves in ǁXegwi like a canonical manner of articulation on the vertical feature axis, in other languages it is better integrated as a generalized allophonic property of some plosives.

Table 4.34 gives a possible analysis of the data on ǁXegwi consonants.

TABLE 4.34 THE CONSONANT SYSTEM OF ǁXEGWI

(48 egressives + 22 ingressives)[1]	EG	EG	EG	EG	IG	IG	IG	IG	EG	EG	EG
	Lb	Al	Pl	Lt	Lt	Dt	Al	Lb	Vl	Uv	Gl
Non-nasal sonorants (4)	w	r~l	y	l							
Fricatives (10)											
Plain		s	ʃ	hl					x		h
Voiced	ß	z	j	dl							ɦ
Simple stops (15+7)											
Plain		t		kl	ǁ	ǀ	!	ʘ	k	q	ʼ
Voiced	b	d	ɟ		ǁg	ǀg	!g		g	G	
Affricate		ts	tʃ						*kx*		
Voiced affricate		dz	dj								
Complex stops (14+4)											
Plain + As	ph	th	ch	klh	ǁŋh	ǀŋh			kh	qh	
Plain + Gl		t’	c’	kl’	ǁ’	ǀ’			k’	q’	
Affricate + Gl		ts’	tʃ’						kx’		
Stop clusters (1+7)											
Plain + /x/		tx			ǁkx	ǀkx	!kx	ʘkx			
Plain + /kh/					ǁkh	ǀkh	!kh				
Nasals (4+4)											
	m	ŋ	ɲ		ǁŋ	ǀŋ	!ŋ	ʘŋ	ŋ		

Note: 1 *Italic* segments only in Traill (1997: 4).

Finally, Lanham and Hallowes (1956) mention for ǁXegwi the frequent labialization of obstruents. Its systematic status remains unclear and it is therefore not shown in Table 4.34; it should be mentioned, though, that many lexical items listed with this feature appear to have cognates with an initial back-rounded vowel in other Tuu languages (see above).

3.3.2.7 Notes on ǀXam transcriptions

Bleek and Lloyd’s complex transcriptions of ǀXam are not fully reproduced in this and later relevant sections (Güldemann, this volume). The transliteration employed instead tries (a) to represent individual linguistic items consistently, (b) to match better the phonological relations between individual segments, (c) to be more comparable with

TABLE 4.35 TRANSLITERATION OF SOME TRANSCRIPTIONS IN THE BLEEK–LLOYD CORPUS

Bleek and Lloyd	Phonological analysis	Transliteration
Egressive consonants (*k* stands for any egressive type, if not indicated otherwise)		
kk	not distinct from plain consonant	*k*
y	ejected velar stop (affricate)	*kx'*
*n̊**	velar nasal	*ng*
Ingressive consonants (*!* stands for any ingressive click type, if not indicated otherwise)		
!k (*Θp*)	simple voiceless click	*!*
!g (*Θb*)	simple voiced click	*g!*
!n (*Θm*)	simple nasal click	*n!*
!	simple voiceless click + glottal stop	*!'*
!y	simple voiceless click + ejected velar stop (affricate)	*!x'*
!k'	unclear	*!k'*
Vowel features (*a* or *u* stands for any vowel quality)		
ā	sequence of two identical vowels	*aa* (but see next)
āū	sequence of two non-identical vowels without lengthening	*au*
ãã	nasalization (only marked on the first vowel in a sequence)	*ãa*
aä	glottalization	*a'a*
ḁa	pharyngealization	*ḁa*

widely established uses in writing Khoesan languages, and (d) to make less use of diacritics. Table 4.35 presents the major changes of this transliteration.

While this transliteration generally maintains the relative oppositions between the different orthographic symbols of the Bleek–Lloyd corpus, one group of orthographic signs has largely been omitted, namely various diacritics marking vowel qualities other than the five basic ones, different degrees of vowel length, and such seemingly suprasegmental features as "raised tone", "musical intonation", etc. (Meriggi 1928/29: 120ff.). This is justified by the fact that this kind of marking is the most inconsistent in the corpus, so that its omission is unlikely to obscure any important and clearly identifiable distinction in the present limited analysis of ǀXam. Note that the transliterated orthography cannot do away with the problems concerning the actual phonological shape of individual lexemes and thus should be evaluated for the purpose of comparative work with the same care as the original transcription by Bleek and Lloyd.

3.4 Eastern ǂHoan

Henry Honken†

3.4.1 Vowels

As is common in Khoesan, Eastern ǂHoan (EH) has five vowels: *a, e, i, o, u*. In addition to modal voicing, these may occur in three other colourings: laryngeal, pharyngeal and breathy. Since little instrumental work has been done on this language, the description given here is likely to be incomplete. For example, it is not clear from the citations in the various sources whether breathy voicing is distinctive. However, laryngealized and pharyngealized vowels certainly contrast with vowels showing modal voicing.

All of these vowels may also occur nasalized though there appear to be restrictions on the vowel sequences. In particular, EH seems to share with the other Khoesan languages a distinctive type of root structure in which clicks occur only in initial position and internal consonants are largely limited to a set of four: *b*, *r*, *m*, *n*. In this canonic structure, the optimum stem form is CVCV as in *|kobo* 'jump'. In disyllables, the vowel immediately following the initial consonant is normally *a* or *o*. If the final vowel is high, *o* is raised to *u*, as in *!kui* 'rot'. The vowel *a* may also be raised and fronted to *e* or *i* in this position, if the initial consonant is dental or palatal or the final vowel high, a quirk possibly borrowed from |Gui. Examples are *gyeo* 'road' and *ts'iu* 'tooth' (cf. Northern Khoesan *ts'ao* 'tooth').

3.4.2 Consonants

The consonantal system of EH, as in all Khoesan languages, is divided into two subgroups: egressive (non-click) and click consonants. The greater part of items in the lexicon begin with clicks. One's first impression is that the EH phonological inventory forms a subset of the !Xóõ inventory, differing from it primarily in the absence of prevoicing (see Traill 1980). Like !Xóõ, EH has a labial click series, a uvular stop as well as clicks with uvular accompaniment and a distinction between nasal clicks and preglottalized nasal clicks. Aside from the lack of prevoicing, the other differences seem to be areal – palatalization of the dentals, for example.

Among the more interesting properties of the EH phonological system is the presence of two series of affricates (most Khoesan languages have only one) and a tonal system with four level tones and one rising tone, features that link EH to Northern Khoesan.

3.4.2.1 Egressive consonants

With regard to places of articulation, plosives are found in six positions: labial, palato-alveolar, palatal, velar, uvular, and glottal. Fricatives have four places of articulation: palato-alveolar, velar, palatal, and glottal. The non-click subsystem is shown below:

TABLE 4.36 EGRESSIVE CONSONANTS IN ǂHOAN

	Labial	Palato-alveolar		Palatal	Velar	Uvular	Glottal
PLOSIVE							
Voiceless	p			ky	k	q	ʼ
Voiced	b			gy	g		
Aspirated				kyh	kh	qh	
Ejective				ky'	(k')	q'	
Prenasalized						nq	
Affricate + vcl.		ts	tc				
Affricate + voiced		dz	dj				
Affricate + aspirated		tsh	tch				
Affricate + ejective		ts'	tc'		kx'		
Affricate + fricative		tsx	tcx	kyx			
Affricate + ejective fricative			tcx'				
FRICATIVE		s		c	x		h
LIQUID		r	l				
NASAL	m			ɲ			
GLIDE	w			y			

Like the majority of Khoesan languages, EH is weak in labials. Most occurrences of initial *p* appear to be loanwords and no examples have been recorded of aspirated or glottalized *p'*. Both *b* and *m* are common as internal consonants but rare as initials.

It is not clear from the data given how to interpret the palatal series. Traill writes these obstruents as palatal stops. This discussion follows Gruber in writing the palatal series as *ky*, *gy*, etc. although it is clearly historically derived from the dental series. In fact, Traill (1980) notes that the Tshila dialect has dentals in these words. The shift of *t*, *d* to palatals appears to be an areal feature, also found in ǀGui and Southern languages like ǂKhomani and ǀ'Auni.

Unlike the surrounding languages, EH has two affricates, *ts* and *tc*. This is relatively rare in Khoesan, recorded otherwise only in some Northern Khoesan languages and ǁXegwi.

There is a contrast, also found in !Xóõ, between velar and uvular stops. The voiced uvular stop appears to be prenasalized as in !Xóõ.

There is a single lateral, realized as [r] before a high vowel and [l] elsewhere.

Initially, there are two nasals: labial and palatal, but in final position only *-m* is found.

There are four fricatives: palato-alveolar *s*, palatal *c*, velar *x* and glottal *h*. Since no instrumental data are available, the exact point of articulation for these sounds is not clear. From the data given, *c* appears to be much more common than *s*.

Laryngeal obstruents are limited to *h* and the glottal stop. The initial aspirate is frequently absorbed into the vowel. Finally, there are two glides, *w* and *y*.

3.4.2.2 Clicks

EH has five clicks: labial, dental, palatal, alveolar and lateral, found with thirteen accompaniments as in Table 4.37 below (taken from Bell and Collins 2001: 127).

TABLE 4.37 CLICK CONSONANTS IN ǂHOAN

Labial	Dental	Alveolar	Palatal	Lateral
ʘk	ǀk	!k	ǂk	ǁk
ʘg	ǀg	!g	ǂg	ǁg
nʘg	nǀg	n!g	nǂg	nǁg
'ʘn	'ǀn	'!n	'ǂn	'ǁn
nʘn	nǀn	n!n	nǂn	nǁn
ʘx	ǀx	!x	ǂx	ǁx
ʘx'	ǀx'	!x'	ǂx'	ǁx'
ʘq	ǀq	!q	ǂq	ǁq
ʘqh	ǀqh	!qh	ǂqh	ǁqh
ʘq'	ǀq'	!q'	ǂq'	ǁq'
nʘq	nǀq	n!q	nǂq	nǁq
ʘh	ǀh	!h	ǂh	ǁh
ʘ'	ǀ'	!'	ǂ'	ǁ'

The data in Table 4.37 are based on material collected by Gruber and show the general outline of EH click phonology. The EH system has one of the more complex systems found in the Khoesan area, showing features reminiscent of both !Xóõ and ǀGui. The click system of EH resembles that of !Xóõ in possessing a labial click, a uvular series and a contrast between preglottalized and prenasalized clicks but it lacks voicing lead. However, in recent work by Bell and Collins (2001) this picture has changed to some extent. The main points of difference are summarized here. In general, their analysis follows that of Gruber except for the nasal and aspirated series.

Bell and Collins present evidence to show that EH has a three-way contrast in the aspirated clicks: velar aspirated, uvular aspirated and delayed aspiration. A similar set of contrasts is found in ǀGui (Nakagawa 1996b). Clicks with delayed aspiration are similar to those found in Juǀ'hoan and Nama. Vowels preceding the click are slightly nasalized, presumably due to the nasal venting that characterizes this type of accompaniment, and the aspiration builds slowly rather than starting immediately after the click.

There also appears to be a contrast between aspirated clicks with velar release and aspirated clicks with uvular release as in *kǀha* 'to stuff in' and *qǀha* 'women'. In the latter type, there is an audible uvular release just after the click burst and the aspiration begins immediately after the uvular closure is released.

Bell and Collins suggest that the accompaniment described by Gruber as a prenasalized velar release is actually a variant of the voiced uvular release, which is normally prenasalized as in !Xóõ. For example, they record Gruber's *nǀgai* 'maiden' and *nǀgoi* 'mock' as *NǀGai* and *NǀGoi*. If this analysis is correct, then EH patterns with other San languages in lacking the contrast between plain nasal and prenasalized voiced velar releases so characteristic of Central Khoesan.

3.5 Kwadi[5]

Tom Güldemann

Westphal's tentative hypotheses on Kwadi vowels have been a four- or six-vowel set with oral and nasal variants. His notes suggest that there are vowel height assimilations across morpheme boundaries and a possible distinction between stem-initial vowels with and without a glottal onset (the transcription fluctuates between *a*, *ha*, and *wa*).

The most remarkable fact about Kwadi regarding consonants is the rarity of clicks both in terms of the number of distinctive segments and their frequency across the lexicon. Although Westphal considers four influxes in his drafted consonant charts, only dental clicks constitute a fairly secure series in his recorded material; the palatal click is only found in a few lexical items, the lateral click has just one token as a variant transcription, and the alveolar click is missing altogether.

The exact articulation places of egressives, especially in the post-alveolar region, must remain unclear. In his two preliminary consonant charts, Westphal alternates between one and two palatal series; some of his earlier palatals are represented in Westphal (1971) as laterals; and finally some palatals even fluctuate in their transcription with velars. The solution in Table 4.38 is a palatal and a lateral series.

TABLE 4.38 THE (TENTATIVE) CONSONANT SYSTEM OF KWADI

	Labial	Dental	Alveolar	Lateral		Palatal		Velar	Glottal
	EG	IG	EG	EG	IG	EG	IG	EG	EG
Nasals	m	ŋǀ	n			ny (ɲ)		ŋ	
Voiceless stops	p	ǀ	t	tɬ	ǁ	c	ǂ	k	’
Voiced stops	b~ß		d			ɟ		g	
Aspirated stops	p(f)ʰ	ǀʰ	t(s)ʰ	tɬʰ		cʰ		k(x)ʰ	
Ejectives		ǀ’		tɬ’			ǂ’	k(x)’	
Plain + /x/		ǀx							
Fricatives	f		s	ɬ		ʃ		x	h
Approximants	w		l~r			y			

While a number of assimilatory processes seem to occur in morphologically complex word forms, generalizations cannot be made due to the rare and often irregular attestations.

NOTES

1 These vowels involve contact between the epiglottis and the pharyngeal wall, as was shown by Traill (1985: 78ff.).
2 I have used the orthographic symbols for these sounds, although they are really voiceless aspirated nasals (see Ladefoged and Traill 1994). Dickens calls the labial voiceless nasal an aspirated syllabic consonant.
3 Which comes from *CVNV. The N as sonorant can still function as a syllable (and tone-bearer).
4 The unpublished field notes of the Bleek family and E.O.J. Westphal are hosted by the "Manuscripts and Archives Department (University of Cape Town)".
5 All data stem from Westphal's unpublished notes, hosted by the "Manuscripts and Archives Department (University of Cape Town)". He took them down on the occasion of analyzing Kwadi audio recordings by a Portuguese anthropologist in 1956 and 1959 and his field trip to southwestern Angola in 1964/65. Since he did not refurbish his material systematically, the considerable transcriptional variation cannot be evaluated conclusively and all analyses must remain very tentative.

REFERENCES

Beach 1938; Bell and Collins 2001; D.F. Bleek 1928–30, 1936, 1956, 2000; W.H.I. Bleek 1875; Bleek and Lloyd 1911; Collins 2001; Dickens 1994, 1996; Doke 1936; Elderkin 1988; Gruber 1973, 1975; Güldemann 2001; Haacke 1988, 1989, 1999; Haacke *et al.* 1997; Hagman 1977; Halle 1995; Heikkinen n.d.; Heine and König 2012; HIPA 1999; Ito and Mester 1986; Kilian-Hatz 2008; Köhler 1981; König and Heine 2008; Ladefoged and Traill 1994; Lanham and Hallowes 1956; McCarthy 1991, 1994; Meinhof 1930; Meriggi 1928/29; Miller 2007, 2010, 2011; Miller *et al.* 2011; Miller-Ockhuizen 1999a, 1999b, 2000, 2003; Miller-Ockhuizen and Sands 1999, 2000; Müller 1888; Nakagawa 1996a, 1996b, 1998, 2006; Nama/Damara Language Committee 1977; Sands 2010; Sands and Miller-Ockhuizen 1999, 2000; Sands *et al.* 1996; Snyman 1970, 1975a, 1975b, 1997; Story 1999; Traill 1980, 1985, 1986a, 1994, 1995a, 1997, 1999; Traill and Nakagawa 2000; Traill and Vossen 1997; Tucker *et al.* 1977; Visser 2001; Vossen 1986b, 1991, 1997a; Westphal 1971; Widlok 1997; Winter 1981b.

CHAPTER FIVE

TONOLOGY

1 HADZA

Bonny Sands

Hadza contrasts high and low tone on syllables (cf. Sands *et al.* 1996). There seem to be no phonotactic constraints on the possible combinations of high and low tone in nominal roots of 1–3 syllables, as shown in Table 5.1. With longer forms, it is difficult to tell whether or not one is dealing with a single root, but apparent 4-syllable roots have a wide range of patterns, e.g. LHLH [pàtákùʃé-] 'palm, sole (m)', HHLL [ǀ'úkúmàjè-] 'elbow (f)'; HLLH [ʔáwànìká-] 'mouth (m)', etc. Verb roots (Tables 5.2–5.3) usually have one surface high tone. There is no strong evidence for lexical tones in Hadza apart from low and high. Mid tone surfaces in certain environments (Tucker *et al.* 1977), but it does not appear to be contrastive at the word level. Falling tones seem only to occur in phrase-final position (especially with final devoiced or deleted 'V sequences) and on surface vowels that have underlyingly VV sequences.

The analysis of Hadza tone must be able to account for the number of different realizations of surface tone in different frames. It is difficult to proceed with analyses of Hadza tonology when few words have been recorded in more than a few frames, and given that there are few tonal minimal pairs in the language. However, it is clear that high tone must be lexically specified for lexical and grammatical morphemes. As in the

TABLE 5.1 HADZA SURFACE TONE PATTERNS ON NOUN ROOTS OF 1–3 SYLLABLES IN LOW TONE FRAME 'Is a___': root + copula *à* + 3SG gender marker (Ø M, -*kʰò* F)

H	*ŋ!é-*	'leopard' (M)	L	*ǁ'è-*	'liver' (F)
HH	*tʀ' álá-*	'dust' (F)	LL	*!ùmà*	'club' (F)
HL	*tʀ'ápò-*	'dove' (F)	LH	*ʔàkhwá*	'eye' (F)
LLL	*fifimò-*	'tiger snake' (M)			
HHH	*nák'ómá-*	'buffalo' (F)			
LLH	*gùmbùlú-*	'water monitor lizard' (M)			
HHL	*mángólò-*	'white-necked raven' (F)			
HLH	*ʔáthàmá-*	'blood' (M)			
LHL	*bèk'áhù-*	'elephant' (F)			
HLL	*ǁá'ànò-*	'dog' (M)			
LHH	*nùmbílí*	'vervet monkey' (M)			

TABLE 5.2 HADZA SURFACE TONE PATTERNS ON MONOSYLLABIC VERB ROOTS IN SEVERAL VERB FRAMES

H	[tʃʰí-àmè]	'they (M) ran'	L	[ǁʰù-ámè]	'they (M) stood still'
H	[tʃʰí-ámò]	'they (M) ran'	H	[ǁʰú-ámò]	'he stood still'
H	[tʃʰí-ʔí]	'You (SG) run!'	H	[ǁʰú-ʔú]	'You (SG) stand still!'
H	[tʃʰí-sì]	'You (M.PL) run!'	L	[ǁʰù-sí]	'You (M.PL) stand still!'

TABLE 5.3 HADZA – MAIN SURFACE TONE PATTERNS ON VERB ROOTS (IN TWO FIRST PERSON FUTURE VERB FRAMES)

Type 1:

H/H	[ʔìnà tʃʰí, tʃʰí-ːtà]	'I will run'
HL/LH	[ʔìnà ʔásè, ʔàsé-ːtà]	'I will sleep'
	[ʔìnà húkwà, hùkwá-ːtà]	'I will fly/jump'
LHL/LLH	[ʔìnà ʔòmóʔò, -ʔòmòʔóːtà]	'I will give birth'

Type 2:

H/L	[ʔìnà ǁʰú-, ǁʰù-hétà]	'I will stand still'
LH/LL	[ʔìnà kwè!é, kwè!è-hétà]	'I will return quickly'
	[ʔìnà ʔùmú, ʔùmù-hétà]	'I will drown'
	[ʔìnà ǀiká, ǀikà-hétà]	'I will hiccup'
LHL/LHL	[ʔìnà ɬàkákà, ɬàkákà-hétà]	'I will slip'

example below, if we consider L to be underlyingly specified as well, we can explain why H is sometimes blocked from spreading and sometimes is able to spread rightward.

```
     H                    H  L
    / \                   |  |
[ǀ'èts'é-kʰó]    vs.   [ǀ'èts'é-jà-kʰo]
tick-3F.SG             tick-copula-3F.SG
'a tick'               'is a tick'
```

It may be that the metrical structure interacts with tone at the phrase level in a way not seen at the word level. Tucker *et al.* (1977) point to the presence of mid tone in nouns in one frame, preceding the verb [bàhè-à] 'there is (3M.SG)'. Nouns realized with a variety of tones (e.g. LLH, HLH, HHH) when preceding the copula and agreement marker are noted as having a flat mid tone in this environment, e.g., [nāk'ōmā bàhèà] 'there is a (M) buffalo' vs. [nák'ómá-à-kʰò] 'is a (F) buffalo'. Other roots, however, are unaffected by the change in frame and retain their original tones, e.g., [sésèmé bàhèà] 'there is a (M) lion' vs. [sésèmé-ja] 'is a (M) lion', and [kʰálìmò bàhèà] 'there is an animal' vs. [kʰálìmò-wà] 'is an animal'. Clearly, much work remains to be done on Hadza tonology.

2 SANDAWE

Edward D. Elderkin

2.1 Basic tones

Sandawe has two tonal values, high and low. Each mora has one of these values. Thus the mora not only relates to duration in time, but is also the tone-bearing unit. E.g.:

(1)	HH	*tsí*	'I'
	HL	*tû*	'to come out'
	LL	*kʰwà*	'to return'
	HHH	*k'éː*	'to cry'
	HHL	*ǀ'ấːⁿnà*	'above'
		k'êsi̥	'I'll cry'

With closure:

(2) HH L *tóẁ* 'to finish'
LL H *ǀ'èẃ* 'buffalo'
HL L *kêẁtò* 'wild pig'
LL L *kùtùm̀té* 'to kneel'

A rising pitch (LH) is not allowed on the final two moras of the vowel in a syllable. HL as the final two moras of a long vowel are not found followed by a closure. We can now refer to a morphological category, the word, but continue a discussion of phenomena related to pitch.

2.2 Tone within a word

The realisation of tone depends on its position within a word. A short vowel has two moras, a long vowel has three moras. Sequences of formatives can give a longer vowel of four moras. A syllable closure has one mora.

2.2.1 Low tones

A low mora immediately following a high mora is raised nearly to the pitch level of that high. A following low mora is also raised, but not so much.

(3)

dzìgídàsà
dzìgídà sà
heart 3F.SG
'she heart'

2.2.2 Downstep

Usually, a syllable-final h and a following syllable-initial h have identical realisations. Downdrift occurs when highs are separated by one or more low moras.

(4)

ʔísòlí
'arrow type'

On occasions, downstep has to be analysed.

(5)

ǂ̥í'pó
'you don't come'

Downstep occurs before a low tone.

(6)

ʔíꜜʔwàː
'give (multiple)'

Downstep is always transparently the result of the loss of a low toned syllable.
We can now discuss relations of pitch obtaining between words in an utterance.

2.3 Words in sequence

2.3.1 Keys

A word has a pitch range within which its high and low moras are realised. This range is dependent on the relative pitch of the first high mora. The high and low moras of a following word will be realised within a pitch range; its first high mora will be realised either higher than, identical to or lower than the first high mora of the preceding word. I refer to these relative pitch ranges as "keys", and number them from the highest to the lowest. The key of a word is shown in the transcription by a superscript number initial to the word. The following example illustrates this.

(7)

¹ʔèʔéː ²tl'àbísõ̂ː ³wàré ¹kúm̀gâː
ʔèʔéː tl'àbísó ȉ wàré kúm̀ gê àː
that time stomach SPEC friend hurt DEC 3M.SG
'that stomach problem, it's really hurting, friend'

Words with all lows fit uneasily into the system of keys, but can be accommodated. It does not make sense descriptively to attempt to merge downstep, which happens within a word, and this system of keys.

2.3.2 Utterances

An utterance may be realised with pitch ranges higher than expected, transposed upwards by about one key. Such an utterance is then interpreted as a question. It sometimes happens that there is a raising of the pitch of a key on a constituent and this supplements other, syntactic, methods of giving informational prominence. Especially towards the end of utterances, after the last marked constituent, the allocation to keys in the transcription becomes phonetic rather than phonemic.

3 SOUTH AFRICAN KHOESAN

3.1 Northern Khoesan

Amanda L. Miller

As with other aspects of Northern Khoesan, Ju|'hoan tonology is better described than other NK languages. Elderkin (1988) and Miller-Ockhuizen (1998) have documented the different tone patterns, and offered phonological accounts for why non-existent patterns do not occur. Okongo !Xung is the next best described, with Heikkinen's (1986) work marking tone patterns, but she does not describe the tonal system in detail. There has been virtually no description of the tonal systems of other Northern Khoesan varieties such as Gobabis !Xung, Mangetti Dune !Xung, Angolan !Xung varieties and ǂAu‖en. Doke (1925) describes the basic details of the tonology of Grootfontein !Xung, but his descriptions are preliminary.

The Ju|'hoan tonal system is composed of four lexical tones, called Super Low, Low, High and Super High, based on Snyman's (1975a) original Afrikaans names *Super Laag*, *Laag*, *Hoog*, and *Super Hoog*. There are seven tone patterns that occur on Ju|'hoan roots: four level tones, as well as three tone sequences, each of which is shown in (8) below on the vowel [a]:

(8) Seven lexical tone patterns in Ju|'hoan

abbreviation	tone name	tone symbol
SL	Super Low	ȁȁ
L	Low	àà
H	High	áá
SH	Super High	a̋a̋
SL–L	Super Low–Low	ȁà
L–H	Low–High	àá
H–L	High–Low	áà

Miller-Ockhuizen (1999c) demonstrates that there is no vowel length contrast in Ju|'hoan, and that all monosyllabic rimes are bimoraic, based on the fact that there is no significant vowel length difference associated with words that Dickens (1994) and Snyman (1975a) mark as CV vs. CVV. Heikkinen (1986: 19) transcribes bitonal roots and diphthongs in Mangetti Dune !Xung with two vowels, but monotonal monophthongal vowels as monovocalic, and notes that there is no vowel length contrast in that language, but that this is an orthographic practice. Doke (1925: 137) claims that there is a vowel length contrast in Grootfontein !Xung, citing minimal pairs.

The tone-bearing unit, the unit that tones associate to, can be either the mora as argued by Miller-Ockhuizen (1998), the syllable, or the root, as argued by Traill (1985: 32) for !Xóõ. Monosyllabic and bisyllabic roots show the same tone patterns, as shown in (9):

(9) Tone patterns on monosyllabic/bisyllabic roots

a. Six tone patterns on monosyllabic roots

<u>SL</u>
kə̏ȕ^h 'to light a fire'

<u>L</u>
|xə̀ì 'to spit'

<u>H</u>
n|óá 'to cook'

<u>SH</u>
!ə̋ű 'to move house'

<u>SL–L</u>
n|^{h}ȕì 'to take'

<u>L–H</u>
g|kx'ùí 'to twist'

b. Seven tone patterns on bisyllabic roots

<u>SL</u>
n‖ȍ.βȍ^h 'orphan'

<u>L</u>
n‖ò.βò 'orphan'

<u>H</u>
g!ú.βú 'to bubble up'

<u>SH</u>
g!ő.βe̋ 'hare path'

<u>SL–L</u>
!ə̏.βì 'to colour'

<u>L–H</u>
n|ò.βá 'to walk fast'

<u>H–L</u>
dcáhà 'edible, plum-shaped fruit'

Note that the H–L pattern only occurs on bisyllabic nouns in the language, and most roots bearing this tone pattern are loanwords from Central Khoesan languages.

The fact that monosyllabic and bisyllabic roots bear maximally two lexical tones requires a separate distributional constraint under the mora, syllable and root as tone-bearing unit analyses. Within the moraic analysis, this limitation is explained if there is a constraint requiring only one tone per tone-bearing unit. This cannot be a universal constraint, since there are many languages, such as Kenyang, which allow contour tones on a single mora (Odden 1995: 451). Syllable and root as tone-bearing unit approaches allow two tones per tone-bearing unit, but have a constraint limiting the number of tones on the root to two, in order to rule out tritonal patterns on bisyllabic roots. Trisyllabic roots, shown in (10), support the mora as tone-bearing unit approach, since these contain contrastive association of bitonal patterns, and one tritonal pattern.

(10) Tonal patterns exhibited on trisyllabic roots

<u>L H H</u>		<u>L L H</u>	
nǀ^{h}à.bí.té	'duck'	*ǁʔ^{h}ò.rò.kó*	'hornbill'
<u>L H L</u>			
gà.rí.sà	'tree snake'		
<u>H L L</u>		<u>H H L</u>	
húhà^{q}rà	'flamingo'	*búrúkhè*	'trousers' (< Afr. *broek*)

Miller-Ockhuizen (1999a, 2003) gives supporting evidence from reduplication which favours the moraic analysis. In partial reduplication in Juǀ'hoan, there is a disparity in the amount of material copied from the base in bisyllabic words, depending on whether the root is monotonal or bitonal. As shown in (11a), if the root is monosyllabic, the entire root is copied. As shown in (11b), in bisyllabic monotonal roots, only the first syllable of the base is copied. As shown in (11c), if the base is bisyllabic and bitonal, both vowels are copied.

(11) Partial reduplication in Juǀ'hoan

a. Monotonal and bitonal monosyllabic roots

cə̀ò	'to be wide'	*<u>cə̀ò</u>.cə̀ò*	'to widen'
!ə́ṹ^n	'to be sick'	*<u>!ə́ú^n</u>.!ə́ṹ^n*	'to make ill'
nǀù'í	'to be shiny'	*<u>nǀù'í</u>.nǀù'í*	'to cause to be shiny'

b. Reduplicated forms of monotonal bisyllabic roots

ǂʔ^{h}ù.βì	'to be crowded'	*<u>ǂʔ^{h}ù</u>.ǂʔ^{h}ù.βì*	'to cause to crowd together'
gǂkx'ò.rò	'to pour'	*<u>gǂkx'ò</u>.gǂkx'ò.rò*	'to empty out'

c. Reduplicated forms of bitonal bisyllabic roots

tsxə̀.βí	'to grab'	*<u>tsxə́í</u>.tsxə́.βí*	'to grab forcefully'
nǂà^q.ró	'to find s.th.'	*<u>nǂà^{q}ó</u>.nǂà^q.ró*	'to find a lost object'

If the mora is the tone-bearing unit and there is a distributional constraint requiring there to be only one tone per tone-bearing unit, these facts are explained. The root and syllable theories cannot explain these facts.

3.1.1 Constraints on tone combinations

All of the tone sequences found in Juǀ'hoan are of tones similar in fundamental frequency. Miller-Ockhuizen (1998) argues that a scalar tone feature is necessary in order to state this distributional constraint in the phonology. With a scalar tone feature, all tone sequences in the language involve tones that are one tone feature specification apart. This analysis predicts that H–SH and SH–H and L–SL should also be attested, but these are not found. The lack of sequences involving SH tone then could be due to its scarcity overall. Alternatively, the fact that the fundamental frequency of SH~H tones is not equidistant as sequences of SL, L and H tones are, could lead to the unacceptability of H–SH sequences. For example, in a study of six speakers' productions of all lexical tone patterns, Miller-Ockhuizen (in progress) found that the SH tone was about 50 Hz higher than H, while H~L and L~SL are only about 25 Hz apart. Thus H and SH tones are not phonetically similar enough to be allowed to co-occur on a single root.

The absence of the L–SL sequence is due to the historical origin of SL–L and L–H tones in phonetic perturbation due to initial voiced aspirated, nasal aspirated and voiced consonants. The high frequency of these consonant types with SL and SL–L patterns is supportive of this view.

Heikkinen's (1987) wordlist of Okongo !Xung contains roots bearing most tone sequences as shown in (12), illustrating that this language does not have a constraint on tonal similarity.

(12) Lexical tone patterns in Okongo !Xung

SL		L	
börö	'bottle'	*!òm*	'sew'
H		SH	
!óβé	'backbone'	*ts'a̋u*	'urinate'
SL–L		L–H	
tsäǹà	'to scratch the ground'	*tsàʔá*^{n}	'sauce'
SL–H		H–SH	
kö^{q}*βé*	'ground'	*n‖óʔű*^{n}	'play'
L–SH		SL–SH	
dəű	'valley'	*'nǂärű*	'to give'
H–L			
ts'ámà	'bird'		
SH–H		SH–L	
khűkhú	'hen'	*ǀ'ű̃sà*	'tree species'

The only patterns that are not attested are H–SL, L–SL and SH–SL. These gaps do not appear to be principled; however, they might be explained by the historical origin of SL tone, which is related to initial depressor consonants, since all missing combinations involve SL. Grootfontein !Xung (Doke 1925: 149ff.) is only claimed to have three lexical tone levels.

3.1.2 Tone – phonation type dependencies

Depression of tone is not only connected to initial depressor consonants, but also to vocalic phonation type contrasts. Breathy and epiglottalized vowels only co-occur with the two lower tones. Elderkin (1988) connects the lack of co-occurrence between laryngeal specifications of consonants and laryngeal specifications of vowels, and the high co-occurrence of similar consonant and vowel features with certain tonal patterns historically. While his diachronic analysis is plausible, there are too many exceptions to warrant any synchronic connection between these two separate constraints.

Synchronically, epiglottalization is the only vocalic phonation type which shows systematic depression of fundamental frequency. Epiglottalized vowels are about 30 Hz lower than modal vowels bearing the same lexical tone, but there are no differences in fundamental frequency in modal and breathy vowels bearing the same tone (Miller-Ockhuizen 2003).

3.1.3 Phrasal tonology

Little is known about the phrasal tonology of any Khoesan language. In Ju|'hoan words in isolation always have an approximately 50 Hz drop in pitch over the last 25 per cent of the word. Since this plunge in fundamental frequency is found with all tone patterns, it is likely that this is a separate edge effect. This might be due to final lowering or a phrasal edge tone, but investigation of pitch patterns in phrases will be necessary to determine its nature. Mangetti Dune !Xung exhibits different edge tones. There are some words that have H edge tones, where the Ju|'hoan cognate has an L edge tone. This property is seriously under-described, and in need of further research.

3.2 Central Khoesan

3.2.1 Namibian Khoekhoe

Wilfrid H.G. Haacke

Khoekhoegowab (N.Kh.), like all Khoesan languages, is a true tone language. Each syllable of a root is associated with a distinctive register (level) tone. Four surface tones – /˵/, /ˋ/, /ˊ/ and /˝/, here dubbed "double low", "low", "high" and "double high" – pair into feet to form six major (and some further five rare) tonal melodies, three rising, two falling, one level. Syllable and tone are isomorphic. All roots are basically disyllabic, diachronically based on a CVCV skeleton, and hence associate isomorphically with the bimoraic tonal melody. The skeleton may, through deletion of C_2 or V_2, have been reduced to CVV, Cṽṽ or CVN. Yet it stays disyllabic. The melody of the few trisyllabic roots that do exist, consist of a bimoraic foot combined with a single tone. Roots (here quoted with a nominalising *-s* to achieve uniformity) have a citation form and a sandhi form that occurs in particular contexts:

Citation	Sandhi	Gloss
!ȍm̀(-s)	*!òm̏(-s)*	'to butt, push'
!ȍḿ-s	*!ȍḿ-s*	'udder'
!òm̀(-s)	*!òm̀(-s)*	'force exit from burrow'
!óm̀(-s)	*!òm̏(-s)*	'coagulate; remove thorn'
!òm̋-s	*!òm̀-s*	'pollard'
!őḿ-s	*!óm̀-s*	'fist'

While the citation form occurs at the beginning of tonological domains, e.g. sentence-initially or phrase-initially, the sandhi form occurs in non-initial positions of a tonological domain; e.g.

tàrȁs ge	'it is a woman'	citation form of *taras*
|khara tàràs ge	'it is a different woman'	sandhi form of *taras*

N.Kh. has, through tonogenesis (tonal depression caused by especially voiced consonants and subsequent devoicing of such consonants), developed an additional tone, the "double low" tone, which in turn has created two new major citation melodies: /˵ˋ/ from /ˊˋ/ and /˵ˊ/ from /ˋˋ/.

Of the three main areas representing tone languages (American Indian, African, and Sino-Tibetan with South-East Asian), N.Kh. tonology is typologically most akin to the South-East Asian type. It uses paradigmatic displacement of melodies rather than syntagmatic feature-changing rules. Another type of perturbation, shared with, *inter alia*, Chinese, is flip-flop, whereby the above citation forms pair off to interchange the respective members in certain contexts as follows:

weak		resilient
/˵ˋ/	and	/˵ˊ/
/ˊˋ/	and	/ˋˋ/
/˝ˊ/	and	/ˋ˝/

In cases where "bilateral" flip-flop applies, both weak and resilient members of a pair exchange; in cases of "unilateral" flip-flop only the weak members change to the resilient members, but not *vice versa*.

While sandhi applies in lexical as well as post-lexical tonology, flip-flop is confined to lexical tonology. Within the lexical tonology sandhi, flip-flop and other tone rules can interact cyclically within the same domain; e.g., in causative formation flip-flop applies to the first root and the "drop" rule (inserting a /ˋ˵/ melody) to the second. Within a post-lexical context where this word does not stand phrase-initially, the sandhi equivalent of the flipped melody of the first root appears:

root:	*ǀgűí*	'one'	citation form
causative (duplication)	*ǀgùí̋ǀgùȉ*	'unite'	flip-flop + drop
	. . . *ǀgùìǀgùȉ*	'unite'	sandhi of flip-flop, + drop

Tone can have derivational functions, apart from causative formation, e.g. intransitive verb formation with /ˋˋ/ or /˵ˊ/: *ȁwó* 'dent' > *àwò* 'become dented'; noun formation (mostly by flip-flop), e.g. *ǁhäwú* 'flare up (v.intr.)' > *ǁhäwùb* 'flame' (n.).

Grammatical formatives, which mostly are monosyllabic, bear a single tone. Such tones, not being constituted as feet, are not subject to the rules of the lexical melodies.

3.2.2 Kxoe subgroup: Khwe, ǁAni

Rainer Vossen

Köhler's (1981: 488ff.) complex analysis of the tonal system of Khwe consists of nine syllabic tones: three register and six contour tones. Table 5.4 indicates their occurrence on mono-, di- and trisyllabic lexical stems:

TABLE 5.4 LEXICAL TONE PATTERNS IN KHWE (AFTER KÖHLER 1981)

Syllabic tone	Monosyllabic stems	Disyllabic stems	Trisyllabic stems
H(igh)	+	+	+
M(id)		+	+
L(ow)		+	
H–M	+		
H–L	+		
M–H_1	+	+	
M–H_2	+	+	
L–H_1	+		
L–H_2	+		

Mid and low tone may also occur on monosyllabic grammatical morphemes.

With regard to (a) di- and (b) trisyllabic lexemes, the following tone patterns derive from the combination of syllabic tones:

(a) L–LH; L–H; H–L; H–M; H–H; MH_1–M; MH_1–H;
(b) H–M–M.

When taking the mora as a basic unit of the phonological structure into account, Köhler's tone combinations can probably be traced back to essentially three register tones: High, Mid, and Low (cf. Vossen 1997a: 97). This coincides exactly with what Kilian-Hatz (2008: 24f.) has proposed recently.

In ǁAni, tonal behaviour appears to comply with the mora principle; i.e., at least two tonal segments – High and/or Low – are assigned to lexical morphemes. On both mono- and disyllabic stems the tonal sequences H–H, H–L, and L–H are found, whereas L–L is attested for one item only. As has already been observed by Köhler (1981) for Khwe, lexical items with identical tonal surface structure are often characterised by morpho-tonological differences. In ǁAni this applies to verbs in particular. Verbal roots containing H–H and L–H sequences can be sub-divided into two classes each. As a result, five verbal tone classes obtain. It should also be noted here that the tonal behaviour of ǁAni verbs is influenced by stress (see Vossen 2004).

3.2.3 Naro

Hessel Visser

Tone is distinctive in Naro. It is carried by vowels and /*m*/. Three tonemes can be distinguished: H(igh), M(id) and L(ow). High tone is marked by an acute accent (/*á*/), low tone by a grave accent (/*à*/), mid tone will be unmarked (/*a*/).

Seven tone melodies are identified for Naro words with two tone-bearing units:

Tone melodies	High	Mid	Low
High	H–H		H–L
Mid		M–M	M–L
Low	L–H	L–M	L–L

The tone melodies H–H and M–M are level: the tone remains the same. H–L, M–L and L–L are falling tone melodies: the tone drops from a higher to a lower frequency. L–M and L–H are rising tone melodies: the tone rises from a lower to a higher frequency. These tone melodies may occur on roots with CVV, CVN and CVCV patterns.

3.2.3.1 Environment

A voiced consonant usually has a lowering effect on the tone of the first vowel: the tone on the first vowel is low. The only exceptions that have been found so far are *bóò* 'to see' (cf. Proto-Bantu *-bón-) and *bíì* 'milk' (Proto-Bantu *-bícì or *-bícį 'fresh milk').

Vowels after an ejective consonant usually have high or mid tone. Low tones are never found after an ejective consonant.

3.2.3.2 List of contrasts

The longest list of minimal pairs of tone melodies in Naro is found on the CVV combination *ǁae* and *!ao*:

H–H	*!áó*	'leftover, half'	*ǀáé*	'we (three or more men)'
H–L	*!áò*	'long'	*ǀáè*	'to breed, sit on s.th.'
M–M	*!ao*	'near' (not a noun/verb)	*ǀae*	'to chew'
M–L	*!aò*	'to choose; to come up'	*ǀaè*	'to watch'
L–L	*!àò*	'palm-nut vulture (*Gypohierax angolensis*)'	*ǀàè*	'to scrape (a hide)'
			ǀàè	'to shelter (against wind)'

Additional examples for the seven tone melodies can be found in the following minimal pairs.

H–L H–H	*kx'áò*	'male'	*kx'áó*	'arrow'
	!xóò	'pipe'	*!xóó*	'to hold'
L–L L–M	*g!òm̀*	'to blow'	*g!òm*	'to shave'
	ǀòò	'to follow'	*ǀòo*	'forehead'
L–M L–H	*ǁgùu*	'breast'	*ǁgùú*	'to make fire'
	ǁnàu	'meerkat sp.'	*ǁnàú*	'to shave'
L–M M–M	*ǀìi*	'wild dog'	*ǀii*	'song'
	ǂòm	'bag'	*ǂom*	'honest'
M–M M–L	*ǀ'am*	'point'	*ǀ'am̀*	'to gossip'
	!uu	'dancing skirt'	*!uù*	'tree'
M–L H–L	*!aò*	'to rise'	*!áò*	'tall'
	!'om̀	'lower abdomen'	*!'óm̀*	'strike'
H–H M–M	*!úú*	'to lift on head'	*!uu*	'dancing skirt'
	káí	'many'	*kai*	'old'
M–L L–L	*koò*	'to chase away'	*kòò*	'to sweep'
	ǁaè	'to watch'	*ǁàè*	'to scratch hide'

3.2.4 ǁGana subgroup: ǀGui

Hirosi Nakagawa

This section outlines ǀGui tonology based on the result of my research on the Xade dialect, which is presently spoken mainly in "New Xade", Ghanzi District, Botswana. Tonal systems of other ǁGana languages and dialects have not been investigated systematically. Judging from my occasional observations on other ǁGana dialects (presently or formerly spoken in Xade, Molapo and Thomelo), however, there is no remarkable difference in tonal type between these and ǀGui.

ǀGui tonology shows a typological similarity to Khoekhoe, which is best documented by Haacke (1999). In the following account I will use a number of Haacke's terms, such as "(tonal) melody", "flip-flop" and "flip-flop pair", for convenience of reference.

3.2.4.1 Two tonological domains

ǀGui has two types of tonological domains which involve different contrastive tone levels. Henceforth, I refer to the two domains as DOM_1 and DOM_2. DOM_1 includes bimoraic roots, the first two morae of trimoraic roots, the first component of reduplication constructions and the first and the second components of lexical reduplication. Note that these forms are all bimoraic. This domain involves three contrastive tone levels: H(igh), M(id) and L(ow).

On the other hand, DOM_2 includes monomoraic and bimoraic non-root elements, such as affixes, postpositions and other grammatical morphemes, the second component of reduplication constructions and the final mora of trimoraic roots. Unlike DOM_1, this domain involves only two contrastive tone levels, i.e. H and L.

It should be noted that in addition to the difference in numbers of contrastive tone levels between DOM_1 and DOM_2, there are two differences in prosodic properties. First, forms falling into DOM_1 are always pronounced with prominence, while those falling into DOM_2 are pronounced without prominence. Second, the pitch range between H and L of DOM_2 is narrower and tends to be lower than that of DOM_1.

3.2.4.1.1 TONAL MELODIES OCCURRING IN DOM_1

All forms belonging to DOM_1 have the structure of CVCV, CVV or CVN (N = /*m*/ or /*n*/) consisting of two morae, i.e. two tone-bearing units (TBU) in my interpretation. In this domain six contrastive pitch patterns occur. I will refer to these pitch patterns as "(tonal) melodies", whether they are level or contour (rising and falling). The six melodies are illustrated with minimal sextuplets in Table 5.5.

TABLE 5.5 SIX TONAL MELODIES IN ǀGUI

	Tonetic labels for melodies	Tonal interpretation	Minimal sextuplet	Gloss
(1)	High level	/H/	*ǀáé*	'to teach'
(2)	Mid level	/M/	*ǀāē*	'to watch'
(3)	Low level	/L/	*ǀàè*	'to be a shelter'
(4)	H–M falling	/HM/	*ǀáē*	'to chew'
(5)	H–L falling	/HL/	*ǀáè*	'to brood'
(6)	L rising	/LM/	*ǀàē*	'to curse'

There are three level melodies exemplified in (1–3) in Table 5.5. Words with such level melodies are interpreted as having a tone H, M or L which is multiply associated with the two morae in DOM_1. Two melodies falling and one rising (4–6) are interpreted as sequences of two tones, i.e. HM, HL and LM respectively. In words with such contour melodies the first tone is associated with the first mora, and the second tone with the second mora.

3.2.4.1.2 TWO-WAY TONAL DISTINCTION OCCURRING IN DOM_2

Unlike DOM_1, DOM_2 shows only two contrastive tone levels, i.e. H and L, and does not have any contour pitch patterns even if forms of DOM_2 are bimoraic. Examples (13–16) illustrate the two-way tonal contrasts in DOM_2. Note that in bimoraic elements like (15) and (16) a tone is multiply associated with two morae.

(13) *cí* 'my'
H

(14) *cì* 'habitually' [aspect marker]
L

(15) *c^h^áná* 'like' [postposition]
H

(16) *kʰùnà* 'as' [postposition]
L

3.2.4.2 Tonal alternations

There are two types of tonal alternations. One type is switching of tonal melodies, which is labelled as "flip-flop"; the other type is a tonal dissimilation found in three verbal suffixes.

3.2.4.2.1 FLIP-FLOP

Flip-flop is a morphotonological rule which switches one melody to another between a certain pair of melodies. There are three regular pairs of melodies which are involved in flip-flop ("flip-flop pairs"), as shown in Table 5.6.

TABLE 5.6 THREE REGULAR FLIP-FLOP PAIRS IN ǀGUI

(1)	/H/	—	/HM/
(2)	/HL/	—	/M/
(3)	/L/	—	/LM/

Flip-flop occurs in the following three contexts: (i) compound verb construction, (ii) three types of reduplications, and (iii) transitive verb derivation of lexical reduplication. Example (17) illustrates a flip-flop involved in the compound verb construction. In the formation of the compound verb the tonal melody of the first verb switches from H to HM. Note that flip-flop occurs only in the first element, the second retaining the tone of citation form.

(17) Citation form / Compound verb

kǀáá	+	*mâã*	→	*kǀáā-mâã*
H		HL		HM-HL
'skin'	+	'give'		'skin for someone'

Examples (18a–c) illustrate three types of reduplication, namely verb-deriving reduplication in (18a), causative reduplication in (18b) and iterative, pluractional action reduplication in (18c). In all three types the first element of reduplication involves flip-flop, and the second element has L. As mentioned previously, the second element falls into DOM_2 and is pronounced without prominence.

(18a) Citation form / Verb-deriving reduplication

súm̀	→	*sūm̄-sùm̀*
HL		M–L
'shade' (noun)		'make shade' (verb)

(18b) Citation form / Causative reduplication

qàù	→	*qàū-qàù*
LL		LM–L
'melt'		'cause to melt'

(18c) Citation form → Iterative/pluractional action reduplication

ǂqʰábā	→	*ǂqʰábá-ǂqʰàbà*
HM		H–L
'flap'		'flap repeatedly'

Flip-flop occurs also in the transitive derivation of a class of intransitive verbs describing various food textures. Since these verbs have the appearance of reduplication and their components do not occur independently, I call them verbs of lexical reduplication. They all have the same reduplicated tonal melodies, namely HL-HL, and are regularly changed into their transitive counterparts by applying flip-flop, HL → M, to the second component (its semantic effect is 'eat while feeling the texture of __'), as exemplified in (19a–b).

(19a) *ǀqx'âũ-ǀqx'âũ*
HL-HL
'have a crispy texture' (intransitive)

(19b) *ǀqx'âũ-ǀqx'āũ*
HL-M
'eat while feeling crispy texture' (transitive)

3.2.4.2.2 TONAL DISSIMILATION

The other type of tonal alternation found in ǀGui is involved in three verbal suffixes. They are the reflexive suffix, *-sì* ~ *-sí*, the suffix with a semantic effect 'do in the face/surface of', *-qx'áí* ~ *-qx'àì*, and the suffix with a semantic effect 'do in search of, do heading for' *-ǀx'àè* ~ *-ǀx'áé*. (The second suffix is a grammaticalized form of the word *qx'áí* 'face, front, far'.)

Unlike other suffixes in ǀGui, the tones of these suffixes are predictable from the preceding tone in the suffixed verb, as exemplified in (20). The tone of the suffix is L in (20a–d) where the preceding tone in the verb is non-L, while it is H in (20e–f) where the preceding tone is L. This also applies to the other two suffixes. In my interpretation the tones of the three suffixes are determined by a dissimilation process which avoids the LL sequence in the boundary between the verb stem and these three suffixes.

(20a) *ǀáé* *-sì* 'teach oneself'
H –L

(20b) *ǀháē* *-sì* 'stab oneself'
HM –L

(20c) *c'ūnī* *-sì* 'pinch oneself'
M –L

(20d) *gùī* *-sì* 'lift oneself'
LM –L

(20e) *ŋ!áò* *-sí* 'hide oneself'
HL –H

(20f) *cùã* *-sí* 'peel oneself'
L –H

It is worth mentioning that this alternation is relevant to the issue of how to interpret contour melodies. According to Clements (2000: 157f.), contours in Khoesan languages "tend to behave as units", and the analysis which decomposes contours into sequences of H and L "seems less appropriate". In the tradition of Khoe tonology this issue is controversial: Beach (1938) interpreted contours as units (unit analysis), and Haacke (1999) regarded them as sequences of level tones (decomposition analysis). In this context the tonal dissimilation found in |Gui is important evidence in favour of the decomposition analysis, because the interaction between the tone of the suffix and the preceding tone on the verb is transparently expressed under decomposition analysis, and not under unit analysis.

3.2.5 Shua subgroup: Cara, Deti

Rainer Vossen

Very little is known about tone systems in Shua languages. In Cara, surface analysis has established H(igh) and L(ow) as essential level tones combining to H–H, L–L, H–L, and L–H as tonal sequences on CVCV, CVV and CVN lexical roots. A more thorough analysis of the suprasegmental structure of Cara verbs has shown that these four sequences each represent two tone classes. The distinction of two classes for each tonal sequence derives from diverse tonal behaviour in the finite verb forms, as follows.

Tone classes 1 and 2 are distinguished on the basis of finite verb forms in the two past tenses, *-tá* (recent past) and *-ha* (imperfect). All other paired distinctions, i.e. of tone classes 3 and 4, 5 and 6, as well as 7 and 8, rely upon diverging tonal patterns in the imperfect forms. (The linker element */a/* between the verbal root and the tense suffix, which is sometimes zero, can play an important part in the overall tonal pattern. Unmarked M(id) tone is considered to be a result of morphotonology.) Cf. the examples in (21):

(21)	Tone class	Sequence	Verb	Recent past	Pattern	Imperfect	Pattern
	1	H–H (I)	*xáĩ* 'swell'	***xáĩ**-á-tá*	**HH**-H-H	***xáĩ**-á-ha*	**HH**-H-M
	2	H–H (II)	*|'áé* 'fall'	***|'àè**-tá*	**LL**-H	***|'àé**-ha*	**LH**-M
	3	L–L (I)	*tsòǹ* 'glide'			***tsóń**-á-ha*	**HH**-H-M
	4	L–L (II)	*ǁgàm̀* 'love'			***ǁgàm̀**-à-há*	**TT**-T-H
	5	H–L (I)	*ts'âã* 'steal'			***ts'áã**-ha*	**HH**-M
	6	H–L (II)	*dzírà* 'suffer'			***dzíra**-ra-há*	**HM**-M-H
	7	L–H (I)	*ts'àó* 'milk'			***ts'àó**-á-ha*	**LH**-H-M
	8	L–H (II)	*khùí* 'lift'			***khùì**-à-há*	**LL**-L-H

In Deti, the same tonal sequences on disyllabic lexical roots have been observed as in Cara. Again, an in-depth study of verbs resulted in the distinction of several tone classes with superficially, at least partly, identical citation forms. However, the findings appear to be less evenly balanced than in Cara, as three L–H and two H–L but only one H–H and L–L class each have been determined. Compare the examples in (22):

(22)

Tone class	Sequence	Verb	Perfect	Pattern	Imperfect	Pattern
1	H–H	*ǀíí* 'sing'	*ǀíí-a-tó*	HH-M-H	*ǀíí-á-ha*	HH-H-M
2	L–L	*tàǹ* 'stand up'	*tàǹ-à-tó*	LL-L-H	*tàǹ-à-há*	LL-L-H
3	H–L (I)	*yáà* 'dance'	***yáà**-tó*	**HL**-H	***yáá**-ha*	**HH**-M
4	H–L (II)	*tóè* 'move away'	***tòè**-à-tó*	**LL**-L-H	***tòè**-há*	**LL**-H
5	L–H (I)	*xǎĩ* 'swell'	***xàĩ**-à-tó*	**LL**-L-H	***xàĩ**-á-ha*	**LL**-H-M
6	L–H (II)	*ǀgàí* 'run'	***ǁgàì**-à-tó*	**LL**-L-H	***ǁgai**-a-ha*	**MM**-M-M
7	L–H (III)	*ɲǔũ* 'sit'	***ɲúũ**-á-tó*	**HH**-H-H	***ɲúũ**-á-ha*	**HH**-H-M

When comparing the above listed tonal patterns, we note differences between tone classes 1, 3 and 7 in the perfect (*-tó*) finite forms but identical sequences in the imperfect (*-ha*) constructions. More remarkable seems the formal agreement between tone classes 2, 4 (for *-tó* and *-ha*), 5 and 6 (for *-tó* only), because 2 and 4 show exactly the same sequences although class 4 verbs contain H–L sequence in isolation, as against class 2 verbs which have L–L.

3.2.6 Tshwa subgroup

Rainer Vossen

Information on tone in this subgroup is extremely scant. Four surface sequences on disyllabic lexical roots have been observed in Kua and Tsua: H–H, L–L, H–L, and L–H. A more detailed investigation of verbal tone in Kua has led to the establishment of five tone classes, as shown in (23):

(23)

Tone class	Sequence	Verb	Present	Pattern	Imperfect	Pattern
1	H–H	*ǀáó* 'shoot'	*kùà ǀáó*	LL HH	*ǀá-ró-hà*	H-H-L
2	L–L	*ǀgàũ* 'spread (a hide)'	*kùà ǀgàũ*	LL LL	*ǀgàũ-á-hà*	LL-H-L
3	H–L	*píì* 'suck'	*kùà píì*	LL HL	*píí-á-hà*	HH-H-L
4	L–H (I)	*tshàó* 'dig'	*kùà tshàó*	LL LH	***tshà**-ró-hà*	**L**-H-L
5	L–H (II)	*xùń* 'grind'	*kùà xùń*	LL LH	***xúń**-hà*	**HH**-L

It is interesting to note that in present tense constructions the sequences of tone classes 4 and 5 coincide, whereas tone classes 2 and 4 on the one hand, and 1, 3 and 5 on the other, agree with one another in imperfect constructions. Significant for the distinction of classes 4 and 5, however, are the different sequences in the imperfect finite forms.

3.3 Southern Khoesan: !Xóõ

Amanda L. Miller

!Xóõ lexical tonology is described by Traill (1985: 28–55; 1977a: 11–47) as having four phonological contour tones, while Miller-Ockhuizen (1998: 220–23) offers a decompositional analysis with four level lexical tones, and phrasal edge tones accounting for the phonetic fall at the right edge of roots in isolation.

3.3.1 Lexical tonology

Traill's analysis of !Xóõ is that there are four tone melodies, one of which is a phonological contour tone (MF), represented as in (24). He notes that the H(F) melody is phonetically contoured, but since there is no contrastive level H melody, it is possible to view this as a level tone.

(24) Traill's (1985, 1994) lexical tone melodies

High	H(F)	*ǀqhúũ*	'white person'
Mid	M	*!ōo*	'knife'
Mid falling	MF	*tâa*	'a San person'
Low	L	*sòo*	'medicine'

Traill (1985: 31ff.) argues that the MF melody cannot be reinterpreted as a sequence with the second tone being phrasally determined, because there would be no explanation for the lack of fall at the right edge of the M melody. In fact, the fundamental frequency (F0) traces of the four !Xóõ melodies given in Figure 2 of Traill (1985: 30) show that both the right and left edges of M and MF melodies differ. The M melody starts lower than the MF melody, and has a lower peak F0.

Traill claims that the MF melody must be a phonological contour since it occurs on monomoraic roots. Miller-Ockhuizen (1998: 222f.) notes that the only monomoraic roots listed in Traill (1994) are grammatical words that tend to occur at the right edge of a phrase, and she attributes the fall to the phrasal tonology.

Traill also notes that positing four lexical tones, and allowing tone sequences, predicts sixteen possible tone melodies, but only four are attested. If the fall found on roots is due to phrasal prosody, then no tone sequences are allowed in !Xóõ. If it proves impossible to interpret the fall as phrasal, then a decompositional analysis would require plausible constraints on tone sequences, similar to what Miller-Ockhuizen (1998: 225ff.) has suggested for Juǀ'hoan.

3.3.2 Phrasal tonology

Traill (1994: 23f.) claims that nouns are lexically marked for one of two tone classes that determine the tone melody of concordially dependent items such as demonstrative pronouns that I refer to as clitics. Traill (1994) lists approximately 200 class I nouns, 1,500 class II nouns, and about sixty nouns that are class I in their alienated forms, but class II in their possessed forms. Tone class I nouns co-occur with level toned clitics, while tone class II nouns co-occur with falling toned clitics. The tone class is claimed not to be predictable from the tonal melody or the noun class. There are several scenarios that are consistent with these facts. Class I nouns might have a floating L tone that is realized on the clitic, which class II nouns lack. Alternatively, there may be two tonally distinct, but segmentally identical clitics, which are selected for by semantic or syntactic properties. No plausible classes have been identified, but further research may prove insightful.

3.4 Eastern ǂHoan

Henry Honken†

Only the briefest account can be given of tone in Eastern ǂHoan. According to Gruber (1973), Eastern ǂHoan has five tones: high, lower high, low, lower low (these are all level or slightly falling), (low) rising. The tones are mapped as contours onto the entire stem. Gruber notes (1973: 432) that "the stress pattern for one root [is] stress on the final syllable."

REFERENCES

Beach 1938; Clements 2000; Dickens 1994; Doke 1925; Elderkin 1988; Gruber 1973; Haacke 1999; Heikkinen 1986, 1987; Kilian-Hatz 2008; Köhler 1981; Miller-Ockhuizen 1998, 1999a, 1999c, 2003; Odden 1995; Sands *et al.* 1996; Snyman 1975a; Traill 1977a, 1985, 1994; Tucker *et al.* 1977; Vossen 1997a, 2004.

CHAPTER SIX

MORPHOLOGY

1 HADZA

Bonny Sands

1.1 Sources of data

All the findings here are based primarily on my own fieldwork, conducted over a few months in 1992 and 1997. Previously published information about Hadza morphology is limited to a few paradigms (e.g. Bleek 1931a, 1931b; Obst 1912; Tucker 1967a, 1967b). The orthography used here (as from section 3.1) follows Bala (1998) and has a number of differences from the IPA, e.g. *y* is used instead of [j], *hl*, *tl* and *tl'* are used instead of [ɬ, tʎ, tʎ'] and ' is used in place of [ʔ]. Tone, stress and aspiration are not marked.

1.2 Root shape

All syllables in Hadza are open, i.e. CV or CVV. Grammatical morphemes are typically one syllable in length, while lexical morphemes are most often disyllabic or trisyllabic, though longer roots are also frequent. For instance, Elderkin (1978) found in a corpus of 446 noun stems that 48 per cent had two syllables, and 39 per cent had three syllables. Many of the roots with three or more syllables are either borrowings, or may potentially be reconstructed with more than one morpheme.

1.2.1 Consonant patterns

All consonants can occur in initial position, and most (including clicks) can occur in medial position as well. But Elderkin (1978) notes that some consonants, e.g. */ts' tʎ' ɦ tʎ ʔ mp^h ɲ/*, are more frequent in initial than in medial position; and that others, e.g. */tʃ' k'w dz ndʒ/*, are more frequent medially than initially. Consonants */p' mp^h nt^h ŋk^h ɲ ŋ ntʃ ndʒ nts ndz ŋw/* are less frequent than others. Clicks are quite common (i.e. they occur in ~28 per cent of verb roots), though less common than in other Khoesan languages.

Certain classes of consonants are more likely to co-occur in roots than others. For instance, Elderkin (1978) notes that */ɦ/* is especially frequent in initial position where the second syllable consonant is an ejective or sonorant, and initial */ʔ/* is often followed by a fricative or voiceless plosive in C_2 position.

1.2.2 Vowel patterns

Only a small percentage of roots contain both mid and high vowels, or both front and back vowels. There is no constraint on the co-occurrence of the low vowel */a/* with any other vowel.

Very few roots violate the constraint on */e i/* or */o u/* within a root. Somewhat more violate the constraint on the co-occurrence of */u e/*, */u i/*, */o e/* or */o i/* within a root. Many of the roots that violate these constraints are obvious borrowings, e.g. */t^{h}umbat^{h}e/* 'tobacco', */dʒiroŋgoda/* 'soda', */diroda-be/* 'west'. Still others may be internally reconstructed with more than one morpheme, e.g. */ɬekaniʔa-p^{h}e/* '(are) the two muscles on either side of the spine (back meat)', /ɬemaʔo-pe/ '(are) the flesh on one's side, starting at the back', /ɬeka-pʰe/ 'back (part of the body)', and /ɬeka/ 'spine' all contain a common element /ɬe/ which was probably once a separate morpheme. However, other roots, such as /ʔutʃ'e-/ (F) 'egg', /ɦaine/ 'Haine, God', and /mise-/ (F) 'top stick in fire-drill', do not have obvious sources in other languages, and include some basic vocabulary.

1.2.3 Semantic basis of the noun classes

The gender of a noun cannot be predicted based on the root shape. With the exception of terms referring to people or animals which can be specified for natural gender, the majority of noun stems cannot occur with either gender. Nevertheless, there are a few patterns of limited lexical distribution we can comment on. For instance, most trees and shrubs are feminine, while products derived from them often have the same root in the masculine gender. For instance, *k'araɦai-kʰo* '*Opilia* sp. of shrub' (F) refers to the plant itself while *k'araɦai* (M) refers to some fruit of the plant. While *k'ada-kʰo* (F) refers to the '*Adenium obesum* desert rose', *k'ada* (M) refers to the poison derived from it.

A number of stems are augmented when taking masculine gender, as in (1).

(1) a. *tʃ'oma-* 'head' (F) F.SG *tʃ'oma-kʰo* 'head'
M.SG *tʃ'oma* 'person with a big head' (i.e. proud)

b. *ʔepa-* 'buttock' (F) F.SG *ʔepa-kʰo* 'buttock'
M.PL *ʔepa-be* 'big buttocks'

c. *haŋ̊!'a-* 'rock' (F) F.SG *haŋ̊!'a-kʰo* 'rock, top grinding stone'
M.SG *haŋ̊!'a* 'large rock, bottom grinding stone'

In some cases, there is no basis for assuming the feminine is more basic, yet the masculine form is still larger, as in (2). But, a number of forms have the larger object in the feminine gender, e.g. *ts'ok'o-kʰo* 'big fire, far-off fire' (F), *ts'ok'o* 'fire' (M); *ʔukʰwa-kʰo* 'arm' (F) and *ʔukʰwa* 'finger' (M); and *muʔa-kʰo* 'big, thick stick' (F) and *muʔa* 'thin stick, twig, whip' (M).

(2) a. F.SG *ʔupʰukʰwa-kʰo* 'foot'
M.SG *ʔupʰukʰwa* 'leg, upper leg'

b. F.SG *ts'aɦo-kʰo* 'tail' (short, e.g. of giraffe, eland, cow)
M.SG *ts'aɦo* 'tail' (long, e.g. of lion, rat, monkey)

There are other shifts in meaning associated with a shift in gender, as in (3).

(3)

	F.SG	M.SG
ts'itʰi-	'tree'	'stick'
ŋ̊ǁ'uk'wa-	'larynx'	'voice'
k̊ʰoʔo-	'rifle'	'bow'
ʔatʃu-	'bowstring'	'sinew'

1.3 Nominal agreement

Hadza nouns are either masculine or feminine, and occur with agreement morphology, bare or with a copula enclitic. The latter were taken to be citation forms, e.g. *n!e-ya* '(is

a) leopard', *!'amats'i-yako* '(is a) louse', *ts'uku-pi* '(is) firewood', *hots'o-pe* '(are) ashes'. The person–gender–number (PGN) markers and the predicate nominal copula enclitic are shown in (4). There are no morphemes marking definiteness, and case is only noted on certain pronominal forms. Agreement morphemes other than those in (4) can be found in locatives, diminutives, possessives, and dead animal terms.

(4)

Noun class	PGN	Copula
F.SG & collective	*-ko*	*-ako*
F.PL & paucal	*-be'e*	*-pe'e*
M.SG & collective	*-Ø*	*-a*
M.PL & paucal	*-bi'i*	*-pi'i*

Although the terms singular and plural are used here, so-called singular forms may also be used as collectives, as shown in (5). The collective reading is very common in narrative texts. A mixed gender group of people will typically take the feminine ending, as the root *hadza-* '(Hadza) person' is grammatically feminine.

(5)

a.		*bek'ahu-*	'elephant' (F)
	M.SG	*bek'ahu-Ø*	'single male elephant'
	M.PL	*bek'ahu-bi'i*	'few male elephants' (2–10)
	F.SG	*bek'ahu-ko*	'one female or unspecified gender elephant; many elephants, large group of elephants'
	F.PL	*bek'ahu-be'e*	'a few elephants' (2–10)
b.		*n!e-*	'leopard' (M)
	M.SG	*n!e-Ø*	'single male or unspecified gender leopard; many leopards or large group of leopards'
	M.PL	*n!e-bi'i*	'few leopards' (2–10)
	F.SG	*n!e-ko*	'single female leopard' (not collective)
	F.PL	*n!e-be'e*	'few female leopards' (2–10)

Nouns without agreement morphology are relatively infrequent, but do appear in contexts where the gender is a given, such as when the noun is preceded by a demonstrative, e.g. *Kwako boko tl'akwe-Ø kwakwa 'akwe sam-iya* 'The girl had not eaten' (Bala 1998: 20). Agreement markers are often phonetically reduced, e.g. [pʰe'] for *-pe'e*, [kʰo̥] for *-ko*.

1.3.1 Other agreement morphology

1.3.1.1 Diminutives

The diminutive is formed in Hadza by attaching a *nakwV-* morpheme to the stem. It occurs with the copula as in (6), or without the copula, as in *Hama 'ola-nakwe-Ø k'u-k'umi-ya* 'These (little) children are small' (Bala 1998: 32). Note the M.PL agreement marker *-te*, which is distinct from the PGN markers in (4).

(6)

	ǁa'ano-	'dog' (M)
F.SG	*ǁa'ano-nakwi-ko*	'female puppy'
F.PL	*ǁa'ano-nakwe-be*	'female puppies'
M.SG	*ǁa'ano-nakwe-te*	'(male) puppy'
M.PL	*ǁa'ano-nakwi-pi*	'(male) puppies'

1.3.1.2 Dead animals

Gender markings occur on a set of lexical items referring to certain dead animals. Only those animals which are hunted with bows have a special form for when the animal is dead. I was not able to elicit a distinction between singular and plural. These forms are sometimes used as vocatives, such as when calling out to the animal when one is tracking it. The majority of these forms take an *-'i* affix in the feminine and an *-'e* in the masculine, as shown in (7). But some forms have a labiovelar on-glide [w] rather than a glottal stop, some vowel harmony, and some have a single form for both masculine and feminine.

(7)

Feminine	Masculine	Gloss
hubu-'i	*hubu-'e*	'dead lion/eland'
hanta-'i	*hanta-'e*	'dead zebra'
huku-'i	*huku-'e*	'dead rhino'
hawa-'i	*hawa-'e*	'dead giraffe'
n!oko-wi	*n!oko-we*	'dead baboon'
hushu-we	*hushu-we*	'dead ostrich'
tihli	*tehle*	'dead buffalo'

1.4 Other nominal inflection

Nominals (as well as verbs, adverbs and demonstratives) can be marked for emphasis with a reduplicated first syllable, as shown in (8).

(8) *Iche- be'e ng'a- ng'ambi- yako.*
some- 3F.PL EMPH- temporary.camp- 3F.SG.COP
'Some people were at a temporary camp.' (Bala 1998: 18)

1.5 Adjectives

Most concepts that would be adjectives in English occur with PGN enclitics in Hadza. An example of an adjectival predicate is *Hama 'ola-nakwe-Ø k'u-k'umi-ya* 'These (little) children are small' (Bala 1998: 32). Comparative constructions are shown in (9). The order in the most commonly occurring type of comparative construction in the texts is quality–marker–standard, as in (9a), but other constructions occur, as in (9b–c).

(9) a. *Sengane pakapa'a-a isha ha!'a-ko nako.*
man's name big-3M.SG.COP COMP rock-3F.SG DEM
'Sengane was as big as the boulder there.' (Berger 1943: 113)

b. *bek'ahu-ko k'umi-yako duduk'e-nina*
elephant-3F.SG small-3F.SG.COP duduk'e-3M.SG.LOC
'(An) elephant is small, (compared) to a Duduk'e.'

c. *ǀuwi-yako k'umi-ko n!apa-ko pakapa'a-ako*
mosquito-3F.SG.COP small-3F.SG ndorobo-3F.SG big-3F.SG.COP
'(A) mosquito is small, Ndorobo fly is big.'

Adjectives take nominal morphology, such as the PGN markers in (1). Many qualities are grammatical verbs rather than adjectives and take the endings shown in (24), e.g. *tl'iki-neko* 'I am bad'. But *tl'iki-'e-na'a* 'I was bad', and *tl'iki-'e-he:ta* 'I will be bad' take past and future tense enclitics, respectively, after a stative marker.

1.6 Numerals

Numerals (cf. 10) take the same types of copula enclitics as nouns and adjectives, as given in (26), and agree with their head nouns. The stems *'ichame-* 'one' and *'ikumi-* 'ten, -teen' take singular endings (*-ya, -yako*), while other numerals (except 'hundred') take plural endings (*bi'i, be'e, pi'i, pe'e*). Stems for 'two', 'four', and 'five' show vowel height harmony with following suffixes. Numerals 'six–nine' are Swahili borrowings, while 'two', 'four', 'five' and 'ten' appear to be borrowed from some other Bantu language.

(10)

1	*'ichame-*	
2	*piye-, piyi-*	
3	*samaka-*	
4	*bone-, buni-*	
5	*botano-, botanu-*	
6	*sita-*	
7	*saba-*	
8	*nani-*	
9	*tisa-*	
10	*'ikumi-*	
11	*'ikumi-ya 'a 'ichame*	(i.e. 10 + 1)
20	*'ikumi-bi piyi-bi*	(i.e. two tens)
100	*!unguwe*	(cf. *!unguwe* 'Maasai')
200	*!unguwi piyi-pi*	(i.e. two hundreds)

Numerals and other quantifiers typically come after the noun they are modifying, as in (11a–b). The quantifier *wa'ina-* 'all' takes agreement marked for oblique case (e.g. *-ma* 3M.SG, *-sa* 3F.SG, *-icha* 3M.PL, *-eta* 3F.PL), as in (11c), similar to English 'all of X'. But the reverse constituent order can be seen with a Swahili borrowing *kila* 'every' in (11d).

(11) a. Haka-mo *ǁa-ǁa-chana* *pa'anakwete* *'ichame . . .*
go-3M.SG.PAST EMPH-hunt-ing old.person one
'One old person went hunting . . .' (Bala 1998: 16)

b. *Iso* *ch-eta* *shilingi-be* *'aso-be'e.*
3M.F.SG.FUT get-3PL.F.DO shilling-3PF many-3PF
'He'll get many shillings.'

c. *Tuma-ko* *mana-ko* *habi* *ts'ifi* *wa'in-echa.* [< *wa'ina-icha*]
where-3F.SG meat-3F.SG 3M.PL.DEM night (M) all-3M.PL
'Where is the meat all these nights . . .' (Bala 1998: 26)

d. *Kila* *gashenga* *ǀ'o-ǀ'ose-ya.*
every thing (M) EMPH-fill-3M.SG.COP
'Everything is filled up.' (Bala 1998: 22)

1.7 Pronouns

1.7.1 Personal pronouns

As with nouns, pronouns can occur with or without a copula, as in (12). Gender is marked on pronouns of all persons and numbers, and an inclusive/exclusive distinction is marked in the first person plural forms.

(12)

	Independent pronouns	Predicate pronouns
1M.SG	*'ono*	*'one-ne'e* (e.g. 'It is I.')
1F.SG	*'onoko*	*'one-neko*
2M.SG	*te*	*te-te'e*
2F.SG	*teko*	*te-teko*
3M.SG	*bami*	*bami-ya*
3F.SG	*boko*	*boko-wako*
1PL.INCL.M	*'unibi'i*	*'unibi'i*
1PL.INCL.F	*'onebe'e*	*'onebe'e*
1PL.EXCL.M	*'ubi'i*	*'ubi-upi'i*
1PL.EXCL.F	*'obe'e*	*'obe-ope'e*
2M.PL	*'itibi*	*'itibi*
2F.PL	*'etebe*	*'etebe*
3M.PL	*bi'i*	*pi'i*
3F.PL	*be'e*	*pe'e*

1.7.2 Demonstrative pronouns

Demonstrative pronouns (see 13) mark gender and number, and distinguish (a) near speaker, (b) far from speaker and hearer, (c) near hearer, and (d) heard but not seen by speaker. Similar roots occur in some of the locative forms: *hamana* 'here', *nana* 'there', *be'ena* 'there near you, there just mentioned', */i'ina* 'over there'.

(13)

'this, these' [near speaker]	'that, those' [distal]	'that, those' [near hearer]	'that' [unseen, but heard]
hama	*hina*	*bami*	*himik'e*
hako	*nako*	*boko*	*hik'iko*
habi'i	*nabi'i*	*bi'i*	(not elicited)
habe'e	*nabe'e*	*be'e*	(not elicited)

1.7.3 Possessive marking

1.7.3.1 Genitives

Genitive markers, as in (14), agree with both the head and the dependent in number and gender. Either the possessor or the possessed can be the head, as shown in (15). Genitives have a *t/n* masculine/feminine singular contrast, and a *n/ch* in the masculine plural, but do not contrast in the feminine plural (*t/t*). The *-bi-* plural marker is not a part of the genitive marker that attaches to pronominal stems, as they are already marked for number. A possessed noun can also be made into predicate by adding the predicate nominal markers after the possessive markers, e.g. *ha!'a-ti-yako* 'the rock (F) is hers', *ha!'a-te-pe'e* 'the rock (F) is theirs (F)', *ha!'a-bi-ti-yako* 'the rocks (F) are hers', *ha!'a-bi-te-pe'e* 'the rocks (F) are theirs (F)'.

(14)

Dependent / Head	M.SG	F.SG	M.PL	F.PL
M.SG	*-ne*	*-te*	*-bi(-)che*	*-bi(-)te*
F.SG	*-ni*	*-ti*	*-bi(-)chi*	*-bi(-)ti*
M.PL	*-ni*	*-ti*	*-bi(-)chi*	*-bi(-)ti*
F.PL	*-ne*	*-te*	*-bi(-)che*	*-bi(-)te*

(15) a. *hits'a* *bek'ahu-* *biche*
fat (3M.SG) elephant- GEN(M.SG.HEAD, M.PL.DEP)
'the fat of the elephant' (Berger 1943: 115)

b. *A* *hadisi-ko* *kota* *bahe* *Iyeye-* *ni-ko.*
and story-3F.SG 3F.SG.PAST end Iyeye (3M.SG-)GEN-3F.SG
'And the story of Iyeye is finished.' (Bala 1998: 32)

1.7.3.2 Independent possessive pronouns

Independent possessive pronouns (see 16) have three distinct parts: a root, genitive marker, and a copula showing agreement with the possessed, e.g. *'one-ne-ya* 'it (3M.SG) is mine (1M.SG)'. The roots are different from the independent pronouns in that only 3SG is distinguished for gender. Except for 3M.SG and 3F.SG, all roots agree in vowel height with the following affix – mid vowels for 3M.SG and 3F.PL possessed, and high vowels for 3F.SG and 3M.PL possessed. The genitive markers on the independent possessive pronouns are identical to the genitive markers used on nouns, except that they do not take the *-bi-* plural marker, as plurality is shown on the pronoun stem. Independent possessive pronouns can also occur without the copula, e.g. *'i-ta-na boko kitabu-ko uni-ni-ko* 'I saw that book of mine'. Past or future possession is indicated with a relative clause.

(16)

	Possessed			
	Singular		Plural	
	Masculine	Feminine	Masculine	Feminine
1M.SG	*'one-ne-ya*	*'uni-ni-yako*	*'uni-ni-pi*	*'one-ne-pe*
1F.SG	*'one-te-ya*	*'uni-ti-yako*	*'uni-ti-pi*	*'one-te-pe*
2M.SG	*te-ne-ya*	*ti-ni-yako*	*ti-ni-pi*	*te-ne-pe*
2F.SG	*te-te-ya*	*ti-ti-yako*	*ti-ti-pi*	*te-te-pe*
3M.SG	*bami-ne-ya*	*bami-ni-yako*	*bami-ni-pi*	*bami-ne-pe*
3F.SG	*boko-te-ya*	*boko-ti-yako*	*boko-ti-pi*	*boko-te-pe*
1PL.INCL.M	*'unibi-che-ya*	*'unibi-chi-yako*	*'unibi-chi-pi*	*'unibi-che-pe*
1PL.INCL.F	*'unibi-te-ya*	*'unibi-ti-yako*	*'unibi-ti-pi*	*'unibi-te-pe*
1PL.EXCL.M	*'ubi-che-ya*	*'ubi-chi-yako*	*'ubi-chi-pi*	*'ubi-che-pe*
1PL.EXCL.F	*'ubi-te-ya*	*'ubi-ti-yako*	*'ubi-ti-pi*	*'ubi-te-pe*
2M.PL	*'itibi-che-ya*	*'itibi-chi-yako*	*'itibi-chi-pi*	*'itibi-che-pe*
2F.PL	*'itibi-te-ya*	*'itibi-ti-yako*	*'itibi-ti-pi*	*'itibi-te-pe*
3M.PL	*bi'i-che-ya*	*bi'i-chi-yako*	*bi'i-chi-pi*	*bi'i-che-pe*
3F.PL	*bi'i-te-ya*	*bi'i-ti-yako*	*bi'i-ti-pi*	*bi'i-te-pe*

1.7.3.3 Oblique possession

A common way of indicating possession is with the oblique marker. In (31) are the oblique markers, which are added after PGN agreement on the nouns. Examples include: *seme-kwa* 'my food', *seme-na* 'your (SG) food', *seme-sa* 'her food', *seme-ma* 'his food', *seme-'ona* 'the food of us all', *seme-ya* 'the food of just us', *simi-ina* 'your (PL) food', *seme-eta* 'their (F) food', *simi-icha* 'their (M) food'. This type of possession may be combined with locatives, e.g. *'its'a-tina-ma* 'in his house', and *ets'a-na ma bami* 'at his house'. Possession may also be indicated with the verb *chokwa-* 'to hold, grasp', but this is atypical.

1.7.3.4 Inalienable possession

A few kinship terms mark possession with a suppletive root (see 17). Singulars of these kinship terms can take oblique marking agreeing with the possessor (e.g. *aso-ma* 'his father', *asu-ko-ma* 'his mother', *pa'a-ko-na* 'your (F) mother', *pa'a-ko-ena* 'your (M) mother'), and plural forms are marked with an accompaniment marker preceding the oblique marker, e.g. *bawa-mi-pi-kwa* 'my "fathers"'. The terms *pakwa-* 'your grandfather', and *pakachoko-* 'your grandmother' also occur alongside *'akaye-* 'grandfather' and *'amama-* 'grandmother', which appear to be used more generally. Traces of a *p-* 2nd person possessive prefix remain, and traces of another prefix exist in the freely varying *'atits'i-* / *mits'i-* 'sibling, cousin'.

(17)

	'my'	'your'	'his/her'
'father, father's brother'	*bawa-*	*pahle-*	*aso-*
'mother'	*'aiya-*	*pa'a-*	*asu-*
'son'	*wa'a-*	*pakwete-*	*'akwete-*
'daughter'	*wa'a-*	*pakwi-*	*'akwi-*

1.7.4 Relative pronouns

Relative pronouns (18) are based on a pronoun stem and a relativizer, and what appears to be an aspect marker. The relatives differ in tense/aspect, but examples (19) are too few to make the distinctions clear.

(18)

	REL 1	REL 2	REL 3
M.SG	*meto*	*meto-*	*ma'a*
F.SG	*(ko)to*	*(ko)ta-*	*(ko)'a*
M.PL	*cho*	*chu-*	*'a*
F.PL	*to*	*to-*	*'a*
1M.SG	*'ono-meto*	*'ono-meto-na*	*'ono-ma'á*
1F.SG	*'onoko-to*	*'onoko-ta-na*	*'onoko-'á*
2M.SG	*te-meto*	*te-meto-si*	*te-ma'á*
2F.SG	*teko-koto*	*teko-ta-ko*	*teko-'á*
3M.SG	*bami-meto*	*bami-meto-so*	*bami-ma'á*
3F.SG	*boko-koto*	*boko-kota-ko*	*boko-ko'á*
1PL.INCL.M	*'unibi-cho*	*'unibi-chu-si*	*'unibi-'a*
1PL.INCL.F	*'onebe-to*	*'onebe-to-se*	*'onebe-'a*
1PL.EXCL.M	*'ubi-cho*	*'ubi-chu-si*	*'ubi-'a*
1PL.EXCL.F	*'obe-to*	*'obe-to-se*	*'obe-'a*
2M.PL	*'itibi-cho*	*'itibi-chu-si*	*'itibi-'a*
2F.PL	*'etebe-to*	*'etebe-to-se*	*'etebe-'a*
3M.PL	*bi'i-cho*	*bi'i-chu-si*	*bi'i-'a*
3F.PL	*be'e-to*	*be'e-to-se*	*be'e-'a*

(19) a. *Bami* *meto* *hi!'e-ta.*
3M.SG.PRO REL1.3M.SG come.out-1SG.PRES
'This story came from me.' (Bala 1998: 16)

b. *Tame* *meto* *kwe-hena* *bami* *tl'o'a?*
who REL1.3M.SG give-2SG.OBL 3M.SG.DEM cloth (3M.SG)
'Who gave you that cloth?'

c. *Bami* *meto-so* *!'a'i-cha* *tsuku-bi.*
3M.SG.PRO REL2-3M.SG throw-PROG firewood-3M.PL
'It is he who is throwing firewood./It is he who will throw firewood.'

d. *"Hama* *seme-Ø* *wa'ina-ma* *tame meto-so* *sa-ka-ma?"*
3M.SG.DEM food-3M.SG all-3M.SG.OBL who (REL2-3SM) eat-DISTR-3M.SG.OBL
'"Who will be the one to eat all this food?"' (Bala 1998: 22)

e. *!Onga* *ma'a* *'a'a-ne.*
hare REL3.3M.SG ahead-LOC/STAT
'It is hare who leads.'

f. *Onoko-* *'a* *'ela-ta* *kitabu-ko.*
1F.SG.PRO REL3 make-3F.SG.DO book-3F.SG
'It is I who made the book.'

1.7.5 Interrogative morphemes

Many of the question morphemes in Hadza begin with an aspirated *t*, and can occur with or without a copula, or tense/aspect marking (cf. 20).

(20)
tumu'usha 'when'
tume'ika, tum- 'where'
tashe- 'how much, what size'
tashi- 'do what'
tashina 'how'
taka- 'how many'
ta- 'who'
'oma Yes-no question particle
'akwadza 'who/what'
'aku 'what kind, who, which'

1.8 Verb inflection

Most Hadza affixes are suffixes, though there is emphatic reduplicative prefixation. It is questionable whether the prefixes seen in some Bantu loans (e.g. *na-sema* 'I say') have become productive. Hadza predicates can be emphasized by reduplicating the initial syllable of the stem, as in (21).

(21) a. *Hinge!* *|i-|i-ye'e.*
EXCLAM EMPH-see-IMP
'Hey, (just) look!' (Bala 1998: 22)

b. *Kaki* *haka* *ha-hama* *se-seme.*
3M.SG.PAST.HAB go EMPH-sit EMPH-eat
'Then he would just sit down to eat.' (Bala 1998: 22)

Suppletion is rare, but infixation is quite common, as in (22). A distributive plural subject or distributed action is marked by the presence of a *kV* syllable after the initial syllable of the root, where V is a copy of the first syllable vowel. Infixation occurs with both intransitive and transitive roots. Some verbs (e.g. *pats'i-* 'to spit') are obligatorily distributive when plural, but others can take either collective or distributive plurals.

(22)	Verb	Singular/collective subjects	Distributed subjects
	'to spit'	*pats'i-*	*pa-ka-ts'i-*
	'to blow'	*bu'ita-*	*bu-ku-'ita-*
	'to vomit'	*kwaǀa-*	*kwa-ka-ǀa-*
	'to sweat'	*ǀats'i-*	*ǀa-ka-ts'i-*
	'to remember'	*'ehlawi-*	*'e-ke-hlawi-*

In a few cases, the *-kV-* infix refers to a repetitive or intensified action, e.g. *ts'i-ki-ts'i-* 'to sprinkle something' (cf. *ts'i'i-* 'to pour, spill something'), *n!i-ki-n!i-* 'to push something a lot' (cf. *n!ihi-* 'to push something'), *'akakase-* 'to sleep, nap' (cf. *'ase-* 'to sleep, lie down'), and *sakame-* 'to devour' (cf. *seme-*, *sama-* 'to eat'). In these cases, the infixed stem can be used with singular or plural subject agreement markers.

1.8.1 Derivation processes affecting verbs

The reduplication of an initial syllable of a verb can be used to create an agentive noun, as in (23). A less productive process occurs with some verbs that take an *hV-* prefix to create an agentive noun (e.g. *hats'ake* 'thief', cf. *ts'ake-* 'to steal'), where V is identical to the vowel in the initial syllable of the stem. In at least one case, an agentive noun is created from a suppletive form (e.g. *ǀo* 'to kill', *ǀ'aǀ'ashe* 'killer'). In some cases, (an) unpredictable syllable(s) occur(s) stem-finally (e.g. *huts'a-* 'to clean', *huhuts'abo* 'a cleaner'), which must historically be part of the verb stem as they also occur in other derived forms.

Yet another nominalization can be derived from an agentive noun to create a noun meaning 'one who is really Mr. Verb', that is, someone really known for being the 'owner' of that verb. The "Mr. Verb" nominals are derived by adding *-ngu* to the agentive stem, though there are often unpredictable phonological differences between the forms.

(23)	Verb	'X' (verb root)	'one who does X, really does X'	'really Mr./Ms. X'
	'to farm'	*tohle*	*to-tohle*	*totohle-ngu*
	'to hunt'	*ǀaǀa*	*ǀa-ǀaǀa*	*ǀaǀaǀa-ngu*
	'to whistle'	*nǀehe*	*nǀe-nǀehe*	*nǀenǀehe-ngu*
	'to beg'	*!osho*	*!o-!osho*	*!o!osho-ngu*
	'to steal'	*ts'ake*	*ha-ts'ake*	*hats'ake-ngu*
	'to clean'	*huts'a*	*hu-huts'abo*	*huhuts'aba-ngu*

Participles can be formed from verbs, with the final vowel of the stem replaced by a stative *i* or *e* vowel, e.g. *ts'eheya!'u'u!'u'u-we nǀehe-yamo* 'The squatting child whistled'; *bami ts'u'ai-ye nǀehe-yamo* (or, *bami nǀehe-yamo ts'uts'u'ai-ye*) 'The child leaving whistled'. Often, the agentive or nominalized form is used, cf. *chu'-iye* 'the pulled (one)', *chu-'e* 'the pulling (one)', *chuchu'ukwa* '(the one) who pulled'. Unpredictable phonological differences between participles and verb stems occur, as with the agentive nouns, e.g. *huts'a-be* '(who) cleans' (cf. *huts'a-* 'to clean'), *tlukwa-che* '(who) cleans' (cf. *tlukwa-* 'to clean').

1.8.2 Tense, aspect, mood

Tense and aspect (there are no known mood markers in Hadza) cannot be discussed apart from subject (i.e. nominative) marking. The past and "present" particles (see 24) can occur as enclitics or as separate auxiliaries (cf. 25), but the future particle can only occur as a separate auxiliary. The "present" particle can represent non-past (present or future) when it occurs as an enclitic.

(24)

Subject	"Present"	Past	Future (Essive)	Copula	Conditional
1SG	*ta*	*na('a)*	*tana*		
M				*-ne'e*	*-ne'e*
F				*-neko*	*-nikwi*
2SG	*tita*	*ta('a)*	*titata*		
M				*-te'e*	*-te'e*
F				*-teko*	*-tikwi*
3M.SG	*(y)a*	*(a)mo*	*yaso*	*-a*	*-eso*
3F.SG	*(ya)ko*	*(a)kwa*	*koko*	*-ako*	*-eko*
1PL.INCL	*bita*	*ba'a*	*bitaba*		
M				*-bibi'i*	*-be'e*
F				*-bebe'e*	*-bikwi*
1PL.EXCL	*ota*	*'a'a*	*otaya*		
M				*-upi'i*	*-ukwi*
F				*-ope'e*	*-'e'e*
2M.PL	*tita*	*ti'a*	*titatiti*	*-titi*	*-si*
2F.PL	*teta*	*te'a*	*tetatete*	*-tete*	*-te*
3M.PL	*pi('i)*	*(a)mi*	*pisi*	*-pi'i*	*-isi*
3F.PL	*pe('e)*	*(a)me*	*pese*	*-pe'e*	*-ese*

(25) a. *dza-na'a* 'I came.'
dza-mo 'He came.'
dza-ta 'I will come.'
dza-tita 'You (SG) will come.'

b. *"Mu-musi-kwa-tita 'ono."*
EMPH-annoy-1SG.DO-2SG.PRES 1M.SG
'"You really annoy me", said the chief.' (Bala 1998: 24)

c. *Kamo mzee: "Tume'ika 'otaya 'ase?"*
3M.SG old.man where 1PL.EXCL.FUT sleep
'The Mzee baboon said: "Where will we sleep?"' (Bala 1998: 22)

Various morphophonological processes occur when subject pronominals are cliticized to verb stems. Though these cannot be described in detail here, some examples are given in (26). Depending on various factors, stress shift, vowel lengthening or *-hV-* insertion may occur. For instance, if a verb has a final accent in the frame: *'ina* ___ 'I'll ___', then it will have a *-he-* syllable when preceding the 1SG present *-ta*, because this enclitic causes stress shift, where the accent must move one syllable to the right, and the final syllable of the verb stem must be accented. Thus, we have the apparently epenthetic *-he-* syllable. The vowel will raise if followed by a syllable with a high vowel, and the *h* will be deleted if preceded by a front vowel. These *hV* syllables are distinct from the *he* syllable that marks the habitual, e.g. *chi-he-ta* 'I run (habitually)', *lu-he-he-ta* 'I stand still (habitually)'.

(26)

Subject	*ǀu-* 'to stand still' Past	"Present"	*chi-* 'to run' Past	"Present"
1SG	*ǀu-na'a*	*ǀu-heta*	*chi-na'a*	*chi-ta*
2SG	*ǀu-ta'a*	*ǀu-tita*	*chi-ta'a*	*chi-tita*
3M.SG	*ǀu-amo*	*ǀu-heya*	*chi-amo*	*chi-yeya*
3F.SG	*ǀu-akwa*	*ǀu-yako*	*chi-akwa*	*chi-yako*
1PL.INCL	*ǀu-ba'a*	*ǀu-bita*	*chi-ba'a*	*chi-bita*
1PL.EXCL	*ǀu-'a'a*	*ǀu-'ota*	*chi-'a'a*	*chi-'ota*
2M.PL	*ǀu-hiti'a*	*ǀu-hitita*	*chi-ti'a*	*chi-itita*
2F.PL	*ǀu-hete'a*	*ǀu-heteta*	*chi-te'a*	*chi-yeteta*
3M.PL	*ǀu-ami*	*ǀu-hipi'i*	*chi-ami*	*chi-ipi'i*
3F.PL	*ǀu-ame*	*ǀu-hepe'e*	*chi-ame*	*chi-yepe'e*

Subjects and their tense/aspect may be marked with a narrative particle. These particles are very frequent in narrations and are used to initiate or link clauses. They can be translated variously, e.g. 'and', 'and then', 'so', 'so then'. The narrative particles (cf. 27) probably derive from the verb *'ika* 'to stand' followed by a pronominal. Examples are given in (28).

(27)

Subject	Past	Past habitual	Past habitual	"Present"	"Present" habitual	Future
1SG	*kana*	*kani*	*na'a'a*	*kata*	*ta'a*	*('i)na*
2SG	*kena*	*kene*	*ta'a'a*	*kenata*	*tita'a*	*('i)ta*
3SM	*kaka*	*kaki*	*mo'a*	*kato*	*ya'a*	*('i)so*
3SF	*kota*	*koti, kuti*	*kwa'a*	*katikwa*	*ko'a*	*('i)ko*
1PL.INCL	*kaba*	*kabi*	*ta'a'a*	*kabita*	*bita'a*	*('i)ba*
1PL.EXCL	*ka'a*	*ka'i*	*'a'a'a*	*ka'ota*	*'ota'a*	*('i)ya*
2M.PL	*kina*	*kini*	*ti'a'a*	*kinata*	*tita'a*	*(t)iti*
2F.PL	*kina*	*kini*	*te'a'a*	*kinata*	*teta'a*	*(t)ete*
3M.PL	*kicha*	*kichi*	*mi'a*	*kichata*	*pi'a*	*('i)si*
3F.PL	*keta*	*kete*	*me'a*	*ketata*	*pe'a*	*('e)se*

(28) a. *Ono haka-ta 'ina 'ase.*
1M.SG go-1SG? 1SG? sleep
'I am going off to sleep.' (Bala 1998: 24)

b. *Kaka ǀhele dzu'a be'ena.*
3M.SG wake.up big-3M.SG then
'Then the head man woke up.' (Bala 1998: 24)

Pronominals also frequently occur in their relativized forms, as in (29). They probably derive from the verb *kwa-* 'to give' followed by a pronominal. In addition to being used when relativizing a nominal, the relative particles can be used to indicate 'when/where', e.g. *Hakaata kwaako ishoko* 'I go to the sun' (Berger 1943: 105); *Kwete tlatla-kwa dzane-hena bami seme* . . . 'When you pick and bring to me this food . . .' (Bala 1998: 22).

(29)

Subject	Past	Past habitual	"Present"	Future	Conditional
1SG	*kwana'a*	*kwahena'a*	*kwata*	*kwene('e)*	*k(w)anikwi*
2SG	*kwata'a*	*kwaheta'a*	*kwatita*	*kwete('e)*	
M					*kwe'ena*
F					*kwatikwi*
3M.SG	*k(w)amo*	*kwaheto*	*kwaya*	*kweso*	*kweso*
3F.SG	*k(w)akwa*	*kwahitikwa*	*kwako*	*kweko*	*kweko*
1PL.INCL	*kwebe'e*	*kwaheba'a*	*kwabita*	*kwebe('e)*	*kwabikwi*
1PL.EXCL	*kwe'e('e)*	*kwahe'a'a*	*kwa'ota*	*kwe'e('e)*	*kwa'ukwi/kwa'okwi*
2M.PL	*kwiti('i)*	*kwahiti'a*	*kwatita*	*kwiti('i)*	*kwiti*
2F.PL	*kwete('e)*	*kwahete'a*	*kwateta*	*kwete('e)*	*kwete*
3M.PL	*kwisi*	*kwahiti*	*kwapi('i)*	*kwisi*	*kwi'icha*
3F.PL	*kwese*	*kwahete*	*kwape('e)*	*kwese*	*kwe'eta*

Apart from the *-he-* habitual marker, it is difficult to determine how various aspects are grammaticalized. There appears to be a *-cho-* progressive or participial marker, e.g. *kota fa-ka-cho komati-ko* 'elands were drinking', as well as a participial *-chana*, which is probably a progressive *-cha-* particle (cf. *-cho-*), followed by the locative *-na*, i.e. *haka-mo ǀa-ǀa-chana* 'he went a(t)-hunting'. But also cf. *-chana-* apparently used as an imperfective in *taǀ'i-chana-na'a* 'I was/am almost dead', or as an infinitival affix in *hupe-te'e haka-chana* 'after a bit, you go'. The *-nV-* particle can be translated as 'must' (e.g. *chi-ni-ne'e* 'I (M) must run/it is I who runs'; *dza-ne-ya* 'he must come/it is he who comes'), or as an inchoative (e.g. *dza-ne-ya* 'he is coming/on his way'), but is probably better considered as a locative, or perhaps, comitative, grammaticalized as an aspect marker.

There is little morphological marking of mood, or non-declarative speech acts. But conditional mood can be marked (cf. 24), e.g. *Natikosa haka-'a'a Endamagha kwa'ukwi ǀi-ya Pandisha chi-ya-'e'e* 'Yesterday we went to Endamaghan; if we had seen Pandisha, we would have brought him'. And imperatives are regularly formed with a *-'V* suffix in the singular, with V being a reduplication of the stem-final vowel, *-si* in the masculine plural, and *-te* in the feminine plural, as in (30). Direct objects can be marked on imperatives, but complete paradigms have not been elicited, but cf. *!e'e kalamu!* 'you (SG) cut a pen (M.SG)', *!o'o ts'iti-bi* 'you (SG) cut trees (M.PL)!', *!eta-si nyanya-ko* 'you (M.PL) cut tomatoes (F.PL)!'.

(30)

dza-'a	'Come!'	(2SG)	*chi-'i*	'Run!'	(2SG)
dza-si	'Come!'	(2M.PL)	*chi-si*	'Run!'	(2M.PL)
dza-te	'Come!'	(2F.PL)	*chi-te*	'Run!'	(2F.PL)

1.9 Grammatical relations

1.9.1 Object enclitics: overview

Subjects are marked with the particles discussed above, which are pronominal arguments to the verb. These particles do not distinguish between subjects of transitives and subjects of intransitives. Agents and experiencers are both typically treated as subjects. Other nominals act as adjuncts to the verb.

Grammatical relations other than subject/agent are marked with pronominal enclitics on the verb, as in (31). Pronominal particles occur that mark direct objects, or the relationship between a patient and a verb, i.e. the accusative case relation. Relations such as recipients, goals and sources are marked with an oblique or applicative particle. One or other type of object clitic may be obligatory for one verb but not for another.

(31)

Object	DO1	DO2	APPL	OBL1	OBL2
1SG	*kwa*	*kwa*	*tikwa*	*kwa*	*ko'o*
2M.SG	*ena*	*ena*	*ena*	*ena*	
2F.SG	*na*	*na*	*tina*	*na*	
3M.SG	*a*	*na*	*ta*	*ma*	*ma'a*
3F.SG	*ta*	*ta*	*tita*	*sa*	*si'i*
1PL.INCL	*ona*	*ona*	*ona*	*ona*	*'a*
1PL.EXCL	*oba*	*oba*	*oba*	*oba*	*ya'a*
2M.PL	*ina*	*ina*	*ina*	*ina*	
2F.PL	*ina*	*ina*	*ina*	*ina*	
3M.PL	*icha*	*icha*	*icha*	*icha*	*ichi'i*
3F.PL	*eta*	*eta*	*eta*	*eta*	*ete'e*

Subject clitics can be cliticized to the object clitics, e.g. *kwe-kwa-mo* 'he gave to me', *kwi-sa-ta* 'I will give to her', *kwi-hicha-ta* 'I will give them (M.PL), *ǀ'-eta-mo* 'he kissed them (F.PL)', *ǀ'o-ta-na'a* 'I kissed her', *ǀ'-a-na'a* 'I kissed him'.

1.9.2 Direct object enclitics

The majority of verbs that can subcategorize for a direct object take DO1 marking, but a large number take DO2 marking instead, e.g. *gosanga-* 'to find', *'apa'a-* 'to follow', *tuǀ'a-* 'to pluck (feathers)', *ta'a-* 'to close', *'ishi'a-* 'to help', *tl'akwa-* 'to carry in arms', *ǀa-* 'to tie'. The class of DO marking must be specified in the lexicon, as any semantic distinction between the particles is now lost, cf. *bahla-* 'to break' + DO2, but *potl'o-* 'to break' + DO1.

Verbs differ in how the clitics attach to the stem, as in (32). In some, the final vowel is replaced by the first vowel of a vowel-initial clitic. In others, the vowels are added after the stem, often with [y], [w] or [h] hiatus between the stem-final vowel and the clitic-initial vowel. There is presumably a relationship between this behaviour and the accent pattern of the verb root and clitic, though this has not yet been investigated.

(32) Direct object enclitics

	3M.SG.DO	3F.SG.DO	3M.PL.DO	3F.PL.DO
DO1 final V replaced:				
ǀ'o- 'to kiss'	*ǀ'-a*	*ǀ'o-ta*	*ǀ'-eta*	*ǀ'-icha*
hi!'e- 'to remove'	*hi!'-a*	*hi!'e-ta*	*hi!'-icha*	*hi!'-eta*
!e- 'to cut'	*!-a*	*!e-ta*	*!-icha*	*!-eta*
no final V replacement:				
!uma 'to fold'	*!uma-(h)a*	*!uma-ta*	*!uma-icha*	*!uma-eta*
kwachacha- 'to peel'	*kwachacha-a*	*kwachacha-ta*	*kwachacha-icha*	*kwachacha-eta*
potl'o- 'to break'	*potl'o-a*	*potl'o-ta*	*potl'o-wicha*	*potl'o-weta*

	3M.SG.DO	3F.SG.DO	3M.PL.DO	3F.PL.DO
final V replaced (except in 3F.SG):				
chu'u- 'to pull'	*chu'-a*	*chu'u-ta*	*chu'-icha*	*chu'-eta*
DO2				
lewa- 'to sharpen'	*lewa-na*	*lewa-ta*	*lew-icha*	*lew-eta*
APPL no final V replacement:				
!'api- 'to dry'	*!'api-ta*	*!'api-tita-*	*!'api-icha*	*!'api-yeta*

1.9.3 Indirect objects and oblique enclitics

Some verbs allow the applicative (cf. 31) to increase the number of arguments taken by the verb. The pronominals represented by the applicative can have a variety of meanings, including causative and benefactive, as in (33).

(33) *!ats'i-tita-na'a* 'I sweated *because of her*.' (cf. *!ats'i-* 'to sweat')
titl'i'-i-tita-na'a 'I startled *her*.' (cf. *titl'i'a-* 'to be startled')
musi-tita-na'a 'I was bothered *by her*.'
hla'a-tita- 'want/like *her/it*' (cf. *hla'a-* 'to like, love, want')
hukwa-tita- 'stand *it/her* up' (cf. *hukwa-* 'to stand up')
biki-tita- 'scare *it/her* into running away' (cf. *biti-* 'to scare into running away')
tisi-tita- 'raise *it/her* up' (cf. *tisi-* 'to grow up')
huti'i-tita- 'make *her* late' (cf. *huti'i-* 'to delay, be late')
'ehlawi-tikwa-mo 'he reminded *me*' (i.e. 'he *caused me* to remember')

Another kind of applicative occurs in a few stems with a *-ke* affix, e.g. *tuts'i-ke-* 'to urinate on someone', cf. *tuts'i-* 'to urinate'; *ts'e'a-ke-* 'to shit on someone/something', cf. *ts'e'a-* 'to shit'; *tsi'a-ke-* 'to have diarrhoea on something/someone', cf. *tsi'a-* 'to have diarrhoea'; *we-ke-la-* 'to hurry (to do) something', cf. *wela-* 'to hurry'; *'e-ke-ke-la* 'to work on something', cf. *'ela-* 'to make, build'.

The number of arguments taken by a verb may be decreased with the use of the morpheme *-iya-*, which is used for both passives and reflexives, e.g. *k'was-iya-na'a* 'I was hit', *k'was-iya-ami* 'they (M.PL) were hit'; *chakw-iya-* 'to choke' (cf. *chakwi-* 'to strangle').

The most common way indirect objects are indicated is with the oblique 1 particles (cf. 34). As mentioned earlier, possession or association are often noted with the oblique particle. The oblique particles are marked for person, gender and number, e.g. *!a'ana-sa-ta hagu-ko* 'I am in the centre of the maize (3F.SG)', *!a'ana-ma-ta !'ets'a* 'I am in the centre of camp (3M.SG)'; *etletle-sa-na'a gali-ko* 'I moved aside for/because of the car'.

(34) *!a'ana-* + OBL1 'to be in the centre *of something*' (*!a'ana-* 'to be in the centre')
tets'e- + OBL1 'to return something *to someone*' (*tets'e-* 'to return, reply')
chokwa- + OBL1 'to follow *someone*' (*chokwa-* 'to hold')
akanabe- + OBL1 '*of someone*, to be called'
!ikwibi- + OBL1 '*of someone*, to sleep'
pa'a- + OBL1 'greeting *to* long-lost *someone*'
bahe- + OBL1 'to be ready *for someone*'

shaka-	+ OBL1	'to turn over *because of someone/something*'
etletle-	+ OBL1	'to move aside *for/because of someone/something*'
!V-	+ OBL1	'to cut something *for someone*'

The oblique 2 (cf. 31) enclitics are a special form of the oblique clitics used only in 2SG imperatives (cf. 35). For instance, *he-te'e* 'you (SG) tell them (F.PL)', combines the 1SG and the 2SG ending, while *h-eta-si* 'you (M.PL) tell them (F.PL)' keeps the morphemes distinct.

(35)	*Te, !e-ma'a*	*kalamu Gudo.*	'You (SG), cut the pen for Gudo.'
	Te, !e-se'e	*kalamu Boni-ko.*	'You (SG), cut the pen for Bonny.'
	Te, !i-si'i	*kalamu-bi Boni-ko.*	'You (SG), cut the pens for Bonny.'
	Te, !i-ma'a	*kalamu-bi Gudo.*	'You (SG), cut the pens for Gudo.'

For at least some verbs, when the verb takes an oblique particle, there is a different kind of agreement with the number and gender of a direct object (i.e. [e] for masculine singular and feminine plural, and [i] for feminine singular and masculine plural). Examples are given in (36). These are probably participial forms, e.g. 'Sewing-it is what he did for her'. There are no clear examples of 3-place predicates from non-elicited speech.

(36)	*!'ap-e-ma-mo tl'o'a.*	'(He) sewed a cloth (3M.SG) for him.'
	!'ap-e-sa-mo tl'o'a.	'(He) sewed a cloth (3M.SG) for her.'
	!'ap-i-ma-mo tl'o'a-ko.	'(He) sewed a cloth (3F.SG) for him.'
	!'ap-i-sa-mo tl'o'a-ko.	'(He) sewed a cloth (3F.SG) for her.'
	!'ap-i-ma-mo tl'o'a-bi.	'(He) sewed cloths (3M.PL) for him.'
	!'ap-i-sa-mo tl'o'a-bi.	'(He) sewed cloths (3M.PL) for her.'
	!'ap-e-ma-mo tl'o'a-be.	'(He) sewed cloths (3F.PL) for him.'
	!'ap-e-sa-mo tl'o'a-be.	'(He) sewed cloths (3F.PL) for her.'

1.9.4 Locatives

The locative *-na* can be used without preceding agreement, particularly when directionality is already clear, e.g. *tlehe-na* '(is) below', *'ato-na* '(is) behind', *chiki-na* 'inside', as in (37a–b), or with preceding agreement, as in (37c–d).

(37) a. *Puhlu-na'a* *hi!'e-na'a* *Amelika-na*
arrive-1SG.PAST come.from-1SG.PAST America-LOC
'I arrived here coming from America.'

b. *Haka-kwa* *|ets'a-na* *ma* *Davidi.*
go-3F.SG.PAST house-LOC OBL3M.SG David
'She went to David's house.'

c. *||'aka-na'a* *ts'okwana* *nkolo-ti-na.*
shoot-1M.SG.PAST giraffe-3M.SG heart-GEN-LOC
'I shot a giraffe in the heart.' (Bala 1998: 16)

d. *Bocho* *hamana* *hi!'e* *bada-ni-na*
come.here here come.out hole-GEN-LOC
'Come out of the hole.'

1.9.5 Instrumental

The instrumental case is noted with a preposition marked for gender of the instrument, as in (38a–b). There are no examples of a grammatically plural (i.e. distributive) instrumental. Berger's (1943) texts show *nina* used as an instrumental for both masculine and feminine instruments, so the instrumentals in (38a–b) are perhaps a recent development, possibly based on Swahili *na* 'and, with', and an instrumental/genitive *-ni-*, which functions as an instrumental in (38c).

(38) a. *Handika'eheta ne-na kalamu.*
write-2F.SG.UT INSTR-M pen (M.SG)
'I will write with a pen.'

b. *Ela-ta-ta mulinga-ko ne-ta gundida-ko.*
build-3F.SG.DO-1F.SG.UT beehive-3F.SG INSTR-F hammer-3F.SG
'I will build a beehive using a hammer.'

c. *'Aku 'ihi'a ni-yako hako panga?*
what.kind thing (3M.SG) INSTR-3F.SG.COP this (3SG.F) machete (3SG.F)
'What are you using this machete for?'

1.9.6 Comitative and accompaniment markers

Comitative is identical to the genitive case, but agreement is only with the noun that is cliticized. The markers are *-ne* (F.SG), *-te* (M.SG), *-che* (M.PL), *-te* (F.PL), e.g. *'one-ne* 'with me (F.SG)', *'one-te* 'with me (M.SG)', *mu'a-ne* 'with a thin stick (M.SG)', *mu'a-te* 'with a thick stick (F.SG)', *kalamu-biche* 'with pens (M.PL)', *nyanya-bite* 'with tomatoes (F.PL)'. The comitative can also be used to increase the valence of a verb, as in (39).

(39) *Etletle-na'a ne-na gali-ko.*
move.aside-1SG.PAST COM-M car-3F.SG
'I moved aside for/because of the car.'

Distinct from the comitative and genitive is the accompaniment marker. The affixes *-me-* (feminine) and *-mi-* (masculine) appear to function as accompaniment markers in sentences such as *!ichana Tabashi mibi* 'I saw Tabashi and his cohorts/friends'. This marker is obligatory for plurals of certain kinship terms. For instance, we have *'edze* 'husband', *'edzi-mi-pi* 'husbands'; *nitame-a-kwa* 'my brother in law', *nitami-pi-kwa* 'my brothers in law'.

1.10 Summary

Hadza has a variety of morphological processes including (en)cliticization, partial (prefixal) reduplication, infixation, and suffixation. The basic structure of the noun is:

N–(Diminutive)–(Agreement)

The basic structure of the verb is:

V–(Direct object clitic)–(Indirect object clitic)–(Subject/tense clitic)

2 SANDAWE

Edward D. Elderkin

2.1 Definition of a word

The essential criteria which define a word in Sandawe are given below. They have to refer to phonology and to the phonetic realisation, but also to syntax.

(a) Syllables

A word consists of an integral number of syllables.

(b) The realisation of low tone

Before the first high-toned mora in a word, sequences of low-toned moras are on a level pitch.

Within a word, sequences of low-toned moras initial in a syllable following a high-toned mora are realised on a falling pitch; where sequences of low-toned moras following a syllable-final high-toned mora are realised on a level pitch, there is a word boundary after that high, unless downstep can be demonstrated.

(40)

tsí mànàkéːꜜtsʰé.
tsí *mànà* *kéː* *tsʰì* *sé*
1SG know DEC$_1$ NEG 1SG
'I don't know.'

(c) Successive highs

Sequences of high-toned moras within the same word are on the same pitch.

(41)

mátó
gourd

Where sequences of high-toned moras are realised on different pitches, the change from one pitch to another indicates a word boundary, unless the criterion of integrity of structure can be invoked. The following example shows a word boundary:

(42)

tsáː ǀ̥í.
'I came.'

(d) Unity of structure

But where the same pitch pattern as in (42) occurs and integrity of structure in terms of the realisation in sequence of formative classes can be stated, the structural criterion prevails. In (43), the formative *pó* '2SG', is not known to appear in word-initial position, and the downstep, ꜜ, indicates the underlying presence of *tsʰè*/*tsʰì* negative, which cannot appear word-finally. The whole is one word.

(43)

k'éːꜜpó.
k'éː *tsʰì* *pó*
cry NEG 2SG
'You didn't cry.'

(e) Substitution

There are occasions when substitution is needed. The sequence

(44) 
xẽ́ːǀ̥í
xéː *ː̃́* *ǀ̥í*
bring and come (SG.S)

is shown to be two words by substituting ǀ̃àtí for ǀ̥í.

(45) 
xẽ́ːǀ̃àtí
xéː *ː̃́* *ǀ̃àtí*
bring and come (PL.S)
^{2}xẽ̂ː ^{2}ǀ̃àtí

The realisation of the low tone on the second syllable shows that there is a word boundary before ǀ̃àtí. The example also shows downdrift in this construction.

The situation is a little more delicate than can be described here. Within lexical items substitution cannot usually be applied, for example to distinguish downstep within a word and a word boundary within a lexical item where the second word is in a lower key. I am also inclined to take reduplications of a stem as nevertheless being parts of one word in which there is a change of key. Syntactically, in (46) *^{1}!'ìné^{2}!'ìné* functions as the verb stem in the VP to which *sípònè* is added. So no word boundaries are to be found within a verb stem.

(46) ^{1}!'ìné^{2}!'ìnésípònè ?
!'ìné *!'ìné* *sí* *pò* *nè*
hunt hunt SÍ 2SG Q
'You do some hunting?'

The result is that, except for the anomalous clitics and examples such as this, all of a word is in the same key.

Any *état de langue* is caught between an idealised past system and an idealised future system, and therefore can be expected to show indeterminacies of analysis and practice. For example, *jóː* as clause-final, is often in Key 1 (see 51), but may become part of the word, as in (55) below; *léʔ̥̀*, used to indicate that the speaker does not know something, is found both as a word clitic and as an independent word (usually then in Key 1).

(47) ^{1}há!̥àpôjnèléʔ̥̀?
há!̥à *pò* *j̀* *Ø* *nè* *léʔ̥̀*
call 2SG IRR 3M.SG Q
'Is he going to call you I wonder?'

(48) ^{1}hèwé ^{2}dògósúnè ^{1}léʔ̥̀?
hèwé *dògósú* *nè* *léʔ̥̀*
3M.SG sister Q
'His younger sister is she perhaps?'

2.2 Formative classes within words

The component formative structure of a word can be divided into three layers:

(a) clitics (in Sandawe always final);
(b) inflectional affixes (in Sandawe usually suffixes);
(c) derivational affixes (within the stem).

The boundaries between these classes are not always sharp.

2.2.1 Clitics

Clitics are not tied to any word or formative class; they are syntactically phrase or clause suffixes and are found attached to the word which corresponds to the last part of the syntactic phrase or clause, extending that word. There are four anomalous clitics, whose anomality lies in their usually having a key specification independent of the key of the word to which they are clitics. It could be argued that these are extra-syntactic. These are treated first.

2.2.1.1 Anomalous clitics

There are four clitics which are anomalous in their behaviour.

(49) *jóː* 'duration'
ôː 'finality'
ṽ̌ː^{1} 'something else is coming'
ṽ̂ː 'affirmation'

jóː appears as *óː* after *i* and *e*, and as either *jóː* or *óː* after *a*; after a nasalised vowel, *góː* is heard. Except for some forms of *jóː*, the clitics begin with a vowel, and no word begins with a vowel. Those which have an oral vowel cause the epenthesis of *g* after a nasalised vowel, and those anomalous clitics which have a nasalised vowel extend their nasality back onto a previous oral vowel. They behave as words in that they have a specification of key which is independent of the key of word to which they are attached; the key which they carry is 1, although *óː* has been found on a lower pitch.

(50) ^{1}híà ^{2}ǁ'àkíóːìːʔ̥̀
hí *à* *ǁ'àkí* *óː* *j̀ʔ̥̀*
'when . . .' 3M.SG descend '. . . when'
'when he'd got right to the bottom'

(51) ^{1}mìníkíwàsúsũ̀ː^{1}góː.
mìníkí *wà* *sí* *sũ̀ː* *óː*
know MLT sí 1PL
'We'd got to know that.'

(52) ^{1}ts'éxì̥sé^{1}ts'é^{1}óːôː.
ts'éxì̥ *sé* *ts'é* ^{1}*óː* ^{1}*ôː*
alone 1SG NEG
'It's not me alone.'

(53) ^{1}ǁ̃ĕːsípõ̀^{1}õ̂ː.
ǁ̃ĕː *sí* *pò* ^{1}*ṽ̂ː*
arrive *sí* 2SG
'So you've got here then.'

(54) ^{1}tsı̃́ː^{1}ı̃̌ː
tsí *ṽ̌*
1SG
'now me, I . . .'

Example (52) has shown also that *óː* has been used together with *ôː*. *óː* has also been found integrated into the structure of a word as in (50) and the following example.

(55) ^{1}wèréóːsà.
wèré *óː* *sà*
walk 3F.SG
'She went on walking about.'

It would be difficult to analyse these anomalous clitics as anomalous words, anomalous in not having an initial consonant, from which the other phonetic phenomena derive.

As a type of hesitation phenomenon, lengthening of the final vowel of a word on its end pitch is sometimes used whilst the speaker is recalling something. It does not have the urgency and floor-holding properties of *ṽ̌ː* 'something else is coming'.

(56) ^{1}hóts^{h}ǒː^{2}hóts^{h}ǒːkíːːːː
hóts^{h}ǒː *hóts^{h}ǒː* *kí*
what what as.well
'and some other things as well like . . .'

2.2.1.2 Ordinary clitics

These are here grouped subjectively into those which express an attitude on the part of the speaker or give perhaps additional information about the phrase they follow (non-syntactic clitics) and those which are part of the syntactic structure (postpositions).

2.2.1.2.1 NON-SYNTACTIC

kí 'as well, too, even'

(57) ^{1}l̃ěːgòː ^{2}téɬà ^{2}k^{h}ǒ̃ːːìʔ`̥kí.
l̃ěːgòː *téɬà* *k^{h}ǒː* *ı̃̀ː* *ts'ì* *kí.*
we.arrived completely house SPEC PP even
'We even reached right up to the house.'

(58) ^{1}láːʔèxì̥ ^{1}ɬùbǎːkíːkíáː ^{2}wàmǒːkí.
láːʔèxì̥ *ɬùbǎːkíː* *kí* *áː* *wàmǒːkí*
the.hare.among.others spider too NOM make.friends
'The hare and the spider made friends.'

kô ná. The exact import of these is not clear, they seem approximately equivalent to English uses of 'now', 'so', 'then'.

(59) ^{1}ʔútáːgìːná ^{1}jáʔ´̥bỗː ^{2}bǎːràːkéː.
ʔútáː *gê* *ì* *ná* *jáʔ´̥bỗː* *bǎːràː* *kéː*
ago DEC$_2$ 2SG that.work begin.it DEC$_1$
'So a long time ago it was that you began work.'

(60) ^{1}mànǎːsàkô ^{3}xáré ^{1}ʔárè ?
mànǎː sà kô xáré ʔárè
know 3F.SG perhaps true
'She knew about it perhaps, didn't she now?'

síʔ̥` 'as far as is concerned'

This is locative in origin (see discussion of *sí* below at 107) and is sometimes used to show the topic of the conversation.

(61) ^{2}swê . . . ^{1}hétékȁːkí ^{2m}bȍːsíʔ̥` ^{1}híkàː ^{2}ʔíé ?
swê hétékȁː kí ^{m}bȍː síʔ̥` híkí à ʔíé
now that.marrying too that.matter how 3M.SG stay
'Now, that matter of marriage, what happened?'

(62) ^{1}hèwéxéːsíʔ̥` ^{1}ǁ'wěː$^{!}$pó ?
hèwéxéː síʔ̥` ǁ'wěː$^{!}$pó
those.things you.didn't.try
'You didn't try that?'

léʔ̥` indicates that the speaker does not know (see 47 and 48).

káʔ̥` indicates reporting, either of speech, or of a presumed event which the speaker does not entirely vouch for.

(63) ^{1}ɬǎː ^{1}ts'éxègáʔ̥`káʔ̥` ^{1}tsʰěː.
ɬǎː ts'éxè gáʔ̥` káʔ̥` tsʰěː
goat one DEC$_2$ ʔ̥` absent
'There's one goat then it seems, it's not there.'

(64) ʔáːkáʔ̥`
ʔáː káʔ̥`
N.CONJ.3PL
'and they said'

Subject PGN:

The subject PGN is one of two systems of PGN formatives, the second is the nominal PGN suffix, treated later. PGN abbreviates person, gender and number. The subject PGN is attached to the last constituent of any phrasal category, without entering the constituency of that phrase. The forms with the imperative/optative are also given.

(65)

	Basic	Imperative/optative
1SG	*sì̥*	*èʔ*
2SG	*ì*	*kò*
3M.SG	*à*	*kwà*
3F.SG	*sà*	*xì̥sa*
1PL	*ò*	*òʔ*
2PL	*è*	*kwè(rá)*
3PL	*ʔḁ̀ [áʔ̥]*	

(66) ^{2}sáː ^{1}dzágònàsà ^{2}tʰâ
sáː dzágò nà sà tʰâ
N.CONJ.3F.SG net to 3F.SG run
'and she runs into the net'

For a 3MLT subject, the 3M.SG form is used as subject PGN. However, a plural verb must be used with a MLT subject.

(67) [1]hǎːxwè [1]mùtʰùgũ̀ː [1]ǁ̥óʔàː [2]ɬéː.
hǎːxwè *[1]mùtʰùgũ̀ː* *[1]ǁ̥óʔ̥* *à* *ɬéː*
those (MLT) poor.people there 3M.SG stand (PL)
'The poor ones stood on that side.'

(Suppletion is sometimes used to differentiate a singular subject verb stem and a plural subject verb stem. Compare the verb above with that in 70; see also 44 and 45).

2.2.1.2.2 SYNTACTIC

méː 'for the sake of, because of':

(68) [1]màkǎːměː [2]máːmè
màkǎː *méː* *máːmè*
things uncle
'friendship for the sake of gain'

A fuller form is *kímé:*

(69) [1]hótsʰǒːkímàː [2]hàpú [3]ʔíò [4]bìkʰéːsú ?
hótsʰǒː *kíméː* *à* *[2]hàpú [3]ʔíò* *bìkʰéːsú*
what 3M.SG your.mother leave.her
'Why did he leave your mother?'

xêʔ̥̀ 'like':

(70) [1]ʔíxàː [1]sìⁿgǎːnàxéʔàː [2]ǃ̬érȇː [2]ǀ̃úmé.
ʔíxì̥ *àː* *sìⁿgǎːnà* *xêʔ̥* *à* *ǃ̬éré* *ȉ̃* *ǀ̃úmé*
thus 3M.SG needle 3M.SG prick and stand (SG)
'It stays pricking (me) there like a needle.'

ʔȉː 'with':

(71) [1]ǀ̥àníʔȉː [2]ǃ'ínóː
ǀ̥àní *ʔȉː* *ǃ'ínóː*
bow hunting
'hunting with a bow'

(72) [1]láːʔè [1]nàʔásȍːʔȉːgà [2]ʔâⁿzǎː . . .
láːʔè *nàʔásò* *ȉ̃* *ʔȉː* *à* *ʔâⁿzà* *ȉ̃*
hare fruit.sp. SPEC 3M.SG begin and
'the hare started with the fruits and (. . . finished a rich man)'

(73) [1]tʰékélȅːȉ kwáː [1]ts'ǒːts'íʔȉːgà [2]ǁ'ô
tʰékéléː *ȉ̃* *kwáː* *ts'ǒːts'í* *ʔȉː* *à* *ǁ'ô*
hyena SPEC N.CONJ.3M.SG hunger PP 3M.SG sleep
'and the hyena slept hungry'

ts'ì̥ can be suffixed under certain conditions to the NP_0 standing as object of an imperfective verb.

(74) ³kwáxi̥ ¹hík'à: ¹|'ĕ:¹ó: ¹ɬă:xẽ̌:ì̃ts'à:
kwáxi̥ hík'ì à |'ĕ: ó: ɬă: xì é: ì̃: ts'ì à
N.CONJ. go and look. at 'duration' goat MLT 3M.SG SPEC 3M.SG
3M.SG
'and straightaway he went and looked at the goats'

|'àʔ̥̀:

(75) ¹nŏ:ⁿdòa‖'àʔìsi̥ ²ʔútá: ²dɮòmó ¹ɬă:ʔì̃:¹sî̃:.
nŏ:ⁿdòà |'àʔ̥̀ sì ʔútá: dɮòmó ɬă: ʔì̃: sì ¹v̂̃
Nondoa 1SG ago buy goat with 1SG 'affirmation'
'I bought (it) long ago from Nondoa, for a goat.'

Locatives:

tà:

(76) ²hèwé ²kìdzídzì̃:tà
hèwé kìdzídzì̃: tà
that village
'in that village'

nà:

(77) ¹hèwé ²!'úmánà ³xé:swì:ts'énè.
hèwé !'úmá nà xé: sú ì Ø ts'énè
3M.SG land bring 3F.SG IRR 3M.SG NEG.Q
'He would take her to his country, wouldn't he.'

ts'ì:

(78) ¹‖̥ŏ:ts'áʔ̥̀ ²|'ô.
‖̥ŏ: ts'ì ʔà |'ô
road 3PL sleep
'They slept on the way.'

kù̥ appears only as a relic, in *hákù̥* 'where' and *ts'ă:kù̥* 'at home' (cf. *ts'ă:nà* 'to home').

(79) ²swê ¹hákù̥ ²|'ôsì̃: ?
swê hákù̥ |'ô ` sì̃:
now sleep IRR 2PL
'Now where are you going to sleep?'

(80) ¹núásà ²mâⁿtsʰàwà ²ts'ă:kù̥.
núá sà mâⁿtsʰà wà ts'ă:kù̥
ugali 3M.SG eat MLT
'She used to eat *ugali* at home.'

tsʰè 'privative' is always followed by a nominal PGN.

(81) ¹ts'ă:kù̥tsʰèsi̥ ¹ɬá:si̥ ²hẵ:gà.
ts'ă:kù̥ tsʰè si̥ ɬá: si̥ hẵ:gà
at home PRIV 1SG well 1SG arise
'I was all right when I left home.'

The previous example has also shown how locative postpositions can be piled up. In the next example, *tè* can be taken as an alloform of *tà*, and *ʔ̥̀* of *ts'ì*.

(82) [1]ʇ̃èmêsú [1]têsúsì̥ [2]síésú [1]dèdúʔ̥̀tètsʰèsùsì̥.

ʇ̃èmêsú	*têsú*	*sì̥*	*síésú*	*dèdú*	*ʔ̥̀*	*tè*	*tsʰè*	*sù*	*sì̥*
woman	another	1SG	took.her	Dedu	LOC	LOC	PRIV	3F.SG	1SG

'I married another woman, one from around Dedu.'

A verbal clause has been found preceding a postpostition.

(83) [1]hòsáː [1]ʇ̃î̃ːgàʔ̥̀ [2]ʇ̃íní.

hèsó	*áː*	*ʇ̃î̃ː*	*ʔà*	*ʇ̃íní*
they	NOM	meat	3PL	eat.meat

'They ate meat.'

[1]hòsáː [1]ʇ̃î̃ːgàʔ̥̀ [2]ʇ̃íníʔ̥̀tè
'at the place where they ate the meat'

2.2.2 Nominals

2.2.2.1 Inflexional affixes

Nominal PGN:

The nominal PGN is technically considered a suffix, as it is immediately preceded by a nominal stem. However, several different structures can function as nominal stem, which gives the nominal PGN a somewhat clitic-like ability. It needs to be quoted twice, once with a high tone, once with a low tone, because of the segmental differences in 1SG and 3SG. Choice of tone seems often to depend on the tone of the item to which it is suffixed. Its form is related to that of the free-standing pronoun, which is also quoted here.

(84)

	Nominal PGN		Free-standing
	High	Low	PRO/DEM
1SG	*sé*	*sì̥*	*tsí*
2SG	*pó*	*pò*	*hàpú*
3M.SG	*éː*	*Ø/m̀/ẁ/è*	*hèwé*
3F.SG	*éːsú/sú*	*sù̥*	*hèsú*
1PL	*sṹː*	*sũ̀ː*	*sṹː*
2PL	*sĩ́ː*	*sĩ̀ː*	*sĩ́ː*
3PL	*só*	*sò*	*hèsó*
3MLT			*hèwéxéː*

There are other forms which it is convenient to list here, but which are never found suffixed to simple nominal stems.

(85)

3C.SG		*ʔ̥̀*
3MLT	*ʔ̥̀wá*	*ʔ̥̀wà*

The 3C.SG (common) form is only found in certain syntactic uses, and fossilised in a few items; the use of "common" derives from the label for a cognate form in Central Khoesan languages, and does not describe the semantics of the Sandawe form.

The nominal PGN multiple forms include the formative *wà* (see also 102); the free-standing pronoun has *xì̥*. Multiple forms relate to humans and non-humans, plural forms to humans only.

The formative *xì̥*:

Suffixed to a noun stem, *xì̥* indicates the referent of that noun stem, plus others of a similar kind. It is multiple.

(86) ^{1}séːᵑgèréxì̥ ^{2}tʰǒːts'éː
séːᵑgèré xì̥ tʰǒːts'éː
Sengere MLT brother
'the brother of Sengere and of the others'

It can be followed by a nominal PGN:

(87) ^{1}ts'éxì̥sé^{1}ts'é^{1}óːôː ^{1}ʔáɬànìxì̥sű̃ː.
ts'éxì̥ sé ts'é óː ôː ʔáɬànì xì̥ sű̃ː
one 1SG NEG 'duration' 'finality' monitor.lizard MLT 1PL
'I'm not alone, I'm with Monitor Lizard' (we are Monitor Lizard and other(s)).

(88) ^{1}hèsúxì̥kísĩ́ːnè ?
hèsú xì̥ kí sĩ́ː nè
3F.SG MLT too 2PL Q
'Are you still with her? (are you (PL) she and other(s))'

Nominative:

The nominative marker is *áː*. In 1PL, *sóː* is used as well as *sű̃ːgáː*. The nominative marker is usually preceded by a nominal PGN (which in 3M.SG is *Ø*) (see 90).

2.2.2.2 Specifier

The specifier *ĩ̀ː* follows something functioning as a nominal, and is itself followed by a low-toned nominal PGN (see 90).

2.2.3 Nominal stems

Both noun stems and adjective stems are associated with a person, gender and number. One difference is that 3MLT is marked by *ʔ̥wa* with adjectives (tones predictable from those on the preceding stem), but unmarked (or shown with *xì̥*) with nouns.

2.2.3.1 Noun stems

Noun stems are typically monomorphemic.

(89) *ǃ̥èẃ* 'buffalo'
tʰěː 'tree'

The vast majority of the uses of nouns are in the third person, and as such, there is usually no nominal PGN present as the appropriate 3M.SG suffix is *Ø*. However, nouns may be used in other persons.

(90) ^{1}tsáː ^{1}láːʔèsĩ̀ːsáː ^{2}tûkáts'í
tsí áː láːʔè sì ĩ̀ː sì áː tûkáts'í
1SG NOM hare 1SG SPEC 1SG NOM show.oneself
'. . . and then me, the hare, I'll show myself'

(91) [1]ʔókʰò [2]ɬǎːpò
ʔókʰò ɬǎː pò
oi goat 2SG
'oi, you goat, . . .'

Some noun stems, however, do have what seems a fossilised or idiosynractic PGN suffixed to them.

(92) *ts'ǒːẁ* '(someone's) younger brother' cf. *ts'ǒː* 'to get small' (SG.S)
ʔǒːẁ '(someone's) son'
ʔǒːsṳ '(someone's) daughter'
ʔǒːkótsʰí 'daughters'
ʔǒːkó 'children'
ʔèmésé: 'male human'
ʔèmêsú 'female human'
ʔòmósò 'humans'
ʔèmêsű: 'we humans'
ʔúm̀sú 'wife'

The use of *é:* (M) and *sú* (F) is especially found with kinship terms, but also with nouns referring to humans by characteristic.

(93) *bàlímáé:* 'brother in law'
bàlímású 'sister in law'
bènégé: 'rich person, employer'
máxàé: 'husband, man' (cf. *máxà* 'young male')
wàgé: 'Swahili speaker' (cf. *wàgó* 'Swahili speakers')
ɬísú 'sister'

The 3M.SG high-toned nominal PGN form, *é:*, is used to form a nominal stem, following a noun stem; all my textual examples are followed by the specifier *ȉ:*.

(94) *màrímòé:* 'the one who's a teacher'

(95) [1]m̀dzûⁿgḛ̂ːːsíʔ̥̀ [2]hàᵐbḛ̌ː ?
m̀dzûⁿgṳ é: ȉ: síʔ̥̀ hàᵐbě: í:
European 3M.SG SPEC PP where 3M.SG
'The European, where is he?'

It is found after a postpositional phrase (see example (66) in Chapter 7) and in the following examples.

(96) [1]wàrȇ: [1]ts̰'ǎːkṳ̂ȇːː
wàré ȉ: ts'ǎːkṳ é: ȉ:
fellow SPEC home 3M.SG SPEC
'that fellow from home'

(97) [1]hěːxwèná [1]kíbáʔ̥̀xȇ: [2]tsʰâ̰ː
hěːxwè ná kíbà ʔ̥ xì é: ȉ: tsʰâ:
that (MLT) 'so' hearth LOC MLT 3M.SG SPEC fat
'that fat on the hearth'

Nominals can be formed from verb stems by adding *ó:*. All tones are high.

(98) *ɬómóː* *ɬòmé* 'to cultivate'
ʔámóː *ʔàmé* 'to rear (child)'

The suffixes *ʔò* and *sà* are used to form nominals from VPS.

(99) ^{1}t^{h}ám̀ts^{h}ú ^{2}síésàméː ^{1}tátẫː ^{1}p^{h}álàgáʔ`̥ ^{2}pěː.
t^{h}ám̀ts^{h}ú sié sà méː tátẫː p^{h}álà gê ʔà pěː
woman take PP first pledge DEC$_{2}$ 3PL put
'To get married, they first give a pledge.'

(100) ^{3}sáː ^{1}ɬăː ^{2}ʔísì̥ ^{1}núá ^{2}mẫ^{n}ts^{h}àʔòsà
sáː ɬăː ʔísì̥ núá mẫ^{n}ts^{h}à ʔò sà
N.CONJ.3F.SG goat refuse *ugali* eat 3F.SG
'and the goat refused to eat the *ugali*'

One frequent way of forming a noun stem is with the suffix *sí*. It is found suffixed to an NP and to a VP. *sí* is followed by a nominal PGN suffix, low-toned, which agrees with the noun, overt or covert, to which the new stem ending in *sí* relates.

Following an NP the translation equivalent in English uses the verb 'have'.

(101) ^{1}tsí ^{1}bógěːsísì̥gáʔ`̥.
NP$_{T}$ NP$_{C}$
tsí bógěː sí sì gáʔ`̥
1SG brother in law 1SG DEC$_{2}$+3C.SG
'I have a brother in law.'

To indicate a plurality (or multiplicity?) of the nouns, *wà* is placed between the noun and the *sí*.

(102) ^{1}mĭː^{n}dzówàsúsȕ̃ːkáʔ`̥.
mĭː^{n}dzó wà sí sȕ̃ː káʔ`̥
journey MLT 2PL EVID
'We have some journeys apparently.'

Following a VP where V is imperfective, the translation equivalent is being able to do something, a characteristic.

(103) ^{1}!̥wẵ̀ː ^{1}h̰èwé ^{1}mànàsísì̥ ^{2}mŏːtóʔ`̥.
!̥wăː ĩ̀ː hèwé mànà sí sì̥ mŏːtò ts'ì
place SPEC that know 1SG Moto OBL
'I know that place. I know Moto.'

(104) ^{1}!^{h}ăːk'ȕ̃ː ^{1}hèwéʔ`̥ ^{1}ǀ̃íǹwàsê, ^{1}tsí ^{1}ǀ̃íǹsísì̥ts'é.
!^{h}ăːk'ú ĩ̀ː hèwé ts'ì ǀ̃íǹ wà sí è tsí ǀ̃íǹ sí sì̥ ts'é
vervet SPEC that OBL eat MLT 3M.SG 1SG eat 1SG NEG
'He eats vervet, I don't eat it.'

Following a VP where the V is perfective, the translation equivalent is having succeeded in doing something.

(105) ^{1}t^{h}íːmésísì̥.
t^{h}íːmé sí sì̥
cook (PERF) 1SG
'I've cooked it.'

sí occurs in the form used as equivalent to 'to be (locative)', that is, after *kóː* (SG.S) and *něː* (PL.S).

(106) ^{1}ts'ǒːts'í ^{1}kóːsè^{1}ẽ̂ː.

ts'ǒːts'í	*kóː*	*sí*	*è*	*ṽ̂*
hunger	be.at		3M.SG	'affirmation'

'Yes, there's a famine.'

Where the subject of the nominal clause is a locative PP, *sí* is followed by *ʔ̥̀*.

(107) ^{2}swê ^{1}tsí ^{2}sâkwè ^{2}ts'ǎːkṳ̀ ^{1}k'àmésíʔ̥̀ ^{2}ʔ̃êːʔ̥̀.

swê	*tsí*	*sâkwè*	*ts'ǎː*	*kṳ̀*	*k'àmé*	*sí*	*ʔ̥̀*	*ʔ̃ê*	*ː̂*	*ʔ̥̀*
now	1SG	uncle	home	LOC	beer		3C.SG	day	SPEC	PP

'There's beer at my uncle's today.'

The subject, NP_T, of the Sandawe sentence is *^{1}tsí ^{2}sâkwè ^{2}ts'ǎːkṳ̀*; the NP_C is *k'àmésíʔ̥̀*, which agrees with the PP which stands as subject by using *ʔ̥̀*, the 3C.SG form of the nominal PGN. *síʔ̥̀* seems also to function as a non-syntactic clitic (see 61 and 62). It can also serve as a marker of subordination (see Chapter 7).

2.2.3.2 Adjective stems

The adjective stems, quoted in 3M.SG form, include:

(108)

ts^{h}ěː	'being in a state of absence'	
tlàkî	'being in a state of not possessing'	
nê	'this'	
nâ	'that'	
láːẁ	'good'	*láːʔ̥̀wà* 3MLT
ǁ̥àé	'new'	*ǁ̥ǎːsú* 3F.SG (e.g. 'coin')
ǀ'áːm̀	'worn out'	*ǀ'ẫːsṳ̀* 3F.SG
hà^{m}bě	'being in which place?'	*hà^{m}bésú* 3F.SG

Adjectives take *ʔ̥wa* as the 3MLT formative. Note that the stems *nê* and *nâ*, although here translated into English by demonstratives, are adjectives.

(109) *nâsò* 'those people'

(110) ^{1}láːʔè ^{1}nê

láːʔè	*nê*	*Ø*
hare	ADJ	3M.SG

'this hare'

(111) ^{1}tl'àk'ḭmé . . . ^{1}néʔ̥̀wà

tl'àk'ḭmé	*nê*	*ʔ̥̀wa*
these.shoes	ADJ	MLT

'these shoes'

2.2.3.3 Demonstratives

There are three different forms with an initial *h-*. Forms with the 3MLT *xḭ̀* are found.

(112) 3M.SG *hě:ǹ* *hèwé* *hǎ:ẁ*
3F.SG *hě:sṳ̀* *hèsú* *hǎ:sṳ̀*
3PL *hě:sò* *hèsó* *hǎ:sò*
3MLT *hě:xwè* *hèwéxé:* *hǎ:xwè*

The interrogative form is:

(113) *hàwé*

2.2.3.4 Numerals

There are five numerals. The first four are usually quoted in isolation followed by the formative *xì̥*: Its use with numbers two to four is multiple; the reason for the appearance of *xì̥* as part of the stem for 'one' seems accidental.

(114) 'one' *ts'éxì̥*
'two' *kísòxì̥*
'three' *sóḿkíxì̥*
'four' *hàkáxì̥*
'five' *kwǎ:ʔ̥ná*

The interrogative also shows *xì̥*:

(115) *hánèxì̥* 'how many?'

(116) wàdzûⁿgṳ̀ kísòsòsì̥ ǀ̥á'ʔĩ́:.
wàdzûⁿgṳ̀ kísò sò sì̥ ǀ̥â ʔĩ́:
Europeans two 3PL 1SG see 1PL
'I saw two Europeans.'

Numbers 'six–nine' are formed by adding to 'five':

(117) ¹ĩ̀ő:kó ¹kwǎʔ̥̀ná ¹dá:ⁿdà ²hàkáxì̥
ĩ̀ő:kó kwǎʔ̥̀ná dá:ⁿdà hàkáxì̥
children five other four
'nine children'

A Bantu loan is used for ten: *kó:mì̥*.

ts'éxì̥ is often translated by 'alone'; it takes a PGN nominal. The form *ts'éxè* probably shows a 3M.SG nominal PGN.

(118) ¹híkì: ²ts'éxì̥pó ²kʰwǎ̃: ²ǀ̥í ?
híkí ì ts'éxì̥ pó kʰwà ĩ̃: ǀ̥í
how 2SG one 2SG return and come
'Why have you come back alone?'

2.2.4 Verbs

The essential verb has a verb stem, which can be accompanied by formatives which indicate aspect, formatives which seem comparable to what are called extensions in Bantu languages, and agreements with oblique constituents of the predicate. The formative *wà* is sometimes present.

2.2.4.1 Oblique agreements

The object agreement is a high-toned nominal PGN.

(119)

1SG	*sé*
2SG	*pó*
3M.SG	*éː*
3F.SG	*(ː)sú*
1PL	*sű̃ː*
2PL	*sĩ́ː*
3PL	*ʔĩ́ː*
3MLT	*ʔ̥ˊwá(ː)*

(120) ^{1}mòkòlàʔĩ́̀ːpòts'é.
mòkòlà ʔĩ́ː ˋ pò ts'é
greet 3PL IRR 2SG NEG
'You won't greet them.'

(121) ^{1}síésûsi̥gáʔˋ̥ ^{2}hèsú.
síé sú ˋ sì gáʔˋ̥ hèsú
take 3F.SG IRR 1SG DEC$_{2}$+3C.SG 3F.SG
'I was going to marry her, that one.'

2.2.4.2 The formative *wà*

This has already been met with in the 3MLT form *ʔ̥wa*, and as a pluraliser with *sí* (see 102). With a verb it indicates a multiplicity or plurality in the application of the meaning of the verb, its precise meaning for its position after or before the object agreement has not been worked out, and can be expected to relate to matters of aspect and multiplicity, pluractionality, frequentative, habitual and the like.

After object agreement:

(122) ^{1}ʔúràː ^{2}fâːséwà.
ʔúrì̥ à fâː sé wà
strength 3M.SG suit 1SG MLT
'They (shoes, multiple)'ll really be of use to me.'

Before object agreement:

(123) ^{1}ts^{h}íàsó ^{1}ɬáːsò ^{1}máxàná ^{1}hétékàwàʔĩ́ː$^{!}$ts^{h}ó
ts^{h}íà só ɬáː sò máxà ná hétékà wà ʔĩ́ː ts^{h}è só
all 3PL good 3PL male 'so' marry MLT 3PL NEG 3PL
'They're all well, they're not married yet.' (Lit.: Men have not taken them.)

2.2.4.3 Derivational affixes

It is assumed that when derivational affixes are suffixed to a verb stem, the whole functions as a verb stem.

Extensions:

The systematisation of the extensions is not straightforward; they are listed here with short comments and examples.

kù/xì̥ gives a benefactive meaning:

(124) ^{2}swê ^{1}t^{h}í:méxì̥pôsò.
swê *t^{h}í:mé* *xì̥* *pó* ` *sò*
now cook.it 2SG IRR 3PL
'Now they'll cook it for you.'

(125) ^{3}swá: ^{1}ǀ̃úm̀swá: ^{2}ǃ̃á:kwè
swá: *ǀ̃úm̀sú* *á:* *ǃ̃á:* *kù* *è*
N.CONJ.3M.SG wife NOM hold 3M.SG
'and his wife held it for him'

ká seems to imply accompaniment or instrument:

(126) ^{1}t^{h}âkŏ̃: ^{1}ʔèʔé̤: ^{2}mìrîgĩ̀: . . . ^{2}ǀ̥íká: !
t^{h}â *kò* *ĩ̌* *ʔèʔé:* *mìrîgĩ̀:* *ǀ̥í* *ká* *:*
run IMP and that.time medicine come 3SG
'Run and bring that medicine!'

(127) ^{1}t^{h}áwẫ: ^{1}t^{h}á̤wáwàká:ʔẵ: !'ŏ:k^{h}á.
t^{h}áwá *ĩ̂* *t^{h}áwá* *wà* *ká* *:* *ʔà* *ĩ̌* *!'ŏ:k^{h}á*
feather SPEC feather MLT 3SG 3PL and ready
'The feathers, they had already feathered (arrows) with them.'

ts'i following a verb stem gives a stem whose translation equivalent is passive, stative or the like.

(128) ^{1}só: ^{2}hàbáts'ìʔ`̥tè
só: *hàbá* *ts'ì* *ʔ`̥tè*
1PL+NOM bear PP
'at the place where we were born'

(129) ^{1}hĕ:sù̥ ^{1}ǁ̥wá:ts'ì̥sà.
hĕ:sù̥ *ǁ̥wá:* *ts'ì̥* *sà*
3F.SG hide 3F.SG
'She hid herself.'

(130) ^{1}mákàts'ígâsì̥.
mákà *ts'í* *gâ* ` *sì*
make.happy DEC$_{2}$ IRR 1SG
'I will be pleased.'

What seems the same formative is found with noun stems; the whole functions as a verb stem.

(131) ^{1}hèwéts'à: ^{2}bènégéts'í.
hèwé *ts'ì* *à* *bènégé* *ts'í*
3M.SG PP 3M.SG rich.man
'For that reason he became a rich man.'

The tone and the uses of this suffix require more attention.

Causatives:

The situation with causatives seems to be complex. There is clearly quite an old suffix, *kù̥*.

(132) [1]ts'éxi̥sáː . . . [2]mâⁿtsʰàkṳ.
ts'éxi̥ sì áː mâⁿtsʰà kṳ
one 1SG NOM eat
'I alone feed (her).'

This suffix is found with a preceding *sú*:

(133) [1]ɬúbáràkí [2]ɪ̃èsúkṳts'ɛ̀ːgàʔ̥̀ [2]xɛ̃́ː [2]ɪ̃àtí.
ɬúbárà kí ɪ̃è(ɪ̃ěː) sú kṳ ts'è ɪ̃ ʔà xéː ɪ̃ ɪ̃àtí
foam too enter REL SPEC 3PL bring and come (PL.S)
'They've brought that thing which breathes out contagion (lit.: causes foam to enter).'

And, with *sú*, followed by an object agreement:

(134) [1]kókɔ̂ːgà [2]si̥âː [1]ɬǎːtànà [2]ɪ̃èsúkèː
kókó ɪ̃ à síé à ɬǎː tànà ɪ̃è sú kṳ èː
cockerel SPEC 3M.SG take and goat PP enter 3M.SG
'He took the cockerel and put him in with the goats.'

(135) *hǎːgàsúkèː* 'woke him'
hǎːgà 'get up'

This sequence is also found suffixed to a noun stem.

(136) [1]mǒːtòts'òː [2]twěːsúkṳ.
mǒːtò ts'ì ò twěː sú kṳ
Moto LOC 1PL night
'Night came on us at Moto.'

I accept Dempwolff's (1916: 37) explanation of the origin of this. The *sú* is *sí* (which can be suffixed to nominals and verbs); the present-day status of *sí* is that it is a noun-forming suffix (see 101–107). However, the historical suffixation of *kṳ* produced a verb stem, the vowel quality of *sí* became *sú* by assimilation and any vowel-initial object agreement replaced the original vowel of *kṳ* completely.

As well as this complex of causative forms, there is a simpler *sé*. All tones in the verb stem before *sé* are low.

(137) *náʔ̥̀* 'to be alight' *nàʔ̥̀sé* 'to light'
ɬákáʔ̥̀ 'to be lost' *ɬàkàʔ̥̀sé* 'to lose, bury'
kʰwà 'to come back' *kʰwàsé* 'to cause to return'

Very often *sé* is found in verb stems without the preceding part being transparently an independent morpheme.

ːⁿkí/ɪ̃ːkí could be called reciprocal, although the idea of performing together is often more appropriate.

(138) [1]ǁ̥àkáts'àwâːkîsṹː.
ǁ̥àkáts'à wà ːⁿkí ` sṹː
ask MLT IRR 1PL
'We'll ask each other.'

(139) *wèré* 'to walk'
wèrèmé 'to walk a lot'
wèrèmɛ̃́ːkí 'to walk a lot together'

It can appear without the nasality:

(140) *!'ŏː* 'to get, meet'
!'ŏːkí 'to meet one another'

Aspect:

Verb stems often have two forms, one perfective and the other imperfective. The perfective form takes object agreements, and it is not yet clear to me what the connection is between the presence of an object agreement and the interpretation as a perfective meaning. (I have heard the Swahili object prefix being used by speakers of Sandawe with the intention of giving a perfective interpretation.) A frequent perfective formative is the mere lengthening of a verb stem-final vowel.

(141) *bìkʰé* *bìkʰéː* 'to leave'

With some disyllabic stems, the lengthening is of the first vowel:

(142) *tʰímé* *tʰíːmé* 'to cook'
!'ìné *!'ĭ̃ːgé* 'to hunt'
ǁ̥áwé *ǁ̥áːwé* 'to pour'

A few verbs show a different vowel:

(143) *ǀ̃wéː* *ǀ̃wáː* 'to take food off fire'
ts'éː *ts'áː* 'drink'

And a few verbs show seeming prefixation:

(144) *k'wéː* *wák'wà* 'to kill'

The systematisation is at present incomplete because of overlap with categories whose semantic areas, or morphological realisation, have not been established, but can be approximated by terms such as frequentative and habitual.

mé:

Several instances of *mé* are associated with perfective stems; all tones before *mé* are low. *mé* is associated with the idea of multiple occurrences.

(145)	*ʔìsá*	'to steal'	*ʔìsàmé*
	ǀ̃ùpʰá	'to blow, to smoke (cigarette)'	
	ǀ̃ùpʰáː	'to blow' (PERF)	
	ǀ̃ùpʰàméː	'to smoke'	
	kʰwà	'to come back'	
	kʰwàmsé	'to cause to return (many things)'	
	náʔ̥̀	'to be alight'	
	nàʔ̥̀sé	'to light (one thing)'	
	nà̆ᵐʔ̥̀sé	'to light (many things)'	

It is frequently found with *ʔ̥wa*, which is typically multiple:

(146) ¹tɬ'àk'ḭmẽ̂ːsíʔ̥̀ ¹bìkʰìméʔ̥́wáxḭsêpòts'é ?

tɬ'àk'ḭmé	*ː̃̀*	*síʔ̥̀*	*bìkʰé*	*mé*	*ʔ̥́wá*	*xḭ*	*sé*	*`*	*pò*	*ts'é*
shoe	SPEC	'then'	leave		MLT	BEN	1SG	IRR	2SG	NEG

'Those shoes then, you won't leave them for me?'

3 SOUTH AFRICAN KHOESAN

3.1 Northern Khoesan

The description of the morphology of !Xun is incorporated in the Chapter 7.

3.2 Central Khoesan

3.2.1 Namibian Khoekhoe (Nama/Damara)

Wilfrid H.G. Haacke

Khoekhoe (N.Kh.) is strictly a suffixing language and is of a predominantly isolating type. The verb stem is not inflected in accordance with the subject. Nominals are specified according to person, gender and number (PGN).

3.2.1.1 The PGN marker

Khoekhoe categorizes nouns according to first, second and third person; masculine, feminine and neuter or communal gender; and singular, dual and plural number. PGN formatives on nominals are conventionally but erroneously treated in the literature as suffixes. They should be viewed, however, as post-clitics, and as such as the true pronouns of the language. The PGN marker has two paradigms, the nominative paradigm for underlyingly subjectival function (Table 6.1; here loosely called PGN marker because of its predominant occurrence), and one for objectival function (Table 6.3; here called object marker, O^{m}). The subjectival PGN marker serves *inter alia* as "suffix" on surface nominals; the O^{m} follows immediately on the verb and serves exclusively as pro-form for the object. In certain syntactic contexts the nominal with the PGN marker will appear in the oblique form with the suffix *-a* (Table 6.2; cf. Chapter 7). The term "pronoun" will not be used here because of the confusion in the literature.

TABLE 6.1 PGN MARKERS OF N.KH. (NOMINATIVE PARADIGM)

Person	Masculine			Feminine			Neuter		
	I	II	III	I	II	III	I	II	III
Singular	*ta*	*ts*	*b/mi/ni*	*ta*	*s*	*s*	–	–	*-i*
Dual	*khom*	*kho*	*kha*	*m*	*ro*	*ra*	*m*	*ro*	*ra*
Plural	*ge*	*go*	*gu*	*se*	*so*	*di*	*da*	*du*	*n*

TABLE 6.2 PGN MARKERS OF N.KH. IN OBLIQUE FORM (+ *a*)

Person	Masculine			Feminine			Neuter		
	I	II	III	I	II	III	I	II	III
Singular	*ta*	*tsa*	*ba/ma/na*	*ta*	*sa*	*sa*	–	–	*-e*
Dual	*khoma*	*kho*	*kha*	*ma*	*ro*	*ra*	*mo*	*ro*	*ra*
Plural	*ge*	*go*	*ga*	*se*	*so*	*de*	*da*	*do*	*na*

TABLE 6.3 OBJECT MARKERS OF N.KH. (+ *i*)

Person	Masculine			Feminine			Neuter		
	I	II	III	I	II	III	I	II	III
Singular	*te*	*tsi*	*bi/mi/ni*	*te*	*si*	*si*	–	–	*-i*
Dual	*khom*	*kho*	*kha*	*mi/im*	*ro*	*ra*	*mi/im*	*ro*	*ra*
Plural	*ge*	*go*	*gu*	*se*	*so*	*di*	*da*	*du*	*ni/in*

The PGN marker for the third person masculine singular is realized as *b* after vowels (which is the most frequent occurrence) and assimilates to preceding consonants (which in original Khoekhoe words can only be *m* or *n*); e.g. *ao-**b*** 'man', *xam-**mi*** 'lion', *!an-**ni*** 'despair', *skol-**li*** 'school'.

3.2.1.2 Nouns

Surface nouns consist of a stem with a PGN marker, e.g.

(147) *tara-s* 'woman' (3F.SG)
tara-ta 'I, a/the woman' (1SG)

For explicatory purposes stem and PGN marker are separated by a hyphen, here. The stem provides (part of) the lexical specification of an NP. As an elementary knowledge of the basic syntactic structures is essential for the understanding of Khoekhoe nominal morphology, the reader should refer to section 3.2.1.1. in Chapter 7.

3.2.1.2.1 GENDER ALLOCATION

In animate nouns (including proper nouns and surnames) masculine and feminine gender is assigned according to biological sex. Neuter is used for non-specific or unknown sex or for generic and indefinite references; in the dual and the plural, neuter gender also designates common or collective, i.e. masculine jointly with feminine gender.

In inanimate nouns masculine nouns tend to signify relatively large or elongated objects, while feminine nouns tend to signify relatively small, shorter, concentric or roundish objects, e.g.

(148)

Masculine		Feminine	
!ā-b	'river'	*!ā-s*	'village, town'
hai-b	'stick; tall, narrow tree'	*hai-s*	'plant; bush, tree (in general)'
dao-b	'path, way, track'	*dao-s*	'doorway'
om-mi	'large building'	*om-s*	'hut, house'

Infinitives (especially action nouns) and nominalizations of phrases are formed with the third person feminine singular *s*, e.g.

(149) *sîsen* 'work, operate' (v.t.) → *sîsen-**s*** 'working, to work' (n.)
cf. *sîsen-ni* 'work, labour' (n.)
*kantors !nâ tekaos ase ra sîsen-**s*** NP: 'working in an office as a typist'

3.2.1.2.2 THE STRUCTURE OF NOUN STEMS

Stems can consist of single or multiple roots, with or without grammatical formatives. Single roots may be true nominal roots, or they may belong to other categories that are nominalized in various ways:

(a) common nouns, by mere addition of a (mostly masculine or neuter) PGN marker;
(b) infinitives, from verbal roots with the feminine PGN marker *s*;
(c) concrete nouns, from verbal roots by tonal derivation and PGN marker;
(d) abstract nouns, by means of the sole derivational suffix *-si* with PGN marker *b* or *s*.

Examples:

(150) Noun root

khoe-i	'person'
khoe-b	'male person = man'
khoe-s	'female person = woman'

(151) Verb root

	gowa	'argue, quarrel'	→
infinitive	*gowa-s*	'to argue, arguing'	→
common noun	*gowa-b*	'language'	

(152) Tonal derivation (flip-flop, see Chapter 5)

göá	v.i.	'foam'	→
göà.s	n.	'foam'	cf. infinitive
göá.s		'foaming'	

(153) Abstract nouns

!gam	'deep'	→
!gamsi-b	'depth, deepness'	
!gā	'become visible'	+ *-sa* ADJ suffix →
!gāsasi-b	'clarity; clearness'	

Compound noun stems may comprise a wide variety of word category combinations, be they basic or derived themselves. Here are just a few examples:

(154) Noun + noun

!apu-s 'rifle' + */uri-s* 'iron, metal' → *!apu/uri-s* 'bullet'

Verb + noun

sîsen 'work' + *ao-b* 'man' → *sîsenao-b* 'labourer, worker'

Adjective + noun

ǂkham 'young' + *khoe-i* 'person' → *ǂkhamkhoe-i* 'youth, juvenile'

!anu 'clean' + *o* 'without' + *!nâ* 'in' + *om* 'build/house' → *!anuo!nâ-om-s* 'brothel'

Multiple combinations

gaxu 'long' + *!nâ* 'in' + *-be* 'ADJ suffix' + *-si* 'abstract nominal suffix' → *gaxu!nâbesi-b* 'long duration'

|guri 'alone' + *|gui* 'one'+ *mî* 'say' + *am-s* 'mouth' + *!nâ* 'in' → *|guri|guimî-am!nâ-s* 'the sole say/authority'

Verbs incorporating objects combined with noun stems

!apu-s 'rifle' + *kuru* 'make' + *ao-b* 'man' → *!apukuru-ao-b* 'gunsmith'

Diminution and augmentation

Diminution is achieved with the general diminutive suffix *-rò*, which is also used with verbs and other word categories (with tonal differentiation, though). With nouns it denotes primarily small size, but also endearment, insignificance/derogation or junior status.

(155)	*ani-s*	'bird, fowl'	→	*ani**ro**-s*	'chicken, fledgling; small bird/fowl'
	mama-s	'mother'	→	*mama**ro**-s*	'dear mother; junior aunt (mother's younger sister)'

The augmentative suffix *-kàrà* is used with nominals rather than verbs:

(156) *ao-b* 'man' → *ao-**kara**-b* 'a colossal man'

3.2.1.3 Distribution test for verbs, adjectives and noun stems

As all categories of stems can serve as predicate- or NP-heads, it is occasionally claimed that verbs and adjectives in particular, but also nouns, are difficult to differentiate in Khoekhoe. A distribution test with the following three aspects (in the present tense), however, allows reliable differentiation, bearing in mind an exceptional closed group of stative verbs.

(157)		Verb	Adjective	Noun
Inchoative/progressive	*ra*	+	+	–
Stative	*a*	–	+	+
Perfect	*hâ*	+	+	–

Examples:

(158)	a.	Verb	*Taras ge **ra** !anu.*	'The woman is cleaning.'
			*Taras ge **a** !anu.	
			*Taras ge !anu **hâ**.*	'The woman has cleaned.'
	b.	Adjective	*Taras ge **ra** !anu.*	'The woman is getting clean.'
			*Taras ge **a** !anu.*	'The woman is clean.'
			*Taras ge !anu **hâ**.*	'The woman has become clean.'
	c.	Noun	*Taras ge **ra** !anu-ao.	
			*Taras ge **a** !anu-ao.*	'The woman is a cleaner.'
			*Taras ge !anu-ao **hâ**.	

The test is redundant for other lexical categories like numerals, as their semantic nature is sufficiently overt.

3.2.1.4 Adjectives

Adjectives, demonstratives, articles, numerals, possessives and relative clauses can be subsumed under the category "qualifier", as they all have the same syntactic behaviour within a noun phrase (see Chapter 7 for attributive, appositive and pronominal function, and for relative clauses).

Adjectives may be simple, compounded from roots, or derived by means of derivative morphemes.

(159)	a.	Simple	*kai* 'big'		
			ǂkhari 'small'		
			!gâi 'good'		
			ǀawa 'red'		
	b.	Compound	*ǂnū!ao* 'black-necked'	cf.	*ǂnū* 'black' + *!ao-b* 'neck'
			!âu!huni 'tan-coloured (like hyrax)'	cf.	*!âu-s* 'hyrax' + *!huni* 'yellow'
	c.	Derived	*-xa* 'denoting abundance/ frequentness'		
			ǁkhūxa 'thorny'	cf.	*ǁkhū-b* 'thorn'
			ǁnâuǀnamxa 'obedient'	cf.	*ǁnâu* 'hear' + *ǀnam* 'love, like'
			-o 'denoting privation'		
			mario 'pennyless'	cf.	*mari-b* 'money'
			-sa corresponding to past participial		
			-sà̈ with transitive verbs		
			-sa̋̈ with intransitive verbs	cf.	Haacke (1999)
			ǂnâsa 'dry, dried'	cf.	*ǂnâ* 'dry' (v.i.)
	d.	Complex	*!gammekhôa**xa*** 'adulterous'	cf.	*!gamme-b* 'matrimony' + *khôa* 'break'

Adjectives can take certain verbal extensions, e.g. *!gâi**ba*** 'good for', and also the diminutive, e.g. *!gom**ro*** 'somewhat heavy/difficult'.

3.2.1.5 Demonstratives

Three demonstratives occur: *nē* 'this', *ǁnā* 'that', *nàű* 'yonder, esp. invisible'. The latter demonstrative, *nàű*, should not be confused with the tonally distinct adjective *nấú* 'other'. The first two demonstratives have a deictic and a referential 'the said . . .' denotation, which causes tonally distinctive behaviour on any following qualifier, e.g.

(160) *nē* ***ǂàù*** *ǀhȍä.b* 'this tame cat here' vs.
nē ***ǂàű*** *ǀhȍä.b* 'this said tame cat'

3.2.1.6 Articles

Khoekhoe has four lexemes, *ti* [tìí̋], *si* [sìí̋], *sa* [sàá̋] and *ǁî* [ǁìì], which in the literature persistently are taken to be pronoun roots/stems used to form the "full" form of the pronoun with the PGN marker, the latter of which often is taken to be the reduced version of the pronoun. This is an erroneous approach, which came about through the fact that these qualifiers are most often used in pronominal rather than attributive position so as to precede the post-clitic PGN marker in lieu of another constituent.

These deictic lexemes, here dubbed articles because of the definite rendering they impart, evade direct translation. They reflect communicatory status (not to be confused with person), which can best be expounded by means of a feature analysis. (Unless animals and inanimate nouns are personified, the feature [human] is redundant next to [+speaker] and [+addressee].) *ǁÎ* furthermore serves to categorize people, apart from forming ordinal numerals, e.g. *Xristeǁ**î**-n* 'Christians', *!khūn**î**-b* < *!khūǁ**î**-b* 'wealthy man'.

(161)	*ti*	*si*	*sa*	*ǀî*
	+definite +speaker +human +singular	+definite +speaker –addressee +human –singular	+definite +addressee +human	+definite +discussed

Examples:

(162)	*si-khom*	'we two males'	(someone other than addressee and I)
	sa-khom	'we two males'	(addressee and I)
	ǀî-khom	'we two males'	(someone else referred to previously and I)

3.2.1.7 Numerals

Khoekhoe has a decimal numeral system. Units are added to tens with the suffix *-ǀa*.

(163)	*ǀgui*	'1'	*koro*	'5'	*khoese*	'9'
	ǀgam	'2'	*!nani*	'6'	*disi*	'10'
	!nona	'3'	*hû*	'7'	*kaidisi*	'100'
	haka	'4'	*ǁkhaisa*	'8'	*ǀoadisi*	'1,000'

Example:

(164)	'2,983'	*ǀgam-ǀoadisi (tsî)*	*khoese-kaidisi (tsî)*	*ǁkhaisa-disi*	*!nona-ǀa*
		2 1,000s (and)	9 100s (and)	8 10s	3-+

Ordinal numerals are formed by appending the article *ǀî*, e.g. *disiǀgamǀa**ǀî*** 'twelfth'. Only "first" has a special lexeme: *ǂguro*.

3.2.1.8 The possessive construction

Khoekhoe has two genuine possessive pronouns (not to be confused with the tonally distinct articles): *ti* [tı̋í] and *sa* [sa̋á], e.g. *ti ari-b* 'my dog'. All other possessives, whether nominal or pronominal, have the structure NP + *di*. The NP is structured internally according to the normal rules pertaining to NPS (see Chapter 7). The possessive marker *di* is likely to be omitted as redundant after simple possessive NPS, as the sandhi tone of the head noun obligatorily indicates the qualifying function of the possessive NP. The lexically least marked form, amounting to that of possessive pronouns in English, uses the article as lexical specification of the NP.

(165)	*si-da* ***di*** *goma-n*	'our cattle'
	nē kaira ao-s ***di*** *xoa!am-mi*	'the pen of this old woman'

Possessives can have a descriptive denotation, e.g. *ǁHui!gaeb (di) abel-n* 'Cape apples'.

3.2.1.9 The associative

The associative (ASS), or comitative, is irregular in its structure, as it does not fit into the same syntactic patterns as the other qualifiers. In the associative with two lexically specified NPS, the head is the possessor, while in the possessive construction the head is the possession.

(166)	*|awa*	*|gawa-s*	*â-i*	*tara-s*$_{\text{head}}$	'the woman with the red hat'
	red	hat	ASS	woman	
	tara-s	*di*	*|apa*	*|gapa-s*$_{\text{head}}$	'the woman's red hat'
	woman	POSS	red	hat	

The construction *â-i* is invariable if the head is a full (i.e. lexically specified) noun. It may cautiously be assumed that this construction is an orthographic misrepresentation. The associative would be more plausible if it is assumed that the construction is a relative clause with an object-NP in the oblique with *-a* followed by a fossilized verb *î* 'have, own', thus:

(167) *|awa |gawa-sa î tara-s (lit.: 'The woman who has a red hat.')

In the pronominal construction, however, *î* does not occur. The PGN marker following *â* refers to the possessor (qualifier). Only if this PGN marker refers to the first person singular (*ta*), can the PGN marker of the possession be repeated after the head:

(168) *|gawa-s* ***â-ts*** 'your hat'
ǂâi-s ***â-ta(s)*** 'my idea'

This is the only case where two PGN markers may be directly adjacent to each other. In all likelihood the two constructions that are traditionally subsumed as "associative", viz. the former one based on *NP a î NP, and the latter one NP *â*+PGN, are independent constructions that have been erroneously lumped together through the wrong spelling that uses nasal *â* for both.

3.2.1.10 Verbs

Verb (stems) can consist of single or multiple roots, with or without suffixes.

(169)	*kōō*	'look'	+	*!ganu*	'penetrate'	*kō!ganu*	'see through something' (lit. and fig.)
	mû	'see'	+	*ǂan*	'know'	*mûǂan*	'recognize'

3.2.1.10.1 VERBAL EXTENSIONS

Khoekhoe uses a limited number of productive suffixal verbal extensions that affect the valency or the basic meaning of the verb, viz. the applicative, reciprocal, reflexive, passive and ventive extensions. Combinations of these are possible.

3.2.1.10.1.1 APPLICATIVE ***-BA***

The applicative extension increases the transitivity of the verb by one, thus intransitive verbs become transitive (170), monotransitive verbs ditransitive (171), ditransitive verbs tritransitive (172).

(170) *Ari-b ge go ǂ**nûba te**.* 'The dog sat down for me.'

(171) *Petru-b ge* ***sîǂkhani-sa Ana-sa*** *ra xoa**ba***.
'Peter is writing a letter to/on behalf of Anne.'

(172) *Sats ge* ***sari-ao-na dao-ba*** *nî* ***|gauba da***.
'You must show the way to the visitors on our behalf.'

Doubled applicative:

(173) *Tara-s ge* ***tita*** ***|gôa-na mâi--e*** *ra sâi**baba**.*
'The woman is cooking porridge for the children on my behalf.'

3.2.1.10.1.2 RECIPROCAL -GU

The reciprocal indicates that the action of "transitive" verbs is reciprocated between the agents of the dual/plural subject.

(174) a. *Khoe-n ge ra tawede**gu**.*
'The people are greeting each other.'

b. *Ana-s tsî Petru-b tsîra ge sî‡khani-de ra xoaba**gu**.*
'Anne and Peter are writing letters to/for each other.'

3.2.1.10.1.3 REFLEXIVE -SEN

The reflexive reverts the action of (transitive) verbs to the subject.

(175)	*|ā*	'wash'	***|āsen***	'wash oneself'
	‡homi	'prepare'	*‡homi**sen***	'prepare oneself'
			*‡homi**senba***	'prepare oneself for something'
			*‡homi**basen***	'prepare something for oneself'

3.2.1.10.1.4 PASSIVE -HE

(176) a. *Tara-s ge piri-sa ra |ao.*
'The woman is milking the goat.'

b.

Piris	*ge*	*taras*	***xa***	*ra*	*|ao-*	***he**.*
goat	IND	woman	by	TAM	milk-	PASS

'The goat is milked by the woman.'

The passive is readily used in oral literature. A variant suffix *'e* is found especially in the Damara dialects.

3.2.1.10.1.5 VENTIVE -XA

The ventive is confined to verbs of movement as it indicates movement towards the speaker. It is derived from the verb *xā* 'attack in a group/with pincer movement'.

(177)	*‡gâ*	'go in'	*‡gâ**xa***	'come in'
	‡oa	'go out'	*‡oa**xa***	'come out; rise (sun)'

3.2.1.10.1.6 CAUSATIVE -SI

The causative extension *-si* is no longer productive and is confined to a limited number of verbs, e.g.

(178)	*‡û**si***	'(spoon-)feed'
	*bā(**si**)*	'dye (tanned skin)'
	*ō**si***	'feed (carnivore) a carcass'
	*khā**si***	'head off (animal)'
	*!û**si***	'let graze'
	*dai**si***	'suckle'
	*!hū!noma**si***	'uproot'
	*ā**si***	'water (animal)'

3.2.1.10.2 DERIVATIONS INVOLVING REDUPLICATION

The three types of verbal reduplication that exist are distinguished through their tonal behaviour. All involve flip-flop (see Chapter 5) on the first root to a certain extent, with a distinctive melody on the second root.

3.2.1.10.2.1 CAUSATIVE VERBS

Causative verbs are formed by means of reduplication with flip-flop, and a low-falling melody /`"/ on the second root. Reduplication is the main strategy for forming causatives.

(179) *!áò* 'fear' *!àò!àö* 'cause to fear, i.e. frighten'
ǂắń 'know' *ǂàn̋ǂàn̈* 'let know, inform'

3.2.1.10.2.2 PROGRESSIVE VERBS

Progressive verbs are formed from noun stems and denote change/development/degeneration into something. They are formed by means of reduplication with (unilateral) flip-flop, and a low-level melody /``/ on the second root. While causative verbs are transitive, progressive verbs are intransitive.

(180) *ǀnöré-b* 'ghost' *ǀnörèǀnòrè* 'turn into a ghost'
!nàrȅ-b 'ice, hail' *!nàrȅ!nàrè* 'freeze, turn into ice' (v.i.)

3.2.1.10.2.3 VERBS OF PRETENCE

Verbs of pretence denote that the action is feigned. The reflexive suffix *-sen* is added to the reduplicated verb and (mostly unilateral) flip-flop is followed by a high-rising melody /`"/ on the second root.

(181) *tsàű* 'become tired' (v.i.) *tsắútsàűsèn* 'pretend to become tired'
tàrắ-s 'woman' *tàrắtàrắsèn* 'act as adult woman (of: girl)'

*3.2.1.10.2.4 DIMINUTIVE VERBS WITH **-RŐ***

(182) *sîsen* 'work' *sîsen**ro*** 'work a little'

3.2.1.10.3 INCORPORATION AND BICLAUSAL VERBS

Khoekhoe belongs to the type of language that can incorporate object nouns, postpositions and (simple) postpositional phrases into the verb (cf. Haacke 1995), e.g.

(183) *Ao-b ge !ari-sa ra !au.* → *Ao-b ge ra !ari!au.*
man IND steenbuck TAM hunt
'The man is hunting steenbuck.'

Noun ... ***!khai-e*** *ra !khō* → ... *ra* ***!khai****!khō* 'catch a cold'

Postposition ... *dai-e* ***sūs !nâ*** *ra ǁhō* → ... *dai-e* ***sūsa*** *ra ǁhō****!nâ***
'pour milk into a pot'

pp-phrase ... *xaiba* ***[daob ai]****$_{PP}$ ra ko* → ... *xaiba ra kōdao-ai*
Kudu track on TAM look 'follow a kudu on its track'

Khoekhoe contains a limited number of biclausal compound verbs, where the first root refers to the action of the subject and the second root to the action of the object, e.g.

(184) *mû!goaxa* 'see (someone) approaching'
!khoeǀgoe 'run towards (someone) lying'

3.2.1.10.4 STATIVE VERBS

A very limited number of stative verbs occur. Most of them appear in pairs of antonyms. Such verbs appear only with the stative, but not the inchoative or perfect aspects.

(185)	*ǂan*	'know'	*ǀū*	'not know, be ignorant of'
	hâ	'exist, be present'	*ǀkhai*	'be absent'
	!khana	'teem'	*anu*	'be worthy of'

3.2.1.11 Adverbs

Next to original adverbs – e.g. *ti* 'so', *ǀnai* 'already', *ǁkhawa* 'again' – derivations by compounding and by suffixation occur.

(186)	Compounding:	*ǁkhāti*	'also'	cf.	*ǁkhā* ADJ 'same' + *ti* 'so'
		nētsē	'today'	cf.	*nē* 'this' + *tsē-s* 'day'

Adverbial suffixes: *-se* is the most productive one, forming adverbial extensions of manner. Next to adverbial clauses (see Chapter 7) it forms adverbs, the latter from adjectives, e.g.

(187)	***kaise***	'very'	cf.	*kai*	'large, big'
	ǀamose	'endlessly'	cf.	*ǀam-s*	'end' + *o* adjectival privative suffix 'without'

Other, less productive suffixes are *-be* (semantically indistinct, denoting periodicity with *koro*), e.g. *tsēkorobe* 'daily'; *-ga* (forming adverbs of time or place), e.g. *ǁgoaga* 'tomorrow morning', *!auga* 'outside'; *-pa* (forming adverbs and adverbial clauses of place), e.g. *nēpa* 'here', cf. *nē* 'this', *mapa?* 'where?', cf. *mâ?* 'which?'.

3.2.1.12 Postpositions

Khoekhoe uses postpositions rather than prepositions, which is accounted for by the fact that several are derived from (head-last) possessive constructions or from verbs (following the lexically specified object).

(188)	NP *ai* 'on (place); at (time)'	cf.	*tā-b di* ***ai-s*** (lit.: 'face of the table')
	NP *ǁkha* 'with'	cf.	*khoe-b di* ***ǁkhā-b*** (lit.: 'man's body')
	NP *!aroma* 'because of'	cf.	*!khai-s di* ***!aroma-s*** (lit.: 'reason of the matter')
	NP *(-a) !oa* 'to, towards'	cf.	NP- *a ra* ***!oa*** 'meet/encounter'
	NP *-a xu* 'from'	cf.	NP- *a ra* ***xū*** 'leave/abandon'

Postpositions can also be compounded and derived by suffixing:

(189)	*xōǁkhā*	'next to'	cf.	*xō-b* 'cheek', *ǁkhā-b* 'body' → 'with'
	mûǁae	'in full view of'	cf.	*mû-s* 'eye', *ǁae* 'come together'
	!nāga	'inside'	cf.	*!nā-b* 'stomach, interior' + *-ga* 'adverbial suffix'
	kōse	'until'	cf.	*kō* 'look' + *-se* 'adverbial suffix'

3.2.1.13 Conjunctions

Original conjunctions are monomorphemic:

(190)	*tsî*	'and'	*hina/hîa*	'while'
	xawe	'but'	*î*	'so that'
	o	'and then'		

Certain conjunctions are derived and mostly have postpositional character, e.g.

(191)	*amaga*	'because'	*ǁnā-amaga*	'therefore, for that reason'
	(ǁnā)!nūbai	<	*ǁnā !nū-b ai*	'on that instance, i.e. immediately'
	. . . xuige	*. . . xū-i ge*	'it is the thing that, i.e. since, for' (to justify commands)	
	tamas ka io	'should it not be so, then', i.e. 'or'		

For a detailed discussion of co- and subordination, see Chapter 7.

3.2.2 !Gora

Wilfrid H.G. Haacke

Perhaps the most conspicuous difference between the structure of !Gora and that of Namibian Khoekhoe (N.Kh.) is the apparently erratic use of grammatical formatives in !Gora, especially the frequent omission of them. As the available descriptions by Meinhof (1930) and Maingard (1962) date from a time when the language was well into its demise, it suggests that the records no longer reflect the original usage but, rather, atrophied forms symptomatic of language death. Maingard's grammatical analysis is, indeed, based on texts recorded by Lucy Lloyd as early as 1879. But as the tribe of the Kai !Goran, to which the informant belonged, ceased to exist not long afterwards, it may be assumed that the language and cultures were already disintegrating then.

3.2.2.1 The PGN marker

In Table 6.4 those forms of !Gora that differ from N.Kh. appear in bold. (The spellings of Maingard and Meinhof are retained here, apart from certain insignificant diacritics.) As Meinhof (1930: 33) points out, !Gora has preserved some older forms that no longer exist in N.Kh. (i.e. Nama dialects). In certain of the !Gora PGN markers, two morphemes can still be recognized. In the first person singular, masculine and feminine forms *r*(*e*) and *ta/te* respectively are distinguished, while N.Kh. only has one form, *ta*. In the third person masculine singular the PGN marker *bi* is not always assimilated to a preceding nasal, e.g. *xam+**mi*** or *xam+**bi*** 'lion', or *ti!kâ-p ǂxam-**p*** (Maingard 1962: 16; cf. N.Kh. *ti !gâb ǂkham**mi***). According to Wuras (1920: 57), assimilation did not even occur with the alveolar nasal: *sisîn**b*** 'work' (cf. N.Kh. *sîsen**ni***). This phenomenon was also recorded in rare instances in the dialects of the ǂĀkhoe and Haiǁom, e.g. *tam+**ba**/nam+**ba***, *nam+**bi*** 'tongue', and Sesfontein *nam+**bo**-o* (apparently the equivalent of accreditive sentence type marker *kom . . . o*).

TABLE 6.4 PGN MARKERS OF !GORA (NOMINATIVE PARADIGM)

Person	Masculine			Feminine			Neuter		
	I	II	III	I	II	III	I	II	III
Singular	***r**(e)*	*ts*	*b(i)/mi/ni*	*ta*	*s*	*s*	–	–	*-i*
Dual	***ka**+m,* ***kha**+m*	***kha**+ro*	***ka+ra**,* ***kha+ra***	***sa**+m*	***sa**+ro*	***sa**+ra*	*m*	***kha**+o*	***ka**,* ***kha***
Plural	*kie/tje*	***ka**+o,* ***ka+u***	*ku, gu* *kui*	***si**, se*	***sa**+o,* ***sa+u***	*di*	*da*	*du*	*n/**ni***

Tables 6.5 (PGN markers in oblique form) and 6.6 (object markers PGN+*i*) are fragmentary, as forms that are not attested in the available literature have been omitted. The reader can, however, derive the probable forms from the above paradigm for the nominative.

TABLE 6.5 PGN MARKERS OF !GORA IN OBLIQUE FORM (+*a*)

Person	Masculine			Feminine			Neuter		
	I	II	III	I	II	III	I	II	III
Singular	*tsa*	*ba/ma/(na)*		*sa*	*sa*	–	–	*-e*	
Dual									
Plural			***ku+a***			*de*			*na*

TABLE 6.6 OBJECT MARKERS OF !GORA (PGN + *i*)

Person	Masculine			Feminine			Neuter		
	I	II	III	I	II	III	I	II	III
Singular	***re***	*tsi*	*bi/(mi/ni)*	*te*	*si*	*si*	–	–	*-i*
Dual	*kham*	***kharo***		***sam***	***saro***				
Plural	*tje*	***kao***				*di*	*da*	*du*	*ni/(in)*

The use of the PGN marker with nouns is not adhered to as rigorously in !Gora as it is in N.Kh. If !Gora nouns are elicited in isolation, the stem is often offered alone (Meinhof 1930: 34). Alternatively, if cited with PGN, then nouns may be cited in the oblique form with *-a* (i.e. as a sentence in the predicative rendering, see Chapter 7). If the context is clear, the PGN marker may also be omitted in NPS in a sentence, e.g. *|ui_ tsî hai_ tsî~**ku*** 'stones and trees'. Where in short sentences the subject-NP consists of a PGN only, the entire NP may be omitted, especially if in the third person; e.g.

(192) a. *ǂnau tsi **r** ko̭a.*
hit you I PAST+JUNCT
'I hit you.'

b. *ǂnau re _ ko̭a.*
hit me PAST+JUNCT
'He hit me.' (See Chapter 7 for the occurrence of "junctures".)

Maingard (1962: 14) notes that the latent vowel *i*, which appears in the nasal assimilations of the third person masculine singular (*mi, ni*) occasionally also surfaces in nouns with *b*, e.g. *kwep-**bi** ko |kam|o* (= *khoeb**i** go |gam|ō*). Meinhof (1930: 37) interprets such constructions differently, in so far as he states that the single PGN marker may follow the subject noun as separate morpheme:

(193) He *haib bi na ham.*
this tree PGN TAM smell
'This tree (it) smells.'

Although Maingard's spelling of *bi* as additional morpheme reflects an approach similar to that of Meinhof, Maingard seems to treat *bi* as variant PGN: "*-bi* functions as subject or object." It would seem that Meinhof's interpretation is more apt. In terms of the analysis proposed for N.Kh., according to which the lexical specification of a noun is introduced by means of an embedded sentence, equi-NP deletion does not take place in !Gora. (See Chapter 7 for an interpretation as deposed subject.) Vossen (1997a: 200) furthermore reports that in ǁAni, Buga and |Ganda the nominal object is repeated ("wiederholt") on the verb as an object concord ("Objektkonkordant"). These data all corroborate the sentential hypothesis, according to which (surface) nouns in N.Kh. are derived from underlying sentences and, hence, are embedded in the main sentence virtually as subordinate clauses. This hypothesis should, *mutatis mutandis*, also apply to other Central Khoesan languages.

The *i* is much more common in the bare PGN marker, i.e. without a stem. As such it is also common in the Damara dialects of N.Kh., e.g. *Mû **i**ts ta?* 'Do you see?' As discussed in Chapter 7, !Gora differs also from N.Kh. in that the object NP as well as deposed subjects often do not take the oblique marker *-a*, e.g.

(194) *Mû-r ko̭-a xam-**mi**.* cf. N.Kh.: *Mû ta ge go, xam+**ma**.*
see-I PAST+JUNCT lion+NOM
'I saw the/a lion.'

On the other hand, Maingard (1962: 14) cites two instances where the nominative *-bi* was used for objects, e.g. *Ats !guixats ko !kam kweb-**bi*** 'You, rascal, have killed a man.'

3.2.2.2 Nouns

The structure of !Gora nouns is essentially similar to that of N.Kh. and hence need not be elaborated on here. This pertains to gender allocation, as well as to the structure of compound stems. A few examples from Meinhof (1930: 57) may serve for illustration:

(195) *|xa-|xa-kx'ao-b* 'teacher' cf. N.Kh. *|khā|khā-aob*
khoe-!am-kx'ao-b 'murderer' cf. N.Kh. *!gamaob*

Diminutives are formed with *da*, rarely with *ro* (as in N.Kh.), e.g. *kx'ani**da**-b* 'little bird'. For case marking, see under !Gora syntax.

3.2.2.3 Adjectives

Adjectives can syntactically be subsumed with demonstratives, articles, numerals, possessives and relative clauses as qualifiers. All of them precede the noun without PGN marker in attributive function, follow the noun with PGN marker in appositive function, and represent the noun with PGN marker in pronominal function.

(196) Attributive: *gai-da 'ao-**b*** 'old man'
Appositive: *'ao-**b** gai-da-**b*** 'old man'
Pronominal: *gai-da-**b*** 'the old one'

Adjectives may be simple, compound or derivative. The derivative suffixes for adjective formation are largely the same as for N.Kh. (Meinhof 1930: 59):

-xa denotes affluence or frequentness in denominal or deverbal adjectives:

(197) *|habi-xa* 'guilty'
||kx'ore-xa 'sinful'

-o denotes privation:

(198) *|'am-'o* 'endless'
hâ-!xaî-'o 'restless'

-sa corresponds to a past participial in English:

(199) *!nō-sa* 'silent'
|kx'obe-sa 'lazy'

!Gora had, in compounds that consist of an adjective with a noun stem, largely maintained the etymon *-xa* (the derivative suffix denoting affluence) in its full pronunciation. In N.Kh. only *-a* has survived, bar a few exceptions:

(200) !Gora N.Kh.
*!ai-**xa**-ǂao* 'gladness' *!gâi**a**ǂgaob* 'gladness'
but: *!ai̯-a-ǂao* 'rejoice'

3.2.2.4 Demonstratives

Three demonstratives are said to occur (Maingard 1962: 22):

(201) *hi/he* 'this'
|na 'that; the said'
hou 'that in the distance'

Meinhof (1930: 46) states that *he* may be doubled, e.g. *hehe ǂ'ûb* 'this food'. He does not state the semantic effect, though.

3.2.2.5 Articles

!Gora distinguishes the same four morphemes as N.Kh., morphemes that are usually mistaken to be pronoun stems. Again, it is more apt to refer to these morphemes as (definite) articles, as they serve to render a noun definite or to emphasize it. For a semantic analysis refer to N.Kh.

(202) *ti*
sa
si
|'aĩ, |'îi

As in N.Kh., *|îi* (or *|'aîb*) serves to form ordinal numbers: *!nona |'aîb* 'the third one'.

3.2.2.6 Numerals

!Gora has the same decimal numeral system as N.Kh., apart from minor differences in the pronunciation of certain of these numerals (here according to Maingard 1962: 16):

(203)	*/kui*	'1'	*haû kx'û*	'7'
	/kam	'2'	*//khaisi*	'8'
	!nwona	'3'	*khoesi*	'9'
	haka	'4'	*disi/tjisi*	'10'
	koro	'5'	*kaidisi*	'100'
	!nani	'6'	*/oadisi*	'1,000'

In two numerals the phonotactic structure appears to be deviant in both N.Kh. and !Gora: *haka* is exceptional in having a velar plosive *k* as C_2; *disi* is only apparently exceptional in having an alveolar fricative *s* as C_2. On the strength of the suffix *-si* in !Gora, *//khai**si***, *khoe**si***, it can be concluded that the original root of 'ten' was *dii* or *tjii*, i.e. with a doubled or "long" vowel. This is corroborated by the tonal melody in N.Kh., which is *dìísí*. Old Cape dialects had a velar plosive as C_1 (Nienaber 1963: 168 paradigm).

3.2.2.7 The possessive construction

The possessive construction is essentially the same as in N.Kh.:

(204) $[\text{NP}]_{\text{possessor}}$ *(di)* $[\text{NP}]_{\text{possession}}$

The possessive morpheme *di* that marks the initial NP as qualifier, being the "possessor", is said to be optional (Meinhof 1930: 40). From this can be concluded that, as in N.Kh., the possessive relationship between the juxtaposed NPS must also have been consistently expressed though tonal perturbation: the head of the NP, it can be assumed by analogy to N.Kh., receives sandhi tone as it is preceded by a qualifier (cf. Haacke 1998: 114). As with all qualifiers, three functions are possible:

(205) Attributive: *xoasao-b (di) kx'o-b*
leopard POSS meat
'the leopard's meat'

Appositive: *kx'o-b xoasao-b di-b*
'the leopard's meat'

Pronominal: *xoasao-b di-b*
'the leopard's'

It can be taken for granted that the possessive marker *di* is optional only in the attributive form, as in the appositive and pronominal form the post-clitic PGN marker (*b*) of the head noun must join onto it. As in N.Kh., the head of the possessive NP can be represented by any pronominal construction, in particular the pronominally used article (often wrongly referred to as "full" or "personal pronoun"), e.g.

(206) *ti-r ti ûa-i*
ART+1 POSS child
'my child' (Maingard 1962: 19)

In constructions where the possessor refers to the first or second person singular, however, N.Kh. does not use the pronominally used article, but instead the only two true possessive pronouns of the language: *ti* [tı̋í] 'my' and *sa* [sa̋á] 'your'. This strategy is optional in !Gora:

(207) *Ti* *(di)* *'ôa-tse!*
my POSS son+VOC
'You my son!' (Meinhof 1930: 45)

These possessive pronouns should not be confused with the articles *ti* [tìı̋] (speaker) or *sa* [sàa̋] (addressee). In !Gora the existence of four possessive pronouns, *ti* 'my' (not gender-specific), *tsa* 'your' (M), *sa* 'your' (F) and *ii* 'its', is attested by Maingard (1962: 21). The neuter form *ii* is syntactically different, however, as it follows the head noun: */xonu-p **ii*** 'its finger'. The absence of further examples does not permit an explanation of the structure.

3.2.2.8 The associative

The associative or comitative constructions with *a-* appear to function as in N.Kh., judging by the scant material available. If, in the pronominal construction, the possessor refers to the first person, the PGN marker of the head is also repeated after the qualifier:

(208) *kx'um-**mi*** *a-**re-p***
house+3M.SG ASS+1SG+3M.SG
'my house'

3.2.2.9 Verbs

Verb construction follows the same principles as in N.Kh. The same verbal extensions occur: passive (*-he*), applicative (*-ba*), reciprocal (*-gu*), reflexive (*-sen/-sin/-sn*) and ventive (*-xa*). While the variant [ʔe] is common both in N.Kh. and !Gora next to *-he*, the glottal fricative is liable to (partial) assimilation in !Gora: after front vowels it can form a palatal glide (*/xuri+**je*** 'was stalked'); after back vowels a labial glide (*habu+**we*** 'was eaten up'); after nasal consonants *h* assimilates fully (*//'an//'an+**ne*** 'be cooked').

The ventive extension *-xa*, which has been consistently overlooked in the literature on N.Kh., also occurs in !Gora, e.g. *ǂkx'oa+**xa*** 'come out'. Historically the ventive is a compound verb instead, using *xáà* 'attack, close in on' as modifying verb (cf. Haacke 1998: 143.)

Reduplication is used for the causative, e.g. *ǂhanuǂhanu* 'correct'. Although the data are not conclusive, it is apparent from Meinhof's (1930: 47) observations that *mutatis mutandis* the same tonological principles apply as in N.Kh. It appears that Meinhof has recognized the existence of the intransitive "progressive" verbs (1930: 138f.), but has misunderstood their semantic import. In N.Kh. they generally have a meaning 'turn/ degenerate into . . .', e.g. *!nàrȅb* 'ice' → *!nàrȅ!nàrè* 'turn into ice'. Flip-flop in N.Kh. occurs only on certain melodies, i.e., it is unilateral, and the repeated root has a low-level melody /` `/. This may have prompted Meinhof (1930: 47) to observe that the pitches are changed by the reduplication in some words but not others. He translates these presumably progressive words, though, simply as (stative) adjectives, e.g. */kx'uri-/kx'uri* 'schmutzig' (his tone marks), instead of 'verschmutzen' (v.i.).

It is also apparent that the third use of reduplication must also have existed in !Gora, viz. in verbs of pretence (Haacke 1998: 135). Such verbs have, in N.Kh., a high rising melody on the repeated root, which is then followed by the reflexive extension *-sèn*, e.g. */o/o+sin* 'to feign death' (Maingard 1962: 6, 58).

Incorporation (mainly of object nouns into verbs) is as prevalent in !Gora as in N.Kh. (cf. Haacke 1995), e.g. *!ou+!xo* 'fish + catch = catch fish, fish', *kx'o+//huru+!nâ* 'meat + thrust + in = thrust into the meat' (Maingard 1962: 16).

3.2.2.10 Adverbs

The derivation of adverbs in !Gora is essentially identical to that in N.Kh. The general suffix for deriving adverbs of manner especially from adjectives is *-se*: *kai* 'big' > *kai+se* 'very', *ǂhanu* 'straight, correct' > *ǂhanu+se* 'correctly'. Adverbs of place are, likewise, formed with the suffix *-pa*: *he* 'this' > *he+pa* 'here'. Derivations with *-ka* occur also: *ǂ'ana+ba+ka* 'intentionally'. Noun stems can be used adverbially either in the oblique form (*hoa tsē+ku+**a*** 'daily') or merely as stem without PGN marker (*hē+tsē* 'today').

It may be noted that in both languages negative imperatives are formed with the adverb *ta* 'never'. !Gora: *Ta /kx'a!* 'Never steal, i.e. don't steal!'; cf. N.Kh.: *Tā /â!* 'Never pilfer, i.e. don't pilfer!' The adverbial nature is more obvious in the more explicit version *tātsē* 'on no day, i.e. never ever' of N.Kh.

3.2.2.11 Postpositions

Postpositions are formed according to the same principles as in N.Kh., and are largely based on the same morphemes. Constructions are mostly based on possessive constructions without the possessive particle *di*. The original possessor noun appears without PGN marker and so assumes an adverbial function. As such it grammaticalizes into a postposition, e.g. */harub* **kx'ai** 'on a mat', cf. */harub (di) kx'ais* 'surface/face of a mat'. Postpositions that require the oblique form of the noun (in both languages) have been derived from a verb with its object: *i tje /xa hai+s+**a** **!oa** ha* 'and he came to the same bush' (lit.: 'and he came meeting the same bush').

3.2.2.12 Conjunctions

Conjunctions operate essentially as in N.Kh.: co-ordinating conjunctions precede the second sentence; subordinating conjunctions follow the embedded sentence. A conjunction exclusive to !Gora appears to be *i* 'and, when'. It is said to appear especially in front of PGN markers, e.g. ***I** du ra /habuse ham xūp hoapdi* 'And you (PL) foolishly do everything.'

3.2.3 Hai//om

Thomas Widlok

3.2.3.1 Nouns

3.2.3.1.1 INFLECTION

The inflection of Hai//om and ǂAkhoe nouns follows closely the structure that has been described for Namibian Khoekhoe (N.Kh.). Differences occur in the terminology used for the description and in some details of forms but these do not affect the structure as such. What Haacke (this volume) outlines for the relevance and function of the PGN marker in N.Kh. holds for Hai//om and ǂAkhoe as well. Tables 6.7–6.9 use Haacke's template (this volume: Table 6.1) for mapping data collected by Heikkinen and by myself onto the categories identified for N.Kh. Entries in brackets indicate N.Kh. grammatical forms which are at variance from the Haiǁom data or which could not be verified by Heikkinen. These gaps appear in the dual number and the neuter gender (see Heikkinen n.d.: 21). Heikkinen's terminology is added in italics.

TABLE 6.7 PGN MARKERS OF HAIǁOM (SUBJECT PARADIGM) – NON-FINAL CASE

Person	Masculine			Feminine			Neuter (Collective/ Communal)		
	I	II	III	I	II	III	I	II	III
Singular	*ta*	*ts*	*b* *(mi/ni)*	*ta*	*s*	*s*	–	–	*-i*
Dual	*tsum (khom)*	– *(kho)*	– *(kha)*	*m*	– *(ro)*	– *(ra)*	*m/tsum* *(m)*	– *(ro)*	– *(ra)*
Plural	*ge*	*go*	*gu*	*se*	*so*	*di*	*da*	*du*	*n*

TABLE 6.8 PGN MARKERS OF HAIǁOM IN OBLIQUE FORM (+ *a*) – FINAL CASE

Person	Masculine			Feminine			Neuter (Collective)		
	I	II	III	I	II	III	I	II	III
Singular	*ta*	*tsa*	*ba* *(ma/na)*	*ta*	*sa*	*sa*	–	–	*-e*
Dual	*tsuma* *(khoma)*	– *(kho)*	– *(kha)*	*ma*	– *(ro)*	– *(ra)*	*ma/tsuma (ma)*	– *(ro)*	– *(ra)*
Plural	*ge*	*go*	*gua (ga)*	*se*	*so*	*de*	*da*	*do*	*na*

TABLE 6.9 OBJECT MARKERS OF HAIǁOM (+ *i*) – MINIMAL OBJECT PRONOUNS

Person	Masculine			Feminine			Neuter (Collective)		
	I	II	III	I	II	III	I	II	III
Singular	*te*	*tsi/tsa*	*bi/ba* *(mi/ni)*	*te*	*si/sa*	*si/sa*	–	–	*-i*
Dual	*tsum/* *tsuma* *(khom)*	– *(kho)*	– *(kha)*	*m/ma* *(mi/im)*	– *(ro)*	– *(ra)*	*m/tsum/* *ma/tsuma* *(mi/im)*	– *(ro)*	– *(ra)*
Plural	*ge*	*go*	*gu/gua*	*se*	*so*	*di*	*da*	*du/do*	*n/na (ni/in)*

Note: The alternative forms for the object marker given for Haiǁom and ǂAkhoe are those which occur in compound verbal structures (see Heikkinen n.d.: 22).

The gender allocation in nouns in Haiǁom and ǂAkhoe follows the same pattern as in N.Kh. As for inanimate nouns, feminine noun endings are used to signify relatively small or roundish objects whereas masculine noun endings are used to signify large or elongated objects. It is noteworthy that wherever the shape is changeable speakers make the nouns drift from one class to the other; e.g., a 'termite mound' may turn from *ǀaras* to *ǀarab*, a 'shelter' from *ǀgaos* to *ǀgaob*, a 'local group' from *ǁgâus* to *ǁgâub*. This also applies to abstract nouns such as *!khaeb* and *!khaes* 'darkness', which can be said to increase or decrease (see Heikkinen n.d.: 19). Allocation of gender also at times exhibits the intentions and inclinations of speakers. For instance, a 'grove of mangetti trees (*Ricinodendron rautaneni*)' may be referred to as *|gom-haide* (F.PL) which highlights the fruit-bearing female trees as against the equally numerous male mangetti trees that are not of interest from the perspective of a food collector.

3.2.3.1.2 DERIVATION

As in N.Kh., a wide variety of word category combinations are possible in Hai‖om and ǂAkhoe, including noun+noun, noun+verb, noun+adjective and multiple combinations. Speakers of Hai‖om and ǂAkhoe generally allow the derivation of new nouns from existing stems in regular patterns to a degree that goes beyond the practice of forming compound nouns common in Indo-European languages. Numerous examples from Heikkinen's and my own data allow the following systematization of noun derivation.

3.2.3.1.2.1 DIMINUTION AND AUGMENTATION

As in N.Kh., the suffixes *-ro* 'diminutive' and *-kara* 'augmentative' are widely used. Especially *-ro* is used not only with nouns but also with verbs and other word categories. It is also an important marker of young age since the personal name of children and of young childless persons as well as some of the kin categories are augmented with *-ro* (Widlok 1999a: 182ff.), e.g. *Seirob* (personal name of a man who is now called *Seib* since he is father of two children), *somrob* 'a little bit of shade', *haikarab* 'tall tree'.

3.2.3.1.2.2 LOCALIZATION

The root *ai* 'place' is being used as a suffix to label fixed places and regions in the Hai‖om environment, as in *|Gomais* (the Mangetti farms north of Tsumeb); but also for more general terms such as *|nanu-aib* 'sky, heaven'. Examples: *!aaib !na* 'in/near the riverbed', *haiaib !na* 'in the bush'.

3.2.3.1.2.3 AGENT FORMATION

The morpheme *ao* 'agent' is being attached to verbs or adjectives, and sometimes to other nouns, to designate the people associated with an activity or a state of affairs, e.g. *aaon* 'drinker, alcoholics', *|aeaon* 'sick people, patients'.

3.2.3.1.2.4 ABSTRACTION

The abstractive suffix *-si* can be used to differentiate essences and general states of affairs from concrete entities, such as corporations from natural persons, but it may also be applied to lexemes that already describe a non-tangible feature and make it more abstract. The suffix is extensively used by Khoekhoe-speaking politicians to express concepts of national politics and by missionaries attempting to translate some of the core concepts of Christianity, e.g. *gaosib* 'reign, domination' from *gaob* 'king' and *!gariǂaosis* 'braveness'.

3.2.3.1.2.5 INSTRUMENTATION

The instrumentative morpheme *ube* is employed to create nouns, mostly for objects, which are utilized to achieve something, to create an effect, e.g. *ǂnau-ubes* 'thing to hit with', *!nari-ubes* 'vehicle'.

3.2.3.1.2.6 COLLECTIVIZATION

In some cases it is possible to collectively name a group of people by adding the suffix *-xa* to an existing category (e.g. a kinship category) or to the name of a person who for some reason and in some particular context forms the focal point of a group. Examples: *|gûxan* 'forefathers and -mothers', *Pauluxage* 'Paul and us, the other men who are with him'.

3.2.3.1.2.7 ASSOCIATION

The associative suffix *-sa* is semantically similar to the collective *-xa* but clearly distinguished because the association with a third person is the focus and the preceding stem indicates those who are associated with that person rather than those with whom others are associated. Furthermore, unlike *-xa*, which may be applied to persons and objects, *-sa* always indicates a personal relationship. Hagman (1977: 27, 166) has labelled this morpheme the noun root derivational suffix "personal relationship" for N.Kh., e.g. *|goasakua* 'his/her sons', *aisasa* 'his/her elder sister'.

3.2.3.1.2.8 CAUSATION

The causative suffix *-sabe* is possibly an extension of the above-mentioned *-sa* with the semantics of being more or less a passive victim of some action. Again, the suffix occurs only with persons, not with things, e.g. *!khosabekua* 'those that are caught, i.e. prisoners', *|namsabeb* 'the one that is loved, i.e. lover'.

3.2.3.1.2.9 PRIVATION

The privative suffix *-o* is commonly used in Hai||om (as in N.Kh.) not only with nouns but also with verbs (see below). It adds the meaning "lacking" to the root and is used in many creative ways, also by missionaries as exemplified by the second example which is taken from Heikkinen's wordlist (see Widlok n.d.), e.g. *Domokhoeb* 'name of a man who lost his voice/who has a hoarse voice', *|habiokhoeb* 'man without sin'.

The productiveness of some of these suffixes cuts across word categories as the outline of derivation of adjectives and verbs below shows.

3.2.3.2 Adjectives

ǂAkhoe adjectives are qualifiers which occur either in nominal structures (preceding or following the nominal head) or as complements to a predicate. Some adjective roots only occur in nominal structures:

(209)	*am-*	'right'	as in	*am|khab*	'right-hand side'
	||are-	'left'	as in	*||are|khab*	'left-hand side'
	aoro-	'male'	as in	*aoro|gôab*	'boy, male child'
	tare-	'female'	as in	*tare|gôas*	'girl, female child'

Examples for simple adjectives are: *|â* 'wet', *|a* 'sharp', *ǂnu* 'black', *|aba* 'red', *au* 'bitter'. Examples for noun-derived adjectives are: *ǂnanin* 'Kwanyama', *|naben* 'Owambo'.

Derivational suffixes to form adjectives are (see Heikkinen n.d.: 24):

(210)	*-ai*	*mboro-ai*	'foolish'
	-be	*amabe*	'good, true'
	-hâ	*ǂgihâ*	'blind'
	-!na	*||gai-!na*	'lazy'
	-ro	*ǂoro*	'rather narrow'
	-ko	*ndokoro*	'only this big'
	-sa	*tsâiasa*	'weak'
	-si	*||gaisi*	'ugly, bad'
	-xa	*khaxa*	'generous'
	-xu	*gaixu*	'long'

3.2.3.3 Numerals

Haiǁom numerals follow the same decimal pattern, using the same lexemes, as has been described for N.Kh. Heikkinen (n.d.: 25) has reported on additional alternative lexemes used by ǂAkhoe people in counting. These are:

(211)	*ǀgui!om*	'one fist' for 'five'
	ǀguiǂondo	'one finger [and a fist]' for 'six'
	ǀgamǂondo or *ǀgamǂonnobwa*	'two fingers [and a fist]' for 'seven'
	!nonaǂondo or *!nonaǂonnobwa*	'three fingers [and a fist]' for 'eight'
	ǀgamsa or *ǁhaisa*	'ten'

3.2.3.4 Demonstratives

The demonstratives *nou*, *nde* and *ǁna* either accompany a noun, as in *nou ǀgôan* 'those children', *nde khoeb* 'this man' or *ǁna khoes* 'that woman', and do not change their form, or they are employed in the place of a noun and receive a PGN marker as the noun would, as in *ǁnab ge* 'that's him', *nouna dire* 'ask those ones', *ndesa?* 'this one?'.

3.2.3.5 Possessive and associative

Haiǁom and ǂAkhoe share the possessive pronouns of N.Kh., namely *ti* and *sa*. The associative or comitative described for N.Kh. (see above) also occurs in Haiǁom and ǂAkhoe.

3.2.3.6 Interrogatives

Questions are formed in a similar way as described for N.Kh. (see Chapter 7 and Hagman 1977: 141ff.), but interrogative pronouns do differ between Haiǁom and ǂAkhoe on the one side and N.Kh. on the other.

The two interrogatives *tari* 'animate' and *tare* 'inanimate' that were identified for N.Kh. (Hagman 1977: 50) occur in Haiǁom in the roots *tai* 'who' and *tae* 'what' followed by a noun or a PGN marker. Examples (Heikkinen n.d.):

(212)	*Taiba ndeba?*	'Who is this?'
	Taitsa satsa?	'Who are you?'
	taeba?/tae xuba?/tae-e?	'what?'
	Tae xuba ndeba?	'What is this?'
	Tae-e tsa hî-e?	'What are you doing?'
	taeb ǀkha?/taeb !aroma?	'why?' (lit.: 'because of what?')

The two interrogative demonstratives *mâa* ('what' in noun phrases with indefinite PGN suffix, 'which' in noun phrases with any other gender) and *ham* 'who', 'only' (with animate unknown referents) that were identified for N.Kh. (Hagman 1977: 51f.) occur in ǂAkhoe in forms that seem to freely switch between these two morphemes. Examples (Heikkinen n.d. and my own field data):

(213)	*mati?*	'what?'
	Hamati ra mî?	'What does it mean?'
	ma ǁaeba?	'at what time?'
	hama ǁae?/hambo?/hamatiko ǁaeb ai?	'when?'

maba? 'where?'
Hamas go !gû?/Hamabas go !gû? 'Where did she go?'
hame?/hambi?/hamba? 'who?'

The interrogative roots may also be used in a declarative sense, as in (214):

(214) *hamatses hoasa* 'every day'
hamab hoaba 'everyone'

3.2.3.7 Verbs

As with words in other Khoekhoe variants it is useful to distinguish Hai‖om event verbs from non-event verbs. Non-event or stative verbs signify a state of affairs and have to be accompanied by the aspect markers *a* (or *i* in some tenses) or *hâ* which would both be translated as 'be', e.g.:

(215) *|U ta a.* 'I don't know.'
ǂAn ta a. 'I know.'
|Â toma ta ge hâ. 'I have not had enough food.'
!Gam-e, maba ra hâ? 'Where is the water?'

A, *hâ* and *i*, together with a few other roots, have been classified as auxiliary verbs (Heikkinen n.d.: 25) or as tense/aspect markers (Haacke, this volume). They fulfil the same functions in Hai‖om as they do in other variants of Khoekhoe.

3.2.3.7.1 INFLECTION

Heikkinen (n.d.: 30) provides the overviews that elaborate on the inflection of Hai‖om verbs (see Tables 6.10–6.14, orthography and terminology adapted to Standard Khoekhoe).

TABLE 6.10 HAI‖OM VERB IN PRESENT TENSE CONSISTING OF VERB STEM + PGN MARKER + ASPECT MARKER (*ra/a*)

Person	Masculine			Feminine			Neuter		
	Singular	Dual	Plural	Singular	Dual	Plural	Collective	Dual	Plural
I	*-ta ra*	*-tsuma*	*-ge re*	*-ta ra*	*-ma*	*-se re*		*-tsuma/-ma*	*-da ra*
II	*-tsa*	–	*-go ro*	*-sa*	–	*-so ro*		–	*-do*
III	*-ba*	–	*-gua*	*-sa*	–	*-de*	*-e*	–	*-na*

TABLE 6.11 HAI‖OM VERB IN PAST TENSE CONSISTING OF VERB STEM + PGN MARKER + TENSE MARKER (*go/ge*) + ASPECT MARKER (*ra/a*)

Person	Masculine			Feminine			Neuter		
	Singular	Dual	Plural	Singular	Dual	Plural	Collective	Dual	Plural
I	*-ta go(ro)*	*-tsum go(ro)*	*-ge go(ro)*	*-ta go(ro)*	*-m go(ro)*	*-se go(ro)*		*-(tsu)m go(ro)*	*-da go(ro)*
II	*-tso(ro)*	–	*-go go(ro)*	*-kho(ro)*	–	*-so go(ro)*		–	*-du go(ro)*
III	*-b bo(ro)*	–	*-gu go(ro)*	*-kho(ro)*	–	*-di go(ro)*	*-i go(ro)*	–	*-n go(ro)*

TABLE 6.12 HAI‖OM VERB IN FUTURE TENSE CONSISTING OF VERB STEM + PGN MARKER + TENSE MARKER (*si ra/si ni/sa ra/(î)ka hî*)

Person	Masculine			Feminine			Neuter		
	Singular	Dual	Plural	SG	Dual	Plural	Collective	Dual	Plural
I	*-ta si ra*	*-tsum si ra*	*-ge si ra*	*-ta si ra*	*-m si ra*	*-se si ra*		*-(tsu)m si ra*	*-da si ra*
II	*-tsi si ra*	–	*-go si ra*	*-si si ra*	–	*-so si ra*		–	*-du si ra*
III	*-bi si ra*	–	*-gu si ra*	*-si si ra*	–	*-di si ra*	*-i si ra*	–	*-n si ra*

TABLE 6.13 NEGATIVE VERB IN HAI‖OM

Person	Masculine			Feminine			Neuter		
	SG	Dual	Plural	Singular	Dual	Plural	Collective	Dual	Plural
I	*-ni tita*	*-ni ti tsum(a)*	*-ni tige*	*-ni tita*	*-ni tim(a)*	*-ni tise*		*-ni ti(tsu)-m(a)*	*-ni tida*
II	*-ni titsa*	–	*-ni tigo*	*-ni tisa (-ni ti khe)*	–	*-ni tiso*		–	*-ni tidu (-ni tido)*
III	*-ni tiba*	–	*-ni tigu (-ni tigua)*	*-ni tisa (-ni ti khe)*	–	*-ni tidi (ni tide)*	*-ni ti-i (-ni ti-e)*	–	*-ni tin (-ni tina)*

In the present tense the negative verb consists of *ta* + PGN marker + aspect marker + verb stem (see above); in the past tense of *ta* + PGN marker + tense marker + aspect marker + verb stem (see above); in the future tense of verb stem + tense marker *(ni)* + *ti/te* + PGN marker.

TABLE 6.14 NEGATIVE VERB IN HAI‖OM (PERFECTIVE FORM WITH *tama*) IN THE PRESENT TENSE CONSISTING OF VERB STEM + *tama* + PGN MARKER + *hâ*; IN THE PAST TENSE OF VERB STEM + *tama* + PGN MARKER + TENSE MARKER (*go/ge*) + *hâ*

Person	Masculine			Feminine			Neuter		
	Singular	Dual	Plural	Singular	Dual	Plural	Collective	Dual	Plural
I	*-tama-ta(ke) hâ*	*-tama-tsum(ge) hâ*	*-tama-ta(ge) hâ*	*-tama-da(ge) hâ*	*-tama-m(ge) hâ*	*-tama-se(ge) hâ*		*-tama-(tsu)m (ge) hâ*	*-tama-da(ge) hâ*
II	*-tama-tsi/ tse hâ*	–	*-tama so(ge) hâ*	*-tama-si/ khe hâ*	–	*-tama-so(ge) hâ*		–	*-tama-du(ke) hâ*
III	*-tama-bi/ -tamab be hâ*	–	*-tama-gu (ge) hâ*	*-tama-si/ khe hâ*	–	*-tama-di(ge) hâ*	*-tama-i (ge) hâ*	–	*-tama-n(ge) hâ*

3.2.3.7.2 DERIVATION

Haiǁom resembles N.Kh. in a number of derivational strategies (compare Heikkinen n.d. with Haacke, this volume, and Hagman 1977).

Ergative derivation is achieved through repetition of the verb stem, e.g.

(216)	*ǂkhaiǂkhai*	'to wake up'	←	*ǂkhai*	'awake'
	ûiûi	'to heal, make alive'	←	*ûi*	'live'

Double verbs are constructed by joining two verb stems, e.g.

(217)	*!gûsi*	'to go and arrive'	←	*!gû* 'to go' and *si* 'to arrive'
	!khokhâi	'to pick up'	←	*!kho* 'to take, grab' and *khâi* 'to rise'

Compound verbs are constructed by combining a verb root or any other root to create a new verb stem, e.g.

(218)	*tarekhoekabe*	'to look for a wife'	←	*tarekhoes* 'woman' and *kabe* 'to search'
	mûdao	'to track'	←	*mû* 'to see' and *dao* 'path, track'

Many verbs are derived from verb or noun roots with the help of a number of suffixes. Among the most common are the following:

(219)		Suffix	Example	
	Reciprocal	*-gu*	*ǀgoegu*	'to swear at one another'
	Diminutive	*-ro*	*aro*	'to drink a little'
	Benefactive	*-ba*	*ǁgaeba*	'to tell someone'
	Causative	*-kai*	*mâkai*	'to stop someone/something'
	Reflexive	*-sun*	*ǀasun*	'to wash oneself'
	Passive	*-he*	*mahe*	'to be given'
	Proactive	*-re*	*ǀaere*	'to go and look for firewood'
	Completative	*-!a*	*mî!a*	'to explain, translate'
	Transformative	*-si*	*!gaiaosi*	'to become a medicine man/healer'

3.2.3.8 Adverbs

In parallel with N.Kh. Haiǁom adverbs may be classified as either simple or derived adverbs. Simple adverbs are *ndiri* 'today', *tsu* 'only', *ǀnîsi* 'maybe'; derived adverbs are *ǁgoaka* 'in the morning', *!nuka* 'far', *aibe* 'at first', *kanube* 'yet', *gâise* 'well' and *ǂhanuse* 'straight'.

3.2.3.9 Interjections

There are a number of lexemes that may be used as both adverbs and interjections. These include *am'a* 'really' expressing emphasis, *goma* 'supposedly' expressing evidence, or lack thereof, *hîa* 'see' expressing persuasion, *hana* 'so' expressing surprise or disbelief.

The elaborate use of some of these interjections in fixed syntactic constructions, for instance in the case of *goma* (see Widlok 1995), justifies a separate categorization of some of these interjections, in the case of *goma*, for instance, as an 'evidential'. Other interjections are less wide-ranging in their use and their semantic meaning. These include simple interjections such as *mboko* and *akua* (both expressing disagreement).

3.2.3.10 Conjunctions

Conjunctions fall into two categories, introductory and suffixed (see Chapter 7). The most common conjunctions to open a sentence are *o* 'and/but then' and *i* 'and then suddenly'. These two conjunctions may also be used sentence-finally, but then their meaning is best glossed as 'when, if' (for *-o*) and 'while' (for *i*).

3.2.4 Kxoe subgroup

Rainer Vossen

This section begins with a brief overview of the lexical structure of Khwe, which may to a certain extent be representative of Kalahari Khoe languages in general. Since Khwe is the best-documented Kxoe variety (cf. Köhler 1981, Kilian-Hatz 2008), the following subsections on morphology will focus on two less-known languages: Buga and ǁAni. Their description is based largely on published (Heine 1999, Vossen 1997a) as well as unpublished data (Vossen).

3.2.4.1 Lexical structure: Khwe

Mathias Schladt[†]

Words and their underlying concepts are associated with others in two ways: in terms of taxonomies and in terms of partonomies. Both are hierarchical systems consisting of a set of elements related to each other in a characteristic way. They are structured primarily by two relations: vertically by a relation of dominance where a superordinate taxon/parton includes the subordinates (in a Western ethnobotanical hierarchy, for example, the taxon 'tree' includes 'oak, beech, elm'), and horizontally by a relation of difference where taxa/parta of the same level are different with respect to some feature ('oak, beech, elm' are taxa of the same level). As a consequence, concepts of the same level are distinct and do not overlap. Both taxonomies and partonomies may violate the logic of relations and exhibit prototypical structures (see, e.g., Lakoff 1987, Taylor 1989).

As the language of a traditional hunter-gatherer society, the lexical structure of Khwe exhibits numerous features originating from the subsistence system of its speakers.

The two main fields of experience are the animal and the plant world. The system of the plant world is virtually synonymous with wild plants as the Khwe have only recently become sedentary and have started to cultivate to a yet very limited extent plants such as 'millet', *khòàvà* (*Sorghum bicolor*); 'pumpkin', *kyánúnukà* (*Cucurbita pepo*); and 'cow-peas', *kui-ǃ'am* (*Vigna unguiculata*).

The Khwe do not have a label for an overall concept "plant". Asking a Khwe what exists on earth, (s)he would typically answer:

(220) *ŋú 'ó-ka tȉĩ yì-dji, kx'oxò-dji, càá, dòá, ǂ'íyo, khóé-na, ǀ'é, xòḿ, nǁūgóá, xàḿ, ǀòàvá, ǂóḿ-ǂom . . .*
'In the world there are trees, edible animals, water, grass, snakes, people, fire, soil, stones, lions, pythons . . .'

Yet, the absence of a linguistic expression says nothing about the existence of a concept (Berlin *et al.* 1968). Indications for the presence of the concept are a number of words exclusively applicable to plants:

(221) *tòâ* 'root, tuber'
tcóró 'outer bark of a tree', also 'skin of a grass'
ǀx'ṹ 'smooth bark of a tree'
ǀgȁ̃á̃ 'leaf'
ǀxùí 'seed (corn), pip'
gyèí 'stump of a tree'
ǀàm 'thorn'

Furthermore, among colour categorization, Khwe has six expressions corresponding to the category "green", three of which are only used in connection with plants:

(222) *ǀx'á* 'green (of leaves)'
ǂqóm 'evergreen'
kx'óà 'green, unripe'

Khwe makes a clear distinction between the labels *yìi* and *dóà*, in the literature (cf. Köhler 1989, 1991) commonly translated as 'tree' and 'grass'. Typical trees such as *gyȁ̃ĩ́-yì* (*Acacia arenaria*) or *khɛ̀ɛ́* (*Combretum collinum*), with high straight stems, branches, leaves and fruits, are excellent members of *yìi*; and *tcóvó-tcòvò* (*Panicum maximum*) or *ǂ'áà* (*Phragmites australis*), which consist of a single culm, have no wood and are of no use except for roof-thatching and foraging, are clear members of *dòá*. But there are a number of other plants which are difficult to categorize. Informants refuse to label them a member of one or the other category. Among them are tuberous plants such as *díngà* (*Tylosema esculentum*) and *nǀárá* (*Urginea sanguinea*), which do not show clear features of one or the other life form. They have the status of unaffiliated generics, there is no superordinate taxon which includes some of them at a higher level.

Among wild plants both under-specification and over-specification do occur. An example of the former is *ǀxȍ̃á̃-dóá* 'eland-grass' which denotes *Heteropogon contortus*, *Schizachyrium jeffreusii* and *Sorghastrum friesii*. They are *Poaceae* species with a very similar morphology. The identical uses of the three grass species (Schladt 2000) suggest that people do not differentiate between them. Similarly *ǂ'átà-ǂ'evu* 'stick-hold tight' denotes a number of plants (as they are identified by Western botanists): *Cenchrus biflorus*, *Elytrophorus globularis*, *Setaria verticillata*, *Tragus berteroniamus*. They all have one feature in common: they are burdocks. This suggests that the term *ǂ'átà-ǂ'evu* is a cover-term for a number of plants, a super-generic in the terms of Berlin *et al.* (1974). This is also supported by the fact that there is another plant named *ǂ'évú* (*Croton gratissimus*) which shows the same features as the others but is at the same time more prominent in terms of morphology, size and use. It must be taken as a prototypical member or a very good example of the mentioned category.

Over-specification is also frequent. It is the case when two or more vernacular names exist for the same botanical species. It can be caused by a number of reasons: one botanical species may occur once as a shrub and once as a tree in the same area. It will still be given one scientific name, but be differentiated as two distinct plants by the people. Again, the same plant may have a different morphology depending on the season. It may be given different names whether it is bearing fruits or not, male or female, bearing leaves or not. In addition, several names for one plant can be caused by dialect variants.

One example of over-specification is the case of *Acacia arenaria*: *gyȁ̃ĩ́-yì* 'steenbok-tree', *ǀxúni-yi* 'crocodile-tree', *ǂxóá-yì* 'elephant-tree'. This acacia species may occur as a climber, as a shrub or as a tree of up to ten metres' height (Coates Palgrave 1997: 231). Whereas for the botanist it is one species, for the Khwe they are different plants.

The second pillar of the Khwe subsistence system, the animal world, is more complex in structure. There is reason to doubt that there exists an overall category in Khwe that corresponds to English "animal".

The term *kx'óxò* is clearly derived from *kx'ó-xù* 'to eat meat-thing' (see below). This implies, in opposition to evidence from parallel studies within other cultures, that the utilitarian aspect of the classification is essential to the Khwe. *kx'óxò* includes all the birds – even those like the 'vulture' *kx'ấĩ* which are rarely eaten – and 'fish' *ǁ'éu*, as well as all the mammals that are not said to have a strong negative power when consumed. On the other hand, insects are excluded due to the fact that they cannot provide a full dish for the people. It is worth discussing whether the "edibility" of a certain animal has an extraordinary status for a hunting and gathering people as compared to herders or farmers. Similar observations have been made by researchers working on societies related to the Khwe:

> "Meat is <u>the</u> food, . . . one too many a day of solely plant foods and people will actually feel deprived and crave for meat".
>
> (Tanaka 1996)

A twofold classification of the domain is suggested:

First, there is a utilitarian classification based on the edibility of animals. It is subclassified by the habitat. This makes sense since the location of a source of food is the most important information.

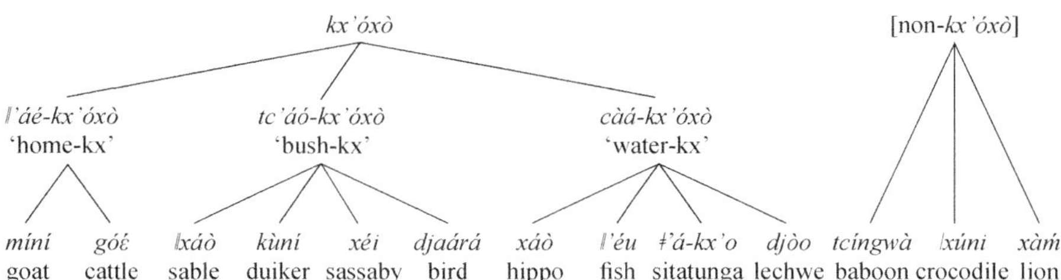

The classification based on morphological features includes both *kx'óxò* and non-*kx'óxò* animals and corresponds closely to hierarchies encountered elsewhere (see, e.g., Brown 1984).

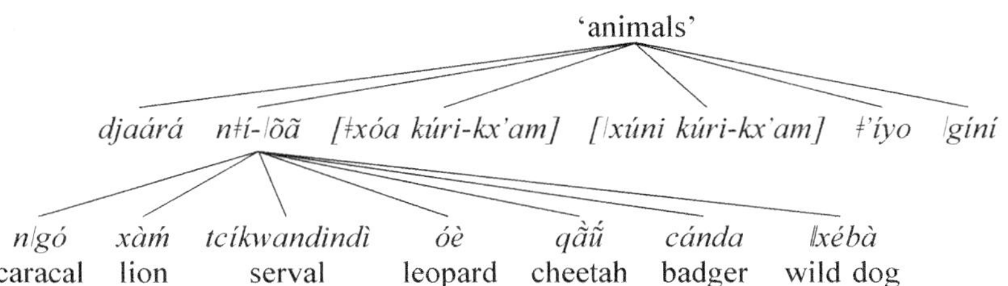

Looking at the lexical structure of "verbs of eating/digesting" previous works state that there is a dichotomy of *ǂ'ű̃* 'eat veldkost' and *kx'ó* 'eat meat'. In Köhler (1991: 72–161, 313–482, 496–523) Khwe informants describe the use, habitat and preparation of wild and cultivated plants and animals. With respect to wild plants in seventy texts Köhler uses the German equivalent of English 'eat' 190 times. The original texts reveal that seven different lexemes are used in Khwe:

(223)

Lexeme	Translation	Occurrences	Percentage
ǂ'ű̃	'eat (non-meat)'	109	57.4
ǀáé	'chew (gen.)'	62	32.6
ǀxòm	'chew something hard'	6	3.2
kx'ó	'eat meat'	5	2.6
tàmà	'ladle out'	4	2.1
ǀnôm	'suck out'	3	1.6
ǀâm	'taste'	1	0.5

The distribution is best described with a prototype model. *ǂ'ű̃* is the most general word for eating plant food. It is better translated with 'eat non-meat' as it is also used with, e.g., the eating up of bone marrow (Köhler 1991: 220) and birds' eggs (Köhler 1991: 427). *ǀáé* is of some importance especially with nuts.

With the description of cultivated plants the distribution is more refined:

(224)

Lexeme	Translation	Occurrences	Percentage
ǀáé	'chew (gen.)'	17	41.4
ǂ'ű̃	'eat (non-meat)'	15	36.6
qaḿ	'chew and spit out the inedible residue'	3	7.3
gyaánù	'throw into one's mouth'	2	4.9
ǀxòm	'chew something hard'	2	4.9
!qóm	'eat along with meat' [*Beikost*]	2	4.9

With animals, *kx'ó* is almost exclusively used for all animals, be it frequently hunted (e.g. *doá* 'kudu'), rarely hunted (e.g. *khúnu* 'African wildcat') or animals which are taboo (e.g. *ǀxúni* 'crocodile'). Besides mammals, the list also includes birds, fish, shells, termites and grasshoppers.

Hierarchical structures influenced by the subsistence system are also found in other fields of Khwe experience. As an example of a partonomical relationship the structure of body-part names is given. When associating a certain body part conceptually and linguistically with another, Khwe uses strategies that have been proved to be universal (Schladt 1997).

Metaphor and metonymy are the two main naming strategies within the domain of body parts. In detail the following strategies can be observed:

Metaphors: parts of the lower body are associated cognitively and linguistically with parts of the upper body:

(225)

'lower part'		<	'upper part'	
(kyaáre) tòm	'sole'	<	*tòm*	'palm'
(tĩ́ĩ̀) ǀgéí	'calf'	<	*ǀgeí*	'cheek'
(kyaáre) ǀàa	'toenail'	<	*ǀàa*	'fingernail'
(kyaáre) cèù	'toe'	<	*cèú*	'finger'

The specifications in parentheses are optional and only used by the speakers if it is not clear from the context which body part is meant. It is always the body part of the upper region which is left unmarked.

Metonymies: the name of a part denotes the whole.

(226)	'part'	>	'whole'
tı̃̂̀ı̃ 'thigh'		>	*tı̃̂̀ı̃* 'leg'
ã́ 'forehead'		>	*ã́* 'face'

An invisible body part is associated with its container. In a loose sense this can be regarded as a part–whole relation as well. The direction of development is not as clear as in the other strategies, since visibility may counteract against the proposed part–whole hierarchy.

(227) 'contained' 'container'

ǀaá 'stomach' <> *ǀaá* 'belly'

A notable feature is polysemy, involving body-part names applicable to both humans and animals, where the direction of borrowing cannot be clearly determined:

(228)	Human	Animal
khòo	'skin'	'garment'
ǁã́ã	'nail'	'claw'
ǀ'ṹũ	'hair'	'feather'
tc'óḿ	'lip'	'beak'
kx'áḿ	'mouth'	'snout'
ǂóm̀	'hip-bone'	'flank'

A final note on loanwords: as a consequence of Khwe loan-work in South Africa from the 1960s onwards and of the participation of Khwe people on the side of the South African Defence Force against SWAPO, numerous loanwords especially from Afrikaans entered the language. More recently, English loans seem to be predominant since the privilege of English is estimated much higher than that of Afrikaans.

Some older loanwords change their meaning; e.g., *bùrúkwè* [cf. Mbukushu *vùrúkwè*, Afrikaans *broekie*] entered into Khwe at a time when traditional clothes were still in use. Its original meaning was '(European) trousers' in opposition to *kyáe* 'fore-apron'. Today, no Khwe wears aprons. The term *kyáe* is therefore available and used for 'trousers (gen.)'. *bùrúkwè* today means 'shorts'.

3.2.4.2 Nouns

Rainer Vossen

As mentioned earlier, Kalahari Khoe languages in general mark nominal stems for person, gender and number (PGN) by enclitics ("suffixes") whose employment is not obligatory in Kxoe varieties. There are three genders – masculine, feminine and common ("neuter") – and three numbers: singular, dual and plural. PGNs are represented by a single formative. The common gender implies the features [masculine + feminine].

The head noun and its qualifiers agree with respect to PGN. The latter are adjectives, numerals, demonstratives, possessives, and nominalized finite verbs functioning as "relative constructions". Moreover, agreement occurs in "genitive" constructions (nominal possession), and in ǁAni and Buga, there is also object agreement encoded in the finite verb (cf. Vossen 1985).

The use of PGN markers concerns both animate and inanimate nouns. With animate nouns the PGN corresponds to the natural sex of the *signifié*, e.g. ǁAni *khóé-**mà*** 'man' vs. *khóé-**hɛ̀*** 'woman'. With inanimate nouns the speaker's choice of the PGN may be arbitrary or semantically conditioned.

The PGN enclitics of ǁAni and Buga are given in Table 6.15:

TABLE 6.15 PGN ENCLITICS OF ǁANI AND BUGA

	ǁAni				Buga		
	SG	DU	PL		SG	DU	PL
M	*-mà*	*-tsà*	*-ǀùà*	M	*-mà*	*-tsà*	*-ǀù*
F	*-hɛ̀*	*-sà*	*-dzì*	F	*-sì*	*-sà*	*-dzì*
C	–	*-khùà*	*-nà*	C	–	*-khyà*	*-nà*

3.2.4.3 Pronouns

The gender–number distinction as described for noun stems reappears throughout the subgroup in the pronominal paradigms. However, in the singular the first person is gender-neutral, and in ǁAni and Buga the second and third persons have no common form.

There are subject and object forms that are largely identical in shape; the latter pronoun, however, is mostly (ǁAni) or optionally (Buga) extended by a particle *'à* which is also used with nominal objects. A significant distinctive feature of the two paradigms is tone. Whereas subject pronouns are high-toned (except for third persons and the second feminine dual form), pronominal objects follow a high-falling tonal pattern.

A specific characteristic of both ǁAni and Buga (but not Khwe) consists in the occurrence of object agreement markers encoded in the finite verb; the conditions of their employment are not entirely clear yet except that, at least in ǁAni, previous mentioning and marking (by *'à*) of the syntactic object are required (see under "Verbs"). Object agreement markers largely resemble the subject forms in shape but are tonally low throughout.

Table 6.16 gives a synoptic overview of the subject, object and object agreement forms discussed above.

The existence of equivalents for the first and second person feminine and common plural has strongly been denied by my consultants.

3.2.4.4 Adjectives

Genuine adjectives are very few, if existent at all. While Kilian-Hatz (2008: 195) claims for Khwe that there is no "proper word class of adjectives", Heine (1999: 39) lists a handful of lexemes for ǁAni, e.g. *kún* 'small' and *ǀéú* 'big'. These also occur in Buga. However, adjectival concepts are mostly expressed by verbal adjectives of the English "to be X"-type, and this holds true even for Heine's above-mentioned examples. Nonetheless, in simple predication expressing condition or shape they tend to be used uninflected and no copula is used in such cases; cf. (229):

(229) a. *Tí di ŋúú-hɛ **ǀáú**.*
1SG POSS house-F.SG big
'My house is big.'

TABLE 6.16 THE PRONOMINAL PARADIGMS OF ǁANI AND BUGA

	ǁAni			Buga	
	SUBJECT	OBJECT	OAGRM	SUBJECT	OAGRM
			SINGULAR		
1	*tí*	*tí, tíà.'à*	*-tì-*	*tí*	*-tì-*
2M	*tsá*	*tsáè(.'à)*	*-tsì-*	*tsá*	*-tsì-*
2F	*há*	*háè(.'à)*	*-sì-*	*há*	*-sì-*
3M	*'â.mà*	*'â.mà(.'à)*	*-m̀-*	*'á.ḿ*	*-m̀-*
3F	*'â.hɛ̀*	*'â.hɛ̀(.'à)*	*-sì-*	*'á.sì, 'â.sì*	*-sì-*
			DUAL		
1M	*tsóḿ*	*tsóm̀, tsómà.'à*	*-tsòm̀-*	*tsám̀*	*-tsàm̀-*
1F	*sóḿ*	*sóm̀, sómà.'à*	*-sòm̀-*	*yám̀*	*-yàm̀-*
1C	*kháḿ*	*khám̀, khámà.'à*	*-khàm̀-*	*khám̀*	*-khàm̀-*
2M	*tsáó*	*tsáò, tsáóà.'à*	*-tàò-*	*tsáó, tsáò*	*-tsàò-*
2F	*sáo*	*sáò, sáóà.'à*	*-sàò-*	*yáó, yáò*	*-sàò-*
2C	*kháó*	*kháò, kháóà.'à*	*-khàò-*	*kháo, kháò*	*-khàò-*
3M	*'â.tsà*	*'â.tsà(.'à)*	*-tsà-*	*'é.tsà, 'â-tsà*	*-tsà-*
3F	*'â.sà*	*'â.sà(.'à)*	*-sà-*	*'é.sà, 'â.sa*	*-sà-*
3C	*'â.kh(ù)à*	*'â.khà(.'à)*	*-khà-*	*'é.khà, 'â.khà*	*-khà-*
			PLURAL		
1M	*ǀé*	*ǀê, ǀéà.'à*	*-ǀè-*	*ǀé*	*-ǀè-*
1F	*sé*	*sê, séà.'à*	*-sé-*	*yé*	–
1C	*té*	*tê, téà.'à*	*-tè-*	*té*	–
2M	*ǀáó*	*ǀáò, ǀáóà.'à*	*-ǀàò-*	*ǀáó*	*-ǀàò-*
2F	*sáó*	*sáò, sáóà.'à*	*-sàò-*	*yó*	–
2C	*tó*	*tô, tóàà.'à*	*-tò-*	*tó*	–
3M	*'â.ǀùà*	*'â.ǀùà.(.'à)*	*-ǀù-*	*'é.ǀù*	*-ǀù-*
3F	*'â.dzì*	*'â.dzìà(.'à)*	*-dzì-*	*'é.dzì*	*-dzì-*
3C	*'â.nà*	*'â.nà(.'à)*	*-ǹ-*	*'á.ń, 'á.ɲ*	*-ǹ-*

b. *Nǀnámí-hɛ* ***ǀáú*** *bé,* ***kúũ.***
pangolin-F.SG big NEG small
'A pangolin is not big, it is small.'

c. *Té di-n nǀnàbó-na* ***kx'óà****?*
1C.PL POSS-3C.PL$_{AGR}$ shoe-3C.PL new
'Are our shoes new?'

(229c) is an interrogative clause which can be reformulated with the "adjective" inflected for the (present) tense, as in (229d):

(229) d. *Té di-n nǀnàbó-na* ***kx'óà-tè****?*
1C.PL POSS-3C.PL$_{AGR}$ shoe-3C.PL new-PRES
'Are our shoes new?'

As shown above, predicative "adjectives" follow the head noun. When used as attributives, they precede the head noun:

(230) a. *N!ábì n‖náò.* 'The giraffe is old.'
b. *n‖náò n!ábì* 'an old giraffe'

Throughout the subgroup, PGN marking is not obligatory. Both noun and "adjective" can be marked or left unmarked, but the qualifier can only take a PGN marker if the head noun, too, is marked:

(231) a. */áú xàm̀* 'a big (male) lion'
b. */áú xàḿ-**mà*** 'a big male lion'
c. */áú-ḿ xàḿ-**mà*** 'a big male lion'

3.2.4.5 Numerals and quantifiers

Cardinal numbers 'one' through 'four' are expressed by lexical stems (see 232); from 'five' onwards, periphrastic constructions can be formed; these are not much used, though. (For examples from ‖Ani, see 233.)

(232)

	‖Ani	Buga
'one'	*/úí*	*/úí*
'two'	*/ám̀*	*/ám̀*
'three'	*n!nóànà*	(not obtained)
'four'	*hàtsá*	(not obtained)

(233) 'five' */úí tshèù khúrì* ['one hand is finished']
'seven' */úí tshèù khúrí ǂám̀-ànà /ám̀* ['one hand is finished, two on top of it'] (Heine 1999: 37)

Heine (1999: 38) reports for ‖Ani that "Ordinal numerals are formed by suffixing the locative/instrumental postposition *kà* (. . .) to the numeral. In the case of 'first', the verb *n!ám* 'start' is used instead of */úí*":

(234) 'first' *n!ám-kà*
'second' */ám̀-kà*
'third' *n!óànà-kà*
'fourth' *ɦàtsá-kà*

(235) *Tí n!óànà-ka khòè-rà.*
1SG three-LOC person-1SG
'I am the third person.'

Numerals precede the governing noun and can, like other qualifiers, be marked optionally for PGN, e.g.

(236) a. *Tsá /ám̀-tsà /'õã-tsà-kà tĩĩ.*
2M.SG two-2M.DU$_{AGR}$ leg-2M.DU-with exist
'You have two legs.'

b. *Tí /úí /gɛ́ɛ́-khoe-hɛ̀ /xoà nǂnũĩ.*
1SG one female-person-3F.SG with sit
'I have (only) one wife.'

Quantifiers other than numerals are:

(237)		ǁAni	Buga
	'every, all'	*kóò-kà.xà*	*kóó.xà-kà*
	'many, much'	*thíyà*	*thíyà*
	'some'	*ǀú* (Heine 1999: 39)	
	'few'	*ǀx'óâ*	*ǀx'óɛ̀*

3.2.4.6 Demonstratives

ǁAni distinguishes at least four demonstrative categories, two of which are complex. If speaker or addressee are present (and therefore visible) during a given speech act, the near referent (next to speaker) is described by *nǀné* while the distant referent (next to addressee) is referred to by *nǀné-tè*. The use of *'á* 'that (one) mentioned' indicates mere referentiality, i.e., the referent is invisible. A higher degree of distance is expressed by *'á-tè* 'that yonder' which can even be extended by the adverb *'ákà* 'far', thus: *'á-àkà-tè* 'that yonder (far away)'.

In my data, head noun and demonstrative agree grammatically with one another in more than 90 per cent of recorded cases. The agreement markers are derived from the nominal PGN enclitics, e.g.: *-m̀* (M.SG), *-ǁù* (M.PL), *-hɛ̀* or *-s(ì)* (F.SG), *-dzì* (F.PL), *-ǹ* (C.PL). Some examples are given in (238).

(238)	*nǀné-**sì***	*khóè-**hɛ̀***	'this woman'
	nǀné-tè-m̀	*xàḿ-**mà***	'that lion'
	*'á(-àkà)-tè-**dzì***	*khóè-**dzì***	'those (absent) women'
	*'á-**ǁù***	*khóè-**ǁùà***	'those men (mentioned previously)'

The description in Heine (1999: 34–37) differs considerably from my own observations and, therefore, may indicate dialectal variation.

Little is known about demonstratives in Buga, as only *nǀné* 'this' and *nǀné-ha* 'that' have been recorded as proximal and distal demonstrative forms. More often than not head noun and demonstrative agree with one another grammatically.

3.2.4.7 Possessive

Throughout the subgroup *di* (Buga *da*) is used as general possessive marker. It allows some syntactic flexibility, as illustrated in (239) for ǁAni.

(239)	a.	*tí*	*dì*	*ǂúú-**hɛ̀***	'my head'
		1SG	POSS	head-F.SG	
	b.	*tí*	*dí-**hɛ̀***	*ǂúú-**hɛ̀***	
		1SG	POSS-F.SG$_{AGR}$	head-F.SG	
	c.	*ǂúú*	*tí*	*dí-**hɛ̀***	
		head	1SG	POSS-F.SG$_{AGR}$	

As a rule, the possessive marker is placed after the personal pronoun; in this order the two may precede (239a–b) or follow (239c) the head noun. The possessive marker optionally agrees with the head noun (239a–b); this may happen even if the head noun itself is not marked for PGN (239c). When used in connection with kinship terms, the possessive marker can, but need not, be omitted (juxtaposition); e.g.: *'â.sì (dì) dàmàsi-hɛ̀* 'her younger sister'.

In Buga, possessives behave almost in the same way as in ǁAni except that juxtaposition appears to be permitted for any noun, thus: *tí dà dzàbá* ~ *tí dzàbá* ~ *dzàbá tí dà* 'my house'.

3.2.4.8 Interrogatives

In ǁAni, the most common interrogatives are *ma* 'who?' (with variable tone), *né* 'what?', and *ná* 'what?, which?'. In combination with certain elements they also serve for creating other question words such as *mà-ká* 'where?' or *ná-tâ* 'how?' (cf. Heine 1999: 66f.). It seems, however, that only *ma* can be marked for PGN (compare the examples in 240).

(240) a. *Nǀné-m̀* *kx'áò-khòè-mà* *má-**mà**?*
DEM-M.SG$_{AGR}$ male-person-M.SG who-M.SG$_{AGR}$
'Who is this man?'

b. *Tsáè.'à* *má* *ǀ'áó-tsì-tà?*
2M.SG$_{OBJ}$ who insult-2M.SG$_{AGR}$-PAST$_{RECENT}$
'Who insulted you?'

c. *Nǀné-mà* *né?*
DEM-M.SG what
'What is this?'

d. *Tsá* *ná* *nǁnáà-tà?*
2M.SG what say-PAST$_{RECENT}$
'What did you say?'

When followed by the possessive marker *di*, *ma* 'who?' conveys the meaning 'whose?', e.g.

(241) *Nǀné-ǹ* *khòó-nǁnàbó-nà* *má* *dì?*
DEM-C.PL$_{AGR}$ skin-shoe-C.PL who POSS
'Whose shoes are these?'

Likewise, when followed by the object marker *'à*, *ma* takes on the meaning 'whom?'.

The interrogatives *ma* 'who?, which?' and *ná* 'which?' are also attested for Buga which lacks the form *né*, though. Instead *ndú* is used to express 'what?'; it can also mean 'why?'. In my data *ná* never occurs alone but only as a component of the complex form *ná.ko* meaning 'how many/much?'. There is no indication of agreement marking in Buga. Some examples:

(242) a. *Tsá* *dà* *ǀx'ûĩ* *má?* 'What's your name?'
2M.SG POSS name who

b. *Ndú* *tsa* *ǂ'úũ-sà* *yábà-tè?* 'What do you want to eat?'
what 2M.SG eat-F.SG wish-PRES

Like in ǁAni, the possessive interrogative 'whose?' is expressed by *má dì*:

(243) *Nǀné* *dzàbá* *má* *dì* *rè?* 'Whose house is this?'
DEM house who POSS INT

3.2.4.9 Verbs

Throughout Kalahari Khoe the verb in its infinite form is identical with the verbal root which as such can represent both the infinitive (verbal base) and the imperative. In order to create finite verb forms, at least the verbal base and a tense/aspect marker are needed. However, most tense/aspect markers require a verbal linker, the so-called juncture. Besides derivative verbal extensions, the passive marker, object agreement markers and the negative formative form part of the verb phrase. Personal pronouns are never bound to the finite verb but are syntactically independent.

The segmental morphological sequence structure of the verb consists of five slots:

(244)

verbal base –	derivative suffix(es) –	• juncture • passive – • (OBJ$_{AGR}$)	tense/aspect –	negation
1	2	3	4	5

Most commonly, slots 1, 3 (juncture) and 4 are filled.

Derivative suffixes (slot 2) are plenty and can be combined to a certain extent. They trigger semantic modifications on the basic verb and impact on its valence.

Slot 3 is usually filled by the juncture; in passive constructions, the juncture is replaced by the passive formative. If object agreement is required, the respective marker takes the place of the juncture. In other words, the filling of slot 3 is governed by syntactic devices. Some examples:

(245) ǁAni

a. *Tí ŋúú-kx'am* ***ǁoéré-sán-à-tà-bé***.
1SG house-mouth open-REFL-JUNC-PAST$_{RECENT}$-NEG
'My door hasn't opened by itself.'

b. *'Érìkù* ***ǁx'áḿ-è-tè***.
dog beat-PASS-PRES
'The dog is beaten.'

c. *Tsá tí di ŋúú-mà.'à* ***mûũ-m̀-tè*** *rè?*
2M.SG 1SG POSS house-M.SG.OBJ see-M.SG.OBJ$_{AGR}$-PRES INT
'Do you see my house?'

Buga

d. *Kx'áò-khòè-mà* ***tòé-xú-tà***.
male-person-M.SG move.away-TERM-PAST$_{RECENT}$
'The man has moved away (for ever).'

e. *Tí* ***'á-ná-hà-bé***.
1SG know-JUNC-PERF-NEG
'I don't know.'

f. *ǀóã* ***ǁúù-ì-tà***.
child give.birth-PASS-PAST$_{RECENT}$
'A child was born (today).'

g. *Khóé-ǁùà.'à tí* ***mûũ-ǁù-tè***.
person-M.PL.OBJ 1SG see-M.PL.OBJ$_{AGR}$-PRES
'I see the men.'

3.2.4.9.1 DERIVATIVE SUFFIXES

A considerable number of functions have been observed throughout the subgroup. Some (e.g. reflexive, causative$_1$, dative, reciprocal) are more productive than others (e.g. inclinative, comitative). Table 6.17 below gives an overview.

TABLE 6.17 DERIVATIVE SUFFIXES IN ǁANI (A) AND BUGA (B)

Function	Suffix	Lg.	Basic verb	Gloss	Extended verb	Gloss
Causative$_1$/	*-kà*	A	*ǂǔũ̃*	'buy'	*ǂǔũ̃-kà*	'sell'
Instrumental		B	*dáò*	'burn'	*dáò-kà*	'roast, grill'
Causative$_2$	*-si*	A	*ǀx'óɛ̀*	'be full'	*ǀx'óɛ́-si*	'fill'
Causative$_3$	REDUPL	A	*ǀóḿ*	'suck'	*ǀóḿ-ǀòm̀*	'suckle'
		B	*'áã*	'know'	*'áã-'àã*	'consult, inform'
Repetitive	REDUPL	A	*ǂxáà*	'split'	*ǂxáà-ǂxàà*	'split up'
		B	*xóó*	'hold'	*xóó-xòò*	'touch'
Dative	*-mà*	A	*khóò*	'gather'	*khóò-mà*	'gather for s.b.'
		B	*yíà*	'climb'	*yíà-mà*	'dress up for s.b.'
Reflexive	*-sàn*	A	*ǁáé*	'instruct'	*ǁáé-sàn*	'learn'
	-hànì	B	*qòḿ*	'bend s.th.'	*qòḿ-hànì*	'bend over'
Reciprocal	*-kù*	A	*ǂ'úũ*	'eat'	*ǂ'úũ-kù*	'copulate'
		B	*séè*	'take'	*séè-kù*	'marry'
Inclinative	*-kx'àò*	A	*ts'âã*	'steal'	*ts'âã-kx'àò*	'be kleptomaniac'
Negative	*-ŋã*	A	*káá*	'want'	*káá-ŋã*	'not want'
Locative	*-'ò*	A	*dàbí*	'turn'	*dàbí-'ò*	'turn inside out'
		B	*qáá*	(unknown)	*qáá-'ò*	'dip/dive in(to)'
Alternative	*-(xà)kú*	A	*tshǎã*	'cultivate'	*tshǎã-(xà)kú*	'cultivate in turns'
Comitative	*-ǀx(ò)à*	A	*ǁqáró*	'paddle'	*ǁqáró-ǀx(ò)à*	'paddle jointly'
	-ǀxòà	B	*túú*	(unknown)	*túú-ǀxòà*	'greet'
Terminative	*-xú*	A	*tshèé*	'chase away'	*tshèé-ré-xú*	'expel'
	-xu	B	*ǀx'áé*	'fall'	*ǀx'áé-xù*	'collapse'
Intentional	*-ǀxɛ̀*	A	*nǁáà*	'tell'	*nǁáà-ǀxɛ̀*	'want to tell' (Heine 1999: 51)
	-sà	B	*ǂxàá*	'give'	*ǂxàá-sà*	'in order to give'

Comments: (1) Strictly speaking, reduplication is not a case of derivation; it has here been included because of the parallel paradigmatic patterns that derive from reduplicated verbs as compared to verbs extended by suffixes. The functions "repetitive" and "causative" often overlap or cannot clearly be distinguished. Thus, ǁAni *ǀóḿ-ǀòm̀* not only means 'suckle' but also 'suck continuously' which, of course, is inherent in the process of suckling. (2) More often than not, dative verb stems convey benefactive meaning. (3) The *-ré* formative contained in ǁAni *tshèé-ré-xú* 'expel' (terminative) links the derivative suffix *-xú* to the basic verb. It corresponds morphologically to the juncture morpheme which normally links tense/aspect markers and not derivative suffixes to (simple or extended) verbs. For an attempt at an historical explanation of this phenomenon, see Vossen (2010). (4) Heine (1999: 48–53) adds a "still" function (*-tsà*) to the paradigm of extensions which is said to be a borrowing from Tswana. He gives the following example (p. 52):

(246) *Tí* *ɦakányà-tsà-tè* *kx'éí-hɛ̀* *khó-mà* *tsa-a-tè.*
1SG think-still-PRES QUOT (?) person-M.SG be.sick-JUNC$_1$-PRES
'I still think that the man is sick.'

Heine (1999: 48) also considers the passive morpheme to be a verbal extension. However, I strongly believe that it does not belong to the same structural slot as derivative suffixes.

Here are two examples for the combined occurrence of verbal extensions:

(247) ǁAni *tàó-ŋã-sàn-à-mà-kx'àò* 'dislike to behave properly'
teach.manners-NEG-REFL-JUNC-DAT-INCL
Buga *ǂhὲέ-kù-kà* 'mix up'
mix-REC-CAUS$_{I}$

3.2.4.9.2 JUNCTURE

In the majority of finite verb forms, structural slot 3 is filled by the juncture, which links the (simple or extended) verb stem to the following tense/aspect marker. On a synchronic level this element has no recognizable meaning nor does it reveal a definite grammatical function. The most one can safely say is that it occurs in non-passive constructions. While Heine (1986) argues that the juncture is to be seen as a grammaticalized copula, Elderkin (1986b) advocates the hypothesis that this element derives historically from a conjunction. (For a state-of-the-art discussion of the juncture in Khoe, see Vossen 2010.)

Although we are fairly aware of the major steps involved in the grammaticalization process, the verbal juncture has not yet been investigated in all its contexts. From Köhler's (1981) description of Khwe it becomes clear that the juncture first existed for the past tenses (juncture II) and only later developed for non-past tenses (present and future; juncture I) as well. A concomitant feature of the juncture consists in its complex morphological variability, i.e., there are extensive series of allomorphs for both juncture I and II, largely conditioned phonologically or by word structure. The full range of allomorphs is, however, restricted to the Khwe language. In ǁAni, juncture I occurs only in the future tense (always as /*a*/) whereas in Buga, it appears to be represented by zero (/∅/) throughout. Table 6.18 gives an overview of juncture allomorphs in Kxoe; their use in ǁAni is exemplified in Table 6.19.

TABLE 6.18 JUNCTURE ALLOMORPHS IN THE KXOE SUBGROUP

	a	*ε*	*wa*	*ya*	*ye*	*ɲa*	*ɲe*	*ra*	*rε*	*re*	*ro*	*na*	∅	*e*	*o*
Khwe	+	+	+	+	+	+	+	+	+	+	+	+	+		
ǁAni	+	+						+	+	+	+	+	+	+	+
Buga								+	+	+	+	+	+		

TABLE 6.19 JUNCTURE EMPLOYMENT IN ǁANI (EXAMPLES)

a. Juncture I (non-past)

CVV		CVCV	
ǀíí-∅-tè sing-JUNC-PRES	present	*ǀxúrú-∅-tè* vibrate-JUNC-PRES	present
táó-∅-ǁòè pound-JUNC-HAB	habitual	*xúnú-∅-ǁòè* snore-JUNC-HAB	habitual
péè-∅-nǂnùà jump-JUNC-INGR	ingressive	*nǁnánì-∅-nǂnùà* build-JUNC-INGR	ingressive
*ǀíí-**á**-gòè(nè)* sing-JUNC-FUT	future	*ǀxúrú-**á**-gòè(nè)* vibrate-JUNC-FUT	future
*táó-**à**-gòè(nè)* pound-JUNC-FUT	future	*xúnú-**à**-gòè(nè)* snore-JUNC-FUT	future
*péé-**a**-gòè(nè)* jump-JUNC-FUT	future	*nǁáni-**a**-gòè(né)* build-JUNC-FUT	future

TABLE 6.19 (*cont'd*)

b. Juncture II (past)

CVV		CVCV	
*ǁóé-**é**-tà* sleep-**JUNC**-PAST$_{RECENT}$	past$_{recent}$	*ǀxúrú-**ná**-tà* vibrate-**JUNC**-PAST$_{RECENT}$	past$_{recent}$
*kx'ò-**ró**-tà* eat.meat-**JUNC**-PAST$_{RECENT}$	past$_{recent}$		
*káá-**á**-ǁ'òm̀* want-**JUNC**-PAST	past	*xúnú-**ná**-ǁ'òm̀* snore-**JUNC**-PAST	past
*kx'è-**ré**-ǁ'òm̀* cry-**JUNC**-PAST	past		
*!ãĩ-**a**-hĩĩ* be.healthy-**JUNC**-PAST$_{REM}$	past$_{remote}$	*!hùrí-**ná**-hĩĩ* sprout-**JUNC**-PAST$_{REM}$	past$_{remote}$
*dzúú-**à**-hàã* skim.off-**JUNC**-PERF	perfect	*nǀnáni-**na**-hàã* build-**JUNC**-PERF	perfect

3.2.4.9.3 PASSIVE

The passive marker is *-e* (*-ɦè*/*-è* according to Heine 1999: 48) in ǁAni and *-i* in Khwe and Buga. It replaces the juncture in slot 3 in passive constructions.

3.2.4.9.4 OBJECT AGREEMENT MARKER

Within the subgroup, object agreement marking occurs in slot 3 and is confined to ǁAni and Buga. In ǁAni, it appears to be obligatory if a pronominal or PGN marked nominal object is related to the verb. No conditions for its occurrence have so far been found in Buga. Here, according to my consultants, the object is never resumed on the verb if it is a pronoun of first or second person feminine or common plural. Examples:

(248) ǁAni

Nominal object

a. *ǀúí-ḿ* *!'úí-**mà**(.'à)* *tí* *mûũ-**m̀**-tà.*
one-M.SG leopard-M.SG(.OBJ) 1SG see-OBJ$_{AGR:M.SG}$-PAST$_{RECENT}$
'I saw one leopard (today).'

Pronominal object

b. ***Tô*** *tí* *mûũ-**tò**-tè.*
PRO:OBJ$_{2C.PL}$ 1SG see-OBJ$_{AGR:2C.PL}$-PRES
'I see you (PL).'

Buga

c. ***Há'à*** *tí* *mûũ-**sì**-tè.*
PRO:OBJ$_{2F.SG}$ 1SG see-OBJ$_{AGR:2F.SG}$
or
Há'à *tí* *mûũ-∅-tè.*
'I see you (SG).'

For an overview of object agreement markers, see Table 6.16.

3.2.4.9.5 TENSE/ASPECT MARKERS

From a morphological point of view it is hardly possible in Kxoe to distinguish between tense and aspect (TA). Grammatical markers expressing temporal/aspectual relations

TABLE 6.20 TENSE/ASPECT MARKERS IN KXOE

TA category	Khwe	ǁAni	Buga
Remote past	*-hĩĩ*	*-híĩ*	
Past	*-tĩ, ǁ'òm̀*	*-ǁ'òm̀*	
Recent past	*-tà*	*-tà*	*-ta*
Perfect	*-hãã*	*-hàã*	*-hà*
Present	*-tè*	*-tè*	*-tè*
Habitual	*-ǁòè*	*-ǁòè*	
Ingressive	*-nǂnùè*	*-nǂnùà*	
Future	*-gòè*	*-gòè(nè)*	*-gòè*

(see Table 6.20) occur in slot 4 exclusively and can never be combined. Most TA markers derive from former verbs, some of which are still in use.

The remote past is mostly used in narratives. The past marker relates to actions that took place between roughly two and five days ago. The recent past indicates today's or yesterday's actions. The term "ingressive" is used here preliminarily; Heine (1999: 20f.) labels this category "progressive" and speaks of "proximative" in the case of "be about to"-actions.

3.2.4.9.6 NEGATION

The predicate is generally negated by verb-final *-bé(é)*. Remember, however, that there is also the option to negate the verbal base by means of derivation, e.g. ǁAni *xáń* 'sew' vs. *xáń-ŋã* 'not sew'.

3.2.5 *Naro*

Hessel Visser

3.2.5.1 Noun phrase (NP)

The head of the NP is usually a noun. The NP-head is normally put in the last position of the NP. The class of nouns can be subdivided into proper nouns and names. Examples of the simplest NP are:

(249) *!nuu* 'hut' *!Xoma* (name)

PGN markers are used to mark person, gender, and number on the noun. They can be compared with articles and pronouns in other languages. There is agreement between the NP-head and the NP-peripheral. An example of an NP with only its head and PGN marker would be:

(250) *!nuu* *ba* 'hut'
HEAD PGN

Adjectives, demonstratives, anaphoric words, and numerals can be used as peripheral elements in the NP. The NP-peripheral qualifies the NP-head and usually, but not necessarily, precedes the NP-head. An example of a NP with noun and peripheral element plus PGN markers (where each element receives its own PGN marker) is:

(251) *|'ẽem !nuu ba* 'another hut'
or
!nuum |'ẽe ba 'another hut'

The last element of the NP, whether it is head or peripheral, is followed by the masculine singular marker.

Extended with another peripheral element:

(252) *|'ẽem !nuum tiri ba* 'my other hut'
other hut my PGN

The structure of the NP is as follows:

(253) (element PGN-8) (element PGN-8) element (PGN-7)

The elements can be the NP-head or an NP-peripheral. Although no formal distinction can be made between NP-head and NP-peripheral, there is a strong tendency for a different behaviour between NP-head and NP-peripheral. For that reason, they are distinguished here in the traditional way.

Usually the peripheral element precedes the nucleus, as in (254):

(254) *!ãèm khóè ba* 'the good man'
good man PGN

But it may also follow the nucleus, as in (255):

(255) *khóè-m !ãè ba* 'the good man'
man good PGN

In this order, the meaning becomes more specific, so that in English the definite article should be used. Note that there is no relationship between "strength" of the PGN marker and the fact of whether it is placed with the nuclear or the peripheral element. It only has to do with the order: the strong marker appears at the end of the NP, the weak marker appears on the peripheral elements.

The weak marker can be repeated as many times as wanted:

(256) *|úí-m kaia-m !'úú-m !n̠oara-m khóè-ba* 'one big white handicapped
one- man-PGN man'

If the NP has more than one peripheral element, the order of these elements is as follows:

(DEMONSTRATIVE) (POSSESSIVE) (NUMERAL) (ADJECTIVE) (ADJECTIVE)

The order of the peripheral element may be important for the meaning. For example, if *|úí* follows the head of the NP, it is used adverbially and has the meaning 'only'. If it precedes the head of the NP, it means 'one':

(257) a. *Ùù-s |úí sar ko kúrú.* 'I only do naughty things.'
only

b. *|úí-s ùù sar ko kúrú.* 'I do one naughty thing.'
one-

The head of the NP may consist of a noun (either a simple noun or a nominalised word) or a name. The head of the NP can assume different forms. It can consist of one morpheme or a combination of a noun plus suffix. Most nouns consist of only one morpheme, e.g.

(258) *!nuu* 'hut' *khóè* 'person'

Words of other categories can be nominalised and thus function as head of the NP, e.g.

(259) adjective: *|x'áré ba* 'the small one'
demonstrative: *|nẽe ba* 'this one'
verb: *!õò sa* 'the going'
PGN marker: *tsáá tsi* 'you'
interrogative: *dìí ba* 'who?'

Other NP heads consist of noun words with suffixes. There are several processes in use for these derived forms.

Nominalisation by *-ku*. A noun can be derived from a verb by adding the suffix *-ku*:

(260) *|nàm̀* 'to love' *|nàm̀-ku* 'love'

Nominalisation by *-!'oo*. A noun can be derived from a quantifier or adjective by adding *-!'oo*:

(261) *kái* 'many' *kái-!'oo* 'amount'
!áò 'long' *!áò-!'oo* 'length'

Nominalisation by adding *xúù*. A verb can be nominalised by adding the word *xúù* ('thing'). The tone on this word is lowered to LL:

(262) *hûa* 'to put on' *hûa-xuu* 'something to put on, dress'

Diminutive: N + *|òà*. The diminutive form of a noun is formed by adding *|òà* to the noun word:

(263) *!nuu* 'house' *!nuu-|oa* 'small house'

Augmentive: N + *ǁgòò*. The augmentive form of a noun is formed by adding *ǁgòò* to the noun word:

(264) *khóè* 'person' *khóè-ǁgòò* 'giant'
áí 'my mother' *áí-ǁgòò* 'my "big mother", my mother's older sister'

Locative: N + *kx'ai*. A combination of a noun plus *kx'ai* indicates the place where somebody or something can be found, or where something is done. Example with a noun:

(265) *!nari* 'God' *!nari-kx'ai* 'heaven (the place where God dwells)'
tshàa 'water' *tshàa-kx'ai* 'the water-place'
ǁnàà ('certain tree') *ǁnàà-kx'ai* 'place with many *ǁnàà*'
ǁ'oo 'death' *ǁ'oo-kx'ai* 'place of death/where funeral is held'

Example with a verb:

(266) *ǁxaa-ǁxaase* 'to learn' *ǁxaa-ǁxaase kx'ai* 'a place to learn'

Note that the tone on this *kx'ai* is low. A noun can also be combined with *kx'áí* 'lid', but then it is a possessive construction:

(267) *suu kx'áí* 'lid of pot'

Specialist: N + *kx'ao*. This combination denotes someone who usually does something, or is specialised in it.

(268)	*ǀxaa-ǀxaase*	'to learn'	*ǀxaa-ǀxaase kx'ao*	'student'
	xóá	'to write'	*xóá-kx'ao*	'writer'

Verb + *khoe*. Combinations of verb + *khoe* usually indicate a person with the mentioned quality.

(269) *ǀnàm̀* 'to love' *ǀnàm̀-khoe* 'love-person' > 'friend'

N + *kx'am*. Combinations of noun + *kx'am* usually indicate a certain place with a hollow form, especially body parts; e.g.

(270) *hîe ta kx'am* 'hollow above collar bone'
ǀxoa ta kx'am 'lowest point of breastbone'

In these examples, the combination is a fixed one. The phenomenon is productive as well, as can be seen in the following examples:

(271) *!x'áó kx'am* 'back part of the neck'
ǀáó kx'am 'hollow of the throat'

Beside body parts, it can also nominalise a verb,

(272) *ǀ'áè* 'to tell, command' *ǀ'áè-kx'ám̀* 'message'

or be used otherwise:

(273)	*xúù*	'thing'	*xúù-kx'ám̀*	'type of thing'
	ǀxào	'knife'	*ǀxào-kx'ám̀*	'scar caused by knife'

The head of the NP may consist of a combination of two or more words. There are several possibilities for the relationship between these words.

In the first construction, the second word is the nuclear one, being modified by the first (peripheral) one. There is no connection word between the two nouns. So the construction goes as follows:

(274) Peripheral Nuclear

khóè *ǂúú* 'a person's head'
person head

bìi *ǀgene* 'horse-fly'
horse fly

ǀxoo *ǀnoe* 'gemsbok squirrel' (squirrel with colour like gemsbok)
gemsbok squirrel

A noun word may also be modified by a verb word:

(275) *ǀhãe* *ǀxào* 'spear'
stab knife

A variant of this process connects the two words by a PGN marker:

(276) *!nuu-m* *ǂobe* 'the hut's roof, the roof of the hut'
house-PGN roof

A somewhat more complicated process is the combination of a noun with a nominalised verb:

(277) *hã̱a* *xuu* 'dress'
put.on something

dongi *hã̱a* *xuu* 'a donkey harness'
donkey put.on thing

This process can be repeated as well. The composite noun form is then embedded into a second composition as a peripheral element:

(278) *ǂuì* *dòm̀* 'the corridor of the nose'
nose corridor

ǂuì *dò-m̀* *kò-m̀* 'the nostril'
nose corridor-PGN hole-PGN

The combination *ǂuì dò-m̀* 'nose corridor' is embedded into the combination with *kò-m̀* 'hole'.

(279) *hìi* *sore* *!xóò* 'a wooden tobacco pipe'
wood tobacco pipe

This example shows that a modifying noun may receive an adjectival meaning: *hìi* is not the owner, but the source; or rather: it qualifies/indicates the material. In English, an adjective 'wooden' or 'of wood', also a "possessive" construction, is used for this.

Verb + object: a combination of a verb with an object may also function as head of the NP. The verb is the central element.

(280) *horo* *!x'áó* 'necklace'
put neck

A somewhat more complicated process is the combination of a verb with a nominalised verb:

(281) *ǂnõo* *xuu* 'chair'
sit thing

!abi *ǂnõo* *xuu* 'saddle'
ride sit thing

These two processes can be combined:

(282) *kx'áà* *xuu* 'a drink-container'
drink thing

kx'áà *xuu* *!xóó* 'a drink-container holder, a can holder'
drink thing hold

The combination *kx'áà xuu* has become the object of the verb *!xóó* 'hold'.

Embedding of process I in process II:

(283) *ǂãa* *ǂúú* 'a necklace'
enter head

!xore *ǂãà* *ǂúú* 'a necklace made of ostrich eggshell'
ostrich.eggshell enter head

The combination *ǂãà ǂúú* is the central element, and is modified by the element *!xore* 'ostrich eggshell'.

Combination of process I with process II:

(284) *|ẽé* *tsao* 'wildebeest tail'
wildebeest tail

horo *!'om* 'a wrist band'
put wrist

|ẽé tsao *horo !'om* 'a wrist band made of wildebeest tail'
wildebeest.tail wrist.band

3.2.5.1.1 POSSESSIVE CONSTRUCTIONS

There are three types of possessive construction. (i) In this construction, the word *di* is used in the following way:

(285) possessor-PGN *di* possessee

The PGN marker following the possessor is in agreement with the possessor. The PGN-8 marker is used:

(286) *khóè-m* *di* *!nuu* 'the man's hut'
man-PGN hut

The possessed thing may also be accompanied by PGN markers. In that case, the weak PGN marker is put after *di*, while the strong PGN marker comes at the end:

(287) *khóè-m* *di-s* *!nuu-sa* 'a man's hut'
man-PGN POSS-PGN hut-PGN

The possessor may also be indicated by the PGN marker only. In that case, the PGN-5 marker is used:

(288) *xa-m* *di-s* *xúù-sa* 'his thing'
xakha-m *di-s* *xúù-sa* 'our thing'

This construction can also be used to indicate a certain quality or property.

(289) *too* *|'õò* *toro* *|u* *di-m* *tsoo ba* 'the man with "the stringed together hair"'

(ii) The second construction can be considered as a shortened version of the first one. The same pattern is followed, but *di* is not used:

(290) *sáá* *ǂárà-ba* = *sarim* *ǂárà-ba* 'your peer'
sikham *||'áé* = *sikham* *di* *||'áé* 'our yard'
tíí *!'õo* = *tirim* *!'õo* 'my boss'

With respect to the last example above, however, a construction like *gakhao q'õò* is not acceptable. In such cases, the word *ka* is used: *gakhao ka q'õoseba* 'your boss'.

(iii) In the third possessive construction, the PGN marker follows the thing that is owned and is connected to it by *-a*. In this construction, only PGN-6 can be used:

(291) Possessee *-a* Possessor

xúà *-a* *ba* 'his thing'
|uì *-a* *te* 'my nose'
xoo *-a* *tsi* 'your half face'

Words can be joined by *ka*. This usually indicates relationships. The morpheme *-se* is added to the relationship word:

(292) *Tsebes ka !õè-se-sa* 'Tsebe's younger sister'
Tsebe younger sister-?-PGN

3.2.5.1.2 NAMES

A separate class of nouns consists of proper names. They act like simple nouns. They are usually accompanied by their corresponding PGN marker. Example:

(293) *|x'ase ba* 'Cg'ase'
|x'ase tsara 'the (two) Cg'ases, or: Cg'ase and his (male) companion'
|x'ase khara 'Cg'ase and his (female) companion'
|x'ase ra 'I, Cg'ase'

3.2.5.1.3 PGN MARKERS

The first extension of the NP to discuss is the PGN markers. To mark person, gender and number on the noun, a so-called PGN marker is added to the noun. PGN markers can be compared with articles in other languages, but sometimes act like pronouns.

First, the PGN marker indicates which person is involved. The NP can refer to

- the speaker (and others): first person;
- the addressee (and others): second person, or
- a person/persons is/are not included in either first or second person: third person.

Examples:

(294) *khóè ra* 'I person' *khóè ta* 'we persons'
khóè tsi 'you person' *khóè tu* 'you persons'
khóè ba 'he person' *khóè ne* 'they persons'

Second, the PGN marker indicates gender. The head of the NP can be 'male', 'female' or 'common'. See section 3.2.5.1.4 for more details on gender, e.g.

(295) *khóè tsi* 'you male person'
khóè si 'you female person'
khóè ba 'he male person > a/the man'
khóè sa 'she female person > a/the woman'

Third, the PGN marker indicates number. The head of the NP can be single, dual or plural. Examples:

(296) *khóè ba* 'man'
khóè tsara 'two men'
khóè |u 'men (more than two)'
khóè ra 'I, man'
khóè tsam 'we, two men'
khóè |ae 'we men (more than two)'
Thama ba 'Thama'
Thama tsara 'he and Thama'
Thama |u 'Thama and his companions'

PGN markers have different forms, depending on their function. The markers will be indicated by number, corresponding with the column in which they can be found. In general, the forms do not differ much. Only for the third person singular do the forms differ greatly. For a complete overview of PGN markers, see the appendix on p. 205.

PGN-1, general subject. This formative marks a subject of a clause in general, e.g.:

(297)	*Bóò*	*-m*	*ko.*	'He sees.'
	!Õò	*i*	*ko.*	'It goes.'
	V	PGN	TAM	

PGN-2, nominal subject. The PGN marker may also function as a nominal subject. In this case, the last phoneme of this nominal subject is repeated:

(298)	*!Ãè*	*me e.*	'He is good.'
	!Ãè	*si i.*	'She is good.'
	!Ãè	*e.*	'It is good.'
	V	PGN	

PGN-3, emphasised person. The PGN-3 marker emphasises a person, either used as subject or as object. In the first and second person singular construction, a corresponding PGN-(1 or 4) marker must be added:

(299)	*tíí . . . ra*	'I' (subject, sometimes even as object)
	tíí . . . te	'I/me' (object)
	tsáá . . . tsi	'you' (M)
	sáá . . . si	'you' (F)

Subject emphasised:

(300)		*Xaba*	*ko*	*bóò.*	'He sees.'
	Tíí	*ra*	*ko*	*bóò.*	'I see.'
		PGN			

Xata	*r*	*ko*	*tíí*	*méé.*	'That's what I say!'
PGN					

Object emphasised:

(301)	*Bóò*	*te*	*tsi*	*ko*	*tíía?*	'Do you see me?'
	Bóò	*(me)*	*tsi*	*ko*	*xaba?*	'Do you see him?'
	Tíí		*tsi*	*ko*	*bóò te.*	'You see me.'
	Tíí	*a*	*tsi*	*ko*	*méé te?*	'Do you mean me?'
	Tíí	*ra*	*tsi*	*ko*	*méé?*	'Do you mean me?' (*ra* as object!)
	Tsáá	*r*		*ko*	*bóò tsi.*	'I see you.'
	Tsáá		*tsir*	*ko*	*bóò.*	'I see you.'

Both subject and object emphasised:

(302) *Tsáá tsi ga tíí |x'õo te.* 'You will kill me.'

PGN-4, object. The PGN-4 marker functions as object:

(303)	*Bóò*	*me*	*r*	*ko.*	'I see him.'
	Bóò	*o*	*r*	*ko.*	'I see it.'

PGN-5, construction with postposition. When a postposition is following a PGN marker which refers to a person (in other words, the PGN marker is used as a pronoun), the PGN-5 marker is used.

Possessive construction (i). The owner (in the form of PGN-5) precedes the thing that is possessed:

(304) *xam* *dis* *xúù* *sa* 'his thing'
xakham *dis* *xúù* *sa* 'our thing'

Postposition:

(305) *xam* *|xoa* 'with him'

PGN-6, possessive construction (ii). In the second possessive construction, the PGN marker follows the thing that is owned and is connected to it by *-a*. Example:

(306) *xúùa* *ba* 'his thing'
|uìa *te* 'my nose'

PGN-7, strong article. The PGN-7 marker can be called a "strong" article. This article appears at the end of the NP, e.g.

(307) *khóè* *ba* 'the man'

PGN-8, weak article. The PGN-8 marker can be called a "weak" article. The first elements of the NP carry the weak article, while the last element is followed by the strong article:

(308) *!ãèm* *khóè* *ba* 'a good man'

With derivations, the combinations are seen as a unit so that in these instances, the dependent PGN marker does not occur after the noun but after the whole unit; e.g., in a combination with *|gòò* 'big' or *|òà* 'small'

(309) *brukhoe* *|gòò* *sa* 'trousers'

one would expect a dependent PGN marker *-s* after *brukhoe*, but it does not occur there. Compare:

(310) *kaisas* *brukhoe* *|goo* *sa* 'big trousers'

It may happen that the PGN marker is reduplicated. This usually happens in constructions with *wèé* 'all, both', e.g.

(311) *Wèé* *khao* *khaos* *ǂ'ēya.* 'She resembles both of you.'
Wèé *tsa-tsara* *!ãè* *tsara a.* 'They are both OK.'

3.2.5.1.4 NOUN GENDER

Gender is marked by the PGN marker. The question that will be answered in this section is: What makes nouns male, female or common? In fact, it is not really gender that the PGN marker indicates. We could equally well say that "general information" about shape is communicated. We thus might rename the PGN marker a *pin*-code: person–information–number marker! But as the term PGN marker is in use, we will not confuse readers by introducing another term.

With animate nouns, the gender is clear:

(312) *khóè* *ba* 'man'
khóè *sa* 'woman'
dùù *ba* 'male eland'
dùù *sa* 'female eland'

However, if someone is talking about an animal in general, the female gender is used:

(313) *!Gãe si i.* 'It is a steenbok.'
gòè zi 'cows, cattle'

This even applies if somebody knows that male animals are around:

(314) *xàm zi* 'lions'

With objects, the following rule applies: objects that are long and/or strong are male, objects that are round and/or weak are female.

(315) *hìi ba* 'stick'
hìi sa 'tree'

From these examples it is obvious that size does not decide gender (trees are bigger than sticks, but that does not make them male): it is the shape that is important.

With insects, it is often difficult to know the gender. Probably the same rule as for objects in general applies: they are said to be female if they are round, and male if they are long:

(316) *bìi-|gène sa* 'horse-fly'
!no̱o ba 'worm'
ǂo̱ma-ǂo̱ma ba 'ant'

The same probably applies to trees and plants. If it is round, it is seen as "female", if it is tall, it is called "male".

(317) *ǂ'óò ba* 'a hardekool-tree that is tall'
ǂ'óò sa 'a hardekool-tree that is more round'

Some nouns are neuter, or common, e.g.

(318) *tshàa ne* 'water'

Abstract nouns usually receive a female PGN marker:

(319) *tseexu sa* 'truth'
|nàm̀ku sa 'love'
!ãè sa 'goodness'

Nominalised verbs take the neuter gender:

(320) *|aoa ne* 'to shoot (shooting)'

Body parts are usually male:

(321) *ǂúú ba* 'head'
ǂxáí ba 'eye'
ǂee ba 'ear'
|'õá ba 'leg'
ǂ'õà ba 'arm'
tshàu ba 'finger'

but:

(322) *|om sa* 'navel'
kx'ám̀ sa 'mouth'

The navel is round, so that may be the reason why it is considered "female". The mouth may also be seen as round, but one may ask: why not the ear and the head?

Objects in the sky have different gender. The 'sun' is female: *ǀáḿ sa*, but the moon is male: *ǁnoe ba* (perhaps because it can appear in non-round shape?). Stars may be either male or female: *ǂo̱no ba* or *ǂo̱no sa*. The Pleiades (called 'seven sisters' in other languages) are female: *xòe zi*, and so is the morning star Venus: *!'úú ǂo̱no sa*. The winter star, however, is male: *!xài ǂo̱no ba*. The rain is sometimes male (*túú ba*), especially when it is a heavy rain, and sometimes it is female (*túú sa*): when it is a soft rain.

PGN markers can be used to indicate slight distinctions. To indicate that something is small, one can change the male PGN marker into a female one:

(323) *!nuu ba* 'hut'
!nuu sa 'small hut'

To translate the English word 'sea' into Naro, one may change the common PGN marker with the word for 'water' into a male one:

(324) *tshàa ne* 'water'
tshàa ba 'sea, river'

3.2.5.1.5 PERIPHERAL ELEMENTS

Adjectives, demonstratives, anaphoric words and numerals can be used as peripheral elements.

Adjectives are usually placed before the noun, with accompanying PGN-8 marker, e.g.

(325) *!ãè-m khóè ba* 'a/the good man'
good-PGN.8 person M

The adjective may, however, also follow the noun. In that case, the accompanying PGN-7 marker is used (because it follows the last element of the NP).

(326) *khóè-m !ãè ba* 'the good man'
person-PGN.1 good M

There is agreement between the noun and the adjective, the noun being the head:

(327) *!ãè m khóè ba* 'a good man'
!ãè tsara khóè tsara '(two) good men'
good PGN person PGN

Demonstratives are deictic in nature. They refer to a nearby or close distance, *ǀnẽe* 'this', or to relative distance (usually near the addressed person), *ẽe*, *ãa* 'that', or to great distance, *ẽesihãa* 'that there'. Demonstratives behave like adjectives: they usually are placed before the noun to which they belong.

(328) *ǀnẽe-m khóè ba* 'this man'
ẽe-m khóè ba 'that man'
ẽesihãa-m khóè ba 'that man there'
DEM-PGN.8 person PGN.7

But they may also be put after the noun:

(329) *khóè-m ǀnẽe ba* 'this man'

A peripheral element in the NP can even consist of a noun word, qualified by an adjective. The phrases *ǀno̲as bìi sa* 'red horse' and *!'úú kx'áí* 'white face' can be combined in the noun phrase

(330) *ǀno̲as bìis !'úú kx'áí sa* 'a red horse with a white face'

where *!'úú kx'áí* qualifies the noun *bìi*.

Adjectives can be derived from verbs by way of reduplication. In this process, the tone on the second part of the reduplication is the same as the tone on the first part.

(331)	*!'ae*	'to get a fright'	→	*!'ae-!'ae*	'terrible'
	ǂom	'to trust'	→	*ǂom-ǂom*	'reliable, trustworthy'

A participle can also be a peripheral element in the NP.

In Naro, there are only three original numerals: *ǀúí* 'one', *ǀám̀* 'two', and *!noana* 'three'. The other numerals are borrowed from other languages (Nama and English). Nama numbers may be used from '4' up to '6' or '10', but in practice English numerals are used from '4' upwards. There is agreement between the noun and the numeral, the noun being the head:

(332)	*ǀúí-m*	*khóè*	*ba*	'one man'
	ǀám̀-tsara	*khóè*	*tsara*	'two men'
	!noana-ǁu	*khóè*	*ǁu*	'three men'
	four-ǁu	*khóè*	*ǁu*	'four men'
	NUM-PGN.8	person	PGN.7	

Anaphoric words refer to a noun that was mentioned before, e.g.

(333)	*xaa*				'that' (the one that was mentioned)
	ǁnaa				'the one that I talked about'
	xaa-m	*ǀx'áré-ba*			'that little one'
	. . . me	*ǁnaa-ba*	*ǁ'aixa-ba*	*kúrú*	'. . . and that one (that was mentioned before) became chief'

Compound NPS have three possible structures:

In structure 1, the first and any subsequent conjoined NP is closed with *hẽé naka*, the final NP of a conjoined series terminates with *hẽethẽé*, perhaps additionally completed by *e*. We may summarise this structure as follows:

NP1 *hẽé naka* (NP2 *hẽé naka . . .* NP_n *hẽé naka*) NP_{n+1} *hẽethẽé (e)*

(334)	*khóè ba hẽé naka*	*khóè sa hẽethẽé e*	'the man and the woman'
	!Xoma ba hẽé naka	*Ti!'ae sa hẽethẽé e*	'Qgoma (a man) and Tiq'ae (a woman)'

In the second structural possibility of conjoined NPS, the PGN marker of the conjoined NPS is placed at the end of every NP. This structure may be summarised as follows:

noun (combined PGN) + noun (combined PGN) + (. . .) + (combined PGN)

(335)	*!Xoma*	*khara*	*Tiq'ae*	*khara*	'Qgoma and Tiq'ae'
	N.SG	PGN.DU	N.SG	PGN.DU	

In the third construction, a combination of the two previous constructions is also possible. In this case, each NP has its own PGN marker, the NPS are combined by *hẽé*, while at the end of the series, the PGN marker of the combined NPS appears. The structure is as follows:

NP$_1$ *hẽẽ́ naka* + (NP$_2$ *hẽẽ́ naka*) . . . (NP$_n$ *hẽẽ́ naka*) NP$_{n+1}$ *hẽethẽẽ́* (combined PGN)

(336)	*khóè ba hẽẽ́ naka*	*khóè sa hẽethẽẽ́*	*khara*	'the man and the woman'
	!xoma ba hẽẽ́ naka	*Ti!'ae sa hẽethẽẽ́*	*khara*	'Qgoma and Tiq'ae'
	NP1	NP2	PGN.DU	

3.2.5.2 Verb phrase (VP)

The elements of the VP will be briefly introduced. After discussing the head of the VP, and the peripheral elements of the VP such as tense markers and aspect markers, the different modes will be outlined, concluding with complex verb phrases.

The head of the VP is usually a verb, indicating actions. These verbs form an open class with many members, *tséé* 'work', *!õò* 'go, walk'.

Agent markers, tense markers, aspect markers and the marker *kò* can be used as peripheral elements in the VP. The VP-peripheral qualifies the VP-head. An example of a VP with verb and peripheral element plus PGN marker:

(337)	*!Õò*	*tsi*	*ga*	*kò*	*ko.*	'You would be going.'
	go	PGN	T	kò	ASPECT	

The structure of the VP cannot easily be summed up. The different options will be discussed in the subsections of mood.

The verb can consist of more than one morpheme. Passive markers, reflexive markers, causative markers, etc. can be added to the verb root. The order is as follows:

verb (reciprocal) (reflexive/causative) (passive) (aspect)

Examples:

(338)	a.	*//'ama*	*-xu*	*-è*	*-a*	'sold'
		buy	CAUS	PASS	a	
	b.	*/ùri*	*-ku*	*-kaxu*	'follow each other'	
		follow	REC	CAUS		

The unmarked form of the verb has an active meaning, e.g.

(339) *tséé* 'work'

The set of verbs can be divided into transitive verbs and intransitive verbs. Usually, the form of the verb does not indicate whether it is transitive or intransitive. Sometimes, however, (in)transitivity of the verb is indicated by tone. The following intransitive verbs differ from their transitive counterparts only by their tone:

(340)	*dàò*	LL	'burn' (tr.)
	dào	LM	'burn' (intr.)
	ǂnàá	LH	'pour' (tr.)
	ǂnàa	LM	'pour' (intr.)

Passive: to indicate that the subject is undergoing an action, Naro adds the suffix *-è* to the verb phrase (the verb or the verb unit). This suffix has low tone and has a lowering effect on the tone of preceding words:

(341) *Tséé* -*è* *r* *ko*. 'I am being sent.'

ǂ'õó -*è* *r* *ko*. 'I am being eaten.'

VERB PASS PGN

The passive construction is very common in Naro.

(342) *ǂIi* -*è* *tsi* *ko*. 'You are called.' (or: so and so is calling you)

VERB PASS PGN

ǂNõo *sao* *méé* -*è*. 'It is said that you must sit down.' (said when you convey a message from somebody else)

N-ǀama *i* *ga* *xaa* *za* *!õò* -*è?* 'When do they go there?' (lit.: when is it being gone there?)

Reflexive: to make a verb reflexive in meaning, Naro adds the suffix -*se* to the verb (unit). The meaning can also shift somewhat from a pure reflexive one:

(343) *kubu* 'beat, break into pieces'

kubu *se* 'hurt yourself on something > fall down (in pieces)'

ǀxaa-ǀxaa 'teach'

ǀxaa-ǀxaa *se* 'teach yourself > learn'

kóḿ 'to hear'

kóḿ *se* 'hear (for) oneself > understand'

Or the meaning can become intransitive:

(344) *kúrú* 'to do, make'

kúrú *se* 'happen'

Some verbs prefer the form with -*se*:

(345) *naru* 'unknown'

naru *se* 'swing'

Addition of -*se* to a verb unit:

(346) *ǀxóà* 'be angry'

ǀxóà *ǀxae* 'be angry toward'

ǀxóà *ǀxaeser* *ko*. 'I am angry with myself.'

Causative: to indicate an action that causes the state of the unmarked verb, Naro adds the suffix -*kaxu*:

(347) *tséé* 'work'

tsee *kaxu* 'make work > use, make use of'

kai 'be big'

kai *kaxu* 'make big > respect, honour'

Reciprocal: the suffix -*ku* makes a verb reciprocal in meaning. Sometimes there is a shift in meaning:

(348) *hùi* 'to help'

hùi *ku* 'to help each other'

kóḿ 'to hear'

kóḿ *ku* 'to hear each other > agree'

Agent markers: to indicate the agent, Naro uses a set of PGN markers. This set was discussed in section 3.2.5.1. These PGN markers are more function words than inflections, because they are usually not attached to verbs. They are only attached to the verb if the PGN marker does not contain a vowel. In fact, they can be considered to be pronominal forms and thus are not part of the verb phrase. They are just mentioned here in passing:

(349)	*Tséé*	*tsi*	*ko.*	'You are working.'
	!Õò	*ta*	*ko.*	'We (M.PL) are going.'
	!Õò	*r*	*ko.*	'I am going.'
		PGN		

Tense markers: to indicate when an action takes place, Naro distinguishes five tenses: distant past, intermediate past, immediate past, present, and future. These are marked as follows:

(350)	*ǁx'a*	distant past
	thu	intermediate past
	ǀna	immediate past
	Ø	present
	ga	future

The markers for the three past tenses usually precede the verb, while the future tense marker usually follows the verb:

(351)	*ǁX'a*	*r*	*tséé.*			'I worked (long ago).'
	Thu	*r*	*tséé.*			'I worked (yesterday, last week).'
	ǀNa	*r*	*tséé.*			'I worked (today, or maybe yesterday).'
			Tséé	*r*	*ko.*	'I am working.'
			Tséé	*r*	*ga.*	'I will work.'
	T	PGN	work	PGN	T	

To indicate a future action, Naro may also make use of an auxiliary verb like *síí* 'go':

(352)	*Síí*	*r*	*ko*	*tséé.*	'I am going to work.'
	go	PGN	T	work	

See more on this in section 3.2.5.2.1.

Aspect markers: to indicate the quality of a certain action, Naro makes use of some aspect markers: neutral, continuative, perfective, imperfective and counter-expectation. These aspects are marked as follows:

(353)	*ẽ*	neutral
	-ko	continuative (in the present)
	-a	perfective
	-a hãa	imperfective
	a-	counter-expectation

All of these markers usually follow the verb.

The neutral aspect focuses on the content of the action rather than on its duration. It does not occur with the present tense, so the near past tense form was used here.

(354)	*ǀNa*	*r*	*tséé.*	'I worked.'
	A	PGN	work	

The most common form of the verb is the continuative. It indicates that an action is ongoing:

(355) *Tséé* *r* *ko.* 'I am working.'
work PGN A

The perfective aspect indicates that an action is finished:

(356) *Tsee* *a* *ra.* 'I have worked.'
work A PGN

The imperfective aspect marker is a discontinuous morpheme, allowing the PGN to be attached after the *a* and before the *hãa*. The aspect focuses on the fact that an action was ongoing.

(357) *Tsee* *a* *ra* *hãa.* 'I was working.'
work A PGN A

The aspect called "counter-expectation" has some notion of surprise, but it may have other nuances as well.

(358) *Tséé* *a* *r!* 'I work!'
work A PGN

Some verbs use the perfective form *-a*, while the meaning is 'present'. Note that with some verbs, some morphological changes occur when adding the *-a*, e.g. *!'ãa + a*.

(359) *ǀ'úú* 'not know'
ǀ'uu *a* *ra* 'I don't know.'
not.know A PGN

!'ãa 'to know'
!'a *na* *ra.* 'I know.'
know A PGN

kò: in addition, Naro has a marker *kò*, which can occur with most tense and aspect markers. It has some general past tense meaning, but needs further research. It may also indicate a condition – the marker *kò* is often found in a conditional clause:

(360) *Tséé* *r* *kò.* 'I worked.'
work PGN PAST

ǀAba khao kò ko ne ǀóá zi bìrí na zi ǀ'ee ǂgùu.
'If you are hungry, tell the girls to light the fire.'

The tense markers, *kò* and the aspect markers can be combined with each other, with the only restriction that *-a* (counter-expectation) does not combine with any tense marker. The following overview may suffice for a general indication of the possible combinations:

(361)

Tense	kò	Aspect
ǀx'a		*ẽ*
thu		*-ko*
ǀna	*kò*	*-a*
Ø		*-a hãa*
ga		*(a-)*

We will first discuss the forms without *kò*. Five tense markers times five aspect markers theoretically give rise to 25 possibilities. However, the combination of present tense + neutral aspect does not occur, which makes it 24. As the counter-expectation marker *-a* only occurs in the present tense, the theoretically possible combinations are reduced to twenty. The combination with *kò* will be discussed later.

(362)

ǁx'a									
ǁX'a	*r*		*tséé.*						'I worked (long ago).'
ǁX'a	*r*	*ko*	*tséé.*						'I was working (long ago).'
ǁX'a	*r*		*tsee*		*a.*				'I have worked (long ago).'
ǁX'a	*r*		*tsee*		*a*			*hãa.*	'I was working (long ago).'
thu									
Thu	*r*		*tséé.*						'I worked (intermediate past).'
Thu	*r*	*ko*	*tséé.*						'I was working (intermediate past).'
Thu	*r*		*tsee*		*a.*				'I have worked (intermediate past).'
Thu	*r*		*tsee*		*a*			*hãa.*	'I was working (intermediate past).'
ǀna									
ǀNa	*r*		*tséé.*						'I worked (immediate past).'
ǀNa	*r*	*ko*	*tséé.*						'I was working (immediate past).'
ǀNa	*r*		*tsee*		*a.*				'I have worked (immediate past).'
ǀNa	*r*		*tsee*		*a*			*hãa.*	'I was working (immediate past).'
							Ø		
			Tséé	*r*			*Ø*	*ko.*	'I am working.'
			Tsee		*a*	*raa*	*Ø.*		'I worked.'
			Tsee		*a*	*r*	*Ø*	*hãa.*	'I have been working.'
			Tséé		*a*	*r*	*Ø.*		'I worked!'
							ga		
			Tséé	*r*			*ga.*		'I will work.'
			Tséé	*r*			*ga*	*ko.*	'I will be working.'
			Tsee		*a*	*r*	*ga.*		'I will have worked.'
			Tsee		*a*	*r*	*ga*	*hãa.*	'I will have been working.'

Some combinations hardly differ in meaning from each other. The difference between immediate past tense plus neutral aspect and immediate past tense plus perfective aspect can be exemplified as follows:

(363) *ǀNar !õò.* 'I have gone (you may still be going).'
ǀNar !õòa. 'I have gone (you have finished the process).'

The difference between immediate past tense plus continuative aspect and immediate past tense plus perfective aspect can be exemplified as follows:

(364) *ǀNar ko tséé.* 'I was working (immediate past, I was in the process).'
ǀNar tseea hãa. 'I was working (immediate past, I have finished).'

Combination with *kò*: each of the above-mentioned combinations can further be combined with the marker *kò*. In theory, this would lead to another twenty possibilities. Not all of these possibilities are found, however. The marker *kò* is put after the tense marker and before the aspect marker. The combination of *kò* + *ko* can be abbreviated as *kòo*. The meaning of these verb forms may be one that expresses uncertainty: 'I might, maybe I did . . .', 'I would have . . .'. The verb forms are sometimes used in conjunctive sentences.

(365) *ǀx'a*

ǀX'a	*r*	*kò*		*tséé.*							'I was working (long ago).'
ǀX'a	*r*	*kò*	*ko*	*tséé.*							'I was working (long ago).'
ǀX'a	*r*	*kò*		*tsee*		*a.*					'I had worked (long ago).'
ǀX'a	*r*	*kò*		*tsee*		*a*				*hãa.*	'I had been working (long ago).'
thu											
Thu	*r*	*kò*		*tséé.*							'I was working (intermediate past).'
Thu	*r*	*kò*	*ko*	*tséé.*							'I was working (intermediate past).'
Thu	*r*	*kò*		*tsee*		*a.*					'I had worked (intermediate past).'
Thu	*r*	*kò*		*tsee*		*a*				*hãa.*	'I had been working (intermediate past).'
ǀna											
ǀNa	*r*	*kò*		*tséé.*							'I was working (immediate past).'
ǀNa	*r*	*kò*	*ko*	*tséé.*							'I was working (immediate past).'
ǀNa	*r*	*kò*		*tsee*		*a.*					'I had worked (immediate past).'
ǀNa	*r*	*kò*		*tsee*		*a*				*hãa.*	'I had been working (immediate past).'
								Ø			
				Tséé	*r*			*Ø*	*kò*	*ko.*	'I was working.'
				Tsee		*a*	*raa*	*Ø*	*kò.*		'I have worked.'
				Tsee		*a*	*r*	*Ø*	*kò*	*hãa.*	'I was working.'
				Tséé		*a*	*r*	*Ø*	*kò.*		'I work?'
								ga			
				Tséé	*r*			*ga*	*kò.*		'I would work.'
				Tséé	*r*			*ga*	*kò*	*ko.*	'I would be working.'
				Tsee		*a*	*r*	*ga*	*kò.*		'I would have worked.'
				Tsee		*a*	*r*	*ga*	*kò*	*hãa.*	'I would have been working.'

3.2.5.2.1 AUXILIARY VERBS

The verbs *síí* 'to go' and *hàà* 'to come' may be used as auxiliary verbs, giving the meaning of something that will be done in future. It depends on the orientation of the speaker whether *síí* or *hàà* will be used. The above-mentioned tense and/or aspect markers are used for the auxiliary verb, which may then be combined with the main verb:

(366) *Hàà r ga nta hẽ̃è?* 'What will I come and do?'
Síí r ga nta hẽ̃è? 'What will I go and do?'
AUX PGN A do Q

ǂ'ãa ne ga hàà tentan !áú. 'The wind will come and throw over the tents.'
ǂ'ãa ne ga síí tentan !áú. 'The wind will (go and) throw over the tents.'

3.2.5.2.2 MORPHOPHONEMIC CHANGES

The suffix *-a* has a lowering effect on the tone of preceding words:

(367) *Tsééa raà.* 'I have sent.'

Before the suffix *-a* the PGN-1 marker for third person masculine singular changes into *b*:

(368) *!Õòa ra.* 'I went.'
*!õòa ma → *!Õòa ba.* ('He went.')

|'uua ra. 'I don't know.'
*|'uua ma → *|'uua ba.* ('He doesn't know.')

With the same suffix *-a*, some verbs show forms that are different from V + *-a*. A verb like *!'ãa* 'to know' has the form *!'ana* in perfective aspect.

3.2.5.2.3 MOOD

Indicative: to make a statement, the indicative mood is used. The examples mentioned up till now were all in the indicative mood; the structure was discussed above.

Infinitive: the infinitive is the simplest form of the verb, e.g. *hàà* 'to come'.

Present participle: a present participle is formed by adding *ko* to the verb. The verb together with *ko* thus becomes a peripheral element in the NP, which may carry the accompanying PGN marker:

(369) *Tséé ko s khóè si i.* 'She is a working person.'
Tséé ko m khóè me e. 'He is a working person.'
work PART PGN person PGN

|'àà ko |'úú zi 'bright colours'
|ùri ko ba 'the following/next'

The past participle is formed by the verb plus the (im)perfective aspect marker:

(370) *!Õò -a s khóè sa dìí sa?* 'The woman that has gone,
go -IMPF PGN person PGN PGN who is it?'

Imperative: to issue a command, one may just use the verb form. Usually, some emphasis is added to the pronunciation of the word. The imperative has the following structure:

verb (PGN marker) (*-o*)

(371) *ǂ'õo* 'to eat'
ǂ'õo! 'Eat!'

Another way to express a command is by adding the suffix *-o* to the verb form, e.g.

(372) *hàà* 'to come'
Hàà -o! 'Come!'

The suffix *-o* may also be added to another element in the clause, e.g. to the PGN marker:

(373) *ǂIi me -o!* 'Call him!'
ǂXobekx'am te -o! 'Open (for) me!'

It may even be added to a combination of clauses:

(374) *|Xobe ter ǂhuuse -o!* 'Give it so that I can dry myself!'

To make explicit that more than one person is addressed, the PGN marker for the respective group can be added:

(375) *ǂ'õo tu!* 'You (mixed, PL), eat!'
Hàà khao -o! 'You (mixed, dual), come!'

Interrogative: to ask something, the tone on the PGN marker is changed to mid:

(376) a. *!Õò tsì ko.* 'You are going.'
!Õò tsi ko? 'Are you going?'
go PGN TAM

b. *!'áá-!'aa mè |áé ga.* 'We'll divide it.'
!'áá-!'aa me |ae ga? 'Will we divide it?'
PGN

c. *Hàà |àè ga.* 'We will come.'
Hàà |ae ga? 'Will we come?'
come PGN TAM

d. *Bóò |àè ga.* 'We will see.'
Bóò |ae ga? 'Will we see?'
see PGN TAM

The difference between these two clauses is minimal. To make clear that it is a question, one may add the suffix *-a* to the PGN marker:

(377) *!Õò tsi ko.* 'You are going.'
!Õò tsi -a ko? 'Are you going?'
go PGN -Q TAM

To stimulate a response, an adhortative construction can be used. The most common one is the one with *hàà* 'come' → 'let':

(378) *Hàà ta !õò !* 'Let us go!'

One can even say this to oneself:

(379) *Hàà na r tshàa tookx'ai!* 'Let me put on the water!'

Another adhortative construction is the one in which the verb is repeated:

(380) *!Õò ta !õò!* 'Let us go!'
ǀHóà naka ta ǀhóà! 'Let us converse!'

A similar construction with slightly different meaning – it sounds more like asking permission – is the one with verbs like *ǀnaa* 'go out of the way, give permission' and *!ãà* 'wait':

(381) *ǀNaa te r tshàa tookx'ai!* '(Permit) let me put on the water!'
!Ãà te r tshàa tookx'ai! '(Wait) let me put on the water!'

3.2.5.3 Negation

To indicate that a certain action does not take place, Naro has different mechanisms:

a. use of *tama*
b. use of *ta*
c. use of *tite*
d. use of *táá* and/or *xuu*

Negative indicative:

a. The word *tama* is added after the verb. The following changes take place in the clause: if the aspect marker *ko* was used, this marker is deleted (the marker *kò* is not deleted). In present continuous forms, *-a* is added after the PGN marker. The structure of the present negative construction may be summarised as follows:

 verb negation PGN *-a*

 (382) *!Õò tama tsi -a.* 'You are not going.'
 go NEG PGN TAM

 Summary structure (past):

 (tense) PGN verb (aspect) (negation)

 (383) *ǀNa tsi tséé Ø tama.* 'You have not worked.'
 ǀNa tsi tséé -a hãa tama. 'You have not been working.'
 T PGN work A NEG

b. The word *ta* is added after the verb. The same changes as in the first option take place. This option might be seen as an abbreviation to *ta*, but sometimes only *ta* can be used, so it is seen here as a different option.

 Summary structure (same as negative indicative):

 verb negation PGN *-a*

 (384) *!Õò ta tsi -a.* 'You are not going.'
 go NEG PGN -a

 but:

 (385) *Máà te ta xa tsia.* 'You didn't give it to me.'
 *máà te tama xa tsia '(You didn't give it to me.)'

c. The word *táá* is added before the verb. The PGN marker is put in second position in the clause.

Summary structure (past):

tense PGN negation verb

(386) *|Na tsi táá tséé.* 'You have not worked.'
T PGN NEG work

Summary structure (counter-expectation):

negation PGN verb

(387) *Táá tsi tséé.* 'You didn't work.'
NEG PGN work

d. In future forms, the word *tite* is used. This word usually comes in the place of *ga*, but they may occur together. Summary of the structure:

verb PGN negation (tense)

(388) *!Õò tsi ga.* 'You will go.'
!Õò tsi tite Ø. 'You will not go.'
!Õò tsi tite ga. 'You will not go.'
go PGN NEG A

Negative infinitive: to make a negative infinitive, either the word *tama* is added after the verb, or the word *táá* before the verb. Summary structures:

(389) *hàà tama* 'not to come'
come NEG

or:

(390) *táá hàà* 'not to come'
NEG come

Negative imperative: to issue a negative command, one may add the word *táá* and/or the word *xuu* to the verb. At least one of the two words must be used. Summary structure:

(táá) verb *(xuu)*

(391) *Tséé!* 'Work!'
Táá tséé! 'Don't work!'
Táá tséé xuu! 'Don't work!'
Tséé xuu! 'Don't work!'

A PGN marker can be added. This is placed between the verb and *xuu*, e.g.

(392) *Mẽeku tu xuu!* 'Don't fight!'

In the negative imperative, the suffix *-o* is not used:

(393) *tséé* 'to work': *táá tséého! 'Don't work!'

Other examples:

(394)	*Táá*	*méé*	*tsi*	*kúrú*	*u*	*xuu!*	'You must not do that!'
	ǀNẽeǀáḿka	*méé*	*ǁu*	*táá*	*tséé!*		'They must not work today!'

The negative interrogative in the present is formed from the negative statement by raising the tone on the PGN marker. Summary structure (present):

verb negation PGN with raised tone *-a*

(395)	Statement	*!Õò*	*tsi*	*kò.*	'You are going.'
	Negative statement	*!Õò*	*tama*	*tsia.*	'You are not going.'
	Negative question	*!Õò*	*tama*	*tsía?*	'Are you not going?'

The negative interrogative in the past is formed from the negative statement by changing the intonation, or preferably by adding *-a* to the PGN marker.

Summary structure (past):

(TENSE) PGN *-a* verb (ASPECT) (NEGATION)

Example:

(396)	*ǀNa*	*tsi*	*-a*	*tséé*	–	*tama.*	'Have you not worked?'
	ǀNa	*tsi*	*-a*	*tséé*	*-a hãa*	*tama.*	'Have you not been working?'
	T	PGN	-a	work	A	NEG	

The negative interrogative in the future is formed in the same way:

(397)	*!Õò*	*tsi*	*-a*	*tite.*	'Will you not go?'
	go	PGN	A	NEG	

Verbs can be combined with other verbs to form a sequence. The verbs are usually connected by the particle *a*,

(398)	*ǁoe*	*a*	*tsàa*	'lie sick'
	lie		sick	

but they can also just be juxtaposed:

(399)	*!áé*	*ǀnoo*	'fasten (strong, stiff)'
	fasten	strong	

Verbs that consist of two or more verbs can be seen as a sequence, but very often the combination results in a change of meaning in comparison with the individual meanings. In the following example, the actions in the first and second element can be seen as a sequence:

(400)	*!xoo*	*gùi*	'pick up'
	hold	lift	
	koma	*!'ãa*	'understand'
	hear	know	

In the following example, the first modifies the second element,

(401)	*!a̱o*	*ǂnoe*	'sit in the way of *qao*'
		sit	

while in the following example, the second element modifies the first:

(402) *kx'uia* *ǀháé* 'stutter, not talk nicely'
speak have problem

Verb combinations are not fixed, but combining verbs is a productive process. When two verbs are combined, some phonological changes may occur, e.g.

(403) *!aa a máá* > *!ara máá*
bóò !'oo > *bóòn !'oo*

The newly formed verb can be split up by other words which may be put in between, e.g., the PGN marker:

(404) *kuru* *bóò* 'try'
Kuru r ko bóò. 'I am trying.'

However, the combination of verbs can also act as a unit:

(405) *Kúrú bóò r ko.* 'I am trying.'
ǀNàì r ko ǀx'o a. 'I jump out.'
ǀNàì ǀx'o a r ko. 'I jump out.'

Some verbs are quite productive as second element, often in a specific meaning, usually postpositional. *Dìbi* 'go back', for example, gives the meaning 'back(wards), out':

(406) *ǂnõoa dìbi* 'sit back'
sono dìbi 'breathe out'

Xuu 'leave' gives the meaning 'away':

(407) *ǀ'ama xuu* 'sell'
buy leave

Máá, derived from 'to give' with a tone change from HL to HH, gives the meaning 'for, to':

(408) *!ãe-ǂao* *máá* 'thank'
be happy give

kxoara *máá* 'allow'
loosen give

!'aa 'divide' gives the meaning 'apart':

(409) *!nàre* *!'aa* 'cut apart'
cut divide

ǀãà 'enter' gives the meaning 'into':

(410) *!hòma* *ǂãà* 'break into (cut/break meat into a pot)'
break enter

ǀx'oo or *ǀx'oa* 'take, come out' gives the meaning 'out':

(411) *ǀnàì ǂx'oa* 'jump out'
ǀnara ǂx'oo 'choose (from other things)'

ǀx'ae 'meet' gives the meaning 'together':

(412) *!õòa ǀx'ae* 'walk together'
ǁnara ǀx'ae 'compare'
count meet

Some verbs incorporate a noun. That it is a unit can be seen from the fact that the verb together with the noun can be handled as one element. For example, the verb plus the noun together are put before *ko*:

(413) *kubu tshaù* 'to hand-beat'
Kubu tshaù tem ko. 'He slaps me.'

Also, the passive marker *-è* is put at the end of the combination:

(414) *ẽem ko kóḿ Tsebe sa ǀx'uri-ǀx'uri ǀx'õè è a sa . . .*
Tsebe PASS
'when he heard that Tsebe's name was defiled . . .'

Combinations in which the first element is a noun:

(415) *ǀÚú tsi ǁgom!* 'Nod your head!'
head PGN nod

Combinations in which the second element is a noun:

(416) *!hàe ǁhòne* 'lie/sleep resting on elbow'
!hàe !úrù 'kneel down'

Some verbs incorporate postpositions.

(417) *ǀxae* 'to' → *sau ǀxae* 'be ashamed, shy'
ǀxoa 'with' → *!õò ǀxoa* 'go with' (see structure clause)
!'oo 'inside' → *bóò !'oo* 'look into, choose'
→ *!õò !'oo* 'go'
→ *!Õò !'ooa tsi ga?* 'Are you going?'

A last combination is that of a verb word plus *te* (usually connected by *-a*), with a distributive and/or iterative meaning:

(418) *!õoa te* 'walk around'
!Õoa tsi ko te. 'You are walking around.'

3.2.5.4 Postpositional phrase

Beside nominal phrases and verbal phrases, Naro has PPS: postpositional phrases. The PP usually consists of an NP and a postposition. The NP is modified in the sense that the last PGN-7 marker is replaced by a PGN-8 marker. If the noun is absent, a PGN-5 marker can be used instead of the PGN-8 marker.

The two possible structures of a PP are:

(419) *!nuu -m koe* 'at/in the house'
house PGN-8 PP

If the postposition is added to a pronoun, this pronoun takes the form of a PGN-5 marker:

(420) *tíí ǀxoa* 'with me'
PGN-5 PP

The PP can also consist of an embedded clause with a postposition:

(421) *ǀ'óm̀ r ko koe* '(at the place) where I sleep'

The function of a PP depends on the postposition that is used.

(422)	locative:	*!nuum*	*koe*	'in the house'
	adverbial:	*ǀàbà*	*ǀxoa*	'with hunger'
		ǀ'ẽe dàò	*ka*	'maybe'
	temporal:	*ǀnẽe*	*ǀám̀ ka*	'today'

The PP as a unit can function as a postposition in itself: the word *!ãá* 'back' can be combined with the postposition *koe*. It would then literally mean 'at the back', but this unit *!ãá koe* has come to mean 'behind':

(423) *!nuum !ãá koe* 'behind the house'

Similarly, *!ãá !'oo* would mean 'in the back', but the unit has come to mean 'after':

(424) *ǀnẽem ǀám̀ !ãá !'oo koe* 'after this day'

3.2.5.5 Adverbial phrase

The adverbial phrase (AP) qualifies a verb or an adjective. It consists of an adjective and an adverbialiser *-(sa)se*. The structure of the AP is as follows:

(425) ADJECTIVE *-(sa)se*
!ãè -se 'well'
good ADVERBIALISER

The AP can also be formed by combining a numeral with the element *-a*:

(426) NUMERAL *-a*
ǀúí -a 'by myself'
one ADV
ǀÚí-a-r teea mááse. 'I stand by myself.'

APPENDIX: OVERVIEW OF PGN (PERSON-NUMBER-GENDER) MARKERS IN NARO

			1	2	3	4	5	6	7	8
			general S	nominal S	EMPH person	object	construction-1	construction-2	strong article	weak article
			bóò ko	*!ãè*	*ko bóò*	*bóò "S" ko*	*dis xúù sa*	*lx'èa*	*khóè*	*!ãè khóè . . .*
			. . . see	he (etc.) is	. . . see	see(s) . . .	my (etc.) thing	my (etc.) name	the (etc.) person	the good person
'I'	1 M/F	SG	r = ra	ra (a)	tií ra	te	ti	te	ra	r
'you'	2 M	SG	tsi	tsi (i)	tsáá tsi	tsi	tsa	tsi	tsi	tsi
'you'	2 F	SG	si	si (i)	sáá si	si	sa	si	si	si
'he'	3 M	SG	m	me (e)	gaba	me	gam	ba	ba	m
'she'	3 F	SG	s	si (i)	xasa	si	xas	sa	sa	s
'it'	3 N	SG	i	Ø (V)	??	(V)	??	??	ne	Ø
'we'	1 M+F	DU	kham	kham (m)	xakhám̀	khàm̀	xakhám̀	kham	kham	kham
	1 M	DU	tsam	tsam (m)	xatsám̀	tsàm̀	xatsám̀	tsam	tsam	tsam
	1 F	DU	sam	sam (m)	xasám̀	sàm̀	xasám̀	sam	sam	sam
	1 M+F	PL	ta	ta (a)	xatá	tà	xatá	ta	ta	ta
	1 M	PL	ǁae	ǁae (e)	xaǁáé	ǁàè	xaǁáé	ǁae	ǁae	ǁae
	1 F	PL	se	se (e)	xasé	sè	xasé	se	se	se
'you'	2 M+F	DU	khao	khao (o)	xakháó	khàò	xakháó	khàò	khao	khao
	2 M	DU	tsao	tsao (o)	xatsáó	tsàò	xatsáó	tsàò	tsao	tsao
	2 F	DU	sao	sao (o)	xasáó	sàò	xasáó	sàò	sao	sao
	2 M+F	PL	tu	tu (u)	xatú	tù	xatú	tù	tu	tu
	2 M	PL	ǁao	ǁao (o)	xaǁáó	ǁàò	xaǁáó	ǁàò	ǁao	ǁao
	2 F	PL	sao	sao (o)	xasáó	sàò	xasáó	sàò	sao	sao
'they'	3 M+F	DU	khara	khara (a)	xakhárá	khàrà	xakhárá	khàrà	khara	khara
	3 M	DU	tsara	tsara (a)	xatsárá	tsàrà	xatsárá	tsàrà	tsara	tsara
	3 F	DU	sara	sara (a)	xasárá	sàrà	xasárá	sàrà	sara	sara
	3 M+F	PL	ne	ne (e)	xané	nè	xané	nè	ne	ne
	3 M	PL	ǁu	ǁu (u)	xaǁú	ǁù	xaǁú	ǁù	ǁu	ǁu
	3 F	PL	zi	zi (i)	xazí	zì	xazí	zì	zi	zi

Examples of PGN use:

1	General subject	*bóò-m ko*	'he sees'	5	Construction-1	*xam dis xúù sa*	'his thing'
2	Nominal subject	*!ã̋è me e*	'he is good'	6	Construction-2 (possessive)	*xúùa ba*	'his thing'
3	Emphasised person	*xaba ko bóò*	'he sees'	7	Strong article	*khóè ba*	'the man'
4	Object	*bóò mer ko*	'I see him'	8	Weak article	*!ã̋èm khóè ba*	'a good man'

TENSE \ ASPECT	NEUTRAL *Ø*	CONTINUATIVE *ko*	COUNTER-EXPECTATION *a-*	PERFECTIVE *-a . . . (-a)*	IMPERFECTIVE *-a hãa*
PRESENT					
Ø		*tséé tsi ko* 'you are working'	*tséé a tsi* 'you work!'	*tseea tsia* 'you worked'	*tseea tsi hãa/tseea tsia hãa* 'you have been working'
Ø + kò	*tséé tsi kò* 'you worked'	*tséé tsi kò ko* 'you were working'			*tseea tsi kò hãa* 'you had been working'
PAST					
ǀna-thu-ǁx'a	*ǀna tsi tséé* 'you have worked'	*ǀna tsi ko tséé* 'you have been working'		*ǀna tsi tsééa* 'you have worked'	*ǀna tsi tseea hãa* 'you have worked'
ǀna-thu-ǁx'a + kò	*(= ǀna tsi ko tséé)*	*ǀna tsi kò ko tséé* 'you had been working'		*ǀna tsi kò tseea (ne)* 'you had worked'	*(ǀna tsi kò tseea hãa)*
FUTURE					
ga	*tséé tsi ga* 'you will work'	*tséé tsi ga ko* 'you will be working'			*tsééa tsi ga hãa* 'you will have been working'
ga + kò	*(= tséé tsi ga ko)*	*tséé tsi ga kò ko* 'you would be working'			*tsééa tsi ga kò hãa* 'you would have been working'

3.2.6 ǀǀGana subgroup

Rainer Vossen

3.2.6.1 Nouns

Most of what has been said about noun characteristics of Kxoe (see 3.2.4.2 above for details) also applies to ǁGana languages. A major difference is that there is no object agreement encoded in the finite verb. Nominal stems are marked rather regularly for person, gender and number (PGN) by enclitics ("suffixes"). There are three genders – masculine, feminine and common ("neuter") – and three numbers: singular, dual and plural. PGNs are represented by a single formative.

The PGN enclitics of ǁGana, ǀGui, and ǂHaba as given in Table 6.21 exhibit a high degree of formal homogeneity within the subgroup:

TABLE 6.21 PGN ENCLITICS OF ǁGANA SUBGROUP VARIETIES

	SG	DU	PL
M	*-mà*, ***-bà***	*-tsèrà*	*-ǃùà*
F	*-sà*	*-sèrà*	*-dzè*, ***-dzì***
C	–	*-khoàrà*, *<u>-khòrà</u>*	*-nà*

Forms in bold type are confined to ǂHaba, the underlined suffix occurs in ǀGui only. The masculine and feminine singular as well as common plural formatives are reduced occasionally to *-m̀*, *-s̀*, and *-ǹ* respectively.

3.2.6.2 Pronouns

The gender–number distinction as described for noun stems reoccurs throughout the subgroup in the pronominal paradigms. In the singular, however, the first person is gender-neutral, and the second and third persons have no common form. Table 6.22 gives a synoptic overview of the subject and object forms.

In ǁGana, all pronouns except first and second person singular present themselves as complex forms consisting of a pronominal element plus PGN marker. The high-toned formative *ú* of the second person dual and plural contrasts with the high-toned *í* of the first person dual and plural. Likewise, low-toned *'ì* representing third person masculine and feminine plural forms a contrast to low-toned *'è* of the third person dual. Phonologically, subject and object pronouns differ from one another through (i) vocalic change of final *e/a* in the first and third person singular, dual, and plural (with very few exceptions), (ii) *b* ~ *m* alternation in the third person masculine singular and the first person dual, and (iii) *r* ~ *n* alternation in the third person masculine plural. Tonologically, the first and second person object pronouns of dual and plural remain unchanged as compared to the subject forms, but in the third person of all number categories they show low tone as against high tones in the first and second person singular.

In ǀGui, all subject pronouns except the second person singular forms are complex and consist of the same structural components as in ǁGana. The object pronouns correspond essentially to the low-toned PGN markers of the subject forms, combined with the consonantal and vocalic alternations as described for ǁGana in (i) through (iii) above.

TABLE 6.22 THE PRONOMINAL PARADIGMS OF ǁGANA SUBGROUP VARIETIES

	ǁGana		ǀGui		ǂHaba	
	SUBJECT	OBJECT	SUBJECT	OBJECT	SUBJECT	OBJECT
			SINGULAR			
1	*tê*	*tíá*	*tí.rè*	*tìà*	*tí*	*tì*
2M	*tsâ*	*tsá*	*tsí*	*tsà*	*tsâ*	*tsà*
2F	*sâ*	*sá*	*sí*	*sà*	*sâ*	*sà*
3M	*'á.bè*	*'à.mà*	*'à.bè*	*mà*	*'é.bà*	*'è.bà*
3F	*sáè*	*'è.sà*	*'ɛ̀.sí*	*sà*	*'é.sà*	*'è.sà*
			DUAL			
1M	*í.tsèbè*	*í.tsèmà*	*hí.tsèbè*	*tsèmà*	*tsám̀*	*tsàm̀*
1F	*í.sèbè*	*í.sèmà*	*hí.sèbè*	*sèmà*	*sám̀*	*sàm̀*
1C	*í.khèbè*	*í.khàmà*	*hí.khèbè*	*khèmà*	*khám̀*	*khàm̀*
2M	*ú.tsàò*	*ú.tsàò*	*hí.tsàò*	*tsàò*	*tsáò*	*tsàò*
2F	*ú.sàò*	*ú.sàò*	*hí.sàò*	*sàò*	*sáò*	*sàò*
2C	*ú.khàò*	*ú.khàò*	*hí.khàò*	*khàò*	*kháò*	*khàò*
3M	*'è.tsérì*	*'è.tsèrà*	*'é.tsèrà*	*tsèrà*	*tsérà*	*tsèrà*
3F	*'è.sérì*	*'è.sèrà*	*'é.sèrà*	*sèrà*	*sérà*	*sèrà*
3C	*'è.khórè*	*'è.khòrà*	*'é.khoàrà*	*khoàrà*	*khórà*	*khòrà*
			PLURAL			
1M	*í.ǀáè*	*í.ǀà*	*ha.ǀà*	*ǀà*	*ǀâ*	*ǀà*
1F	*í.sê*	*í.sà*	*há.sè*	*sè*	*sê*	*sè*
1C	*í.tê*	*í.tà*	*há.tà*	*tà*	*tâ*	*tà*
2M	*ú.ǀàò*	*ú.ǀàò*	*hí.ǀàò*	*ǀàò*	*ǀáò*	*ǀàò*
2F	*ú.sàò*	*ú.sàò*	*hí.sàò*	*sàò*	*sáò*	*sàò*
2C	*ú.tò*	?	*hí.tò*	*tò*	*tô*	*tò*
3M	*'ì.ǀóè*	*'ì.ǀùà*	*hí.ǀù*	*ǀùà*	*ǀóà*	*ǀòà*
3F	*'ì.dzê*	*'ì.dzè*	*'é.dzè*	*dzè*	*dzî*	*dzì*
3C	*'á.rè*	*'à.nà*	*'á.rè*	*'à.nà*	*nâ*	*nà*

ǂHaba contrasts with both ǁGana and ǀGui, in that it lacks complex forms almost entirely. With the exception of the first person singular, subject and object forms are distinguished generally by tone only. While subject pronouns show a high-falling pattern, object pronouns are low-toned throughout.

3.2.6.3 Adjectives

As in most Kalahari Khoe languages, the number of adjectives proper is very small. Some examples are given in Table 6.23.

TABLE 6.23 SOME ADJECTIVES IN ǁGANA SUBGROUP VARIETIES

Gloss	ǁGana	ǀGui	ǂHaba
'short'	*ǀòm̀*	*ǀoàm̀*	*ǀóm̀*
'heavy'	*!óḿ*	*!oáḿ*	*!úḿ*
'bad'	*ǀx'áǹ*	*ǀx'áǹ*	*ǀx'áǹ*

More often than not, adjectival concepts are conveyed by verbal adjectives of the English "to be X"-type. Predicative adjectives are placed after and attributive ones before the head noun. PGN marking is not obligatory.

3.2.6.4 Numerals and quantifiers

Cardinal numbers 'one' through 'four' are expressed by lexical stems; however, the paradigms in (427) are not complete due to lack of information. That numbers higher than 'four' are constructed periphrastically, as in some other Kalahari Khoe languages, remains to be verified.

(427)	ǁGana	ǀGui	ǂHaba
'one'	*ǀúí*	*ǀúí*	*ǀúí*
'two'	*ǀám̀*	*ǀám̀*	*ǀám̀*
'three'	*ŋúnà*	(not obtained)	*ŋóná*
'four'	(not obtained)	*hátsà*	(not obtained)

Numerals precede the head noun and can optionally be marked for gender.

I have no data on ordinal numbers. Quantifiers such as 'much, many' and 'few' tend to be expressed by the adjectives 'big' and 'small', respectively. For 'all' the stem *úé-* was found to be used in ǁGana and ǂHaba.

3.2.6.5 Demonstratives

All varieties have a proximal and a distal demonstrative (see Table 6.24). While the former is formally homogeneous throughout the subgroup, varying shapes have been found for the latter, which is complex in itself.

TABLE 6.24 DEMONSTRATIVES IN THE ǁGANA SUBGROUP

	Proximal		Distal	
ǁGana	*nǀné*		*'á.séá*	
ǀGui	*nǀné*	'this'	*nǀnè.sí.háã̃*	'that'
ǂHaba	*nǀné*		*'à.sá.hà*	

Demonstratives precede the governing noun. PGN agreement markers are more rigidly used in ǁGana than in ǀGui or ǂHaba. In ǁGana, they are reduced in the masculine and feminine singular (*-m̀*/*-s*) as well as in the masculine and common plural (*-ǀù*/*-ǹ*). Examples:

(428) a. *nǀné-ś* *!xóó-sà* 'this pipe'
DEM-AGR:F.SG pipe-F.SG

b. *'á.séá-dzè* *yìí-dzè* 'those trees'
DEM-AGR:F.PL tree-F.PL

c. *séá-ǀù* *ǀóã-ǀùà* 'those boys'
DEM-AGR:M.PL child-M.PL

In (428c) the demonstrative has lost its initial element *'a*; this seems to be the case as a rule if the demonstrative is placed sentence-medially (rather than initially).

3.2.6.6 Possessive

In ǁGana, *di* and *ka* alternate as possessive markers. Juxtaposition is not attested in my data but may nevertheless be practised. In the first person singular *kí* is used instead of the subject pronoun *tê*. Whether it is a genuine possessive pronoun or not remains to be investigated. The examples in (429) illustrate that agreement on the possessive marker appears to be optional and is not conditioned by syntactic positioning:

(429)	*kí*	*dì-m̀*	*ŋúú-mà*	'my house'	*ŋúú-mà*	*kí*	*dì-m̀*
	1SG	POSS-M.SG	house-M.SG		house-M.SG	1SG	POSS-M.SG
	kí	*kà*	*ŋúú-mà*		*ŋúú-mà*	*kí*	*dì*
	1SG	POSS	house-M.SG		house-M.SG	1SG	POSS

Possessive constructions in ǀGui look in principle the same as in ǁGana except that juxtaposition appears to be quite common, e.g. *tí m̀'m̂* 'my head'.

3.2.6.7 Interrogatives

ǁGana and ǀGui have cognate forms for 'who?' and 'which?' but differ with regard to 'what?' (see Table 6.25). All interrogatives except ǀGui *yìí* 'what?' agree with the referent optionally, as in (430).

TABLE 6.25 INTERROGATIVES IN ǁGANA SUBGROUP VARIETIES

	ǁGana	ǀGui
'who?'	*máà*	*mâã*
'which?'	*dí*	*dí*
'what?'	*nùú*	*yìí*

(430) ǁGana

a. *Nǀné-ś khóè-sà má-s̀ 'è?*
DEM-F.SG person-F.SG who-F.SG INT
'Who is this woman?'

b. *Dí-nà kùà tíá kx'âĩ?*
which-C.PL PRES PRO:OBJ$_{1SG}$ laugh
'Which (one) is laughing at me?'

c. *Nǀné nùú-dzè 'è?*
DEM what-F.PL INT
'What is this?'

ǀGui

d. *Nǀné-ǀù kx'áò.khòè-ǀù máã-ǀù 'è?*
DEM-M.PL male.person-M.PL who-M.PL INT
'Who are these men?'

e. *Tsí kè dí-mà ḿm̀?*
2M.SG PRES who-M.SG see
'Whom do you see?'

f. *N!né yìí xóò-dzè 'è?*
DEM what thing-F.PL INT
'What is this?'

In possessive contexts, interrogatives are followed by the possessive marker *dì* (ǁGana) or *kà* (ǀGui):

(431) a. *Kx'áó-dzè má.xà-ǀù dì?*
arrow-F.PL who.?-M.PL POSS
'Whose arrows are these?'

b. *N!né dí-ń kà nǁnàbó-dzè 'è?*
DEM which-C.PL POSS shoe-F.PL INT
'Whose shoes are these?'

3.2.6.8 Verbs

The segmental morphological sequence structure of the verb consists of six slots:

(432)	tense/aspect	verbal base	derivative suffix(es)	• juncture • passive	tense/aspect	negation
	1	2	3	4	5	6

In ǁGana and ǀGui, the imperfect is the only tense that occurs post-verbally. For ǂHaba the same holds true of the indefinite past (slot 5). All other tense/aspect markers precede the verbal base as free morphemes (slot 1). As a consequence, slots 1 and 5 cannot be filled simultaneously. The juncture (slot 4) is restricted to non-passive constructions. In ǂHaba, tense/aspect marking seems to be non-obligatory, as the example in (433) illustrates:

(433) *Tí kúù-tímá.* 'I shall not go/did not go.'
1SG go-NEG

The following sentences exemplify the filling of slots:

(434) ǁGana

a. *Tìè **kùà** tsháà-sà.'à kx'áà-**tàmà**.*
1SG PRES water-F.SG.OBJ drink-NEG
'I don't drink water.'

b. *Khóè-m̀ súbu-bè ǂ'óḿ-sà **nǀnàm̀-á-hà**.*
person-M.SG indolent-M.SG$_{AGR}$ sleep-F.SG like-JUNC-IPT
'An indolent man likes sleeping.'

ǀGui

c. *Khóé-nà **nǀgáḿ-kú-á-hã̄**.*
person-C.PL love-REC-JUNC-IPT
'People love each other.'

d. *'Á.rè **ǁ'áà-kú-témá**.*
3C.PL fight-REC-NEG
'They don't fight one another.'

ǂHaba

e. *ǀX'ɛ̃ɛ̃.khòè* ***tséé-é-hã̄.***
stranger send.away-PASS-PAST$_{INDEF}$
'The stranger was sent away.'

f. *Tí* ***tsxám̀-kàxú-á-hã̄.***
1SG greet-CAUS-JUNC-PAST$_{INDEF}$
'I sent my regards.'

3.2.6.8.1 DERIVATIVE SUFFIXES

Throughout the subgroup derivation serves to diminish or increase the valence of verb stems and, thus, impact on the syntax of verbal phrases. It also triggers semantic modifications. Some functions (e.g. reflexive, causative$_1$, dative, reciprocal) are more productive than others (especially inclinative). Table 6.26 below gives an overview.

TABLE 6.26 DERIVATIVE SUFFIXES IN ǁGANA SUBGROUP VARIETIES

Function	Suffix	Lg.	Basic verb	Gloss	Extended verb	Gloss
Causative$_1$	*-kà.xú**	A	*tsxám̀*	'greet'	*tsxám̀.kà.xù*	'let greet'
		B	*kx'áà*	'drink'	*kx'áà.kà.xú*	'water, let drink'
		C	*ǀúm̀*	'suck'	*ǀúm̀.kà.xú*	'suckle'
Causative$_2$	REDUPL	A/C	*ǀx'óè*	'be full'	*ǀx'óé.ǀx'òè*	'fill'
Repetitive	REDUPL	A	*!óò*	'knock'	*!óó.!òò*	'knock out'
		C	*ǁâã*	'separate'	*ǁâã.ǁàã*	'winnow'
Dative	*-mâ*	B	*tsâã.xù*	'cook'	*tsâã.xù.à.mâ*	'cook for s.b.'
	-mà	C	*nǁnáì*	'sing'	*nǁnáì.mà*	'sing for s.b.'
Reflexive	*-hè*	A	*ḿm̀*	'see'	*ḿm̀.hè*	'see o.s., be visible'
	-sì	B	*kúa'm*	'hear'	*kúa'm.sì*	'hear o.s.'
	*-si**	C	*ǁx'áà*	'wash'	*ǁx'áà.si*	'wash o.s.'
Reciprocal	*-kù*	A	*k'óà*	'separate'	*k'óà.kù*	'part company'
		B	*nǀgáḿ*	'love, like'	*nǀgáḿ.kù*	'love/like each other'
	*-ku**	C	*séè*	'take'	*séè.kù*	'marry'
Inclinative	*-kx'àò*	C	*kx'ùí*	'speak'	*kx'ùí.kx'àò*	'be talkative'
Locative	*-'ò*	A	*ǀ'úbí*	'?'	*ǀ'úbí.'ò*	'weed (out)'
	*-k'o**	C	*!ãĩ*	'shake'	*!ãĩ.k'ó*	'shake out'
Terminative	*-xò*	A	*ǁóé*	'lie'	*ǁóé.xò*	'lie down'
	-xù	B	*ǂx'óà*	'go out'	*ǂx'óà.xù*	'go away'
	-xú	C	*gúm̀*	'blow'	*gúḿ.á.xú*	'blow out'
Intentional	*-à*	B	*!ûũ*	'go'	*!ûũ*	'in order to go'

Notes: A = ǁGana; B = ǀGui; C = ǂHaba.

Comments: (1) Derivative suffixes marked by an asterisk are tonologically flexible; they do not take a fixed tone but rather vary in their tonal behaviour in accordance with the tonal pattern of the verb stem. (2) Verbs marked for intentional function in ǀGui cannot be conjugated. (3) For an explanation of the linker element *-a-* in the examples for dative (B) and terminative (C), see comment (3) in 3.2.4.9.1.

3.2.6.8.2 JUNCTURE

The data available for ǁGana subgroup varieties are definitely not sufficient to clarify all the regularities of occurrence of the basic element *-a* and its allomorphs. Formally, there are more correspondences than differences vis-à-vis Kxoe varieties (especially ǁAni), as described in 3.2.4.9.2. The difficulty of predicting the juncture of a given verb form would suggest notifying the respective form(s) with each verb in the dictionary. However, two general observations are worth mentioning here. First, the juncture is used only in connection with past tenses (*-ha* or *-hã*), i.e., no non-past juncture has yet developed in this subgroup. Second, zero junctures are employed very frequently. In ǂHaba, the allomorph *-na* was found to occur extraordinarily often after disyllabic verbs ending in a mid-vowel.

Table 6.27 gives an overview of juncture allomorphs in the ǁGana subgroup.

TABLE 6.27 JUNCTURE ALLOMORPHS IN THE ǁGANA SUBGROUP

	a	*ɲa*	*ra*	*re*	*ro*	*na*	∅
ǁGana	+		+	+	+	+	+
ǀGui	+		+	+	+	+	+
ǂHaba	+	+	+	+	+	+	+

3.2.6.8.3 PASSIVE

The passive marker is *-e* throughout. It replaces the juncture in slot 4 in passive constructions.

3.2.6.8.4 TENSE/ASPECT MARKERS

From a morphological point of view it is hardly possible, as in Kxoe, to distinguish between tense and aspect (TA). Grammatical markers expressing temporal/aspectual relations occur in slot 1 or 5 (see 432 above) and can never be combined. TA markers largely correspond formally to one another between different varieties, but the precise grammatical content may vary considerably from variety to variety, as the following table illustrates.

TABLE 6.28 TENSE/ASPECT MARKERS IN THE ǁGANA SUBGROUP

TA formative	ǁGana	ǀGui	ǂHaba
-ha ~ -hã	imperfect	imperfect	indefinite past
tu	near past		near past
ke	nearest past	present	nearest past
nǀgè		near past	
nǀne			past
ko	present		present/future
kua	present	present (progressive)	
ga ~ ka ~ ∅	future		
kx'àwà		future	

-hã or *-ha* is the only tense/aspect marker that is immediately suffixed to the verb base through the juncture, as in the following ǂHaba example:

(435) *Tí* *kúũ-á-hã.* 'I went.'
1SG go-JUNC-PAST$_{\text{INDEF}}$

The particle *tu* is attested for ǁGana and ǂHaba (cf. 436) as near past marker:

(436)	*Tú.kà*	*tìrè*	*tú*	*tsháá-sà*	*kx'áà.*	'Yesterday I drank water.'
	yesterday	1SG	PAST$_{NEAR}$	water-F.SG	drink	(Köhler 1962: 543)

In ǁGana and ǂHaba (cf. 437a), *ke* stands for nearest past whereas in ǀGui (437b) it represents present tense:

(437)	a.	*Nǀné-ḿ*	*qúú-m̀.kà*	*tìrè*	*kè*	*tsháá-sà*	*kx'áà.*
		this-M.SG	today	1SG	PAST$_{NEAREST}$	water-F.SG	drink

'This morning I drank water.' (Köhler 1962: 543)

	b.	*Tírè*	*kè*	*tsà*	*ḿm̀.*
		1SG	PRES	PRO:OBJ$_{2M.SG}$	see

'I see you.'

ǀGui *nǀgè* and ǂHaba *nǀnè* appear as preteritive forms whose employment is expressed only hazily in (438a) and (438b), respectively:

(438)	a.	*'Á.bè*	*nǀgè*	*tìà*	*ḿm̀.*	'He saw me recently.'
		3M.SG	PAST$_{NEAR}$	PRO:OBJ.1SG	see	
	b.	*Tí*	*nǀnè*	*kûũ.*		'I have gone.'
		1SG	PAST	go		

The expression of future causes considerable irritation. While it seems to be lacking entirely in ǂHaba, Maingard (1957: 68) claims *ka* to be used in ǁGana; my own data, however, show no indication of future formation for this variety. The formative *kx'àwà* seems to be restricted to ǀGui:

(439)	*'Á.bè*	*kx'àwà*	*tìà*	*ḿm̀.*	'He will see me.'
	3M.SG	FUT	PRO:OBJ.1SG	see	

Finally, the ǀGui sentence in (440) contains a particle *hĩ* which seems to express the near future or even "subjunctive" and resembles strikingly the remote past marker in Kxoe (cf. section 3.2.4.9.5). Since it occurs only once in my data I have left it out from Table 6.28 above.

(440)	*ǀXáá-dzè*	*tírè*	*hĩ*	*kx'óó.*	'I shall/should eat meat (now).'
	meat-F.PL	1SG	hĩ	eat	

It is obvious that much research remains to be done on the TA system of the ǁGana subgroup varieties. The present description can be no more than tentative.

3.2.6.8.5 NEGATION

Verbs are negated by means of phrase-final *-tama* (ǁGana), *-tema* (ǀGui) and *-tima* (ǂHaba). For examples, see (433) and (434a/d) above.

3.2.7 Shua subgroup

Rainer Vossen

3.2.7.1 Nouns

By and large, the PGN enclitics of the subgroup varieties appear to be homogeneous; however, ongoing reduction of the nominal marking system is unmistakable. The extreme case is Deti, which has maintained a masculine–feminine distinction in the singular only but does not make use of it in productive ways; on the contrary, such PGN enclitics are confined to some lexicalized forms such as *'ádé**sá*** 'my mother', *sídè**sá*** 'your mother' or *'àbà**má*** 'my father'. In ǀXaise, the masculine plural is expressed periphrastically ("many Xs"), and generally speaking, not much weight is laid on the use of PGN markers except in Ts'ixa. Table 6.29 contains the nominal formatives of Ts'ixa and Danisi.

TABLE 6.29 PGN ENCLITICS OF TS'IXA AND DANISI

	Ts'ixa			Danisi		
	SG	DU	PL	SG	DU	PL
M	*-mà*	*-tsèrà*	*-ǀùà*	*-ma*	*-tsàrà*	*-kùà*
F	*-sa, -sì*	*-sèrà*	*-dzà, -dzì*	*-sa*	*-sàrà*	*-dzà*
C	–	*-khòrà*	*-nà*	–	*-khoàrà*	*-nà*

In Ts'ixa, the masculine singular and plural as well as common plural markers can occur as shortened *-m̀*, *-ǀù* and *-ǹ* respectively; in Danisi, such reduction has only been observed in the masculine singular (*-m*). In my data Ts'ixa *-sì* (F.SG) is employed more frequently than *-sa*. Köhler (1962: 535) gives only *-kua* for masculine and *-dzi* for feminine plural, which he had obtained in Danisi, too.

TABLE 6.30 PGN ENCLITICS OF CARA AND ǀXAISE

	Cara			ǀXaise		
	SG	DU	PL	SG	DU	PL
M	*-mà*	*-dzàrà*	*-kùà*	*-mà*	*-tsàrà*	–
F	*-sà*	*-sàrà*	*-dzì*	*-sà*	*-sàrà*	*-dzà*
C	–	*-khòrà*	*-nà*	–	*-khòrà*	*-nà*

3.2.7.2 Pronouns

With the exception of Deti, Shua personal pronoun systems are largely coherent. The most conspicuous commonalities may be seen in (i) the complex formation of the third person pronouns with the pronominal formative *'é* (plus PGN marker), (ii) the tonal patterns "high" in the first and second and "high-low" in the third person, and (iii) the marking of pronominal objects by means of *'à* which follows the subject form. Table 6.31 gives a synoptic overview of the subject forms only (except Deti).

TABLE 6.31 THE PRONOMINAL PARADIGMS OF SHUA SUBGROUP VARIETIES

	Cara	ǀXaise	Ts'ixa	Danisi	Deti	
	SUBJECT				SUBJECT	OBJECT
			SINGULAR			
1	*tá*	*tá*	*tí*	*tá*	*tá*	*tá*
2M	*tsá*	*cá*	*tsá*	*tsá*	*tsá*	*tsá*
2F	*sá*	*sá*	*sá*	*sá*	*sá*	*sá*
3M	*'é.mà*	*'é.mà*	*'é.mà*	*'é.mà*	*'é.mà*	*'é.mà*
3F	*'é.sà*	*'é.sà*	*'é.sà*	*'é.sà*	*'é.sà*	*'é.sà*
3C	*'í*	–	*'î*	–	–	–
			DUAL			
1M	*dzáḿ*	*tsáḿ*	*tsúḿ*	*tsúḿ*	*'à.tsáḿ*	?
1F	*sáḿ*	*sáḿ*	*súḿ*	*súḿ*	*'à.kháḿ*	?
1C	*kháḿ*	*kháḿ*	*khúḿ*	*kháḿ*	*'à.kháḿ*	?
2M	*dzáró*	*tsáró*	*tsóró*	*tsóró*	*'à.tsáró*	?
2F	*sáró*	*sáró*	*sóró*	*sóró*	*'à.kháró*	?
2C	*kháró*	*kháró*	*khóró*	*kháró*	*'à.kháró*	?
3M	*'é.dzàrà*	*'é.tsàrà*	*'é.tsérà*	*'é.tsárà*	*'é.tsàrà*	?
3F	*'é.sàrà*	*'é.sàrà*	*'é.sérà*	*'é.sárà*	*'é.khoàrà*	?
3C	*'é.khòrà*	*'é.khòrà*	*'é.khórà*	*'é.khórà*	*'é.khoàrà*	?
			PLURAL			
1M	*jé*	*ké*	*ǁé*	*ké*	*'à.cé*	*'à.cá*
1F	*sé*	*sé*	*sé*	*sé*	*dzé*	*dzá*
1C	*dzé*	*tsé*	*tsé*	*tsé*	*'à.cé*	*cá*
2M	*gáó*	*káó*	*ǁó*	*káó*	*gáó*	*gáóá*
2F	*sáó*	*sáó*	*só*	*sáó*	*dó*	*dóá*
2C	*dó*	*tó*	*tó*	*tó*	*dó*	*dóá*
3M	*'é.kùà*	*'é.kùà*	*'é.ǁùà*	*'é.kùà*	*'é.kùà*	*'é.kùà*
3F	*'é.dzì*	*'é.dzì*	*'é.dzà*	*'é.dzà*	*'é.nà*	*'é.nà*
3C	*'é.nà*	*'é.nà*	*'é.nà*	*'é.nà*	*'é.nà*	*'é.nà*

Note: 3C.PL in Cara and Ts'ixa is to be interpreted as "neuter".

The formal differences between the paradigms are merely of phonological nature. In Ts'ixa, Kxoe influence can be determined in the first person singular and in the first, second and third person masculine plural.

Deti contrasts sharply with other Shua varieties in that it shows indications of linguistic change which may partly be considered as characteristic of moribund languages. Many of its pronominal forms are complex rather than simple. The neutralization of all feminine and common pronouns in the dual and the second and third person feminine and common pronouns in the plural as well, is very peculiar and shows, from a comparative perspective, that the original feminine pronouns got lost. My consultants strongly denied the existence of dual pronouns such as *'à.sáḿ* (1F.DU), *'à.sáró* (2F.DU) or *'á.sàrà* (3F.DU) which one would expect here instead of *'à.kháḿ*, *'à.kháró* and *'é.khoàrà*, respectively. Also in the first person plural there is a double representation of forms (masculine and common) that breaks an otherwise rigidly distinctive system. Subject and object pronouns do not differ from one another in the singular and in the third person plural. Missing object pronouns in the dual paradigm are due to data gaps.

3.2.7.3 Adjectives

More often than not, adjectival concepts in Shua varieties are conveyed by verbal adjectives of the English "to be X"-type. There are, however, limited sets of proper adjectives, some of which have been compiled in Table 6.32.

TABLE 6.32 SOME COMMON ADJECTIVES IN SHUA SUBGROUP VARIETIES

Gloss	Cara	ǀXaise	Ts'ixa	Danisi	Deti
'old (of things)'	*nǁgáò*	*nǁnáò*	*nǁgáò*	*nǁgáò*	*nǁnáò*
'bitter'	*k'àú*	*k'àú*			*k'àú*
'hard'	*kárí*		*kárí*	*kárí*	*kárí*
'short'	*ǁòḿ*	*ǁòḿ*	*ǁóm̀*	*ǁòḿ*	*ǁóm̀*
'new'	*k'óá*		*k'óà*		*k'óá*
'sour'	*tsárú*	*tsárú*		*tsárú*	*tsárú*
'red; brown'	*ǀòá*	*ǀòá*		*ǀòá*	*nǀgóá*
'good; sweet'	*káĩ*	*kâĩ*	*kâĩ* 'good'	*kâĩ* 'good'	*káĩ*
'good; clean'	*t'úĩ* '+ correct'	*t'ûĩ* 'good'	*t'ûĩ*	*t'ûĩ*	*t'úĩ*
'small . . .'	*ǀ'áré* 'narrow'			*ǀ'áré* 'small'	*ǀ'àré* 'thin'

Predicative adjectives are placed after and attributive ones before the head noun. PGN marking is practically non-existent.

3.2.7.4 Numerals and quantifiers

Cardinal numbers 'one' through 'four' are lexical stems (see 441). Numerals above 'four' are constructed periphrastically in most varieties, as in Kxoe (cf. 3.2.4.5).

(441)

	Cara	ǀXaise	Ts'ixa	Danisi	Deti
'one'	*ǀúí*	*ǀúí*	*ǀúí*	*ǀúí*	*ǀúí*
'two'	*ǀám̀*	*ǀám̀*	*ǀám̀*	*ǀám̀*	*ǀám̀*
'three'	*ǁóbé*	*ŋónà*	*ǁóbé*	*ǁóbé*	*ǁóbé*
'four'	*hàtsá*	*ǁóbé*	*fóò* (< Engl.)	(not obtained)	*hátsà*

The numerals 'three' and 'four' in ǀXaise require a brief discussion. Obviously, 'four' is the same form as 'three' in the other subgroup varieties, while 'three' is a reflex of Proto-Khoe that is also found in Tshwa subgroup varieties (cf. 3.2.8.4). One might speculate upon this curiosity in various ways; however, since nothing is known about the origin of *ǁóbé*, this would be nothing but guesswork.

Ordinal numbers are shaped by a particle inserted between the cardinal number and the governing noun. This particle is *ǁ'àì* in Cara (442a) and Deti (442b) and *kà* in Ts'ixa (442c). There are no data on Danisi and ǀXaise.

(442) a. *ǀÁm ǁ'àì xam tsá-'à múũ-á-ha.*
two PTCL lion 2M.SG-OBJ see-JUNC-IPT
'The second lion saw you.'

b.

Hátsá	*ǁ'àì*	*biye*	*hùú-sà*	*gàò-sè-hà(ò).*
four	PTCL	horse	DEM$_{DIST}$-F.SG	see-F.SG.OBJ$_{AGR}$-IPT

'The fourth horse saw her.'

c.

ǀÓbe	*kà*	*dí-ḿ*	*dòâ-kà*	*'é.mà-'à*	*múũ-nà-tà.*
three	PTCL	POSS-M.SG	kudu-POSTP	3M.SG-OBJ	see-JUNC-PAST$_{NEAR}$

'The third kudu saw him.'

It seems that in Ts'ixa the particle *kà* must be employed in combination with the possessive marker *di* (see 3.2.7.6); at the same time the governing noun is followed by the postposition *kà* 'with'. The reason for this is still unclear.

All numerals precede the head noun and are hardly ever marked for gender.

The most common quantifiers found are 'many, much', 'few' and 'all':

(443)

	Cara	ǀXaise	Ts'ixa	Danisi	Deti
'many, much'	*thíyà*	*ǀxárá*	*thíyà*	*thíyà*	*gùrí*
'few'			*'úré*	*'óré*	*cúĩ*
'all'	*'yé*	*'íye*	*'íyé*	*'ìyé*	*wè*

3.2.7.5 Demonstratives

Shua varieties have a proximal and a distal demonstrative:

TABLE 6.33 DEMONSTRATIVES IN THE SHUA SUBGROUP

	Proximal		Distal	
Cara	*ìí*		*ùú*	
Ts'ixa	*nǀné*	'this'	*mé*	'that'
Danisi	*ĩĩ*		*ùú*	
Deti	*hĩĩ*		*hùú*	

In both categories the Ts'ixa forms diverge from the other varieties. While the proximal demonstrative corresponds to what is commonly found in West Kalahari Khoe languages (and may therefore be borrowed), the distal *mé* cannot be explained at present.

As a rule, demonstratives precede the governing noun. Note, however, that in Ts'ixa the opposite order is possible but not common. In Cara and Ts'ixa, demonstratives agree optionally with the head noun. In contrast to this, no indication of agreement was found in Danisi and Deti. Some examples:

(444)	Cara	*ìí(-mà)*	*khóé-mà*	'this man'
		DEM(-AGR:M.SG)	person-M.SG	
		ùú(-sà)	*khóé-sà*	'that woman'
		DEM(-AGR:F.SG)	person-F.SG	
	Ts'ixa	*mé-ḿ*	*'ábá-mà*	'this male dog'
		DEM-AGR:M.SG	dog-M.SG	
	or:	*'ábá-mà*	*mé-ḿà*	
	Danisi	*ĩĩ*	*xáḿ*	'this lion'
		DEM	lion	
		ùú	*dóá*	'that kudu'
		DEM	kudu	

3.2.7.6 Possessive

The possessive marker is *di* (in Danisi *ka*, in addition) throughout the subgroup. However, juxtaposition appears to be the preferred construction, e.g.: Cara *tí tshàú* 'my hand', Danisi *tsá dòŋgí* 'your donkey'.

When the possessive marker *di* (or *ka*) is used syntactic variation is possible, as in the following Danisi examples for 'your donkey': *dòŋgí tsá dì* ~ *dòŋgí.mà tsá kà* ~ *tsá dì (~kà) dòŋgí.mà*. The possessive marker is not subject to agreement. In Cara, the first and third person subject pronouns change in possessive constructions as follows: 1SG *tá* → *tí*; 3F.SG *'é.sà* → *'é.sì*; 3M.SG *'é.mà* → *'é.m̀*.

3.2.7.7 Interrogatives

The following interrogatives have been found so far (Table 6.34):

TABLE 6.34 INTERROGATIVES IN SHUA SUBGROUP VARIETIES

	Cara	Danisi	Ts'ixa	Deti
'who?'; 'which?'	*máá* ~ *náá*	*máá* ~ *máé*	*máá* ~ *máé*	*máá* ~ *má.n(à)*
'what?'	*ndú*	*ndú*	*néé*	*dúú*

All varieties have a [+animate] and a [−animate] class of interrogatives. In the former class there are alternative forms whose use does not appear to be constrained in any way. In Cara and Ts'ixa, they optionally take on agreement markers, but in Danisi this applies to *máá* only. As a rule, inanimate interrogatives do not agree with the referent, and Deti shows no agreement marking whatsoever. Examples:

(445) Cara

a. *Máá(-dzì) 'è ùú ǁgáà-khòè(-dzì)?*
who(-F.PL) INT DEM_{DIST} female-person(-F.PL)
'Who are those women?'

b. *Tsá ndú k'ùì-à-tá?*
2M.SG what say-JUNC-$\text{PAST}_{\text{NEAR}}$
'What did you (just) say?'

Danisi

c. *Máé tsá kà káà-xù-sá 'è?*
which 2M.SG POSS cut-thing-F.SG INT
'Which is your knife?'

d. *Ndú kè tsá ǀ'ãĩ 'yàń?*
what PRES 2M.SG buy want
'What do you want to buy?'

Ts'ixa

e. *Máé-'à tsá kùè ǂíí?*
who-OBJ 2M.SG PRES call
'Whom are you calling?'

f. *N|né née?*
DEM$_{PROX}$ what
'What is this?'

Deti

g. *Hĩĩ k'á-khòè má.nà 'è?*
DEM$_{PROX}$ male-person who INT
'Who is this man?'

h. *Hĩĩ dúú 'è?*
DEM$_{PROX}$ what INT
'What is this?'

In possessive contexts, interrogatives are followed by the possessive marker *dì* except in Ts'ixa, where juxtaposition occurs:

(446) Cara

a. *Ìí jíbè má.n dì 'ì?*
DEM$_{PROX}$ axe who POSS INT
'Whose axe is this?'

Danisi

b. *Máé dì 'è n|gábé-s ĩĩ-sà?*
who POSS INT pipe-F.SG DEM$_{PROX}$-F.SG
'Whose pipe is this?'

Deti

c. *Hĩĩ |ábà má.ń dì 'è?*
DEM$_{PROX}$ hat who POSS INT
'Whose hat is this?'

Ts'ixa

d. *Máé ká-xù n|née?*
who cut-thing DEM$_{PROX}$
'Whose knife is this?'

3.2.7.8 Verbs

In principle, there is a high degree of similarity in the formation of finite verbs across the subgroup. Table 6.35 gives an overview.

Except for Ts'ixa, all varieties have two slot structures: one for present and future tenses (type A) – in |Xaise only present –, and another one for negated present tense and past (type B). In Ts'ixa, slots 1 and 5 exclude each other, and the same applies to Danisi as regards slots 1 and 6 (type A). Here slot 5 (negation) can only be filled if the verb appears in the future tense, whereas in type B the negation slot refers exclusively to the preterite.

In Cara, mutual exclusion is noted for slots 1 (tense only) and 6 (type A). If slot 1 is filled by a negation marker, then the verb appears in the future tense and, in addition, the negated present marker must show up in slot 6. If the negation marker fills slot 5, then again the verb appears in the future tense and its marker can go either to slot 1 or 6. Type B permits simultaneous filling of all five slots.

TABLE 6.35 VERBAL SLOT STRUCTURE IN SHUA SUBGROUP VARIETIES

Ts'ixa						
	TA – [–preterite] [–negated present]	verbal base –	derivative suffix(es) –	• juncture • passive –	TA – [+preterite] [+negated present]	negation
	1	2	3	4	5	6
Danisi						
Type A (present & future)	TA –	verbal base –	derivative suffix(es) –	passive –	negation –	TA
	1	2	3	4	5	6
Type B (negated present & past)	verbal base –	derivative suffix(es) –	• juncture • passive –	TA –	negation	
	1	2	3	4	5	
Cara						
Type A (present & future)	• TA • negation –	verbal base –	derivative suffix(es) –	passive –	negation –	TA
	1	2	3	4	5	6
Type B (negated present & past)	verbal base –	derivative suffix(es) –	negation – [preterite]	• juncture • passive –	TA	
	1	2	3	4	5	
ǀXaise						
Type A (present)	TA –	verbal base –	derivative suffix(es) –	passive –	negation –	TA
	1	2	3	4	5	6
Type B (negated present & past)	verbal base –	derivative suffix(es) –	• juncture • passive • negation –	TA		
	1	2	3	4		
Deti						
Type A (present & future)	• TA • negation –	verbal base –	derivative suffix(es) –	• passive • *-na* –	TA	
	1	2	3	4	5	
Type B (negated present & past)	verbal base –	derivative suffix(es) –	• juncture • passive • (OBJ$_{AGR}$) –	negation –	TA	
	1	2	3	4	5	

In ǀXaise (type A), slots 1 and 6 exclude each other. Slot 5 (negation) is only filled when the tense marker in slot 1 or 6 implies a future perspective. Type B permits simultaneous filling of all four slots. The verb is negated in slot 3 only if it occurs with the indefinite past marker.

Finally, in Deti (type A) the tense slots 1 and 5 are filled alternatively. The juncture allomorph *-na* in slot 4 is restricted to the future tense (in slot 1 or 5). All five slots can be filled simultaneously. In type B the rules largely resemble the situation as found in ǁAni (cf. 3.2.4.9). However, if the negation marker (slot 4) is used no juncture must appear in slot 3. If slot 5 is filled by the negated present tense the juncture in slot 3 is zero.

In (447) below the filling of slots is briefly exemplified.

Ts'ixa

(447) a. *Tí khoe ǀxòà* ***ǁ'áé-ku-na-tà-íté.***
1SG person with meet-REC-JUNC-$\text{PAST}_{\text{RECENT}}$-NEG
'I have met nobody.'

b. *Tí* ***gèrɛ̀*** ***ǁ'ám̋-ɛ-íté.***
1SG FUT beat-PASS-NEG
'I shall not be beaten.'

Danisi

c. (A) ***Kùà ǁgàm̀-kú-é-bé.***
FUT love-REC-PASS-NEG
'People will not love each other.'

d. (B) *Máé tsá kà mà-má.'à* ***gádzé-ká.xù-à-hà?***
who 2M.SG POSS head-M.SG.OBJ hurt-CAUS-JUNC-PRET
'Who has hurt your head?'

Cara

e. (A) *Tsá* ***ke*** *'yánù* ***'yǔũ.***
2M.SG PRES porridge eat
'You eat porridge.'

f. (B) *Tsá ǀgaba* ***ts'áã-e-há.***
2M.SG bow steal-PASS-IPT
'Your bow was stolen.'

ǀXaise

g. (A) *Tá* ***ké*** *hĩĩ-a* ***ǀìí-hĩĩ-m̂.***
1SG PRES make-JUNC (= "FUT") shave-REFL-NEG
'I shall not shave myself.'

h. (B) *Ń.tshè tá 'ábà* ***'yùũ-ká.hu-tà.***
today 1SG dog eat-CAUS-PRES.NEG
'I don't feed the dog today.'

Deti

i. (A) ***Tshénà*** *tá* ***ǁ'âã-kù-tà.***
NEG.FUT 1SG fight-REC-PRES.NEG
'I shall not fight.'

j. (B) *'É.nà* ***yáà-yàà-mà.nà-tó.***
3C.PL dance-REP-NEG-PERF
'They have danced time and again.'

3.2.7.8.1 DERIVATIVE SUFFIXES

Deverbal derivation by means of suffixes is very common in Shua. At least a dozen functions with partially varying forms occur throughout the subgroup. Some (e.g. reflexive, causative, dative, reciprocal, terminative) are more productive than others (e.g. inclinative, comitative). Table 6.36 below gives an overview.

TABLE 6.36 DERIVATIVE SUFFIXES IN SHUA VARIETIES

Function	Suffix	Lg.	Basic verb	Gloss	Extended verb	Gloss
Causative$_1$	*-ka.xu*	Ts'	*ǀáì*	'run'	*ǀái-ka.xu*	'let run'
		Da	*ǁ'áǹ*	'build'	*ǁ'áǹ-ká.xù*	'let build'
	-xu	Ts'	*dáó*	'burn' (intr.)	*dáó-xù*	'burn' (tr.)
		Da	*kx'áà*	'drink'	*kx'áà-xú*	'water'
	-ka.hu	Ca	*hàá*	'come'	*hàá-kà.hú*	'bring'
		ǀX	*ǁ'áì*	'buy'	*ǁ'áì-kà.hù*	'sell'
	-ka.xu	De	*nǁgáì*	'sing'	*nǁgáì-kà.xù*	'let sing'
Causative$_2$	REDUPL	Ts'	*ǀ'óɛ̀*	'be full'	*ǀ'óɛ́-ǀ'òɛ̀*	'fill'
		Ca/ǀX	*ǀ'áé*	'fall'	*ǀ'áé-ǀ'àè*	'let fall'
		De	*ǀ'àé*	'fall'	*ǀ'àé-ǀ'àè*	'let fall'
Repetitive	REDUPL	Ts'	*khúù*	'blow'	*khúù-khùù*	'keep blowing'
		Da	*ǁ'áḿ*	'slap'	*ǁ'áḿ-ǁ'àm̀*	'clap, applaud'
		Ca	*c'èé*	'cry'	*c'èé-c'èè*	'weep'
		ǀX	*káó*	'knock'	*káó-kàò*	'keep knocking'
		De	*khùḿ*	'cut'	*khùḿ-khùm̀*	'cut open'
Dative	*-ma*	Ts'	*sóò*	'forge'	*sóo-ma*	'forge for'
	-má	Da	*nǀgóá*	'cook'	*nǀgóá-má*	'cook for'
	-ma	Ca	*gàò*	'look at'	*gàò-má*	'look at for'
		ǀX	*ǀíí*	'sing'	*ǀíí-má*	'sing for'
		De	*hĩĩ́*	'work'	*hĩĩ́-mà*	'work for'
Reflexive	*-sì*	Ts'	*yábà*	'love'	*yábà-sì*	'love oneself'
	-si	Da	*ǁ'áà*	'wash'	*ǁ'áà-si*	'wash oneself'
	-sin	Ca	*ǁ'òḿ*	'cut'	*ǁ'òḿ-sin*	'cut oneself'
	-hĩ	ǀX	*ǁ'úm̀*	'cut'	*ǁ'úm̀-hĩ*	'cut oneself'
	-sin	De	*ǀgàm̀*	'love'	*ǀgàm̀-sín*	'love oneself'
Reciprocal	*-ku*	Ts'	*ǁ'áḿ*	'beat'	*ǁ'áḿ-ku*	'fight with s.o.'
		Da	*sĩĩ́*	'work'	*sĩĩ́-kú*	'work together'
		Ca	*'ám̀*	'agree'	*'ám̀-kú*	'agree with each other'
	-kú	ǀX	*ǀám̀*	'hear'	*ǀám̀-kú*	'hear one another'
	-ku	De	*káá*	'help'	*káá-ku*	'help each other'
Inclinative	*-kx'àò*	Da	*'yũ̌ũ*	'eat'	*'yũ̌ũ-kx'àò*	'eat greedily'
Locative	*-'o*	Ts	*péè*	'jump'	*pé-ré-'ò**	'jump over'
		Da	*kũ̂ũ*	'go'	*kũ̂ũ-'ò*	'go to'
		Ca	*hàá*	'come'	*hàá-'ò*	'fetch, call for'
		ǀX	*k'áà*	'drink'	*k'áà-'ò*	'drink from'
		De	*ŋábí*	'turn'	*ŋábí-'o*	'turn inside out'

TABLE 6.36 (*cont'd*)

Function	Suffix	Lg.	Basic verb	Gloss	Extended verb	Gloss
Iterative	*-ká.sì*	Da	*ǁgâĩ*	'run'	*ǁgáĩ-a-ká.sì**	'jog'
Comitative	*-ǀxòà*	Da	*kûũ*	'go'	*kûũ-ǀxòà*	'go with somebody'
Terminative	*-xu*	Ts'	*ǁ'ŏã*	'pour'	*ǁ'ŏã-xú*	'pour away'
	-xú	Da	*!xóé*	'scratch'	*!xóé-á-xú**	'scratch off'
	-hu	Ca	*ɲàà*	'put'	*ɲáá-hu*	'put down'
		ǀX	*cùú*	'wipe'	*cùù-á-hu**	'wipe off'
	-xu	De	*ɲúũ*	'put'	*Òúũ-á-xú**	'put down'
Intentional	*-a*	Ca	*kûũ*	'go'	*kúũ-à*	'in order to go'
	-'à	De	*kûũ*	'go'	*kûũ-'à*	'in order to go'

Notes: Ts' = Ts'ixa; Da = Danisi; Ca = Cara; ǀX = ǀXaise; De = Deti.

Comments: (1) Strictly speaking, reduplication is not a case of derivation; it has here been included because of the parallel paradigmatic patterns that derive from reduplicated verbs as compared to verbs extended by suffixes. The functions "repetitive" and "causative" often overlap or cannot clearly be distinguished. Likewise, repetitive and iterative in Danisi appear to be the same semantically. (2) More often than not, dative verb stems convey benefactive meaning. (3) Verbs containing the intentional suffix cannot be conjugated. (4) Extended verb forms marked by an asterisk contain the juncture morpheme which normally links tense/aspect markers to the verbal base, and not derivative suffixes. For an attempt at an historical explanation of this phenomenon, see Vossen (2010). (5) Derivative suffixes left unmarked in the "Suffix" column lack inherent tone and are tonally dependent on the verbal base. (6) Combinations of verbal extensions are possible throughout the subgroup.

3.2.7.8.2 JUNCTURE

Shua varieties make use of the juncture only if the verb occurs in a past tense form. The base of the juncture is /a/, allomorphs are relatively few (see Table 6.37 below) and their distribution does not always seem to be clearly conditioned.

TABLE 6.37 JUNCTURE ALLOMORPHS IN THE SHUA SUBGROUP

	a	*ɲa*	*ra*	*rɛ*	*ro*	*na*	∅
Ts'ixa	+			+	+	+	+
Danisi	+					+	
Cara	+		+			+	+
ǀXaise	+	+	+			+	+
Deti	+		+			+	+

In Ts'ixa, the juncture is most frequently represented by the allomorph *-na*, whose occurrence seems hardly predictable; this applies to the base form, too. A small number of verbs take no juncture at all while others employ the (presumably historically motivated) allomorphs *-ro* and *-rɛ*. Like in Kxoe varieties, the use of the juncture correlates with the tense/aspect form of the verb, as illustrated in (448):

(448) *k'òò-**rò**-tà* vs. *k'òò-**ná**-ha*
eat-JUNC-PAST$_{\text{RECENT}}$ eat-JUNC-PAST$_{\text{REMOTE}}$

However, since *k'òò-**ró**-ha* is also possible for the remote past one may eventually interpret the formation with *-na* as an indication of *-na* gradually becoming a kind of standard juncture in Ts'ixa. Such an hypothesis would be supported, for instance, by (449) below, where the use of *-na* following a high back nasal vowel contradicts clearly our general observation in Kalahari Khoe languages.

(449) *mûũ-**nà**-tà* vs. *ǀ'úũ-**à**-tà*
see-JUNC-PAST$_{\text{RECENT}}$ kill-JUNC-PAST$_{\text{RECENT}}$

In Danisi, the only known allomorph of the base form of the juncture is *-na*. While the base form can, in principle, follow any verb-final vowel except *ã* and must be used after nasal consonants, *-na* occurs sometimes after *ã* and frequently after back oral vowels in disyllabic verb stems. Out of the ordinary is the employment of the juncture on the verbs *khùí* 'lift, raise' and *ǁ'àm̀* 'hit, strike' (450):

(450) *khùí-**na**-tá* vs. *khùì-**à**-há*
lift-JUNC-PRET lift-JUNC-PRET
*ǁ'àm̀-**nà**-tá*
hit-JUNC-PRET

Here, the verb *khùí* appears in the two preterite forms of Danisi with different junctures. Possibly the distinction correlates with the tense/aspect form of the verb, as in Kxoe. Other verbs, however, do not behave in this way. As for the construction of 'hit' in (450), the use of *-na* following the nasal consonant is against any rule in Kalahari Khoe languages.

In Cara, the base form /*a*/ of the juncture occurs after nasal consonants and any verb-final vowel except *ã*. For as yet unknown reasons, some verbs fill the juncture slot with zero. The use of *-ra* after verb-final *a* and of *-na* following *ã* is verb-specific.

ǀXaise largely follows the Cara pattern. On all CVCV and a few CVN verbs the juncture is zero. In some instances, the allomorph *-ɲa* has been observed following the high front nasal vowel, e.g.: *ǀxûĩ* 'vomit' → *ǀxú-**ɲá**-ha* vs. *tsĩĩ* 'sneeze' → *tsì-**à**-tá*.

In Deti, the juncture most frequently appears in its base form irrespective of word structure and phonological environment. On just a few verbs *-ra* (after verb-final *a*) and *-na* (following *ã*) are used.

3.2.7.8.3 PASSIVE

The passive marker is *-e* throughout the subgroup. Alternatively, *-ɛ* and *-ye* can be used in Ts'ixa and Deti respectively.

3.2.7.8.4 OBJECT AGREEMENT MARKER

Within the subgroup, object agreement marking appears to be restricted to one language: Deti. Moreover, according to my limited data, it is attested only for pronominal objects. One may assume, however, that nominal objects, too, can be encoded in the finite verb, as in the Kxoe varieties ǁAni and Buga (cf. 3.2.4.9.4).

Within the morphological sequence structure (type B) the object agreement marker falls into slot 3. It is largely unclear under which conditions it must be used or can be omitted. Even the fact that in my data its occurrence is confined to verbs in the negated present or in the past tense does not prove in principle its strict non-occurrence in connection with other tense/aspect forms (type A).

The use of object agreement markers in Deti is illustrated in (451):

(451) a. *Kái xàm̋ **tá** gàò-**tè**-hà.*
big lion 1SG.OBJ look.at-1SG.OBJ$_{AGR}$-IPT
'The big lion looked at me.'

b. *|ám̀ xàm̋ **hùú.tsàrà** gàò.**tsè**.hà.*
two lion 3M.DU.OBJ look.at-OBJ$_{AGR:3M.DU}$-IPT
'Two lions looked at them (i.e. two male persons).'

3.2.7.8.5 TENSE/ASPECT MARKER

Given the scantiness of data, it is hardly possible in Shua to distinguish between tense and aspect (TA). Occurring forms are therefore treated jointly.

Throughout the subgroup, present, past and future represent primary temporal levels. The negated present is expressed by a verbal suffix of its own. Secondary temporal levels, which are attested for the past in the subgroup as a whole, cannot always be determined semantically due to the weak data basis.

Cross-linguistically, formal identity of TA markers prevails over differences, although a certain degree of variation must be admitted concerning the semantic attribution. This is reflected in the following chart (Table 6.38).

TABLE 6.38 TENSE/ASPECT MARKERS IN SHUA

TA category	Ts'ixa	Danisi	Cara	ǀXaise	Deti
Remote past	*-ha*				
Preterite		*-tá, -ha*			
Recent past	*-tà*		*-tá*	*-tá*	*-tá*
Perfect					*-tó*
Imperfect			*-ha*		*-ha*
Indefinite past				*-ha*	
Present	*ko, kue*	*ke*	*ke*	*ke*	*ce*
Negated present	*-tã*	*-tà*	*-tà*	*-tà*	*-tà*
Future	*gèrè*	*kua*	*kùà, ke hĩĩ-a*	*ke hĩĩ-a*	*kua*
Gerundive			*(-sì)*		*-si*

The occurrence of two distinct present formatives in Ts'ixa cannot be explained sufficiently. More frequently employed is *kue*, whereas *ko* corresponds to progressive usage in some examples. The negated present formative *-tã* is likely to be related etymologically to *-tà* in the other varieties.

A high degree of functional variation is exhibited by the formative *-ha*. Future research must clarify the exact status of this element across the subgroup. In Danisi, a semantic distinction between *-tá* and *-ha* is not discernible.

To express future action Cara offers two options: *kùà* and *ke hĩĩ-a*; the latter can also be used in reverse order, i.e. *hĩĩ-a ke*. At any rate *ke hĩĩ-a* represents the only way of expressing future action in ǀXaise. Since *ke* is the present tense formative in Shua, it can be concluded that there no longer exists a genuine future form in this variety. In Deti, the future formative *kua* often shows up in connection with verb-final *-na*.

Gerundive *-si* and *-sì* in Cara and Deti, respectively, have not been found elsewhere in Shua.

For examples of TA employment in Shua, see 3.2.7.8 (447).

3.2.7.8.6 NEGATION

All varieties share the negated present formative *-tè* (*-tã* in Ts'ixa). Verbs in the past and future use *-ítě* in Ts'ixa and *-bé* (most likely a borrowing from Kxoe) in Danisi. In the other varieties the negation strategies are of complex nature.

Cara has one joint and also separate negation markers for the two past formatives. The joint marker is *-ma.na*, a compound element of uncertain origin immediately suffixed to the verbal base:

(452) a. *Tá k'òò-hú k'òó-**mà.nà**-tá.*
1SG eat.meat-thing eat.meat-NEG-PAST$_{\text{RECENT}}$
'I have not (yet) eaten meat (today).'

b. *Tá k'òò-hú k'òó-**má.ná**-ha.*
1SG eat.meat-thing eat.meat-NEG-IPT
'I didn't eat meat.'

With separate markers the constructions in (452) are as follows:

(453) a. *Tá k'òò-hú k'òó-**tòm̀.tám̀**.*
1SG eat.meat-thing eat.meat-NEG-PAST$_{\text{RECENT}}$
'I have not (yet) eaten meat (today).'

b. *Tá k'òò-hú k'òó-**tòm̀**-(á-)-ha.*
1SG eat.meat-thing eat.meat-NEG-(JUNC-)IPT
'I didn't eat meat.'

The negation in (453a) presents itself like a negated (recent past) tense form in its own right, comparable to the negated present. One might hypothesize that the *tá* component in *-tòm̀.tám̀* is the recent past formative as such and, hence, the negation marker is rather *-tòm̀ . . . m̀*. The negation marker *-tom* in (453b) can optionally be followed by the juncture.

Future constructions in Cara, again, can be made in two ways: by means of the trisyllabic (!) particle *tátánà* in combination with the negated present *-tà* formative, e.g.

(454) a. *'é.nà **tátánà** |íí n‖gáì-**tà**.*
3C.PL NEG song sing-PRES.NEG
'They will not sing a song.'

or with the aid of the suffix *-m̀*:

(454) b. *Tá kùà híĩ-**m̀**.*
1SG FUT make-NEG
'I shall not do it.'

In |Xaise, the suffix *-tom* negates the two past tense formatives while in future constructions the present tense marker *ke* combines with the verbal suffix *-m*, as in (455):

(455) ***Kè** tá tsìĩ-m̂.*
PRES 1SG sneeze-NEG
'I shall not sneeze.'

Deti (like Cara) makes use of the suffix *-mà.nà* in past constructions. In the future tense, the negation particle *tshénà* is employed in combination with the negated present marker *-tà*.

3.2.8 Tshwa subgroup

Rainer Vossen

3.2.8.1 Nouns

The two varieties described here, Kua and Tsua, exhibit similar but not identical person–gender–number (PGN) enclitics (see Table 6.39). As in the Shua subgroup, ongoing reduction of the nominal marking system is unmistakable. This process appears to be more advanced in Tsua than in Kua. In my data on the latter variety, the masculine plural and feminine singular markers, *-si* and *-ku* respectively, no longer occur on nouns themselves but are substantiated through agreement only. Tsua, on the other hand, has given up nominal PGN marking completely in everyday discourse; however, at least the dual forms and the feminine plural could be elicited, if only by means of structured questionnaires.

TABLE 6.39 PGN ENCLITICS OF KUA AND TSUA

	Kua			Tsua		
	SG	DU	PL	SG	DU	PL
M	*-bè*	*-tsérà*	*(-ku)*	–	*-tsèdè*	–
F	*(-si)*	*-sérà*	*-dzà, -dzì*	–	*-sèdè*	*-dzè*
C	–	*-khórà*	*-rà*	–	*-khòdè*	–

3.2.8.2 Pronouns

Even the little data available tend to stress the unity of Kua, Tsua and Cua as against the Shua varieties (cf. 3.2.7.2), in particular in the first person dual forms. Table 6.40 shows the pronominal subject paradigms deriving from my own data (Kua, Tsua) and from Köhler's pioneering article (1962: 540f.) in which he offers two minimally diverse sets for Cua ("Tywa") from different locations (Nata and Letakana).

In Kua and Tsua, a short and an extended form have been noted for the first person singular pronoun. The same seems to hold true of Cua since Köhler obtained a short form from Letakana and a long one from Nata. Apart from that, complex forms are confined to third person pronouns in all three numbers. They consist of the pronominal element *'é* (*'í* in Kua) followed by a PGN marker.

Object pronouns have been elicited in Kua only. They end regularly in the vowel *a*. In comparison with the subject pronouns no formal discrimination exists in the second person singular, the third person dual, and the first person masculine plural (see Table 6.41).

3.2.8.3 Adjectives

More often than not, adjectival concepts in Shua varieties are conveyed by verbal adjectives of the English "to be X"-type. There are, however, limited sets of proper adjectives, some of which have been compiled in Table 6.42.

TABLE 6.40 PRONOMINAL SUBJECT PARADIGMS OF TSHWA SUBGROUP VARIETIES

	Kua	Tsua	Cua	
			Nata	Letakana
		SINGULAR		
1	*kyé, kyédì*	*kyé, kyédè*	*tyírè*	*tyé*
2M	*tsá*	*tsá*	*tʃá*	*tsá*
2F	*sá*	*sá*	*ʃá*	*sá*
3M	*'í.bè*	*'é.bè*	*'é.bè*	*'é.bè*
3F	*'í.sì*	*'é.sì*	*'é.ʃì*	*'é.sè*
3C	*'í.xùè*	–	–	–
		DUAL		
1M	*tsábè*	*tsábè*	*tsábè*	*tsábè*
1F	*sábè*	*sábè*	*sábè*	*sábè*
1C	*khábè*	*khábè*	*khábè*	*khábè*
2M	*tsárò*	*tsárò*	*tsáró*	*tsáró*
2F	*sárò*	*sárò*	*sáró*	*sáró*
2C	*khárò*	*khárò*	*kháró*	*kháró*
3M	*'é.tsèrà*	*'é.tsèdè*	*'é.tsàrà*	*'é-tsàrà*
3F	*'é.sèrà*	*'é.sèdè*	*'é.sàrà*	*'é.sàrà*
3C	*'é.khòrà*	*'é.khòdè*	*'é.khòrà*	*'é.khòrà*
		PLURAL		
1M	*kâ*	*ká*	*ká*	*ká*
1F	*sí*	*síè*	*síè*	*sí*
1C	*tsí*	*tsíè*	*tsíè*	*tsí*
2M	*káó*	*káó*	*káó*	*káó*
2F	*dzáó*	*sáó*	*sáó*	*sáó*
2C	*tó*	*tó*	*tó*	*tó*
3M	*'é.kùè*	*'é.kùè*	*'é.kùè*	*'é.kùè*
3F	*'é.dzì*	*'é.dzì*	*'é.dzè*	*'é.dzè*
3C	*'é.rè*	*'é.dè*	*'é.nàè*	*'é.rè*

Note: 3C.SG in Kua is to be interpreted as "neuter".

TABLE 6.41 OBJECT PRONOUNS IN KUA

	SINGULAR	DUAL	PLURAL
1M	*kyá*	*tsábà*	*kâ*
1F	*kyá*	*sábà*	*síà*
1C	–	*khábà*	*tsíà*
2M	*tsá*	*tsáròà*	*káóà*
2F	*sá*	*sáròà*	*dzáóà*
2C	–	*kháròà*	*tóà*
3M	*'í.bà*	*'é.tsèrà*	*'é.kùà*
3F	*'í.sà*	*'é.sèrà*	*'é.dzà*
3C	*'ì*	*'é.khòrà*	*'é.rà*

TABLE 6.42 SOME COMMON ADJECTIVES IN KUA AND TSUA

Gloss	Kua	Tsua
'heavy'	*kóḿ*	
'stupid'	*bèè*	
'big'		*ǀûũ*
'short'	*ǀòḿ*	*ǀúm̀*
'new'		*nǀgáò*
'sour'		*tsádú*
'red'		*(w)údú*
'hard'		*kádí*
'cold'		*hùrú*
'small, little'		*ǀ'àré*

Predicative adjectives are placed after and attributive ones before the head noun. PGN marking is practically non-existent.

3.2.8.4 Numerals and quantifiers

Cardinal numbers 'one' through 'three' are lexical stems (see 456). As in other Kalahari Khoe branches, numerals above 'three' are constructed periphrastically, e.g.: Kua 'four' *k'áò-tsàù* (lit.: 'male hand' = 'index finger').

(456)

	Kua	Tsua
'one'	*ǀúí*	*ǀúí*
'two'	*ǀám̀*	*ǀám̀*
'three'	*ŋúnà*	*ŋónà*

Neither ordinal numbers nor the use of numerals, be it morphological or syntactical, are documented in my data collection.

The most common quantifiers found are 'many, much' and 'all':

(457)

	Kua	Tsua
'many, much'	*gùrí-'òè*	*tshíyáà*
'all'	*wúé*	*'úéè*

3.2.8.5 Demonstratives

Both Kua and Tsua have two proximal demonstratives, *ìí* and *nǀní*, and one distal demonstrative, *ùú*. Agreement with the head noun is largely optional and is marked by the nominal PGN forms (cf. Table 6.39). In the masculine singular the exceptional PGN *-bè* (of Kua) is replaced by the more common *-ma* enclitic, here reduced to the bilabial nasal, i.e. *-m*.

As a rule, demonstratives precede the head noun. Some examples from Kua:

(458) *ìí(-ḿ)* *k'áò-khò-bè* 'this man'
DEM(-AGR:M.SG) male-person-M.SG

ùú *'ábà* 'that dog'
DEM dog

*N*ǀ*ní-m̀*	*k'árò-*ǀ*'òã.*	'This is a boy.'
DEM-AGR:M.SG	boy-child	
*N*ǀ*ní-dzì*	ǁ*gàé-*ǀ*'òã.*	'These are girls.'
DEM-AGR:F.PL	female-child	

3.2.8.6 Possessive

The scant data on Tsua seem to suggest that juxtaposition is the only strategy in this variety; e.g. *kyé kàí* 'my house', *tshòé kàí* 'a person's house' (with *rectum–regens* word order). In contrast to this, Kua can make use of both juxtaposition and the possessive particle *di*; e.g. *tsá máà* or *máà tsá dì* 'your (M.SG) head'. The possessive marker always follows the personal pronoun. With nominal possession, juxtaposition appears to be the only strategy (at least in my limited data); e.g. *cxóà máà* 'the elephant's head', *k'áro káà.xù* 'the boy's knife'.

3.2.8.7 Interrogatives

In Kua, the following interrogatives have been found: *maa* ~ *nàá* 'who?, which?' and *nâ.ũ* 'what?'. Their employment is exemplified in (459):

(459) a. *Ǐi* *máá* *k'áò-khòè?*
DEM$_{PROX}$ who male-person
'Who is this man?'

b. *Nâ.ũ* *tsá* *kùà* *káà?*
what 2M.SG PRES want
'What do you want?'

c. *Nà.ré màà* *tsá* ǀ*'àm̀-á-hà?*
who 2M.SG beat-JUNC-IPT
'Who has beaten you?'

Example (459c) demonstrates that *maa* and *nàá* may co-occur, in which case the second vowel in *nàá* is replaced by an enclitic *.re* that takes its high tone.

In possessive contexts, interrogatives follow the juxtaposition strategy whereby the interrogative *nàá* replaces the last vowel by high-toned *.ń*:

(460) *Nà.ń* *júá* *tsá* *kùà* *káà?*
who stick 2M.SG PRES want
'Whose stick do you want?'

3.2.8.8 Verbs

In principle, the verbal slot structures of Kua and Tsua diverge only slightly from the situation in Shua (cf. 3.2.7.8). For Kua, the following morphological sequence has been noted:

(461)

• TA • negation –	verbal base –	derivative suffix(es) –	• passive • juncture –	TA
1	2	3	4	5

Maximal filling of slots is only possible if the tense/aspect marker falls into slot 5 and, at the same time, the statement is negative, in which case the negation marker occurs in slot 1. Such a constellation is given only if the verb is marked for either the negated preterite or negated future. If slot 1 is filled with the present or future marker, slot 5 can never be filled simultaneously. The juncture in slot 4 is restricted to the (non-passive) preterite.

In (462) below the filling of slots is briefly exemplified.

(462) a. ***Xóénà kûũ-è-tà.***
NEG go-PASS-PRES.NEG
'One will not go.'

b. ***Kùà hìĩ.á kûũ-'ò-è.***
FUT go-LOC-PASS
'One will go on.'

c. *Sá* ***kyúù-ká.xù-rù-hì.***
2F.SG buy-CAUS-JUNC-PRET
'You sold.'

Tsua has almost the same slot structure as Kua except that no negation marker must occur in slot 1, thus:

(463)	TA –	verbal base –	derivative suffix(es) –	• passive • juncture –	TA
	1	2	3	4	5

While slot 1 can only be filled by the present or future tense marker, in slot 5 the verb is marked for the preterite or negated present tense. The juncture (slot 4) is used in non-passive constructions. Examples:

(464) a. *Kyé* ***xòé-xù-à-hà.***
1SG run-TERM-JUNC-PRET
'I ran away.'

b. *Kyé* ***kùà*** ***ǀíí-è-tà.***
1SG PRES sing-PASS-PRES.NEG
'I did not sing.'

Example (464b) shows that the preterite is negated by the combination of present *kùà* (slot 1) and negated present *-tà* (slot 5).

3.2.8.8.1 DERIVATIVE SUFFIXES

Deverbal derivation by means of suffixes is less common in Tshwa than in Shua. Only eight functions with partially varying forms have so far been identified; all of them appear to be productive. Table 6.43 below gives an overview.

Comments: (1) Strictly speaking, reduplication is not a case of derivation; it has here been included because of the parallel paradigmatic patterns that derive from reduplicated verbs as compared to verbs extended by suffixes. The functions "repetitive" and "causative" often overlap or cannot clearly be distinguished. (2) More often than not, dative verb stems convey benefactive meaning. (3) Derivative suffixes left unmarked in the "Suffix" column lack inherent tone and are tonally dependent on the verbal base. (4) Combinations of verbal extensions are possible throughout the subgroup.

TABLE 6.43 DERIVATIVE SUFFIXES IN TSHWA VARIETIES

Function	Suffix	Lg.	Basic verb	Gloss	Extended verb	Gloss
Causative$_1$	*-ka.xu*	Kua	*káì*	'recover'	*káì-kà.xù*	'cure'
		Tsua	*thŭũ*	'hurt'	*thùũ-ká.xù*	'cause pain'
Causative$_2$	REDUPL	Kua	*|'óè*	'be full'	*|'óè-|'òè*	'fill'
Repetitive	REDUPL	Kua	*k'éé*	'cry'	*k'éé-k'èè*	'weep'
		Tsua	*xùń*	'grind'	*xùń-xùǹ*	'keep grinding'
Dative	*-ma*	Kua	*t'àá*	'carve'	*t'àá-mà*	'carve for'
	-mà	Tsua	*xòó*	'hold'	*xòó-mà*	'hold for'
Reflexive	*-hì*	Kua	*k'áń*	'cut'	*k'áń-hì*	'cut oneself'
	-hi	Tsua	*|'íí*	'shave'	*|'íí-hì*	'shave oneself'
Reciprocal	*-ku*	Kua	*k'ûĩ*	'live'	*k'ûĩ-kù*	'live together'
	-tsu	Tsua	*khàé*	'spear'	*khàé-tsù*	'spear each other'
Locative	*-'o*	Kua	*kûũ*	'go'	*kûũ-'ò*	'go on'
		Tsua	*ǁ'àḿ*	'beat'	*ǁ'àḿ-'ò*	'knock out'
Terminative	*-xù*	Kua	*'úè*	'break' (tr.)	*'úè-xù*	'smash'
		Tsua	*xòé*	'run away'	*xòé-xù*	'run away from'

3.2.8.8.2 JUNCTURE

Tshwa varieties make use of the juncture only if the verb occurs in the preterite form. The base of the juncture is /a/, allomorphs are relatively common, particularly in Kua (see Table 6.44 below).

TABLE 6.44 JUNCTURE ALLOMORPHS IN THE TSHWA SUBGROUP

	a	*ɲa*	*ra*	*re*	*ro*	*ru*	*na*	*∅*	*e*	*o*
Kua	+	+	+	+	+	+	+	+	+	+
Tsua	+	+		+	+		+			

In Kua, the base of the juncture occurs irrespective of the end of the verb; in Tsua its employment is restricted to verbs ending in a nasal consonant or high vowel. The zero juncture is frequently used in Kua after verbs ending in a vowel sequence. The allomorph *-na* often, but not always, follows verbs ending in a low nasal vowel and some verbs having a CVCV structure. In both varieties the allomorph *-ɲa* was found to occur exclusively after verbs ending in a high front and nasal vowel; there are, however, some exceptions to this rule as, for example, in Kua:

(465) *tsĭĩ* 'sneeze' *tsìĩ-**á**-hì*
sneeze-JUNC-PRET

vs.
xûĩ 'be pregnant' *xùù-**ɲá**-hì*
be.pregnant-JUNC-PRET

A phenomenon exclusive to Kua is assimilation of the juncture base /a/ to the verb-final vowel; it is confined to the mid-vowels /e/ and /o/, in which case the juncture allomorphs are also [e] and [o] respectively.

3.2.8.8.3 PASSIVE

The passive marker is *-e* throughout the subgroup.

3.2.8.8.4 TENSE/ASPECT MARKER

In view of the fragmentary data collection available on Tshwa it seems impossible to distinguish between tense and aspect (TA). Occurring forms are therefore treated jointly.

Throughout the subgroup, present, past (preterite) and future represent firmly attested temporal levels. Present and preterite appear as particles, while the future marker is a complex form. The negated present is expressed by a verbal suffix of its own. Table 6.45 gives a brief overview of TA markers in Tshwa.

TABLE 6.45 TENSE/ASPECT MARKERS IN TSHWA

TA category	Kua	Tsua
Preterite	*-hì*	*-hì, -ha*
Imperfect	*-hà*	
Present	*kùà*	*kùà, kò*
Negated present	*-tà*	*-tà*
Future	*kùà hĩĩ.á*	*kùà hĩĩ.á*

The occurrence of two distinct present formatives in Tsua can presently not be explained sufficiently. Perhaps *kò* is a result of reciprocal vowel assimilation in *kùà*. Likewise, the accurate usage of *-ha*/*-hà* and *-hì* largely remains to be seen. The future marker is formed by a combination of present tense *kùà* plus *hĩĩ.á*, which in itself may consist of the verb *hĩĩ* 'make' plus the base of the juncture. All in all, the data at our disposal are too meagre to provide deeper insight into the TA system of Tshwa varieties.

For examples of TA employment in Tshwa, see 3.2.8.8 (462 and 464).

3.2.8.8.5 NEGATION

Both varieties share the negated present formative *-tà*. Preterite and future constructions employ composite forms by making use of the negated present formative *-tà* as a general negation marker that is indirectly preceded by a TA marker (Tsua) or a particle of as yet unknown origin (Kua) (see 466).

(466)

	Kua	Tsua
Preterite	*àkà . . . -tà*	*kùà (tûũ) . . . -tà*
Future	*xóénà . . . -tà*	*hĩĩ.á . . . -tà*

3.3 Southern Khoesan (Tuu)

Tom Güldemann

3.3.1 Taa (East !Xoon dialect)[2]

3.3.1.1 Introduction

East !Xoon shows a fairly neat distinction between lexical stems and grammatical morphemes (alias grams) regarding their phonotactic pattern. Stems have a strong preference for the shape C(C)V(C)V; grams have a simpler CV-form and their initial consonants are relatively low on the strength hierarchy (Traill 1985: 173ff.). The majority of word forms are constituted by either one lexical stem or one gram; in both cases the final vowel can be subject to certain inflectional changes (*inter alia* important for transitive verbs). Parts of speech referring to nominal entities more often involve one or more suffixes. In general, the language has relatively little bound morphology and the majority of grams are particles.

3.3.1.2 Pronouns

Pronouns mostly come in two series, an unmarked and an emphatic variant. There are six pronoun categories for speech-act participants, as given in Table 6.46 (the allomorphs in the first person plural can be reconstructed as an earlier inclusive–exclusive distinction).

TABLE 6.46 PRONOUNS FOR SPEECH-ACT PARTICIPANTS IN EAST !XOON

	Singular	Plural	Dual
1st person	*n̄('n̄)*	*īh('ī), 'īsî*	*ǂnáĩ('i)*
2nd person	*āh('a)*	*ūh('ū)*	*ǂnûm('ū)*

A set of five pronouns is used to encode third persons; these are exponents of agreement classes which constitute a rather complex system of noun categorization (see 3.3.1.3.1). These classes are also indexed by concords in certain inflected word forms. The forms of class indices are given in Table 6.47.

TABLE 6.47 THIRD PERSON PRONOUNS AND CONCORD FORMATIVES IN EAST !XOON

	Free pronoun	Enclitic concord	Corresponding noun ending
Class 1	*ìh*	*-i*	*-i, -li, -bi*
Class 2	*ã̀h('ã̀)*	*-ã*	*-ã, -n(a), -m(a)*
Class 3	*èh('è)*	*-e*	*-(j)e, -le, -be*
Class 4	*ùh('ũ)*	*-u*	*-u, -lu, -bu*
Class 5	*ǹh(ǹ)*	*-n*	none

The dual pronouns are apparently related to the numeral *ǂnûm* 'two' (see Güldemann 2004a); plural pronouns in general can co-occur with the stem *ǀâe* 'three'.

All pronouns substitute for nouns in major syntactic contexts, functioning as subject, object, adjunct and possessor. After certain parts of speech they are supplemented or replaced by the enclitic concord forms (see Chapter 7, section 3.3.1.5). Deictic, relative and interrogative markers are not expressed by way of canonical pronominal elements and thus are not treated here.

3.3.1.3 Nouns

3.3.1.3.1 GENDER

The five agreement classes established by the above pronominal elements pattern according to the number categories singular and plural, thereby creating a system of genders, which are mostly pairs of singular–plural classes. This is sketched in Figure 6.1 (cf. Güldemann 2000b).

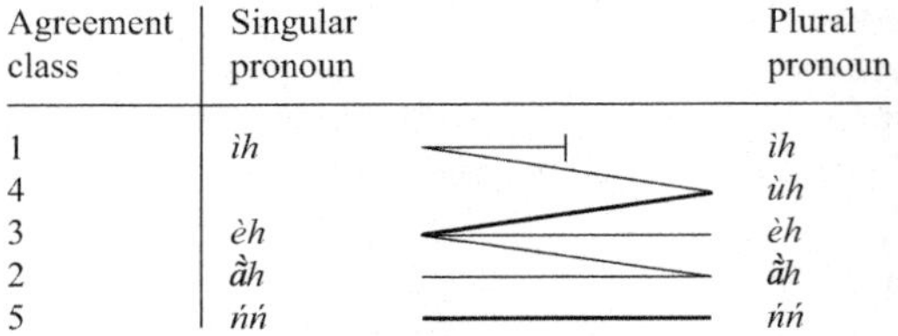

Agreement class	Singular pronoun	Plural pronoun
1	*ìh*	*ìh*
4		*ùh*
3	*èh*	*èh*
2	*ã̀h*	*ã̀h*
5	*ńń*	*ńń*

FIGURE 6.1 AGREEMENT CLASSES AND NON-INQUORATE GENDERS IN EAST !XOON

Note: Bold lines indicate inter-sententially relevant genders.

East !Xoon has two gender systems, one for *inter*-sentential contexts, and the other for *intra*-sentential contexts. The first one is simple and appears to have conflated the genders of the second, more complex system into a binary distinction according to animacy. The system holding for gender agreement within the clause is highly lexicalized and neither the meaning nor the form of a noun needs to betray its gender assignment. It is also important to recognize for this second system that the majority of agreement classes do not imply a number feature. That is, a class can refer with one noun to the singular, with another to the plural. This fairly free mapping of classes over number is one reason for the fact that there are fewer agreement classes than genders (alias class pairs). The preliminary analysis of gender assignment for a part of the nominal lexicon is given in Table 6.48.

TABLE 6.48 NOUN GENDERS IN EAST !XOON (PRELIMINARY)

Class pair	Number of items	Discernible assignment criteria (with number of items in brackets)
Intra-sentential agreement		
1	8	noun ending *-i* (4)
1/2*	1	
1/3*	1	
1/4	53	noun endings *-li*/*-lu* (18) and *-i*/*-ba* (8)
2/(2)	118	parts of a whole including body parts (53); offspring (2) and all diminutives; nationalities and other social groups (6); all deverbal *sà*-nominalizations (singular); harmful ~ dangerous things (12); human activity and associated objects (11)
3/2	25	noun endings *-e*/*-m* (16)
3/(3)	113	liquids and other entities without a fixed form (14); edible plants (especially those eaten for moisture) (8); 'meat' and alienated body parts (12); other non-count nouns (5); recent loanwords (39); all place names (singular)
3/4	11	terms of kinship and social relations (9); all personal names (singular)
5/2*	1	'thing'
Inter-sentential agreement		
3/4		animate
5/5		inanimate

Notes: * possibly inquorate gender; *n*/*(n)* gender with uni- and/or trans-numeral items, relevance of assignment criterion unclear.

The class pairs marked in Table 6.48 by an asterisk seem to be lexical exceptions (cf. Corbett's "inquorate genders", 1991: 170–75), so the number of productive genders is likely to be lower than ten. In the class pairs comprising relatively many items one can discern groups of nouns which share a particular feature in meaning or form. These sets of nouns can be viewed as gender cores and reflect criteria that were, and/or still are, productive for the assignment of a noun to a particular gender. However, there are many exceptions to these generalizations so the categorization system as a whole appears to be rather arbitrary.

One type of assignment is morphonological in nature: quite a few noun forms demonstrate a correlation between their inflectional ending (last column of Table 6.47) and the agreeing pronoun. However, since the majority of nouns do not show such a correspondence, nominal gender marking is mostly "covert".

3.3.1.3.2 NUMBER

Although there are only two categories, singular and plural, number marking on nouns is a complex matter in East !Xoon, because the formal alternations are quite diverse and irregular across the lexicon. Owing to this fact, and possibly also due to under-analysis, the following information can only be a list of marking devices and not a final set of morphological rules.

Some nouns do not change their form and are perhaps best analysed as not partaking in the number distinction, for example, the noun *ǀgá̰m* '*Crotalaria damanensis*'. A typical feature of Tuu languages in general is that a restricted set of nouns has different suppletive stems co-varying with number. Compare the following (agreement class in brackets):

(467)	SG	*tâa* (3)	*tâa qáe* (2)	*tâa à̰a* (2)	*!ùm* (3)
	PL	*tûu* (4)	*ǀà̰ã* (2)	*ǁxàã* (2)	*Θàã* (2)
		'person'	'woman'	'man'	'eland' (T94: 154, 78)

As mentioned above, a noun form can display a recognizable inflectional ending. This often changes with number; its form may or may not correlate with the agreement class. For example, while the pair of endings and the class indices correspond with *ǁgá.bi* (SG, class 1), *ǁgá.bu-tê* (PL, class 4) 'woman's rear apron', there is no such correlation with *ǀà̰h.m* (SG, class 1), *ǀà̰h.ma-tê* (PL, class 4) 'violet-eared waxbill'.

Since number is so poorly integrated with gender, it is not surprising that this feature is expressed on many nouns by a separate set of true number suffixes. The default plural marker is *-tê*, because it occurs with the large majority of nouns. Other plural suffixes are *-nî*, *-sá*, *-sâ̰* and *-tû*. Sometimes, a plural suffix replaces a separable suffix of the singular form; such possible singular markers are *-sì/-sí*, *-sè/-sê*, *-kú*, *-ká*, *-bà* and *-bè*. Some suffixes imply a particular agreement class; for example, plurals with *-tû* consistently go into class 4 (see 3.3.1.3.3 for a historical explanation).

Changes of suffix, inflectional ending, and the stem can all co-occur. For example, the singular form of 'beetle' *ǀgà̰h.i-sí* (class 1) is changed to plural *ǀgà̰h.m-sá-tê* (class 2), which has a different ending and even two suffixes; the plural changes of *Θnṵ́ũ* (class 1) 'louse species' to *Θnàã-tê* (class 4) consist of adding a suffix as well as altering both stem (note the lost pharyngealization) and ending.

It is difficult to represent transparently the complexity and interaction of marking gender and number in the interlinearization of examples. The following conventions are applied, if found relevant: (a) a discernible inflectional ending of a noun form is set off from the rest of the stem by a dot, (b) relevant agreement classes are given in the gloss line, also separated by a dot from the preceding meaning gloss. The second principle results in a two-digit number, the first digit for the singular class, the second for the plural one; the translation and the possible presence of a number suffix disambiguate which of the two agreement classes is relevant. Some nouns only occur in one number category and accordingly only have one glossed agreement class. These conventions convey the noun's gender, allow one to check whether noun ending and class correspond with each other, and finally help to identify agreement triggers within a syntactic phrase. Class markers on elements other than nouns either serve as pronouns or mark agreement: in the first case the glossed class number is followed by the gloss PRO, in the second case the class number is preceded or followed by an arrow which points towards the agreement trigger.

3.3.1.3.3 DERIVATION

The sparseness of affixal morphology is balanced by the existence of productive processes of noun compounding, conveying nominal concepts such as sex, shape ~ size, and social-group membership. The compounds are based on semantically generic human nouns as the head of the complex nominal.

(468) *ǀá̰i ǂgá̰i* — lion female — 'female lion'; *ts'óo ǀ'óã qáe* — bottle female — 'a wide shaped bottle' (T94: 107, 177)

(469) *tâa à̰a* — person male — 'man'; *ǀà̰ba à̰a* — thorn plant male — 'long thin thorn'; *!ōo à̰a* — knife male — 'spear' (T94: 195)

(470) *ǀ'àã Θàa* — fire child — 'a small/distant fire'; *!xóɲa-tê Θ'âni* — PROP-PL children — 'the !Xoon people' (T94: 47)

There are also many lexicalized compounds expressing a great variety of concepts; their constituents do not always occur in isolation. A recurrent and semantically partly transparent pattern, especially frequent for body part terms, is found with certain relational nouns as compound heads such as *ǀnàn* 'fruit, head, tuber', *tshôe* 'inside', etc.

As can be expected, the gender of such compounds is that of the head noun (see Güldemann 2000b for a discussion of the seemingly problematic case of *à̰a*- and *qáe*-compounds). This is mostly gender 2/2, because the head nouns of compounds are inherently relational ('part of whole', 'child of', etc.) and such nouns on their own usually go into this gender (cf. Table 6.48). Somewhat more remarkable is the number marking of compounds in that both head and modifier are subject to relevant formal alternations, as with the double marking on the plural counterparts in (471) and (472).

(471) SG *ǀxá.n tshô.e* (2)
PL *ǀxá.na(-tê) tshô.ã-tê* (2)
'floating ribs, flank' (T94: 59)

(472) SG *kâ ǀà̰.li Θàa* (2)
PL *(kâ) ǀà̰.lu-tê Θ'âni* (2)
'baby blue wildebeest' (T94: 53)

Compound heads can grammaticalize into semantically opaque and/or more productive suffixes. This can explain grammatical features of certain complex words. For example, human plural nouns ending in *-tû* belong to class 4; the suffix is likely to be derived from an earlier compound head *tûu* 'people' which still exists as a class 4 noun.

Other phenomena related to derivation and morphologically complex nouns are still poorly understood. For example, Traill (1994: 24f.) mentions irregular lexicalized diminutives in addition to the productive diminutive compound; these often involve a prefix *kâ-* and/or a suffix *-bà*. A particle *kâ* is also attested as a lexicalized formative with non-diminutive nouns, for example, *kâ !ā̠he*, a name for a plant species. The existence and kind of denominal derivation processes also need further study. At least some nouns appear to be converted into verbs by adding the MPO marker *kV*.

3.3.1.4 Nominal modifiers

The majority of elements which can function as attributive modifiers of nouns show a grammatical behaviour similar to canonical verbal lexemes. They take tense–aspect markers as the nucleus of a predicative expression; they can undergo deverbal nominalization; and they must occur in a relative clause as nominal attributes. On account of these morphosyntactic characteristics, such items do not seem to constitute a word category in its own right – although called "adjectives" by Traill (1994: 33) –, they are best classified instead as stative verbs. Lexemes belonging to this group also serve to express notions that in other languages are taken care of by pronominal elements. In (473), the stem *āh'ã* is the predicative nucleus of a relative clause and conveys the meaning 'which' in conjunction with the sentence-initial interrogative marker *ǀa*.

(473)	*ǀā-n*	*ǂ'âa*	*kēē*	*ǁû.a*	*tēē*	*āh'ã*	*kē?ē?*
	Q-1SG	shoot	MPO:3>	springbok.32	REL:3	be.which	REL:<3

'Which springbok should I shoot at?' (T94: 195)

Two demonstratives can also be viewed as such attributive predicates, as they have the form of canonical relative clauses: *t*-concord-*jà* *k*-concord (proximate) and *t*-concord-*sàk*-concord (remote).

(474)	*tûu*	*tú'uu-sà*	*kù*
	people.4	REL:4PRO-REM.DEI	REL:<4

'those (remote) people' (T94: 20)

Cardinal numerals as a set are heterogeneous regarding their word category status. There are three such items: *ǂ'ûã* 'one', *ǂ'nûm* 'two', *ǁâe* 'three'. When followed by the MPO marker *kV*, they are used as verbs and then mean 'be at one with', 'pair up with', 'make a threesome', respectively. As attributive modifiers, the stems for 'two' and 'three' directly follow the noun without any formal change – a behaviour that is identical to that of a head noun in a genitive construction. The stem for 'one' is different in that it agrees with its noun in class by way of stem-final concord changes. This is parallel to a few other post-posed nominal attributes like *!xaV* 'big, senior, many', *ǁàhV* 'old', and the deictics *tV'V*, *tVV* and *'VV* (the last two are exemplified here).

(475)	*tâa*	*tēe*	*ǀqhúũ*	*'àã*
	person.3	DEI:<3	white.person.2	DEI:<3
	'this person'		'this white person' (T94: 154, 197)	

Modifiers of the last type constitute a separate small class of adjectives, which is different from both verbs and nouns.

3.3.1.5 Verbs

3.3.1.5.1 NOMINAL CROSS-REFERENCING

Verb stems are not subject to morphological changes with one important exception: transitive verbs show object cross-reference, brought about by indexing the object's noun class in the inflectional ending. With some verbs, this change not only affects the second syllable peak, usually a vowel, but also the C_2-position of the stem in that the consonants *b* or *j* are inserted vis-à-vis the neutral form. The consonant seems to correlate with the quality of the second vowel: the labial *b* occurs in stems with a rounded V_2 and the front glide *j* in stems with a non-rounded V_2 (compare the verb table in T94: 28).

Another type of non-morphological concordance between verb and noun can be identified: parallel to number marking on nouns, some basic verb meanings are expressed by a pair of suppletive stems, which co-vary with the number feature of an associated nominal (see also the discussion by Dickens and Traill 1977). The subject determines the stem form of intransitives, the object that of transitives.

(476)	Singular	Plural	Plural distributive		
	tshûu	*!'áã*		'sit'	(T94: 271)
	ǀ'ûi	*ǀq'án-tâ*		'be small, few, thin'	(T94: 272)
	ṵ̂lu		*!gâ'o*	'enter, plant'	(T94: 226, 258)
	ǀùa	*ǀhàõ*	*!áu*	'take, catch'	(T94: 215)

3.3.1.5.2 TENSE, ASPECT, MODALITY AND OTHER CLAUSE OPERATORS

Verbal categories like tense, aspect and modality are not encoded in the verb; instead, independent markers precede (and in one case follow) the verb or verb sequence. These are either auxiliary verbs or lexically opaque particles; a clear-cut distinction between the two cannot always be drawn, though, because the latter can emerge from the former via grammaticalization. The following functional characterizations of predicate markers are only tentative; a more conclusive analysis must await a careful examination of a larger number of tokens in their discourse contexts.

Two markers stand out regarding their position vis-à-vis the predicate: (a) *ǀĩi*, marking resultative/perfect/stative and derived from the verb 'be present, here', occurs phrase-finally; (b) *bà*, possibly an imperfective gram, tends to occur immediately before the main verb and, thus, is normally preceded by all other predicate markers. Other verb grams are: *ǀqhúa* negation, *à* past, *ē* root possibility, *qúma* (also *qóma*, *qúba*, *qóba*) hearsay evidence; the marker *ńń* remains functionally unclear. It possibly encodes modality or sentence type.

3.3.1.5.3 DERIVATION

Valence-changing derivation is accomplished by particles or periphrastic constructions. The collocation of a verb and the MPO marker leads to an increase in valence, for example, *ǀnûu* 'run (S)' > *ǀnûu kV* 'cause to run away' (T94: 31). Passivization is achieved by placing the patient in subject position and putting the particle *kâ* before the transitive verb. The agent can be expressed in an adjunct phrase established by means of the MPO marker.

(477) *èh ń bà tā̰-e tâa.* ⇒
3PRO ? IMPF hear-3> person.3
'He hears the person.'

tâa *ń* *bà* *kâ* *tą̄ã* *kè.*
person.3 ? IMPF PASS hear MPO:3PRO
'The person is heard by him.' (T94: 31)

A particle *kâ* before the verb stem does not always render a passive derivation. In some cases, this element is an obligatory part of a complex lexical item (T94: 33), occurring with both intransitive and transitive verbs. Some examples are: *kâ qáɲa* 'be beautiful (P)', *kâ ǂ'āõ* 'be short (P)', *kâ !nābu* 'stagger, shake, shiver', *kâ !nṳhũ sV* 'remove'; the plural meaning with stative verbs is a partly regular semantic phenomenon (cf. Gruber 1975 and Collins 1998 regarding the similar effect of *kí* in ǂHoan).

Fixed collocations of stem+particle, stem+stem, or even stem+particle *kâ*+stem are a generally pervasive phenomenon in the East !Xoon verb lexicon (T94: 31ff.). Their existence can be explained partially as a result of lexicalization and semantic specialization of serial verb constructions or sequences of verb+relational gram.

Verbal derivation is also accomplished by verbal periphrases: causatives of stative verbs can be formed by the verb *'àhn* 'do' and a deverbal nominalization as in (478):

(478) *n̄n̄* *ń* *bà* *'àh-na* *ǂ'āba-sà.*
1SG ? IMPF do-2> be.short-NOM.2
Lit.: 'I am making shortness, i.e. shortening (it).' (T94: 149)

Processes of category-changing derivation are also attested. Deverbal nominalizations are formed in two ways (T94: 29ff.): (a) the basic stem is converted without any morphological change into a noun of class 1 or 3, and (b) the enclitic *-sà* is attached to the last element of a verb phrase (see Chapter 7, section 3.3.1.3.2). The distinction between the two appears to be abstract vs. process nominalization, respectively. Deverbal adverbializations of intransitive stative verbs are accomplished by means of the pre-posed particle *té* (T94: 18f.).

3.3.2 |Xam[3]

3.3.2.1 Introduction

Orthographic words in Bleek and Lloyd's |Xam data can show considerable length and phonetic substance. Since the basic phonotactic patterns typical for Tuu languages, namely C(C)V(C)V for lexical stems and CV for grams, are also largely applicable to |Xam (B28–30: 86f.), it is clear that such complex words (e.g. those with a non-initial strong consonant) involve more than one meaning-bearing unit from a synchronic or diachronic viewpoint.

However, nothing definitive can be said regarding the actual status of an orthographically bound morpheme as a suffix, particle, or even free word. It is not clear which word concept underlies the transcription and there exists considerable variation, in that one and the same element can be written as a bound or free form. In general, the degree of agglutination or isolation in |Xam cannot conclusively be ascertained. From an areal perspective, isolation is more likely, but it is nevertheless possible that phonological words in |Xam were more complex than in other languages.

A second problem in the analysis of |Xam morphology relates to the identification of particular items, because a number of functionally different grams have an identical or similar orthographic form. For several reasons, these are often difficult to distinguish. Most importantly, the available text translations frequently fail to reflect the semantic-functional subtleties that are necessary to disambiguate the effect of a certain element in different contexts. Moreover, morphotactic clues for gram identification are rare as virtually all inflectional or derivational changes occur host-finally. Also, while morphology differs in many languages across major parts of speech like nouns, verbs, etc., ǀXam grams are to a considerable extent similar or identical between nominal and verbal expressions, in spite of the fact that there seems to exist a noun–verb distinction. The same similarity or identity of grammatical morphemes holds from a historical perspective: a form which is a grammatically productive morpheme with some stems occurs in other lexemes as an obligatory element that appears to have become petrified and lost any independent meaning. Finally, the lack of prosodic information as well as morphonological gram alternations can also blur certain underlying distinctions. As will be demonstrated below, the above remarks apply in particular to the three morphological devices of stem reduplication, suffixation of *-ken*, *-gen*, *-ten*, *-ng*, and suffixation of *-a*.

3.3.2.2 Pronouns

ǀXam displays a distinction between unmarked pronouns used in subject, object and possessor function and oblique forms, which are the pronominal counterparts of nominal adjuncts and are possibly composed of a preposition and the unmarked form.

There are five pronominal categories for speech-act participants; the inclusive–exclusive distinction is absent in the oblique series.

TABLE 6.49 PRONOUNS FOR SPEECH-ACT PARTICIPANTS IN ǀXAM

	Unmarked series		Oblique series	
	Singular	Plural	Singular	Plural
1st person inclusive		*i*		*hii*
1st person exclusive	*ng*	*si*	*ki*	*hii*
2nd person	*a*	*u*	*haa*	*huu*

The two sets of third person pronouns are given in Table 6.50. These can be mistaken as reflecting a canonical number opposition due to the fact that one of them is associated always with the singular and the other predominantly with the plural. In reality, they are exponents of agreement classes which encode two number and two gender categories.

TABLE 6.50 THIRD PERSON PRONOUNS AND RELATED AGREEMENT FORMS IN ǀXAM

	Unmarked pronoun	Pronoun + declarative *-ng*	Oblique pronoun	Deictic pronoun	Relative focus marker
Class 1	*hã, ha*	*hang*	*ãa*	*ha*	*aa*
Class 2	*hĩ, hi*	*hing*	*ĩi*	*he*	*ee*

The two variants of the unmarked pronouns are free allomorphs, or rather allographs, according to the available data. Their reduplication yields emphatic variants. The deictic pronouns occur either as independent pro-forms or together with post-posed appositional nouns; they combine back-reference with some form of pragmatic salience (topicality or focality) of the referential entity. The class-sensitive relative focus marker is used in relative and cleft-like constructions. (For further information, see Chapter 7.)

3.3.2.3 Nouns

3.3.2.3.1 GENDER

According to Güldemann (2000b), |Xam is a gender language. Its system is, however, restricted in having two genders only: gender I with an overt singular–plural distinction contains the majority of the nominal lexicon including all animate nouns; gender II has relatively few items, but among them unexpectedly many body parts (see Figure 6.2). The only agreement targets are the pronominal items listed in Table 6.50.

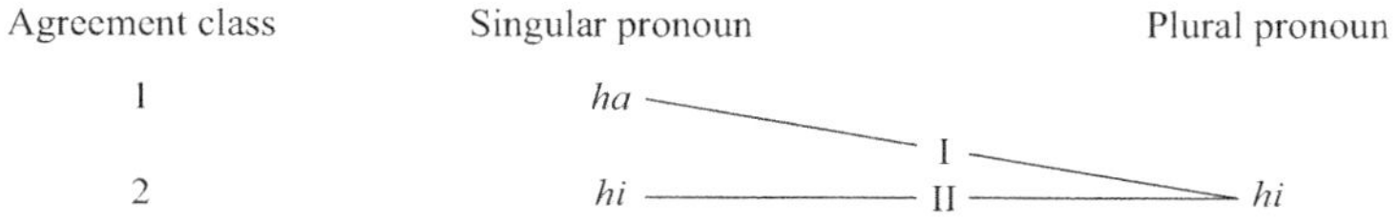

Agreement class	Singular pronoun		Plural pronoun
1	*ha*	I	
2	*hi*	II	*hi*

FIGURE 6.2 AGREEMENT CLASSES AND GENDERS

3.3.2.3.2 NUMBER

Nominal number is highly irregular across the |Xam lexicon (see the overview in B28–30: 88–92). In view of this situation and the possible semantic complexity of this domain in some other Khoesan languages (see, e.g., Gruber 1975 and Collins 1998 regarding ǂHoan), it is unclear whether the functioning of number marking will ever be recovered fully from the Bleek–Lloyd corpus.

From a formal point of view, the following marking patterns can be identified: there are quite a few nouns which are not subject to any, at least segmental, changes in the plural (particularly frequent with animal terms). Concerning segmental number changes it is useful to distinguish between simple and complex formations. Simple devices are:

(a) lexical suppletion (with a range of items comparable to East !Xoon of Taa),
(b) full and partial reduplication of the noun, and
(c) addition or replacement of a suffix.

Compare some examples from D.F. Bleek's lists (discernible morpheme breaks marked by hyphens):

(479)	SG	*!ui*	*tu*	*|ã*	*mama*	*!x'ui*	*g!wa-ra*
	PL	*!k'e*	*tu-tu*	*|an-de*	*mama-gu*	*!x'ui-ten*	*g!wa-ten*
		'person'	'mouth'	'brother'	'mother'	'sieve'	'metal knife'

Among the plural suffixes shown in (479), *-gu* has a special status because it is an "associative plural": it can occur with kinship terms and all personal names and then means 'X and his/her people'.

The majority of nouns employ more than one of the above strategies including additional stem-final mutations. Virtually every combination of different number changes (a notable exception is suppletion+reduplication) and order of their application appear to be attested. Compare the selection of singular–plural pairs in (480).

(480)	SG	*ǀwa-ra*	*!xaa*	*ǀũ-ru*	*kum*
	PL	*ǀwa-ǀwa-ra*	*!xa-!xaa-de*	*ǀu-ǀu-di*	*ku-kum-i*
		'mother animal'	'brother-in-law'	'fingernail'	'story'

The suffixes *-ken*, *-gen*, *-ten*, *-ng* as number markers deserve special treatment. They are frequent and combine even more freely with other devices as shown in (481).

(481)	SG	*ǀao*	*gǀo-gǀo*	*xu*	*g!ui-ten*
	PL	*ǀao-ken-ǀao-ken*	*gǀo-ken-gǀo-ken*	*xu-xuu-ken*	*g!ui-g!ui*
		'hill'	'whirlwind'	'face'	'silver jackal'

(482)	SG	*ǀua-ten*	*gou-ru*	*ko-ro*	*!au'u-ken*
	PL	*ǀua-ǀua-ten*	*gou-gou-ten*	*ko-ten-ko-ten*	*!au-!au-wa-ng*
		'star'	'blister'	'jackal'	'body'

(483)	SG	*ǀkha*	*gǀeri-ten-ti*	*ǀha*	*gwai*
	PL	*ǀkhai-ten*	*gǀeri-ten-de*	*ǀhau-ken-gu*	*tu-ken(-gu)*
		'stick'	'little bird'	'spouse'	'male'

The status of such suffixes in individual word forms is a serious problem of analysis. Suffixes with identical orthographic shapes occur in a variety of morphotactically similar, but functionally different contexts, making it difficult to identify the appropriate function of a given suffix. D.F. Bleek (*ibid.*) sometimes equates in fact a suffix of a plural noun with the subject enclitic *-ken* – her "emphatic nominative" (see Chapter 7, section 3.3.2.2.1). This analysis (applied, e.g., to the plural pattern of *ǀao* 'hill' in 481) is unlikely because it implies an awkward scope of plural reduplication. Moreover, a different allomorphic variation between the subject enclitic and the formally similar number suffix indicates that number markers like *-ken*, *-ten*, etc. are morphemes in their own right. Another problem is that such suffixes occur in some singular noun forms; this could partly be due to yet another suffix, *-ken*, found in derivational processes (see below). Since the status of plural *-ken*, *-ten*, etc. is not always clear, these may be glossed occasionally as ?PL.

3.3.2.4 Derivation

Derivational noun compounding in ǀXam has a functional range largely similar to East !Xoon: the nouns 'man, male' and 'woman, female' after the modified noun express the sex of animates; small size is conveyed by the noun 'child, offspring'.

(484)	*to'i*	*gwai*	*to'i-ta*	*tu-ken*
	ostrich	male	ostrich-?	males-?PL
	'male ostrich'		'male ostriches' (B28–30: 96)	

(485)	*to'i*	*ǀ'aiti*	*to'i-ta*	*ǀaa-gen*
	ostrich	female	ostrich-?	women-?PL
	'female ostrich'		'female ostriches' (B28–30: 96)	

(486)	*ǀho*	*ʘwa*	*ǀho-ǀho-ka*	*!au-ken*
	bag	child	P-bag-?	children-?PL
	'little bag'		'little bags' (B28–30: 95f.)	

As shown in (484–486), the plurals of these grammatically productive compounds are not achieved, as could be expected, by just changing the form of the head noun. Instead, they have the following structure: the head noun is pluralized (this happens to be complex itself involving the *-ken* suffix as well as a suppletive stem); the modified stem, too, occurs in the plural form as far as such exists; and an element *ka, ta* (segmentally identical with the genitive marker) occurs between the two.

Another pluralizing pattern holds for lexicalized compounds with body parts as head: only the modifier is marked for plural, while the head remains unchanged as in (487):

(487)	*n!oa-n!oa-ng*	*xu*	*!au-!au-ten*	*tu*
	PL-foot-?PL	face	PL-?-?PL	hole (< mouth)
	'soles'		'bellies' (BL11: 12f., 153)	

Provided Bleek and Lloyd did not miss non-segmental changes marking plural, this is identical to what Collins (1998: 17–23) calls in ǂHoan "plural inheritance", or rather to a particular case thereof. The general phenomenon is that the syntactic head in a complex nominal with plural interpretation "inherits" the number feature of the satellite. In the particular case of a body part as head, this "plural inheritance" is grammaticalized, i.e., number marking on the body part noun is obligatorily absent.

Derivational changes of a noun to another category have not yet been identified. Deverbal nominalizations and such elements as *ǂamΘwa* 'gently, a little' and *ǂumΘwa* 'subsequently', which have the form of diminutive nominals, encode manner in a predicate slot before the propositional main verb. Since this syntactic phenomenon is not accompanied by formal changes in the items concerned, and since there is no recognizable lexical category of adverbs, it does not necessarily reflect the conversion of nouns into adverbs; it can also be viewed as the employment of nominals in a non-typical context.

3.3.2.5 Nominal modifiers

Some lexical stems are used predominantly as modifying attributes of nouns; these all occur post-nominally. This functional and structural commonality aside, they reveal hardly any other characteristic in morphological design or grammatical behaviour which would justify subsuming them under the unitary lexical category "adjective". On the contrary, most items show features indicating their alignment with either of the two basic categories, nouns and verbs. The suppletive or morphologically complex plural forms of some of the most frequent adjective-like items cannot resolve the problem, because such number marking devices apply primarily to nouns and verbs.

One group of modifiers follow the noun asyndetically. They are difficult to distinguish formally from nominal head nouns of derivational compounds; some items even show nominal properties: *korekore* (SG), *koritenkoriten* (PL) 'round' is also or even primarily a noun meaning 'ball'; the phrase with *kuu* 'all, whole' betrays the syntax of genitive constructions, because it is linked to the modified noun via *ka, ta*, as in (488).

(488)	*ha-ng*	*n|e*	*tãi*	*g!wãxu*	*ka*	*kuu.*
	3PRO-PSE	IMPF	walk	sky	GEN	whole
	'It travels across the whole sky.' (BL11: 44f.)					

However, some such items may meet the criterion of sufficient morphosyntactic distinctness from a synchronic perspective and could represent the core of an incipient class of adjectives. The formative *Θwa* (SG) 'small' can be mentioned here: while its origin in the noun 'child' is clear from a comparative perspective, it does not occur as an independent lexeme in |Xam. This also seems to apply to such items as *!eri* (SG), *!e!eten* (PL) 'big' and *koo* (SG), *kuiten* (PL) 'other'.

There is another group of adnominal stems expressing qualities, for example, *ǀuri* (SG), *ǀuten* (PL) 'short'; *!u'iya* (SG), *!u'i!u'ita* (PL) 'large, grown, abundant'; and *!xoowa* (SG), *!xo!xooka* (PL) 'tall, high'. When used as attributes, they must occur in a relative clause and they often incorporate the stative suffix *-a*, which indicates their affinity to the word category verb. The deictic element *a*, which seems to encode proximity and is glossed in (489) as 'be here', also belongs partly to this group of nominal modifiers (but see below).

(489)	*!u'i*	*ee*	*a*	*hĩĩ*	*koa̰-ng*	*se*	*ǀo'aken*	*di*	*!oo.*
	ashes.2	REL	be.here	2PRO	OBL-?	SUBJ	do.altogether	become	milky way

'These wood ashes here must for ever become the milky way.' (BL11: 72f.)

Some elements associated with the group of verb-like modifiers show an ambivalent formal behaviour. For example, the only numerals *!oai* 'one' (also 'be alone'), *!uu* 'two', and *n!wona* 'three' appear as attributes in the form of both relative predicates and plain adnominal modifiers. The deictic *ǀee* (compared to *a*, it seems to indicate a greater distance from speaker and/or hearer) also displays a categorial ambiguity: while it can be used in a syntactic slot typical for verbs, as a nominal attribute it follows the noun asyndetically (in this context, it can be extended by the deictic *a* and postural verbs like *s'oo* 'sit' or *taa* 'lie'). A similar ambiguity holds for *ǀa̰ng*: it is used as a transitive verb 'eat raw food' or as an asyndetically linked noun modifier 'new, fresh, raw'.

In general, the data on lexical stems used for the semantic modification of nouns indicate that an incipient closed class of adjectives could exist; at the same time, almost all items concerned still betray the historical fact that they have been recruited from the two major lexical categories, viz. nouns and verbs.

A remark on modifying deictics and determiners should be made here. The functions of such items could not yet be determined conclusively, but some of their structural aspects are fairly clear already. The elements *ha* (class 1) and *he* (class 2), characterized by Bleek (1928–30: 94) as "demonstrative adjectives . . . 'this, these'", are called here on account of the available data "deictic pronouns", for two reasons. First, they are not pre-nominal attributes, but rather independent pro-forms to which a noun can, but need not be adjoined; it is in fact possible that they themselves originate in the unmarked pronouns modified by the deictic *a*, i.e. *ha+a* > *ha* and *hi+a* > *he* (such pronoun modification is attested in other Tuu languages). Second, they have so far been found only with a function referring to the discourse, rather than spatial deixis. All this sets them apart from the post-nominal, attributive deictics *a* and *ǀee*, which themselves differ in certain formal properties (see above). Finally, it can be observed that nominal words can be followed by the suffix *-a*; this is especially clear with nouns ending in the suffixes *-ken*, *-ten*, which then change to *-ka*, *-ta*. More research is needed for a conclusive analysis, but it is possible that such nominals are definite (hence the preliminary gloss ?DEF); that is, the suffix *-a* could represent a grammaticalized determiner, probably going back to the verbal deictic *a*. In general, the encoding of deixis is, parallel to the situation in East !Xoon, distributed over quite diverse morphosyntactic categories with an unexpected importance of verb-like items (see also Chapter 7).

3.3.2.6 Verbs

A verbal lexeme rarely changes morphologically in a word form. The sparseness of verbal affixes implies that the great majority of grams in predicates are auxiliaries and particles. An alternation of the final vowel between *i* and *a* can be observed occasionally with certain verbs. It is attractive to view this as a reflex of cross-referencing the object on the verb, because the two nominal agreement classes have the same vowel distinction. Since this hypothesis is not corroborated by the data, the phenomenon remains unexplained, though.

There exists, however, an identifiable verb suffix *-a*. In the orthographic representation, this replaces final vowels of some short verbs, turns *-ken* and *-ten* into *-ka* and *-ta*, and surfaces as *-ya* and *-wa* after final front and back vowels, respectively. It has different functions which will be discussed below under the relevant headings.

3.3.2.6.1 TENSE, ASPECT, MODALITY AND OTHER CLAUSE OPERATORS

ǀXam possesses a great number of markers that modify the state of affairs in its semantic and pragmatic representation. A more exhaustive and conclusive functional analysis of these grams would require a greater data corpus. The following remarks can only give a first glimpse of a picture of great variability and expressiveness and only consider those elements where the number of encountered tokens allows a first, if still preliminary functional interpretation.

Verb phrases can lack predicate markers completely, that is, only lexical stems occur. Sometimes this results in an *irrealis* meaning, especially after imperatives, as in (490).

(490) *hoo s'aa ki Θhoo !waa ǀee*
take.up come 1SG.OBL branch broken.piece DEI.1
'Bring me that piece of wood over there,

ng !we !ho hĩĩ ng ǁaa !o'ite!
1SG ?put.on.fire put 2PRO 1SG burn grandmother
that I may put (the end of) it (in the fire), that I may burn (it) towards grandmother Sirius!' (BL11: 338f.)

In the majority of cases, especially in narratives, the absence of predicate markers seems to represent the perfective member of an aspect opposition; the imperfective seems to be encoded by *nǀe*, which tends to be placed close to the main verb.

One instance of a verb suffix *-a* appears quite consistently with verbs expressing an achieved state or a quality; such verb forms are sometimes called "participle" by Bleek (1928–30: 168ff.). While this suffix has mostly a resultative and stative function, some examples with dynamic verbs indicate that it could also be a marker of perfect and, in background clauses, of anterior taxis.

This suffix aside, predicate markers occur between subject and verb phrase. Some items only occur in this context and thus represent grammaticalized particles. Some, however, are semantically transparent auxiliary verbs which can also be used in another predicate slot with a lexical meaning or a different grammatical function. The following list gives the most important elements and tries to offer more precise, if still preliminary, functional characterizations compared to those in Bleek (1928–30: 162–67): *kx'au(ki)* negation; *ǀu* past; *s'oo* inferential 'seem'; *kx'o̰a* obligation and inferred certainty (the functionally similar *ko̰aa* is possibly only a transcriptional variant); *do̰a* ability and possibility; *sing* past habitual (also occurring in *irrealis* contexts); *ǁ'aa* or *ǁ'ang* itive 'go and', altrilocal, and future; *s'aa* ventive 'come and' and future; *s'a̰ng* contingent 'would' (also co-occurring with the obligation marker); *se irrealis*-subjunctive.

3.3.2.6.2 DERIVATION

There are several derivations with or without effects for the valence of the verb. With respect to the first case, it is not yet possible to give the precise functional range of the marking devices, because there are already considerable difficulties in ascertaining the primary valence of a verb stem. This is due to two major facts. First, verbs with more than one valence pattern of the basic form seem to exist. Second, nominals often do not immediately follow their controlling verbs (see Chapter 7, section 3.3.1.1), so that in a clause containing more than one verb stem – and this is the unmarked case –, it is often unclear which one controls a given nominal constituent.

One valence-changing derivation with a transitive–benefactive function is, however, clear; this is the second major domain where a verbal suffix *-a* is found.

(491) . . . *hĩĩ se heru-ki ǀait-a hĩĩ ǀõ'ing.*
2PRO SUBJ throw-? go.up-BEN 2PRO sun
'. . . they should throw up the sun for them.' (BL11: 54f.)

It attaches, as in (491), to the last stem in the nuclear verb chain and has the same phonetic (or orthographic) effects as the stative suffix; this often makes it difficult to determine conclusively the function of *-a* in a particular utterance.

A suffix *-a* is also reported by Bleek (1928–30: 170) as a passive marker. Since my data do not contain relevant tokens, I cannot add to this information or evaluate the relation of this suffix to the stative and the valence-increasing *-a*.

Intransitive–causative verb pairs as *ǀara* 'bask' vs. *ǀara-ken* 'make, give warmth' in (493) and *ǂaa* 'be bright' vs. *ǂaǂaaken* 'make bright' also give evidence for a derivational verb suffix *-ken*. This might be a possible explanation for the existence of a number of morphologically complex verb lexemes, which are composed of a stem and a lexicalized suffix *-ken*, *-ten*.

Causativization of intransitive verbs can be achieved as well by periphrasis, as in (492).

(492) . . . *ha tạba ki ǁ'ee !utau au ǀõ'ing-ta ǀaraken-ǀara-ken.*
1PRO make ? enter Sirius MPO sun-GEN NOM-warm.oneself-?CAUS
'. . . he made Sirius come into the heat of the sun.' (BL11: 340f.)

It should also be mentioned in this context that a number of semantic notions are conveyed by lexically complex predicates. Many of them are more or less lexicalized compound-like collocations of two verb stems, related syntactically to serial verbs, for example, *ǀii s'aa* 'take'+'come' > 'bring' and *ǀam ǁ'aa* 'take up'+'go' > 'take away to'. Others appear to be fixed verb+noun combinations like *ta ǁ'ii* 'sense'+'heat' > 'feel, be warm'.

The variable functions of verbal reduplication will be treated at the end of this section. This device is used (a) for the expression of pluractional events with meanings like intensive, iterative, durative, etc.; (b) for causativization (BL11: 151ff.; B28–30: 171); and (c) for the formation of process and non-process nominalizations. Different types of verbal reduplication are reported from Khoekhoe languages and correlate there with distinct prosodic patterns; it is likely but cannot be ascertained from the data that this is also the case in ǀXam.

Examples of nominalization by means of reduplication (c) are *ǀho'aken* 'be black' > *ǀho'akenǀho'aken* 'blackness' and *ǂaken* 'speak' > *ǂakenǂaken* 'speech, language'. Note that the predicate slot before the propositional main verb marking manner allows the occurrence of nominal forms and often contains reduplicated verbs; it is hard to determine at this stage whether these reduplications are deverbal nouns of reduplication (c) or pluractional forms of reduplication (a).

The different derivation strategies can build up complex sets of related words as shown in (493); this also demonstrates how formally similar derivation is to nominal plurals.

(493) Simplex form | *ǀara* | 'warm oneself, bask'
Nominalizing reduplication | *ǀara-ǀara* | 'basking'
Causativization with *-ken* | *ǀara-ken* | 'make, give warmth'
Nominalizing reduplication of *ken*-causative | *ǀaraken-ǀara-ken* | 'warmth, heat'

3.4 Eastern ǂHoan

Henry Honken[†]

Eastern ǂHoan is poorly documented (though information on this language is beginning to accumulate through the studies of Collins and others) and, like many San languages, highly analytic in structure. Because of this poverty of data and relative lack of inflection, we will treat morphology and syntax together in this section.

3.4.1 Nouns

Nouns are inflected only for number and do not have gender (but cf. Collins's position below). There are two numbers, singular and plural, the productive plural suffix being *-qa*. There is a considerable variety of plural formations as illustrated below.

The majority of nouns simply add *-qa* to the base.

(494) a. *ǁka'a* 'thing' *ǁka'a-qa* 'things'
b. *n!nalo* 'chameleon' *n!nalo-qa* 'chameleons'

There is a subsystem of nouns which form the plural by vowel change and shifting the base tone to rising tone. Many of these are body part nouns.

(495) a. *ʘkoa* 'eye' *ʘkoen-qa* 'eyes'
b. *ciu* 'hand' *tceon* 'hands'
c. *ǀna* 'arm' *ǀne* 'arms'
d. *ts'iu* 'tooth' *ts'eon* 'teeth'

Some nouns are used only in the plural (these take, like mass nouns, singular adjectives). Examples are 'milk', 'garbage', 'honey', 'food'.

(496) a. *ʘGo-qa qhãe.* 'The honey is sweet.'
honey-PL sweet:SG

b. *'am-qa nǀna'a.* 'The food is bad.'
food-PL bad:SG

c. *Ma kí-!xai-'a ǁq'o'bu-qa kì !koa na.*
1SG take-SG-PERF garbage PREP house LOC
'I take the garbage out of the house.'

Nouns that refer to natural pairs take the plural formative *nǀne*; these are all inalienable. The formative *nǀne* is also found in plural verb constructions.

(497) a. *ya guru* 'his ankle'
ya guru nǀne 'his ankles'

b. *ǂki-si ǂha"ma* 'the bird's wing'
ǂki-si ǂha"ma nǀne 'the bird's wings'

Finally, a few nouns have suppletive singular and plural forms,

(498) a. *'a"ri-ǁga"i* 'woman' *ǀqha* 'women'
b. *ǂ'am-koe* 'person' *tcon-!ka'e* 'people'

and the diminutive suffix *-si* has a suppletive plural *-ǀka'a*:

(498) c. *gya"m-si* 'child' *gya"m-ǀka'a* 'children'

3.4.1.1 Possession

Eastern ǂHoan distinguishes between alienable and inalienable possession. The possessive construction for alienable possession has the form noun+*ci*+noun, as in (499):

(499) *ǂ'am-koe ci kyeama*
person POSS dog
'the person's dog'

The exact form of the alienable possessive construction depends on the semantic nature of the possessed noun. As in other languages that have this distinction, alienable nouns in Eastern ǂHoan include body parts, kin terms, spatial relations and some miscellaneous nouns.

Collins (1998) divides the alienable nouns into a number of sub-classes: the kin-class, the many-class, the *kí*-plural class and others. The inalienable possession construction does not employ the possessive marker *ci* but it does require in some cases a plural marker *kí* (with high tone) that precedes the head.

3.4.1.2 The kin-class

When the possessed noun is [+human] (this includes all kin terms except *m'zale* 'cousin', a Bantu loanword), the two nouns are juxtaposed without a marker and the head noun is pluralized by *-qa*.

(500) a. *'am gye* 'my mother'
1SG:POSS mother

b. *'am gye-qa* 'my mothers'
1SG:POSS mother-PL

When the noun expresses an aggregate or is a mass noun (per Collins, is in a "many-to-one" relationship with its possessor), the use of *kí* is obligatory with both singular and plural (*-qa* is optional if the head noun is plural).

(501) a. *ǀ'on kí gu* 'the tree's flower'
tree PL flower

b. *ǀ'on-qa kí gu-qa* 'the trees' flower(s)'
tree:PL PL flower-PL

c. *Θ'u kí tc'u* 'the duiker's skin'
duiker PL skin

d. *Θ'u-qa kí tc'on-qa* 'the duikers' skins'
duiker:PL PL skin:PL

Nouns that fall into this class include:

(502) *n‡nu* 'feather'
kya"a 'bone'
gu 'flower'
n|nu 'vein'
|q'i 'blood'
‖ka"e 'meat'

Most of the remaining inalienable nouns fall into Collins's *kí*-plural class. With nouns in this class, *kí* is used only if the head noun is plural.

(503) a. *gyam-si* *!ko* 'the child's stomach'
child-DIM stomach

b. *gya"m-|ka'a* *kí* *!ko* 'the children's stomachs'
child-DIM:PL PL stomach

c. *‡'am-koe* *!koa* 'the person's house'
person house

d. *tcon-!ka'e* *kí* *!koa* 'the people's houses'
person-PL PL house

However, inalienable nouns that refer to natural pairs – 'armpit', 'tusk', 'knee', 'kidney', 'wing', etc. – take a special plural marker *n|ne* and do not permit *ki*; one example is:

(504) *ya guru* 'his ankle'
ya guru n|ne 'his ankles'

3.4.2 Pronouns

The pronominal system shows interesting differences from those of other San languages, which generally have a dental or velar nasal in 1SG, the form [a] in 2SG and contrasting vowels in 1PL and 2PL. The system is set out in Table 6.51.

TABLE 6.51 THE PRONOMINAL SYSTEM IN EASTERN ‡HOAN

1SG	*ma*	1PL:EXCL	*n-!ka'e*
		1PL:INCL	*qa"a*
2SG	*u*	2PL	*dji*
3SG	*ya*	3PL	*tsi*

First person singular and third person singular and plural show some similarities to Northern Khoesan (cf. Ju|'hoan 1SG *mi*, 3SG *ha* and 3PL *si*) but the other forms are unique to Eastern ‡Hoan (though it is possible that 2SG *u* is copied from !Xóõ 2PL *u*[h]*u*). The 1PL:EXCL form appears to incorporate a non-productive plural suffix *-!ka'e*, also found in *tcon-!ka'e* 'people'.

The distinction between inclusive and exclusive first person plural pronouns, also found in Northern Khoesan and !Xóõ, may be an areal feature of San languages. However, Eastern ‡Hoan appears to be unique in having a special possessive form in the first person singular (*'am*); for the other persons, the possessive form is identical to the base form.

Some examples of pronouns in various constructions follow.

Subject and object:

(505) *Tsi* *i* *|qaen* *ya.* 'They hit him.'
PRO:3PL PAST hit PRO:3SG

Possessive:

(506) a. *tsi* *ǁqo'e* 'their child'
PRO:3PL child

b. *'am* *gye* 'my mother'
PRO:1SG:POSS mother

c. *'am ci* *'am-qa* 'my food' (Collins 1998: 35)
PRO:1SG:POSS food:PL

Pronouns may form a reflexive by suffixing *-|'en*, as in (507):

(507) a. *ya-* *|'en* 'he himself'

b. *Ya* *tcxoam-a* *ya-* *|'en.* 'He hides himself.'
PRO:3SG hide-PERF PRO:3SG- REFL

3.4.3 Adjectives

Adjectives constitute a separate form class and are distinguished from verbs in two ways (Gruber 1975: 30). First of all, they are unable to take either the present continuous particle *'a* or the perfect suffix *-à*. Second, plural adjectives are preceded by the particle *kí* (with high tone), e.g.

(508) a. *N!nalo* *'a* *cin.* 'The chameleon is dead.'
chameleon PROG die

b. *N!nalo-qa* *'a* *cin-n|ne.* 'The chameleons are dead.'
chameleon:PL PROG die:PL

but:

(508) c. *ǁKà'a* *kuru.* 'The thing is hot.'
thing hot

d. *ǁKà'a-qà* *kí* *kuru.* 'The things are hot.'
thing:PL PL hot

Some examples of adjectives are *kuru* 'hot', *cu* 'beautiful', *!ka'a* 'red', *!kaun* 'wise', *qhaen* 'delicious', *n|na'a* 'ugly'. According to Gruber (1973: 933), adjectives follow the noun:

(509) *|'óõ* *ǂgào* 'the big tree'
tree big

However, Collins (1998: 35) notes that only a few adjectives can be used attributively.

3.4.4 Quantifiers and numbers

Eastern ǂHoan belongs to that small group of languages which do not have complete number systems. In languages of this type, number words, usually limited to two or three, behave like other quantifiers such as 'some' or 'both'.

Eastern ǂHoan has three such number-like quantifiers: *Θmun* 'one', *Θkoa* 'two', *qaen* 'three'. Like adjectives, these follow the noun.

(510) a. *ki* *ci* *Θmun* 'in one place'
PREP place one

b. *tsi* *Θkoa* 'they two'
PRO:3PL two

The only other quantifier attested in the published data is *'ue* 'all', which also follows its head.

(510) c. *kì* *kx'a* *kí* *na* *'ue* 'in all countries'
PREP ground PL LOC:N all

3.4.5 *Demonstratives*

There are two demonstratives: proximal *ha* and distal *kyoa*. These follow the noun.

(511) a. *'a"ri-djà* *ha* *ó* *'àm* *dza-Θkúi.*
man DEM:PROX COP 1SG:POSS friend
'This man is my friend.'

b. *gyá"m-sì* *kyoa* *kyòan-'á.*
child-DIM DEM:REM shelter-PERF
'That child is sheltering from the sun.'

The enclitic *'u* can be combined with the other demonstratives to produce a remote demonstrative. In this construction, the phrase must be relativized.

(512) a. *!hà'e* *ǀná* *kyè-* *ḿḿ* 'this lion'
lion REL DEI:COP- REL

b. *!hà'e* *ǀná* *kyè-* *'u-* *ḿḿ* 'that lion yonder'
lion REL DEI:COP- REM- REL

3.4.6 *Verbs*

The basic word order is SVO. The verb is normally preceded by particles or auxiliaries which mark tense and aspect. According to Collins (1998), all post-verbal elements aside from the direct object are preceded by the general preposition *kì*. However, the direct object is marked by *kì* in ditransitive sentences to disambiguate it from the indirect object; the normal order is verb–indirect object–direct object.

(513) *Má* *'á* *kí-cí* *ǂ'àm-kòe* *kì* *!kòa.*
SUBJ VERB IO DO
1SG PROG CAUS-see man PREP house
'I am showing the man the house.'

3.4.6.1 Tense and aspect

Tense and aspect are marked by particles which directly precede the verb in most cases. Eastern ǂHoan has the tenses past and future and aspects progressive and perfective. Some aspectual distinctions may also be marked by auxiliary verbs although the perfective is marked by a suffix. The verbal particles are *'a* progressive, *i* past, *qo* future and there are further distinctions of near and remote past and future.

The perfective is marked by the suffix *-a*. This may co-occur with the other tense particles. Valence and other verbal properties may also be marked by prefixes such as *kí-* causative and *kì-* passive, or the suffix *-tcu* repetitive. Auxiliaries may sometimes be derived from full verbs such as *tca*, near future, from the verb *tca* 'to come'.

(514) a. *Ma i ki- ǀkobo gya"m-si.* 'I made the child jump.'
1SG PAST CAUS- jump child-DIM

b. *Ma i Ɵkoa 'ǀna Ɵkoa.* 'I killed the two anteaters.'
1SG PAST kill anteater two

c. *Ma qo ki- tsaxo 'am ǀka"e.* 'I will cook and eat the meat.'
1SG FUT CAUS cook eat meat

d. *Yà ǀkoam- a ki kx'a na.*
3SG kneel- PERF PREP earth LOC:N
'He is kneeling on the ground.'

e. *Yà 'á 'ǀná-á kì ǀ'óõ-qà zá.*
3SG PROG sit:SG PREP tree:PL LOC:N
'He has been sitting by the trees.'

f. *Čòõ-!kà'e í kí-ǀkà- 'á kì !kòa ná.*
people PAST sit:PL- PERF PREP house LOC:N
'The people were sitting in the house.'

3.4.6.2 Other verbal categories

A number of additional verbal categories are marked by particles or affixes. Negative sentences are marked by the form *ǀho'on*, which precedes tense and aspect particles. Benefactive sentences are produced by forming a compound verb with *cu* 'give'. Still other aspectual distinctions may be made by placing auxiliaries before the verb. Examples:

(515) a. *Ya ǀho'on i !hon Ɵ'u.* 'He did not kill the duiker.'
3SG NEG PAST kill:SG duiker

b. *Gya"m-ǀka'a 'a tsaxo- cu "am gye kì ǀka"e.*
child-DIM:PL PROG cook- BEN 1SG:POSS mother PREP meat
'The children cook meat for my mother.'

c. *Jo 'a kì- ǀqhu- ǀ'o kì kx'u na.*
water PROG PASS pour- enter PREP pot LOC:N
'Water is being poured into the pot.'

d. *Ma i kí- ǀkobo kyeama.* 'I made the dog jump.'
1SG PAST CAUS- jump dog

e. *Ɵ'ú-qà qó ǀná kí-kyà"o kì ǀ'ón zá.*
duiker:PL FUT CONT:AUX go PREP tree LOC:N
'The duikers are going by the tree.'

3.4.6.3 Copulas

Eastern ǂHoan has several verbs that function as copulas: the existential verb *'a* 'be located', the impersonal copula *'en* and the general copula *o*.

The form *o* is used in equational sentences to express the idea that the two noun phrases are equivalent.

(516) *Tsi o kyeama xa nǀne.* 'They are the dog's masters.'
3PL COP dog master:PL

The form *'a* is used to express location. It is probably the source of the present progressive tense–aspect marker.

(517) a. *ǁka'a-si 'a ki ǀ'on za.*
thing:DIM LOC:COP PREP tree LOC:N
'The thing is beside the tree.'

b. *Kyeama 'a ki koloi na.*
dog LOC:COP PREP truck LOC:N
'The dog is inside the truck.'

The impersonal copula is used in deictic sentences such as 'Here's a . . . , there are . . .'.

(518) *ǂ'am-koe ki 'Θmun-qa 'en.* 'Here are the person's heads.'
person PL head:PL IMPS:COP

3.4.7 Other word classes

In addition to the major word classes described above, there are a number of minor classes: adverbs, prepositions and interrogatives. The interrogative class is somewhat heterogeneous in that some interrogatives are expressed by adding a suffix to a generalized noun while others are full forms of nominal or verbal origin. As in most languages, adverbs are derived from a variety of sources and are uninflected. The forms which Gruber and Collins call "prepositions" function somewhat differently from prepositions in other languages.

3.4.8 Interrogatives

The basic interrogatives 'who, what' are expressed by adding the interrogative sentence particle *-ya* to the nominal base *'a"ri*, the same base which appears in *'a"ri-dja* 'man', *'a"ri-ǁga"i* 'woman'.

(519) *Ma 'a tsi 'a"ri- ya?* 'Who/what do I see?'
1SG PROG see person- Q

The form *nyima* 'where' seems to be borrowed from ǀGui. According to Gruber (p.c.), predicates other than 'be' predicates require the embedded verb phrase to be converted to a noun phrase by means of the correlative particle *na*.

(520) a. *Θ'ú-qà nyìma?* 'Where are the duikers?'
duiker-PL be where

b. *Nyìma jà kyà"o- 'á -ná?* 'Where has he gone?'
where Q go PERF- CORR

Eastern ǂHoan has two additional interrogatives, *ki-ǁkain* 'which' and *ca* 'how'. Gruber (p.c.) notes that *ki-ǁkain* contains the "inalienable possession particle *ki* which can occur in other determiner-like constructions."

(521) a.

Ú	*'á*	*tsí*	*Θ'ú*	*kí!kùin*	*(-ya)?*
2SG	PROG	see	duiker	which	Q

'Which duiker do you see?'

b.

Cá	*ú*	*'á*	*'aḿ?*
how	2SG	PROG	eat

'How do you eat?'

The interrogative 'how' is frequently linked with other predications such as *ǂ'en* 'appear', *ye* 'be some size', *tc'am* 'feel', *'ao* 'do, become', *ko* 'be many' to translate various senses of the English 'How or what is it like?'

(522)

Cá	*yà*	*yé?*
how	3SG	be (size)

'How big is it?'

Finally, the marker *xe* can be used to topicalize some element in an interrogative sentence, as in (523).

(523)

Θ'ú	*xè*	*'á*	*'ám*	*!qhŭi-qà*	*ià?*
duiker	TOP	PROG	eat	grass:PL	Q

'Is it the duiker eating the grass?'

3.4.9 Prepositions and locative nouns

Collins (1998: 24) notes that Eastern ǂHoan has prepositions. One example is *ke* 'with, and' which also functions as a sentence conjunction.

(524)

ke	*ma*
PREP	1SG

'with me'

Another example is the general preposition *kì*, which is used to mark a wide variety of constructions; in particular, *kì* interacts with a set of postpositions to form locative phrases. In origin, the postpositions appear to be nouns, most commonly body part nouns, a type of construction found in other African languages. Some of them are alienable nouns, as in

(525)

|'on	*ci*	*||q'am*
tree	POSS	top

'on the tree'

but most are inalienable nouns which assign genitive case to their dependent noun, e.g. *'am na* 'in me', *'am !qha'ne* 'near me'. These locative constructions take the form

GEN:PREP + NOUN + LOC:N

as in (526).

(526)

Ya	*tcxoam*	*'a*	*ya*	*|'en*	*ki*	*||ha"a-qa*	*na.*
3SG	hide-	PERF	3SG	REFL	PREP	rock-PL	LOC:N

'He hid himself in the rocks.'

3.4.10 Adverbs

Adverbs are derived from adjectives with the suffix *-sa*. Adverbial elements may precede the verb as in (527).

(527) *Ma qhaen- sa tsaxo- a ǀka"e.* 'I cook the meat well.'
1SG good- ADV cook- PERF meat

If they follow the verb, adverbial phrases are marked by *kì*.

(528) *Koloi ǀgon- 'a kyeama kì ǀq'o- sa.*
car hit- PERF dog PREP hard- ADV
'The car hit the dog hard.'

3.4.11 Some issues in syntax

3.4.11.1 High-toned *kí* and low-toned *kì*

One of the few issues in syntax which has been examined in some detail in the published material is the multifarious uses of the two markers *kí* and *kì*. Gruber and Collins study these two forms in detail and give numerous examples of their uses.

It should be clear from the examples given previously that the two forms occupy a central place in Eastern ǂHoan structure. Both Gruber and Collins agree that all instances of *kí* represent a single morpheme; similarly for *kì*. To give some idea of the range of meaning covered by these two forms, we will begin by listing their functions as described in the published material.

3.4.11.1.1 HIGH-TONED *kí*

(i) Causative. Gruber notes that *kí* may be pre-posed to verbs and adjectives to form causatives as in *cu* 'beautiful', *kí-cu* 'beautify', *tsi* 'see', *kí-tsi* 'show'.
(ii) Plural. High-toned *kí* is used in a number of plural constructions: to mark plurality in adjectives; to mark the plural in some inalienable possession constructions.
Collins has suggested that the *kí* in the inalienable possessive construction can be interpreted as a noun class marker, dividing nouns into several groups according to whether they do or do not take *kí*. In this connection, he has additionally proposed that *kí* is cognate with the Northern Khoesan third person pronoun *ká*, also a gender marker. Collins (1998: 7) notes that "*kí* in ǂHoan and *ká* in Juǀ'hoan each serve as morphological indicators for a non-animate noun class" and claims that "class 5 in Juǀ'hoan corresponds to the combination of the many-class and the *kí*-[PL]-class in ǂHoan."
(iii) Non-productive verbal prefix. High-toned *kí* occurs as a prefix to a subset of verbs with no clear function. These may even include loans, e.g. *kí-kyoam* 'swallow' and *kí-nyibu-ka* 'cover' from ǀGui *tyoam* and *dyibu*, respectively.

3.4.11.1.2 LOW-TONED *kì*

(i) Adjunct marker. Collins (2002) notes that all post-verbal adjuncts except the direct object are marked by *kì*. In ditransitive constructions, *kì* may thus serve to disambiguate the two objects. As we have seen, *kì* is also used in conjunction with a set of specialized nouns to form locative constructions, e.g.

(529) a. *Ya 'a kí- tsi ǂ'amkoe kì !koa.*
SUBJ T VERB DO IO
3SG PERF CAUS- show man PREP house
'He showed the man the house.'

b. *Ma 'i tchi Θ'u kì ǀka"a- qa.*
SUBJ T VERB DO INSTR
1SG PAST shoot duiker PREP arrow PL
'I shot the duiker with arrows.'

c. *Koloi ǀgon- 'a kyeama kì gyeo na.*
SUBJ VERB T DO LOC
truck hit PERF dog PREP road LOC:N
'The truck hit the dog in the road.'

d. *Koloi ǀgon- 'a kyeama kì ǀq'o -sa.*
SUBJ VERB- T DO ADV
truck hit PERF dog PREP hard ADV
'The truck hit the dog hard.'

(ii) Passive. Low-toned *kì* also serves as the passive prefix to verbs.

(530) *ǂ'amkoe kì- ǀgon- 'a ki gyeo na.*
SUBJ VOICE VERB T
person PASS hit PERF PREP road LOC:N
'A person was struck in the road.'

In discussing these forms the researchers make the following points: *kí* and *kì* are different morphemes. All appearances of *kí* represent the same morpheme; likewise for *kì*. *kí* has some connection with plurality, especially distributive plurality.

3.4.11.2 Suppletive plurals in verbs

A small number of verbs have distinct (suppletive) singular and plural forms. This is conceivably an areal feature since it is also found in other San languages (Juǀ'hoan, !Xóõ). In all of these languages, the number of verbs affected is small, the forms are mostly suppletive and they follow an "ergative" pattern; that is, with intransitive verbs, the subject controls the verb but in transitive sentences, the verb agrees in number with the object. Examples are:

(531) a. *Θ'u 'a kya"o.* 'The duiker is going.'
duiker PROG go:SG

b. *Θ'u-qa 'a ki-kya"o.* 'The duikers are going.'
duiker:PL PROG go:PL

TABLE 6.52 VERBS WITH SUPPLETIVE SINGULAR AND PLURAL FORMS

Verb	SG	PL	Verb	SG	PL
'go'	*kya"o*	*ki-kya"o*	'kill'	*!hon*	*Θkoa*
'come'	*tca*	*ki-tca*	'recline'	*ǂqi'i*	*!qhau*
'die'	*cin*	*cin-'ǀna*	'remove'	*ki-!xao*	*ki-nǀnui*
'drop'	*cui*	*gun, qole*	'rise'	*kyu*	*ga*
'enter'	*!'u-co*	*!ka"m*	'run'	*ki-'!no*	*ki-n!qaen*
'fall'	*!q'ao*	*ǂqhe*	'seat'	*ǀ'a*	*ǀ'e-ǁka*
'grow'	*ǀga"a*	*ǀga"a-si*	'sit'	*'ǀna*	*ki-ǁka*
'hang'	*ǀ'i*	*!ga*	'stand'	*!kui*	*ǀgan*
			'take'	*!ku*	*ǂq'ai*

To this group, Collins adds also:

Verb	SG	PL
'cry'	*ǀ'i*	*ki-ǀ'i*
'go from'	*ǂ'o*	*ki-ǂko"o*
'laugh'	*nǀgai*	*ki-nǀgai*

The table has been arranged to group the forms by structure. The following points can be noted:

The set of verbs marked for plurality in Eastern ǂHoan differs in a number of respects from similar sets in other San languages. First of all, the set shows a greater degree of regularity. The prefix *kí-* is used to pluralize in seven cases (though it also appears in the singular in two). The forms 'sit' and 'seat' comprise a mini-paradigm with the plural on the transitive verb derived by vowel change. Both 'die' and 'grow' base the plural on the singular. Second, almost all are intransitive verbs whereas in the other San languages there is a more even balance between transitive and intransitive.

To take Juǀ'hoan as an example, Dickens (1994) cites fourteen transitive and thirteen intransitive verbs. And the only forms that show any structure are 'be long', 'be small', 'be short', all adjectives. A similar situation obtains in !Xóõ.

3.4.12 Larger constructions

There is very little information available on more complex constructions. The examples given below barely scratch the surface.

3.4.12.1 Use of ***ke***

The form *ke*, which can be used as a preposition meaning 'with', can also be used to link nouns. There is an example in Gruber (1975: 43):

(532)	a.	*ǀnobo*	*ke*	*tcon-!ka'e*	'talk with people'
		talk	with	person:PL	
	b.		*ke*	*ma*	'with me'
			with	1SG	
	c.	*'a"ri-dja*	*ke*	*'a"ri-ǁga"i*	'the man and the woman'
		man	with	woman	

3.4.12.2 Complements

As in !Xóõ, complements may be formed by means of the possessive particle *ci*. The verb forming the complement may be accompanied by tense particles.

(533) *Ma 'a tsi tcon-!ka'e ci 'a ki-n!gaen.*
1SG PROG see people POSS PROG run:PL
'I see the people who are running.'

3.4.12.3 Relative clauses

Relative clauses are formed with the relative pronoun *ǀna*; the verb must take relative marking.

(534) a. *!hà'e ǀná kyè- 'ú- ḿḿ*
lion REL DEM- REM- REL
'yonder lion (= the lion which is yonder)'

b. *Ma 'a tsi kx'u ǀna u m- cu-'a ki gya"m-si.*
1SG PROG see pot REL 2SG REL give-PERF PREP child-DIM
'I see the pot which you have given to the child.'

3.4.12.4 Compound verbs

Eastern ǂHoan readily forms compound verbs of a type which have generally been described as serial verbs in other San languages. The first part of the compound carries the basic meaning while the second element has a modifying function. Collins (2001) notes that verbal compounds consist of two adjacent verbs sharing a single tense–aspect marker. All other functions (voice, negation, etc.) are also marked only once. There appear to be restrictions on the nature of the second verb; that is, V_2 is drawn from a small subset of the verbal lexicon.

The voice possibilities are: both intransitive (*ǀkobo-kyu* 'jump up' ← *ǀkobo* 'jump' + *kyu* 'rise'); both transitive (*ǀqhu-ǀ'o* 'pour in' ← *ǀqhu* 'pour' + *ǀ'o* 'put in'); intransitive/transitive (*kala-ka* 'fly to' ← *kala* 'fly' + *ka* 'go to').

For more data and examples, see Collins (2001).

3.4.12.5 Subjunctives

Subjunctive sentences are formed with the particle *ka*, which follows the subject.

(535) *ma ǀkoe na ka ǀhoam-ǀhoam tca*
1SG still AUX SUBJ jog come
'while I was still coming jogging'

This pattern is so similar to !Xóõ that it is likely to be borrowed.

3.4.12.6 Pluractional verbs and other specialised verb compounds

Collins describes two such elements in considerable detail. These are *-tcu*, repetitive, and *-ǀqo*, action performed in several places.

(536) a. *Tsi 'a ki- nǀobo-ǀqo ke tcon-!ka'e.*
3PL PROG PL- talk-around PREP people
'They are going around talking to people.'

b. *Ma ki- ǀq'ao- tcu- 'a ǂam-koe.*
1SG PL- stab REP- PERF person
'I stabbed the person repeatedly.'

The suffix *-ǀqo* (compare the form *-nǀ'ho* in Juǀ'hoan, which has a similar function) gives a sense to the verb of "doing around", that is, performing the same action in different places. The suffix *-tcu* gives a repetitive meaning to the verb. Both of these constructions require the distributive plural morpheme *kí*. According to Collins, the *kí-V-tcu* construction can only be used with transitive verbs of contact such as 'stab', 'shoot', 'hit', 'bite' and so on.

Two additional examples of more specialized compound verbs are *-cu*, benefactive, and *-|'o*, ingressive. Both of these are used as independent verbs: *cu* 'give' and *|'o* 'enter'.

(536) c. *N|gain-|ka'a 'a kyxai- su !xae.*
girl-DIM:PL PROG dance BEN chief
'The girls danced for the chief.'

d. *Ma 'a ǁqhu-|'o jo ki kx'u na.*
1SG PROG pour-enter water PREP pot LOC:N
'I poured water in the pot.'

3.4.13 *Sentence inversion*

As we noted earlier, standard word order in Eastern ǂHoan is SVO with the indirect object preceding the direct and all verbal extensions (other than the direct object) being marked by the generalized preposition *kì*. It is also possible to front post-verbal elements for emphasis or focus.

(537) a. *Ya !koa ya i !hai kì ǁqhwi-qa.*
3SG house 3SG PAST thatch PREP grass:PL
'His house, he thatched with grass.'

b. *ǁqhwi-qa ya i !hai kì ya !koa.*
grass-PL 3SG PAST thatch PREP 3SG house

c. *Gyeo na koloi ǁgon-a kì ǂ'amkoe.*
road LOC:N truck hit-PERF PREP person
'In the road, the truck hit a person.'

Note that in examples b and c, the direct object is marked with the preposition *kì*, presumably for clarity.

Eastern ǂHoan is clearly of great interest in many respects. It is the best candidate for a relationship between two San groups, it may throw considerable light on the history of Northern Khoesan, it has a rich syntactic structure with many unusual constructions such as the various *k*-plurality forms and it challenges several standard assumptions about the Khoesan languages (e.g., that the labial click is restricted to the Southern group). As an endangered language, it deserves intensive study.

3.5 Kwadi[4]

Tom Güldemann

3.5.1 *Pronouns*

Pronominal categories and forms for speech act participants are tentatively as follows:

TABLE 6.53 PRONOUNS FOR SPEECH ACT PARTICIPANTS IN KWADI

Person	SG	PL	DU
1st		*(u)hina* (?INCL.)	*(h)amu*
	ta	*ala* (?EXCL.)	
2nd	*sa*	*u*	*uwa*

They are attested in subject, object and possessor function, however, with the following amendments: the first person singular possessor form is *tʃi*, the object pronouns are followed by *-le*/*-de*, and the first person dual object form is just *mu*.

Third person pronouns seem to consist of a demonstrative base *ha* and the gender–number suffixes *-dɛ*, *-e*, *-wa*, *-u*, *-'ɛ* yielding the five pronouns *hadɛ*, *hɛɛ*, *hawa*, *hau*, and *ha'ɛ* (see below for their distribution over genders). These are only found in the material as subjects and possessors; instead of expected *hadɛ*, only *ha* is attested as possessor.

There are examples of pronouns followed by sex-denoting nouns and of almost all dual and plural pronouns followed by quantifiers like 'two', 'many', or 'all'.

3.5.2 Nouns

Although some phrases suggest that noun stems can be used on their own, nouns are generally followed by the five gender–number suffixes mentioned above. Westphal (1971: 393, 395f.) describes them tentatively as constituting a system of three genders (masculine, feminine, common) and three numbers (singular, dual, plural). The whole range of paradigms in his notes yields a slightly different picture in that there are still other patterns of how suffixes map gender and number. Table 6.54 only gives the securely attested patterns of masculine and feminine genders; there is no gender distinction in dual number (cf. Güldemann 2004b for more discussion).

TABLE 6.54 NOUN GENDERS IN KWADI

	SG	PL	DU
M	*-dɛ*	*-u*	*-wa*
F	*-e*	*-'ɛ*	*-wa*

With some nouns, number appears to be conveyed by stem suppletion, for example, *kie tçe* 'woman' vs. *tala kwa'e* 'women'. There are several cases of agent-noun compounds with the noun *kho-* 'human, person' as head, for example, *tçe'e-kõŋ-kho-wa* 'murderers' [= people-kill-person-DU] and *so-kho-dɛ* 'healer' [= medicine-person-M.SG].

3.5.3 Verbs

Verbal morphology is the most complicated area in the data. Apart from many structurally opaque verb forms, there are also different conjugation patterns, the majority of which are morphologically complex. A basic distinction can be made according to whether the simple stem is used or some extended form thereof.

The simple stem can be found as the only predicate element, apparently functioning as hortative, present, and imperative, as in (538). The form also occurs with prefixes or suffixes in an auxiliary construction with *kõlako* 'going to', with the past marker *kale* as in (539), and as a complement before the verb 'want', as in (540).

(538) *u* *la!*
2PL.PRO leave
'Leave ye!'

(539)

ta	*kale*	*θẽ-na.*	*ta*	*kale*	*ke-la-kx'a.*
1SG.PRO	PAST	cook-?	1SG.PRO	PAST	?-?-drink
'I cooked.'			'I drank.'		

(540)

ta	*kx'o-'e*	*kx'a-la-xe.*
1SG.PRO	water-F.PL	drink-?-want
'I want to drink water.'		

"Extended stem" refers to a form that seems to be elaborated morphologically by segments contained in the simple stem. This elaboration seems to target special syllable patterns as output. Full reduplication occurs with disyllabic stems as in *taŋga-taŋga* 'read'. Reduplication with an intermediate affix, with *la*, *da* as the most frequent form in the data, is found with monosyllabic verbs as with *θẽ-la-θẽ* 'cook'. More complex simple stems are changed to a shape with an affix and partial reduplication as in *hon-da-honeke* 'write'. The extended stem of the trisyllabic verb 'speak' is *la-labala*, for which different analyses could be proposed. Extended stems occur in the material as citation forms and in at least three conjugation forms whose structures seem to be (a) subject + extended stem, (b) subject + *ka* + extended stem, and (c) subject + extended stem-*na*, as shown in (541).

(541)

ta	*la-labala.*	*ta*	*ka*	*la-labala.*	*ta*	*la-labala-na.*
1SG.PRO	EXT-speak	1SG.PRO	FUT	EXT-speak	1SG.PRO	EXT-speak-TA
'I speak.'		'I will speak.'			'I speak.'	

These dimly emerging regularities aside, there are first of all numerous questions for the analysis. This is already indicated by Westphal's (1971: 396) remark about a possible past marker within extended stems. The exact reproduction of the following verb paradigm in the present also demonstrates these problems.

(542)

Subject	Object-*le*	Predicate	
sa	*ta-de*	*munana.*	'You (SG) **see** me.'
sa	*mo"-de*	*mo'nana.*	'You (SG) **see** us two.'
sa	*ala-de*	*munana.*	'You (SG) **see** us.'
ta	*sa-le*	*mondana.*	'I **see** you (SG).'
ta	*"wa-le*	*monanana.*	'I **see** you two.'
ta	*u-li*	*mɔɔna.*	'I **see** you (PL).'

It remains entirely unclear what the above transcriptions convey. Do the differences across the verb forms record irrelevant phonetic details or complex inflectional changes? If the latter were the case, do they index information about subject, object, tense–aspect or yet other categories, or even a composite thereof?

Even more important is the following caveat: all remarks above only apply to a subset of verbs, because many items listed do not have citation forms of the extended-stem design. Since there are virtually no examples with such verbs as predicates, the relevant conjugational rules for a large portion of the verb lexicon remain unknown.

NOTES

1 v indicates a vowel identical in quality to the preceding vowel.

2 East !Xoon is the northernmost variety of the Taa language complex. The major published source is Traill (1994, to be abbreviated as T94). For further analysis, Traill furnished me with three texts (Traill, in prep.): *Uhbuku's spoon and other dangers:*

!Xóõ texts on then and now. He also took time to answer questions and to comment on first drafts, reflecting his research up to about 2000; his subsequent work is not integrated here. My sincere thanks to him for this help, without which this section could not have been written. It goes without saying that any shortcomings of the following presentation are my own.

3 I gratefully acknowledge the contributions by René Kriegler, who prepared with me the |Xam course held at the University of Leipzig in the winter semester 1998/99, and by the students Anja Langer, Jessica Ludwig, Christfried Naumann, and Tatjana Orechkina, who actively participated in bringing a selection of texts on the computer and taking the first steps towards their linguistic analysis. The description is first of all based on the analysis of this text material and is restricted to the Strandberg variety. The transliteration applied here is discussed briefly by Güldemann (this volume). When referring to Bleek and Lloyd (1911) and Bleek (1928–30), the abbreviations BL11 and B28–30, respectively, are used.

4 Sources as in Chapter 4, section 3.5.

REFERENCES

Bala 1998; Berger 1943; Berlin *et al*. 1968, 1974; D.F. Bleek 1928–30, 1931a, 1931b; Bleek and Lloyd 1911; Brown 1984; Coates Palgrave 1997; Collins 1998, 2001, 2002; Corbett 1991; Dempwolff 1916; Dickens 1994; Dickens and Traill 1977; Elderkin 1978, 1986b; Gruber 1973, 1975; Güldemann 2000b, 2004a, 2004b; Haacke 1995, 1998, 1999; Hagman 1977; Heikkinen n.d.; Heine 1986, 1999; Kilian-Hatz 2008; Köhler 1962, 1981, 1989, 1991; Lakoff 1987; Maingard 1957, 1962; Meinhof 1930; Nienaber 1963; Obst 1912; Schladt 1997, 2000; Tanaka 1996; Taylor 1989; Traill 1985, 1994; Tucker 1967a, 1967b; Vossen 1985, 1997a, 2010; Widlok 1995, 1999a, n.d.; Wuras 1920.

CHAPTER SEVEN

SYNTAX

1 HADZA

Bonny Sands

1.1 Constituent order

Published syntactic information about Hadza is extremely limited, being restricted to a few loosely translated narratives (Berger 1943, Bala 1998). This section is largely based on those published accounts and on a small corpus of directly elicited structures collected by the author during short periods of fieldwork in 1992 and 1997. The source of the data must be taken into account as the directly elicited structures tend to follow the Kiswahili prompt SVO order and have more overt nominals than the narrative texts.

1.1.1 Dominant order

Hadza is usually described with basic VSO order (e.g. Heine 1975c: 171), but this analysis is somewhat misleading as overt nominals are relatively infrequent, and sentences with two overt nominals are very infrequent. Hadza is best described as a pronominal argument language (cf. Jelinek 1984). The (en)clitic marking of arguments is less marked than the use of independent pronouns or overt nominals.

1.1.2 Variability in constituent order

In direct elicitation, for sentences in which the agent and patient in a phrase differ in either person, gender or number, any of the constituent orders – SVO, SOV, OSV, OVS, VSO, VOS – were judged by consultants to be equal in meaning and grammaticality. Agreement morphology is sufficient alone to distinguish thematic relations in these cases. The noun which is higher in animacy (cf. Frawley 1992: 92–99) is taken to be the agent, unless the noun lower in animacy is in initial position, in which case it is taken to be the subject, as can be seen in (1). The verb *kwase* 'hit' is marked for a 3F.SG object *-ta-* and 3F.SG past tense subject *-kwa* and does not distinguish between the roles of the participants.

(1) a. *Boni-ko kwase-ta-kwa akwitiko.* (SVO) 'Bonny hit a/the woman.'
b. *Boni-ko akwiti-ko kwase-ta-kwa.* (SOV)
c. *Kwase-ta-kwa Boni-ko akwiti-ko.* (VSO)
d. *Kwase-ta-kwa akwiti-ko Boni-ko.* (VOS)
e. *Akwiti-ko kwase-ta-kwa Boni-ko.* (SVO) 'A/the woman hit Bonny.'
f. *Akwiti-ko Boni-ko kwase-ta-kwa.* (SOV)

Though direct questioning was not able to reveal particular discourse functions associated with different word orders, evidence from the texts suggests that nominals are positioned before the verb when emphasized or brought into focus. In (2), the emphasized *dongo-ko* 'zebras' occur pre-verbally, while the subjects *ichi-ko kalimo* 'some animals', and *komati-ko* 'elands' occur post-verbally.

(2) *Dza-dza-'e* *kota*
EMPH-come-STAT NARR.PAST.3F.SG(collective singular)

fa-fa-ka-cho *ichi-ko* *kalimo.*
EMPH-drink-DISTR-PART some-3F.SG animal
V [S]

Dongo-ko *'a* *fa-ka-cho* *kota* *ts'u'a-iya.*
zebra-3F.SG EMPH drink-DISTR-PROG NARR.PAST.3F.SG remove-REFL
S V

Welapi-na *kota* *dza* *kota*
morning-LOC NARR.PAST.3F.SG come NARR.PAST.3F.SG

fa-ka-cho *komati-ko* *kota* *ts'u'a-iya.*
drink-DISTR-PROG eland-3F.SG NARR.PAST.3F.SG remove-REFL
V S

'Some animals were coming and drinking away. Even zebras came to drink and then left. In the morning, elands came to drink and then left.' (Bala 1998: 26)

In (3), we see pre-verbal positioning of nominals being used to indicate a new topic. For instance, the second sentence has the object, *mana-ko* 'meat', in pre-verbal position, followed by an account of actions performed on the meat. A switch in topic is indicated by the dislocated *a unu* '(and) a person', preceding both the auxiliary *kaka* and the main verb. The noun phrase *bami 'ihi'a* 'this thing' is not pre-verbal and does not indicate a new topic.

(3) ... *"Mahi-te* *'iba* *!eke* *'acho."*
go.with-3F.PL.IMP NARR.FUT.1PL.INCL cut.3M.SG.DO.DISTR skin(3M.SG)
V V O

Mana-ko *yame* *tla-ka-tlatle* *ets'a-na.*
meat-3F.SG NARR.PAST.3F.PL EMPH-DISTR-carry camp-LOC
O V

Yame *lutl'u-ta* *yame* *se-ke-me* *ma-mako-ma.*
NARR.PAST.3F.PL collect-3F.SG.DO 3F.PL.PAST eat-DISTR EMPH-boil-3M.SG.OBL
V V V

A *unu* *kaka* *tl'o-tl'odzo* *"Hamishe'ena*
EMPH person(3M.SG) NARR.PAST.3M.SG EMPH-say maybe
S V

dza-ya *bami* *'ihi'a* *!ama.*
come-3M.SG.PRES 3M.SG.DEM thing(3M.SG) again
V [S]

Hama'isho *ka* *'iiin,* *bahe-yakwa* *'isho-ko."*
today CONJ EMPH finish-3F.SG.PAST sun-3F.SG
V S

'... "Let's go and cut skin." They carried the meat home. They collected it up and boiled it up to eat. Someone said, "Maybe this thing will come again. And today is really ... the sun is finished." (Bala 1998: 32)

Objects typically occur after verbs, but occasionally objects occur before subjects, as in (4). Either the subject *ne'e-ko* 'baboons' is added as an afterthought, or there is a focus on the object, the hut filled with food by the baboons, rather than on the baboons themselves.

(4)

Tla-tlakwa	*ǀ'o-ko-s-eta*	*ǀ'ets'a-be*	*ne'e-ko,*
EMPH-pick	fill-DISTR-3F.PL.DO	hut-3F.PL	baboon-3F.SG
V	V	O	S
paki	*kaka*	*ǀ'okoso*	*yamu'a.*
until	NARR.PAST.3M.SG	fill.DISTR	place(3M.SG)
		V	

'The baboons just picked and picked and filled up the houses until the space was all filled up.' (Bala 1998: 22)

1.2 Major sentence types

1.2.1 Simple sentences

The most commonly occurring type of clause in Hadza narratives is one in which subject marking and tense/aspect are indicated by an auxiliary rather than on the main verb. In (5), we see examples of sentences in which subject agreement is marked on a declarative past auxiliary. In (5a), there is no additional marking on the verb, but (5b) shows direct object agreement, and (5c) shows indirect object agreement.

(5) a.

Kota	*wech'e.*
NARR.PAST.3F.SG	lack

'They were not enough.' (Bala 1998: 22)

b.

Kaka	*wech'e-ya.*
NARR.PAST.3M.SG	lack-3M.SG.DO

'He missed them.' (Bala 1998: 26)

c.

Kaka	*hama-sa.*
NARR.PAST.3M.SG	sit-3F.SG.OBL

'He waited for them.' (Bala 1998: 26)

Verbs may show agreement with more than one nominal, as in (6a), but this is infrequent in the narrative texts. Agreement occurs with or without the overt nominals, as in (6b).

(6) a.

Mu-musi-kwa-tita	*'ono.*
EMPH-annoy-1SG.OBL-2SG.PRES	1M.SG.PRO

'You really annoy me.' (Bala 1998: 24)

b.

A	*'ono*	*tl'impi-'a-na'a*	*hich'i!*	*Tl'impi-'a-na'a.*
EMPH	1M.SG	step.in-3M.SG.DO-1SG.PAST	shit(3M.SG)	step.in-3M.SG.DO-1SG.PAST

'Ah! I stepped in shit! I stepped in it.' (Bala 1998: 24)

Existential constructions with a presentative function are typically verb-initial, as in (7).

(7)

Bahe-yamo	*ǀets'a*	*yeta*	*'akaka'ane-be.*
be.present.-3M.SG.PAST	camp(3M.SG)	of.3F.PL	first.people-3F.PL

'There was a camp of old-time Hadzas.' (Bala 1998: 16)

There is also a negative existential construction, as in (8). The word *ukuwa* 'there.is.no' is usually followed by noun phrases, e.g. *ukuwa shida* 'no problem', but can also occur after a noun phrase, e.g. *ika Hadza ukuwa* 'and there are no Hadza'. The root *'uku-* 'be without' also occurs in constructions such as *Semeyamo 'uku'eta te* 'he ate without you (SG)', and *Semena'a 'ukunama bami* 'I ate without him'.

(8) *Ukuwa 'a 'atama-Ø. Ukuwa 'a mana-ko.*
there.is.no EMPH blood-3M.SG there.is.no EMPH meat-3F.SG
'There is not even any blood. There is no meat.' (Bala 1998: 16)

Predicate locatives can be expressed with a copula cliticized to a preceding noun or adverb, as in (9).

(9) *Ika chikina ǀ'ikititi-yako tafa-ko, 'undushi,*
and inside storeroom-3F.SG.COP sp.berry-3F.SG sp.berry(3M.SG)

nguila-ko, 'embele 'aku seme-Ø.
sp.berry-3F.SG sp.berry(3M.SG) what.kind food-3M.SG

A ets'a-na ma bami hi'iyehe-ya seme.
EMPH home-LOC 3M.SG.OBL 3M.SG.PRO like.thus-3M.SG.PRES food(3M.SG)
'But inside the storeroom there were *tafako* berries, *undushi* berries, *nguilako* and *embele* berries – all kinds of food. Inside it there was food like this.' (Bala 1998: 24)

Predicate nominals (including predicate adjectives) are noted with the copula enclitic on a noun, adjective, or pronoun (cf. 10a and b). Some verbs can take the copula (often after a participial/stative suffix), e.g. *ǀangala-* 'to lie down', *ǀangal-i-neko* 'I (F) was lying down'.

(10) a. *Bami-ya pa'anakwete, 'ashapo sa mana-ko,*
3M.SG-3M.SG.COP old.man expert 3F.SG.OBL meat-3F.SG
'He is an old man; a real meat expert . . .' (Bala 1998: 26)

b. *ǀuhi-yako hako.*
mosquito-3F.SG.COP 3F.SG.DEM
'This is a mosquito.' (Bala 1998: 32)

c. *Hlalakama-te'e, te*
be.crazy-2M.SG.COP 2M.SG.PRO
'You are crazy.' (Bala 1998: 32)

1.2.2 Complex sentences

Clauses may be linked through a variety of devices. Predicates are often co-ordinately linked with auxiliaries, as in (11). As in (11a), clauses in a chain may all take the same narrative particle. Relative particles, as in (11b–d), link clauses subordinately. These particles are typically clause-initial in the narrative texts.

(11) a. *Kaka nǀo'o kaka 'a-'ase.*
NARR.PAST.3M.SG snore NARR.PAST.3M.SG EMPH-sleep
'He just snored and slept.' (Bala 1998: 26)

b. *Kwakwa nǀak'afe 'ishoko kaka chi-'o'o.*
REL.PAST.3F.SG be.late.afternoon sun(3F.SG) NARR.PAST.3M.SG run-EMPH
'When it was the late afternoon, he really ran.' (Bala 1998: 26)

c. *Kwete* *tla-tla-kwa* *dza-ne-hena* *bami* *seme . . .*
REL.FUT.2F.PL EMPH-pick-1SG.IO come-COM-2SG.POSS 3M.SG.DEM food(3M.SG)
'When/if you pick and bring to me this food . . .' (Bala 1998: 22)

d. *Boko* *tl'a'i-yako* *kwako* *niki-'e* *seme.*
3F.SG.PRO sing.STAT-3F.SG.PRES REL.PRES.3F.SG grind-STAT food
'She sings while grinding food.'

Clauses may also be linked in which one predicate takes enclitics while others take auxiliaries. In the narratives, verbs with enclitics marking tense appear to mark the contingency, anteriority, or relevance of the predicate to following predicates, as in (12). Predicates with enclitics are more common than those with auxiliaries in the elicited data, but this appears to be an artefact of the method of elicitation.

(12) a. *Hla'a-tita* *mana-ko* *'ina* *'a* *!o-ta.*
want-3F.SG.OBL meat-3F.SG 1SG.FUT EMPH kill-DO
'I want meat to kill.' (Bala 1998: 28)

b. *Ono* *haka-ta* *'ina* *'ase.*
1M.SG.PRO go-1SG.PRES 1SG.FUT sleep
'I am going off to sleep.' (Bala 1998: 24)

c. *Haka-bita* *ba* *!e-!eke* *'acho.*
go-1PL.INCL.PRES 1PL.INCL.FUT EMPH-cut.3M.SG.DO.DISTR skin(3M.SG)
'We will go and really cut the skin.' (Bala 1998: 16)

Adverbials may be used to make the contingent relations between clauses more explicit, as in (13). Note that *hla'a-* 'want' sub-categorizes for an oblique case marked object rather than an accusative case marked direct object.

(13) *Isa* *hla'a-tita,* *'ina* *'akwe* *!upi.*
as/since want-3F.SG.OBL 1SG.FUT NEG sleep
'Since I want it, I won't sleep.' (Bala 1998: 30)

1.3 Negation

The particle that carries the negative sense, *'akw-*, patterns like an auxiliary in some cases. It can occur clause-initially with marking for tense and person–number–gender, as in (14). The subject enclitics that attach to the negative stem in the negative future are similar to the conditional enclitics, while the ones that attach to the negative past and negative present are similar to the (affirmative) past and "present" enclitics, as can be seen in (15).

(14) a. *Hama* *gashenga* *'akwe-so* *!upi-tikwa.*
3M.SG.DEM thing NEG-FUT.3M.SG sleep-1SG.OBL
'This thing won't let me sleep.' (Bala 1998: 30)

b. *Nasema Mzee,* *'akwe-'e'e* *'obe'e* *tsi'a.* *'A-'ase-'ota.*
I.say, old.man NEG-FUT.PL.EXCL 1F.PL.EXCL.PRO diarrhea EMPH-sleep-1PL?
'I say, Mzee, we won't shit. We'll just sleep.' (Bala 1998: 24)

c. *Akwa-kwa* *talasha* *isho-ko* *kaka* *kenena* *'ela ts'oko.*
NEG.PAST.3F.SG set sun-3F.SG NARR.PAST.3M.SG early build fire(3M.SG)
'The sun hadn't begun to set when he had already built his fire.' (Bala 1998: 26)

d. *'Akwa-ta hla'a-ta tsi'a 'ika he.*
NEG-PRES.1SG like-3M.SG.APPL diarrhea(3M.SG) like so
'I don't like diarrhea like that.' (Bala 1998: 24)

The negative particle *'akw-* can take other endings, but examples of these are few. It can take conditional endings, e.g., *'akwe-ne'e haka* 'I (M) wouldn't go', *'akwa-nikwi* 'I (F) wouldn't go', and copula endings, e.g., *'akwe-ya hak-e-'ehe* 'it is him, he hasn't gone', *'akwe-pe'e hak-e-'ehe* 'it is them (F.PL), they haven't gone'.

(15)

	Negative		
	Future	Past	Present
1M.SG	*'akwe-ne*	*'akwa-na*	*'akwa-ta*
2M.SG	*'akwe-to*	*'akwa-ta*	*'akwa-tita*
3M.SG	*'akwe-so*	*'akwa-mo*	*'akwa-ya*
3F.SG	*'akwe-ko*	*'akwa-kwa*	*'akwe-ko*
1PL.INCL	*'akwe-be'e*	*'akwa-ba*	*'akwa-bita*
1PL.EXCL	*'akwe-'e'e*	*'akwa-'a'a*	*'akwa'ota*
2M.PL	*'akwi-ti'i*	*'akwa-ti'a*	*'akwa-tita*
2F.PL	*'akwe-te'é*	*'akwa-te'a*	*'akwa-teta*
3M.PL	*'akwi-si*	*'akwa-mi*	*'akwa-pi'*
3F.PL	*'akwe-se*	*'akwa-me*	*'akwa-pe'*

In cases where an auxiliary (including relatives and narrative particles) is already present in the clause, the stem *'akwe/'akwa* occurs without marking for person–gender–number or tense, as in (16). However, an inflected negative particle can co-occur with an inflected verb, e.g., *'akwa-na baha-ta hako kazi* 'I have not finished this work', *'akwe-ne baha-ta hako kazi* 'I am not finishing this work'. Note that *baha* is a non-finite verb with a 3F.SG.DO marker.

(16) a. *Kaka 'a 'unu 'akwe tetata'o.*
3M.SG even person not know
'And no one in the camp knew.' (Bala 1998: 18)

b. *Kwako boko tl'akwe kwakwa 'akwe sam-iya*
REL.PRES.3F.SG 3F.SG.DEM girl REL.PAST.3F.SG NEG eat-PASS

paka 'a hama'isho.
until even today/now
'The girl had not eaten up to then.' (Bala 1998: 20)

In imperative sentences, a different negative particle is used, i.e. *takwe* (cf. 17). This is probably the *'akwe* negative particle with a fossilized *t-* second person prefix.

(17) a. *Takwe kukuyi-ta yamu'a-Ø.*
NEG worry-2SG.OBL country-3M.SG
'Don't be bothered with the great outdoors.' (Bala 1998: 26)

b. *Kaka tl'o-tl'odzo, "Takwe 'ihli."*
3M.SG EMPH-speak NEG fear
'He just said, "Don't be afraid."' (Bala 1998: 22)

Existential constructions are negated with the stem *'uku(-)wa'* 'there is no', e.g. *'ukuwa mana-ko* 'there is no meat', *'ukuwa shida* 'no problem', *'uku-weta* 'there is nothing about them (3F.PL)', *ukuwa-yina etebe kazi* 'there is no work for you (3F.PL)'. Relative pronouns can be negated, e.g. *'ono ma'a 'akwe haka* 'it is not me who is going'. Hadza also has a 'not know' verb *'aho*, e.g. *'aho* 'I don't know', *'aho-sa* 'I don't know about her', *a-'aho-wena te* 'I just don't know about you'. More work needs to be done to discover other strategies Hadza may have for negation, such as constituent negation, and the negation of predicate nominals and predicate locatives.

1.4 Questions

Yes/no questions are formed with the use of the question particle, *'oma*, as in (18). The particle typically occurs directly after the predicate and copula or tense clitic, e.g. *Sabena hu-hupe-ya 'oma kwini-chana?* 'Is Sabena still nursing?'; *Teko, hocha-ni-teko 'oma, hama'isho?* 'Are you pregnant now?'; *Haka-bita 'oma?* 'Are we going?' Questions can also be formed with yes/no question intonation alone, e.g. *Bahe-be'e?* 'Are they there?'

(18) *Te,* *hla'a-tita-tita* *'oma* *mana-ko?*
2M.SG want-3F.SG.OBL-2SG.PRES Q meat-3F.SG
'Do you really want meat?' (Bala 1998: 30)

Information questions are typically formed with the question word placed clause-initially, taking predicate morphology (cf. 19).

(19)

		Examples
tumu'usha	'when?'	*Tumu'usha-ya dza?* 'He came when?' *Haka-bita tumu'usha?* 'When will we go?'
tume'ika	'where?'	*Tume'ika-ya Sagilo?* 'Where is Sagilo? *Tume'ika-pe kikombe-be?* 'Where are the cups?' *Sasa, tume'ika-ta 'ono?* 'Now where shall I go?' *Tume'ika 'otaya 'ase?* 'Where will we sleep?'
tum-	'where?'	*Tum-ako mana-ko habi ts'ifi wa'in-echa?* 'Where is the meat all these nights?'
tashe-	'how much?, what size?'	*Tashe-ya sukari kwa-tita dzana?* 'How much sugar is it that you brought?' *'Onoko tashi-neko/'ono tashe-ne?* 'What size am I?' *Habi'i !'ikwi tashi-'i-pi'i?* 'What kind of sleep is this?'
tashi-	'do what?'	*'Onoko tashi-na'a?* 'I did what?' *Tashi-nikwi'/tashi-ne'e?* 'I would do what?' *Tashi-tita?* 'You will do what?' *Nasema teko, tashi teko?* 'I say, what can you do?' *Sasa 'atonena 'iba tashi?* 'Now what will we do?'
tashina	'how?'	*Tashina-ta'a dza?* 'How did you come?' *Tashina-tita hama?* 'How do you sit?'

		Examples
taka-	'how many?'	*taka-'i-pi'i?* 'how many?' *taka-'e-heya 'unu?* 'how many people?' *kwatl'a-be taka-'e-pe?* 'how many shoes?'
ta-	'who?'	*Tami-pi habi'i?* 'Of whose group, these?' *Nasema teko ta-me-ya?* 'I say, what kind of person are you?' *Ta-me?* 'Who are you (2M.SG, 2F.PL)?' *Ta-mi?* 'Who are you (2M.PL)?' *Ta-o?* 'Who are you (2F.SG)?' *Ta-o-ne'e?* 'Who am I?'
'akwadza	'who/what?'	*'Akwadza-a bami?* 'Who is he?' *'Akwadza-neko?* 'Who am I (F)?' *Akanabe-na 'akwadza 'itita?* 'What do you call it?'
'aku	'what kind?, who?, which?'	*'Aku 'unu-wa?* 'Is what kind of person?' *Habi'(i)-'aku-ni-pi'?* 'These are of what?' *'Aku meto dza?* 'Who has come?' *'Aku 'unu-wa kwa-tita* ǀ*i-ya?* 'What kind of/which person did you see?' *Ika bami 'aku gashenga?* 'And what is this thing?'

1.5 NP structure

The basic structure of a noun phrase (NP) is:

N – (agreement) (modifier)
Modifier: genitive, demonstrative, adjective, quantifier, relative

It is possible that at least some modifiers can alternatively occur before the noun. Demonstrative–noun and noun–demonstrative orders both occur in the narrative texts, as does quantifier–noun, e.g. *Yame kotula wa'ina-eta, lobe-be'e, wa'ina-ma* ǀ*'ets'a 'atonena.* 'Then they all started (saying), the big baboons, and the whole camp now.' (Bala 1998: 22).

There is insufficient information available to determine the relative ordering of modifiers within an NP, as there are very few examples of an NP with more than one modifier, as each new piece of information is preferentially introduced in a separate clause. The few examples in (20) show that modifiers may precede oblique markers.

(20)

'Aso-'o'o-	*sa*	*Gwadiso-ko*	*akwadza?*
parent-really-	OBL.3F.SG-3M.SG.COP?	Gwadiso-3F.SG	who(3M.SG.COP?)

'Who is really Gwadiso's father?'

Teko,	*taka-etete*	*pa'a*	*-tina*	*-yina?*
you(3F.SG)	how.many-2F.PL.COP	your.mother	-GEN-LOC	-2F.PL.OBL

'You (3F.SG), how many of you (3F.PL) from your mother are you (3F.PL)?'
(i.e. how many siblings do you have?)

Noun phrases may consist of more than one noun; they may be conjoined with the particle *'a* 'and, even', e.g. *Hadisi-ko kota bahe lola-ni-ko 'a ne'e-ko.* 'Here ends the story of the hare and the baboon.' (Bala 1998: 24); or occur without a conjunction, e.g. *Ko-kopandana-'a'a dza-na ǁ'ekwa, ba'ala-ko, 'aku gashenga.* 'We just found some *ǁ'ekwa* roots and honey and other things to bring to you.' (Bala 1998: 20)

Relative clauses in Hadza are post-nominal. Relatives occur either with a relative pronoun which is marked for person–number–gender and tense/aspect, e.g. *ma'a* (3M.SG relative pronoun) in *!onga ma'a 'a'ane* 'hare is who leads', or with the relativizer *kwa* (cf. 21). Relative clauses with the *kwa* relativizer are headed by a demonstrative (e.g. *hako, hama*), followed by the relativizer *kwa*, which has a pronominal subject enclitic marked for person–gender–number and tense. A noun must be raised to subject status before it can be relativized, and the relative clause is a separate clause, e.g. (21a) 'I saw the woman. It was she who hit Maria.'

(21) a. *ǁI-ta-na'a* *'akwiti-ko* *hako-kwa-kwa*
see-3F.SG.DO-1SG.PAST woman-3F.SG 3F.SG.DEM-REL-3F.SG.PAST

k'wase-ta *Maria-ko.*
hit-3F.SG.DO Maria-3F.SG
[I saw the woman. It was she who hit Maria.] 'I saw the woman who hit Maria.' (subject)

b. *ǁI-ta-na'a* *Maria-ko* *hako-kwa-kwa*
see-3F.SG.DO-1SG.PAST Maria-3F.SG 3F.SG.DEM-REL-3F.SG.PAST

k'was-iya *nena* *'akwiti-ko.*
hit-PASS INSTR woman-3F.SG
[I saw Maria. It was she who was hit.] 'I saw Maria, who was hit by a woman.' (direct object)

c. *ǁI-ya-na'a* *mu'a* *hama-kwa-mo*
see-3M.SG.DO-1SG.PAST stick(3M.SG) 3M.SG.DEM-REL-3M.SG.PAST

k'wase-ta *Maria-ko.*
hit-3F.SG.DO Maria-3F.SG [possibly *-ako*, 3F.SG.COP]
[I saw the stick. It was that which hit her Maria.] 'I saw the stick that was used to hit Maria.' (instrument)

d. *ǁI-ta-na* *hako-kwa-kwa* *bami-ni-ye.*
see-3F.SG.DO-1SG.PAST 3F.SG.DEM-REL-3F.SG.PAST 3M.SG.PRO-GEN-STAT
[I saw it. It was the one of his.] 'I saw that (3F.SG) which is his.' (possessive)

1.6 Clause structure

The basic structure of the verb phrase (VP) is:

V – (direct object clitic) – (indirect object clitic) – (subject/tense clitic) (adjunct)

or

AUX – (subject/tense clitic) V – (object clitic) (adjunct)

Adjuncts include lexical nouns and independent pronouns that are co-referential with direct and indirect object pronominal enclitics on either the auxiliary or verb, or post-positional phrases.

The location of adverbials has not been fully investigated, but there is a set of clitic adverbs that appear close to the predicate they are modifying, even before subject and object clitics, e.g. *Mits'i-kwa mite-'o'o-we-ya*. 'My brother is really getting fatter.'; *!o!o-'o'o-ko* 'really a praying mantis'; *Huma-'o'o-wako!* 'It is really!'; *Nasema mzee ya tumi'ika |'o-'aso'-aso-'eta?* 'I say, Mzee, where will we go when the house is really all filled up?' (Bala 1998: 22). These clitic adverbs attach to the main verb rather than the auxiliary, e.g. *Na 'ela-'ani ts'oko*. 'I'll quickly build a fire.'

1.7 Agreement

Hadza clauses contain subject clitics marked for person–gender–number and tense which agree with any adjoined independent subject pronouns or nouns. Direct and indirect object clitics are marked for person–gender–number and agree with any adjoined full object nominals. Genitives, locatives and other case relations have markings also showing person–gender–number agreement. Agreement is discussed in more detail in sections 1.8 and 1.9 of Hadza in Chapter 6.

2 SANDAWE

Edward D. Elderkin

2.1 Basic syntactic structures

2.1.1 Constituents

As syntactic constituents, the following categories are used:

(22)
NP	noun phrase
PP	postpositional phrase
TEMP	temporal
ADV	adverb
V	verb
VP	verb phrase
CONJ	conjunction

A functional distinction is made between NP_S (subject of a verbal clause) and NP_T (subject of a copula clause), and between NP_O (oblique, in a verbal clause or within a VP) and NP_C (complement, of a copula clause), as necessary.

VP is not analysed here as a constituent of any clause; NP_O and V are taken as separate constituents. But VP is useful in the description because it can stand as a constituent in an NP; this is crucial in the statement of the structure of some nominal clauses, specifically the general negative and the irrealis.

The above categories are placed in a syntactic framework by the use of sequence, grammatical formatives and tone keys, which allow syntactic and informational relationships to be interpreted.

2.1.2 Symbolisation

Tree diagrams are used to illustrate structures, as they are described here; they refer to the surface structure only. They should not be taken as relating to any theory of language.

It should be repeated that the description here relates to an interpretation of what I see as the origin of certain structures: where clause structures derive from the nominal clause, and yet within them have a verb, they are susceptible to interpretation on the analogy of verbal clauses, which are here described as having a verb as a constituent; this reinterpretation has been demonstrated by Eaton (2002).

When what is here called a nominal PGN appears, it is assumed that what precedes it must be something which functions as a nominal stem, and such information is included in the tree diagrams for clarity: so "PP (= NSt)" identifies a postpositional phrase which functions as a noun stem (in that it is followed by a nominal PGN).

2.2 Clause structures

2.2.1 Verbal clause

2.2.1.1 Sequence

The sequence of the major constituents of verbal clause structure is:

(23) NP_S NP_O V

Between the NP_S and the V are found also PPS within the clause. At least one of the constituents is normally marked. Marking is by

either *áː* NOM suffixed to the NP_S
or the subject PGN suffixed to any clause constituent except NP_S
or both of the above.

One or more constituents may be so marked, except that if the verb is marked, no other constituent may be marked.

(24)

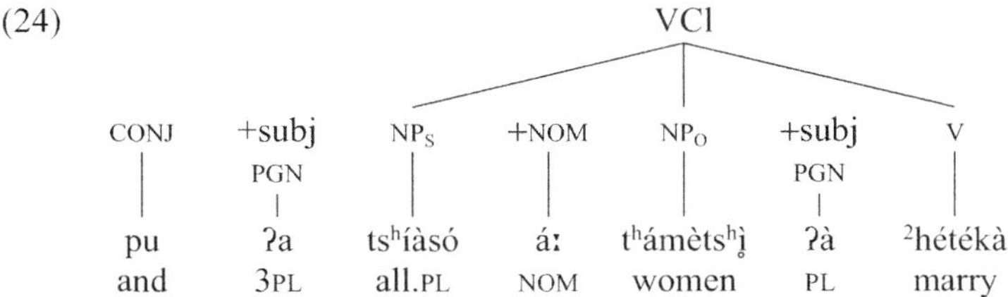

^{3}ʔáː ^{1}tsʰíàsáː ^{1}tʰámètsʰàʔ̥̀ ^{2}hétékà
'and they all had married wives'

Marking brings the constituent marked (except a conjunction) into prominence in the information structure of the clause; marking the verb could be interpreted as bringing the whole clause into prominence. More specifically, Eaton (2005) suggests that it focuses polarity.

2.2.1.2 Keys

NP_S and NP_O have an underlying Key 2, as do PPS; V has an underlying Key 3. A marked constituent is promoted to Key 1. Those unmarked constituents, NPS and PPS, which precede the marked constituent, are also promoted to Key 1. As keys may not be jumped downwards, V after a marked Key 1 is promoted to Key 2, although in practice, where the preceding marked constituent contains a downward key transposition or a downstep, downdrift often causes the Key 2 on V to be heard as Key 3.

(25)

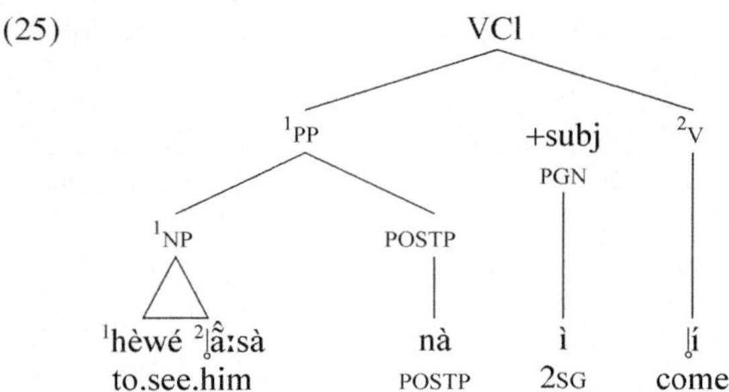

[1]Hèwé [2]ǀ̥ȃːsànìː [3]ǀ̥í.
'You came to see him.'

It is not obligatory that a clause should contain a marked constituent raised to Key 1; the following sentence has two clauses, but only one example of such raised marking.

(26)

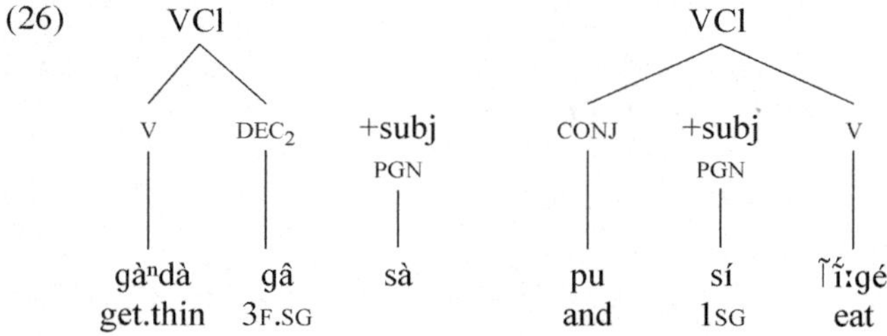

[1]Gàⁿdàgâsà [3]síː [3]ǀ̃ǐ́ːgé.
'It got thin and I ate it.'

In the following example, where three clause constituents are marked, the speaker has had to resort to a phonetic raising of the third constituent (shown by ↑) in order to achieve the prominence she desired.

(27)

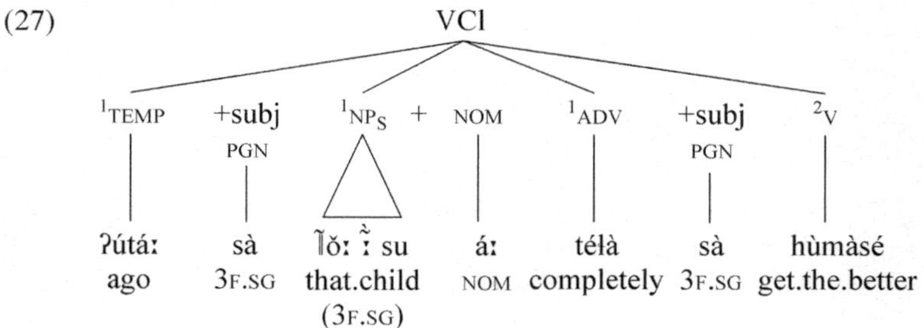

[1]ʔútáːsà [1]ǀ̃ǒːǐswáː ↑[1]télàsà [2]hùmàsé.
'That child *always* used to get the upper hand.'

It is clear that some uses of the system of word keys are syntactic and emic. But in the transcription the allocation of a key to each word includes some decisions which are etic. A fuller statement would possibly explain some key allocations in the framework of an intonational system which related to information structure and other allocations of key to the syntax.

2.2.1.3 Other constituents

A more complete statement needs to include other categories as constituents of the verbal clause: the conjunction, the temporal, and the adverbial (the latter two have been illustrated in the preceding example). It does not seem revealing to attempt to place in sequence the constituents appearing between the NP_S and the V.

(28)

$$\text{CONJ} \quad \text{TEMP} \quad \text{NP}_S \quad \begin{Bmatrix} \text{NP}_O \\ \text{ADV} \\ \text{PP} \end{Bmatrix} \quad \text{V}$$

There is much extrapositioning in conversation. Material following the verb should be considered as extrapositioned. As a rule of thumb, material should be considered to be preposed if it appears before the narrative conjunction, before a temporal (if no conjunction is present) or before the first marked constituent (if neither conjunction nor temporal is present before it). There is nevertheless also scrambling within the clause itself.

The first of the following two sentences has a fairly unmarked constituent sequence; in the second, *hèwéts'ḭ* 'for that reason' is given more prominence by preceding *ʔútáː*.

(29) a. *^{3}póː ^{2}ʔútáː ^{1}hèwéts'òː ^{1}mǒːtònòː ^{2}k'ómé*
pó: ʔútáː hèwé ts'ì ò mǒːtò nà ò k'ómé
N.CONJ.1PL ago 3M.SG POSTP 1PL Moto LOC 1PL move
'and at that time we moved to Moto for that reason'

b. *^{3}póː ^{1}hèwéts'òː ^{2}ʔútáː ^{2}níʔ̥̀*
póː hèwé ts'ì ò ʔútáː níʔ̥̀
N.CONJ.1PL 3M.SG POSTP 1PL ago go (PL.SUBJ)
'and for that reason we went at that time'

2.2.1.4 Temporal

ʔútáː in these examples is one of a small number of clause constituents, usually monomorphemic, which relate to time and which have an underlying Key 3. They often appear towards the beginning of a clause preceding the marked constituent where they are promoted to Key 2. They are nouns, but when used with this underlying Key 3 within clause structure, can be considered as a distinct constituent category, temporals.

(30) *ʔútè* 'yesterday'
ʔútáː 'some time ago'
swê 'now'

(31) *^{2}ʔútè ^{1}hàpú ^{2}ts'ăːkùsà ^{3}ǁ̃ĕː.*
ʔútè hàpú ts'ăːkù sà ǁ̃ĕː
2SG home 3F.SG arrive
'Yesterday she arrived at your house.'

2.2.1.5 Narrative conjunction

It is convenient to refer to the word which contains the conjunction *pu* followed by a subject PGN as the narrative conjunction. Despite the presence of a subject PGN, the narrative conjunction is never promoted to Key 1. It is usually heard on Key 3, although occasionally it seems to have Key 2, especially where the following key is Key 1.

(32) *^{2}kwáː ^{1}łúpàː ^{2}tł'ăː*
kwáː łúpà à tł'ăː
N.CONJ.3M.SG grass 3M.SG take
'and he took the grass'

But the fact that the narrative conjunction contains a subject PGN does mean that the verb of the clause may not be so marked. To achieve the same effect as marking, the verb can be brought to an early part of the clause and given Key 1.

(33) *^{3}kwáː ^{1}ǁ'àtá ^{2}láːʔȅː*
kwáː ǁ'àtá láːʔè ȉː
N.CONJ.3M.SG be.tired hare SPEC
'and the hare got tired'

2.2.1.6 Imperative

The imperative is a verbal clause. The nominative suffix *áː* can appear with an imperative PGN. (For the imperative PGN system, see Chapter 6, p. 128 (65).)

(34) *^{1}Dàrímòxì̥sà ^{2}ʔíts^{h}àwà.*
dàrímò xì̥ sà ʔíts^{h}àwà
field.shelter 3F.SG look.for (IMPF)
'Let her look for a hut in the bush.'

(35) *^{1}Hísà ^{2}gằ^{n}dàjʔ̥̀ ^{1}ǂ̃íːgékò ^{1}hàpáː.*
hí sà gà^{n}dà jʔ̥̀ ǂ̃íːgé kò hàpú áː
'if . .' 3F.SG get.thin '. . if' eat 2SG NOM
'If it gets thin, you eat it.'

2.2.2 Exclamatory clause

The clause constituents found in a verbal clause may be used in the subject-initial, verb-final, sequence with *ts'ì* marking any object, and without either subject PGN or the nominative *áː*. All constituents are given Key 1. The import of such a clause is surprise or praise.

(36) *^{1}Tàtá ^{1}t^{h}ékáts'ì ^{1}!'ìné!*
tàtá t^{h}éká ts'ì !'ìné
father leopard OBL hunt
'Father can really hunt leopards!'

ts'ì suffixed to an object is also found in the basic sentences; the correlations of this are not yet understood (see also Chapter 6, p. 134 (104)).

2.2.3 Nominal clause

The structure of the nominal clause is

(37) NP_T NP_C

The straightforward interpretation is as a copula. Each constituent is in Key 1.

(38)

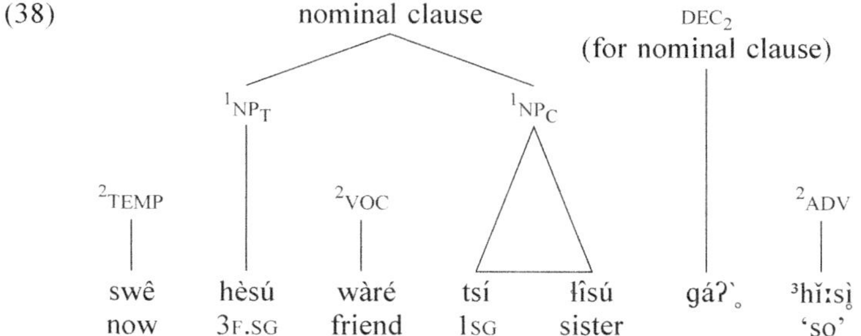

^{2}Swê ^{1}hèsú ^{2}wàré ^{1}tsí ^{2}łîsúgáʔ`̥ ^{3}hǐːsį̊.
'She's my sister you know.'

The nominal clause forms the basis of the irrealis clause and of the general negative clause.

2.3 Phrase structure

Three categories of phrase may be distinguished:

(39) NP noun phrase
PP postpositional phrase
VP verb phrase

2.3.1 Noun phrase

It is difficult to give a sequenced structure for the NP; the following constituents are found dominated by NP:

(40) nominal
demonstrative
pronoun

A nominal may be followed by the specificiser *ḭ̀̂*. Nominals have the structure NSt + N.PGN. As the specificiser has the structure *ḭ̀̂* + N.PGN, it might be better to consider it syntactically a separate constituent within a phrase, although morphologically it forms one word with the preceding nominal.

2.3.1.1 Genitive

A genitive relationship between a noun and another constituent is achieved by using tone keys, the key of the noun is one key below that of the other consituent, which precedes the noun. The noun can be considered to be the head noun. The other consituent is an NP, the genitive constituent. In the following examples, ^{n} represents a key number, determined syntactically.

(41) ^{n}NP + $^{n+1}$N

This structure stands as a noun.

(42)

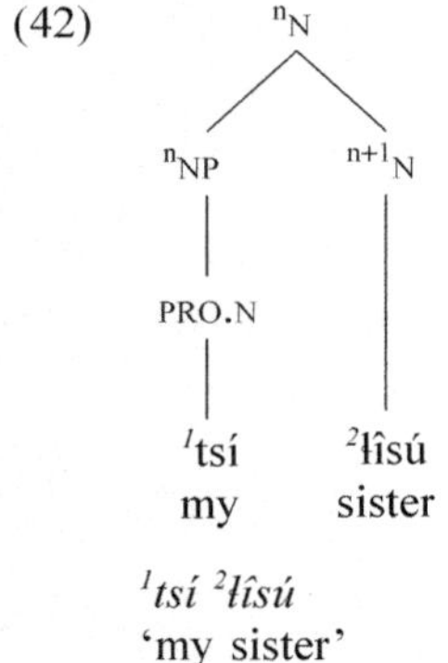

¹tsí ²ɬîsú
'my sister'

The NP in this genitive structure may itself consist of a genitive construction:

(43)

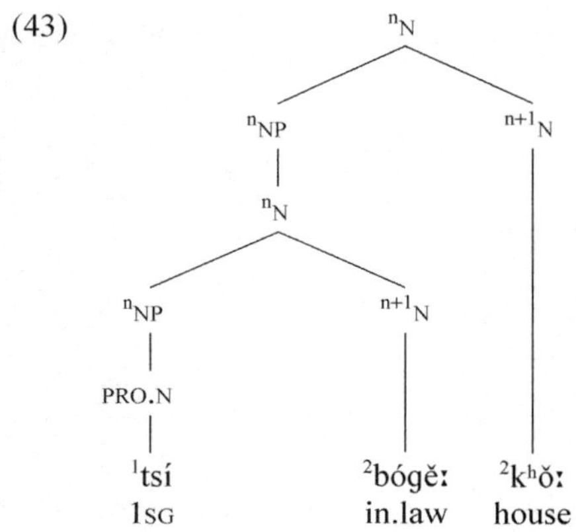

¹tsí ²bógěː ²kʰǒː
'my in-law's house'

Items otherwise used as TEMP, being nouns, may be found as the genitive constituent:

(44) *¹ʔútáː ²ǃ̃êsi̥ . . . ²ǀ̥í.*
ʔútáː ǃ̃ê si̥ ǀ̥í
ago day 1SG come
'I came the day before yesterday.'

(45) *¹ʔèʔéː ²mìrîgĩ̀ː*
ʔèʔéː mìrîgì ĩ̀ː
that.time medicine SPEC
'the remedy of that time (the one which I showed you)'

A PP can also be used in the genitive position:

(46) *¹ⁿdêgèʔĩ̀ː ²mĩ̌ːdzỗː*
ⁿdêgè ʔĩ̀ː mĩ̌ːdzó ĩ̀ː
plane POSTP journey SPEC
'travel by air'

2.3.1.2 Genitive with pronominal head

The head noun in NP + N may be pronominalised. Its PRO form is *j̀*, which is morphologically cliticised to the last word of the preceding constituent; *j̀* is in the key of the preceding constituent, that is, there is no change of key.

(47) ^{1}*hàpî:ts'é*
hàpú j̀ ts'é
2SG NEG
'that's not your (job)'

(48)

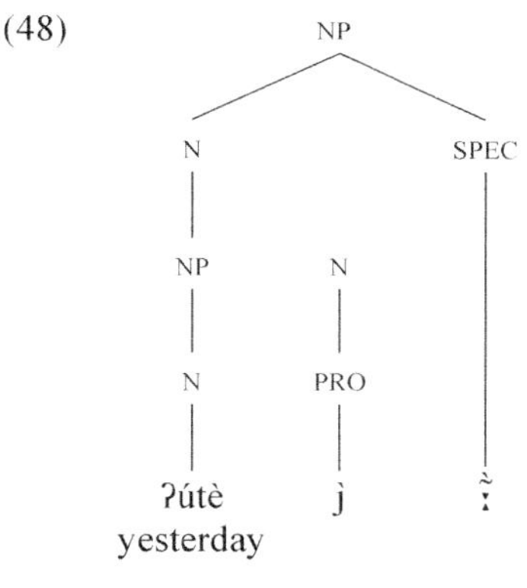

(^{2}*ĩ̃ŏ:ì*) ^{2}*ʔútȅjj*
'(that child,) that one of yesterday'

This construction is the basis for one type of relative clause and clauses introduced by *hí*; see (88) and (93).

2.3.2 *Postposition phrase*

The PP has the structure

(49) NP + POSTP

More than one postposition can be found (see examples in the Chapter 6, p. 131f. (81) and (82)): the structure of the PP can then be taken as PP + POSTP.

There is one postposition which has only been found as final constituent in a PP which functions as a noun stem in that the PP is always followed by a nominal PGN suffix. This postposition is *ts*^{h}*è/ts*^{h}*ì̥* 'from' (privative), which is identical to the negative marker *ts*^{h}*è/ts*^{h}*ì̥* and cognate with the nominal stem *ts*^{h}*ĕ:* 'being in a state of absence', both of which are also followed by a nominal PGN suffix. The nominal and the preposition are illustrated in the following examples; for the negative, see examples (69–75).

(50) Nominal stem: *tsʰěː*

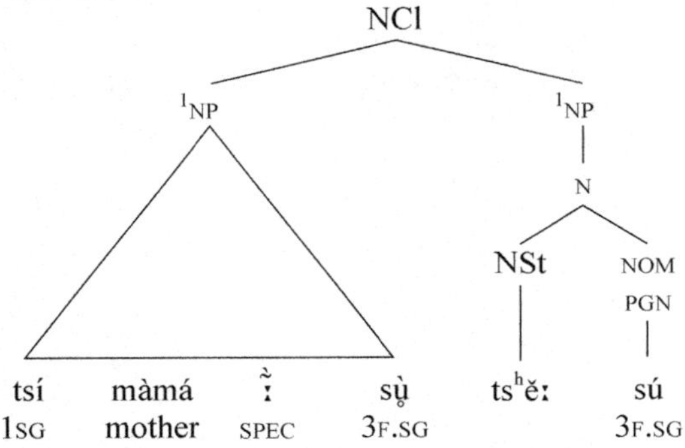

^{1}Tsí ^{2}màmâːsṳ̀ ^{1}tsʰěːsú.
'My mother wasn't there.'

(51) Postposition:

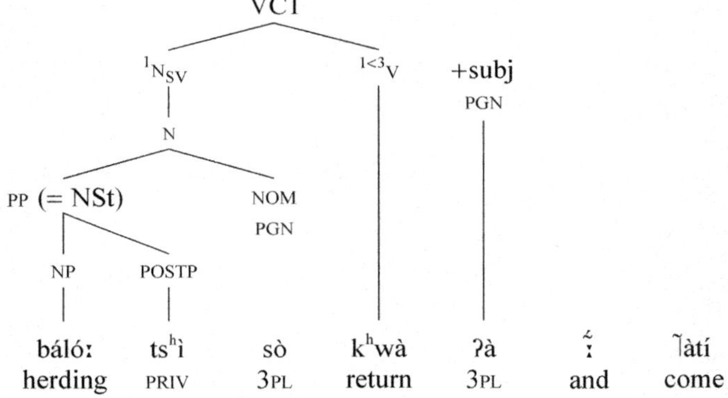

^{1}Bálóːtsʰìsò ^{1}kʰwàʔăː ^{2}ǀàtí.
'They returned from herding.'

The form with the nominal PGN for 3M.SG is *tsʰè*.

(52) *^{1}ǀèmésé: ^{1}têáː ^{1}sà^{n}dàwěːtsʰèáː . . . ^{3}ḽí.*

ǀèmésé:	tê	áː	sà^{n}dàwěː	tsʰè	áː	ḽí
person	other	NOM	Sandawe	PRIV	NOM	come

'Another person, from Usandawe, came.'

With 3MLT, a *wà* has been noted before the postposition (the PP, with a 3MLT NP, as in (53), takes the 3M.SG nominal PGN).

(53) *^{1}Hěːxwèná ^{1}kíbáʔ̥xě̂ː ^{2}tsʰâː ^{1}hákṳ̀wàtsʰè?*

há	kṳ̀	wà	tsʰè	Ø
Q	POSTP	MLT	PRIV	3M.SG

'Where's that fat on the hearth from?'

Such an N, that is with PP + NOM PGN, can stand, as would be expected, as an NP followed by the nominative marker or followed by the subject PGN in the normal way, as in the following example:

(54)

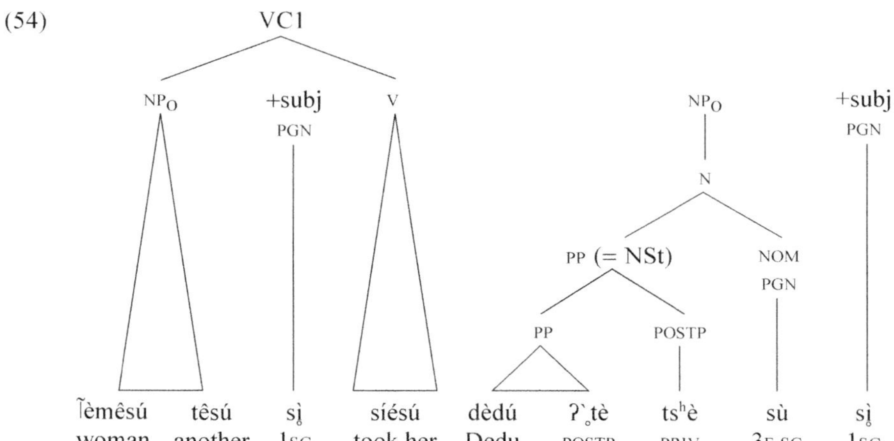

¹Ĩèmêsú ¹têsúsį̀ ²síésú ¹dèdúʔ`̥tètsʰèsùsį̀.
'I married another woman, from the Dedu area.'

2.3.3 *Verb phrase and the irrealis*

A VP consists of a series of one or more NP$_O$s, one or more PPs, and finally, a V; only V is obligatorily present, and none of the NPs is the NP$_S$. It is, in other words, the predicate of a clause, that is, a clause without any NPs which constitute the subject, and without any subject PGN.

The VP, as it has been used in the present analysis, always stands in an NP; VP is used in the present analysis to explain the structure of two clause types, the irrealis, described in this section, and the general negative, for which see section 2.5.1 below. As the VP stands as a nominal, it may, in other uses, be followed by the specificiser ː̃̀.

(55)

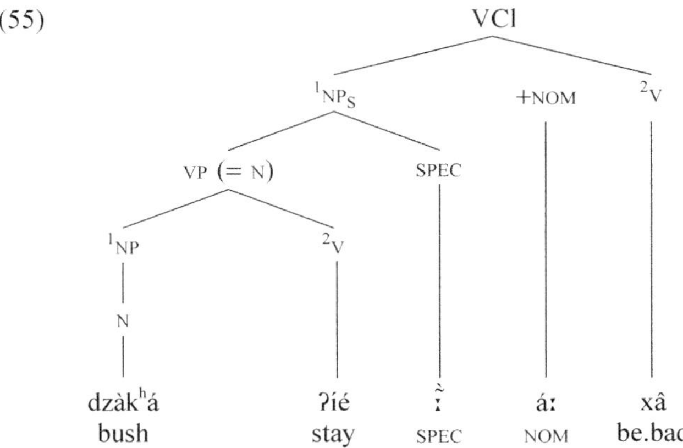

¹dzàkʰá ²ʔíễːgáː ²xâ.
'Staying in the bush is bad.'[1]

A VP can stand as the NP in a genitive construction, where the head N is a PRO form.

(56)

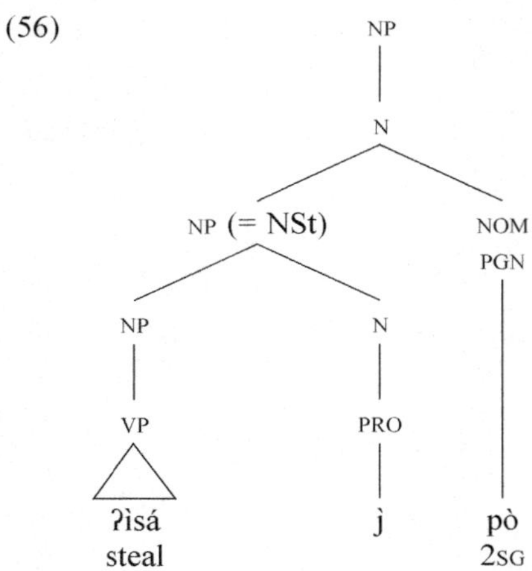

ʔìsâjpò.
'(You are) somebody who steals.'

As a nominal, this can take the specifier.

(57) *ʔìsâjpȍːpò.* '(You are) that one who steals.'

However, this structure is further developed; if the PRO form is merely `, that is, the lowering of an immediately preceding high mora, the clause becomes an irrealis clause, used for future events and events that did not happen. (The fuller form, *j̀*, is retained in the 3M.SG.)

(58)

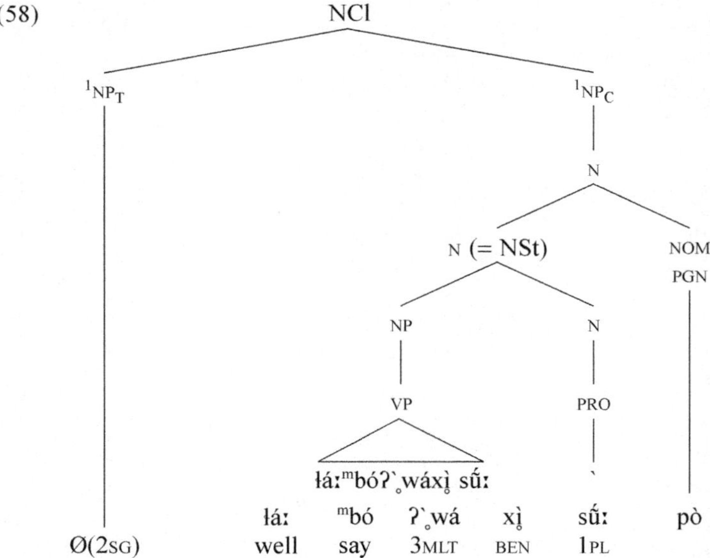

^{1}ɬáː ^{2m}bóʔ`̥wáxì̥sű́ːìpò.
'You will tell us properly.'

2.4 Declarative *gê ké:*

There are two forms, which seem likely to share a common origin: DEC$_1$ *ké:* and *gê/gâ*. *ké:* always retains this form, except when the final mora is lowered in the irrealis.

(59) *^{1}Tlǎ:si̥ké:̀pò.*
tlǎ:si̥   ké: ̀   pò
die   IRR   2SG
'You will die.'

ké: is found suffixed to constituents in verbal and in nominal clauses.

(60) *^{1}Hôké:á: ^{2}xế: ^{2}ǀ̥í?*
hô   ké: á: xé: ̋:   ǀ̥í
who   NOM   bring   and   come
'Who came and brought it?'

(61) *^{1}Sű: ^{2}jáʔ̥̀bȍ:kíná ^{1}téɬàké:gò: ^{2}ʔútèsíʔ̥̀ ^{3}tóẁ.*
sű: jáʔ̥̀bȍ: kí   ná   téɬà   ké: gê   ò   ʔútèsíʔ̥̀   tóẁ
our work   even   'so'   completely   DEC$_1$ DEC$_2$ 2PL   yesterday   finish
'As far as our work is concerned, we completely finished it yesterday.'

gê is found in the verbal clause, suffixed to a constituent other than the subject, where it is followed by a subject PGN.

(62) *^{1}Tsí ^{1}sèʔégàsi̥ ^{2}mě:nà: ^{2}hě:ẁ ^{2}mâ^{n}ts^{h}ȁ:.*
tsí   sèʔé   gâ   si̥   mě:nà: hě:ẁ   mâ^{n}ts^{h}ȁ:
1SG   much   1SG   like.it   this   food
'I really like this food.'

It is also used within the following structure to form a nominal:

(63)

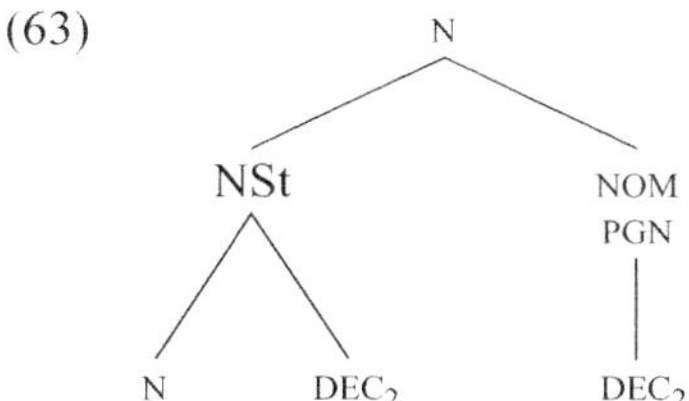

(64) *ʔárá:gê!* (ʔárá:gè) (with 3M.SG as Ø)
'It's true!'

This structure is also found with demonstratives, as in

(65) *nêpògêpó*
'you (2SG) there'

and with more complex nominals:

(66) *^{1}Tsí ^{2}wàré ^{2}swê ^{1}hǎ:ẁ ^{1}sȁ^{n}dàwě: ↑^{1}màgàsi̥tá:ts'i̥ế::̀si̥gâsi̥.*
tsí   wàré   swê   hǎ:ẁ   sà^{n}dàwě: màgàsi̥tá:ts'i̥ẽ::̀si̥gâsi̥
1SG   friend   now   that   Sandawe
'Now, friend, I'm that sort of Sandawe, a man from Mangastaa.'

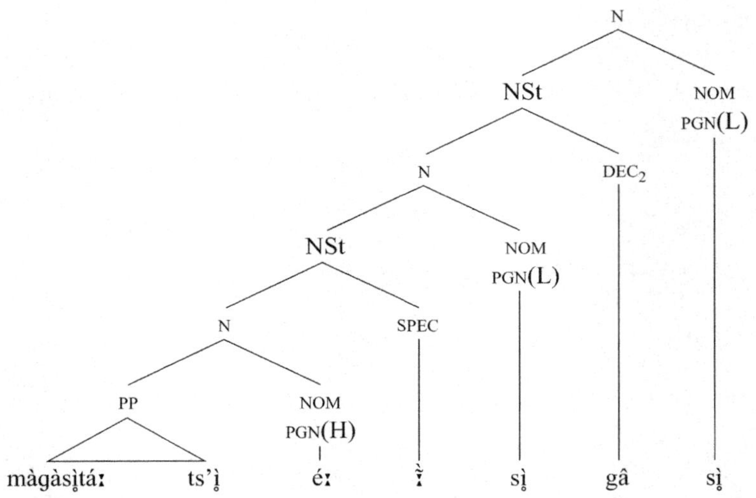

Where *gê*/*gâ* is suffixed to a nominal clause, the nominal PGN agrees with the clause. The appropriate nominal PGN for this is 3C.SG, *ʔ̥̀*, giving the form *gáʔ̥̀*.

(67) *^{1}ʔútáːsíʔ̥̀ ^{1}síésûsi̥gáʔ̥̀ ^{2}hèsú.*

ʔútáːsíʔ̥̀	síé	sú	`	sì	gáʔ̥̀	hèsú
long.ago	take	3F.SG	IRR	1SG		3F.SG

'I really was going to marry her a long time ago, that one.'

(68) *^{1}Tsí ^{1}bógěːsísi̥gáʔ̥̀.*

tsí	bógěː	sí	sì	gáʔ̥̀
1SG	uncle		1SG	

'I've got an uncle.'

2.5 Negative

As a clause, a verbal clause is not directly negated; a different structure, the general negative, is used for this purpose.

The negative formative is *tsʰè*/*tsʰi̥*; just as the cognate homophonous postposition (cf. Chapter 6, p. 131f.), it is always followed by a nominal PGN.

2.5.1 Negative clause

2.5.1.1 General negative

The general negative serves as the negative to the verbal clause; its structure is that of a nominal clause, in which the complement is a noun whose stem is a postposition phrase. This can be stated as:

(69) ^{1}NP$_T$ ^{1}VP tsʰi̥ NOM PGN

This constituency is illustrated below:

(70)

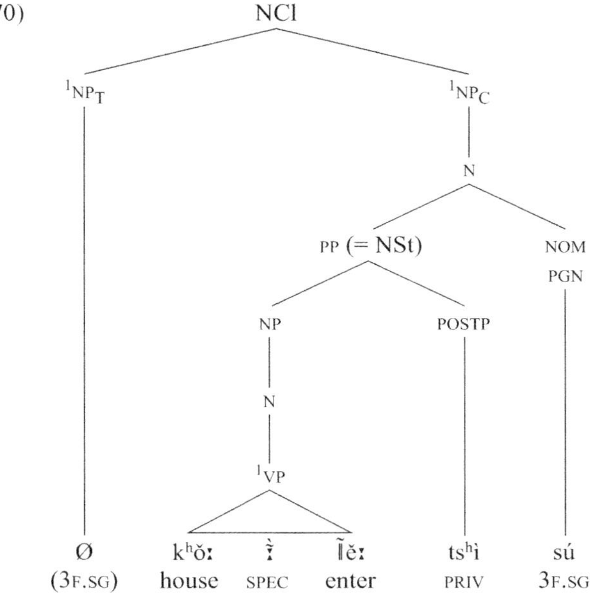

¹Kʰǒ̀ː ²ǁ̃ěːˈtsʰú.
'She did not enter the house.'

As the complement is an NP, it is not surprising that an NP with an identical structure should stand at other places. Compare the two following clauses:

(71) *¹Mâⁿtsʰàtsʰìpó.* or mâⁿtsʰàpó (= mâⁿtsʰàˈpó) 'You do not eat.'
¹Mâⁿtsʰàtsʰìpáː ²ǁ'ô. 'You sleep without eating.'

In the first clause, *mâⁿtsʰàtsʰìpó* stands as NP_C, the NP_T is absent, but, as the nominal PGN suffix in the NP_C shows, the absent NP_T is 2SG. In the second clause, *mâⁿtsʰàtsʰìpó* is the NP which is the subject of a verbal clause, and is suffixed with the nominative marker, *áː*.

2.5.1.2 Negative of nominal clause

In dealing with the declarative, it was noted that the nominal PGN suffix agreement for a clause is 3C.SG, *ʔ̥̀* (see 2.4). Negation of a nominal clause is achieved as follows:

(72) NCl + *tsʰè/tsʰḭ̀* + *ʔ̥̀*

The two last constituents coalesce to form *ts'é*.

(73)

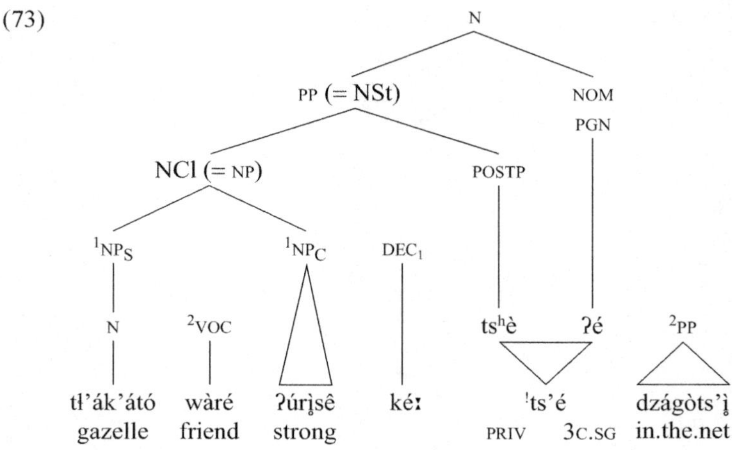

[1]Tł'ák'átó [2]wàré [1]ʔúrḭsêkéː'ts'é [2]dzágòts'ḭ.
'A gazelle has no strength in the net.'

There is a fuller form of *ts'é*, which is *ts'èʔé*, in which the 3C.SG PGN is retained, but the *tsʰè* nevertheless appears as *ts'è*.

(74) *[2]Swêsíʔ̥̀ [1]ʔíxíː ts'èʔé.*

swê	síʔ̥̀	ʔíxíː	ts'èʔé
now	'then'	thus	

'So now, it's not like this.'

2.5.1.3 Irrealis negative

Not surprisingly, as the irrealis clause is based on the structure of a nominal clause, it forms its negative in the same way as a nominal clause, by postposing *'ts'é*.

(75) *[1]Hěːẁ [1]kókỗː [1]wáʔ̥̀máːtà [1]ǁ'ôjts'é.*

hěːẁ	kókó	ː̥̃̀	wáʔ̥̀máː	tà	ǁ'ô	j̀	Ø	ts'é
3M.SG	cockerel	SPEC	companions	POSTP	sleep	IRR	3M.SG	NEG

'This cockerel doesn't sleep with his kind.'

2.5.1.4 Imperative negative

The negative in an imperative is *měː*.

(76) *[1]Měːkò [2]ʔísḭ!*

měː	kò	ʔísḭ
	2SG	refuse

'Don't refuse!'

Note that in an affirmative clause, *měː* is to be understood as 'nearly'.

(77) *[1]ǀ'wǎ̃ː [1]měːgàː [2]séléʔ̥̀kô [2]gùᵐbǔːts'ḭ.*

ǀ'wǎ̃ː	měː	gê	à	séléʔ̥̀	kô	gùᵐbǔː	ts'ḭ
millet		DEC_2	3M.SG	be.missing	'so'	Gumbu	POSTP

'There nearly wasn't any millet at Gumbu.'

2.5.2 Negative phrase

A phrase is negated *qua* nominal clause, and not *qua* phrase. If a phrase were negated as a phrase, it would be expected that the nominal PGN suffix which followed the negative marker *tsʰè*/*tsʰi̥* would be in agreement with the PGN of the phrase. A phrase is negated with *ts'é*, which incorporates the 3C.SG *ʔ̥̀*. But the object agreement in the verb of the next example seems to demonstrate that the PGN characteristics of the NP are retained in the agreement.

(78) ^{1}*ʔ̃èmêsũ̏:ts'ê:* ^{2}*l̥ȃ:sű:.*

ʔ̃èmêsũ̏:	ts'é	è	l̥ȃ:	sű:
person.1PL	NEG	2PL	see	1PL

'You won't consider us to be (proper) people.' (lit.: you see us as being not (proper) people)

As a form negated with *ts'é* is a nominal, it can be followed by the specificiser. The following example contains the fuller form of the negative, *ts'èʔé*.

(79)

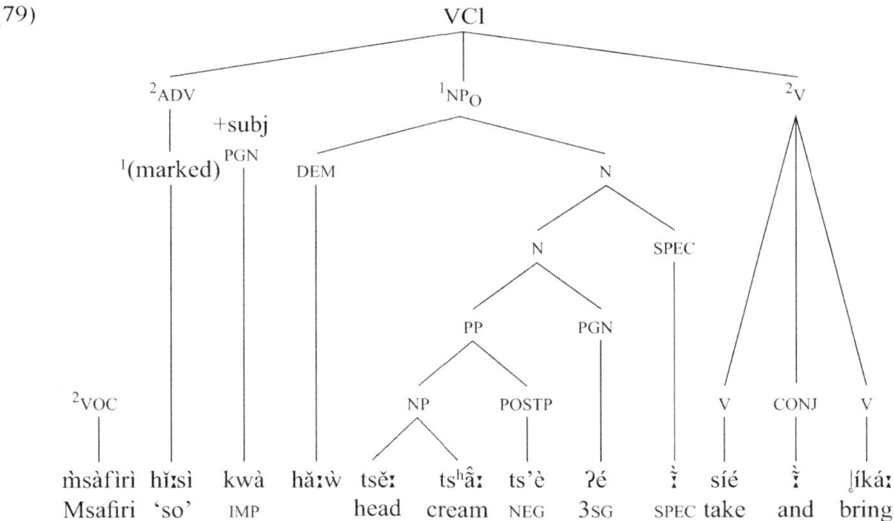

^{2}*m̀sàfîrì* ^{1}*hǐ:si̥kwà* ^{1}*hǎ:ẁ* ^{1}*tsě:* ^{2}*tsʰȃ:ts'èʔê̋:* ^{2}*síê̋:* ^{2}*l̥íká:.*
'Msafiri, go and get the cream which isn't hair cream.'

2.6 Interrogative

Interrogative constituents are characterised by an initial *h-*. Syntactically the only one deserving comment here is *híkí* (sometimes recorded as *hìkí*) 'how', which, normally adverbial, in the irrealis has been noted used seemingly as a verb.

(80) ^{1}*Híkìsũ̏:* ^{1}*léʔ̥̀.*

híkí	`	sũ̏:	léʔ̥̀
	IRR	1PL	'don't.know'

'I don't know what we should do.'

2.6.1 Yes/no interrogative, affirmative

The yes/no interrogative has *nè*, which is suffixed to the constituent which is questioned. The categorial status of that constituent is not changed. In verbal sentences, that constituent is marked by the subject PGN or the nominative suffix.

(81)	TEMP	VOC	NP_C		
	^{2}ʔútá:	*^{2}lé:bà*	*^{1}ts^{h}ĕ:pónè?*		
	ʔútá:	lé:bà	ts^{h}ĕ:	pó	nè
	absent	Leeba	not.be	2SG	Q

'At that time, Leeba, were you absent?'

(82)	NP_S	ADV	V		
	^{1}Ts^{h}íàná:	*^{1}ɬá:*	*^{2}ǁ'ôǁ'ô?*		
	ts^{h}íà	nè	á:	ɬá:	^{2}ǁ'ôǁ'ô
	all	Q	NOM	well	sleep

'Had they all slept well?'

(83)	V			
	^{1}K^{h}éʔéwànì:?			
	k^{h}éʔé	wà	nè	ì
	hear	MLT	Q	2SG

'Have you heard (of it)?'

2.6.2 Yes/no interrogative, negative

The negative interrogative marker is *ts'énè* (for *ts'é*, see above). However, its use is often more of emphasis than of interrogation. It can be used in verbal clauses, where it can be seen as negating and querying a phrase, or even the verb itself.

(84)	V	NP_O		
	^{1}Mànă:^{1}ts'énà:	*^{1}ǁ'ínéwàts'ȅ:^{2}ǃȇ:?*		
	mànă:	ts'é nè	à	(see 89)
	know	NEG Q	3M.SG	

'He knew, didn't he, when they'd be ripe?'

(85)	NP_S	ADV	V		
	^{1}Hèwé	*^{1}ǁ̥ŏ:xı̥̀ts'énà:*	*^{2}ʔíḛ́:^{2}ǁ'ô?*		
	hèwé	ǁ̥ŏ:xı̥̀	ts'é nè	à	ʔíé ː̰ ǁ'ô
	DEM	still	NEG Q	3M.SG	stay and sleep

'He was *still* asleep?'

In an example such as the following, *hàpúts'énè* is taken as a nominal stem, suffixed with the 2SG *po*. As a clause on its own, *hàpúts'énè* would be taken as a nominal clause: 'It's not you, is it?'

(86)		NP_S			VOC		NP_O	V	
	Hàpú	*ts'énè*	*pó*	*á:*	*wàré*	*tsí*	*nàʔásò*	*xwánȉ:*	*wà?*
	2SG	NEG.Q	2SG	NOM	friend	1SG	fruit.sp	scrape	MLT

^{1}hàpúts'énèpá: ^{2}wàré ^{2}tsí ^{3}nàʔásò ^{4}xwánȉ:wà

'It's you isn't it who've grubbed up my fruits?'

The putative origin of *ts'é* given above is such that it would be expected to be final in a third person nominal. But in its use in *ts'énè*, it seems to have shed all status as a third person nominal; its suffixation, as the suffixation of *ne* alone, does not alter the categorial or PGN characteristics of the preceding constituent.

2.7 Parameters within a clause

Perfective and imperfective forms of verbs have different syntactic possibilities. With an imperfective verb stem, the NP_O has the possibility of being suffixed with a *ts'ḭ̥* under circumstances unclear to me. With intransitive verbs, where no overt exponent of the perfective has been noted, how, or if, any system of perfectivity is extended to them remains to be researched.

The question of agreements with multiple NP_s and the relationship between the ideas of multiple, pluriactional, frequentative and habitual and the like have yet to be disentangled; Kießling (2002) is a start.

2.8 Coordination and subordination

2.8.1 Coordination

The frequent marker of coordination is *ĩ́*, for which longer versions *hĩ́ː* and *nĩ́ː* exist. *à* is also found conjoining verbs or clauses; the whole word which includes this *à* is often in Key 1, as below.

(87) *¹ʔóʔàː ¹ǀ̥âː ²!'ŏːsű̃ː.*
ʔóʔ`̥ à ǀ̥í à !'ŏː sű̃ː
here 3M.SG come meet 1PL
'He came and met us here.'

2.8.2 Relative clauses

Where other languages might use a subject relative clause, Sandawe has the construction with *sí* (see Chapter 6). Two structures have been noted equivalent to non-subject relative clauses.

2.8.2.1 Pronominal genitive with clause

With a pronominalised N, the genitive constituent may be a verbal clause; the translation equivalent in English has a relative clause.

(88)

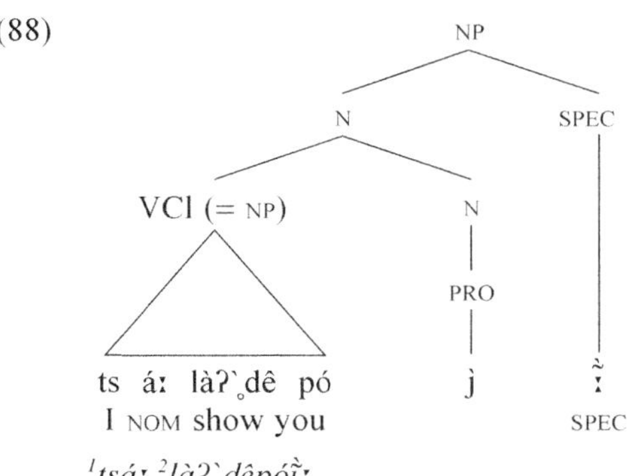

¹tsáː ²làʔ`̥dêpóĩ̃ː
'that one which I showed you'

2.8.2.2 Relative clause with *ts'è*

I do not yet understand the structure or origin of the use of *ts'è* in relative clauses. Three examples are given here.

(89) *¹ǁ'ínéwàts'ȅː ²ǃ͂ễː*
ǁ'íné wà ts'è ȉ ǃ͂ê ȉ
ripen MLT SPEC day SPEC
'the day they would be ripe'

(90) *¹Sű́ː ¹ǃ̥wăː ¹ǁ'ôts'èò ²ʔítsʰà.*
sű́ː ǃ̥wăː ǁ'ô ts'è ò ʔítsʰà
1PL place sleep 1PL look.for
'We're looking for a place to sleep.'

(91) *¹Hòsáː ²ǂ͂wéːwàts'ȅː mànàːsípò?*
hòsó áː ǂ͂wéː wà ts'è ȉ mànàːsípò
3PL NOM do MLT SPEC you.know.it
'Have you got to know what they do there?'

2.8.3 Temporal and hypothetical clauses

2.8.3.1 *hí . . . ʔ̥̀*

Such a clause is introduced by the conjunction *hí*, which must be followed by the subject PGN. It is closed by *j̀* followed by *ʔ̥̀*.

(92) *¹híà ²ǃ͂ĕːj̀ʔ̥̀* 'when he arrived'

Any number of clauses may appear between *hí* and *j̀ʔ̥̀*.

Where the subordinated clause is a nominal clause, the subject PGN agreement is not available. Here, the subject PGN agreement relates to the whole clause; we have seen that the appropriate nominal PGN to refer to whole clauses is the 3C.SG *ʔ̥̀* (its use in *gáʔ̥̀* and in the formation of the negative *ts'é*). There is no special 3C.SG subject PGN: the 3M.SG *à* is used. The following analysis assumes a conjectural analysis for *j̀ʔ̥̀* as pronominal in a genitive, (*j̀*), plus a locative, (*ts'ȉ̥ > ʔ̥̀*). The presence of *j̀* with a basic clause is probably historically parallel, but synchronically opaque.

(93)

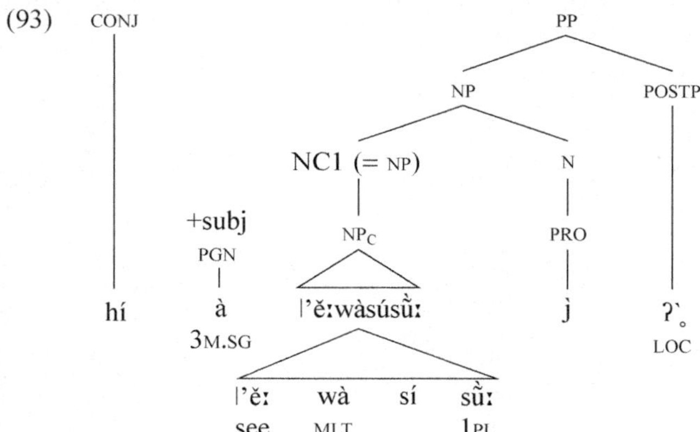

¹híà ²ǀ'ĕːwàsúsű̀ːgìːʔ̥̀
'when (if) we are capable of seeing (i.e. if we are alive)'

(94) *^{1}Hèwéxéːkí ^{1}híà ^{1}tlàkîpôjʔ̥̀ ^{1}hákụ̊?*
hèwéxéː kí hí à tlàkî pó j̀ ʔ̥̀ hákụ̊
DEM.3MLT too 3M.SG lack 2SG where
'Those things, if you haven't got any, what is there to do?'

2.8.3.2 *síʔ̥̀*

síʔ̥̀ (see discussion of *sí*, p. 134f.) is also found suffixed to a clause to show a subordinate status.

(95) *^{1}Kǒ^{n}dóànàsi̥ ^{2}hík'i̥ ^{1}lîvùáː ^{2}ts^{h}ĕːkísíʔ̥̀.*
kò^{n}dóà nà sì hík'i̥ lîvù áː ts^{h}ĕːkí síʔ̥̀
Kondoa POSTP 1SG go vacation NOM be.finished
'I went to Kondoa when the holidays were over.'

(96) *^{1}Wàgéːáː ^{2}síésúsíʔ̥̀ . . . ^{1}hèwé ^{2}!'úmánà ^{3}xéːswìːts'énè*
wàgéː áː sié sú síʔ̥̀
stranger NOM take 3F.SG
'If an outsider marries her,

hèwé !'úmá nà xéː sú j̀ Ø ts'énè?
3M.SG land POSTP bring 3F.SG IRR 3M.SG NEG Q
he would take her to his country, wouldn't he?'

3 SOUTH AFRICAN KHOESAN

3.1 Northern Khoesan: !Xun[2]

Bernd Heine and *Christa König*

3.1.1 Introduction

The orthography used here is essentially that proposed by Dickens (1991, 1994). There are a few cases where, for phonetic and comparative consistency, we propose alternative symbols (with one exception, they involve ejective plosives). The relevant cases are presented below:

Dickens	Heine	Dickens	Heine
ang	ŋ	ǀk	ǀkx'
dc	dc'	ǂk	ǂkx'
ds	ds'	!k	!kx'
kx	kx'	ǁk	ǁkx'
tj	tc'		
tz	ts'		

Tone marking differs from one author to another. The marking used here is essentially the one used by Köhler (1971a, 1973) but differs slightly from that proposed by Dickens (1994, 2005) and Heikkinen (1986, 1987). The correspondences in tone marking are:

Tone	Label	Köhler (1971a, 1981)	Dickens (1994, 2005)	Heikkinen (1986, 1987)	Snyman (1997: 35)	Heine/ König
extra-high	EH	a̋				á
high	H	á	ááá	a̋	á	á
mid	M	ˈa	á	á	ˈa	ā
low	L	à	à	à	à	à
extra-low	EL	ȁ	a (unmarked)	ȁ	ā	ȁ

Following Heikkinen (1986, 1987), contour tones are described as combinations of two register tones, e.g., *áà* [â] high-low. (Since vowel length is not distinctive, using double vowels for tone marking does not cause a problem in !Xun.)

In the course of the present treatment, starred forms (e.g., *mí 'I') are used to refer to sets of etymologically related forms. Three different kinds of sets are distinguished: Proto-!Xun (*X), Proto-Northwestern !Xun (*NW), and Proto-Southeastern !Xun (*SE). While the starred forms have been set up using established approaches of diachronic reconstruction, comparative !Xun studies are still in their infancy and the reconstructions proposed have to be taken with care. The reader is therefore advised to treat the starred morphs as no more than convenient reference items for sets of what appear to be etymologically related forms.

Past studies of !Xun have been strongly biased in favour of one particular dialect, namely E1. But there do not appear to be any intrinsic reasons for this preference: E1 is neither sociolinguistically nor linguistically in any way special. One of the main goals of the present sketch is to draw attention to the need that exists to embark on a cross-dialectal study of this language (cf. Miller-Ockhuizen and Sands 1999).

In view of requirements of space, the present treatment can do no more than provide a skeleton survey of !Xun morphology and syntax, with emphasis on presenting inventories of structural paradigms rather than grammatical descriptions. There are fairly reasonable grammatical accounts of E1, E2, W1 and W2 (see chart above) and the reader is referred to these works for further details and exemplification. In the present treatment an attempt is made to furnish examples most of all from dialects for which no or no appropriate data have been published. This applies in particular to N, for which no published information whatsoever exists.

3.1.2 The clause

!Xun is a fairly isolating-analytic language having primarily a head-dependent order of constituents (but see below), and a noun class system. The basic word order is subject–verb–object (SVO), irrespective of whether pronominal or nominal participants are involved, e.g.

(97) E2 *Mī kú shē 'āà.*
1SG PROG see 2SG
'I see you.'

(98) N1 *[. . .] ta n!hēí !hm̄m̄ ke n|āò pòhó [. . .]*
. . . and then leopard PAST treat.well jackal . . .
'[. . .] and then the leopard treated the jackal well [. . .]'

Certain matrix verbs taking nominal complements, such as 'want' (N1 *tū*, E1 and E2 *àrè*, W1 *káré*, W2 *kàlè*, K *kèrè*), require the object to precede the verb; hence, in such cases there is verb-final constituent order (see also Snyman 1970: 127; Köhler 1973: 63; Heikkinen 1987: 49f.; Heine and König 2012), e.g.

(99) E2 *Mi ǀōa àrè g!ú-à-kè tcì.*
1SG NEG want water-TR-DEM drink
'I don't want to drink this water.' (Köhler 1973: 63)

There is no grammaticalized case system. Case relations are marked in particular by means of the following:

(a) word order, used in particular to distinguish between subject and object;
(b) the transitive suffix *-a (TR; see 3.1.3.5);
(c) the transitive preposition (TR) (*ke in *NW and *kò in *SE; see 3.1.5.2);
(d) postpositions (see 3.1.5.2); and
(e) verbal derivational forms (see 3.1.6.2).

These generalizations, however, do not take care of the many pragmatically determined variations that are possible. For example, participants expressing either topic or focus may be placed clause-initially, e.g.

(100) E2 *!Àŋ-à-kè mi ǀōa kú ǁòm.*
tree-R-N4:DEM 1SG NEG PROG cut
'This tree, I don't cut it.' (Köhler 1973: 63)

3.1.3 Verb phrase

3.1.3.1 Introduction

Ignoring question words, adverbs and auxiliary elements that may also appear in the verb phrase, the order of main constituents is as summarized in Table 7.1.

TABLE 7.1 THE MAIN CONSTITUENTS OF THE VERB PHRASE IN SIX !XUN DIALECTS

N1	NEG	ASPECT	TENSE	V		object NP
W1	NEG	ASPECT	TENSE	V		object NP
W2	NEG	ASPECT		V		object NP
C1	NEG		TENSE	V	-PROG	object NP
E1	TENSE	ASPECT	NEG	V		object NP
E2		NEG	ASPECT	V		object NP

Note: ASPECT stands for categories such as imperfective, habitual, progressive, while TENSE stands for past and future.

In W2, and to some extent E3, declarative main clauses are marked for topic: the topic marker *má* is placed at the end of the topic constituent, which typically is the subject noun phrase but may also be an adverbial phrase or a subordinate clause:

(101) W2 *Hà má to'ḿ ǀ'àn ǁáé.*
N1 TOP be.near with die:SG
'He is about to die.'

No conclusive evidence is available on dialects other than the ones listed in Table 7.1. The listing takes care of the most common uses only. What it suggests is that Northwestern !Xun differs from Southeastern !Xun in its linear arrangement of verb phrase constituents, e.g.

(102) N1 *Yà má /ōā ú-á tcí ǹdī?*
N1 Q NEG come-R come never
'Will he ever come?'

(103) N1 *Yà /ōā kē tcí.*
N1 NEG PAST come
'He has not yet come.'

(104) N1 *Yà g/úye ha ke ū-ā.*
N1 yesterday PROG PAST come-R
'He was going yesterday.'

In E1, the negation marker */óá* follows the aspect marker *kú*, but in habitual negation ('never') the negation marker precedes:

(105) a. E1 *Ē kú /óá 'm !há.*
1PL:EX PROG NEG eat meat
'We are eating meat.'

b. *Ē /óá kú 'm !há.*
1PL:EX NEG PROG eat meat
'We never eat meat.' (Dickens 2005)

3.1.3.2 Suppletive verbs

All !Xun dialects have a set of suppletive verbs. These verbs have two different forms each, where one form refers to a singular and the other form to a plural participant. Which participant this is depends on the verb class concerned. In the case of intransitive verbs, there is number agreement between subject and verb: whether the singular or the plural stem of the verb is selected depends on the number of the *subject* noun. The following is an example of an intransitive suppletive verb (for complete lists in E1, E2, W1 and W2, see, respectively, Snyman 1970: 110; Köhler 1973: 28; Heikkinen 1987: 76; Heine and König 2012):

(106)

	SG	PL	Meaning
N1	*tchú*	*g/á*	'lie down'
W1	*sú*	*g/à*	
E1	*cú*	*g/à*	
E2	*cúú*	*g/àà*	

(107) a. E2 *!Àŋ-ā-kè kú !òàh.*
tree-R-DEM:N4 PROG break:SG
'The tree there is breaking.'

b. *!Àŋ-s-à-kè kú kx'ùm.*
tree-PL-R-DEM:N4 PROG break:PL
'The trees there are breaking.'

Transitive verbs show number agreement with the *object* noun: whether the singular or plural stem is selected depends on the number of the clausal object, e.g.

(108)

	SG	PL	Gloss
N1	*!hún*	*ǁ'úàn*	'kill'
W1	*!hún*	*'n!ǎhbì, ǁ'áŋ*	
E1	*!hún*	*!'óán*	
E2	*!hun*	*!'ōān*	

(109) a. E1 *n!hǎì* *!hún* *gúmí* 'The lion killed the cow.'
lion kill:SG cattle

b. *n!hǎì* *!'óán* *gúmí* 'The lion killed the cattle.'
lion kill:PL cattle

3.1.3.3 Aspect and tense

Divergences among !Xun dialects are particularly obvious in the case of marking tense and aspect. First, with one exception there is no tense–aspect form which can be reconstructed safely back to Proto-!Xun. Second, there are some differences with regard to the tense–aspect concepts distinguished. For example, whereas Northwestern !Xun dialects have a habitual category, there is none in Southeastern !Xun. Third, even if the same category exists in different dialects, there are considerable differences in the frequency of occurrence. For example, while all dialects have a past tense, its use is obligatory only in N (*kē*), while neither W1 (*kē*), W2 (*kē*) nor E1 (*kǒh*) mark past actions consistently by using the past tense form.

Table 7.2 summarizes the main tense–aspect categories that are distinguished. Note that our interpretation and terminology do not necessarily coincide with that of other authors. Note further that we have included only categories that are distinguished in at least two different dialects.

TABLE 7.2 THE MAIN TENSE–ASPECT CATEGORIES IN !XUN

Concept	N1	N2	W1	C1	E1	E2
Incompletive	zero	zero	zero		zero	zero
Imperfective (IMPF)	–	–	*ā*	*tí*	*kú*	*kú*
Progressive (PROG)	*hā*	*a*	*-ā*	*tí*	*kú*	*kú*
Habitual (HAB)	*ká*	*ke, ki*	*kí*		–	–
Completive (COMPL)	*ǂānì, tòàn*	*toa*	*òh-ā*		–	*ǂānì, tōān*
Past (PAST)	*kē*	*ka, ke*	*kē*	*go*	*kǒh*	
Future	*ú, ò-tā*	*o*		*o(ga)*		*úú*

With the exception of the completive markers in N1 and E2, all markers are placed *before* the main verb. Whether they form proclitics or prefixes is unclear in most cases. Combinations of markers are possible; in E1, for example, *kǒh* and *kú* may combine to indicate a habitual action in the past, e.g.

(110) E1 *Sì-* *!á* *kǒh* *kú* *'m* *!há* *n|è'ésí.*
3PL -PL PAST PROG eat meat only
'They used to eat meat only.' (Dickens 2005)

3.1.3.3.1 INCOMPLETIVE

This is the default tense–aspect category in !Xun. With reference to E1, Dickens (2005) says that the verb is never inflected for time and that tense is often determined by real-world context. Thus, sentence (111) can have any of the translations given; to express distinctions of time, adverbs are added, as in (112).

(111)	E1	*Hà*	*ú-á*	*Tc'ùm!kúí.*
		N1	go-TR	Tsumkwe

a. 'He goes to Tsumkwe.'
b. 'He went/has gone to Tsumkwe.'
c. 'He will go to Tsumkwe.'

(112) a. E1 *Hà goàq‡'àn ú-á Tjùm!kúí.*
'He went to Tsumkwe yesterday.'

b. *|Ámà hè hà ú-á Tjùm!kúí.*
'Today he goes to Tsumkwe.' (Dickens 2005)

These uses are characteristic of the incompletive aspect in E1. In other dialects they also show a wide range of uses, even if not nearly as wide as in E1.

3.1.3.3.2 IMPERFECTIVE

Köhler calls the imperfective marker *kú* in E2 the "time marker" (1971a: 497) or "Aktionspartikel" (1973: 52). The function of this particle, which is placed between subject and verb, is largely unclear. Köhler (1973: 52) says that it serves "eine Handlung des Subjekts einzuleiten, seltener ein Prädikat als Vorgang (Adjektivverben)" (to introduce an action of the subject, less frequently a predicate as a process (verbal adjectives)). Dickens (2005) treats E1 *kú* as an imperfective marker used "to show that an action is continuous or habitual or unfinished". Southeastern !Xun *kú* is best characterized as a continuative morpheme which includes the functions of a progressive and an inchoative.

(113)	E2	*Kā*	*|ām*	*kú*	*n‡hàò*	*zō*	*kú*	*cè*	*kà*	*úú*	*ts'āā.*
		when	sun	IMPF	set	bees	IMPF	return	and	go	sleep

'When the sun sets the bees go back to sleep.' (Köhler 1973: 16)

(114)	E1	*N!úí*	*n!a'àn.*	*N!úí*	*kú*	*n!a'àn.*
		moon	be.big	moon	AP	be.big
		'The moon is big.'		'The moon is getting big.'		

The imperfective marker *kú* corresponds to the incompletive marker *āā* in W1 (Heikkinen 1987) and to *tí* in T (Vedder 1910/11).

3.1.3.3.3 PROGRESSIVE

All !Xun dialects have some grammaticalized notion of a progressive:

(115)	N1	*Yà*	*|éyà*	*hā*	*tsí.*
		N1	today	PROG	come

'He is coming today.'

(116)	N3	*!Xe*	*a*	*tci*	*g|u.*
		dog	PROG	drink	water

'The dog is drinking water.' (Bleek 1956: 3)

3.1.3.3.4 HABITUAL

Only in Northwestern !Xun is there a distinct category of a habitual. In N1, *ká* is used obligatorily for habitual actions or events:

(117)	N1	*ǀÁm*	*wúcè*	*mā*	*ká*	*gǀā*	*ī*	*kè*	*gǁúū.*
		day	all	1SG	HAB	give	2PL	TA	water
		'Every day I give you (PL) water.'							

The W1 marker *kí* serves as a marker of both habitual and continuous actions (Heikkinen 1987: 88).

3.1.3.3.5 COMPLETIVE

The marker *òh-ā* of W1 expresses a "complete, continuous state"; it is etymologically the same as the equative copula (see 3.1.3.5).

The verbs *ǂannì and *toan, both meaning 'finish, be finished', also serve to express a completive aspect in N1, N2, and E2, e.g.

(118)	N1	*Mí-*	*'ŋ̄*	*kē*	*'ḿ*	*tòàn*	*ǁhà.*
		1SG-	DEM:PROX	PAST	eat	COMPL	meat
		'I have eaten meat.'					

(119)	N2	*Cuula*	*ki*	*cin*	*ǁ'á*	*toa*	*tci,*	*toa*	*ǂxa.*
		arrow	PAST	?	?	finished	come	let	fly
		'The arrow is shot off, let fly.' (Bleek 1956: 206)							

(120)	E2	*Mi*	*'m*	*!hā*	*ǂānnì.*
		1SG	eat	meat	finish
		'I have eaten the meat.' (Köhler 1973: 52)			

3.1.3.3.6 PAST

The use of the past tense marker *kē* in N1 is obligatory when past actions or events are involved while in E1 it is not consistently used for past actions (see above).

(121)	N1	*Mà*	*kúlímà*	*kē*	*ū-ā*	*kú-*	*ndú'à.*
		1SG	long.ago	PAST	go-R	LOC-	DEM:DIST
		'I went there long ago.'					

3.1.3.3.7 FUTURE

The most common, though not the only means of expressing future events is by using some grammaticalized form of the verb *X *ú 'go'. No future tense appears to exist in W1 and E1.

(122)	N	*Yà*	*ǀōā*	*ú-*	*á*	*tcí.*
		N1	NEG	FUT	-R	come
		'He will not come.'				

3.1.3.4 Negation

Verbal negation is fairly uniform across all dialects: (a) There are two markers, each associated with a clearly defined range of functions. (b) Negation markers are preverbal clitics (when there is a verb). (c) The negation markers are *ǀōā (general negation) and *kora (negative existence), their distribution across dialects is summarized below. Concerning the position of the negation marker, see 3.1.3.1.

*X	*ǀōā	*kora
N1	*ǀóá, ǀqá*	*kūlā, kùla*
N2	*ǀwa, ǀwí(n)*	*kula*
W1	*ǀōā*	*kōrā*
W2	*ǀōā*	*kwàlā*
K	*ǀōā*	*kōrā*
C1	*ǀoa*	
E1	*ǀóá*	*kòàrà*
E2	*ǀōā*	*kōārà*

*ǀōā cannot stand on its own, it requires a following predicate. *kora, on the other hand, has a verb-like status, i.e., it occupies the slot of a main verb. The phrase *ǀōā* + *kú* (progressive) is often shortened to *ǀú* in Southeastern !Xun.

3.1.3.5 Copulas

There are a number of copula-like elements, but only two are of major significance: *gè and *òh 'be, be somewhere, exist'. Both have a range of overlapping functions, with that range differing from one dialect to another. In E1, for example, only *gè* appears to be locative (Dickens 2005); in E2, *gèè* expresses existence and *gè-à* ('exist' + transitive suffix) location ('be somewhere'), but *'o* is used for location as well (Köhler 1973: 59). The reflexes of these items are summarized below. Note that in Northwestern !Xun, *òh almost invariably takes the transitive suffix *-a. There is a verb *òò* 'do, make' in E1 which is presumably related to *òh (cf. Dickens 2005).

*X	*gè	*òh
N1	*gè*	*wa* (< *òh-a)
N2	*ge, gɛ̀*	*o, o-a, w-a*
W1	*gè*	*òh-ā*
W2	*gè*	*òhā*
K	*gē*	
C1	*ge*	*-ua*
E1	*gè(-à)*	*ō*
E2	*gèè*	*'ō*

(123) N1 *G!ōà mā gè-ā kú- ndū'à?*
tobacco Q COP-R LOC- DEM:DIST
'Is there tobacco?'

(124) N1 *Tcí-dē kā-ndū'à wā nǀāq-dē.*
woman N4-DEM:DIST COP bush-woman
'That woman is a Kxoe.'

3.1.3.5.1 THE TRANSITIVE SUFFIX *-*A* (TR)

The transitive suffix could be treated in virtually any other section on !Xun grammar since it has a range of functions that relate in much the same way to verbal and to nominal morphosyntax, to derivation and to inflection. The transitive suffix, called the qualifying copula ("Qualifikationskopula") by Köhler (1973: 18), the transitive suffix by Heikkinen (1987: 5), and the transitive suffix *-a* by Dickens (2005) is added to verbs and nouns to express a number of different functions, including transitivity, and derivation. Its reflexes are presented below.

*X	*-a
N1	*-ā*
N2	*a*
W1	*-ā*
W2	*-ā*
K	*-ā*
E1	*-a*
E2	*-a*

The transitive suffix has a number of allomorphs, which usually take the following forms (cf. Snyman 1970: 71, 113; Köhler 1973):

-wa	following back vowels (*o, u*),
-ya	following front vowels (*e, i*),
-nya	following front nasal vowels (*en, in*),
-an	following a low nasal vowel (*an*),
-Ø	following a,
-a	following consonants.

Since the distribution of these allomorphs is predictable, we follow Dickens (1994, 2005) in ignoring them in the present orthography, hence N1 [ʼú-wá] 'going' will be written *ú-á*. In E1, the tone of this particle is the same as the last tone of the preceding item to which *-a is suffixed (Dickens 2005), but the situation is more complex in other varieties. Note in this connection that Dickens (1997: 108ff.) distinguishes two markers *-a-*: one that has low tone and serves as a relative clause marker (see 3.1.8.2), and another whose tone is a copy of that of the preceding syllable, which is used (a) as a transitivity marker and (b) as a suffix of compounds, marking the head of a compound (see 3.1.6.1).

3.1.4 Noun phrase

The noun phrase consists essentially of either a pronoun or a noun with or without modifiers. While modifiers almost always follow their head nouns, some precede. The basic order of noun phrase constituents tends to be as follows (see 3.1.4.3 below):

PRE-NOMINAL MODIFIER NOUN (ADJ) (NUM) (DEM) (relative clause)

3.1.4.1 Pronouns

Table 7.3 contains a complete list of personal pronouns. Note that third person singular personal pronouns are identical with the noun class markers of class 1 (N1). For a list of noun class markers, see Table 7.5.

The items listed in Table 7.3 are used as subject and object pronouns, and – with few exceptions – also as possessive attributes (see 3.1.4.4.5). As subjects they precede the verb, as objects they follow the verb, and as attributival modifiers they precede the noun they modify.

The number suffixes *-tsan and *-!ao (Table 7.4) differ from personal pronouns and noun class markers in that they do not stand on their own; rather they are suffixed to the former, or else to nouns or other noun phrase elements. The dual forms *-tsan (number suffix) and *sa (personal pronoun) can both be assumed to represent grammaticalized

TABLE 7.3 PERSONAL PRONOUNS IN !XUN

	Singular			Dual	Plural			
	1	2	3 (N1)		1:EX	1:IN	2	3
*X	*mí	*à	*hȁ	*sa	*è	*m̀	*ì	*sŋ̏
*NW	*mí, *mā	*à	*hȁ	*sa	*è, *dju	*m̏hm	*ì	*cŋ̏
N1	*mí, mā*	*à, ā*	*yȁ*	*cā*	*djū*	*m̏hm̏*	*ì*	*cŋ̏*
N2	*mi, ma*	*a*	*(h)a*	*sa*	*e*		*i-hi*	*i, si*
W1	*mí, mā, nā*	*à, bà*	*hȁ*	*sā*	*è, zù*	*m̏hm̀*	*ì, yà*	*sŋ̏, sȅ*
W2	*mí, mā*	*à, bà*	*ɦȁ*	*cā*	*è, djù*	*m̏hm̀*	*ì, yà*	*cŋ̏, yīí*
W3	*mí, nā*	*à*	*hȁ*	*sā*	*è*	*m̏m̀*	*ì*	*sŋ̏, yīí*
K	*mí, mā, mé'ē, nā*	*à*	*hà*		*è, djūú*		*ì*	*s(ì)ŋ*
C1	*mi, na*	*a*	*hà*		*e*	*m'*	*i*	*sn*
*SE	*mi	*à	*hȁ	*sà	*è	*m̀	*ì	*sì
E1	*mí*	*à*	*hȁ*	*sà*	*è*	*m̀*	*ì*	*sì*
E2	*mī*	*'āà*	*hà*		*'ēè*	*m̀*	*'īì*	*sì*
E3	*mī, m̄*	*à*	*hȁ*	*sà, sā*	*è*	*m̏*	*ì, ī*	*sì*

forms of the numeral *tsan 'two'. Dual pronouns are obligatorily used in conjoining constructions such as the following:

(125) E1 *E- tsá mí tsú kú !ȁ qè g!ò'é.*
1EX:PL- DU:1SG uncle PROG hunt oryx
'My uncle and I (lit.: we-two my uncle) were hunting oryx.' (Dickens 2005)

TABLE 7.4 !XUN NUMBER SUFFIXES

	Dual	Plural
*X	*-tsan (< *tsan 'two')	*-!ao (< *!ao 'three')
*NW	*-tcá	*-!áó
N1	*-tcá*	
N2	*tsa*	*!o*
W1	*-tsā, -sāŋ*	*-!āō, -!ō*
W2	*-tcá*	
K		*-!ó*
C1	*dsaan*	*g!ao* (trial and plural)
*SE	*-tsá	*-!a
E1	*-tsá*	*-!á*
E2	*-tsá*	*-!ā*

Throughout the !Xun-speaking area, the simple personal pronouns (or noun class markers) are normally used; however, in Southeastern !Xun personal pronouns tend to occur in a "strengthened" form, as in the following example from E2, where plurality is expressed three times in the subject pronoun *'ìì-!ā-s-à-ɦè*:

(126) E2 *ɦà tc(ī)-ēè rēē 'īì- !ā- s- à- ɦè kòqà?*
why Q 2PL- PL- PL- R- DEM fear
'What are you (PL) afraid of?' (Köhler 1973: 42)

There are a number of particles that can be placed after the personal pronouns to express specific textual functions. Perhaps the most common one is *$h\grave{\eta}$* (EMPH), which immediately follows the first noun or pronoun of the clause, thereby "emphasizing" that NP, where "emphasizing" in many cases means expressing contrastive focus ('X, rather than Y'). The cross-dialectal forms this pronoun takes are listed below.

*X	*hŋ̀
N1	*-hŋ̄*
N2	*-hŋ, -hn*
W1	*-hŋ̀*
W2	*-hŋ̀*
C1	*-xn*
E2	*hŋ̀*

(127) N1 *Djū- hŋ̄ djū* *ǀ'ē-xà kē ō kā.*
1PL:EX- EMPH 1PL:EX EMPH:REFL PAST do N4
'We *ourselves* did it.'

In all dialects there is also a pattern whereby personal pronouns are "strengthened" by adding any of the demonstratives listed below (see 3.1.4.4.1). The main function of this strategy is to provide the hearer with deictic information on the location of the referent concerned, e.g.

(128) a. N1 *Yà- 'ŋ̄.* 'S/he (right here).'
N1- DEM:PROX

b. *Yà- ndū'à.* 'S/he (over there).'
N1- DEM:DIST

The structure these pronouns take is the following (where PRO = personal pronoun, TR = transitive suffix, DEM = demonstrative attribute):

N1	PRO + DEM
W1	PRO + DEM
W2	PRO + DEM
E1	PRO + TR + DEM
E2	PRO + TR + DEM

The reflexive pronouns appear to be derived from a noun *ǀ'ae 'body' (see below). In E2, the noun *!x'a* 'heart', preceded by a possessive attribute, serves as "emphatic self", e.g., *mi !x'a* 'I myself' (lit.: 'my heart').

*X	*ǀ'ae 'oneself' (REFL)
N1	*ǀ'é*
W1	*-ǀ'ē*
W2	*ǀ'ē*
E1	*ǀ'àè*
E2	*ǀ'ēē*

(129) N1 *Yà kēē !hún yà ǀ'é.*
N1 PAST kill:SG N1 REFL
'He has killed himself.'

The forms of the reciprocal pronoun, conceivably derived from the noun *khòè 'places' (SG: *kò, cf. Köhler 1973: 50), are listed below. The verb preceding *khoe must have the transitive suffix *-a on it in all dialects.

*X	*khoe
N1	*khōē, khòè*
W1	*-khōē* (emphatic marker), *-kòè*
W2	*kòè, khòè*
W3	*kòè*
C1	*goe*
E1	*khòè*
E2	*khwè*
E3	*khöë, köëë*

(130) N1 *Cŋ̀ kē !òlì- ǀá'ā khòè.*
3PL PAST fight- BEN REC
'They fought each other.'

3.1.4.2 Nouns

Nouns are marked neither for case nor for indefinite or definite reference, in Northwestern !Xun they also tend to be unmarked for number. Definiteness may be expressed by the demonstrative *ǁ'än (see 3.1.4.4.1), and specific (presentative) reference by *nǀúí 'a certain'. Many verbs are what Köhler (1973: 26) calls "bivalent" (cf. Dickens's [2005] distinction between "verb" and "deverbal nominalization without change"), that is, they can be used as verbs or nouns, e.g.

(131) E2 *'m* (a) 'eat', (b) 'food, fruit'
'm- sì 'veldkost'
eat PL

There are considerable differences in the treatment of nominal number marking. While in Southeastern !Xun count nouns are pluralized by adding the suffix *-sì*, nouns are essentially transnumeral in Northwestern !Xun, that is, they normally have no formal number marking, e.g.

N1 *g!áùn* 'tree, trees'
n!éú 'old man, old men'

To emphasize plurality or for disambiguation, however, plural suffixes can be used, e.g.

N1 *g!áùn-cŋ̀* 'trees'
n!éú-cŋ̀ 'old men'
djú bā-cŋ̀ 'our fathers (i.e., not yours)'

The following are the predominant means of marking number distinctions:

(a) Suppletion, e.g.

	SG	PL	Gloss
E1	*!'hò àn*	*nǀà qè*	'man'
	dà'ámá	*dà'ábí(-sì)*	'child'
	jù	*jú*	'person'

(b) *-sì; see below:

*X	*sì					
N1						
W1	*së*					
C1	*se*					
E1	*sì*	e.g.,	E1	*tc'ù*	PL	*tc'ù-sì* 'house'
E2	*sì*					

(c) *-sin; see below:

*X	*sin
N1	*cŋ̈*
N3	*siŋ*, *sŋ*
W1	*sä ŋ*, *hä ŋŋ*
C1	*sn*
E1	*sín*
E2	*sin*

	SG	PL	Gloss
C1	*dsàò*	*dsàò-sn*	'woman'
	gome	*gome-sn*	'cattle'

(d) *-mà, PL *-m̈hè

Diminutive nouns take the singular suffix *-mà, which they exchange for *-m̈hè in the plural (see section 3.1.6.2).

(e) Transnumeral nouns

Names of plants, animals, and inanimate items normally have no formal singular/plural marker on them.

3.1.4.3 Noun class system

A typological characteristic of !Xun is the presence of a noun class system. The system is covert, that is, nouns do not have any formal class marking on them. There are four individual noun classes, more precisely, agreement classes. Class membership can be derived only from pronominal exponents referring to nouns. The pronominal exponents of noun classes and their dialect distribution are summarized in Table 7.5.

There is a slightly different set of agreement markers used as possessee pronouns (POSS:PRO), which are presented in Table 7.6. Possessee pronouns are suffixed to the possessor noun or pronoun, e.g.

(132) N1 *Tc'ú kā-'ŋ̄ wā Dúmbà-gā.*
home N4-DEM COP Dumba-POSS:PRO:N4
'This home is Dumba's.'

While these class distinctions are found across dialects, there are a few individual differences. N1 differs from the other dialects in having replaced the N1 marker *hä by *yà* and by having lost class 2 (N1), and the Southeastern !Xun dialects (E1 and E2) have merged N1, N2, and N3 to one marker (*hè*) in their proximal demonstrative forms, so that there remains only a two-way distinction *hè* non-N4 vs. *kè* N4.

TABLE 7.5 !XUN NOUN CLASS MARKERS (CF. TABLE 7.3)

	N1	N2	N3	N4
*X	*hȁ	*sì	*yi	*kā
*NW	*hȁ		*yīí	*kā
N1	*yà*[1]		*yīí	*kā*
N2	*ha, a*	*si*	*i, hi*	*ka*
W1	*hȁ*	*sȅ*	*yīí*	*kā*
W2	*ɦȁȁ*		*yīí*	*kā*
K	*hà*			
C1	*hà*	*se*		*ga*
*SE	*hȁ	*sì	*yì	*ka*
E1	*hȁ*	*sì*	*yì, hì*	*ká*
E2	*ɦà*	*sì*	*yì, hì*	*kā*

Note: 1 N1 *yà* is probably an innovation, which replaced Proto-!Xun *hȁ.

TABLE 7.6 POSSESSEE PRONOUNS IN !XUN ACCORDING TO NOUN CLASSES

	N1	N2	N3	N4
*X	*wà	*hì	*yìí	*gā
N1	*-wà*		*-wīí*	*-gā*
W1	*-wa, -ya*		*-yīí*	*-gā*
W2	*-yȁ*		*-yīí*	*-gā*
W3	*-wà*		*-yīí*	*-gā*
C1	*-hà*			*-gà*
E1	*mà*	*hì, yìí*	*yìí*	*gá*
E2	*-mà*	*-yìí*	*-yīí*	*-gā*
E3	*mȁ*	*hȉ-sì*	*hȉ-sì*	*-gā*

Some of these classes combine into class pairs or genders (Güldemann 2000b). Depending on their association with noun classes, nouns can be said to belong to any of the genders listed below (cf. Köhler 1973: 29; Heikkinen 1987: 67ff.; Dickens 1994: 20; 2005). As shown below, there are altogether five genders, of which three have no formal number distinction.

*X	*N1/N2	*N1/N3	*N1	*N3	*N4
N1		N1/N3	N1	N3	N4
W1	N1/N2	N1/N3	N1	N3	N4
W2		N1/N3	N1	N3	N4
E1	N1/N2	N1/N3	N1	N3	N4
E2	N1/N2	N1/N3	N1	N3	N4

Since N1 and W2 have lost class 2, there is only one paired gender.

Nouns are inherently marked for class membership. For a detailed classification of nouns in E1, see the entries in the dictionary of Dickens (1994). A number of generalizations on membership of genders have been proposed (see especially Köhler 1971a; 1973: 31–35 for E2; Heikkinen 1987: 67f. for W1; Güldemann 2000b for E1). The following are a few salient number and meaning characteristics of genders across the various dialects. Note that Köhler (1973) treats *N1/N2 plus *N1/N3 as one gender (his "I. Klasse") in E2; accordingly, this gender includes not only human nouns but also animal names.

Gender	Number	Salient meanings
*N1/N2	singular/plural	human nouns
*N1/N3	singular/plural	many animals, inanimate nouns
*N1	transnumeral	many plants and plant products, inanimate nouns
*N3	transnumeral	mostly inanimate nouns
*N4	transnumeral	inanimate nouns, body part nouns, abstract nouns

3.1.4.4 Nominal modifiers

Nominal modifiers follow their head noun, with the exception of the following, which precede:

(a) the referential demonstrative *ǁ'àn (see 3.1.4.4.1),
(b) pronominal possessive attributes (see 3.1.4.4.6),
(c) two of the three main patterns of nominal attributive possession (see 3.1.4.4.5).

(133) W1 (a) *Mā sē kē- txà hä- ǁ'àn !'hòm.*
1SG INT PAST- shoot 3SG DEM leopard
'I was going to shoot that leopard.' (Heikkinen 1987: 18)

There is some variation in the way modifiers are placed relative to one another, both across dialects and within a given dialect (see, e.g., Köhler 1973: 66f. for E2). In Southeastern !Xun, though not in Northwestern !Xun, noun modifiers can be divided into two types: attributive and predicative modifiers. While the former are added to the head noun without any formal linkage, the latter require the relative suffix *-a*, PL *-sa* (see 3.1.3.5) as nominal (or pronominal) suffixes. The main characteristics of attributive and predicative modifiers in Southeastern !Xun are summarized roughly below:

	Attributive modifiers	Predicative modifiers
Linking element	*-Ø*	*-a*, PL *-sa*
Kinds of modifiers	adjectives, numerals, quantifiers	verbs of state, demonstratives, relative clauses

The following overview is confined to a few categories only to illustrate the structure of nominal attribution; for more details the reader is referred to a detailed treatment in Heine and König, 2012.

3.1.4.4.1 DEMONSTRATIVES

With the exception of (e) below, demonstrative attributes follow the noun they qualify; their use tends to be accompanied by appropriate demonstrative gestures (Snyman 1970: 114). The primary demonstratives distinguished are listed below. Note, however, that various dialects have strategies to form additional demonstratives to express more deictic distinctions. Dickens (1997) observes with reference to E1 that demonstratives are verbal in nature.

	Proto-!Xun form	Primary meaning	Conceptual label	Abbreviation
(a)	*-'è	'this (here)'	proximal, contrastive	PROX
(b)	*-'ŋ̀	'this (right here)'	here	HERE
(c)	*-to'à	'that (visible)'	distal	DIST
(d)	*ú + (a), (b) or (c)	'that (out of sight)'	far	FAR
(e)	*ǁ'àen	'that (mentioned earlier)'	reference	REF

The meanings given are the ones most commonly associated with these categories; there is some variation both among different dialects and within one and the same dialect. Category (b) is only found in Northwestern !Xun (N1, W1, W2), while (e) is not found in N1. (e) appears to be used in E1 to some extent as a definite article. There is considerable variation in the form these demonstratives take; space limits do not allow us to describe this variation here.

Examples from N

(134)	N1	*tcí-/xòà*	*kā-*	*'ēē*			'this person'
		person	N4-	DEM:PROX			
	N1	*g!áún*	*kā-*	*'ŋ̄ ŋ̄*			'this tree'
		tree	N4-	DEM:HERE			
	N1	*g!áún*	*kā-*	*ndū'à*			'that tree'
		tree	N4-	DEM:DIST			
	N1	*Dè'bè*	*yīí*	*ú*	*yīí-*	*ndū'à*	'the children (far away)'
		children	N3	go	N3-	DEM:FAR	

In Southeastern !Xun, demonstratives require the preceding head noun to take the transitive suffix *-a* (see 3.1.3.5), and the noun class markers have merged with the proximal demonstrative:

hà + 'è	>	*hè*	'this'	N1
hì + 'è	>	*hè*	'this'	N3
ká + 'è	>	*ké*	'this'	N4

(135)	E2	*dzháú-*	*à*	*h-*	*è*	'this woman'
		woman-	TR	N1-	DEM:PROX	

In Northwestern !Xun there appears to be a "nasal extension" in the distal demonstrative, that is, there is a nasal element, the diachronic basis of which remains unclear (CL = noun class marker):

*X	*-to'à
N1	CL + *ndū'à*
W1	CL + *ndò'à*, or CL + *-tò'à*
W2	CL + *ndù'à*
K	CL + *tō'à*
C1	*(n)doaa* ("locative particle"; Vedder 1910/11: 15)
E2	-TR + *tòàh*

(136)	a.	W2	*tcháú*	*ɦà-*	*ndū'à*		'that woman'
			woman	N1	DEM:DIST		
	b.	E2	*dzháú-*	*s-*	*à*	*tòàh*	'the women there'
			woman-	PL-	TR	DEM:DIST	

3.1.4.4.2 LOCATIVE PRONOUNS

There is a locative root (LOC) *NW *ku, *SE *kò which combines with the set of demonstratives to form locative pronouns or adverbs. Frequently, the root is linked with the demonstrative by means of the transitive suffix *-a. The shape this root takes is as follows (see also under 3.1.7.2, 'where?'):

*N	*ku				
N1	*kū-, kw-á-*	e.g.,	*kw-é-'ēē*	'here'	(PROX)
N2	*kw-a*	e.g.,	*kw-á-'ŋ̄ŋ̄*	'here'	(HERE)
W1	*kū-, ngū-*				
W2	*kū-, kw-ā-*				
K	*kū-*				
C1	*go*				
E1	*kò-à-*				

3.1.4.4.3 ADJECTIVES

The treatment of adjectives is one of the more complex areas in !Xun grammar (see Heine and König 2012); for none of the dialects does there exist a satisfactory description. There are only few adjectives in the dialects. Most notions that translate as adjectives in other languages are treated as verbs of state.

(137)	N1	*ǁHá*	*kā-*	*'ŋ̄*	*tcŋ́.*	*Mā*	*cŋ́*	*ǁhā*	*tcŋ̄.*
		meat	N4-	DEM:HERE	fat	1SG	see	meat	fat
		'This meat is fat.'				'I see fat meat.'			

With reference to E1, Dickens (2005) observed that there is a small class of adjectives, while in another work (Dickens 1997: 110) he had argued that adjectives do not exist in E1. What other authors call "adjectives" (Köhler's "regelmäßige Adjektive") or "descriptive adnouns" is referred to by him as *verbals* – a category that also includes demonstratives. The main reason for setting up such a category is that all these items require the head noun or pronoun to take the relative clause marker *-à* as a suffix. Dickens acknowledges, however, that there is a separate category of what others call "unregelmäßige Adjektive" or "irregular descriptive adnouns". These are nominal in nature and differ from verbals in a number of ways; some have suppletive plural forms:

E1	*g!òq*	PL	*nǁàqè*	'male'	(see also under 3.1.6.2)
	n!à'àn	PL	*!àè(!àè)*	'adult, grown-up'	

It would seem, however, that there is a cline between adjectives and verbals in most !Xun dialects: these two groups can be arranged along a scale extending from items behaving largely like nouns to items behaving like verbs which are added to nouns in the form of relative clauses. From the data available it is hard to determine the exact status of a given item. Adjectives and quantifiers follow their head noun and take the plural marking, while the preceding head noun loses its plural marking (Dickens 2005; see also Heikkinen 1987: 16):

(138)	E1	*dshàú*	*gè-*	*sín*	'the remaining women'
		woman	other-	PL	

3.1.4.4.4 NUMERALS

Table 7.7 gives a list of cardinal numerals. Counting from '5' onward is possible, there are somehow productive patterns in all dialects. As a matter of fact, numerals above '5' are rarely used. Numerals are placed after the head noun without inflectional markings (see Köhler 1973: 68f., Heikkinen 1987: 19f., Heine and König 2012). In E2, nouns that otherwise would take a plural suffix do not do so after any of the numerals '2', '3', and '4', e.g. *Gòbà n!nannì* 'three Mbukushu people'.

TABLE 7.7 CARDINAL NUMERALS IN !XUN

	1	2	3	4
*X	*n|è'e	*tsan	*!áo 'more than 2', '3'	*tsan ka òh(-a) tsan ('2 + 2')
N1	*n|ē'ē*	*tcā*	*!áō*	*tcā-kā-yà-tcā; bīnē*
N2	*n|eé*	*tsa*	*!ao*	
W1	*n|e'ē*	*tsa*	*!ao*	*tsā-kā-òh-ā-tsā*
W2	*n|è'è*	*tcā*	*!āō*	*tcā-kā-yà-tcā; ǁàḿ*
C1	*|ee*	*dsaan*	*g!ao*	*dsan-sá-dsan*
E1	*n|è'é*	*tsàqn, tsán*	*n!ànnì*	*tsán-ká-tsán*
E2	*n|ēh*	*tsān*	*n!ānnì*	*tsān-kò-tsān*

(139)	W1	*Khómè*	*hà̈*	*n|ǜì̈*	*hà̈*	*ǁ'hān*	*tsā.*
		tomorrow	N1	take:PL	N1	son	two

'The next day he took his two sons.'

(140)	W1	*Sàŋ*	*!āō*	*má*	*!āō.*
		3PL	three	TOP	three

'They are three.'

3.1.4.4.5 ATTRIBUTIVE POSSESSION

There are three types of possessive constructions, which are:

	Construction type	Proposed label	Lectal distribution
(a)	possessor–possessee	Juxtaposition	N1, N2, W1, E1, E2
(b)	possessor–POSS–PRON–possessee	Specification	N1, E1, E2
(c)	possessee–REL–COP–possessor	Relativization	N1, W1, E1, E2

The possessive particle (POSS) has the following forms:

*X	*ǁ'àn
N1	*ǁ'ē*
W1	–
E1	*ǁ'àn*
E2	*ǁ'ā*

With the exception of (b), which does not occur in W1, all constructions are found in all dialects for which there is a grammatical description. Note that while (a) and (b) have the possessor before the possessee, the possessee precedes in (c). The copula requires the transitive suffix *-a in N1 and W1 but not in E1 and E2. More research is required on how these three constructions differ from one another in their functions (see Heine and König 2012). On the whole, however, they are used interchangeably, e.g.

(141) N1 (a) *Dúmbà tc'ú* 'Dumba's home'

(b) *Dúmbà ǁ'e yà tc'ú*
Dumba POSS N1 home

(c) *tc'ú kā- 'ŋ̄ wā Dúmbà- gā*
home N4- DEM:HERE COP Dumba- POSS:N4

In E1 and E2, these forms receive the suffix *SE *-sì when there is a plural referent, while N1 and W1 do not distinguish number.

Köhler (1973: 67) notes that construction (b) is used for inalienable possession in E2; neither in E1 nor in any other dialect is there any restriction of this kind. Furthermore, Köhler (1973: 22) mentions a construction [POSSESSOR–POSSESSEE–TR], presumably a variant of (a), which, he says, is also used for inalienable possession in E2:

(142) E2 *tsxáú g!ū- ā*
waterhole water- TR
'water of the waterhole'

3.1.4.4.6 PRONOMINAL POSSESSIVES

The forms used for a pronominalized possessor precede the possessee without formal linkage, e.g.

E2 *mī !ú* 'my name'
ɦà !ú 'his, her name' (N1)

They are identical with the personal pronouns (see 3.1.4.1, Table 7.3). But there are a few exceptions:

(a) The first person singular attribute is *mí (frequently shortened to *m; see below) rather than *ma in N1 and W1.
(b) In some W1 (western) varieties, the second person singular attribute is *bà*, rather than *'à*.
(c) The first person pronoun *mí is shortened to *m̀ preceding the noun *ba 'father' and other kinship terms:

N1 *m̀ bā* 'my father'
N2 *m bá* 'my father' (Bleek 1956: 221)
E2 *m̀ bāà* 'my father' (Köhler 1973: 43)

In the same way as the possessor can be pronominalized, so can the possessee. A pronominal possessee (POSS:PRO) is suffixed to the possessor noun or pronoun. The forms it takes in the various dialects are listed in Table 7.6, section 3.1.4.3.

(143) a. N1 *Wā mí- gā.*
COP 1SG- POSS:PRO:N4
'It is mine.' (referring to a noun of class 4, e.g. *khìndä* 'cup')

b. *Wā mí- wà.*
COP 1SG- POSS:PRO:N1
'It is mine.' (referring to a noun of class 1, e.g. *dà'bà* 'child')

3.1.5 Adverbial phrase

In most cases, adverbial phrases are not structurally different from noun phrases. Locative, temporal and some other adverbial participants are in most cases unmarked, but there is what may be called a multi-purpose postposition *ŋ́!ŋ́ (see below) that can be used (see also under 3.1.6.2).

3.1.5.1 Adverbs

!Xun has a minimum of inflectional morphology and expresses a number of concepts by means of adverbs. The language is therefore rich in what corresponds to the functional notion of an adverb. Adverbs, especially temporal adverbs, tend to be placed between subject and verb, but they also occur elsewhere, especially clause-initially or clause-finally. Like nouns, adverbs can be clause participants, taking the transitive preposition (TR; see 3.1.5.2), e.g.

(144) N1 *Mā kēē 'm̄-ā ǀhā kē kúlímà.*
1SG PAST eat-TR meat TR long.ago
'I ate meat long ago.'

Many verbs, as well as some nouns, may function as adverbs (cf. Heikkinen 1987: 44), e.g.

(145) N1 *Gǀú mā ú.*
night 1SG go
'I leave at night.'

(146) E1 *Ká khòècà ká dà'ábí kàqà 'm 'm-sì.*
N4 seem COMPL children already eat food
'It seems that the children have already eaten the food.'

Perhaps one of the main sources for adverbial concepts is verbs of state used in an adverbial function. Some of these have turned into verbal suffixes:

(147) E2 *'Ī ì tsā gūù-tāqm-ā.* cf. *tāqm* 'to miss a target' (cf. 3.1.6.2)
2PL DU take-miss-TR
'You two don't grab it properly.'

3.1.5.2 Adpositions

Dickens (2005) says that there are no prepositions in E1. On the basis of cross-linguistic observations one may in fact call !Xun a postpositional language. Still, as we will see below, there are also items that one feels justified to call prepositions.

There is a multi-purpose postposition, *ŋ́!ŋ́ 'in, at', which has the following dialectal distribution:

*X *ŋ́!ŋ́ 'in, at'

N1 *n!ŋ̄*
N2 *n!i*
W1 *n!ŋ́*
W2 *ŋ́!ŋ́*
T *!n*
E1 *n!ŋ́*
E2 *n!ŋ*

The primary meaning of *ŋ́!ŋ́ is probably 'inside' and, in fact, this item has uses as a relational noun or adverb where it takes this meaning, cf.

N1 *tc'ù* 'home'
tc'ù-n!ŋ̄ 'house' (lit.: the home's inside)

(148) N1 *Yà gè- ā n!ŋ̄.*
N1 stay- TR inside
'S/he is inside.'

In addition there is what Dickens calls "locative nouns used in possessive construction", which can with equal justification be interpreted as postpositions, and we will refer to them as secondary postpositions. With few exceptions they are etymologically transparent, that is, they can be used as nouns and postpositions. Many of them require to be headed by the primary postposition *ŋ́!ŋ́.

(149) N1 *Khǜndä ge- a ǁäxü !'úlí.*
cup COP- TR stool back
'The cup is behind the stool.'

The only dialect that appears to have a range of prepositions is N2; note that this is the dialect that has been influenced most strongly by the (prepositional) Bantu languages.

(150) N2 *A gu n!ai, a hn da na ha tcu.*
N1 take lion N1 EMPH carry? LOC N1 home
'(He) took the lion and then carried it home.' (Bleek 1956: 62)

In addition there is what we propose to call the transitive preposition (TR) *N *ke, *S *kò, called the "transitive particle" by Dickens (2005), the "Objektergänzungspartikel" by Köhler (1973: 19), and the "multi-purpose-oblique" (MPO) by Güldemann and Vossen (2000). It has the following distribution across dialects:

*N	*ke	*S	*kò
N1	*kē*	E1	*kò*
W1	*kè*	E2	*kò*
W2	*kè*	E3	*kò*
K	*kē*		

This marker has properties of an oblique case preposition; it is used to increase the valency of the verbs by being preposed to some extra-participant, mostly but not only locative, temporal, or instrumental noun phrases or adverbs. The syntactic slot occupied by the transitive preposition is preceding the second participant after the verb. This can be shown by reversing the order of the two participants – a rule that is observed across dialects, e.g.

(151) W1 *Hä ǀ'ū- ā tōq kè ǂà.* or
N1 put.in- R honey TR pot

Hä ǀ'ū- ā ǂà kè tōq.
N1 put.in- R pot TR honey
'He put (the) honey into a/the pot.'

3.1.6 Compounding and derivation

3.1.6.1 Compounding

Compounding is highly common and can be said to belong to the typological characteristics of this language. What appears to be the predominant pattern is that the last constituent is likely to be the semantic and syntactic head while the preceding one assumes the role of a modifier (cf. Köhler 1973: 37; Heikkinen 1987: 7f.; Heine and König 2012). Compounding may involve nouns and nouns, nouns and verbs, or verbs only (note that there is a partly productive pattern of deriving nouns from verbs without any formal marking). In certain cases, the transitive suffix (TR) is required on the second item.

(152) a. E2 *kx'ōò-* *ts'í* 'opening of a pot'
pot- mouth

b. W1 *gà'ō-* *khúí* 'daytime'
sun- be.hot

c. W1 *Mā gù 'à tà ǀ'hè- ǀē.*
1SG take 2SG and pound- die:SG
'I take you and pound you to death.'

3.1.6.2 Derivation

Both nominal and verbal derivation, achieved by means of enclitics or suffixes, are fairly common and productive mechanisms. The following treatment is confined essentially to a listing of the main derivative exponents.

The main nominal derivational enclitics or suffixes are:

	Proto-!Xun form	Meaning
(a)	*-a	deverbal abstract nouns (NOMIN)
(b)	*-de	female (F)
(c)	*-kòè	reciprocal (REC)
(d)	*-kx'àò	agent nouns (AGENT)
(e)	*-mà, PL *-m̀ɦe	diminutive (DIM)
(f)	*-sí	deverbal nouns (NOMIN)
(g)	*-gǁöq, PL *-nǁëè	male (M)

(a) *-a deverbal abstract nouns

E1	*jäqm*	'be thin'	*jäqm-a*	'thinness'
W1	*'ú*	'go'	*'ū-ā*	'visitor, journey'

(b) *-de female. This suffix appears to be derived from a noun for 'mother'.

N1	*!xó*	'elephant'	*!xó-dé*	'female elephant'
W1	*ǂù*	'wedding'	*ǂù-dē*	'bride'

(c) *-kòè reciprocal. This nominal extension, which must not be confused with the verbal reciprocal marker (see 3.1.4.1), does not seem to be productive. It is found exclusively in Northwestern !Xun, always preceded by the transitive suffix *-a.

(153) N1 *ǀúí-* *ā-kwè* *tcá* '(two) sisters'
elder.sister- TR-REC DU

(d) *-kx'àò agent nouns

N1	*ts'áà*	'steal'	*ts'á-kx'āò*	'thief'
E1	*!äqè*	'hunt'	*!äqè-kx'àò*	'hunter'

(e) *-mà, PL *-m̀fie diminutive. This suffix still occurs as a relational noun 'child'. Its dialectal distribution is as follows:

	SG	PL
*X	*-mà	*-m̀fie
N1	*-mà*	*-mfièē*
N2	*ma*	*me*
W2	*-mà*	*-m̀hè*
E1	*-mà*	*-mhí*
E2	*-mà*	*-mfiìí*

N1	*g!áún*	'tree'	*g!áún-mà*	PL	*g!áún-mfièē*	'small tree'

(f) *-sí deverbal nouns. This suffix has three main functions: (a) place, (b) manner, and (c) instrument. Nouns formed in this way are allocated to class 4 (N4).

	Verb	Meaning	Noun	Meaning
N1	*tc'â*	'sleep'	*tc'â-cí*	'sleeping place'
	'ḿ	'eat'	*'ḿ-cí*	'eating place, eating utensil'
E1	*gè'é*	'sing'	*gè'é-sí*	'way of singing'

(g) *-g!öq, PL *-n‖äqè 'male'. This suppletive suffix has the following dialectal distribution (see also under 3.1.4.4.3):

	SG	PL
*N	*-g‖öq	*-n‖äqè
N1	*-‖òq*	*-n‖ae*
N2	*g‖o*	
W1	*-g‖öq*	*n‖äqe*
E1	*g!öq*	*n‖äqè*

N1	*!xó-‖òq*	PL	*!xó-n‖āē*	'male elephant'
	!hm̄-‖òq	PL	*!hm̄-n‖āē*	'male leopard'

The main verbal derivative affixes are listed below. It remains, however, unclear in most cases whether, or to what extent, we are in fact dealing with affixes rather than clitics, or even with independent words.

(a) *-a — transitive suffix (TR)
(b) *-khoe — reciprocal (REC)
(c) *-ra — 'away' andative (AND)
(d) *-sóè — 'out' elative (ELA)
(e) *-taqm-a — frustrative (FRU)
(f) *tí — passive (PASS)
(g) *-|a'a, *-|'àn — benefactive suffix (BEN)
(h) *-|x'oa 'with' — comitative (COM)
(i) *nǂú, *nǂáí — causative proclitic (CAUS)
(j) *-ǂòà 'like' — similative (SIM)

(k) *-nǁhöò 'aimlessly'
(l) *-ǁx'áé 'together'

With the exception of the causative marker (i), all derivational elements follow the verb.

(a) *-a transitive suffix

This item, which was mentioned already in section 3.1.3.5 and elsewhere, also acts in some way as a derivational device in that it extends *inter alia* the transitivity pattern of the verb: when added to a verb it allows for an extra participant.

(b) *-khoe reciprocal

(154) N1 *Yà ǀàü mí.* / N1 like 1SG / 'S/he likes me.'
Cŋ̈ ǀàü-à khōē. / 3PL like-TR REC / 'They like each other.'

(c) *NW *-ra 'away' andative

This suffix appears to be confined to Northwestern !Xun. Note that in Angolan varieties of Northwestern !Xun it tends to be realized as *-la*:

PN *-rā

N1 *-lā*
N2 *-la*
W1 *-rā*
W2 *-lā*

N1 *gǀà* 'put' PL *gǀà-lā* 'throw away (PL)'

(d) *NW *-sóè 'out' elative. This suffix, too, appears to be confined to Northwestern !Xun:

N1 *!xóè* 'chase' *!xóè-cúè* 'chase away'
W1 *tsàq* 'pour' *tsàq-sòè* 'pour out'

(e) *-taqm-a frustrative

Except for E2, it is unclear whether this item is a derivative suffix or an independent verb **taqm* 'to miss a target'.

(155) E1 *Hä !àqè tàm- à g!ò'è.* / 3SG hunt FRU- TR oryx / 'He hunted the oryx in vain.' (Dickens 2005)

(f) *NW *tí passive

A genuine passive morpheme is found only in W1 and W2 (see Heikkinen 1987: 32, 83), e.g.

(156) W1 *Zù xáŋ nǀūún nǀùhì- sòè- tí tà xáŋ tè!'àn tà kū'àŋ.ŋ* / 1PL:EX then just take:PL- ELA- PASS and then bring and here / 'We were then just taken out and then brought here.' (Heikkinen 1987: 32)

(g) *-ǀa'a, *ǀ'àn benefactive

The benefactive clitic or suffix is derived from the verb 'give', with which it is homonymous (see Dickens 2005 for E1):

	General benefactive marker	'give me, for me'	Verb 'give'
*NW	*-ǀa'a	*na	*ǀa'a
N1	*ǀá'ā*	*na*	*ǀá'a*
N2	*ǀaa*	*na*	*ǀaa, na*
W1	*-ǀà'ā*	*nā*	*ǀà'a*
W2	*-ǀà'à*	*nà*	*ǀà'à*
C1	*-ǀáàn*	*na*	*ǀáàn*
*SE	*-ǀ'àn	*na	*ǀ'àn
E1	*-ǀ'à(n)*	*na*	*ǀ'àn*
E2	*-ǀ'aà*	*nāà*	*ǀ'āà*

(157) N1 *Ì gù ǀá'ā pòhō kè mī!*
2PL take BEN jackal TR 1SG
'Catch the jackal for me!'

(h) *ǀx'oa 'with' comitative

This suffix replaces the transitive suffix *-a* in E1. Its functions include the marking of comitative, instrumental, and means participants.

(i) *nǂú, *nǂáí causative proclitic

This verbal proclitic or prefix has the following dialectal distribution:

*NW	*nǂú
N	*nǂú*
W1	*nǂú*
W2	*nǁú*[3]
*SE	*nǂáí
E1	*nǂáí*
E2	*nǂéí-, nǂí-*

(158) N1 *Mí- hŋ̄ ĥā nǂú gē'ē- à yà.* cf. *Yà ĥā gē'ē.*
1SG EMPH PROG CAUS sing- TR N1 N1 PROG sing
'I am making him sing.' 'He is singing.'

(159) E1 *Farmakx'àò- sì nǂáí ǂháí- á gúmí.*
farmer- PL make be.many- TR cattle
'The farmers increased the [number of] cattle.'

(j) *-ǂòà similative. This verbal extension is only found in Northwestern !Xun.

(160) N1 *Cŋ̀ ĥāā djŋ̀- ǂōā dē'bē.ē*
3PL PROG think- SIM children
'They think like children.'

(k) *nǁhòò 'aimlessly'. This suffix appears to be confined to Southeastern !Xun. In E1 it occurs as a verb meaning '(wander) about, do something without direction' in Dickens (1994: 257).

(161) E2 *Zō kú n!nòm- nǁhò.*
bee PROG fly- roam
'The bees fly around everywhere.'

(l) *ǁx'áé 'together'

This suffix is derived from the verb *ǁx'áé 'gather, meet'. The various extensions and their lexical sources are summarized below.

	Derivative	Verb	Meaning
*X	*ǁx'áé	*ǁx'áé	'walk together'
N1	-*ǀx'áé*	*ǀx'áé*	'walk together'
W2	*ǀx'āē*	*ǀx'āē*	'meet, find'
E1	*ǀkx'áé*	*ǀkx'áé*	'be together, be assembled'
E2	-*ǀx'áé*	*ǀx'áé*	'gather, meet'

(162) N1 *Djū kē tcí- ǀx'áé.*
1PL:EX PAST come- together
'We came together.'

3.1.7 Interpersonal and textual functions

3.1.7.1 Imperative

Singular imperatives are formed by using the simple verb stem. Not infrequently, the appropriate subject pronoun is added before the verb.

N2 *tòá* 'go away!' (said to children)

(163) N1 *Ì ǀqá tc'á màlí.*
2PL NEG steal money
'Don't (you PL) steal money!'

(164) W1 *m̀hm̀m̀ 'ū- ā ts'ù.*
1PL:IN go- TR home
'Let us go home!'

There are a few verbs having a suppletive imperative stem, especially the verb for 'come':

	Imperative		Elsewhere	
*X	*wohe	'come!'	*tsí	'to come'
N1	*wòhé, tcí*		*tcí*	
W2	*tcí, gǀìí*		*gǀè*	
E1	*hòö*		*tsí*	
E2	*wéè*		*tsí*	

(165) N1 *Wòhé!* or *Tcí- á kwé-'e!* 'Come here!'
come- TR here-PROX

E1 *hòö* 'come!'
E2 *wéè* 'come!'

Negative imperatives are formed by placing the verb *nǁàn 'leave, let go' before the main verb in W1, W2 (*nǀà*), E1 and E2 (*nǀàh (kú)*, short form: *nǀáú*).

(166) W1 *Nǀà nǀùhì n!òm tìí.*
NEG:IMP take:PL stone heavy
'Don't take heavy stones!'

But more commonly, the negation marker *ǀoa is used (see 3.1.3.4), e.g.

(167) N1 *À ǀóá !xóé ǂóà yà- ndū'à!*
2SG NEG chase giraffe N1- DEM:DIST
'Don't chase the giraffe!'

3.1.7.2 Interrogative

A general characteristic of !Xun is that questions invariably require the use of the question particle (Q), irrespective of whether sentence questions or word questions are involved. The various forms the question particle takes are listed below.

*X	*re
N1	*má*
W1	*rā*
W2	*lā*
K	*rā*
C1	*a*
E1	*ré*
E2	*rēē*

The question particle is placed after the first noun phrase of the clause, e.g.

(168) E1 *N!hà ì ré !hún n!ŋ̀?*
lion Q kill:SG eland
'Does the lion kill the eland?'

Like sentence questions, word questions normally require the presence of the question particle. As a rule, interrogative pronouns occupy the clause-initial position. It is not possible to do justice to the wide range of forms and combinations of forms used for word questions. The following are perhaps the most salient categories.

(a) *nè 'which?'. This attributive interrogative follows its head noun. It has the following dialectal distribution:

*X	*nè
N1	*nì*
W2	*lē*
*SE	*nè, *nìn
E1	*nè, nìn*
E2	*nè, nìn*

(169) N1 *Ā má cŋ́ tc'ù nì?*
2SG Q see home which
'Which home do you see?'

(b) 'Who?' The dialectal distribution of this interrogative, which is etymologically derived from the phrase 'which person?', is as follows:

N1	*m-djū (má)*
W1	*m̀-zōē (rā), m̀-zē (rā), m̀-zūsē*
W2	*m̄djē*

E1 *hà-jò-è (ré)*
E2 *ɦà-jū-ē (rēē), ɦà nè (rēē), ɦà nìn (rēē)*

(170) N1 *M-djū dā'bà ma kē ǁ ē?*
who child Q PAST die:SG
'Which child has died?'

(171) W1 *m̀-zōe ra hà̈ 'è?*
who Q N1 DEM:PROX
'Who is this?'

(c) 'what?'

The dialectal distribution of this pronoun, which is etymologically derived from a phrase 'which thing?', is as follows:

N1 *m-tí (má), m-tcí (má)*
W1 *m̀-tsé (rá), m̀-tsí-sè (rá)*
W2 *m̄-tcé (má), tcé (má)*
E1 *hà-tc-é (ré)*
E2 *ɦà-tcí-à nè (ree)*

(172) N1 *M-tí má à tù 'ḿ?*
what Q 2SG want eat
'What do you want to eat?'

(d) 'where?'

The dialectal distribution of this pronoun is as follows (see also 3.1.4.4.2):

N1 *kō'lē (má), tè*
N3 *kuli*
W2 *lē, kū lē*
T *kore-ua*
E1 *kò (ré)*
E2 *kòh (rè), kò ré, kò rè cē rēē*

(173) N1 *Kō'lē má à ú- à?*
where Q 2SG go- TR
'Where are you going?'

(e) 'how?'

The dialectal distribution is as follows:

*NW *ne

N1 *nē*
W1 *nè*
W2 *lē*
E1 *nè, nàùn, nìn*
E2 *nàò, nīn*

(174) N1 *Yà má nē kē ú- á?*
N1 Q how PAST go- TR
'How did he go?'

(175) W1

Yà	*'è-hè*	*òh-*	*ā*	*ǀàē-ǀàē*	*nè*	*òh-*	*ā?*
2PL	here	be-	TR	adult	how	be-	TR

'What are you adults like?'

3.1.8 Clause combining

3.1.8.1 Coordination

!Xun is primarily a coordinating language, that is, concatenating clauses by means of a coordinating conjunction constitutes the primary means of combining propositional contents. But clauses may be, and frequently are, combined without any formal linkage:

(176) N2

Tumba	*bá*	*ki*	*ǀɔle*	*me*	*ǀo,*	*a*	*ǀum,*	*a*	*toan*
Tumba	father	PAST	mark	1SG	forehead	N1	cut	N1	finish

'Tumba's father marked my forehead, cut,

gu	*gǀɔva*	*a*	*ǀ'ɛhn,*	*ki*	*xwa*	*ǀ'ɛ.*
take	leave	and	grass	PAST	rub.in	grass

took leaves and grasses, rubbed in grass.' (Bleek 1956: 262)

There are two main coordinating conjunctions having overlapping functions: *tè and *ka. They belong perhaps to the most perspicuous elements of !Xun discourse structure. While they connect clauses, they may also introduce utterances. In addition to their coordinating functions, they also serve subordinating functions (see 3.1.8.2; see also Heikkinen 1987: 55). Their dialectal distribution is as follows:

*X	*tè 'and'	*ka 'and'
N1	*tā*	*kā-kē*
N2	*ta*	*ka*
W1	*tà*	*kā*
W2	*tà*	*kā*
C1	*te, ɔ(gɔ)*	*ga*
E1	*tè*	*ká*
E2	*tè*	*kā*

*tè 'and' is by far the most frequently used conjunction in !Xun (see, e.g., Heikkinen 1987: 56ff.), and the one expressing the widest range of functions. In addition to marking consecutive (and simultaneous) events, it may also signal subordinate functions such as introducing temporal, adversative, reason, manner and other clauses (see 3.1.8.2), e.g.

(177) N1

Yà-ndū'à	*kē*	*!xòlù*	*dóngí*	*tā*	*dììsá*	*tā*	*'ú.*
N1-DEM:DIST	PAST	mount	donkey	and	be.slow	and	go

'He rode the donkey slowly.'

In some uses, *tè may even express the notion of a relative clause, e.g.

(178) N1

Mā	*kē*	*cŋ́*	*dā'bā*	*tà*	*yà*	*tcí.*
1SG	PAST	see	child	and	N1	come

'I saw a child who is coming.'

*ka is used typically to combine propositions that are conceived as expressing one single event. It also appears to be used for combining simultaneous events or events occurring in quick succession (cf. Dickens 2005), e.g.

(179) E2 *Zō kú cè kā úú ts'á.*
bee PROG return and go sleep
'The bees return and go to sleep.' (Köhler 1973: 26)

Instead of *kā, hè* is used in W1, E1, and E3 to conjoin subordinate clauses (Heikkinen 1987: 52).

In addition, verb serialization constitutes one of the strategies of clause combining. Dickens (2005) distinguishes two kinds of serial patterns in E1: (a) a transitive one (verb + transitive verb + object; see 180) and (b) an intransitive one (verb + intransitive verb + subject; see 181), both illustrated below.

(180) E1 *Dà'àmà khù g/áí- á kàtòngá.*
child jump go.out- TR box
'The child jumped out of the box.'

(181) N1 *(. . .) tā hé pòhó kē !āà ú kē cā tc'ú.*
and then jackal PAST run.away go TR DU home
'(. . .) and the jackal ran away to their common home.'

3.1.8.2 Subordination

3.1.8.2.1 COMPLEMENT CLAUSES

A number of different markers are used to introduce complement clauses, especially *tè and *ka (concerning the dialectal variants of these two markers, see 3.1.8.1), in E1 also *tcá* (< *tcí-à* 'that thing which'; cf. Dickens 2005).

Examples of *tè

(182) a. N1 *Mm̄ n‡hìí tā yà- ndū'à kē cì- là.*
1SG know and N1 DEM:DIST PAST leave- AND
'I know that he has left.'

b. W1 *Hà g/à'è n!ŋ́ tsà'ā tà hà kē /xòm hà.*
3SG birth inside hear and 3SG PAST pity 3SG
'His relatives heard that he had helped him.'

Example of *ka

(183) E1 *Hà g/à'ámá kòàq ká dà'àmà cè tè /kx'àè.*
N1 now fear COMPL child return COMPL be.sick
'He now fears that the child will again be sick.'

In W1, *tà (n/àn) kòè* or *kā (n/àn) kòè* ('and saying') introduce complements after cognition verbs. In E1, *tè kò* or *ká kò* ('and said') are used as quotative markers, and *tcá* (< 'the thing which') serves to introduce complement clauses after verbs of cognition (Dickens 2005).

3.1.8.2.2 RELATIVE CLAUSES

Relative clauses follow their head noun. They are introduced by any of the following markers (or a combination thereof; see below), which are placed between the head noun and the relative clause:

(a) *hè,
(b) demonstrative (see 3.1.4.4.1),

(c) the transitive suffix *-a (see 3.1.3.5),
(d) the coordinating conjunction *tè (see 3.1.8.1).

The distribution of relative clause markers across dialects is typically as summarized below.

Form	(a) *hè	(b) Demonstrative	(c) *-a	(d) *tè
*X	*hè	PRON + DEM	*-a	*tè
N1	*(hè)*	PRON *-ndu'à*, PRON *-'ŋ*	–	*tà*
N2	*e*		*-a*	
W1	*hè*	PRON *-'è*	–	
W2	*-è*			
E1	*hè*	PRON *-è*	*-à*, PL *-sà*	
E2	*ɦè, yè*	*-à tòàh* (DEM:DIST)	*-à*, PL *-sà*	

These forms are not necessarily contrastive ways of expression; rather, they may be combined in some way or other. In the following example, (a), (b), and (c) are combined:

(184) E2 *Mī ǀōā !hā !'òrè tcí- s- à tòàh hè 'āà tānnì.*
1SG NEG know basin thing- PL- R DEM REL 2SG bring
'I don't know the container that you brought.'

(a) and (b) in particular tend to be combined, that is, frequently a demonstrative of (b) may or must be followed by *hè, e.g.

(185) E1 *Jù- à- hè hè !óá mí (. . .)*
person- REL- DEM:N1 REL tell 1SG
'This person, who told me (. . .)'

In the Northwestern !Xun dialects, demonstrative-based relative clause markers (b) appear to constitute the most frequently used means of forming relative clauses.

(186) N1 *Mí ǀōā n‡hìí tán kā- 'ŋ̄ŋ̄ 'ā kē tīnì tcí.*
1SG NEG know container N4 DEM:HERE 2SG PAST bring come
'I don't know the container that you brought.'

(187) W1 *Kùūh ǁām̄m- ā !àē-hàŋ wèēsè yīī- 'è !xūún òh- ā.*
road pass- TR village all N3- DEM !Xun be- TR
'The road went through all the villages where !Xun live.'

The transitive suffix *-à* (PL *-sà* in E1 and E2), figuring in (c), has been discussed elsewhere (especially section 3.1.3.5). It is perhaps the primary means of marking relative clauses in E1, and its use as a relative clause marker is largely confined to Southeastern !Xun, that is, to E1, E2 and E3, although it is also found in N2. In E1, (a) is used for non-restrictive relative clauses. Note that Dickens (1997: 108ff.) distinguishes two markers *-a-*: one that has low tone and serves as a relative clause marker, and another whose tone is a copy of the preceding syllable, which is used (a) as a transitivity marker and (b) as a suffix of compounds, marking the head of a compound (see 3.1.6.1). The plural form *-sà* of E1 and E2 is composed of the plural clitic *sì* and the transitive suffix *-à*, hence *-sì* + *-à* > *-sà*. Synchronically, however, *-sà* behaves like an invariable plural suffix which is used even after nouns such as *jú* 'people' or *n!ŋ̀* 'eland(s)' which ordinarily would not take the nominal plural suffix *-sì*; cf.

(188) E1 *jú- sà mi kx'óá*
people- TR:PL 1SG look.for
'the people I am looking for'

In E1, the use of *-à*, PL *-sà* as relative clause markers appears to have been responsible for a number of grammaticalizations that have become a typological characteristic of this language. Using these markers seems to have become a ubiquitous strategy in !Xun.

Only in N1 can the coordinating conjunction *tè (> *tà*) be used productively to introduce relative clauses (see 3.1.8.1):

(189) N1 *Mā kē cŋ́ dā'bā tà yà tcí.*
1SG PAST see child and N1 come
'I saw a child who is coming.'

3.1.8.2.3 ADVERBIAL CLAUSES

There is a large variety of structures used to present adverbial clauses. Markers used to introduce adverbial clauses are not infrequently derived from, and still resemble to some extent, coordinating constructions involving the conjunctions *tè or *ka (see 3.1.8.1), and it is not always easy to trace a clear boundary between coordination and subordination. The following are a few adverbial clause functions and the most common means to encode them.

Clauses expressing cause tend to be introduced by the following markers (the W1 conjunction *kā'è* is also used for conditional, concessive, and comparative clauses):

N1 *tà (n!hei)* ('and then')
W1 *ösi ka'è, (tsi) ka'è*
W2 *kā-ē . . . má*
E1 *khàmà (. . . tè), khàmà . . . n|á*

(190) N1 *Mí-'ŋ̄ |ōā wūnā 'ḿ tā (n!hēī) mí-'m̄ kūlāā kwá- 'ŋ̄.*
1SG NEG get food and then 1SG NEG:EXIST LOC- DEM:PROX
'I'll get no food because I am not here.'

(191) W1 *Kā'è má öh- ā dàbà- täqē, kāndò'à bà ōō xáŋ tò'à.*
as 1SG be- TR child- mother then 2SG must then go
'Since I am the child's mother, you must go.' (Heikkinen 1987: 28)

Reason clauses are introduced most of all by complex conjunctions such as the following:

N1 *(tà) ká-hŋŋ*
W2 *kā-ē, kā-hŋ̀ ŋ̄ŋ̀, kā-hŋ̀ kùndò'à*
C1 *ga-xn ga*
E1 *khàmà, tè ǁ'à-ká-à-hìn, tè ǁ'à-kò-à-hìn*

(192) N1 *Yà ɦa ǂèhi ta ká-hŋ yà |oa tcí.*
N1 PROG be.sick and therefore N1 NEG come
'He is sick, therefore he can't come.'

The following are the markers used primarily to introduce protasis clauses of conditional sentences:

*X *ká

N1 *ká, kābā*
W1 *kā*
W2 *kā, kā-ē, kē*
C1 *ga*
E1 *ká (. . . ókáà), ká (. . . ǁ'àkáà)*

(193) N1 *Ká à ǀōā cà'à n‡hìí mā n‡á'm̀ ā.*
if 2SG NEG hear know 1SG beat 2SG
'If you don't understand, I'll beat you.'

Purpose clauses are introduced by any of the following conjunctions (concerning the marker *hŋ, see 3.1.4.1; the W1 marker *ahŋ́* is used only in imperative clauses):

*X	*hŋ
N1	*hŋ́, nń, Ø*
N2	*hŋ*
W1	*ō, ahŋ́*
E1	*nǀŋ̀, ǁ'à*
E2	*hŋ̀, nǀŋ, hīn*

(194) N1 *Tā n!héī pòhó kē ú tá ú kē tchŋ̀ gǁúū, tā tán*
and then jackal PAST go and go PAST drink water and container
'And the jackal went and went and he drank water, but there was no container,

kē kùlá hŋ́ yà ‡'è- á gǁú- hŋ̀ tcì- ǀá'ā n!hàé.
PAST NEG:EXIST PURP N1 fetch- TR water- EMPH come- give lion
'so that he could draw the water and take it to the lion.'

3.2 Central Khoesan

3.2.1 Namibian Khoekhoe (Nama/Damara)

Wilfrid H.G. Haacke

3.2.1.1 Basic syntax: the underlying structure of nouns

The simplest sentence of Namibian Khoekhoegowab (N.Kh.), here termed minimal sentence, has only one (lexical) stem. A minimal sentence complies with the minimal requirement of having at least one, but only one lexical stem: it consists of a subject-NP consisting of nothing more than a pro-form, viz. a PGN marker, (a) tense–aspect marker(s) (TA) and a verbal acting as predicate head (VBL). The verbal – the stem – could be a genuine verb or any morphological category that can act as predicate head (see Chapter 6). The sentence can, if a matrix sentence, be marked for mood by a sentence-type marker; in the case of the indicative (IND) by *ge*. Sentence-type markers must, if used, follow immediately on the (subject-)PGN.

PGNs are subject to the surface constraint that, as post-clitics, they cannot stand sentence-initially. Hence, either a conjunction (extraneous) has to precede them, or the lexical specification (see below) of the subject, or any other sentence constituent must be fronted. As a minimal sentence has no additional constituents, fronting is obligatory, leaving two options. TAS, like all grammatical formatives, can also not stand sentence-initially. The present stative marker *a* 'be', being non-specific with regard to time-span, is pivotal for the morphological derivation of surface nouns.

Underlying sentence (predicative):	#PGN		TA	VBL#
	*s	(ge)	a	kaira
	she	(IND)	is	old

Predicative surface strategy:	#VBL	PGN		TA#
	Kaira	*s*	*(ge)*	*a.*
	'She is old.'			

Copulative surface strategy:	#VBL	TA	PGN		#
	Kaira	*a*	*s*	*(ge).*	
	'She is an old one.'				

Crucially, the latter strategy – where the TA as representative of the predicate precedes the subject – receives a nominal interpretation. It is thus conventionally called copulative, alluding to the tradition that copulative sentences express "X be NP". In the copulative strategy the present stative TA *a*, being least marked, can be elided. As embedded sentence (see phrase marker below, thus without sentence type marker *ge*) this minimal sentence will receive a (reduced) relative clause interpretation:

Kaira-s 'She who is an old one' > 'the *or* an old one'

With a noun stem, and conjunctively spelt, the copulative strategy is grammaticalised to a surface noun in the nominative form, while the predicative strategy (without deletion of *a*) is grammaticalised to the oblique form (often erroneously referred to as accusative):

Underlying sentence (predicative):	*s	(ge)	a	tara
	she	(IND)	is	woman
Predicative surface strategy:	*Tara*	*s*	*(ge)*	*a.* >
	'She is a woman.'			
	Tara-sa.	(oblique)		
Copulative surface strategy:	*Taras (ge).* >			
	'She is a woman.'			
	Tara-s.	(nominative)		
	'She who is a woman.' > '(the/a) woman'			

The present derivation accounts plausibly for the fact that N.Kh. surface nouns can, next to the third person, also refer to the first or second person, and that nouns can be overtly marked for tense (T) and aspect (A), positively as well as negatively, e.g.

(195)	***Student***	***ge***	***i-***	***du***	*ge*	*suwuse*	*sîsen-e*	*nî*	*hō.*
	student	T	A-	PGN	IND	readily	work	T	find
	'You who were students will readily find work.'								

As the subject of a minimal matrix sentence consists of a PGN only, any further lexical elaboration on the subject must be added by means of an embedded sentence. This embedded information, which can consist of the noun "stem" or qualifiers or both, is here called the lexical specification of the NP.

Where expedient for explicatory purposes, the following bracketing conventions may be applied:

Braces, curly brackets { } enclose the maximal projection of the NP (including appositions) with PGN markers, as governed by a case marker;

square brackets [ ] enclose the lexical specification of an NP, i.e. the noun stem with any qualifiers as governed by a PGN marker; after a closing square bracket no hyphen is used before the PGN;

parentheses ( ) – if used within square brackets – enclose qualifiers in an NP;

double underlining ___, where used, marks nominal heads, viz. {[(qualifier)(qualifier) noun stem]$PGN_{head\ phrase}$ [(qualifier)]$PGN_{apposition}$}CASE, e.g.

(196) *{[(nē) (kaira) ao]gu} [(sari ra)]gu di*
these old man+PGN visit PRES+PGN POSS
'of these old men who are visiting'

The NP functioning as subject in the initial slot appears in the "nominative" strategy (NOM, with a zero suffix *Ø*). Objects, deposed subjects and subjects of interrogative sentences all appear in the "oblique" strategy (OBL) as parenthetic sentences (cf. below).

[Student]ta ge ra ôa!nâ (I, a student, am investigating)

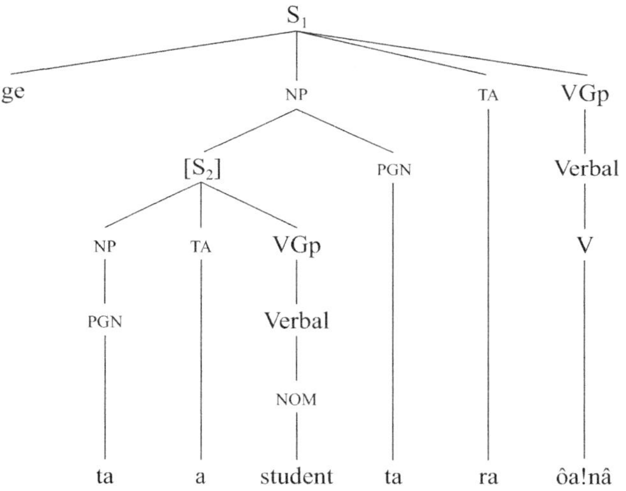

Notes
S_1: tar a ôa!nâ = matrix-S.
S_2: *ta a student > student a ta > student ta (TA deletion) > student (Equi-NP-Deletion)
(VGp = Verbal group. This category is needed, as in more complex sentences the predicate head can consist of more than one word.)

The true noun of N.Kh., therefore, is what is traditionally considered to be the stem of the surface noun (i.e. without PGN), as also is the case in the languages of the Kalahari Khoe branch. Note that the noun "stem" appears without PGN even in N.Kh. when it functions as verbal in the predicate head; it also does so in adverbs, e.g. *nētsē* 'this day = today'. (For implications of the underlyingly sentential origin of nouns, see Haacke 1977, 1979, 1992a, 1992b.)

3.2.1.2 Constituent order

N.Kh. constituent order is very flexible, subject to the following major constraints:

(a) Grammatical formatives (PGNS, TAS, S-type markers) cannot stand sentence-initially.
(b) Only one constituent at a time can occupy the initial slot, i.e. the slot immediately preceding the subject PGN.

The reason for the flexibility is that the initial slot is the principal focus position of the sentence, hence all eligible constituents must be able to be moved into the initial slot.

A minimal sentence can be extended with an object NP consisting of an object marker only. The object marker (o^m), being a type of PGN marker, is post-clitic and must always follow immediately on the verb stem, e.g.

#PGN	TA	VBL	o^m#		
*b	ra	ǂgai	si	'He is calling her.'	underlying
>					
ǂGai	*si~b*	*(ge)*	*ra.*	'He is calling her.'	predicative strategy
[ǂGai	*si ra]b ge.*			'He is the one calling her.'	copulative strategy

The tilde (~) above and elsewhere indicates that the PGN marker does not form a constituent with the preceding morpheme(s). Standard orthographic convention misleadingly prescribes conjunctive spelling of non-vocalic PGN markers (*b, s, ts, m, n*), even if they do not form a constituent with the preceding morpheme. The closing square bracket (]) implies that the immediately following PGN marker does form a constituent with the enclosed lexical specification.

If in N.Kh. the object is lexically specified, then this object NP in the oblique form will be inserted like a parenthetical sentence normally before the TA, and the o^m will be deleted. (In certain Kxoe dialects the o^m is not deleted, thereby corroborating the evidence that Khoe languages underlyingly are SVO languages.) The normal, least marked surface structure of a positive indicative sentence with lexically specified subject, lexically specified object(s) and with (an) adverbial(s) is

(197)	#NP$_{\text{Subject}}$	ge	NP(S)$_{\text{Object}}$	Adverbial(s)	TA	VBL#
	Axa-b	*ge*	*ǀgôa-sa*	*tsaurase*	*go*	*ǂgai.*
	boy	IND	girl	gently	PAST$_{\text{RECENT}}$	call
	'The boy gently called the girl.'					

Adverbials and object NPS have no preferential order. Sentences with lexically specified objects lead to the commonly held assumption that N.Kh. is an SOV language.

3.2.1.3 Sentence permutations: predicative and copulative renderings

Two types of permutation need to be distinguished in N.Kh.: fronting and inversion. During fronting a constituent other than the subject specification is moved into the initial slot for the purpose of focus assignment. Crucially, if a lexically specified subject is present, it is always deposed from this initial slot by the fronted constituent. During inversion, on the other hand, a constituent is put before the (full) subject, without the lexical subject specification being deposed.

Subject deposition here refers to the syntactic process whereby the lexical specification of a subject is displaced from the initial focus position and resurfaces elsewhere in the sentence with a copy of the subject PGN and in the oblique form (*-a*): usually immediately after the indicative marker *-ge*, if present; otherwise at the end of the sentence (then often misconceived as "complement" of a copulative sentence), or – in a hortative sentence – even in front of the focus position.

Co-ordinating conjunctions can appear in the initial slot, or before the entire sentence. If within the initial slot, they likewise trigger subject deposition:

(198)	*Tsî~b*	*ge*	*axa-ba*	*ǀgôa-sa*	*tsaurase*	*go*	*ǂgai.*
	and he	IND	boy+OBL	girl+OBL	gently	PAST$_{\text{RECENT}}$	call
	'And then he, the boy, gently called the girl.'						

3.2.1.3.1 FRONTING

(199) a. Object:

|Gôa-sa$_{\text{FOCUS}}$	*~b*	*ge*	*axa-ba*	*tsaurase*	*go*	*ǂgai.*
girl+OBL	he	IND	boy+OBL	gently	PAST$_{\text{RECENT}}$	call

'The boy called *the girl* gently.'

b. Adverbial: *Tsaurase*$_{\text{FOCUS}}$*~b ge axa-ba |gôa-sa go ǂgai.*
'The boy called the girl *gently*.'

c. Predicate: *ǂGai go*$_{\text{FOCUS}}$*~b ge axa-ba |gôa-sa.*
'The boy *did call* (the girl).'

|Gôa-sa tsaurase go ǂgai$_{\text{FOCUS}}$*~b ge [axa]ba.*
'The boy *gently called the girl*.' [= predicative rendering]

[|Gôa-sa tsaurase go ǂgai]-b ge [axa]ba.
'He, the boy, is one gently calling the girl.' [= copulative rendering]

Sentences in which the entire predicate is fronted, can be re-interpreted as co-referential copulative sentences, i.e. copulative sentences of the type "NP is NP". Such sentences amount to cleft sentences (a sentence divided into two sections, each with its own verbal). This implies that in N.Kh. co-referential copulative sentences are not to be interpreted as consisting of "subject NP" with "complement NP". Rather, the second NP is the deposed subject. In practice, both interpretations are found among speakers, depending on the context.

3.2.1.3.2 INVERSION

Likewise, an inverted sentence (i.e. a sentence in which the order of the predicate and the lexically specified subject in its entirety is inverted, as indicated by the vertical line below) can have a predicative and a copulative reading:

(200) a. *|Gôa-sa tsaurase go ǂgai | [axa]b ge.*
'The boy gently called the girl.' [predicative reading]

b. *|Gôa-sa tsaurase go ǂgai [axa]b ge.*
'It/he is the boy who gently called the girl.' [copulative reading]

The latter, copulative reading is based on the copulative strategy of the minimal sentence discussed above in section 3.2.1.1, but here the verbal group is extended with a relative clause as attributive qualifier (in parentheses; cf. below) next to the head *axa*. Two types of copulative sentences can thus be distinguished:

simplex copulative sentences with one surface NP, e.g.

[Axa]b ge. (minimal)
'It/he is a boy.'

[(|Gôa-sa tsaurase go ǂgai) axa]b ge. (extended)
'It/he is a boy who . . .'

co-referential copulative sentences with two surface NPS, e.g.

[|Gôa-sa tsaurase go ǂgai]b ge [axa]ba.
'He, the boy, is (the) one who gently called the girl.'

Copulative sentences in N.Kh., thus, are not different sentence types underlyingly but are derived from the basic predicative sentence.

3.2.1.4 Compound and complex sentences

While co-ordination of sentences and constituents is accomplished exclusively by means of conjunctions, subordination of sentences can be effected by means of conjunctions, (adverbialising) suffixes, relativisation, complementisation and nominalisation. Subordinated sentences are never marked by sentence type markers (e.g. indicative *ge* or accreditive *kom o*).

3.2.1.4.1 CO-ORDINATION

Co-ordinating conjunctions precede the linked sentence. Hence they stand between the two sentences and are conventionally preceded by a comma, if not a full stop. They appear either before the entire sentence or, more commonly, stand in the initial slot, e.g.

(201) *Sa-ts ge om-sa nî ôa!nâ, tsî ti-ta ge kantor-sa nî ôa!nâ.*
you IND house+OBL T search and I IND office+OBL T search
'You shall search the house and I shall search the office.'

or

(202) *Sa-ts ge om-sa nî ôa!nâ, tsî ~ ta ge (ti-ta) kantor-sa nî ôa!nâ.*
you IND house+OBL T search and IND I office+OBL T search
'You shall search the house and I shall search the office.'

Subordinating conjunctions may be linked to the resumptive referential pronoun *ǁnā*, which refers to the initial sentence. Such combinations then introduce main sentences, e.g.

(203) a. *ǀAesen ~ta hâ amaga ~ts ge ti soa-s ǁnā nî !gû.*
ill I A because you IND my place in T go
'Since I am ill you must go in my place.' [subordinating]

b. *ǀAesen ~ta ge hâ. ǁNā amaga ~ts ge ti soa-s !nâ nî !gû.*
ill I IND A in because you IND my place in T go
'I am ill. Therefore you must go in my place.' [co-ordinating]

3.2.1.4.2 SUBORDINATION

3.2.1.4.2.1 SUBORDINATION BY CONJUNCTION

Subordinating conjunctions follow on the sentence they embed as adverbial clause (with the exception of the conjunction *î* 'so that'). Exclusively subordinating conjunctions are mostly derived and are based on postpositional constructions or complementisers. *!Nūb*, for instance, is a fossilised noun with a meaning like 'occasion', followed by the postposition *ai* 'on':

(204) *Mû bi ta go !nūbai ~b ge khoe-ba go !khoebē.*
see him I T when he IND man+OBL T run.away
'As I saw him, the man ran away.'

Most simple subordinating conjunctions can also have a co-ordinating function, depending on position, e.g.

co-ordinating:

(205) *Ti-ta ge khō-na nî ǀnoro tsî ta ge nî ǁamaxū ni.* ⇒
I IND skins+OBL T tan and I IND T sell them
'I shall tan skins and I shall sell them.'

deletion of joint subject and TA:

(206) *Ti-ta ge khō-na __ ǀnoro tsî __ __ nî ǁamaxū ni.* ⇒
I IND skins+OBL tan and T sell them
'I shall tan skins and I shall sell them.'

subordination:

(207) *Ti-ta ge khō-na ǀnoro tsî ~ ta ge nî ǁamaxū ni.*
I IND skins+OBL tan and I IND T sell them

or:

(208) *Ti-ta ge nî ǁamaxū ni, khō-na ǀnoro tsî.*
I IND T sell them skins+OBL tan and
'As I tan skins, I sell them.'

Compound noun phrases consist not of co-ordinated but of subordinated NPS which are lexical specifications (itemisations) of the "resumptive" PGN that seemingly concludes the compound NP. As the PGNS of the individual NPS are not identical with the all-encompassing PGN (*n*) of the matrix sentence, they cannot be deleted by equi-NP deletion. Hence the minimal copulative sentences that introduce the lexical specifications stay intact, each being followed by the subordinating *tsî*.

(209) *[ǁGû-b tsî ǁgû-s tsî ǀgôa-i*
father and mother and child

tsî] n ge go sī.ī
and ~they IND TA arrive
'They – being father, mother and child – have arrived.'

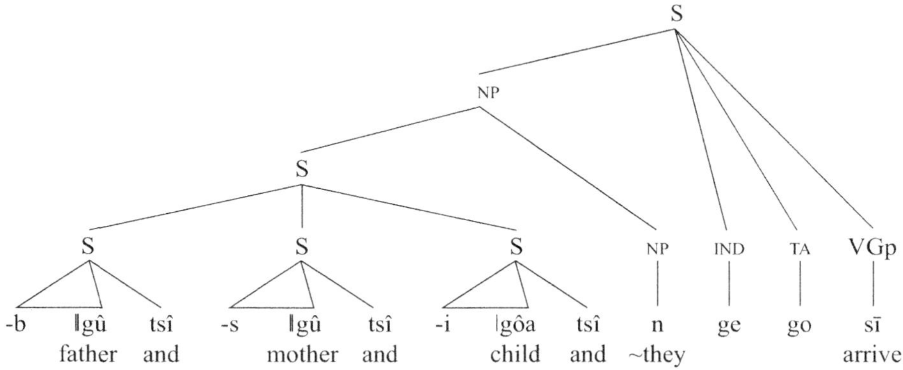

3.2.1.4.2.2 SUBORDINATION BY ADVERBIALISING SUFFIXES

Four suffixes can embed sentences as adverbial clauses:

-se for adverbial clauses of manner (cf. 210);
-!â for adverbial clauses of concession, to express irreconcilability/incompatibility/unexpectedness (cf. 211);
-ga for adverbial clauses of purpose (cf. 212);
-pa for adverbial clauses of place (cf. 213).

Examples:

(210) *!Gû(~s) nî~se ~s ge ǂû-na nî ǀama.*
go.she T ADV she IND food+OBL T buy
'Having to go she will buy food.'

(211) *!Gû(~s) nî~!â s ge ǂû-na nî ǀama.*
go.she T ADV she IND food+OBL T buy
'Although she must go she will buy food.'

(212) *!Gû(~s) nî~ga ~s ge ǂû-na nî ǀama.*
go.she T ADV she IND food+OBL T buy
'In order to go she will buy food.'

(213) *!Gû(~s) nî~pa ~s ge ǂû-na nî ǀama.*
go.she T ADV she IND food+OBL T buy
'Where she will go she will buy food'

If the subject of the adverbial clause is self-evident, it can be deleted in the adverbial clause. Speakers today use both an absolute and a relative tense system in the adverbial clause. In the absolute system the tense is chosen according to the actual speaking time, as for the matrix sentence. In the relative system the tense is chosen relative to the event of the matrix sentence: if the embedded action occurs simultaneously, present tense; if before, past tense; if afterwards, future tense. E.g.

'Yesterday I saw children (they) going into hiding.'

(214) a. *ǀAri ~ta ge ǀgôa-na* ***gau(~n) gose*** *go mû.*
day. removed ~I IND children hide they PAST~ADV T see
[absolute system]

b. *ǀAri ~ta ge ǀgôa-na* ***gau(~n) rase*** *go mû.*
day. removed ~I IND children hide they PRES~ADV T see
[relative system]

3.2.1.4.2.3 SUBORDINATION AS RELATIVE CLAUSES

Relative clauses behave like other N.Kh. qualifiers and can, therefore, appear in attributive, appositive and pronominal function in an NP (cf. below). As they are embedded sentences, sentence type markers will not occur in them. If the antecedent is also the referent of the subject or the (direct) object of the relative clause, it can be deleted in the relative clause; if it is the referent of a postpositional phrase or possessive, it cannot be deleted (see Haacke 1985).

Subject:

(215) *Mû te ~b ge go.* + *[Khoe]b ge a ǀhôakao.*
see me he IND T man IND A scoundrel
'He saw me.' 'The man is a scoundrel.'

⇒ *[Mû te __ __ go khoe]b ge a ǀhôakao.*
see me T man IND A scoundrel
'The man who saw me is a scoundrel.'

Object:

(216) *Mû bi ~ta ge go.* + *[Khoe]b ge a ǀhôakao.*
see him I IND T man IND A scoundrel
'I saw him.' 'The man is a scoundrel.'

⇒ *[Mû __ ~ta __ go khoe]b ge a ǀhôakao.*
see I T man IND A scoundrel
'The man whom I saw is a scoundrel.'

Postpositional phrase:

(217) *Khoe-b ǀkha ~ta ge go !hoa.* + *[Khoe]b ge a ǀhôakao.*
man with I IND T talk man IND A scoundrel
'I chatted with the man.' 'The man is a scoundrel.'

⇒ *[ǁÎ-b ǀkha ~ta __ go !hoa khoe]b ge a ǀhôakao.*
man with I T talk man IND A scoundrel
'The man with whom I chatted is a scoundrel.'

Possessive:

(218) *Khoe-b di !khō-īsi-ba ta ge go mû.* + *[Khoe]b ge a ǀhôakao.*
man POSS photo+OBL I IND T see man IND A scoundrel
'I saw a picture of the man.' 'The man is a scoundrel.'

⇒ *[ǁÎ-b di !khō-īsi-ba ta __ go mû khoe]b ge a ǀhôakao.*
man POSS photo+OBL I T see man IND A scoundrel
'The man whose picture I saw is a scoundrel.'

3.2.1.4.2.4 SUBORDINATION WITH THE COMPLEMENTISER *!KHAI-S*

The noun *!khai-s* 'affair, matter' serves to embed complement sentences, i.e. the equivalent of English "that"-sentences. (See also the fossilised noun *!nūb* 'occasion' in the conjunction *!nūbai* above.) Being embedded in NPS, such complement sentences with *!khai-s* can then serve as subject, object or postpositional phrase in a sentence. Relative clauses and complement sentences have an identical surface structure. However, the difference is that, unlike the antecedent of the relative clause, *!khai-s* underlyingly is not part of the embedded sentence. (As our bracketing conventions refer to surface structure, the complement sentence also appears in parentheses, similar to relative clauses.)

Relative clause:

(219) *Elisabet-s ge [(Eben-ni go !hoatsoatsoa) ǂhôa]sa ra ǂgom.*
Elisabeth IND Eben T tell.begin story+OBL A believe
'Elisabeth believes the story which Eben began to tell.'

Complement sentence:

(220) *Elisabet-s ge [(Eben-ni go !hoatsoatsoa) !khai]sa ra ǂgom.*
Elisabeth IND Eben T tell.begin (matter)+OBL A believe
'Elisabeth believes (it), that Eben started to tell/talk.'

Complement sentences appear either attributively with *!khai-s*, or pronominally, but not appositively; e.g.

attributive:

(221)	*Matheu-b*	*ge*	*go*	*hōǂui*	*[(ǁî-b*	*di*	*khoexabe*	*~di*	*a)*	*!khai]sa.*
	Matthew	IND	T	find.out	he	POSS	relative	they	T	matter

'Matthew found out that they are his relatives.'

pronominal:

(222)	*Matheu-b*	*ge*	*go*	*hōǂui*	*[(ǁî-b*	*di*	*khoexabe*	*~di*	*a)*	*]sa.*
	Matthew	IND	T	find.out	he	POSS	relative	they	T	it

'Matthew found out that they are his relatives.'

In complement sentences the stative aspect marker *a* is not normally grammaticalised into an (oblique) suffix, nor is the copulative strategy possible. Sentences remain in their original predicative form:

(*)Matheu-b ge go hōǂui [ǁî-b di khoexabe-de !khai]sa (NB: di + a → de)
*Matheu-b ge go hōǂui [ǁî-b di khoexabe(a)-di !khai]sa.

Complement sentences serve to embed indirect speech:

(223)	*Dî*	*ni*	*re*	*[(maǀae*	*~n*	*nî*	*!gû)*	*!khai]sa!*
	ask	them	please	when	they	T	go	matter

'Please ask them when they will go!'

Pronominally used complement sentences should be distinguished from nominalised/ infinitive phrases. While both end in *-s*, complement sentences are finite, i.e. they have a subject and specify tense and aspect, while nominalised phrases are non-finite (hence infinitive) as they specify neither a subject, nor tense and aspect.

Nominalisation:

(224)	*[Rem-s*	*ose*	*!nari]*	*s*	*ge*	*a*	*tsū.*
	brakes	without	drive	PGN	IND	TA	bad

'Driving without brakes is bad.'

Complement:

(225)	*[Maria-s*	*rem-s*	*ose*	*go*	*!nari*	*(!khai)]*	*s*	*ge*	*a*	*tsū.*
	Maria	brakes	without	T	drive	matter	PGN	IND	TA	bad

'That Mary drove without brakes is bad.'

3.2.1.4.2.5 SUBORDINATION AS POSTPOSITIONAL PHRASE

Postpositional phrases have an adverbial function and have the structure #NP postposition#. Both complement sentences and infinitive phrases can be embedded as postpositional phrases.

Infinitive phrase:

(226)	*[Audo-ba*	*!narimâi]*	*s*	*khao!gâ*	*~b*	*ge*	*nî*	*ǂganamhe.*
	truck+OBL	park	PGN	after	PGN	IND	T	lock+PASS

'After parking a/the truck it must be locked.'

Complement:

(227)	*[Audo-ba*	*~ts*	*go*	*!narimâi*	*(!khai)]*	*s*	*khao!gâ*	*~b*	*ge*	*nî*	*ǂganamhe.*
	car+OBL	you	T	park	COMPLT	PGN	after	PGN	IND	T	lock+PASS

'After you have parked a/the truck it must be locked.'

3.2.1.5 Mood, tense, aspect

3.2.1.5.1 MOODS

N.Kh. distinguishes five moods, the three normal moods pertaining to statements, questions and commands, but with two further subdivisions. Certain of these moods are explicitly marked by sentence type markers that follow immediately on the PGN of the subject.

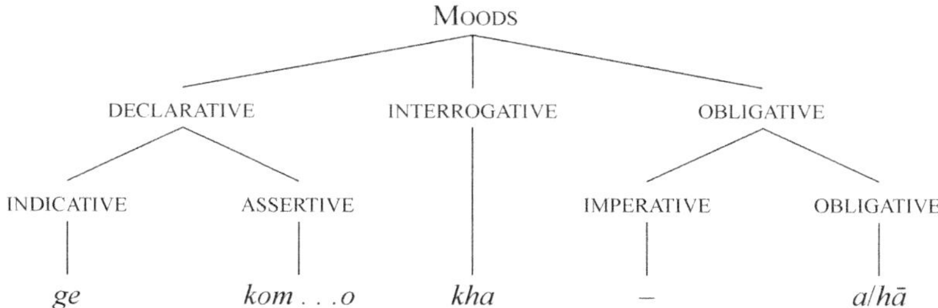

Indicative: The particle *ge* marks indicative main sentences, i.e. ordinary statements.

(228) . . . $PGN_{subject}$ IND . . . TA . . . VBL
Hoan ge ra ǂnā.
'All dance/All are dancing.'

Assertive: The assertive mood is an emphatic type of declarative, often used to remind someone of something that ought to be known.

(229) . . . $PGN_{subject}$ ASST . . . TA . . . VBL-o
Hoan kom ra ǂnā-o.
'Surely then, all dance/are dancing.'

Interrogative: Questions are marked by the interrogative marker *kha* only if surprise or incongruity is to be conveyed. Otherwise the interrogative mood is conveyed by intonation (and the absence of a declarative marker). If the subject is lexically specified (and only then), it appears in the oblique with the case marker *-a*.

With lexically specified subject:

(230) NP-$a_{subject}$ Q . . . TA . . . VBL
Hoana kha ra ǂnā?
'Do all dance, then?/Are all dancing, then?'

Without lexically specified subject:

(231) . . . $PGN_{subject}$ Q . . . TA . . . VBL
Mapa~nØ kha ra ǂnā?
'Where do they dance, then?/Where are they dancing, then?'

Imperative: Imperatives and hortatives do not have sentence type markers like the above that follow immediately on the subject PGN. Unless rudely curt, they are marked by a sentence-final particle *re*, equatable with 'please', and they have no TAS. The imperative addresses the second person, while the hortative normally – but not exclusively – addresses the first and third person. If the subject of the imperative is in the second person singular, it is omitted (unless rendered as address).

(232) VBL (PGN) IMP
ǂNā *re!* 'Please dance!' (SG)
ǂNā ro *re!* 'Will you two please dance!' (DU)

Hortative: The term hortative is a misnomer, as the semantic import is not significantly different to that of the imperative. The name suggests itself by virtue of the fact that such sentences are translated as 'Let us/them . . .'. Hortatives are marked by sentence-initial *a* or *hā* 'come', and – like the imperative – have no TA but the particle *re*. The hortative construction is used primarily for subjects in the first or third person. The subject must always be present.

(233) A PGN VBL re!
A da ǂnā re! 'Please let us dance!'

3.2.1.5.2 TENSE–ASPECT SYSTEM

A main and a subsidiary tense–aspect system can be recognised. Potential tenses with *ka/ga* are best accommodated in a subsidiary system, as they do not fit into the main paradigm. For the main system four tenses combine with four aspects (Table 7.8):

TABLE 7.8 MAIN TENSE–ASPECT SYSTEM: POSITIVE

ASPECT / TENSE	Remote past *ge*	Recent past *go*	Present *Ø*	Future *nî*
Punctual	*ge*	*go*	–	*nî*
Progressive	*gere*	*goro*	*ra/ta*	*nîra*
Perfective	*ge hâ i*	*go hâ i*	*hâ*	*nî hâ i*
Stative	*ge i*	*go i*	*(a)*	*nî i*

Recent past *go*: This tense refers to events not longer than about a day ago, but may also be used to denote relative recentness.

Remote past *ge*: The remote past refers to any event further removed than ones for which the recent past would be used.

Present tense *Ø*: Hagman (1977: 62) has correctly pointed out that the present tense is not marked by a morpheme in N.Kh., contrary to the conventional misconception that *ra* marks the present tense.

Future/compellative tense *nî*: This particle serves to render future tense ('shall/will') as well as obligation ('must').

The above tenses combine with the following aspects:

Punctual aspect *Ø*: This aspect has semelfactive import, as it refers to actions that happen once at a discreet point in time. Note that a punctual present tense **Ø/Ø* does not exist.

Progressive aspect *rV*: This aspect marks iterative or continuous, ongoing action. The morpheme *ra* is subject to vowel assimilation in the past tenses.

Perfective aspect *hâ*: This aspect indicates that an action had been ongoing and was completed before the time the tense refers to, thus having brought about a situation still pertaining; e.g. present perfective *!Â ta ge hâ* 'I have become hungry', i.e. 'I am hungry'. The implication is that this situation had not existed at some earlier stage.

Stative aspect *a/i*: The stative indicates an unchanging situation or state, without implying a beginning or end of this state. No progression or development is implied.

Example: Perfective recent past + punctual recent past:

(234) *Luka-b ge |aesen go hâ i, ǁgâu-s tawa ta go sīo.*
Luke IND become.ill T A A yard at I T arrive+when
'Luke had become (= was) ill when I arrived at the homestead.'

See Chapter 6 for the identification of verbs, adjectives and noun stems according to their distribution with aspects.

Past tenses with the punctual aspect occasionally contain a particle *a* (thus *ge a*, *go a*) which has no obvious function, other than perhaps being more formal. This *a* is not to be confused with the stative aspect marker. Rather, it is a remnant of what is known as junctures in the Kalahari Khoe languages of Central Khoesan. This juncture *a* is also found in !Gora.

The tenses with *ga/ka* dubbed "potential" (POT) here (Hagman: "indefinite") cannot be treated as subjunctive (mood), as they do also occur in the indicative mood of main sentences (cf. IND *ge*) with optative import, e.g.

(235) *!Gû gu ge ga!*
go they IND POT
'If only they would go!'

The main import is to render (subordinate) conditional clauses (hence the allusion to the subjunctive). The present potential implies that occurrence of the event is still possible; the past potential and also the perfective aspect imply that it is no longer possible:

(236) a. *|Api i kao, o . . .*
rain it POT+if then
'Should it rain, then . . .'

b. *|Api i ka hâo, o . . .*
rain it POT PERF+if then
'Had it rained, then . . .'

Only two tenses occur with the potential: present and past (preterite); cf. Table 7.9. The future is expressed periphrastically with a nominalised clause in the future tense, with the present tense. Punctual and progressive aspect are not consistently distinguished.

TABLE 7.9 POTENTIAL TENSE–ASPECT SYSTEM: POSITIVE

TENSE / ASPECT		Past	Present	(Future)
Punctual	*Ø*		*ga*	*[. . . nî . . .]s ka*
Progressive	*ra*	*kara* Vb *i*	*kara* Vb	*[. . . nî . . .]s kara*
Perfective	*hâ*	*ga* Vb *hâ i*	*ga* Vb *hâ*	
Stative	*i/a*	*ga* Vb_{stat} *i*	*ga (a)* Vb_{stat}	

3.2.1.6 Negation

In the negative main paradigm the perfective and stative aspects merge into one, the "non-punctual" aspect (cf. Table 7.10).

TABLE 7.10 MAIN TENSE–ASPECT SYSTEM: NEGATIVE

ASPECT \ TENSE		Remote past *ge*	Recent past *go*	Present *Ø*	Future *nî*
Punctual	*Ø*	*ge tama i*	*go tama i*	*tama*	*tide*
Progressive	*r*V	*tama gere i*	*tama goro i*	*tama ra i*	*tama nî(ra) i*
Non-punctual	*hâ*	*tama ge hâ i*	*tama go hâ i*	*tama (hâ)*	*hâ tidetama nî hâ i*

Negative progressive present:

(237) *ǀÎ-b ge bol-sa !khō tama ra i.*
he IND ball+OBL catch NEG A A
'He never catches the ball.'

Negative punctual remote past:

(238) *Petru-b ge ǀnā mari-e ū tama ge i.*
Peter IND that money+OBL take NEG T A
'Peter did not take that money.'

Negative non-punctual recent past + positive punctual recent past:

(239) *ǂNû tama go hâ i axa-b ge go ǀnamahe.*
sit.down NEG T A A boy IND TA reprimand+PASS
'The boy who had not sat down (= was not sitting) was reprimanded.'

The potential particle has a high or low tone, depending on its position relative to the verb. Hence two spellings occur in the standardised orthography: *ka* for the high tone version, *ga* for the low tone one. See Table 7.11 for the negative of the potential tense–aspect system.

TABLE 7.11 POTENTIAL TENSE–ASPECT SYSTEM: NEGATIVE

ASPECT \ TENSE		Past tense	Present	(Future)
Punctual	*Ø*	*ga* Vb *tama i*		
Progressive	*ra*	*kara* Vb *tama i*		*[. . . tama . . . nî i]s kara* *[. . . tide . . .]s kara*
Perfective	*hâ*	*ga* Vb *tama hâ i*	*ga* Vb *tama hâ*	
Stative	*i/a*	*ga* Vb_{stat} *tama i*		

Negative perfective past:

(240) *ǀÎ-b ga hui te tama hâ io,*
he POT help me NEG A A+if

o ta ge nēsisa ǀnai ga ǀō hâ.
then I IND now already POT dead A
'If he had not helped me, I would already be dead now.'

Negative future:

(241) *[!Khī di tide]s karao, o . . .*
come they NEG.FUT TA+if then
'Should it be the case that they will not come', i.e.
'Should they not come, . . .'

3.2.1.7 NP structure, case

The minimal NP consists of a PGN marker, be it for the subject or the object (cf. section 3.2.1.4). These PGNS are the true pronouns of N.Kh. (see Chapter 6). The referent of this PGN can be more closely identified by means of a lexical specification, which can consist of a nominal head (stem) and/or qualifiers. (Adjectives, demonstratives, articles, numerals, possessives and relative clauses are subsumed here under the category qualifier, as they have the same syntactic behaviour.) The normal position of a qualifier, for the attributive function, is to the left of the head. As such it is governed by the PGN to the right of the entire lexical specification and no further inflection occurs. If a qualifier is added after the head, it functions as apposition and, therefore, needs a copy of the PGN that governs the head. An appositively used qualifier thus has the same structure as a pronominally used qualifier. Both NPS, that of the head (with further optional attributive qualifiers) and that of the apposition, are part of the matrix {NP}, i.e. the maximal projection, the function of which is marked by a case marker morpheme after the matrix NP, if it contains a lexical specification:

{NP}	*Ø*	nominative	for subject in initial slot of declarative sentences;
{NP}	*a*	oblique	for subjects of questions, deposed subjects, objects;
{NP}	*di*	possessive	as qualifier;
{NP}	*e*	vocative	in address;
{NP}	post-position		for adverbials.

The following structural patterns apply for all qualifiers, including relative clauses (but excluding the associative *â-*). The following words are used as representative examples: *nē* 'this', *kai* 'big', *goma-s* 'cow'. The lexically specified NPS are illustrated for the oblique with *-a*.

minimal NP:	{PGN} (for subject) {s} 'she'	{o^{m}} {si} 'her'	(for object)
stem alone:	{[stem]PGN} *{[goma]s}* 'cow'		case *a*
with attributive qualifier(s):	{[(qualifier) (qualifier) stem]PGN} *{[(nē) (kai) goma]s}* 'this big cow'		case *a*
with (attributive and) appositive qualifier(s):	{[(qualifier) stem]PGN$_1$ [(qualifier)]PGN$_1$} *{[(nē) goma]s [(kai)]s}* 'this big cow'/'this cow, the big one'		case *a*

It is evident from the appositive usage that the case marker is not suffixed to a word but rather appended to an entire syntactic constituent, viz. {NP}. The appositive usage can be employed for stylistic reasons (as an afterthought), or it can be obligatory to avoid the wrong reference of another qualifier. This would be required if a second qualifier contains a noun, as in possessives or relative clauses. As any qualifier refers to the first noun to its right (with regular tone rules), such a noun would have to be removed into an apposition to avoid wrong reference:

(242) *nē ǂgāri-ao-b di goma-sa* 'this farmer's cow' *not* *'this cow of the farmer'
{[(nē) goma]s [(ǂgāri-ao-b di)]s}a 'this cow of the farmer', or
{[(ǂgāri-ao-b di) goma]s [(nē)]s}a *ibid.*

3.2.2 !Gora

Wilfrid H.G. Haacke

3.2.2.1 Basic syntax: the underlying structure of nouns

!Gora syntactic structures are essentially the same as for Namibian Khoekhoe (N.Kh.). Hence this discussion of !Gora syntax should be read in conjunction with the discussion of N.Kh. As observed earlier, the apparently irregular use of grammatical formatives and especially the frequent omission of them in !Gora may be the most conspicuous difference between N.Kh. and !Gora grammar, and may have been symptoms of imminent language death.

Further corroboration that the surface noun is derived from an underlying minimal sentence is provided by !Gora through the fact that – contrary to N.Kh. – equi-deletion appears *not* to be applied to the PGN marker of the embedded sentence that provides the lexical specification of the subject. The original PGN markers of both the matrix and the underlying sentence are thus retained, according to Meinhof (1930: 51):

(243) *!Nai-**b*** ***bi*** *tje na hā-ku ǀxa ǁuru-e.*
giraffe PGN IND PRES.PROG horses with chase+PASS
'The giraffe is being chased with horses.'

The lexical specification of the subject NP (*!nai a b 'he/it is a giraffe') is embedded as an S in the subject NP of the matrix sentence, which otherwise consists of only a PGN marker *bi*:

(244) [S]***bi*** *tje na hā-ku ǀxa ǁuru-e*
*!nai-**b***

For bracketing conventions, see 3.2.1.1. The brackets will be introduced here into the examples quoted from various sources. Hyphens from the original quote may then be omitted, though.

In N.Kh. the PGN marker of the embedded lexical specification would be deleted by virtue of equi-NP deletion, in the equivalent sentence *!Nai**b** ge ra hāgu ǀkha !haehe*:

(245) [S]***b*** *ge ra hāgu ǀkha !haehe*
*!nai-(**b**)*

According to Meinhof's transcription the PGN is actually pronounced twice in !Gora, as he also explicitly confirms (1930: 37); cf. also . . . *ha-**b bi** ǀkx'ã-e hã* 'the horse (it) was stolen' (1930: 62), or *he hai-**b bi** na ham* 'this tree (it) smells'. An example of Maingard's (1962: 20) leaves no doubt about the iteration of the PGN: *kx'amma**p îp** kie kei hâ* 'truth is great'.

It is noteworthy that the syllabic PGN marker with the vowel *-i* is also manifested in the northern Damara dialects of N.Kh., e.g. in Sesfontein: *xoe**ni** ge ra ǀō* 'people die'. However, no iterative articulation of the plosive has been observed. In !Gora the PGN with *i* is found not only in the subject but also in the object, according to Maingard (1962: 14):

(246) *Ats !guixats ko !kam kwep-**bi**.* 'You, rascal, have killed a man.'

The total omission of the subject, even the PGN marker, appears to be more frequent in !Gora than in N.Kh. (This is another characteristic that !Gora has in common with the Sesfontein dialects of the Damara cluster; cf. Haacke 1986: 382.) While in N.Kh. it is only likely to occur as response in a dialogue, especially to a question, it seems to be less restricted in !Gora, e.g.

(247) *he_ tje kx'o-**b**-a* (Meinhof 1930: 50)

Note that the indicative marker *tje* here appears even without preceding PGN. But cf. the same sentence elsewhere by the same author (Meinhof 1930: 37):

(248) *He* ***b*** *tje kx'o-**b**-a.* Copulative
this PGN IND meat+OBL
'This is (the) meat.'

(249) *'Ā, !ũ _ tje na.*
yes go (PGN) IND PRES.PROG
'Yes, we are going.' (Meinhof 1930: 76)

While in N.Kh. objects and *deposed subjects* consistently occur in the oblique form (with *-a*), this case suffix is often though not predictably omitted in !Gora (here indicated as *Ø*).

(250) a. *{[ǁ**Na** **ǂxani]s}Ø** ma re.* topicalised object
that book give me/please(?)
'Please (?) give (me ?) that book.' (Meinhof 1930: 77)

b. *Mũ tama da hã* ***{[(gaida) 'ao]b-i}Ø**.* postposed object
see NEG we PERF old man
'We did not see the old man.' (Meinhof 1930: 75)

Likewise the oblique suffix may or may not be omitted in the deposed subject; with oblique:

(251) *Mû re __ ko-* $a_{(,)}$ ***{[(ǁ'aĩ-)] kṷ-} a**.*
see me (they) RECT.PAST+ JUNCT ART+ PGN+OBL
'They saw me.' (Meinhof 1930: 44)

without oblique:

(252) *i-* ***{b}*** *tje* ***{[ǀ'ami]b}Ø*** *mi*
and he REM.PAST(?) ostrich say
'and then he – the ostrich – said' (Meinhof 1930: 37)

Meinhof had correctly recognised that the deposed subject is a lexical specification in the form of an epenthetic *sentence*: "Dies 'Subjekt' ist eine Art Apposition oder *Zwischensatz* zu dem vorhergehenden Subjektspronomen" (This 'subject' is a kind of apposition or *intrasentential clause* to the preceding subject pronoun.) (1930: 38; emphasis added).

The oblique suffix *-a* (derived from the stative aspect marker; cf. N.Kh.) assimilates to *-e* if it follows on PGN markers with *-i*; e.g. Meinhof (1930: 61):

(253) *ǂ'ants* *hã* *{[khoe]* *b}ē* *{[ǁna* *ha* *-b* __
know.you PERF person +PGN-**i** that horse +PGN
+**OBL**

ko *ǀkx'ã* *hã]* *b}**a**?*
RECT.PAST steal PERF PGN+**OBL**
'Do you know the man that had stolen that horse?'

The above example illustrates that the use of the vowel *-i* is erratic with PGN markers. In N.Kh., furthermore, the oblique case marker *-a* will only follow on the very last PGN marker of the all-comprising NP; in this case only on the apposition, not on the preceding head. Cf. the equivalent sentence in N.Kh., where the head noun and the appositive relative clause are part of *one* {NP}:

(254) *ǂAnts a {[khoe]b [(ǁnā hā-b-a go ǀâa hâa)] b}**a**?*
'Do you know the man that had stolen that horse?'

Despite the frequent neglect of the oblique suffix in the "predicative" strategy of a noun, nouns in isolation are frequently cited in the oblique when elicited as answer to the question for a term; e.g.

(255) *Xam+m**a**.* 'It is a lion.' instead of: *Xam+m**i**.*

The habit of using the oblique for citation forms explains the origin of Europeanised ethnonyms like "Koran**a**" < *!Gora+n+**a*** < *n a !Ora or "Namakw**a**" < *Nama+gu+**a***. While in the Nama dialects nouns (today) are never cited in the oblique, the oblique is occasionally used in the relic area on the northern Damara periphery, and in Naro.

3.2.2.2 Constituent order

!Gora, like N.Kh., uses fronting and inversion as focusing strategies. The initial slot in the sentence (i.e. before the subject PGN) is the focus position. A few examples should suffice here:

(256) a. ***!Xo-b-i*** *r* *na* *ǂae.* 'I am smoking a *pipe*.'
pipe+NOM I PRES.PROG smoke (Meinhof 1930: 60)

but

b. ***ǂae*** *r* *na* *!xo-b-i.* 'I *am smoking* a pipe.'
smoke I PRES.PROG pipe+NOM

Copulative constructions are of the same kind as in N.Kh., with apparently one exception. Minimal copulative sentences consist of one NP, which may be extended with attributive qualifiers:

(257) {[*!Guixa* *hâ* *ǀhû]b}* *pi* *kie.*
roguish PERF White+PGN IND (Maingard 1962: 26)

Maingard translates the sentence as: 'The master was or has been a rogue.' In N.Kh., at least, this sentence would have two readings, depending on its internal structure:

Predicative, with subject-predicate inversion (as Maingard): 'The white man has become roguish.'
Copulative (as the above bracketing reflects): 'He is a white man who has become roguish.'

Maingard's spelling reflects a double PGN marker: *p+bi*. This would imply a non-occurrence of equi-deletion, as argued earlier. However, in the present construction the noun stem *ǀhû* is the verbal (i.e. predicate head) of the matrix sentence; hence there can be no question of embedding. Regrettably it can no longer be verified whether the transcription reflects the true syntactic situation.

Maingard's predicative translation

(258) *{[(Tswi ǀkoap* *ko* *mâ* *tsi)* *ga]s}* *kie.*
God RECT.PAST give you cleverness IND (Maingard 1962: 27)

as 'God has given you cleverness' appears to be misguided. The equivalent in N.Kh. would be read as a minimal copulative sentence extended with a relative clause: 'It is cleverness that God has given you'; i.e. 'It is God-given cleverness.'

So-called "Coreferential copulative sentences", i.e. sentences purportedly consisting of two (surface) NPS of the structure {NP}***Ø*** *kie* {NP}***a*** also are on record:

(259) *{[(ǁNa)]ku}****Ø*** ___ *{[ǁxama]ku̱}****a****.* 'Those are hartebeest.'
that+PGN (IND) hartebeest+PGN+OBL (Meinhof 1930: 37)

A more apt reading is one of subject deposition caused by fronting of the predicate head *ǁna*:

(260) **{[*ǁXama*]* ku*}* $\mathbf{Ø}_{\text{Subject}}$ kie a ǁ**na**. >
ǁ**Na**~ {ku} $\mathbf{Ø}_{\text{Subj.PGN}}$ (kie) - {[ǁxama] ku} $\mathbf{a}_{\text{Dep.Subj.}}$
'They – the hartebeest – are *those*.'

The following kind of sentence listed by Meinhof (1930: 38), with the oblique NP occurring *before* the NP in the nominative, does not occur in N.Kh.:

(261) *{[(!Nani)* *tse]ku}****a*** *{[vēkhe]b}****Ø****.*
six day+PGN+OBL week+PGN+NOM
'Eine Woche sind sechs Tage.' = 'A week consists of six days.'

Whether this was a frequent and accepted syntactic construction, or whether it was deviant usage suggestive of language death, can no longer be established. It is conspicuous that in !Gora copulative sentences the indicative marker *kie* is omitted in most instances.

3.2.2.3 Complex sentences

3.2.2.3.1 SUBORDINATION BY CONJUNCTION

As in N.Kh., the principle applies that co-ordinating conjunctions precede the second constituent, while subordinating conjunctions follow on the subordinated constituent.

(262) *Toa ku ta 'o, 'i na ǀ'anu khoede xu-****tsĩ****.* (Meinhof 1930: 63)
'And when they (will) finish, they will return home, leaving the women.'

In order to demonstrate the derivation, the above !Gora sentence is explained by way of its N.Kh. equivalent:

(263) *Toa gu rao, o gu ge ra ǀaru, khoede xū tsî.*
finish they PRES.PERF ~when then they IND PRES.PERF return women leave and

The underlined embedded clause in the above sentence is derived from the following two input sentences:

(264) *O gu ge khoede ~~ra~~ xū tsî ~~gu~~ ~~ge~~ ra ǀaru.*
then they IND women PRES.PERF leave and they IND PRES.PERF return

⇒ *O gu ge khoede xū tsî ra ǀaru.*
then they IND women leave and PRES.PERF return

(derivation via equi-deletion of subject PGN, IND and PRES.PERF)

⇒ *O gu ge ra ǀaru khoede xū tsî.*
then they IND PRES.PERF return women leave and

(derivation by postposing the VP with trailing conjunction)

Tsî in its subordinating function was, in earlier publications, wrongly treated as a suffix both in N.Kh. and !Gora (for a discussion, see Haacke 1992b, esp. p. 191). This explains Meinhof's hyphen before *tsî*.

Compound NPS are constructed in the same way as in N.Kh. (Maingard 1962: 51):

(265) *ǀNâ [ǂxi ra]**p** tsî [ǂnu]**p** tsî~**ka** xa hampa sa diba?*
that shine PRES.PERF +PGN and black+PGN and-PGN from which you POSS+PGN +OBL
'Which one of those two – he being a shining one, he being a black one – is yours?'

3.2.2.3.2 SUBORDINATION BY ADVERBIALISING SUFFIXES

Adverbial clauses can, as in N.Kh., be embedded by means of adverbialising suffixes, e.g. the locative *-pa*:

(266) *ǀXao-da-'i mâ **ba**.* = *ǀXaoda-'i mâ**pa**.* (Meinhof 1930: 62)
lamb+DIM+PGN stand ~ ADV.SUFF '(there) where the little lamb stood'

3.2.2.3.3 SUBORDINATION AS RELATIVE CLAUSES

Relative clauses appear in the typical three functions of qualifiers (in parentheses): attributively (to the left of the head, without PGN marker), appositively (to the right of the head, with identical PGN marker), or pronominally (with PGN marker).

Attributive (Meinhof 1930: 62):

(267) *{[(ǀKx'atse 'ir ko ǀ'ama hã) ha]b} bi ǀkx'ã-e hã.*
yesterday I RECT.PAST buy PERF horse PGN steal+PASS PERF
'The horse that I bought yesterday has been stolen.'

Appositive (Meinhof 1930: 62):

(268) *ǂNou tje ta {[khoe]**b-i** [(ha-b_ ko ǀkx'ã hã)]**b**}**Ø**.*
beat we FUT man horse REC.PAST steal PERF+PGN+NOM
'We will beat the man who stole the horse.'

Note that the above NP should have taken the oblique case suffix *-a* instead of *Ø* after the maximal projection of the {NP}, it being the object of the sentence.

Meinhof (1930: 61) quotes a rare instance (according to N.Kh.) where the oblique case marker also occurs after the internal NP containing the head. This construction should, however, be interpreted as iterative NPS:

(269) *ǂ'ants hã {[khoe]b}**e**(,) {[(ǀna ha-b ko ǀkx'ã hã)]b}**a**?*
know~you PERF man+**OBL** that horse RECT.PAST steal PERF+PGN+**OBL**
'Do you know the man who has stolen the horse?'

Pronominal (Maingard 1962: 36):

(270) *ǁNa re {[(taip kam ta di)]b}**Ø**.*
tell me what we.two FUT do+PGN 'Tell me what we two shall do.'

The above example is actually an instance of a pronominal use with omission of the complementiser noun *!kxeip*. True relative clauses would have a similar surface structure in pronominal usage.

3.2.2.3.4 SUBORDINATION WITH THE COMPLEMENTISER *!KXEIP/S*

Complement sentences, amounting to "*that*-sentences" in English, are formed as in N.Kh.:

Maingard (1962: 36):

(271) *Its kana mubasin {[(!kamme kam na) !xei]**p**}Ø.*
you POT.PROG see+APPL+REFL kill+PASS we-two PRES.PROG matter
'Then you may see for yourself *that we (two) are killed*'

Again, the oblique case marker *-a* is not used to mark the objectival position of the complement sentence. The N.Kh. equivalent of the above sentence would be:

(272) *Ots kara mûbasen {[(!gamhe khom ra) !khai]**s**}**a**.*

3.2.2.4 Mood, tense and aspect

The same moods seem to appear as in N.Kh.

Indicative *tje* (Maingard *kie*):

(273) *i- da* ***tje*** *ǀ'uri-kṷ-a u-hã tama* 'and we have no iron bars'
and we IND iron.bars+OBL take+PERF NEG (Meinhof 1930: 37)

The indicative marker *tje* appears to be omitted more readily in !Gora than *ge* is in N.Kh. (cf. Maingard 1962: 24). (In the N.Kh. equivalent *ge* the palatalisation is no longer reflected in the standardised orthography, as it is predictable before front vowels. The obsolete spelling was *gye*.) On the other hand, *tje* may appear in !Gora even while the PGN marker of the subject is omitted – something not found in N.Kh.:

(274) *{[(He)_]}* ***tje*** *{[kx'o]b}a.* 'This is the meat.'
this+ IND meat+PGN+OBL (Maingard 1962: 24)

Assertive *kum . . . o*:

(275) *its* ***kum*** *ǂkaus ǂũ bi* ***o***
and~you ASST bowl eat it ASST
'and you indeed eat (out of the bowl)' (Maingard 1962: 33)

The example above is fragmentary in that it has no tense–aspect marker and no (oblique) case marker or postposition with *ǂkaus*.

Interrogative *ka*:

(276) *Ham- tsē its* ***ka*** *ta ǀũa-xa?*
which day you Q PRES.PROG come down
'When then will you come down?'

Hortative *a/ha*:

(277) *A- re kx'a.*
HORT I drink
'Let me drink!' (Maingard 1962: 30)

The *tense–aspect system* of !Gora is essentially the same as that for N.Kh. The difference seems to be more of a morphological or phonological nature. The N.Kh. (present) progressive aspect marker *ra*/(*ta*) is !Gora *nã*, with an occasional variant *ra*.

!Gora *ta* (*ra* after vowels) amounts to N.Kh. *nî* for the future tense, according to Meinhof (1930: 52), while !Gora uses *nĩ* to indicate obligation, i.e. 'must'. In N.Kh. *nî* indicates both future *tense* and obligation 'must'. Maingard (1962: 25) has, however, correctly recognised that *nâ* is an *aspect* formative "for the incomplete action", rather than a present *tense* marker, as Meinhof (1930: 51) seems to take it.

It is remarkable that !Gora, like the older Damara dialects, makes use of a juncture *a*, a "juncture" as first described by Köhler for Central Khoesan languages of Botswana. This means that junctures are not as symptomatic for the Kalahari Khoe languages of the family as was hitherto maintained. Rather, it appears to be symptomatic for specifically the Nama dialects of N.Kh. not to use any juncture.

(278) *Mũ-r* ***ko̭-a*** *xam-mi.* 'I have seen the/a lion.'
see I RECT.PAST+JUNCT lion (Meinhof 1930: 52)

Meinhof (1930: 52) reports the doubling of the past tense markers. Regrettably the significance of it is not clear. In one example *ko-ko* appears with the perfect aspect marker *hã*, in the other example with the zero morpheme for the punctual aspect:

(279) a. *Hama- ts* ***ko-ko*** *ǂ'ũ-b hō hã?*
where you RECT.PAST+RECT.PAST food find PERF
'Where did you find the food?'

b. *Xo̭asao-b tsĩ ǀxao-'i tsĩkhara ir* ***ko-ko*** *!am.*
leopard and lamb and~them I RECT.PAST+RECT.PAST kill
'I have killed a leopard and a lamb.'

It is not clear whether Meinhof's example (1930: 4) for the remote past is an instance of duplication or an instance of the indicative marker followed by the (single) remote past tense marker:

(280) *He-he !'a-s kx'ai i-r* ***tje*** ***tje*** *!nae- hã i-r*
this+this place on I **?** REM.PAST be born PERF and~I

tje ***tje*** *he-ba ǀxa-ǀxa-sen hã ǂani-s koba-b.*
? REM.PAST here learn PERF book language
'At this place was I born and have learnt the language of the book.'

Instances of the progressive aspect with the two past tenses and the future (*gere*, *goro* and *nîra* in N.Kh.) do not seem to be on record. A combination with the subjunctive *ka* is on record (Meinhof 1930: 53):

(281) *!Hami !ũ* *kao* ***ka na?*** 'Would you go hunting?'
hunt+go you (M.PL) SUBJ+PROG

Too little information on *negation* is available to allow the establishment of a systematic paradigm. The indicative is said to be negated with *tama* as in N.Kh. (Meinhof 1930: 54). Commands use a positive predication as in N.Kh., which is then negated with the negative temporal adverb *ta* ('never'):

(282) *ǁNa* *dao-b* *kx'ai* *i* ***ta!*** 'Never go on that path!'
that path on go never

In conclusion it may be observed that deviations between !Gora and N.Kh. are mainly of a phonological and morphological (including lexical) nature, while syntactic structures widely concur. Differences that occur in syntax are not systematic but largely amount to irregularities and omissions in !Gora. These irregularities in !Gora seem to be symptoms of imminent language death less than two generations after Meinhof conducted his research. Granting this, it can be claimed that !Gora and N.Kh. share the syntax of a common language, Khoekhoegowab, which is subdivided into dialects – albeit fairly diverging – by virtue mainly of the differences in phonology and morphology.

3.2.3 Haiǁom

Thomas Widlok

The late Terttu Heikkinen has provided an extensive classification of ǂAkhoe sentence types which is summarized here. Since her sample data are almost exclusively derived from narratives, especially from folktales, I have complemented her analysis with conversational data from my own data wherever it seemed useful. More examples for the sentence types described here and more details on the analysis of ǂAkhoe narratives are contained in Heikkinen's unpublished work (Heikkinen, n.d.).

3.2.3.1 Word order

ǂAkhoe word order is flexible to the same degree as word order in Nama (see Moritz 1963: 93–97; Haacke, this volume), which is nevertheless sometimes classified as an SOV language (see Rust 1965: 100).

3.2.3.2 Major sentence types: basic sentences

3.2.3.2.1 POSITIVE DECLARATIVE SENTENCES

According to Heikkinen (n.d.: 40) topic is marked throughout ǂAkhoe discourse with the topic marker *ge*, the "declarative particle" (Hagman 1977: 54), which follows either the subject itself or the PGN marker that refers to it. In narrative speech declarative sentences normally start with the initial conjunctions *o* or *ao* and end with the verb-final particle *e*. In everyday speech ǂAkhoe declarative sentences characteristically end on *i ge* which, as pointed out by Heikkinen (n.d.: 41), "is the result of nominalising the sentence proper with the collective [neuter] class suffix *-i* and topicalizing the sentence as a whole so that it becomes a non-verbal stative sentence".

(283) *Ao da ge ǀêi-i ǀkha kere oa e.*
CONJ 1PL.C DEC it with PAST return PART
'And we returned with it.'

(284) *ǀNati ge ûi ge hâ i ge.*
this 1PL.M live PAST PAST AUX PART
'This is how we lived.'

(285) *ǀÊi ǃasa ge ǂhâba hâ i ge.*
this place DEC need PAST AUX PART
'This place we need.'

3.2.3.2.2 EVENT SENTENCES

The event sentence consists of the following sequence (optional elements are placed in parentheses, constituting parts are placed in square brackets):

> (Pre-Sentence) [Subject (consisting of qualifier and noun)] [Predicate (consisting of adverb, object, verb)] [(Post-Sentence)]

(286) *[O gu ge gôasagua] [hogu ge hâ e] [gôasade i-e].*
CONJ 3PL.M sons marry PAST.PERF daughters too
'His sons were married, and so were his daughters.'

Pre- and post-sentences are optional. A pre-sentence contains a PGN suffix attached to a conjunction, an adverbial or an object. If there is a pre-sentence including the PGN suffix, another subject reference is not required. A post-sentence may contain qualifiers to nouns or modifications to verbs.

3.2.3.2.3 STATIVE SENTENCES

Stative sentences are of two types, either with a copula, *a* 'to be' or *i* 'to become', or without. Stative sentences with a copula may have a pre-sentence to complement the following basic sequence:

> [(Subject)] [Predicate (consisting of (a copula and) a complement)]

(287) [*Khaira-i ge*] [*a ǂui*].
food PART be much
'There is plenty of food.'

Stative sentences without a copula which are non-verbal and consist of the declarative particles *ge* or *go* following the complement may also have an optional subject. The complement may also be an embedded nominalized sentence (see 289 below).

> [Predicate (consisting of a complement)] [Subject]

(288) [*Damagu*] [*di gomadi ge*].
Ndonga-men POSS cows DEC
'They are the Ndonga men's cows.'

(289) [*Arogôa tsu*] [*ta ge i i ge*]?
boy only 1SG PAST be PART
'I was just a boy.'

3.2.3.2.4 MODIFICATIONS OF EVENT AND STATIVE SENTENCES

The simple sentence types described so far may be modified into what Heikkinen (n.d.: 46) called "focus sentences" and "expressive sentences". Focus sentences may be either event sentences or stative sentences which are modified in that a focused element precedes the predicate (see 290). Expressive sentences (291) form a subtype of stative non-verbal sentences and they consist of a complement plus the emphatic declarative *ko mo* (see also Hagman 1977: 54). This is their basic structure:

[(Pre-Sentence)] [Focus] [(Subject)] [Predicate] [(Post-Sentence)]

(290) [*O khe* *aisa*] [*arokhoegu* *tsugua*] [*ra* *ǂna* *si* *e*].
CONJ giraffe-dance men only PRES dance PART
'The giraffe [dance] is danced by the men only.'

(291) [*Nîge di daoba*] [*sa*] [*ǂâ i ko mo*].
we POSS path you go in DEC
'You just pick up our trail.'

3.2.3.2.5 IMPERATIVE SENTENCES

The derivation of imperative sentences from positive declarative sentences entails a number of modifications to the form of the sentence.

The imperative particle *re* is added unless the imperative sentence is already preceded by an imperative sentence. In that case the connective *an(i)* is used instead of *re*.

Particles that mark topic, tense and aspect are dropped, and so is the sentence-final particle *e*.

The PGN marker is dropped in the second person singular (in all other persons it follows the verbal). The subject is only explicitly included for extra emphasis.

(292) *Ha* *re!*
come IMP
'Come!'

(293) *ǁGam-e* *ma* *te* *re* *an* *ta* *a.*
water give me IMP so that I drink
'Give me water so that I can drink.'

There are instances of what Heikkinen calls "imperative equivalents". These are imperative sentences in effect (and intention) but they lack some of the formal features outlined above. In imperative equivalents the imperative particle is dispensable when the sequential connective *an(i)* is in place:

(294) *Ani* *tsi* *tareǀgôate* *tsi* *ôahâ* *xuia* *ǀguisa* *kaoba* *te.*
SEQ 2SG.M daughters 2SG.M have if one give.to.marry me
'If you have daughters, give one to me for marrying [her].'

The imperative particle is also dispensable when the emphatic *ko* and the PGN marker (also in the second person singular) are in place.

(295) *Ma* *te* *tsi* *ko!*
give me you EMPH
'Do give it to me [now]!'

Furthermore, language pragmatics provides ways of expressing imperatives without using the form of a direct demand. Questions that are created with the interrogative particle *o* are often oblique imperatives, 'Is there no water? [... Then get me some!].' Similarly, declarative sentences using the evidential particle *goma* often work in an imperative way, 'I'd like to smoke. [... Do give me some of your tobacco!].' See Widlok (1997) for this and other aspects of the relationship between pragmatics and syntax in ǂAkhoe.

3.2.3.3 Interrogative sentences

ǂAkhoe interrogative sentences may be divided into verbal and non-verbal sentences. Both types of interrogative sentences may be further divided into information questions and polar questions.

3.2.3.3.1 INTERROGATIVE VERBAL SENTENCES

There are two ways of deriving interrogative verbal sentences from positive declarative sentences. Introducing an interrogative pronoun or adverb and dropping the topic marker (declarative particle) *ge* creates an information question. Using the intonation contour of a question (where the pitch does not descend at the end of the sentence) and dropping the topic marker *ge* creates a polar question. Most polar questions of the verbal type end on *-e* with a response usually ending in *i ge* (see above).

(296) *Taib boro om omde ndete?*
who PAST build houses these
'Who has built these houses?'

(297) *Sa gaikhoede hâ tsu di a e !gâise?*
your women be only 3PL.F AUX PART well
'Are your wives well?'

3.2.3.3.2 INTERROGATIVE NON-VERBAL SENTENCES

Interrogative non-verbal sentences are derived from declarative non-verbal sentences by changing the intonation from final into non-final (see above) and by dropping the topic marker (declarative particle) *ge*. Information questions are created by introducing the interrogative particle *o*, 'what about?', at the end of the sentence. Polar questions do not require an interrogative particle but use the oblique form (final case) of the subject or the complement.

(298) *ǀGam-e o?*
water Q
'What about the water? [Is there none?]'

(299) *ǂNanirotsa?*
Kwanyama+diminutive+PGN
'Are you a Kwanyama child?'

3.2.3.4 Negation

The negative particle *ta* appears at the beginning of the verb.

(300) *Tita ge ta ra mû.*
I DEC NEG PART see
'I don't see.'

This also applies in negative imperative constructions.

(301) *Ta du !ao re.*
NEG 2PL.C fear IMP
'Don't be afraid.'

The negative particle *tama* follows the verb and frequently combines with the perfective aspect.

(302) *. . . mû bi taman hâ i.*
see PAST NEG+3PL.C PAST PART
'. . . while they were not looking.'

The negative particles *ti-* and *te-* are used in nominalized sentences. They follow the verb, and tense and aspect markers.

(303) *O khe |gôa-i ia ra ohe tisa.*
CONJ PART children POSTP TAM eat+PASS NEG+3SG.F
'It is not eaten by the children.'

3.2.3.5 Complex sentences

3.2.3.5.1 COORDINATING NOMINAL COMPOUND STRUCTURE

The coordinating nominal compound structure is constructed with the help of the connective *i* which follows each constituent, including the last one. All nouns that are linked in this way appear in the oblique form (the final case, see Chapter 6). The structure is completed at the end with the connective *i* plus a PGN marker.

(304) *!Naukhoroba i Ai‖gûba i tita i ge.*
!Naukhorob and Ai‖gûb and myself and DEC
'It is !Naukhoroba, Ai‖gûba and myself.'

(305) *!Gaiaogu ge |gamgua i-e !nonagua i-e.*
healers DEC two PART-PART three PART-PART
'There are two or three healers.'

Note that in (305) the constituents are listed as alternatives. Instead of *i*, constituents may also be linked with the connective *a* but in this case the connective is only between constituents and not added in a summarizing fashion at the end of the structure. The connective *tsî* 'and' also occurs in the way it is being described for Nama (see Haacke, this volume).

3.2.3.5.2 SUBORDINATING NOMINAL COMPOUND STRUCTURES

Two types of subordinating nominal compound structures may be distinguished, one in which a qualifier may precede a noun and the other in which it may follow a noun. Except for nominal qualifiers, all other qualifiers that precede the noun remain uninflected. Qualifiers that follow the noun are inflected in concord with the noun. Adjectival qualifiers that precede the noun remain uninflected:

(306) *!nu !huba*
far country
'a far-away country'

Adjectival qualifiers that follow the noun are inflected in concord with the noun that is also inflected:

(307) *mari-i hoa-e*
money all
'all the money'

The possessive pronouns remain uninflected when preceding the noun:

(308) *di omsa*
my house
'my house'

There are possessive constructions with *a* in which the qualifier follows the noun and is inflected:

(309) *ǂkhanisi asa*
book her
'her book'

Embedded sentences (relative clauses) may also occur as qualifiers preceding the noun and they, too, remain uninflected:

(310) *Gomade ra kure ǂAkhoerob be.*
cows PRES herd ǂAkhoe.boy DEC
'He is a ǂAkhoe boy who herds cows.'

When the embedded sentence follows the noun as a qualifier, it is also inflected:

(311) *Gaikhoeb be hâ i ke, ǁgâusa ǂnûi hâba.*
man DEC PAST PART PAST house put be.there.3SG.M
'There was a man who had put up a house.'

Preceding nominal qualifiers appear in the non-final case (see Chapter 6):

(312) *ǀîbi gomade*
his cows

Nominal qualifiers following the noun receive the inflection of the noun:

(313) *!ore tisa* (cf. *ti !oresa*) 'my dish'
dish my

Whenever there are two qualifiers, one precedes the noun and the other follows it:

(314) *sa mari-i hoa-e* 'all your money'
your money all

3.2.3.5.3 VERBAL COMPOUND STRUCTURES

All verbal compound structures described here are coordinating. ǂAkhoe and Haiǁom have a considerable number of double verbs which are, however, considered to be one verb. They are clearly distinguishable from coordinate verbs because the elements of the compound verbs are separated from one another by one or more of the following elements:

Aspect or tense marker:

(315) *Aob be ǁgama ra ha e.*
CONJ+3SG.M PAST draw.water TAM come PART
'He drew water and came.'

Object, adverbial or another element of the predicate:

(316)	*Ao*	*ta*	*ge*	*si*	*tarekhoesa*	*ra*	*!gamme*	*e.*
	CONJ	1SG.M	PAST	go.to	woman	TAM	marry	PART
	'I went to marry a woman.'							

Minimal subject (a PGN marker) or minimal object (a pronoun):

(317)	*Ao*	*di*	*ge*	*ǀaegua*	*khau*	*gua*	*gere*	*sâi*	*si*	*e.*
	CONJ	3PL.F	DEC	fires	kindle	them	TAM	cook	her	PART
	'They kindled fires and cooked her.'									

The connective affix *-a* may also be used but it is optional:

(318)	*ǀGunude*	*gu*	*!gaesun-a*	*ra*	*ǂna*	*si*	*i*	*ge.*
	rattles	3PL.M	tie+REFL+CON	TAM	stamp	OBJ	PART	PART
	'They tie rattles (around their ankles) and stamp with their feet (when they perform the dance).'							

The connective *-a* and the aspect marker *ra* may also separate auxiliaries from other elements of a compound verbal structure:

(319)	*Nakalebi*	*gomade*	*ta*	*ge*	*hâna*	*ra*	*kure*	*e.*
	Nakale's	cows	1SG	PAST	AUX	TAM	herd	PART
	'I used to herd Nakale's cows.'							

3.2.3.5.4 ADVERBIAL COMPOUND STRUCTURES

In these subordinate compound structures embedded sentences occur as adverbials. There are two ways of marking the relation between the elements of this compound structure, through introductory connectives or through suffixes that are attached to the embedded sentence (or through both).

Common introductory connectives are *an(i)* (indicating purpose) and *ise-* (indicating manner). Common suffixes are *-ka* (indicating purpose) and *-se* (indicating manner):

(320)	*Aob*	*be*	*ǀgôagua*	*ra*	*ǂkhaiǂkhai*	*e,*	*ani*	*gu*	*ǂûka.*
	CONJ.3SG.M	PAST	sons	TAM	wake.up	PART	so.that	OBJ	eat+SUFF
	'He woke up the sons so that they might eat.'								

(321)	*!Nani*	*tsede*	*tsum*	*gere*	*!gû*	*i*	*ge,*	*!âsa*	*tsuma*	*ǀose.*
	six	days	1DU.M	tam	walk	PART	PART	hunger	PGN	die+SUFF
	'We walked for six days, dying of hunger.'									

After an imperative construction, connectives and suffixes may be dropped:

(322)	*Ha*	*re*	*tsum*	*!gû.*
	come	IMP	1DU.M	go
	'Come so that we may go.'			

3.2.3.6 Clause structure

Apart from the main clause and embedded clauses (see above) ǂAkhoe sentences may have two other clauses which Heikkinen has labelled pre-sentence and post-sentence. The pre-sentences mostly contain an introductory conjunction (or an interjection) and a PGN marker to which a tense and a topic marker may be added. They may also contain an object or adverbial or a vocative (especially in imperative and interrogative sentences).

(323) *Ao bi haiaib âi ra !gû e.*
CONJ 3SG.M bush/forest to PRES go PART
'He goes into the bush/forest.'

The post-sentence, too, may contain a vocative, an adverbial, and appositions or qualifiers that refer to the nominal constituents of the sentence.

(324) *!Gû sa i ke sasa.*
go 2SG.F PART DEC 2SG.F
'You go.'

3.2.3.6.1 NP STRUCTURE

3.2.3.6.1.1 SUBJECT NOUN PHRASE

The subject noun phrase is a simple or a compound nominal structure with or without qualifiers. It is minimally represented by a PGN marker only but it may also contain a topic marker. The noun has two potential forms identified by Heikkinen (n.d.) as "final" and "non-final" and by Haacke (this volume) as "subject paradigm" and "oblique" (see Chapter 6). Heikkinen (n.d.: 71) provides the following summary of the occurrence of these two forms:

The non-final case occurs with most postpositions, in possessive and associative constructions (with or without *di*) and when *ge ka* or *ko* follow.

The final case occurs with some postpositions (e.g. *xu* and *!o*) and as object or indirect object unless *ge ko* or *ka* follow, when anticipated or re-stated in the form of a PGN marker and in interrogative constructions.

(325) *|Gui gaikhoeb be hâ i ge.*
one man (*non-final case*) PAST PAST PART DEC
'There was a man.'

(326) *Aob be gaikhoeb bere hî khomâi ra hî e.*
CONJ 3SG.M man PAST PAST do.as TAM do PART
'He did as the man had done.'

3.2.3.6.1.2 OBJECT NOUN PHRASE

Like the subject noun phrase the object noun phrase consists of a nominal with optional qualifiers that precede or follow it. Also, like the subject noun phrase, the object may be referred to with a minimal pronoun. For a table of ǂAkhoe minimal object pronouns, see Chapter 6.

(327) *Tita hamati du ni hî te?*
1SG what you FUT do OBJ
'What will you do to me?'

(328) *Aob be ta ǁkhaba ra mû si e.*
CONJ 3SG.M PAST NEG see again OBJ PART
'He did not see her again.'

3.2.3.7 VP structure

The predicate of a ǂAkhoe sentence may consist of the following elements: verb, object, adverbial, copula and complement (or non-verbal complement without a copula). Affixed to the verb stem are optional markers for aspect, tense, voice, mood, a minimal object, and the final *-e*. Since the latter two elements have already been discussed above, it should suffice to add some details on aspect, tense, voice and mood.

3.2.3.7.1 ASPECT

Aspect is not obligatory. The completive *a* and the incompletive *ra* are complementary to one another, they cannot occur together. Both are optional and both may be combined with other aspect markers. The habitual *hâna* often co-occurs with the incompletive and the perfective *hâ* with the completive. As the Heikkinen collection of ǂAkhoe folktales shows, the incompletive *ra* is dominant. However, the vowel of *ra* is assimilated to the vowel of the preceding PGN marker as shown in Chapter 6.

3.2.3.7.2 TENSE

The inflection of verbs according to tense has been described above (see Chapter 6). The present tense is unmarked and consists of a verb stem plus a PGN marker and an aspect marker. The immediate past tense with *go* and the distant past tense with *ge* frequently combine with the incompletive *ra* and in a number of cases fuse with the preceding PGN marker (see Tables 6.10 and 6.11). Besides the future tense with *ni* or *ka hî* there are "future equivalents" (Heikkinen, n.d.: 64) created with *si* 'come, arrive' in combination with *ra* or *ni*.

3.2.3.7.3 VOICE

The passive formative *-he* is always suffixed to the verb stem:

(329) *Eliab ge ge ǂnau-he.*
Eliab DEC PAST beat-PASS
'Eliab got beaten up.'

3.2.3.7.4 MOOD

The mood of necessity is expressed with the future particle *ni*:

(330) *Tita ge hî ni tita.*
1SG DEC DO FUT NEG
'I won't do it.'

The conditional mood is expressed with the particle *ka*, which combines often with *ra* but also with *ni*.

(331) *ǁIti kara io, . . .*
this PART.PRES if
'If this is so, . . .'

The imperative mood is expressed with *re* or in expressive imperative sentences with *ko* (see above).

3.2.3.8 Agreement

According to Heikkinen (n.d.: 72), the concord relations in ǂAkhoe may be summarized as follows:

> A subject or object concords with its anticipator, with its qualifiers that follow it, and with nominals that re-state or paraphrase it (usually a PGN marker). Subjects may also concord with the verb which is, however, not always inflected. A complement concords with the subject except when the complement follows the copular 'a' (then it remains uninflected).

3.2.4 Kxoe subgroup: Khwe

Christa Kilian-Hatz

3.2.4.1 Introduction

Crucial for the understanding of Khwe syntax is the fact that Khwe is a discourse oriented language. It appears that there is always at least one constituent emphasized: either a noun phrase or a verb phrase. For that purpose, Khwe uses different syntactic strategies that will be described in the following subsections. Focus is understood here as a syntactic strategy of foregrounding. In Khwe it serves two purposes: to emphasize a certain referent or action in contrast to another possible candidate ("contrasting" or "identificational focus"), or to introduce new information ("informational" or "presentational focus"). In this respect, the main aim of this section is to answer two implicitly interrelated questions. Both have been discussed in the existing literature on Khwe, albeit in different contexts:

(a) Which constituent order types exist in Khwe and what are the conditions for their use?
(b) What is the syntactical function of the marker *a*?

We will begin with a discussion of the different constituent order types. The conditions under which these different types are used will be examined in section 3.2.4.2. Section 3.2.4.3 explains the multiple functions of the marker *à*. In section 3.2.4.4 the formation of predicate focus will be briefly presented. Finally, section 3.2.4.5 sums up the results of the analysis.

3.2.4.2 Constituent order

3.2.4.2.1 BASIC ORDER WITH CORE PARTICIPANTS

Generally, speakers accept three word order types with transitive verbs, namely OSV, SVO, and SOV. In the literature several other word orders are mentioned. Köhler (1973: 85) distinguishes four basic word order types (SVO, OSV, OVS, and SOV); he adds that the SOV order is frequently used and is, therefore, the "standard pattern". Quite a different distribution is given in Köhler (1981: 539), where five basic word orders (OSV, SOV, SVO, OVS, and VSO) are listed. Köhler assumes that the use of a certain word order depends on the kind of morphological markedness of the referents. In his analysis all five word order types may occur with PGN marked nouns but only two types (SOV and SVO) are possible when the nouns are marked with the so-called neuter singular PGN *a*. All five constructions are said to be possible as long as the object is marked with *a*, whereas only SOV and SVO are possible when both subject and object are marked with *a*.

In order to confirm Köhler's assumption that there is an interdependency between word order type and the kind of morphological markedness that nouns bear, a statistical survey was undertaken. The results are summarized in Table 7.12. From a sample of 30 texts collected by Heine (1997) and Kilian-Hatz and Naude (1999) roughly 1,500 sentences have been examined. Despite the fact that only 37 cases showing a strictly basic word order (i.e. declarative sentences with nominal referents) were found, the following distribution was observed and considered as representative.

Although the number of examples in Table 7.12 is low, the following preliminary conclusions can be drawn:

TABLE 7.12 DISTRIBUTION OF BASIC WORD ORDER TYPES IN KHWE COMPARED TO THE MORPHOLOGICAL MARKEDNESS OF THE REFERENTS

	Unmarked subject	Subject + PGN	Subject + PGN + *a*	Subject + *a*
Unmarked object	SOV: 1 SVO: 1		none	none
Object + PGN	SOV: 1	SOV: 2 SVO: 3	none	none
Object + PGN + *a*	SOV: 5 SVO: 1 OSV: 3	SOV: 4 SVO: 5 OSV: 3	none	none
Object + *a*	SOV: 2 SVO: 1 OSV: 1	SOV: 1 SVO: 2 OSV: 1	none	none

(a) Khwe has only three basic word order types: SOV, SVO, and OSV.
(b) Subject and object are never marked simultaneously with *a*, i.e., *a* is restricted to the object.
(c) The occurrence of basic word order types seems to be restricted: as opposed to SOV and SVO, OSV is only possible when the object is marked with *a*.
(d) The occurrence of basic word order types does not seem to depend on whether the referents are PGN marked or not.
(e) Object and subject are identified as follows: the subject is placed sentence-initially (SOV, SVO). Only when the object is marked with *a* may it precede the subject in an OSV order.

Compare examples (332) and (333) where: in (a) both subject and object are PGN marked; in (b) subject and object or just the object is unmarked; in (c) the subject and object or just the object is marked with PGN, in which case the object is marked with *a* or its allomorph *ɛ̀*; and, finally, in (d) the object only is marked with *a*.

SOV:

(332) a. *Táci-mà tcìkúmì xú-m̀ tama xòó-è-gò vé.*
older.brother-3SG.M unsuccessful. hunting thing-3SG.M even get-I-FUT NEG
'The older brother, the unsuccessful one, cannot catch anything.'

b. *ṹã̀ dìǹí ṹ-á-xu-a-ta.*
hare honey go.for-II-COMPL-II-PAST
'Hare went for honey.'

c. *ṹã̀ ǀaá-m̀ à ǂã́ã-na-xu-a-tè.*
hare invitation-3SG.M *à* put.on-II-COMPL-I-PRES
'Hare comes with the invitation.' (lit.: 'Hare puts on the invitation.')

d. *Té djirí-tè té dì ǁáó à gùì-é kṹũ̀-à-tè vé.*
1PL.C monkey-1PL.C 1PL.C POSS heart *à* take-II go-I-PRES NEG
'We monkeys, we do not carry our hearts along with us.'
(Heine 1997: 28)

SVO:

(333) a. *ǀűũ-hɛ̀ cĩ̋ĩ á ǂ'ũ̋-hɛ̀.*
mother-3SG.F cook DEM food-3SG.F
'The mother cooked the food.'

b. *Kyɛ̀hɛ́ ǀ'ée nò wuú cì-gùì-à-xú míní kyàráa ki.*
every day when hyena NEM-take-II-COMP goat corral LOC
'Every day, hyena comes and takes a goat in the corral.'

c. *ǀGàròo yà-gùì-é-tè á ǀ'é-hɛ̀ ɛ̀.*
ostrich come-take-I-PRES DEM fire-3SG.F ɛ̀ɛ̀
'Ostrich comes and takes that fire.'

d. *Tí ũ̋ã̀-rà ǂú-a-ta xó à.*
1SG hare-1SG collect-II-PAST thing *à*
'I myself, the hare, collected something.'

In contrast to this, OSV only appears when the object is either marked with PGN and *a*, as in (334a), or only with *a*, as in (334b).

OSV:

(334) a. *Nǁàtá cámi-m̀ à kóo-a-tè córò.*
thus polecat-3SG.M *à* hold.back-I-PRES rock.monitor
'Thus the rock monitor (tries to) keep back the polecat.'

b. *Tcɛ́m̀ xó à qóro kx'úí-é-tè.*
true thing *à* cock speak-I-PRES
'It is true what the cock says.'

The order of core participants with ditransitive verbs is based on the word order of transitive verbs that are extended by the indirect object. Thus, ten possibilities of word order combinations (see Table 7.14 and examples 445a–j) are found in sentences with three core participants (subject, direct and indirect object). However, only two combinations may be considered as kind of standard: S–O–IO–V and S–V–IO–O (indicated in italics *and* bold); finally, S–IO–V–O (in italics only) is found more frequently than the other six combinations that remain.

The question arises as to which of these word order types is the dominant one. A good candidate seems to be the SOV constituent order, which is reflected in relative clauses and some types of serial verb constructions. The evaluation of about 1,500 sentences in recent text collections (1999) reveals that the SVO order (see Tables 7.13 and 7.14 below; in the latter, it is indicated in italics *and* bold) is used almost twice as often as the two other ones. As shown above, the OSV order occurs only under certain very specific conditions, whereas SOV and SVO orders appear to occur in all environments. In interrogative sentences, SVO order is only used when the subject is asked for or is foregrounded, whereas OSV order is employed when the object is asked for or is foregrounded. In "why"-questions both OSV and SOV are used; and with "how"-questions, where the verbal action is foregrounded, only SOV order is used.

A very similar distribution can be observed in relative clauses where there is a clear basic SOV order. This is the case, for example, in relative sentences where the relativized noun is a sentence-initial, pronominal applicative/benefactive, instrumental, or temporal extension. An OSV order appears – as expected – when the relativized noun is the pronominal object in the relative sentence. When the relativized noun is the indirect object in the relative sentence, both object phrases (i.e. the pronominal indirect object followed by the nominal direct object) precede subject and verb. SVO order is not obtained because the relative pronoun is always suffixed to the finite verb when it is the subject in the relative sentence.

All these observations clearly indicate that Khwe has a dominant SOV word order. SOV is the most neutral order that occurs in all contexts except where, for foregrounding purposes, the object is fronted, thus giving an OSV order. In the case where an SVO order occurs, the subject takes a special emphasis. The fact that the majority of Central Khoesan languages are considered SOV languages (cf. Güldemann and Vossen 2000: 117) tends to support our hypothesis.

3.2.4.2.2 CONSTITUENT ORDERS IN SENTENCES WITH PRONOMINAL REFERENTS

In basic sentences the identification of subject and object presents no particular difficulty. A different situation arises in sentences with purely pronominal, or nominal and pronominal referents. Compare examples (335)–(337) where the meaning is always 'I see a house.' In these cases all three word orders are possible without restrictions or morphological conditions. (a) always indicates a referent that is either marked with *a* or is unmarked, (b) shows the referent with a PGN suffix, and under (c) the referent is marked with a PGN marker plus *a*. Speakers consider the examples under (337) with OSV order as preferred variants.

SVO:

(335)	a.	*Tí*	*ngú*	*à*	*mű̃ũ̀-à-tè.*
		1SG	house	*à*	see-I-PRES
	b.	*Tí*	*ngú-mà*		*mű̃ũ̀-à-tè.*
		1SG	house-3SG.M		see-I-PRES
	c.	*Tí*	*ngú-m̀*	*à*	*mű̃ũ̀-à-tè.*
		1SG	house-3SG.M	*à*	see-I-PRES

SOV:

(336)	a.	*Tí*	*mű̃ũ̀-à-tè*	*ngú*	*(à).*
		1SG	see-I-PRES	house	*à*
	b.	*Tí*	*mű̃ũ̀-à-tè*	*ngú-mà.*	
		1SG	see-I-PRES	house-3SG.M	
	c.	*Tí*	*mű̃ũ̀-à-tè*	*ngú-m̀*	*à.*
		1SG	see-I-PRES	house-3SG.M	*à*

OSV:

(337)	a.	*Ngú*	*(à)*	*tí*	*mű̃ũ̀-à-tè.*
		house	*à*	1SG	see-I-PRES
	b.	*Ngú-mà*		*tí*	*mű̃ũ̀-à-tè.*
		house-3SG.M		1SG	see-I-PRES
	c.	*Ngú-m̀*	*à*	*tí*	*mű̃ũ̀-à-tè.*
		house-3SG.M	*à*	1SG	see-I-PRES

The restriction to three types of word order is also valid for sentences that are not basic. In a sample of 508 sentences with both nominal and pronominal referents, taken from nine narrations (cf. Heine 1997, Kilian-Hatz and Naude 1999) as well as from Köhler's texts (cf. Köhler 1991: 279ff., 428ff., 447ff., 462ff.), no other word order types are found. Thus, in sentences with nominal and pronominal referents, the following picture obtains: SVO is the most frequent word order, followed by OSV and SOV. It must be noted that in narrations the most frequently used sentence type is intransitive SV and/or transitive SV where the object is understood. Similarly, the high frequency of sentences without a subject (i.e., the OV and V types) can be explained by the fact that the subject, as well as the object, are most often elided in narrative sentences when the referent is known either from the context or in subordinated and co-coordinated sentences, when the referent is the same as in the main or preceding sentence (cf. 441 and 442). It must be added that there is no difference in the occurrence of word order types in main and subordinated sentences; subordinated sentences vary in the same way as main sentences. The distribution of word order types (pronominal referents included) is shown in Table 7.13:

TABLE 7.13 FREQUENCY OF WORD ORDER TYPES IN KHWE IN SENTENCES WITH NOMINAL AND PRONOMINAL REFERENTS

Word order type	Number	Percentage
SVO	51	10.04
OSV	35	6.90
SOV	33	6.50
OV	37	7.28
VO	5	0.98
SV	289	56.90
V	58	11.42

Simple neutral sentences in Khwe appear to be a contradiction to our claim that Khwe has a dominant SOV order. Consider (338) which is most representative of sentences of its type. To all appearances we have here an OSV word order. The sentence is normally translated as in (a). If, however, the speaker intends to foreground the object, exactly the same word order appears. We may therefore conclude that in all sentences at least one element must be foregrounded and that the foregrounding of the object is the neutral case.

OSV:

(338) *ǀ'áò à tí ǂxàrò-á-ta Màtìaci-m̀ ki / . . . Màtìaci-m̀ à.*
money *à* 1SG give-II-PAST M.-3SG.M to M.-3SG.M *à*
a. 'I gave the money to Matthew.' or:
b. 'I gave the *money* to Matthew.'

SVO order is chosen when the subject is emphasized:

(339) *Tí ǂxàrò-á-ta ǀ'áò à Màtìaci-m̀ ki.*
1SG give-II-PAST money *à* M.-3SG.M to
'*I* gave the money to Matthew.'

Subject and object precede the verb (SOV) when the verbal action is emphasized:

(340) *Tí ǀ'áò (à) ǂxàrò-á-ta Màtìaci-m̀ ki.*
1SG money *à* give-II-PAST M.-3SG.M to
'I *gave* the money to Matthew.'

In unconnected sentences SVO order is used to emphasize the subject. It also appears when the object is either the elliptic subject or the object of a following sentence, i.e., the referent is identical in both sentences as demonstrated in examples (441) and (442):

(441) *Pòo ú-ó-xu-a-hã xàa wúyàmbò xà-hɛ́ ɛ̀. Cì-khúu-can-*
jackal send-LOC-COMPL-II-PAST DEM arrow DEM-3SG.F *ɛ̀* NEM-return-REFL-

a-kò xóm̀ ki ǁɔ̃̀ã́-é-tè nò pòo ǂĩ.
II-CONV ground LOC descend-I-PRES when jackal be.without.any.voice
'The jackal shot this arrow again. (The arrow) returns and comes down to the ground (but) the jackal doesn't say a word.'

(442) *ǁṹũ-hɛ̀ ǂúu cɛ́-m̀ à, |óɛ́ átaxa ǂ'ṹ.*
mother-3SG.F collect bush.sp.-3SG.M *à* child thus eat
'The mother collects the *cɛ́* fruit, then the child eats (it).'

Thus, the flexibility of word order is primarily a feature of a highly pragmatically determined language where at least one sentence constituent is always emphasized through its position: either the verbal action or one of the referents (the focused constituents are underlined in Table 7.14). The relative frequency of SVO order in narrations can be explained by the fact that either the agent – encoded in the subject – is emphasized (i.e., narrative sentences are more agent-oriented) or the object becomes the elided subject or object in the following sentence. In interrogative sentences SVO order is only used when the subject is asked for or is foregrounded, whereas OSV order is used when the object is asked for or is foregrounded. In "why"-questions both OSV and SOV are used, while in "how"-questions where the verbal action is foregrounded only SOV order is used. Word order is used in particular to respond to "who"-questions and, thus, may express either argument focus or predicate focus. This is illustrated in examples (443a–b), (444a–c), and (445a–j).

TABLE 7.14 KHWE CONSTITUENT ORDER WITH A VERBAL PREDICATE AND CORE PARTICIPANTS

Intransitive	Transitive	Ditransitive	
S–V	S–O–V	***S–O–IO–<u>V</u>***	S–IO–O–<u>V</u>
			<u>S</u>–<u>O</u>–V–IO
	<u>S</u>–V–O	***<u>S</u>–V–IO–O***	<u>S</u>–V–O–IO
		IO–S–V–O	*<u>S</u>–IO–V–O*
	<u>O</u>–S–V	*<u>IO</u>–<u>O</u>*–SV	<u>O</u>–<u>IO</u>–S–V
			<u>O</u>–S–V–IO

(443) a. <u>O</u> S V
|Gàrò-hɛ́ ɛ̀ té yá!
ostrich-3SG.F O 1PL.C look.for
'We have to look for the <u>ostrich</u>!'

b. S O <u>V</u>
Énò |gàròo té à ǁxáo-a-gòè tè!
perhaps ostrich 1PL.C O help-I-FUT now
'Perhaps the ostrich <u>can help</u> us now!'

(444) a. S O V
ǀő̋ã̋-mà bácìkòrò à kyã̋ã-ka-a-tè.
child-3SG.M bicycle O run-CAUS-I-PRES
'The boy rides a bicycle.'

b. O S V
Bácìkòrò à ǀő̋ã̋-mà kyã̋ã-ka-a-tè.
bicycle O child-3SG.M run-CAUS-I-PRES
'The boy rides a bicycle.'

c. S V O
ǀȍã̋-mà kyã̋ã-ka-a-tè bácìkòrò à.
child-3SG.M run-CAUS-I-PRES bicycle O
'The boy rides a bicycle.'

(445) a. S IO O V
Tí Màtìaci-m̀ à ǀ'áò xàrò-á-tà.
1SG Matthew-2SG.M O money give-II-PAST
'I gave the money to Matthew.'

b. S O IO V
Tí Khwe-dam à tcá à ǀáé-è-tè.
1SG Khwe-language O 2SG.M O teach-I-PRES
'I teach you Khwe.'

c. S V IO O
Pólícà-ǀùà ǀéú-á-tà khó-m̀ à dàó à.
police-3PL.M show-II-PAST man-3SG.M O way O
'The police showed the way to the man.'

d. S V O IO
Xà-má cóɛ-rɛ-ma-à-tè yiíceregú à té à.
DEM-3SG.M narrate-II-APPL-I-PRES tale O 1SG O
'He tells us a folktale.'

e. S IO V O
Tí tcá à ǀáé-è-tè Khwe-dam à.
1SG 2SG.M O teach-I-PRES Khwe-language O
'I teach you Khwe.'

f. S O V IO
Tí Khwe-dam à ǀáé-è-tè ǀő̋ã̋-m̀ à.
1SG Khwe-language O teach-I-PRES child-3SG.M O
'I teach Khwe to the boy.'

g. O IO S V
Nǀé xó-djì à tcá à tí dò-á-tè.
DEM thing-3PL.F O 2SG.M O 1SG believe-I-PRES
'As for these things, I believe you.'

h. O S V IO
ǀ'áò à tí xàrò-ná-tà Màtìaci-m̀ à.
money O 1SG give-II-PAST Matthew-3SG.M O
'I gave Matthew the money.'

i. IO S V O
Tcá à tí dò-á-tè nǀé xó-djì à.
2SG.M O 1SG believe-I-PRES DEM thing-3PL.F O
'I believe you these things.'

j. IO O S V
Màtìaci-m̀ à ǀ'áò à tí xàró-á-tà.
Matthew-3SG.M O money O 1SG give-II-PAST
'I gave the money to Matthew.'

3.2.4.2.3 ORDER OF ATTRIBUTES

Khwe has a modifier–head order. Therefore, manner adverbs precede the verb and adjectives and possessor attributes precede the noun. However, in order to emphasize an attribute they are postposed.

3.2.4.2.3.1 OVS AND VSO ORDER? – FORMATION OF VERBAL ADJECTIVES

Khwe does not have a coherent, proper word class of adjectives. It distinguishes formally between verbal adjectives, adjectives derived from nouns, adjectives related to pronouns, and numerals. An adjective in Khwe is defined as an attribute that immediately precedes the head noun which it modifies.

Verbs are the main source for qualifying adjectives. Köhler (1973: 32), therefore, defines adjectives in Khwe generally as verb stems and considers other sources as exceptions. Most adjectives are in fact pure verb stems that precede the head noun. The pure verb stem is otherwise used as a finite tenseless form; it denotes that states or events are not necessarily related to the time of speaking. This tenseless form is typically used with verbs of state or verbs like 'be' or 'live'. An example is provided in (446a), the equivalent use as attribute is given in (446b), and (446c–d) finally illustrate its use as predicate formed with a TAM marker.

(446) a. *Yì á ǀéú.*
tree FOC be.big
'The tree is big.'

b. *ǀÉú yì á.*
big tree COP
'It is a big tree.'

c. *Yì á ǀéú-à-tè.*
tree FOC be.big-I-PRES
'The tree becomes big.'

d. *Yì á ǀéú-a-hã.*
tree FOC be.big-II-PAST1
'The tree became big.' Or: 'The tree is actually big.' Or rarely: 'The tree was big (but it is not big any more).'

Köhler's "adjective" category only comprises the subclass of stative verbs. However, verbs from other verb classes are also used in the same way. Thus, in principle every verb may be used attributively in so far as it is semantically compatible with the head noun. In this respect, the open class of verbs is identical with the subclass of qualifying adjectives. (447a) contains the process verb *djàó* 'work', (447b) the derived reciprocal verb *ǀxúni-ku* 'mix with each other'; in (447c) the negated verb *ǀúu-nya* 'not give birth' is used, while (447d) presents the verb *ngúí* 'praise'.

(447) a. *Tí mṹũ-à-tè djàó ǀȍ̃ã́-hɛ̀.*
1SG see-I-PRES work child-3SG.F
'I see a working girl.'

b. *ǁxúni-ku khóé-nà*
mix-REC person-3PL.C
'mixed people' (i.e. people of different nationalities)

c. *ǁúu-nya ǁgɛ̀ɛ-khòè-hɛ̀*
give.birth-NEG female-person-3SG.F
'infertile/barren woman'
(lit.: 'woman that does not give birth')

d. *ngúí ǀí-mà*
praise song-3SG.M
'hymn of praise'

Not only simplex and derived verbal stems but also complex verbs can be used as adjectives; this is demonstrated in (448) with the serial verb construction consisting of 'die' and 'stand'.

(448) *ǁ'ó-ó-xu-a tı̃̀ı̃ nǁgóɛ́*
die-II-COMPL-II stand moon
'last stage of waning moon'
(lit.: 'dead standing moon')

As shown in the examples above, verbal adjectives are most often verb stems that precede the head noun. There are, however, instances where the attributively used verb occurs in its finite form with a TAM marker. In contrast to the tenseless form, which indicates a timeless quality, the form with a TAM suffix indicates a special temporal relation, as in (449) and (450), and/or an aspectual relation, as in (451): the verb 'do' is used attributively in its tenseless form (451a) and with the verbal TAM suffix *-ǁòè* denoting the habitual in (451b). The verbal adjective *hı̃ı̃́* 'do, act' → 'doing' is furthermore modified by the intensified adverb 'well' which still reflects its verbal-like character.

(449) *ǁ'úu-a-tà càá*
freeze-II-PAST2 water
'ice, ice cream' (lit.: 'frozen water')

(450) a. *Kx'éí nyáḿ-ka khóé-hɛ̀ mà-hɛ́?*
first start-CAUS person-3SG.F who-3SG.F
'Who was the woman who started first?'
(lit.: 'Who is the first starting person?')

b. *Kx'éí nyáḿ-ka-ra-hı̃ khóé-hɛ̀ mà-hɛ́?*
first start-CAUS-II-PAST5 person-3SG.F who-3SG.F
'Who was the woman who started first?'
(lit.: 'Who is the first having started person?')

(451) a. *Xà-má tcɛ́kà-kara hı̃ı̃́ khó-mà.*
DEM-3SG.M good-INTS.ADV do person-3SG.M
'He is the right person.' (lit.: 'He is a very well doing man.')

b. *Xà-má tcɛ́kà-kara hı̃ı̃́-è-ǁòè khó-mà.*
DEM-3SG.M good-INTS.ADV do-I-HAB person-3SG.M
'He is the right person.' (lit.: 'He is a usually very well doing man.')

Example (452) presents a typical predicative noun phrase formed with the copula/presentative *à*. In (452a) the stative verb 'be small' appears in its tenseless form and precedes the noun; it thus qualifies here as a verbal adjective 'small'. In (452b), however, the verb is marked with the TAM suffix *-hã* denoting past tense/resultative. However, here the verb does not form the predicate but is still the attribute to the following head noun. Constructions such as (446b) and (448)–(452) may have triggered the misleading assumption of a fourth and fifth basic word order (OVS and VSO respectively) where a verbal predicate may precede the subject. In fact, a VS order is not allowed in Khwe and not attested in any recent data; constructions like (453a–b) seem doubtful and are probably only found and accepted in sentences which are elicited under rather artificial fieldwork circumstances. A verb preceding the subject always forms its attribute and never its predicate. (Similarly, the verbal adjective and the following noun may form an object noun phrase, as in 447a.)

(452) a. *ǂ'ó dáó à.*
small path COP
'This is a small path.' But NOT: 'The path is small.'

b. *ǂ'ó-ró-hã dáó à.*
small-II-PAST1 path COP
'This is a small path.' (lit.: 'This is a have-become-small path.')
But NOT: 'The path (recently) became small.'

OVS – "rare, but accepted":

(453) a. *Dóá-m̀ à |x'ű-á-hã Khóé-ǁùà.
kudu-3SG.M O kill-II-PAST1 Khwe-3PL.M
'The Khwe have killed a kudu.' (Köhler 1981: 539)[4]

VSO – "in narrations":

(453) b. *|x'ű-á-hã Khóé-ǁùà dóá-m̀ à.
kill-II-PAST1 Khwe-3PL.M kudu-3SG.M O
'The Khwe have killed a kudu.' (Köhler 1981: 539)

3.2.4.2.3.2 POSTPOSED ATTRIBUTES

(a) Possessive attributes

Attributive nouns or pronouns are postposed to lay focus on the possessor in a nominal possessive construction. The regular possessive construction has a strict modifier–head order; the possessor is followed by a possessive postposition and finally by the possessee, as illustrated in (454a) and (455a). The reverse order with a postposed possessor is used in order to emphasize the possessor. Here, the possessor attribute plus the appropriate possessive postposition are postposed as a kind of apposition to the head. Depending on whether the possessee is definite or indefinite, the modifying noun or pronoun is followed by the possessive postposition *di* (with an indefinite possessee), as in (454b) and (455b), by the postposition *ù* plus a PGN suffix (with a definite possessee) which is co-referential to the PGN of the head noun, as in (456) and (457). The possessive postposition is commonly omitted if the possessor noun has a PGN, thus the possessor (N-PGN_1-PGN_2), as in (458a–c).

(454) a. *Yaá-kà tí ki ngú-à dì tcápì à!* possessor–possessee
come-CAUS 1SG LOC house-GEN POSS key O
'Bring me the key of the house!'

b. *Yaá-kà tí dì tcápì à ngú-à dì à!* postposed attribute
come-CAUS 1SG POSS key O house-GEN POSS O
'Bring me the key of the <u>house</u>!'

Possessor–possessee postposed attribute:

(455) a. *té dì ǀáé-è ki*
1PL.C POSS camp-GEN LOC
'in our camp'

b. *ǀáé té dí-è ki*
camp 1PL.C POSS-GEN LOC
'in <u>our</u> camp' (lit.: 'the camp, in ours')

(456) *Tcɛ́ɛ <u>ǀxɛ̀-hɛ̀</u> bàì <u>tí-m̀</u> <u>dàmàci-mà</u> <u>ù-hɛ̀</u>*
really body-3SG.F so 1SG-3SG.M younger.brother-3SG.M POSS-3SG.F

bɛ̀rɛ́-ná-xu-a-hã!
be.left.over-II-COMPL-II-PAST
'That's it! Thus, only the body of <u>my younger brother</u> is left over!'
(lit.: 'The body, my brother's, is left over.')

(457) *Nò á-m̀ tá-khò-mà ǀóé nò*
CONJ DEM-3SG.M be.old-person-3SG.M sleep CONJ

dàmàci-hɛ̀ kx'éí tcɛ́-i yò á-m̀
younger.sister-3SG.F first send-IMPS while DEM-3SG.M

<u>tcɛ́tcɛrɛ-ǀõã-m̀</u> kà <u>xà-cí</u> <u>m̀</u> à tĩ̀-ĩ̀-tá tcɛ́rɛ-ɛ-tè.
rattle-DIM-3SG.M INSTR DEM-3SG.F POSS O stand-II-PAST rattle-I-PRES
'While the old man is sleeping, the younger sister is sent first to stand (near him) and to rattle with <u>her</u> small rattle (lit.: while she is rattling that small rattle, hers).'

Postposed possessor with omitted possessive postposition:

(458) a. *ngúí ǀí-hɛ̀ Càxàríyà-m̀-hɛ̀ (= . . . Càxàríyà-m̀ m̀-hɛ̀)*
praise song-3SG.F Zacharias-3SG.M-3SG.F Zacharias-3SG.M POSS-3SG.F
'<u>Zacharias</u>' praise hymn'

b. *ngúí ǂí-mà Màríyà-cì-mà (= . . . Màríyà-cì ù-mà)*
praise song-3SG.M Mary-3SG.F-3SG.M Mary-3SG.F POSS-3SG.M
'<u>Mary's</u> praise hymn'

c. *wò-ó-hɛ̀ Yícàcì-m̀-hɛ̀ (= . . . Yícàcì-m̀ m̀-hɛ̀)*
birth-LOC-3SG.F Jesus-3SG.M-3SG.F Jesus-3SG.M POSS-3SG.F
'the birth of <u>Jesus</u>'

(b) Adjectives

A verbal adjective is emphasized by copying an emphatic possessive/genitive construction. Thus, in emphatic possession as well as in emphatic qualification the head noun is followed by the copula *à*; it precedes the modifier which itself is followed by the emphatic particle *di à* (examples are given in 459b, 460b, and 461–462):

HEAD *à* MODIFIER *di à*

The construction *di à* is composed of the possessive postposition *di* and the copula *à*. It goes back to an emphatic possessive construction where a modifying noun or pronoun is replaced by a verbal adjective; this can be paraphrased as "It is X, it has the quality of Y". The underlying possessive structure can be schematized thus:

POSSESSEE *à* POSSESSOR *di à* → N/PRON *à* ADJ *di à*

The emphatic qualification still forms an afterthought which is reflected in constructions such as (462); here, the emphasized adjectival stative verb *ǃéci* ('be white') is clearly separated from the preceding pronoun by a pause and, hence, forms an apposition to it. As demonstrated in (461) and (462), emphatic qualification is used particularly to contrast two situations.

(459) a. *kx'óá kx'óxò-djì*
be.raw meat-3PL.F
'raw meat'

b. *kx'óxò à kx'óá dì à*
meat COP be.raw POSS COP
'raw meat' (lit.: 'meat of being raw')

(460) a. *ǁHoḿ tá-khòè à djàò-á-tè.*
be.strong old-person FOC work-I-PRES
'The sprightly elders are working.' (Köhler 1973: 34)

b. *Tá-khòè à ǁhoḿ dì à djàò-á-tè.*
old-person FOC be.strong POSS COP work-I-PRES
'The elders, who are still sprightly, are working.' (Köhler 1973: 34)

(461) *Tcɛ́ka ǂ'ű à tí ǁhɛ̀-ɛ́-ǃoè; ǂ'ű à tc'ó dì à*
be.good food O 1SG pick.up-I-HAB food O be.rotten POSS O

tí ǂhɛ̀-ɛ́-ǃò vé.
1SG pick.up-I-HAB NEG
'I am used to picking up good fruits; I am not used to picking up tainted fruits.' (Köhler 1973: 34)

(462) *Nò xà-má, xàḿ à, xà-ḿ m̀ à, ǃ'éci dì à*
CONJ DEM-3SG.M lion COP DEM-3SG.M POSS O be.white POSS O

gùi nò á ǂqóvoǁhòè ki ǂấã nò ǀqúnu.
take CONJ DEM clay.pot LOC put.in CONJ boil
'And it's him, the lion; he takes his (parts), the white ones (i.e. fat parts of meat), puts them in the clay pot and boils them.'

3.2.4.3 Marking with *à*

The morpheme *à* is common in Central Khoesan languages as object marker as, for example, in Nama, and as copula with presentative function (cf. Heine 1986). It has various functions in Khwe as a presentative marker, as focus and object marker, and finally as a marker of oblique case.

According to Köhler (1981: 514f., 539), there are two different *à* morphemes in Khwe which exclude each other:

(a) Köhler (1981: 514f.) analyses a suffix *à* as a common or neuter singular marker, forming part of the PGN paradigm, as he demonstrates as follows:

	Singular		Dual		Plural	
M	*ǀő̃ấ-mà*	'boy'	*ǀő̃ấ-tcà*	'two boys'	*ǀő̃ấ-ǁùà*	'boys'
F	*ǀő̃ấ-hɛ̀ɛ̀*	'girl'	*ǀő̃ấ-cà*	'two girls'	*ǀő̃ấ-djì*	'girls'
C	*ǀõấ (à)*	'child'	*ǀõấ-khà*	'two children (boy and girl)'	*ǀõấ-nà*	'children (boys and girls)'

The function of the common singular is restricted syntactically to nouns being subject and/or used in the *status constructus* (i.e. a genitival construction with relational nouns and with postpositions). Furthermore, the marker *à* may be omitted

(i) if the PGN suffix does not distinguish natural gender but only grammatical gender;
(ii) if natural gender is expressed alternatively by the modifiers 'male' and 'female' as illustrated below:

khóé	'person, human'	vs.
kx'á-khò-mà	'man' (lit.: male-person-3SG.M)	
kx'á-khòè	'man' (lit.: male-person)	

(b) The second *à* morpheme is defined by Köhler (1981: 539) as a particle marking the direct object of nouns that have a PGN suffix but not the common singular PGN *à*. If, as in Köhler's examples below, subject and object consist of such nouns that are marked with the singular common suffix *à*, a formal object marking with the particle *à* is excluded. In this case, subject and object are identified by word order only, i.e., the subject always precedes the object (in SVO or SOV):

SOV: *Khwé* *à* *doá* *à* *|x'ú-á-hǎ̃.*
Khwe SG.C kudu O kill-II-PAST
'A Khwe has killed a kudu.' (Köhler 1981: 539)

SVO: *Tá-khòè* *à* *ǁhéù-à-tè* *ápà* *à*.
old-person SG.C raise-I-PRES dog O
'The elder raises a dog.' (Köhler 1981: 539)

It must be added here that the marker *à* is not only found in the contexts described by Köhler but also with indirect objects and with nouns that are used as local and temporal adverbials.

Despite the different functions, the marker *à* is in some way incompatible with the negation marker *vé*: in non-verbal clauses the negation marker replaces *à* (e.g., in *Khwé à* 'It is a Khwé' vs. *Khwé vé* 'It is not a Khwe'). In verbal clauses as (463) the negation marker never immediately follows a noun which is marked with *à*; therefore, the clause in (c) is ungrammatical.

(463) a. *Tí* *n|ám̀* *vé* *éruku à.*
1SG like NEG dog O
'I don't like dogs.'

b. *Éruku à* *tí* *n|ám̀* *vé.*
dog O 1SG like NEG
'I don't like dogs.'

but: c. *Tí n|ám̀ *éruku* *à* vé.
1SG like dog O NEG

The syntactic restrictions and the exclusion of a double object marking with *à* (as object and as PGN) reveal that there are not two separate, coincidentally homonymous morphemes *à*. It will be shown that the functions of *à* are closely interrelated so that there is only one multi-functional morpheme.

The hypothesis of a multi-functional morpheme *à* is furthermore supported if we compare the allomorphic distribution, as listed in Table 7.15. Although the form *à* may be used in all contexts, different allomorphic variants exist: *è* and the bound forms *-à* and *-è*. While the nouns have different syntactic functions they may take the same allomorphic variants.

A different scenario arises when looking at the interrelation of PGN and *à* in different sorts of texts provided by Köhler (1989, 1991), Heine (1997) and Kilian-Hatz and Naude

TABLE 7.15 DISTRIBUTION OF THE ALLOMORPHIC VARIANTS OF *à* IN KHWE

Allomorph	Subject	Direct object	Indirect object	Temporal/Locative adverbial
à	+	+	+	+
ɛ̀ after PGN *-hɛ̀*		+	+	+
-à	+	+	+	
-e after final *-i/-e*	(+)	+	+	

TABLE 7.16 MARKING DEFINITE VS. INDEFINITE NOUN PHRASES IN KHWE

	Definite			Indefinite	
	Pronoun	Proper N	Specific N	Generic N	Unspecific N
Subject	+PGN –*à*	–PGN –*à*	+PGN –*à*	–PGN –*à*	–PGN +/–*à*
Direct object	+PGN +/–*à*	+PGN +*à*	+PGN +/(–)*à*	–PGN –*à*	–PGN +/–*à*
Indirect object	+PGN +*à*	+PGN +*à*	+PGN +/(–)*à*	–PGN –*à* ?	+PGN +/–*à*
Local/temporal adverbial N			+PGN +/–*à*		–PGN +/–*à*

(1999). The results are listed in Table 7.16 (where: + = "with"; – = "without"; ( ) = "rarely"; / = "or"). Here it becomes obvious that:

(a) PGN marking with a suffix is only possible on a referent which is identifiable for speaker and hearer, i.e. on pronouns, proper nouns, and specific nouns. In contrast to these, generic and unspecific nouns do not accept any PGN.
(b) Only unspecific subject nouns may take the marker *à*.
(c) *à* is very often used to mark a direct and/or indirect object, but it is not obligatory with all nouns. It is never found on generic nouns and is optional with unspecific object nouns and pronouns; it is the preferred and, therefore, the default marker with specific object nouns; it is only obligatory with proper nouns.

From this we can conclude that there is a crucial distinction between zero marking and PGN marking which corresponds to the grammatical categories indefinite vs. definite, as follows: the PGN markers in Khwe are used like definite articles with specific nouns, whereas unspecific and generic nouns are zero marked and, therefore, indefinite.

As summarized in Table 7.17 below, only one core constituent is marked with *à*: in intransitive sentences it is the subject, in transitive sentences the direct object, and

TABLE 7.17 KHWE MARKING OF PARTICIPANTS BY *à*

	S (of intransitive V)		S (of transitive V)		O	IO	T	L
	Indefinite NP	Definite NP	Indefinite NP	Definite NP			NP	NP
intr.	+/–	–					+/–	+/–
tr.		–	(+)/–	–	+/–		+/–	+/–
dtr.		–	(+)/–	–	+/–	+/(–)	+/–	+/–

in ditransitive sentences the indirect object (the less common case is indicated in brackets); or it is a local/temporal adverbial. This again supports the hypothesis that *à* is a focus marker that foregrounds a contrasted referent or introduces a new referent.

The following sub-sections provide examples for the use of *à* with definite and indefinite noun phrases in different syntactic functions.

3.2.4.3.1 SUBJECT WITH *à*

Only unspecific and, therefore, indefinite nouns that are the subject of intransitive or verbless sentences may be marked with *à*. Here, the marker *à* is very frequently used, although it is not obligatory. It functions as a focus marker which introduces new information. The examples in (464) have an unspecific animal as subject of an intransitive clause. Although they are similar in structure, only the noun in (464b) is marked with *à*.

(464) a. *ǁX'érì ǂã̋ã-a-tè ǁx'áǁx'à-a ki.*
scorpion enter-I-PRES grass.sp.-OQ LOC
'A scorpion is disappearing in the grass.'

b. *Kúcugucugu à ǀgèvùu-à-tè.*
eagle FOC fly-II-PAST
'An eagle is flying.'

The sentences in (465) all begin with a local adverbial followed by a noun and the intransitive posture verb *tɛ́/tĩ̀ĩ* 'stay, stand, be'. While the noun 'store' is unmarked in (465a), the same noun is focused with *à* in (465b). The noun 'school' in (465c) and the nouns in (466) are marked with the allomorphic suffix variant *-a*.

(465) a. *Kyáó ki Búma-m̀ ókà ǀám̀ cìtórà tɛ́-ɛ́-hi.*
later LOC Buma-3SG.M LOC two store be-II-PAST
'Later there were two stores in Buma.' (Köhler 1989: 548f.)

b. *Àndárà ki ǀúi-xa ǁű̃ũ cìtórà à tɛ́-ɛ́-hĩ.*
Andara LOC one-GER be.big store FOC be-II-PAST
'A big store exists only in Andara.' (Köhler 1989: 551f.)

c. *Dìkúndù ki cure-à tĩ̋ĩ.*
Dikundu LOC school-FOC stand
'There is a school in Dikundu.' (Köhler 1989: 534f.)

(466) *Xú à hámbe, nǀám̀-ku-a hámbe, ǁxúi-ku-a ǀéú.*
thing FOC not.be love-REC-FOC not.be hate-REC-FOC be.much
'There is nothing [i.e. bad living conditions], there is no love, [but] there is much hate.'

(467a–b) are verbless sentences. Whereas (467a) contains an indefinite noun phrase 'rainless year' and a generic noun phrase 'year of drought', (467b) has a definite noun 'God' vs. an indefinite, generic verbal noun 'love'. Only the first noun in (467a) can be marked with *à*. None of the subjects in (468) may be marked with *à* because they are definite nouns.

(467) a. *Ó-tú-kúrí à poópo-kúrí.*
PRIV-rain-year COP drought-year
'A year without rain is a year of drought.' (Köhler 1991: 46f.)

b. *Khyànί-mà n|àm̀-ku.*
God-3SG.M love-REC
'God is love.'

(468) *N|àtá Khóé-|ù tamaxa Góává-|ù tamaxa |Gánda-|ù*
thus Khoe-3PL.M also Mbukushu-3PL.M also Mbwela-3PL.M
'So did the Khoe (men), the Mbukushu (men), as well as the Mbwela

tamaxa, tá thángà-m̀ kókàxa tέ-έ hĩ̀ĩ-t-a-hĩ.
also thus tribe-3SG.M all be-II do-FREQ-II-PAST
(men), i.e. all tribes.' (Köhler 1989: 551f.)

3.2.4.3.2 DIRECT OBJECT WITH *à*

3.2.4.3.2.1 INDEFINITE NOUNS AS OBJECTS

The marker *à* is also found with non-specific, indefinite nouns that form the direct object, as shown in typical examples such as (469a–c). The suffixed allomorphic variant *-a* is used in (470). Although the object is marked with *à* in most cases, *à* is not obligatory, as in (471a–b), where it does not occur. The direct object may be unmarked,

(a) if either the subject and object roles are clear from the context, as in (470a–b), where the inanimate objects cannot be the actor;
(b) or if another participant is marked with *à*. This is the case in (471a–b) where the indirect object is marked in (471a), and the possessive in (471b); the latter is already emphasized by its postposed position.

(469) a. *Càá à tí kx'àà-ca yà-à-hã̋!*
water O 1SG drink-PURP come-II-PAST
'I (just) came to drink water!'

b. *Tí kóróta-a-tĩ |'áò à Màtìaci-m̀ ókà.*
1SG borrow-II-PAST money O Matthew-3SG.M LOC
'I borrowed money from Matthew.'

c. *Hã̋ |aá à wò-á-gòè, nò kx'á-|õã à áva-a-gòè.*
2SG.F belly O have-I-FUT CONJ male-child O give.birth-I-FUT
'You will be with a child (lit.: you will get a belly) and give birth to a son.'

(470) *Kyὲhέ-m̀ |úí-mà |àm̀ |àm̀ n|góá-à gùi!*
each-3SG.M single-3SG.M two two stone-O take
'Each one (of you) take two stones!' (Heine 1997: 10)

(471) a. *Tàxúnò ǁháó tamaxa bó tamaxa |xàó tamaxa phókò tamaxa*
then hoe also axe also spear also knife also
'Then they sold hoes, axes, spears, knives,

kyáxù tamaxa ǁèu tamaxa |goó tamaxa
dagger also razor.blade also pointed.iron also
daggers, razor blades, as well as pointed irons,

taá xoá-m̀ yókàxa tέ-έ ǂũ̋ũ-kà-t-a-hĩ.
thus iron-3SG.M all be-II buy-CAUS-FREQ-II-PAST
i.e. all (kinds of) ironmongery.' (Köhler 1989: 447f.)

b. *Pákò, á xó tcá ngúrí-é-ǹ tama!*
never DEM thing 2SG.M lie-I-PROG also
'Never (i.e., it is not true)! That kind of affair you are also lying about!'

(472) a. *Nò xà-ná cèú táva-na-hĩ ǁű̃ũ-m̀ à.*
CONJ DEM-3PL.C hand wave-II-PAST father-3SG.M O
'Then they made signs to his father (lit.: they waved their hands).'

b. *Nàtíu ǀ'é xà-má ǂấã-na-tà á yó dì à?*
why fire DEM-3SG.M put.on-II-PAST DEM size POSS FOC
'Why has he lit such a big fire (lit.: a fire of such a size)?'

3.2.4.3.2.2 DEFINITE OBJECTS WITH *à*

The marker *à* can optionally follow a definite object noun phrase. This includes specific count nouns marked with a PGN suffix, as in (473a–b), pronouns, as in (474) and (475b), as well as proper nouns; the latter are obligatorily marked here with both a PGN suffix and *à*.

Most frequently, the marker *à* is found after a direct object; this may be due to the following facts:

(a) It is problematic to distinguish subject and object roles when both referents are animate, as in (475a–b) and (476a); *à* is used here to avoid ambiguity about subject and object roles, as in (476b–c).
(b) *à* functions to contrast the referents, as demonstrated in (477) where two direct objects are involved: the first object, 'monitor', is a re-called discourse topic which is focused with *à* and contrasted with the second object, 'genet', which is the actual discourse topic of the narration.

Although the general marking of direct objects with *à* appears to be the default case, there are still many contexts where *à* is lacking. This is again observed:

(a) when another referent is marked with *à*, as in (473b);
(b) if subject and object roles are identifiable from the former discourse or extra-linguistic context, as in (473a–b) and (474).

(473) a. *ǀÓɛ́-hɛ̀ átaxa ǂ'ű-à-tè cɛ́-djì à.*
child-3SG.F thus eat-I-PRES bush.sp-3PL.F O
'Thus the child eats the *cɛ́* fruits.'

b. *Tcá dì mbóró à ǀxű ǀxúni-mà.*
2SG.M POSS chance FOC kill crocodile-3SG.M
'It is your chance now to kill the crocodile.' (Heine 1997: 21)

(474) *Kx'ấĩ-éè, kx'ấĩ-è, tí-è ǂgaámá yaáka, tí-è ǂgaámá yaáka!*
vulture-VOC vulture-VOC 1SG-O wings bring 1SG-O wings bring
'Vulture, Vulture, bring me (my) wings, bring me the wings!'

OSV:

(475) a. *Ó-ǀ'ű̃ũ-khòè-tè té khóé-tè xà-má kx'ó.*
PRIV-hair-person-1PL.C 1PL.C person-1PL.C DEM-3SG.M eat
'He has to eat us, the ones without fur.'

SOV:

(475) b. *Khó-mà xà-ḿ ǀxúni-mà à thũ̋ũ̀-kara kyáè-e-hã*
person-3SG.M DEM-3SG.M crocodile-3SG.M O pain-INTS.GER tie-II-PAST
'The man had tied the crocodile on his horse in a way that was very painful;

bèyè-é ki; nǀã̋ã khóáná ki xà-má á-mà kx'ó-ca.
horse-O LOC DEM reason LOC DEM-3SG.M DEM-3SG.M eat-PURP
that is why he (crocodile) wanted to eat him (that man).' (Heine 1997: 20)

OSV:

(476) a. *Tàn tíì tcá tí ú!*
stand.up then 2SG.M 1SG bring
'Stand up, then I may take you!'

SVO:

b. *Tcá tí à kx'ȍã̋!*
2SG.M 1SG O wait
'You have to wait for me!'

OSV:

(476) c. *Yàá! Cáò à tí kyá-rá-hã!*
yes 2DU.F O 1SG love-II-PAST
'That's it! I love you two (women)!'

(477) *Tínù córò-mà-à ǀgàa-khòè-djì nǀgóá-à-tè.*
then rock.monitor-3SG.M-O female-person-3PL.F cook-I-PRES
'Then the women are cooking the rock monitor,

Kx'á-khòè-ǀè tcámba-mà nǀgóá-à-tè.
male-person-1PL.M genet-3SG.M cook-I-PRES
(and) we men are cooking the genet.' (Heine 1997: 36)

From the observations with indefinite and definite objects we conclude that *à* has two functions: on the one hand, it contrasts possible referents in object position; contrasting is again a main function of focus. On the other hand, it serves to avoid ambiguity of the syntactic roles of core participants; at this stage the marker *à* also distinguishes grammatical, rather than purely pragmatic, contrast. This complex function of *à* is the reason why a double marking with a separate focus marker *à* and an object marker *à* is impossible.

3.2.4.3.3 INDIRECT OBJECT WITH *à*

With indirect objects the marker *à* behaves similarly as with direct objects. If the sentence contains an indirect object, this is mostly marked with *à* regardless of its definiteness (see 481a–b). Only a few contexts are found where a sentence contains both a direct and indirect object because a participant is commonly omitted if it is known by the context. If both objects are mentioned, there are three possibilities of marking the referent with *à*:

(a) All objects are marked, as in (479–481a).
(b) Only the indirect object is marked, as in (478).
(c) Only the direct object is marked, as indicated by the brackets in (479) and (480).
(d) No object is marked, as in (481b) and (482); this is, however, rarely found.

(478) *Tíyò nǀĩ̋ĩkà tí yà-à-tá nò, tcá tí-è kwɛ́ɛ xó vé!*
then there 1SG come-II-PAST CONJ 2SG.M 1SG-O refuse thing NEG
'You can't refuse this to me, when I come here!'

(479) *Màtìaci-m̀ (à) ǀ'áò à tí xàró-ná-tà.*
Matthew-3SG.M (O) money O 1SG give-II-PAST
'I gave money to Matthew.'

(480) *ǀGɛ̀ɛ-khòè-djì (à) thàngà-m̀ à ǂũ̀-à-má-t-a-hĩ̃.*
female-person-3PL.F (O) clothes-3SG.M O buy-II-BEN-FREQ-II-PAST
'(We) bought clothes for the women.' (Köhler 1989: 549f.)

(481) a. *Á càá-hɛ̀ɛ̀ tí kx'áà-ca hĩ̃ĩ̀ nò càá à tí à.*
DEM water-3SG.F 1SG drink-PURP do CONJ water O 1SG O

kwɛ́ɛ-ka-t-i-t-a-tè!
refuse-CAUS-FREQ-IMPS-FREQ-I-PRES
'When I want to drink that water, they very often refuse me the water.'

vs. b. *Xà-má á càá-hɛ̀ nǀĩ̃ĩ̀kà té khóé-tè kwɛ́ɛ-ka.*
DEM-3SG.M DEM water-3SG.F there 1PL.C people-1PL.C refuse-CAUS
'We, the humans, refused him that water there.'

(482) *Á ǀ'é-hɛ̀ xà-má áta ǀhùáxu-i-hã nò.*
DEM fire-3SG.F DEM-3SG.M thus take.away-IMPS-PAST CONJ
'One (of us) has taken that fire away from him.'

3.2.4.3.4 LOCAL AND TEMPORAL ADVERBIALS WITH *à*

3.2.4.3.4.1 LOCAL ADVERBIALS

There are two ways to form a local adverbial: either the noun is followed by a local postposition, or the noun is marked optionally with *à* only.

Adverbials of the first type are used to specify and to focus on the kind of positioning, as in (483). This is achieved with three simple and semantically rather vague postpositions: "proximal" *ki* 'in, at, to, on'; "distal" *kà* 'in, at, to, on' and "ablative" 'from'; and *ókà* "distal directional" 'to' and "ablative" 'from'.

In contrast to this, adverbials of the second type are used to focus on the kind of location itself; the location is mostly emphasized by the additional use of the focus marker *à*, as in (484a–b). Similar to the Latin dative case, the local noun in Khwe occurs with an intransitive motion verb or a transitive verb, as in (484b). It does not form the object because it is not depending on the valence of the verb; so passivization is not permitted. Syntactically it is an oblique case, therefore the focus marker *à* is glossed here as oblique "OQ".

(483) *Dìvundu-cì ki ǂx'óá-rá-kò nákò Wínduka kà ǀxáǹ ngú.*
Divundu-3SG.F LOC go.out-II-CONV then Windhoek LOC very far
'It is very far from Divundu to Windhoek.'

(484) a. *M̀ m̀! Cé kũ̃ũ̀-à-tè ŋ́ú à ǀx'án ngúù nò tcá ŋ̀ki ǀóé-è-ǀòè!*
no 1PL.C go-I-PRES land OQ very far CONJ 2SG.M here lie-I-HAB
'Well, we are going to a very distant place, but you are used to lying here!'

b. *Tí ŋ̀ta tí xóm̀ à yaá-à-kó kũ̃ũ̀-à-ǀòè khóé-rà!*
1SG so 1SG ground OQ come-I-CONV walk-I-HAB person-1SG
'This is the way I always walk along/on the ground! That's me!'

c. *Hámbe ǀé hĩ̀-é-kò wèrè-ná-kò càá kx'áà-à-gò vé óo à.*
be.absent 1PL.C do-II-CONV scoop-II-CONV water drink-I-FUT NEG place OQ
'There is no way to scoop water at that place and drink (it).'

3.2.4.3.4.2 TEMPORAL ADVERBIALS

Similar to the formation of local adverbials, temporal adverbials are formed either with a temporal noun that is followed by a temporal/local postposition, as in (485a–b), or with a temporal noun that is optionally marked with *à*, as in (486a–b) and (487a–c).

Adverbials formed with a postposition denote an exact, specific point in time, as in (485a–b). In contrast to this, adverbials without a postposition generally express a temporal extension answering the question 'how long?'. If the time-period is emphasized, it takes the focus marker *à*, as in (487a–c); this is very often the case if the clause contains the intransitive verb *tɛ́* 'stay', as in (486a–b).

(485) a. *Á ǀám-cì kà xà-ḿ m̀ xà-ḿ m̀ daḿ-mà*
DEM time-3SG.F LOC DEM-3SG.M POSS DEM-3SG.M POSS tongue-3SG.M

khòàná-can-a-hĩ.
loosen-PASS-II-PAST
'Immediately (lit.: at that time . . .) his tongue was loosened.'

b. *Xà-ná yà-à-hĩ́ ǀúí cèú koro-kò n!óáma-kà ǀ'ée-m̀*
DEM-3PL.C come-II-PAST one hand plus three-ORD day-3SG.M

ki kṹ ǀɔ̃́ã́-m̀ à nǂgí-ca.
LOC be small child-3SG.M O circumcise-PURP
'On the eighth day they came to circumcise the child.'

Without the marker *à*:

(486) a. *Dìcó-ngyéu thíyà kúrí-nà Djáó ŋú-m̀ ókà*
Dico-young.man many year-3PL.C Botswana country-3SG.M LOC

cií tɛ́-ɛ́-hĩ.
arrive stay-II-PAST
'The younger Dico lived already many years in Botswana.' (Köhler 1989: 551f.)

b. *ǀÚi ǀ'é tɛ́-ɛ̀-hĩ ṹã̀-m̀ tấã pòo-m̀ tấã gúa-m̀ tấã.*
one.day be-II-PAST hare-3SG.M with jackal-3SG.M with hyena-3SG.M with
'Once upon a time (one day) there was the hare, the jackal, and the hyena.'

With the oblique/focus marker *à*:

(487) a. *Kúríkúrí à hấ tɛ́-ɛ̀-gòè kx'ɛ́ à!*
time.time OQ 2SG.F stay-I-FUT how
'You will live like that forever!'

b. *Xà-hɛ́ ǂ'á-rá-hĩ fáèfì nǁgóɛ́ à tɛ́-ɛ́-hĩ.*
DEM-3SG.F hide-II-PAST five month OQ stay-II-PAST
'For five months she remained in seclusion.'

c. *Xà-má té à nǀám-a-hĩ á teiti-hɛ̀ ɛ̀.*
DEM-3SG.M 1SG O love-II-PAST DEM time-3SG.F OQ
'At/during that time, he loved us.'

3.2.4.3.5 MULTIPLE FOCUS

As shown above, morphological marking of subject and object is optional because *à* is not a syntactic but a pragmatic marker. Its main function is to contrast possible candidates.

Whereas the subject of an intransitive or transitive clause is marked with *à* in less than 3 per cent of documented cases, the direct object is marked with *à* in about two thirds of cases; sentences with a focused subject *and* a focused object, as in (488)–(490), are rarely found. This is also due to the fact that most subjects in a narration are definite and do not allow *à*.

Examples where both subject and object are focused with *à* are provided in (488a–c) with definite objects and in (489a–b) with indefinite objects. Examples like the latter ones are exclusively found in elicited, isolated sentences in order to emphasize for didactic reasons; but it is not common in narrations. The sentences in (490) contain a focused subject and a temporal adverbial with *à*, and in (491b) even a focused object.

(488) a. *Mórúrwànì à kyã̋ũ-a-éi-a-xu-a-hĩ dáó-m̀ à.*
border FOC close-II-PERM-II-COMP-II-PAST way-3SG.M O
'A border (fence) barred the way.' (Köhler 1989: 557f.)

b. *Tc'áó-kx'óxò à tú-ca-m̀ à djɛ́xò-kà-à-ǁòè.*
bush-animal FOC rain-water-3SG.M O be.bad-CAUS-I-HAB
'Animals from the bush [new info] spoil the rainwater [old info].' (Köhler 1991: 13f.)

c. *Ndée! Tóm̀tom-xò à ŋ̀kà tí à tóm̀-à-tè.*
my.mother swallow-NOMIN FOC here 1SG O swallow-I-PRES
'Mummy, a swallowing thing (i.e. a python) is here (and it) swallows me!'

(489) a. *Áxàm à pá-à-tè ápa à.*
tick FOC bite-I-PRES dog O
'A tick bites a dog.'

b. *Yì-yéú à yì á yáà-à-tè.*
tree-mouse FOC tree O climb-I-PRES
'A tree-mouse is climbing up a tree.'

(490) a. *Kx'á-khòè à áta thùú à ǂ'óḿ-á-ǁò vé.*
male-person FOC thus night OQ sleep-I-HAB NEG
'A man may not sleep in such a night.'

b. *ǀũ̀ á tcám̀ à yaá-o-ro-xu-a-tà ǀ'ée à!*
war FOC 1DU.M O come-LOC-II-COMPL-II-PAST day OQ
'The/a war has already come to us today!'

3.2.4.3.6 THE EVOLUTION OF *à*

The diachronic evolution of the morpheme *à*, being a genuine copula in Central Khoesan, can finally be reconstructed in four stages. On the one hand, we observe a contextual extension from indefinite to definite nouns, and on the other hand it develops from a marker of pragmatic contrast to a marker of more and more grammatical contrast. (The different functions are each indicated by different labels ("COP", "FOC", "O", and "OQ"). The stages are summarized as follows:

I COP The copulative/presentative use of *à* is restricted in Khwe to indefinite subjects in verbless clauses.

II FOC It becomes a focus marker that introduces new information:
(a) indefinite subjects;
(b) indefinite object participants.

III	O	Extension to new, but definite information encoded in the object(s): (a) contrasting focus; (b) disambiguating syntactic roles.
IV	OQ	Focus for local and temporal adverbials.

3.2.4.4 Predicate focus

In Khwe, the two motion verbs *yaá* 'come' and especially *cií* 'arrive' are used to focus on the verbal action and, thus, indicate that a new episode of narration starts, as in (492) and (493). The verbs are used as first verbs in a serial verb construction to express a "movement towards the stage", as in (491a–b). In many contexts, however, the movement is no longer transparent; here the verbs function as "new-event markers", as in (492).

(491) a. *Djiri yà kx'áà-à-tè.*
monkey come drink-I-PRES
'When coming/arriving, the monkey drinks.'

b. *Djiri cì kx'áà-à-tè.*
monkey arrive drink-I-PRES
'When coming/arriving, the monkey drinks.'

(492) *ǂXoá-mà cì-ǁ'ó-ó-xu-a-hã̀.*
elephant-3SG.M NEM-die-II-COMPL-II-PAST
'(Suddenly) one of the elephants died.'

(493) *Nǀàtá tĩ̀-xá nò córò cì-mũ̋ũ̀-a-xu kũ̋ũ̀-hɛ̀ ɛ̀.*
thus stand-GER CONJ monitor NEM-see-II-COMPL go-3SG.F O
'Thus the rock monitor stands there; and then (he) sees (their) arrival.'

3.2.4.5 Summary

To conclude, only three basic constituent orders are permitted in Khwe: SOV, OSV, and SVO. Thus, a verbal predicate always follows the subject. In this respect, Khwe shares the typological feature of a needed SV constituent order with all other Khoesan languages. In contrast to this, a finite verb (with or without TAM) that precedes the subject forms as a "verbal adjective" is an attribute; this conforms to the strict modifier–head order, with all other kinds of adjectives and with (non-emphatic) possessor constructions.

The variation of the three basic constituent orders is not indicative of a clause type (e.g. interrogations, main or subordinated clauses) but is primarily a feature of an expressive speech style where one sentence constituent is always emphasized: either the verbal action (SOV) or one of the referents (SVO or OSV). Thus, word order in Khwe expresses pragmatic rather than syntactical relations.

Moreover, the use of the three word orders does not depend on the morphological markedness of the nouns, i.e., whether or not they are PGN marked. However, word order does interact with morphological markedness by means of *à*, which functions as a copula, as a focus and as a combined focus-object marker.

The grammatical evolution of *à* can be described in terms of a development from a rather pragmatic function (focus) to a more grammatical, syntactic function (object marking), where the latter is obligatory in basic OSV constructions. During its development *à* undergoes the following stages:

I A focused referent precedes the main clause in a copulative periphrasis with *à*; the referent is identical with the object of the main clause (O *à*, SOV).
II Reinterpretation of the copulative periphrasis as focused and topicalized object of the main clause (O *à* SV).
III Reinterpretation of the focus marker *à* as combined focus-object marker.
IV Expansion of the focus-object marker to objects in SOV and SVO constructions (SO *à* V and SVO *à*).

The syntactic status of subject and object in basic and non-basic sentences can finally be described as in Table 7.18:

TABLE 7.18 CONSTITUENT ORDER TYPES IN KHWE SENTENCES

Constituent order	Description
SV	standard in intransitive clauses and/or clauses with an elliptic object
OSV	topicalized object (partly neutral in isolated sentences, not allowed in basic sentences)
O *à* SV	topicalized object that is focus (obligatory variant in basic sentences)
SVO	emphasized subject
SVO *à*	emphasized subject with object in focus
SOV	emphasized verbal action
SO *à* V	emphasized verbal action with object in focus
"V"S (→ SV)	verbal adjective modifying the subject as its head noun, standard without objects
O"V"S (→ OSV)	verbal adjective modifying the subject as its head noun, topicalized object
"V"SO (→ SOV, SVO)	verbal adjective modifying the subject as its head noun, object not topicalized

It has been demonstrated that focus is an important concept of structuring information in Khwe. Focusing is achieved in two ways: through morphological marking and through the order of the constituents. While the order of the basic constituents always foregrounds one constituent, attributes are foregrounded by postponing. It has been discussed in detail that the use of the focus marker *à* increases the contrasting emphasis on arguments in different syntactic roles. In addition, the new-event marker focuses on the predicate and signals that it contains brand-new information. The different strategies are finally summarized in Table 7.19.

TABLE 7.19 FOCUSING STRATEGIES IN KHWE

Strategy	Semantics	Focus		
		Predicate	Argument	
			Noun	Pronoun
Basic constituent order	informational focus	SO<u>V</u>	<u>O</u>SV, <u>S</u>VO	<u>O</u>SV, <u>S</u>VO
Postposed possessor	contrast and/or emphasis	–	possessor	possessor
Postposed adjective	contrast	–	modifier of noun	–
Marking with *à*	identificational focus contrast	–	indefinite S/O	O
New-event marker	signals brand-new information	+	–	–

3.2.5 Naro

Hessel Visser

3.2.5.1 Sentences

The sentence is defined as a series of elements with a VP as the nucleus. In this chapter, we are going to look at the position of the elements in a sentence that can consist of the following elements:

AP, LP, NP (NP$_S$, NP$_O$ or NP$_{IO}$), TP, VP (which is the head of the sentence).

There is a great deal of flexibility in terms of positioning of elements in the sentence. The general structure of a basic sentence is:

(element 1) (element 2) (element 3) (element 4) (. . .)

This means effectively that there is no fixed order for VP, NP, LP and AP. When the continuous marker *ko* or the future tense marker *ga* occurs in the sentence, it is placed after the first element in the sentence, e.g. (examples are elicited):

(494)

NP$_S$	ko	NP$_O$	LP	VP
Tíí ra	*ko*	*piri ne*	*ǁ'áé koe*	*bóò.*
1SG	*ko*	goats	at.home	see

'I see goats at home.'

If a PGN-1 marker is present in the sentence, this marker is placed between the first element and *ko*:

(495)

NP$_O$	NP$_S$	ko	LP	VP
Piri ne	*ra*	*ko*	*ǁ'áé koe*	*bóò.*
goats	1SG	*ko*	at.home	see

Other PGN markers may be placed here as well, though not necessarily:

(496) a.

LP	NP$_O$	NP$_S$	ko	VP
ǁ'áé koe	*ne*	*r*	*ko*	*bóò.*

but also:

b.

LP	NP$_S$	ko	VP	NP$_O$
ǁ'áé koe	*r*	*ko*	*bóò*	*ne.*

'I see them at home.'

3.2.5.1.1 INTRANSITIVE SENTENCES

3.2.5.1.1.1 INTRANSITIVE SENTENCE STRUCTURE IN THE PRESENT TENSE

The structure of the simplest intransitive sentence in the present tense, containing a VP and an NP$_S$, is as follows:

(element 1) *ko* (element 2)

Since the elements may change position, we have two possibilities: NP$_S$ first (497a), or VP first (497b).

(497) a.

NP$_S$	ko	VP
Khóè ba	*ko*	*!õò.*
the.man	*ko*	walk

b. VP PGN-1 ko NP_S
!Õò m ko khóè ba.
walk he *ko* the.man
'The man is walking.'

Note that a PGN-1 marker is added to the sentence. It takes the position between the first element and *ko*. If the NP_S is left out, this PGN-1 marker obligatorily remains:

(498) VP PGN-1 ko
!Õò m ko.
'He is walking.'

If a further phrase is added, e.g. a locative phrase, the sentence structure is as follows:

(element 1) *ko* (element 2) (element 3)

Theoretically we have six possibilities (499a–f), illustrated for the sentence 'the man is walking home', consisting of the elements *khóè ba* 'the man', *ko* 'continuous marker', *!õò* 'walk' and *ǀ'áé koe* 'home – to':

(499) a. NP_S ko VP LP
Khóè ba ko !õò ǀ'áé koe.

b. NP_S ko LP VP
Khóè ba ko ǀ'áé koe !õò.

c. VP PGN-1 ko NP_S LP
!Õò m ko khóè ba ǀ'áé koe.

d. VP PGN-1 ko LP NP_S
!Õò m ko ǀ'áé koe khóè ba.

e. LP PGN-1 ko NP_S VP
ǀ'áé koe m ko khóè ba !õò.

f. LP PGN-1 ko VP NP_S
ǀ'áé koe m ko !õò khóè ba.

Of course, some constructions are used more readily than others. It is difficult to evaluate, but of these six, (b) and (e) are used often, while (d) is hardly acceptable and (c) and (f) are hardly ever used.

If the NP_S with accompanying PGN-1 marker is taken out, we are left with two options:

(500) a. LP PGN-1 ko VP
ǀ'áé koe m ko !õò.
home.to he *ko* walk

b. VP PGN-1 ko LP
!Õò m ko ǀ'áé koe.
walk he *ko* home.to

If two further phrases are added, e.g. a locative and an adverbial phrase, the sentence structure is as follows:

(element 1) *ko* (element 2) (element 3) (element 4)

In theory, we have 24 possibilities, of which I will mention the most acceptable ones:

(501) a.

NP$_S$	ko	AP	VP	LP
Khóè ba	*ko*	*!háése*	*!õò*	*ǁ'áé koe.*

b.

NP$_S$	ko	AP	LP	VP
Khóè ba	*ko*	*!háése*	*ǁ'áé koe*	*!õò.*

c.

LP	PGN-1	ko	NP$_S$	AP	VP
ǁ'áé koe	*m*	*ko*	*khóè ba*	*!háése*	*!õò.*

d.

AP	PGN-1	ko	NP$_S$	LP	VP
!Háése	*m*	*ko*	*khóè ba*	*ǁ'áé koe*	*!õò.*

Of all of these, (b) is the most acceptable.

In general, there is a tendency for the VP to be put toward the end of the sentence and the NP$_S$ tends to come at the beginning.

3.2.5.1.1.2 INTRANSITIVE SENTENCE STRUCTURE IN THE PAST TENSE

The usual structure of a sentence in the past tense is with the tense marker at the beginning:

(502)

tense	NP$_S$	VP
|Na	*m*	*!õò.*
PAST	he	walk

'He walked.'

It can, however, also be put at the end:

(503)

VP	NP$_S$	tense
!Õò	*m*	*|na.*
walk	he	PAST

We can in fact say that in the past tense, the tense marker functions as an "element". The PGN-1 marker is always put in second position.

3.2.5.1.2 MONOTRANSITIVE SENTENCES

3.2.5.1.2.1 MONOTRANSITIVE SENTENCE STRUCTURE IN THE PRESENT TENSE

The structure of the simplest transitive sentence in the present, with NP$_S$, NP$_O$ and VP as elements, is as follows:

(element 1) (*ko*) (element 2) (element 3)

We will exemplify the structure with *bóò* 'to see', *ko* 'continuous marker' *piri ne* 'goats' and *khóè ba* 'the man', hence: 'The man sees the goats.' The most acceptable sentence structures are:

(504) a.

NP$_S$	ko	NP$_O$	VP
Khóè ba	*ko*	*piri ne*	*bóò.*

b.

NP$_O$	PGN-7	ko	NP$_S$	VP
Piri ne	*m*	*ko*	*khóè ba*	*bóò.*

We see once more that the VP has a tendency to come at the end of the sentence. We may say that this is the default position.

If one additional phrase is added, e.g. a locative phrase, the sentence structure is still the same:

(element 1) *ko* (element 2) (element 3) (element 4)

The most acceptable structures are the following:

(505)	a.	NP$_S$	ko	NP$_O$	LP	VP	
		Khóè ba	*ko*	*piri ne*	*ǀ'áé koe*	*bóò.*	
	b.	LP	PGN-7	ko	NP$_S$	NP$_O$	VP
		ǀ'áé koe	*m*	*ko*	*khóè ba*	*piri ne*	*bóò.*
	c.	NP$_O$	PGN-7	ko	NP$_S$	LP	VP
		Piri ne	*m*	*ko*	*khóè ba*	*ǀ'áé koe*	*bóò.*
	d.	NP$_S$	ko	NP$_O$	VP	LP	
		Khóè ba	*ko*	*piri ne*	*bóò*	*ǀ'áé koe.*	
	e.	NP$_S$	ko	LP	NP$_O$	VP	
		Khóè ba	*ko*	*ǀ'áé koe*	*piri ne*	*bóò.*	

As in the previous examples, the VP is put at the end of the sentence. The NPS are put towards the beginning. NP$_S$ usually precedes NP$_o$.

If two phrases are added, e.g. a locative and an adverbial phrase, the sentence structure is as follows:

(element 1) *ko* (element 2) (element 3) (element 4) (element 5)

Here the additional elements *ǀ'áé koe* 'home – to' and *!háése* 'quickly' are used. The best options are as follows, in order of preference:

(506)	a.	*!Háése*	*m*	*ko*	*khóè ba*	*piri ne*	*ǀ'áé koe*	*bóò.*
	b.	*ǀ'áé koe*	*m*	*ko*	*khóè ba*	*piri ne*	*!háése*	*bóò.*
	c.	*Khóè ba*	*ko*	*piri ne*	*!háése*	*ǀ'áé koe*	*bóò.*	
	d.	*Piri ne*	*m*	*ko*	*khóè ba*	*!háése*	*bóò*	*ǀ'áé koe.*

The options with the LP or AP in first position score high. Again, the VP comes at or towards the end and the NP$_S$ towards the beginning. The AP and also the LP are placed close to the VP. The phrase that is in front has more emphasis.

3.2.5.1.2.2 MONOTRANSITIVE SENTENCE STRUCTURE IN THE PAST TENSE

As with intransitive sentences, the usual structure of a monotransitive sentence in the past tense is with the tense marker at the beginning:

(507) *ǀnar piri ne bóò* or: *ǀnar bóò piri ne*

Because in fact it functions as an element (that can be placed anywhere), it can also be put later in the sentence. The PGN-1 marker, however, is always placed in second position.

(508)	a.	*piri ner*	*bóò*	*ǀna*
	b.	*piri ner*	*ǀna*	*bóò*
	c.	*boor*	*ǀna*	*piri ne*

The construction *X bóòr piri ne ǀna is not accepted.

3.2.5.1.3 DITRANSITIVE SENTENCES

The structure of the simplest ditransitive sentence, with NP$_S$, NP$_O$, NP$_{IO}$ and VP as elements, is as follows:

(element 1) *ko* (element 2) (element 3) (element 4)

Contrary to the monotransitive sentence, however, the order is much more prescribed. The default order is as follows:

(509) NP$_S$ ko NP$_O$ NP$_{IO}$ VP
Khóè ba ko piri ba |óá ba máà.
'The man is giving a goat to the child.'

In the example, the elements *|óá ba* '(the) child', *máà* 'to give', *ko* 'continuous marker', *piri ba* '(the) goat', and *khóè ba* '(the) man' are used. However, the NP$_O$ can be placed after the NP$_{IO}$, with no difference in meaning. The context decides in this case which meaning is intended.

(510) NP$_S$ ko NP$_{IO}$ NP$_O$ VP
Khóè ba ko |óá ba piri ba máà.

When using PGN markers only, the order is as follows:

(511) verb NP$_{IO}$ NP$_O$ NP$_S$ ko
Máà tsi si r ko.
give you it 1SG PRES
'I give it to you.'

If the NP$_{IO}$ consists of a PGN marker only, it is placed after the verb:

(512) *ǁ'ama máá tsi si*
buy give you it
'buy it for you'

The addition of more elements is possible, but more elements will make the sentence quite long. The added elements again can take any position in the sentence, but there is a preference for the beginning or end of the sentence:

(513) a. *Khóè ba ko piri ba |óá ba máà ǁ'áé koe.*
'The man is giving a goat to the child at home.'

b. *Khóè ba ko piri ba |óá ba máà !háése.*
'The man is giving a goat to the child quickly.'

3.2.5.1.4 PASSIVE SENTENCES

Passive sentences follow the same pattern as active sentences. The agent, when present, is indicated by the postposition *ka* 'by'.

Agentless passives:

(514) *Khóè ba ko bóò-è.*
the.man PRES see-PASS
'The man is seen.'

(515) *Bóò-è tsi ko.*
see-PASS you PRES
'You are seen.'

Passives with agents:

(516) *Khóè ba ko xas ka bóò-è.*
the.man PRES her by see-PASS
'The man is seen by her.'

(517) a. *Xas ka-m ko bóò-è.*
her by-he PRES see-PASS

b. *Bóò-è-m ko xas ka.*
see-PASS-he PRES her by
'He is seen by her.'

3.2.5.1.5 AUXILIARY VERBS

In sentences with auxiliary verbs, the VP may be interrupted by other phrases:

(518) *Tsebe sa ko síí tshàan ǀài.*
Tsebe PRES AUX water fetch
'Tsebe is going to fetch water.'

In this sentence, *síí ǀài* is the AUX-verb group. The NP_O *tshàan* 'water' is placed in its centre.

3.2.5.1.6 NOMINAL PREDICATIVE SENTENCES

In a nominal sentence, the last vowel of the PGN marker is duplicated. The structure of a nominal sentence is as follows:

(element 1) (element 2) (element 3) PGN-2 V

Examples:

(519) a. *Bíì i.* 'It is milk.'

b. *Tshúù u.* 'It is bad.'

(520) a. *Tsáá tsi tíí ǀárà tsi i.*
age.mate you you COP
'You are my age mate.'

b. *Tirim ǀnàm̀-khoe me e.*
POSS friend 3SG COP
'He is my friend.'

c. *ǀ'ẽedaoka tsi !ãè tsi i.*
right you may you COP
'Maybe you are right.'

Instead of a noun (as head of NP) a peripheral element of the NP may be used:

(521) a. *ǀX'ãè tsi i.* Adjective
ugly you COP
'You are ugly.'

b. *!Noana ǀu u.* Numeral
three they COP
'They are three.'

c. *!X'ãè !au tsi i.* Noun modified by adjective
bad you COP
'You are bad mannered.'

What is indicated in (521c) is better expressed in English by something one *has* (property/quality) than by something one *is* (equation). In (522) the difference is shown by the PGN marker. Example (522a), where the qualifier is unmarked for PGN, indicates a property, while in (522b) an equation is expressed by the PGN-marked adjective.

(522) a. *T'õè !nõó me e.*
nice country he COP
'He has a nice country.'

b. *T'õè-m !nõó me e.*
nice-PGN country he COP
'It is a nice country.'

3.2.5.1.7 EXCLAMATORY NOMINAL SENTENCES

Some nominal sentences form a kind of exclamation with the structure ADJ – *ee*:

(523) *Tshúù ee!* 'How bad it is!'
!'ooa ee! 'How dry it is!'
!X'ãè ee! 'How ugly it is!'

Compare the last example in (523) with the regular nominal sentence:

(524) *!X'ãè e.* 'It is ugly.'

3.2.5.1.8 EMBEDDING OF SENTENCES

Sentences can be embedded in other parts of speech, e.g. in a NP, where it may function as an adjective. In this section, we will only look at embedded sentences that function as adjectives.

The structure of an embedded sentence is basically the same as that of an independent sentence. The only difference is made by the absence of the PGN marker corresponding to the NP that the embedded sentence refers to. The process of embedding is as follows:

1 Produce the NP with a fictitious adjective instead of the embedded sentence:

(525a) *Khóèm !ãè ba hààra.* 'The good man has arrived.'

2 Produce the sentence that you want to embed as an independent sentence:

(525b) *Mau koe-m xuua.* 'He comes from Maun.'

3 Remove the PGN marker (that agrees with the head in the corresponding noun phrase) in the sentence that is to be embedded:

(525c) *Mau koe-Ø xuua.*

4 Put this sentence instead of the fictitious adjective:

(525d) *Khóèm Mau koe xuua ba hààra.*
'The man that comes from Maun has arrived.'

Notice the difference in the examples between the non-embedded and the embedded sentences to see the absence of the PGN marker:

(525) b. *Mau koe m xuua.* 'He comes from Maun.'

d. *Khóèm Mau koe xuua ba hààra.*
'The man that comes from Maun has arrived.'

In (525d) the PGN *-m* is missing in the embedded sentence. Notice that the PGN marker following the embedded sentence is the same as the one that the fictitious adjective in the same position would have:

(525a) *Khóèm !ãè ba hààra.* 'The good man has arrived.'

3.2.5.1.8.1 OTHER CONSTRUCTIONS WITH EMBEDDED SENTENCES

Sentences can be embedded in other phrases as well, e.g. into a postpositional phrase:

(526) *dàò tsara ko ǁhoabaku koe* 'where the two paths cross'

3.2.5.1.8.2 POSITION OF THE EMBEDDED SENTENCE

The embedded sentence takes the position of the adjective either before or after the noun. The choice probably depends on the length of the embedded sentence. A shorter sentence tends to precede the noun (527a), while a longer sentence tends to be placed after the noun (527b). Thus:

(527) a. *Mau koe xuuam khóèm di |x'õea ne Daxam m.*
'The name of the man who comes from Maun is Dagam.'

but: b. *Khóèm ẽe ko !nuum koe ǁ'ãea ba kòo |xóò zi !ae.*
'The man who lives in the house was hunting gemsbok.'

3.2.5.1.8.3 RELATIVE MARKERS

If a sentence is embedded into e.g. an NP as a peripheral element, it may be connected to the head of the NP with the particle *ẽe* as a relative marker. It functions as the first element of the sentence that is followed by eventual PGN markers and *ko*, after which the other elements of the sentence are placed.

(528) a. *wèé xúùan **ẽe** |ao ko ǃnàe* 'everything that you talk about'
b. *khóèm **ẽe** ko !nuum koe ǁ'ãea ba* 'the man who lives in the house'

3.2.5.1.9 COMPARATIVES AND SUPERLATIVES

Comparatives are formed with the word *ka*, which may be translated as 'than' or 'in comparison with'. The referent with which another one is compared is followed by this *ka*. Together with the referent *ka* forms a postpositional phrase that can be used as an element in a sentence. Unlike in English, the quality being compared has no special marker (cf. *-er* in 'bigg*er*').

(529) a. *Tsáá ka m !áò me e.*
you COMP PGN-1 tall he COP
'He is tall in comparison with you.' > 'He is taller than you.'

or: b. *!Áò me e tsáá ka.*

A superlative is formally not distinguished from a comparative.

(530) *xatá wèé ta ka kaia ba*
'he big one in comparison with all of us' > 'the oldest of all of us'

3.2.5.1.10 VOCATIVE

In order to form the vocative *-è* is added to

(a) a proper name:

(531) *Thama-è!* 'Thama!'

(b) PGN-1 marker,[5] preceded by the prefix *a-*:

(532) a. *A-tse-è!* 'Hey, you!' (SG.M)
b. *A-tsao-è!* 'Hey you!' (DU.M)

(c) a NP, followed by a PGN-1 marker:[6]

(533) a. *|Hõó tse-è!* 'You white person!'
b. *ǁ'áé di tu-è!* 'You people at home!'
c. *Kx'a|nao uù-è!* 'You naughty Kg'anxao!'

3.2.5.1.11 INTERROGATIVE SENTENCES

To make a question in general, the particle *a* can be placed at the beginning of the sentence (534a) or added to the PGN marker (534b):

(534) a. ***A*** *Naro sa tsi ko kx'ui?* 'Do you speak Naro?'
b. *Naro sa tsi-**a** ko kx'ui?*

Interrogative sentences may also be formed with a series of question words. These form a closed class:

dìí 'who?'
dùú 'what?'
dùútsi 'which? what kind of?'
ndaka 'which (of a group)?'
nda 'where?'
n-|ámá 'when?'
nta (ma) 'how?'
nta koo 'how many?'

In interrogative sentences, the NP may consist merely of an interrogative word:

(535) ***Dìí*** *ba ko Xantsi koe !õò?* 'Who is going to Gantsi?'

Other interrogative sentences may have interrogative words that are locative, temporal or qualificatory in nature:

(536) a. *Tsebe sa ko* ***nda*** *!õò?* 'Where is Tsebe going?'
b. ***N-|ámá*** *tsi ga |xaa-|xaa te |aoa ne?* 'When will you teach me to shoot?'
c. ***Dùútsi*** *ǁ'aè ka tsi hààra?* 'At what time have you come?'
d. ***Ndaka****-s ǁ'aa sa tsi ko ǁ'ẽe?* 'Which flower do you want?'
e. *Hààr ga* ***nta*** *hẽé?* 'What will I come to do?'
f. *Tsaris dàra sa ko* ***nta*** *ii?* 'How was your trip/visit?'

The question word *nta ma* consists of two parts. Other elements may be placed between them:

(537) ***Nta*** *tsi* ***ma*** *!'ana?* 'How do you know?'

The particle *ma* may appear twice:

(538) ***Nta ma*** *ra ga* ***ma*** *hòò zi?* 'How will I find them?'

To indicate a question about quantity, amount, length, measure, etc. *koo* is added to the particle *nta*:

(539) a. ***Nta koo*** *se si sáàa?* 'How much have you gathered?'
b. ***Nta koo*** *se tsi kaia?* 'How tall are you?'

Another kind of question word expects a yes/no answer. With *dèè* one asks for affirmation. The answer can be positive or negative.

(540) *Tíí* ***dèè****?* '(Do you mean) me?'

With the particle *ná* one asks for confirmation. The answer is expected to be positive:

(541) *Tíí ra a* ***ná****?* 'It is me, isn't it?'

3.2.5.2 Complex sentences

Naro allows a number of possibilities for combining two or more sentences. These may structurally be divided into those without and those with a conjunction. These in turn allow for a distinction between simple juxtaposition and sentential complementation, where certain verbs require sentential complements. We will discuss the possibilities in turn.

3.2.5.2.1 CONNECTION WITHOUT CONJUNCTION

3.2.5.2.1.1 JUXTAPOSITION

Sentences may be combined by just juxtaposing them. These often involve a series of commands.

(542) *Síí séè!* 'Go (and) get!'

It is not unusual to find a sequential order reflecting the order of events:

(543) *!Õò síí tséé!*
walk go work
'Go and start working!'

When sentences are juxtaposed, it may happen that one sentence gives the background for the other one, to provide a reason for the statement that follows. No conjunction is required in these cases:

(544) *|Áḿ sa |na ǁheè, n-|ámá si ga khárà?*
'The sun has set, when will you make your bed?'

In this example, the first part of the sentence gives the background for the second part. Formally, the sentences are coordinated. Content-wise, however, the first one is subordinated to the second.

3.2.5.2.1.2 REQUESTING VERBS

In sentences expressing a wish or desire, the verb *|'ẽe* is used. If a desire is expressed in connection with an action, however, it is replaced by the verb *kx'oana*, which does not take the continuous marker *ko*. The content of the wish comes to the left of *kx'oana*, indicating a deeper SOV order:

(545) *!Õò kx'oana ra.*
go want 1SG
'I want to go.'

In sentences where a strong request is uttered, the verb *méé* 'must' is used. It usually takes second position in the sentence. Like *kx'oana*, *méé* is a defective verb. Neither takes the tense and aspect markers.

(546) a. *|Óá ba **méé**-m koa ba au te.*
'The boy must give the blanket to me.'

b. *Kúrú **méé**-r.*
'I must do it.'

Content verbs differ from requesting verbs in that they take tense and aspect markers. In sentences with a (general) request, the verb *||gàrà* is used:

(547) *Thama bar ko **||gàrà** konean !nàri.*
'I request Thama to drive cars.'

In sentences that express (absence of) knowledge, either the verb *!'ãa* 'to know' (548a) or the verb *|'úù* 'not know' (548b) is used.

(548) a. *||Nárá ner **!'ana**.* 'I know (how) to read.'
b. *||Nárá ner **|'uua**.* 'I don't know (how) to read.'

In these instances, the verb *||nárá ne* is a nominalised verb. It acts like a noun and is in fact not a combination of two sentences. In the sentence structure it takes the object position.

In a similar way, a construction with *|nàm̀* can be used to express what is liked:

(549) a. *Gãa-toe tsi **|nàm̀a**.* 'You like swimming.'
b. *Kõer **|nàm̀a**.* 'I love playing/I like to play.'

3.2.5.2.2 CONJUNCTIONS BETWEEN SENTENCES

Some conjunctions are always placed between sentences. Generally, it is possible to connect two sentences with *a*. The following changes occur:

(a) The conjunction *a* occurs between the two sentences. It takes the position of the first element in the second sentence.
(b) Elements in the two underlying sentences (like tense markers, PGN markers) that are the same are left out of the second sentence.
(c) As *a* takes the position of the first element in the dependent sentence, the subsequent elements are rearranged.

A construction with *a* may have the following functions.

Content. The second verb may give the "content" of the main verb. This is the case with verbs like 'to know', 'to forget', 'to think', 'to tell'; thus:

(550) *|'uru* ***a*** *táá ǂẽekx'am.* → 'She forgot to close.'
(she.)forget and not.close

Sequence. The construction may also indicate a "sequence":

(551) a. *Tíí ra ko tsxòà* ***a*** *ǀgùú.*
'I strike (a match) and light (the fire).'

b. *ǀNa tsi ǀx'ara* ***a*** *dùú kúrú?*
'What did you do after you had finished?'

Purpose. The construction may also indicate a "purpose":

(552) *Hàà si ga !'úú ka* ***a*** *!xáía te ǀx'aà.*
'You will come tomorrow to wash my clothes.'

Consequence. The construction may also indicate a result. The second sentence gives the consequence of the first sentence:

(553) *Dùú sa tsi ko thu tséé* ***a*** *ǀhõea.*
'What work have you done, so that you became tired?'

Reason. The first sentence may also give the reason for the second one:

(554) *Káà mari si ǀna ii* ***a*** *ko ǀgàrà te.*
'She was without money, so she asked me.'

Hendiadys. The construction with *a* may also result in a meaning that transcends the separate verb meaning. It is a sort of hendiadys:

(555) *Dùú ra ko ǀnẽe koe ǀ'óm̀* ***a*** *kúrú?*
'What is the use of sleeping here?'
[What can I do here, I even have to sleep here then!]

Specific – general. Naro may give specific information first, followed by the more general information. Consider the following example:

(556) *(Thama barko ǂgàrà konean !nari xabà)* *ǀxaa-ǀxaa te tama* ***a*** *ko ǀxuì.*
'(I request Thama to drive cars, but) he refuses[7] to teach me.'

ǀÓé, ǂnõo 'while'. A special class of sentences with *a* uses verbs like *ǀóé* 'to lie' or *ǂnõo* 'to sit'. They usually express an action that is ongoing while something else happens. The verbs *ǀóé* and *ǂnõo* have a sort of auxiliary function.

(557) a. ***ǁÓé*** *a ra ko !õò koes kóné sa punture.*
'While I was travelling, the car had a puncture.'

b. *Duutsa kxãa sa ǀao xáé* ***ǂnõo*** *a* *ko ǀhóà?*
'What news are you (sitting and) talking [about]?'

Naka. Two sentences may be connected by the word *naka*. The changes that occur are:

(a) Placed between the two sentences, *naka* takes the position of the first element in the second sentence.
(b) Elements in the two underlying sentences (like tense markers, PGN markers) that are the same are left out of the second sentence. The markers *ko* and *ga* are also removed.
(c) As *naka* takes the position of the first element in the dependent sentence, the subsequent elements are rearranged.

The action in the second sentence may be the content of the action in the first one, it may follow it, and it can be the result of it.

(558) a. *Kom tsi ar* **naka** *tsi ǁnáè tama.* Content
hear you 1SG and you sing NEG
'I don't hear you singing.'

b. *Hàà* **naka** *tee kx'áà!* Sequence
come and tea drink
'Come and drink tea!'

c. *Xaiǀara kx'ui* **naka** *kóḿ.* Result
again speak so.that hear
'Say (it) again so that (I can) hear.'

Sentences can be connected by *na* 'and'. The same rules apply as in the sentences connected by *naka*. The usual meaning is "content". The verb in the main sentence may be a content verb like 'to tell'.

(559) a. *ǀÓá zi bìrí ǀ'ee zi ko ǁgùú!*[8] ⇒
ǀÓá zi bìrí **na** *zi ǀ'ee ǁgùú!*
'Tell the girls to light the fire!'

b. *Thama ba bìrí nam ǁxaa-ǁxaa tsi!*
'Tell Thama to teach you!'

c. *Sáá méé si ǀ'eea kúrú na i tsãa.*
'You must make the fire so that it will boil.'

To introduce a contrary statement, the word *xabà* or *ixaba(xa)* 'but' may be used.

(560) *Thama ta tsi ma ǂiiè tite,* **ixabaxa** *tsi ga Tshabu ta ma ǂiiè.*
'You will not be called Thama, but you will be called Tshabu.'

3.2.5.2.2.1 SUBSEQUENT SENTENCES WITH IDENTICAL SUBJECTS

In some dependent sentences the subject is marked by a PGN-7 marker (which is otherwise used to mark a "strong article"), preceded and followed by *a*. The two together are placed at the beginning of the dependent sentence. This PGN marker is the most important signal that the two sentences play an interdependent role. It indicates that the subject in the dependent sentence is the same as the subject in the main sentence. Various meanings are possible for this type of subordination. It may be temporal, conditional, or causal.

(561) a. *Thama ba ko kx'om zi nabo,* ***a ba a*** *xam dis khóè sa máà.*
'Thama harvested the berries and gave them to his wife.'

b. *Me Thama !õò,* ***a ba a*** *síí Xantsi koe ǁ'ãè.*
'Thama went and lived in Gantsi.'

3.2.5.2.2.2 CONNECTION BY PGN-1 MARKER

Sentences may be connected by a PGN-1 marker. The dependent sentence does not contain tense or aspect markers. The construction indicates a purpose.

(562) a. *ǂIi mem hàà!* 'Call him to come!'
b. *ǀXobe ter ǂhuuseo!* 'Give it so that I can dry myself!'
c. *ǀXobe ter hòne!* 'Give it so that I can stir!'

In some sentences the subject is marked by a PGN-2 marker (which is otherwise used to mark a nominal subject). It is placed at the beginning of the dependent sentence and is the most important indication that the two sentences play an interdependent role. This PGN-2 marker also shows that the subject in the dependent sentence is different from the subject in the main sentence. Various meanings are possible for this type of sentence.

(563) a. *Thama bar ko ǂgàrà me konean !nàri ǀxaa-ǀxaa te.* Content
'I request Thama to teach me driving cars.'

b. *Xantsi koe ta ko ǀúù ii si kóné sa khõá.* Temporal
'When we were near Gantsi, the car broke down.'

3.2.5.2.2.3 CONJUNCTIONS AT THE BEGINNING OF THE DEPENDENT SENTENCE

The conjunctions in this section are not necessarily placed between two sentences. They may also occur at the beginning of the sentence.

(564) a. *ǀnẽe* 'if': *ǀnẽe ǀgòm̀m ko ne . . .* 'if he agrees . . .'
b. *ẽe* 'when': *ẽem ko kóm̀ẽ̀ . . .* 'when he heard . . .'

Dependent sentences with *ká* indicate the reason for what is done in the main sentence. While *ká* is used at the beginning of the sentence that gives the reason, *khama* and *domka* are placed at the end of the dependent sentence (see also 3.2.5.2.2.4 below).

(565) a. *Si xas dim ǀóá ba Thama ta ma ǁii*
***ká** xas dim ǀõò ba Thama me e **domka**.*
'She called her son Thama because her father was Thama.'

b. ***Ká** xas dim ǀõò ba Thama me e **domkas***
xas dim ǀóá ba Thama ta ma ǁii.
'Because her father was Thama, she called her son Thama.'

c. *Me !aro, **ká** Buxu sa ǀxóà ǀxae mea **khama**.*
'He ran because Bugu was angry with him.'

3.2.5.2.2.4 CONJUNCTIONS AT THE END OF THE DEPENDENT SENTENCE

Several conjunctions are placed at the end of the dependent sentence. This dependent sentence can occur in either first or second position. If it appears in second position (which means that the conjunction comes at the end of the sentence), no changes occur compared with the underlying sentences. If it occurs in first position (so that the conjunction comes between the sentences), the elements in the second sentence are rearranged, as the conjunction is considered to be the first element.

A dependent sentence ending in *khama* 'like, because' indicates the reason for what is mentioned in the main sentence.

(566) a. *!Ãè-ǂaorko ǀna si ka̲bise **khama**.*
'I am happy because (that) you came back.'

or: b. *ǀNa si ka̲bise **khamar** ko !ãè-ǂao.*
'You came back, that's why I am happy.'

A dependent sentence ending in *domka* 'for, because' indicates the reason for what is mentioned in the main sentence.

(567) a. *!Ãè-ǂaorko ǀna tsi hàà **domka**.*
'I am happy because you came.'

or: b. *!Na tsi hàà **domkar** ko !ãè-ǂao.*
'You came, that's why I am happy.'

The conjunction *ke* only occurs with imperatives. The dependent sentence with *ke* gives the reason for the action to be taken.

(568) a. *Xuu te, tsàar ko **ke**!* 'Leave me, (because) I am sick!'
or: b. *Tsàar ko **ke** xuu te!* 'I am sick, (so) leave me!'

The conjunction *ka* indicates purpose or a temporal meaning.

(569) a. *|Nẽes ǂ'õo sar |na ǁ'ama máá khaoa ǂ'õó khao ga **ka**.* Purpose
'I have bought this food for you so that you can eat.'

b. *Thama ba kò 49 kuri ii Xantsi koem ko toe **ka**.* Temporal
'Thama was 49 years old when he moved to Gantsi.'

The content of the main verb in the main sentence may be indicated in a coordinate sentence which ends in the word *sa*. This happens, for example, with verbs like 'to know', 'to forget', 'to think'.

(570) a. *!'ana ra, |nẽes hìi sa ǁ'ooa **sa**.*
'I know that this tree is dead.'

b. *|Nẽes hìi **sa** ǁ'ooa sar !'ana.*
'That this tree is dead I know.'

It appears as if this *sa* is the same word as the PGN marker for 3SG.F. In fact, the dependent sentence as a whole can be considered to be the object of the main verb. Compare the difference between:

(571) a. *|'urua tsia ǁxuka **sa**.* 'Have you forgotten Xguka?'
b. *|'urua tsia ǁxuka si i **sa**.* 'Have you forgotten that it is Xguka?'

Sentences can be connected by the conditional ('if') or temporal ('when') particle *ne*. In a conditional sentence the verb often takes the word *kò*.

(572) a. *!Ãè-ǂaor ko hàà si **ko ne**.*
'I am happy if/when you come.'

or: b. *Hàà si **ko ner** ko !ãè-ǂaor.*
'If/when you come, I am happy.'

3.2.5.2.3 DIRECT AND INDIRECT SPEECH

In Naro, there are direct quotes and indirect speech. Both are usually introduced with the word *(a)máá*, and mostly concluded by the word *témé* (which can be seen as a contraction of *ta méé*).

(573) *Ke méé si **máá**: "Xam dir !õè ra a," **témé**.*
'So you must say: "I am his sister".'

A comparable construction is used for the contents of thoughts. Instead of *témé*, *ta ǂ'ẽea* is used:

(574) *|Nẽetam ko ma ǂ'ẽea: "Msem ga ǁxóà |xae te," **ta ǂ'ẽea**.*
'He thought: "Maybe he is angry with me".'

3.2.5.2.4 MORE COMPLEX SENTENCES

It is possible to have several levels of dependent sentences in one sentence. For instance, a sentence can be subordinate to another sentence while the two together may again be subordinate to yet a third sentence.

(575) *ǂ'ẽe tsi ko !ãè e !nuum ga |nẽe koe tshàoè sa?*
'Do you think it is possible to build a house here?'

It might be expected that the nominal sentence would end in *sa*, but it does not, apparently because it is not necessary to put *sa* in the sentence twice. The *sa* (indicating content of both the "thinking" and the nominal sentence) is placed at the end of the two dependent sentences.

(576) *Hàà nar síí |nẽes xúù* **sa** *tòó nam xabá táá bóò si.*
'Let me go and put this away so that he cannot see it.'

3.2.6 ǁGana subgroup: |Gui

Hirosi Nakagawa

3.2.6.1 Introduction

The syntax of ǁGana subgroup languages is virtually non-described. Syntactic features have sporadically been recorded in the literature (e.g. Güldemann and Vossen 2000, Köhler 1962, Silberbauer 1981, and Vossen 1997a). This section describes selected aspects of |Gui syntax. It is based on the author's field notes on the Xade dialect.

3.2.6.2 Simple sentences

Like other Khoe languages (Güldemann and Vossen 2000: 117), dominant word order of simple sentences is SOV. It shows a wide range of variation. There are five other possibilities: SVO, OSV, VSO, OVS and VOS, which are all accepted as well-formed, although OSV is more common than the other four.

In order to better understand the variability of word order of simple sentences it is essential to consider the position of auxiliaries (AUX) for tense–aspect, which usually occur in simple sentences and concern the constraint of word order variation. If AUX is taken into account, dominant word order is S-AUX-O-V, as illustrated in (577).

(577)		S	AUX		O	V
	Kʰóè	*bì*	*qχ'ó*	*Júù*	*mà*	*múũ̀.*
	person	3M.SG.NOM	PAST.REM	eland	3M.SG.ACC	see

'The man saw a male eland.'

TABLE 7.20 WORD ORDER VARIATION IN |GUI IN TERMS OF S, O, V AND AUX

*AUX–S–O–V *AUX–S–V–O	S–AUX–O–V S–AUX–V–O	S–O–AUX–V S–V–AUX–O	S–O–V–AUX S–V–O–AUX
*AUX–O–S–V *AUX–V–S–O	*O–AUX–S–V *V–AUX–S–O	O–S–AUX–V V–S–AUX–O	O–S–V–AUX V–S–O–AUX
*AUX–O–V–S *AUX–V–O–S	*O–AUX–V–S *V–AUX–O–S	*O–V–AUX–S *V–O–AUX–S	O–V–S–AUX V–O–S–AUX

Note: The varieties marked with * are judged as ill-formed.

A test using sentences like (577) and its potential alternatives reveals a constraint on word order variation which is presented in Table 7.20 above. Note that all ill-formed orders have AUX to the left of the subject. This constraint applies to sentences with different element combinations, such as S–AUX–V, S–AUX–LOC–V and S–AUX–O–O–V.

As becomes clear from (577), the so-called PGN morphemes mark the morphosyntactic category of case of the relevant noun. Note that the two PGN morphemes *bì* and *mà*, both representing 3M.SG, indicate different cases, namely the nominative of S and the accusative of O. In addition to nominative and accusative, ǀGui has genitive case, as will be seen later. Case is implied not only in PGN morphemes but also in personal pronouns (cf., for instance, *cìrè* 'I', *cá* 'me', *cí* 'my'), and it forms the background of word order variation. My preliminary investigation shows that ǁGana, too, has nominal case marking and exhibits a considerable degree of variation.

3.2.6.3 Noun phrase and adpositional phrases

Dominant word order within a noun phrase (NP) is head-final, i.e., the noun head occurs in final position, as illustrated in (578). Modifiers and demonstratives agree with their head noun in terms of person, gender and number. In (578), the PGN morpheme *m̀* agrees with the nominal PGN *mà* (for 3M.SG). Modifier and demonstrative occur in the genitive case within the NP, and the case of the head noun is indicated by the PGN morpheme which follows it.

(578) *ŋǀì* *m̀* *ŋǂúú* *m̀* *dzérá* *mà*
DEM.NEAR 3M.SG.GEN black 3M.SG.GEN bird 3M.SG.ACC
'this black bird'

Regarding possessive expressions, Güldemann and Vossen (2000: 115) state that two types of pronominal possessive constructions are possible in Khoe: (i) "juxtaposition of a personal pronoun and a referential noun" and (ii) "use of the associative particle" or "another morpheme of the same function". ǀGui has both types, as exemplified in (579) and (580).

(579) *ʔésì* *màā*
PRON.3F.SG.GEN head
'her head' (inalienable possession)

(580) *ʔésì* *kà* *ŋ!úū* *mà*
PRON.3F.SG.GEN POSTP hut 3M.SG.ACC
'her hut' (alienable possession)

Example (579) illustrates the juxtaposition type, in which the pronoun occurs in the genitive case. In the other type shown in (580), the pronoun is also in the genitive case and is followed by the postposition *kà*, which functions as associative. In both examples the head noun appears in final position, i.e., the phrase has the possessor–possessee word order.

Note that the head noun does not have a PGN marker in (579). In this construction only the nominative case is marked with a morpheme *è*, other cases are not marked. The semantic distinction between the two types involves alienability: juxtaposition is used typically for inalienable possession, while the associative construction indicates alienable possession. In order to convey the meaning of 'my head aches', for instance, (581a) is grammatically correct, whereas (581b) is ill-formed because "my head" implies inalienable possession.

(581) a. *Cí* *màā* *è* *cʰúű̀.*
PRON.1SG.GEN head (NOM) ache
'my head aches'

b. *Cí kà màā sì cʰúű̀.
PRON.1SG.GEN ASS head 3F.SG.NOM ache

In (579)–(581) the possessors are all pronouns. If possessors are nouns, the constructions are basically the same, as illustrated in (582) and (583). Note that possessor nouns do not agree grammatically with possessee nouns in these constructions.

(582) *kʰóè* *m̀* *màā* *(è)*
person 3M.SG.GEN head (NOM)
'the man's head' (inalienable possession)

(583) *kʰóè* *sì* *kà* *ŋ!úū* *mà*
person 3F.SG.GEN ASS hut 3M.SG.ACC
'the woman's hut' (alienable possession)

All the attested adpositions in ǀGui are postpositional. (There is one locative morpheme, though, which behaves like a preposition.) The basic structure of the postpositional phrase is illustrated in (584). Postpositions are case-governing elements in ǀGui. Note that the PGN morpheme suffixed to the noun is in the genitive case before the postposition. All primary postpositions listed in Table 7.21 govern the genitive case.

(584) *ŋ!úū* *m̀* *wà*
hut 3M.SG.GEN POSTP
'in a hut'

TABLE 7.21 ǀGUI POSTPOSITIONS

Postposition	Gloss
kà	'at, in, on, with', etc.
dá	'to, toward, for'
wà	'in'
ǀχàè	'on'
ǀχòà	'with'
kʰùà	'as'
kʰùnà	'as'
cʰá	'like'
cʰānā	'like'
cà	quotative, mimesis marker

3.2.6.4 Coordination

ǀGui has a coordinating conjunction *á*[9] which can roughly be translated as 'and'. This conjunction is used for clausal and not for phrasal coordination. As illustrated in (585), *á* occurs between the subject and the auxiliary of the second clause. If subject and/or auxiliary in the second clause are the same as those in the first clause, then they are omitted obligatorily in the second clause, as exemplified in (586a–b).

(585) *Qχ'áòkò bì c^{h}ú ǀʔáékú gǀàēkò sì á kì ǀʔóó.*
husband 3M.SG.NOM PAST return woman 3F.SG.NOM CONJ PAST die
'The husband returned home yesterday, and the wife died today.'

(586) a. *Qχ'áòkò bì c^{h}ú ǀʔáékú á kì ǀʔóó.*
husband 3M.SG.NOM PAST return CONJ PAST die.
'The husband returned home yesterday and died today.'

b. *Qχ'áòkò bì c^{h}ú ǀʔáékú á ǀʔóó.*
husband 3M.SG.NOM PAST return CONJ die
'The husband returned home and died yesterday.'

3.2.6.5 Subordination

3.2.6.5.1 COMPLEMENT CLAUSE

A complement clause is illustrated in (587), in which the embedded clause in [ ] functions as the complement (i.e. object) of the main clause. The embedded complement clause is nominalized by means of the feminine singular PGN marker *sà*, which denotes the accusative case for the object of the main clause. Note that the subject in the complement clause is in the genitive case.

(587) *Cìrè kì [k^{h}óè m̀ c^{h}ú àà sà] kúḿ.*
1SG.NOM PAST person 3M.SG.GEN PAST come 3F.SG.ACC hear
'I heard today that the man came yesterday.'

3.2.6.5.2 RELATIVE CLAUSE

Another type of subordinating clause is the relative clause. There are two types of relative constructions in ǀGui. They differ in word order: one involves the pre-nominal and the other one the post-nominal relative clause.

The pre-nominal relative clause is illustrated in (588). The subject in the relative clause is in the genitive case, which is marked by the PGN morpheme. The PGN marker occurring in clause-final position grammatically agrees with the head noun, and the PGN formative attached to the head noun marks the case of this noun phrase.

(588) *[k^{h}óè m̀ qx'ó múũ̀ m̀] dzérá mà*
person 3M.SG.GEN PAST.REM see 3M.SG.GEN bird 3M.SG.ACC
'the bird which the man saw'

The construction with the post-nominal relative clause involves the postposition *kà* as a relativizer, as illustrated in (589). The subject of the relative clause occurs in the genitive case marked by the PGN *m̀*, and the case of this noun phrase is marked by the PGN suffix in phrase-final position.

(589) *dzérá kà [k^{h}óè m̀ qx'ó múũ̀ mà]*
bird POSTP.REL person 3M.SG.GEN PAST.REM see 3M.SG.ACC
'the bird which the man saw'

3.2.6.5.3 ADVERBIAL CLAUSE

Adverbial clauses are formed basically by means of postpositions, such as *kà* (multi-functional: time, conditional, reason, purpose, etc.) and *k^{h}ùnà* (manner), occurring in clause-final position. The subject of the adverbial clause is in the genitive case, like that of complement and relative clauses. An adverbial clause usually occurs before the main clause. Example (590) contains an adverbial clause of manner, as indicated by the postposition *kʰùnà*.

(590)

ʘǃámī	*m̀*	*cì*	*!úũ̀*	*kʰùnà*	*ʔàbì*	*cì*	*!úũ̀.*
pangolin	3M.SG.GEN	HAB	walk	POSTP	3M.SG.NOM	HAB	walk

'He walks like a pangolin walks.'

3.2.6.6 Negation

Standard negation is expressed by means of particles. There are two main negative particles, *cúá* and *cʰēmā*.

(591)

ʔàbì	*cʰú*	*cúá*	*χáńtsì*	*sì*	*dá*	*!úũ̀.*
3M.SG.NOM	PAST	NEG	Ghanzi	3F.SG.GEN	POSTP	go

'He did not go to Ghanzi yesterday.'

The negative particle *cúá* typically follows immediately S–AUX, as shown in (591), but it can also occur sentence-initially and immediately before the verb.

The negative particle *cʰēmā* negates either an entire clause (like *cúá*) or a particular clause constituent. The former instance is illustrated in (592) and the latter in (593).

(592)

ʔàbì	*cʰú*	*χáńtsì*	*sì*	*dá*	*!úũ̀*	*cʰēmā.*
3M.SG.NOM	PAST	Ghanzi	3F.SG.GEN	POSTP	go	NEG

'He did not go to Ghanzi yesterday.'

(593)

ʔàbì	*cʰú*	*xám̄*	*m̀*	*cʰēmā*	*mà*	*múũ̀.*
3M.SG.NOM	PAST	lion	3M.SG.GEN	NEG	3M.SG.ACC	see

'He saw no male lion yesterday.'

In addition to *cúá* and *cʰēmā*, there are other negative particles such as *céè* (always occurring immediately after the verb), *cīī* (used for negative commands), etc.

3.2.6.7 Interrogative sentences

3.2.6.7.1 YES/NO QUESTIONS

Yes/no questions are formed by means of a question marker *m̀* which always occurs immediately after the subject, as exemplified in (594). When this question marker occurs, the subject noun phrase is in the genitive case.

(594)

Kéèxà	*m̀*	*m̀*	*cʰú*	*tsá*	*ɟírā.*
Keexa	3M.SG.GEN	Q	PAST	2M.SG.ACC	visit

'Did Keexa visit you yesterday?'

3.2.6.7.2 QUESTION-WORD QUESTIONS

Question-word questions, so-called wh-questions, are formed by means of simple or complex question words. There are two simple question words, *ìīxò*[10] 'what' and *máā̃*[11] 'how, which', and various complex question words that are combinations of simple question words and other elements such as postpositions, nouns, etc. Some complex question words are synchronically not analysable. In (595) the simple question word *ìīxò* is used as the object of the sentence. In general, question words can optionally occur in sentence-initial position, as in (596).

(595) *Kʰóè bì kì ĩĩxò sà ts'áũ̄*
person 3M.SG.NOM PAST what 3F.SG.ACC do
'What did the man do today?'

(596) *Máã̄ kámā ʔàbì qx'āwā àà.*
which time 3M.SG.NOM FUT.REM come
'When will he come?'

3.2.6.8 Other important constructions

3.2.6.8.1 NOMINAL PREDICATE

Equation is expressed by mere juxtaposition of two noun phrases. In this construction, the subject (i.e. the first NP) is in the nominative and the predicate (the second NP) is unmarked for case, as shown in (597).

(597) *ʔàbì kééxà.*
3M.SG.NOM Keexa
'He is Keexa.'

In addition to this common construction, there are two other equation and identification constructions.

The first construction is formed with the copula *ʔà* in sentence-final position, cf. (598). The subject is always a demonstrative pronoun and the nominal predicate occurs in the accusative case.

(598) *ʔáā kééxà mà ʔà.*
DEM Keexa 3M.SG.ACC COP
'That is Keexa.'

The other construction consists of a single NP with an identification clitic. Examples (599a–c) illustrate this peculiar construction. The noun appears in the nominative case and is followed by the identification "copula" *ʔí* in declarative sentences (599a), or it occurs in the genitive case and is followed by the question clitic *má* in interrogative sentences (599b). This construction may contain a tense–aspect auxiliary in final position, as exemplified in (599c).

(599) a. *Dzérá bì ʔí.*
bird 3M.SG.NOM DECL
'(It) is a bird.'

b. *Dzérá m̀ má?*
bird 3M.SG.GEN INT
'Is (it) a bird?'

c. *Ŋ!úū bì ʔí qx'ó.*
hut 3M.SG.NOM DECL PAST.REM
'(It) was a hut.'

It should be noted that this construction is not the "existential" construction, which consists of a subject and an existential verb, as illustrated in (600).

(600) *Dzérá bì háã̄.*
bird 3M.SG.NOM exist
'There is a bird.'

3.2.6.8.2 COMPOUND VERB CONSTRUCTION

Compounds consisting of two verbs exhibit a peculiar syntactic behaviour, namely the leftward movement of the first component.

As shown in (601a), the basic structure of the compound verb consists of two joined verbs. The first component can be dislocated and moved to the left of the second component across several constituents, as demonstrated in (601b–d). (Note that the first component, *g|ájã*, is bold-faced throughout.)

(601)	a.	*ʔàrì*	*qx'ó*	*g|úī*	*sì*	*wà*	***g‖ájã**-|ʔóó.*
		3C.PL.NOM	PAST.REM	bush	3F.SG.GEN	POSTP	constipate-die

'They were constipated to death in the bush.'

b.	*ʔàrì*	*qx'ó*	***g‖ájã***	*g|úī*	*sì*	*wà*	*|ʔóó.*
c.	*ʔàrì*	***g‖ájã***	*qx'ó*	*g|úī*	*sì*	*wà*	*|ʔóó.*
d.	***G‖ájã***	*ʔàrì*	*qx'ó*	*g|úī*	*sì*	*wà*	*|ʔóó.*

3.2.6.8.3 "FOCUS" CONSTRUCTION

|Gui has a construction in which a particular constituent is marked by the clitic *kí* for a certain pragmatic function that requires future research; I provisionally call it "focus" here. Example (602a) is a sentence without focus marking. In order to mark a constituent for focus, the clitic *kí* must be placed after the noun stem of the focused constituent. (602b–d) show that various constituents can be focused. Note that a clause cannot have more than one focused constituent.

(602)	a.	*Qχ'ārū*	*bì*	*cì*	*ŋ!àbī*	*m̀*	*kà*	*kʰóò*	*sà*	*|qàè.*
		Kx'aru	3M.SG. NOM	PROG	chisel	3M.SG. GEN	POSTP	fur	3F.SG. ACC	scrape

'Kx'aru is scraping fur with a chisel.'

b.	*Qχ'ārū*	*kí*	*bì*	*cì*	*ŋ!àbī*	*m̀*	*kà*	*kʰóò*	*sà*	*|qàè.*
	Kx'aru	FOC	3M.SG. NOM	PROG	chisel	3M.SG. GEN	POSTP	fur	3F.SG. ACC	scrape

'It is Kx'aru who is scraping fur with a chisel.'

c.	*Qχ'ārū*	*bì*	*cì*	*ŋ!àbī*	*kí*	*m̀*	*kà*	*kʰóò*	*sà*	*|qàè.*
	Kx'aru	3M.SG. NOM	PROG	chisel	FOC	3M.SG. GEN	POSTP	fur	3F.SG. ACC	scrape

'It is with a chisel that Kx'aru is scraping fur.'

d.	*Qχ'ārū*	*bì*	*cì*	*ŋ!àbī*	*m̀*	*kà*	*kʰóò*	*kí*	*sà*	*|qàè.*
	Kx'aru	3M.SG. NOM	PROG	chisel	3M.SG. GEN	POSTP	fur	FOC	3F.SG. ACC	scrape

'It is fur that Kx'aru is scraping with a chisel.'

3.2.6.8.4 COMPLEX PREDICATIVE ADJECTIVE

|Gui has yet another uncommon co nstruction involving the predicative adjective with locative information. Example (603) illustrates its structure: the morpheme *à* links a noun to an adjective. It is labelled as LINK here:

(603)	*ʔàbì*	*!áĩ̀*	*jà*	*ǂáó.*
	he	good	LINK	heart

'He is good in the heart.' (= 'He is happy.')

It is worth noting that the noun following *jà* (which is an allomorph of *à*, cf. note 9) is always part of the body of the subject. Thus, 'heart' in the example forms part of the subject 'he'. The semantic effect of this construction should be: adjective-noun-ed (e.g. good-hearted, big-eyed, etc.).

At first sight, *à* would seem to be a preposition, but this element occurs only in this construction, unlike other adpositions (i.e. postpositions) that are used in various contexts. Probably *jà* is a linker which incorporates a noun into a complex adjective.

3.2.7 Shua subgroup

Rainer Vossen

As has already been pointed out in Chapter 6, information on Shua languages is very scarce; therefore, the following notes are limited in size and must be taken as provisional.

3.2.7.1 Word order

The basic order of chief constituents appears to be SOV. By far the majority of examples represent this sequence structure.

(604) a. Cara *Khóé-nà ké kàí |gùì.*
person-C.PL PRES house thatch
'The people are thatching the/a house.'

b. Deti *'ábá ce |'óã k'òò.*
dog PRES bone eat
'The/a dog is eating/eats the/a bone.'

In (604) the object is placed between the tense/aspect morpheme and the verb and is not marked morphologically.

Occasionally, the subject occurs sentence-initially and the object follows the verb, hence SVO (605a–b). In (605c) the object occurs sentence-initially and is followed by the subject and the verb; however, this word order type (OSV) is quite exceptional in my data.

(605) a. Cara *A tsá ké múũ-re ìí k'áḿ-|ge?*
Q 2M.SG PRES see-INT DEM animal
'Do you see this animal?'

b. Danisi *Tsá ké mûũ-rè |ábá tí dì?*
2M.SG PRES see-INT hat 1SG POSS
'Do you see my hat?'

c. Deti *K'òò-xú tá k'òò-á-hà.*
meat 1SG eat-JUNC-IMPERF
'I ate meat.'

Although (605a–b) are interrogative sentences, SVO order does not seem to be restricted to questions.

The two examples from Danisi in (606) illustrate singular instances of VOS (a) and VSO (b) word order:

(606) a. *Mûũ ke tsá 'à tá.*
see PRES 2M.SG OBJ 1SG
'I see you.'

b. *Mûũ ke tsá tá 'à.*
see PRES 2M.SG 1SG OBJ
'You see me.'

Concerning the positioning of adverbials there would seem to be no restrictions. See the following examples of locatives in Cara (607) and Deti (608):

(607) a. *Má-n ǀxòà tsá* ***'áé kà*** *ǁ'àé-kù-à-tá?*
who-C.PL POSTP 2M.SG home POSTP meet-REC-JUNC-PAST.RECT
'Whom did you meet **at the village**?'

b. *ǁGàà-khóé ke* ***gùnu 'ò*** *'á táo.*
female-person PRES mortar POSTP OBJ grind
'The woman is grinding **in the mortar**.'

(608) a. *Káú cè tá* ***'áé kà.***
remain PRES 1SG home POSTP
'I must remain **at home**.'

b. *ǀÁba tí dì* ***'áe kà*** *hàà.*
hat 1SG POSS home POSTP be
'My hat is **at home**.'

c. ***ǁXóḿ 'o*** *hùú-mà kùũ-à-ha.*
river POSTP DEM-M.SG go-JUNC-IMPERF
'He (lit.: that one) has gone **to the river**.'

In three of the five examples above, i.e. (607a–b) and (608b), the adverbial occurs in pre-final position, immediately preceding the verb and always following the subject. In contrast to this, (608a) and (608c) represent cases of sentence-final and sentence-initial positioning, respectively. In the latter example, however, the adverbial is clearly topicalized. Altogether, the five examples illustrate five different word order types: O–S–ADV–V (607a), S–AUX–ADV–V (607b), V–AUX–S–ADV (608a), S–ADV–V (608b), and ADV–S–V (608c).

A partly different picture obtains for temporal adverbials in the examples in (609) for Cara and (610) for Deti:

(609) a. *A* ***'úíka*** *tsá tí ǀõã-ǁgàé múũ-á-hà rè?*
Q yesterday 2M.SG 1SG child-female see-JUNC-IMPERF INT
'Did you see my daughter **yesterday**?'

b. *A tsá* ***'úíka*** *súrì xúń-á-hà rè?*
Q 2M.SG yesterday tobacco grind-JUNC-IMPERF INT
'Did you grind the tobacco **yesterday**?'

c. ***'Ókuri*** *tá 'aká súrì thíyá gòm̀-à-tá.*
last.year 1SG EMPH tobacco much smoke-JUNC-PAST
'**Last year** I smoked a lot of tobacco.'

d. *Tá kùà* ***'úwá*** *'áíyá-khòè sĩĩ-a-ma.*
1SG FUT tomorrow chief work-JUNC-DAT
'I shall work for the chief **tomorrow**.'

(610) *Hùú-nà cé* ***'ùúa*** *ǁnáì.*
DEM-C.PL PRES morning sing
'They (lit.: those ones) sing **in the morning**.'

In (609a) and (609c) the adverbial is placed sentence-initially, followed by the chief constituents in SOV order. The preceding question marker in (609a) is obligatory (see 3.2.7.2.2 below) and does not impact otherwise on the sentence structure. In the remaining examples the temporal adverbial follows the subject and precedes the object (if applicable) and verb; thus: S–(AUX–)ADV–(O–)V.

3.2.7.2 Simple sentences

3.2.7.2.1 DECLARATIVES

Some general examples have already been given in (604), (605c) and (606). The examples in (611) illustrate copulative constructions.

(611) a. Cara *Ìí tí ǀ'on* ***'è.***
DEM 1SG name COP
'This is my name.'

b. *Tá Cárákhòè* ***'è.***
1SG Cara.person COP
'I am Carakhoe.'

c. *Tá ʃúákhòè* ***m̀.***
1SG Shua.person COP.NEG
'I am not Shuakhoe.'

d. *Jé ǀara gùrí* ***'ì.***
1M.PL field large COP
'Our field is large.'

e. Danisi *Ĩ́ĩ tí dòŋgí* ***'è.***
DEM 1SG donkey COP
'This is my donkey.'

f. Deti *Híĩ k'áá-khoe* ***rù.***
DEM male-person COP
'This is a man.'

g. *'àbàmá Dètí* ***rò.***
my.father Deti COP
'My father is Deti.'

They show that the affirmative copula is *'è* in Cara and Danisi; in (611d) it has been assimilated to the final vowel of the preceding adjective. The variation between *rò* and *rù* in Deti is likely to be due to idiolectal speech. (611c) shows the use of the negative copula *m̀* in Cara.

In the following sentence from Cara a paraphrastic 'have'-construction is contained. Note that *hàã* 'exist' is a defective verb:

(612) *ǀÚm-khoe thíyá bee* ***ǀxoa*** ***hàã.***
chief many cattle POSTP ('with') exist
'The chief has many cattle.'

3.2.7.2.2 QUESTIONS

Since wh-questions have already been touched upon in connection with interrogatives in Chapter 6, section 3.2.7.7, the present section will exclusively be devoted to yes/no questions. In Cara these tend to begin, as a rule, with the question marker *à* and end with the interrogative particle *rè*, as in (613).

(613) a. ***À*** *ùú-mà* *tsá* *cahú* ***rè****?*
Q DEM-3M.SG 2M.SG brother INT
'Is that (one) your brother?'

b. ***À*** *ìí* *màà* *tí* *di* ***ri****?*
Q DEM head 1SG POSS INT
'Is this head mine?'

c. ***À*** *tsá* *ke* *dànì* *ǀóã* *'úũ-re-a-má* ***rè****?*
Q 2M.SG PRES honey child collect-JUNC-JUNC-DAT INT
'Are you collecting honey for your children?'

Note that in (613a–b) the interrogative particle would seem to imply copulative function. The form *rì* in (613b) has undergone progressive assimilation to the final vowel of the preceding possessive marker; cf. (611d).

In the following examples, the interrogative particle occurs sentence-medially. While in (614a) it follows the verb immediately, it is separated from the verb by the tense/aspect marker in (614b). The two versions are said to be interchangeable.

(614) a. ***À*** *tsá* *ke* *kóḿ* ***rè*** *tí* *ǀ'on?*
Q 2M.SG PRES hear INT 1SG name

b. ***À*** *kóḿ* *ke* ***re*** *tsa* *tí* *ǀ'on?*
Q hear PRES INT 2M.SG 1SG name
'Do you hear my name?'

Double occurrence of the interrogative particle is observed in (615). The fact that it shows up after *both* predicative adjectives may be further evidence for the assumption of the particle's inherent copulative function (see above).

(615) ***À*** *tsá* *ǀáó-á-ha* *ǀáò* *gùrí* ***rè*** *re* *cúĩ* ***rè****?*
Q 2M.SG shoot-JUNC-IMPERF buffalo big INT CONJ small INT
'Was the buffalo (that) you shot big or small?'

My field notes on Danisi confirm the description for Cara except that medial occurrence of the interrogative particle *rè* is confined to positioning right after the verb, as in (616) and (609b) above.

(616) *Tsá* *'à-ná-hà* ***rè*** *tí* *bà.*
2M.SG know-JUNC-PAST INT 1SG father
'Do you know my father?'

In Deti, sentence-final occurrence of the interrogative particle is the most common pattern:

(617) a. *Tsá* *'úikà* *tá* *gáó-tè-hà* ***re****?*
2M.SG yesterday 1SG see-1SG.OBJ$_{AGR}$-IMPERF INT
'Did you see me yesterday?'

b. *ǀÓã* *kukùrì* *cè* *bátsà* *k'áà* ***re****?*
child all (= PL) PRES beer drink INT
'Do children drink beer?'

The implicit copulative function of the interrogative particle becomes obvious in (618), especially when comparing the question in (618b) with the declarative sentence in (618c) where the interrogative *rè* in (b) takes exactly the position of the copula *rò* in (c).

(618) a. *Tsá Muhura* ***re?***
2M.SG Hura INT
'Are you (a) Hura (person)?'

b. *Xáò káik'i* ***rè?***
hippo big INT
'Is a hippo big?'

c. *Xáò káik'i rò.*
hippo big COP
'A hippo is big.'

3.2.7.2.3 IMPERATIVES

As a rule, simple imperatives consist of the verb stem only in the singular and plural (619a). A second person plural pronoun may be used after the verb stem in order to emphasize plurality, as in (619b).

(619) a. Cara *ǀNáì!* 'Sing!' (SG and PL)
b. Deti *ǀGáí!* 'Run!' (SG) *ǀGáí! tò!* 'Run!' (PL)
run 2C.PL:OBJ

The same applies to imperative sentences with complements, e.g. Cara:

(620) a. *Tsàã ǀnóá!* (SG/PL) 'Cook soup!'
soup cook

b. *Tí ǀxóá hàá!*(SG/PL) 'Come with me!'
1SG POSTP come

c. *Súri 'úú cáá-khoe-kùà ǀ'ĩĩ!*
tobacco give old-person-M.PL POSTP
'Give (SG/PL) tobacco to the elders!'

Negative imperatives are formed by placing the particle *tí* after the verb stem, cf. Deti:

(621) SG *ǀNáì* ***tí!*** 'Don't sing!'
PL *ǀNáì!* ***tí*** *tò!* 'Don't sing!'

3.2.7.3 Complex sentences

3.2.7.3.1 COORDINATION AND SUBORDINATION

Generally speaking, it seems difficult to draw a dividing line between coordination and subordination on the basis of the available data. In most cases, coordinate clauses are not linked by conjunctions but occur in juxtaposition, as in the Cara examples below:

(622) *K'áá-khoe ké 'é.ku ǀõã ǀxòà gùnì 'ó kûũ, ǀgaa-khóé*
male-person PRES 3M.PL child POSTP hunt POSTP go female-person
'The men go hunting with their sons (and) the women

kúk'ari ké 'é.dzi ǀôã ǀxòà 'úũ-re 'ò kûũ.
all (= PL) PRES 3F.PL child POSTP gather-JUNC POSTP go
go gathering with their daughters.'

(623) *Tí ǀàbò k'òá 'è, tí kũĩ-k'ái ǀàbò ǀnáó-ha.*
1SG sandal new COP 1SG sister sandal be.old-IMPERF
'My sandals are new, (but) my sister's sandals are old.'

The sentence in (624) has a subordinate structure in English but is coordinate in Cara:

(624) *'é.mà kúũ-á-ha tóã-m ǀxòà k'òò-hú 'úika,*
3M.SG go-JUNC-IMPERF friend-M.SG POSTP meat yesterday
'Yesterday he went out with a friend (to)

'è.m 'ùũ-á-ha.e 'áé kúũ-á-ha.
3M.SG kill-JUNC-IMPERF home go-JUNC-IMPERF
carry the hunted meat home.'

An intentional meaning is also contained in the following example from Deti, where the subordinate English clause '(in order to) eat meat' is replaced by a postpositional (adverbial) phrase:

(625) *K'áró cé hàà k'òò-xú k'òò 'ò.*
boy PRES come meat eat POSTP
'The boy has come to eat meat.' (lit.: '. . . to the meat eating')

The examples in (626) from Cara (a) and Deti (b) represent subordinate participial constructions. The verb of the dependent clause is always followed by the participial clitic *si* (Cara)/*se* (Deti).

(626) a. *À tsá k'áró múũ-á-ha re k'áró ke k'òò-hú ts'âã* ***sì****?*
Q 2M.SG boy see-JUNC-IMPERF INT boy PRES meat steal PART
'Did you see the boy stealing meat?'

b. *Tá 'aba mùũ-à-há k'òò-xú ce k'òó* ***sè*** *'ába.*
1SG dog see-JUNC-IMPERF meat PRES eat PART dog
'I saw the/a dog eating meat.'

Note that in either sentence the object of the main clause (*k'áró* and *'aba* respectively) is resumed in the dependent clause (as agent of the participial construction), pre-verbally in (a) and post-verbally in (b).

Finally, (627) illustrates an intriguing instance of clause embedding in Cara:

(627) *Tá ke tí cahu-m dànì ká páá-é-hà k'àĩ.*
1SG PRES 1SG:POSS brother-M.SG bee POSTP bite-PASS-IMPERF laugh
'I am laughing (because) my brother has been stung by a bee.'

Literally translated, the sentence reads: "I am |my brother by a bee has been stung |laughing." That is, the embedded clause (representing the subordinate clause) breaks up the verb phrase of the main clause.

3.2.7.3.2 RELATIVE CLAUSES

Shua languages do not have relative pronouns. There exists, however, a post-verbal particle *e* (with varying tone) which is used in relative clause-like constructions; cf. (628a–c) for Cara and (628d–e) for Deti.

(628) a. *Mài tsá tá 'a khàà-à-tá é kùrí-ha.*
egg 2M.SG 1SG OBJ give-JUNC-IMPERF REL finish
'The eggs which you gave me are finished.'

b. *Tá 'à tséé-ma k'áà-khòè xóm 'àã e!*
1SG OBJ send-DAT male-person land know REL
'Send me a man who knows the area!'

c. *Ìí kai tsá ǁ'án-á-ha é t'úĩ 'è.*
DEM house 2M.SG build-JUNC-IMPERF REL nice COP
'This house, which you have built, is nice.'

d. *ǀgàà-khóé tá múũ-á-há è*
female-person 1SG see-JUNC-IMPERF REL
'the woman whom I have seen'

e. *K'áá-khòè ǀõã ǁ'òò-há é kũũ-a-ha.*
male-person child die-IMPERF REL go-JUNC-IMPERF
'The man whose child has died has left.'

3.2.8 Tshwa subgroup

Rainer Vossen

Reliable information on the syntax of Tshwa languages and dialects is practically non-existent. The following observations, which derive from my own data collection, are poor in substance and are confined to the Kua variety of Malatswae in Eastern Botswana.

3.2.8.1 Word order

Like in most Khoesan languages, SOV appears to be the basic order of chief constituents; cf. (629a). However, OSV was also found to be possible, as in the question in (629b), where the sentence-initial position of the object may be due to topicalization because the same sentence can be constructed in SOV order.

(629) a. *Tsá kùà ìí k'óó-xù mûũ.*
2M.SG PRES DEM animal see
'You see this animal.'

b. *Nǀní k'óó-xù tsá kùà mûũ è?*
DEM animal 2M.SG PRES see INT
'Do you see this animal?'

3.2.8.2 Simple sentences

3.2.8.2.1 DECLARATIVES

Two types of copulative sentences occur in my data: while the examples in (630a–b) illustrate the use of the affirmative copula *(r)è*, no copula is used in (631). The conditions for the use or non-use of the copula are still unknown. From a comparison of (630b) with (631b) one might infer that the use is optional.

(630) a. *N/ní-m̀ tsá máá* ***è****.*
DEM-M.SG 2M.SG head COP
'This is your head.'

b. *N/níè kí yĭbè* ***rè****.*
DEM 1SG:POSS axe COP
'These are my axes.'

(631) a. *N/ní-dzì /gàé-/òã.* 'These are girls.'
DEM-F.PL female-child

b. *N/níè kí yĭbè.* 'This is my axe.'
DEM 1SG:POSS axe

3.2.8.2.2 QUESTIONS

A few examples of wh-questions have already been provided in connection with interrogatives in Chapter 6, section 3.2.8.7. Yes/no questions are normally, but not always, marked with a sentence-final particle *è*. (630b) above is an example. In (632) this interrogative particle is missing and the sentence-initial question marker *à* (which in turn is missing in 630b) is used instead. (Remember that in Cara both question marker and interrogative particle must be employed; cf. 3.2.7.2.2.)

(632) ***À*** *tsá kùà kí yĭbè mûũ?*
Q 2M.SG PRES 1SG:POSS axe see
'Do you see my axe?'

Finally, there are also examples without any interrogative elements, as in (633):

(633) *Tsá kí /'ún 'án-á-hà?*
2M.SG 1SG:POSS name know-JUNC-IMPERF
'Do you know my name?'

3.3 Southern Khoesan (Tuu)

Tom Güldemann

3.3.1 Taa (East !Xoon dialect)[12]

3.3.1.1 Structure of unmarked clauses

The basic clause consists of at least a subject followed by a predicate. A complement of a verb immediately follows the verb. Any participant outside the valence of a verb as well as adverbial expressions are normally placed in a final adjunct position and require a relational gram. In the majority of cases, this is the default marker *kâ*, *tâ*, called here "multi-purpose oblique" (MPO) marker, but there are also other elements such as dative */nàa*, comitative *ǂ'á*, and a particle *sà*, the function of which is still unclear. This general syntactic configuration yields a constituent order Subject–Predicate–Object–Adjunct; the adjunct position can occur more than once. The material available does not contain examples with both a nominal object and a nominal adjunct; example (634) only displays a pronominal object cross-referenced on the verb and a dative adjunct.

(634) *āh sîi sâa ǁq̰-be ǂhù-ma ǀnāĩ ǂnáĩĩ*
2SG CONN go chop-3 cut.up-2PRO DAT:1DU> 1DU
'and you go to chop [class 3 concord speech error] it [skin.2] up for us two' (Traill, in prep.)

Clauses with two unmarked post-verbal nominals, that is, ditransitive clauses in the conventional sense, are rare, if existing at all. This is even true for the notion 'give': this is conveyed by (a) *ǀùa* (S), *!áõ* (P) 'take' followed by patient + DAT recipient, as in (T14), or (b) *!qháã* 'give' followed by either recipient + MPO-patient or MPO-patient + DAT-recipient, as in (635).

(635) *!qháã kūū ǂnûm ǁɢûli-tê ǀè dtxó'lu ǀnà-e ǂ'á sq̰ã!*
give MPO:4PRO two genital.22-PL GEN.3 stench.3 DAT-3PRO COM:2 fat.22
'give him their stinking genitals [lit.: stench of their (DU) genitals] with the fat!' (Traill, in prep.)

In general, the order Object–Adjunct is not reversible. While the sentence in (636) seems to be a counter-example, this evidence is inconclusive: the stem *ǁqhúu* and the gram *kV* are a lexicalized collocation rendering together the meaning 'snatch'; moreover, the two post-verbal pronouns could also form a genitive construction 'the one of you = yours'.

(636) *n̄ à ǁqhúu kā'a tán*
1SG PAST snatch:2SG DEI.5
'I snatched it from you.' (T94.118)

Regarding the order of semantic roles, both patient–recipient and recipient–patient are possible, also when expressed as two adjuncts and the recipient is human. While (635) illustrates the first order, (637) shows the second one.

(637) *!qhôo kē ǂābe kē tâa ǂàã*
teach MPO:3> black.person.3 MPO:3> person.3 language.2
'teach the black man person's language, i.e. !Xóõ' (T94.88)

Each of the four major constituents can be structurally complex (for nominals, see below). The predicative nucleus of a clause conveying the state of affairs displays a particularly intricate organization. One reason for this is the existence and extensive employment of serial verb constructions. Such chains of lexical items express a unitary event/situation, whereby one verb stem encodes a particular aspect of the semantically complex state of affairs. The occurrence of other elements before and/or after such a verb series also contributes to the complexity of the predicate nucleus. The different types of semantic components tend to occur in specific structural slots of this larger chain of elements; the available East !Xoon data and comparative evidence from ǀXam suggest the following preliminary generalization for the relative order of such slots.

I	II	III	IV
absolute deixis (spatial/temporal)	manner or concomitant event	main event	relative deixis (path/location/aspect)

This sequence together with non-subject nominals seems to be a syntactic unit, because it falls under the scope of predicate markers and the clause linker *sí*, *í*, and it can be subject to complete repetition for the purpose of marking pluractionality (T10, T15).

The first slot contains such items as *tą́i* 'be far', *ǀàa* 'go off', and deictics like *té'e* or *tā'a*, which all encode the location where the state of affairs holds; even the locative interrogative *āh'ã* occurs in this position (T12). The stem *sâa*, also belonging here and in fact the most frequent in the available material, has variable functions: it can express a spatial meaning of altrilocality or the temporal notion of future, both derived from its primary sense 'go'. Absolute time deixis is also conveyed by items such as *khúbe* 'morning', *ǀnâe* 'then', *qâ̰a* 'long ago'.

Elements of slot I are not necessarily verbs. Some items are inherently ambivalent, being used as a verb or a noun (e.g. *!góa* 'cool down (of sun), afternoon'). Also, stative verbs appear in this slot as bare stems (*tá̰i* 'be far') or in a nominalized form (*!'ám-sà* 'be long' > 'far away'). This means that slot I elements need not be part of a serial verb construction; at the same time, it conforms with Traill's (1994: 18f.) observation that adverbial meaning is expressed in two positions, before and after the nuclear verb (chain).

The same ambiguity regarding word category holds for the elements in slot II encoding manner and concomitant action. While a *sà*-nominalization like *ǀáli-sà* 'often, much' (T94.19) is possible, other items in this position are verbs like *ǀgâã* 'spend day, for a long time', *ǂháni* 'be on top, much', *'áa* 'be alone', and interrogatives and deictics of manner like *āh'āo* 'how', *!āh'u* 'thus', *'áu* 'thus'.

Slot IV is filled by verbs of position and (caused) motion like *ǂná̰la* 'take out ~ off', *tshûu* 'sit ~ on', *ṵ̂lu* 'enter ~ in(to)', *ǀqhûã* 'place ~ at', *ǀûa* 'go around ~ about'. Especially frequent are the verbs *sâa* 'go' and *sîi* 'come', since they express 'thither' and 'hither' respectively; the use of these relative spatial notions depends highly on the speaker's perspective at a particular point in the discourse. Some slot IV verbs appear to convey aspectual notions like stativity or terminativity. The fact that the stative-resultative marker *ǀîi*, which is derived from a verb meaning 'be present, here', also occurs in final position could be related to this phenomenon.

The main event/situation is encoded in slot III. In some sentences it is difficult to determine conclusively which verb in a series constitutes slot III, especially where two adjacent verbs belong to the same semantic domain. Thus, for the sequence *ǀà̰a ǂhùbe* 'chop' + 'cut into pieces' > 'chop up' in example (634), I can only surmise that *ǀà̰a* constitutes slot III and *ǂhùbe* is a slot IV item encoding the patient's affectedness and the final achievement of the cutting. This problem can sometimes be resolved when considering a verb's general behaviour: if it is used frequently and with more flexible semantics, it is less likely to encode the main event in a disputable token. This seems to be the case with the second verb in the sequence *!núm tshûu* 'live' + 'sit' > 'live, settle (for some time)' or in (638) with the first verb in *ǀgâã 'ǀnā̰h'*-, 'spend day' + 'chop out' > 'chop out all day'. The decision is also less controversial in clauses with the imperfective marker *bà*, because as a rule of thumb it directly precedes the main verb (T15, T24, T25, T34).

Since the four predicate slots are hardly ever occupied simultaneously in the available clause tokens, the above order pattern in complex predicates is a synopsis of attested co-occurrences of two or three positions. The situation becomes even more complex because of the possibility of multiple occurrences of one slot. All in all, the above schematic outline must be checked against a far wider range of data and may well turn out to be a generalization which is not valid for all East !Xoon sentences. Nevertheless, the following examples show that the preliminary analysis is capable of accounting for clauses of considerable complexity.

Sequence I–II–III:

(638)	*í*	*qúba*	*sâa*	*ǀgâã*	*'ǀnā̰h'-na*	*sâ'ã*
	CONN	HS	go	spend.day	chop.out-2>	seed.2

'and are said to have chopped out (*tsamma*) seeds all day long' (Traill, in prep.)

Sequence I–III–IV (cf. also T38):

(639)	*sí*	*sâa*	*ǂhābi*	*tshûu*	*ǀîi*
	CONN	go	get.on.top	sit	STAT

'to have gone to get on top' (Traill, in prep.)

Sequence II–III–IV:

(640)	*ǀqhû.je*	*ēh*	*kâ*	*'áu*	*ǀqhâa*	*sîi*
	bee.32	3PRO	BG	thus	build	hither

'when the bees build along this way' (Traill, in prep.)

Some categorical fluctuation for items at the left and right margins of the above predicate core seems to exist, because elements in these positions can grammaticalize into grams that no longer belong to the slot sequence proper. Items in the first slot can end up as markers of tense, aspect, modality, clause linkage etc., which are placed before the nuclear predicate. In a parallel fashion, some oblique markers of valence-external nominals in the adjunct position are likely to be derived from earlier final verbs in serial constructions: dative *ǀnàa* is probably cognate with a verb meaning 'give' in other Tuu languages and comitative *ǂ'ā* seems to originate from the East !Xoon verb *ǂ'au* 'take possession of'. Also, lexicalized collocations between a verb and such an oblique marker may arise, as in (636).

3.3.1.2 Special clause types

3.3.1.2.1 QUESTIONS

All questions involve the interrogative particle *ǀá*; this is placed sentence-initially and incorporates a pronominal concord referring to the subject as in the polar question in (641).

(641)	*ǀé*	*ǀîi?*	'Is he here?' (T94.53)
	Q:3PRO	be.present	

A term question is rendered by the combination of this particle with a clause containing a referentially unbound pro-form in place of the questioned constituent. When asking for both 'who' and 'what', this pro-form is the class 3 pronoun *èh*; hence there is no formal difference between these two interrogative types, as in (642).

(642)	*ǀā*	*ń*	*bà*	*káne*	*ké*	*èh?*
	Q:2SG	?	IMPF	want	MPO:3>	3PRO

'Whom/what do you want?' (T94.18)

In 'where' questions, the notion of place is rendered by a special non-referential locative verb glossed here as 'be somewhere' (T12). Adnominal 'which' is derived from this locative question in using the same verb within a relative clause, as in (643).

(643)	*ǀā*	*ń*	*bà*	*káne*	*ká*	*'âã-sa*	*táã*	*āh'ã*	*kàã?*
	Q:2SG	?	IMPF	want	MPO:2>	eat-NOM.2	REL:2PRO	be.somewhere	REL:<2

'Which food do you want?' (T94.18)

Other content questions are not treated here, as the available information is insufficient. Interrogatives in one-word utterances differ from those in sentential questions: *é èh'è é* 'who (SG)?', *ú ùh'ù ú* 'who (PL)?', and *tán āh'ã kán* 'what?'.

3.3.1.2.2 NOMINAL PREDICATES, COPULATIVES, AND FOCUS

An equational clause, exemplified in (644), displays a clause-medial copulative *kV*, *tV* which agrees in class with the predicate nominal. An invariable clause-final stem *ńnà* serves for identification, as in (645).

(644) *èh* *té'è* *ǹ* *kì* *g!xá'u.*
3PRO DEI.3 ? be:1> south.wind.1
'This one is the south wind.' (T94.87)

(645) *tâa* *ńnà.* 'It's a person.' (T94.19)
person.3 ID.COP

Example (646) shows the possible combination of the two elements triggered by a marked pragmatic configuration; *ńnà* seems to be used here as a predication focus marker 'it is (the case) that' and its omission would yield a non-emphatic clause.

(646) *ǀqhúa* *kē* *tâa* *ńnà.*
NEG be:3> person.3 ID.COP
'It's not a person [lit.: it is, he is not a person], i.e. the person does not behave properly.' (T94.19)

Both equational *kV* and identificational *ńnà* are used in cleft-like term-focus constructions (cf. Güldemann 2010). With *kV*, the focused constituent is fronted and the following *kV* takes an enclitic co-referential with the subject of the background clause (T34, T39). With *ńnà*, the focus occurs between the background clause and the focusing copula, as *āh'ā* 'you' in (647).

(647) *tâa* *tān* *ń* *bà* *!qháã* *tà* *kē* *āh'ā* *ńnà*
person.3 REL:1SG ? IMPF give LOC.PRO REL:3 2SG ID.COP
'the person to whom I am giving is **you**' (T94.87)

3.3.1.3 Clause linkage

3.3.1.3.1 COORDINATE CLAUSES

A clause coordinator of the 'and'-type has not been found in the material. A marker *sî*, *î* before the predicate core indicates a general semantic connection with the preceding sentence and primarily creates textual coherence (see examples in the text). If the subjects across the linked clauses are co-referential, the subject need not surface in the second; then, *sî* ends up as a clause-initial marker. A sequential reading is a frequent but not an inherent feature of this connective, because it also turns up in non-sequential contexts and can co-occur with an explicitly consecutive auxiliary *ǀnâe*. Another clause connector marking (con)sequence is *ǀîi* (*tê*) '(this being) so' (T35, T40).

3.3.1.3.2 COMPLEMENT CLAUSES AND RELATED CONSTRUCTIONS

Traill (1994: 17) describes two complementation types. One involves a true nominalization achieved by attaching *-sà* to the last constituent of the embedded clause, converting it into a class-2 nominal. Since complex verb phrases retain their normal constituent order, *-sà* attaches either directly to the verb as in (648) or to a post-verbal constituent as in (649). The subject role of the subordinate predicate is encoded as an "alienable possessor" of the nominalization. The last word of the initial matrix clause has a pronominal enclitic, which either indexes the entire class-2 nominalization, as in (648), or cross-references, if present, its initial *genitivus subjectivus*, as in (649).

(648)	*ùh*	*ń*	*bà*	*káne*	*kà*	*!qāhe-sà.*
	4PRO	?	IMPF	want	MPO:2>	hunt-NOM.2

'They want to hunt/hunting.' (T94.17)

(649)	*ùh*	*ń*	*bà*	*ǀṵ̄n*	*ǀà*	*ǀùã*	*ǀàũ ǁnàa*	*ǀnēe-sa.*
	4PRO	?	IMPF	refuse:1SG	GEN:2>	give-2>	tobacco.2	DAT:3PRO-NOM.2

'They refuse (disapprove of) my giving him tobacco.' (T94.30)

The second type of complement clause (indicated in the following examples by square brackets) is marked by the final particle *tê* and is even more sentential in that it completely retains normal syntax. Accordingly, the pronominal enclitic on the last element of the matrix clause always indexes the embedded initial subject.

(650)	*n̄*	*ń*	*bà*	*ǂ'án sān*	*ǀnā-e*	*!nūle*	*tê.*
	1SG	?	IMPF	wish [1SG	see-3>	country.3]	COMPLT

'I want to see the country.' (T94.17)

Reported discourse, mostly introduced by *té'ẽ*, does not show any sign of subordination and should not be viewed as sentential complementation proper. This also applies to the intention-proximative construction with the auxiliary *tā*, which precedes a finite clause.

(651)	*ùh*	*ń*	*tú'ù*	*sâa.*
	4PRO	?	INTENT:[4PRO	go]

'They intend going.' [lit.: 'they want, they go'] (T94.154)

3.3.1.3.3 RELATIVE CLAUSES

Relative clauses (indicated in the examples by square brackets) are postnominal and framed by two markers, *tV* before and *kV* after the clause, each incorporating a cross-reference enclitic. In a subject relative clause, both enclitics refer to the head noun, which is simultaneously the relative subject as in (652).

(652)	*tûu*	*tú*	*bà*	*ǀgáã*	*kù*
	people.4	REL:[4PRO	IMPF	work]	REL:<4

'the people who are working' (T94.34)

In non-subject relatives like (653), only the final marker refers back to the head noun.

(653)	*tûu*	*tē*	*tâa*	*bà*	*!nábe sí*	*kù*
	people.4	REL:3>	[person.3	IMPF	argue.with]	REL:<4

'the people with whom the person is arguing' (T94.34)

The following can be generalized from this information: (a) the two relative markers indicate the boundaries of the embedded clause; (b) this clause retains a normal syntax; (c) preposed *tV* always incorporates a cross-reference to the initial subject noun phrase; and (d) postposed *kV* resumes in its cross-reference the head noun of the complex nominal.

3.3.1.3.4 ADVERBIAL CLAUSES

Since the information on adverbial clause linkage is insufficient, only two more frequent devices are mentioned. First, a particle *kâ* between subject and predicate marks the clause as a temporal or conditional background (T28, T32, T35, T47). Second, the verb *bV* 'be (like)' can be used as an initial conjunctive incorporating an enclitic referring to the subordinate-clause subject; the semantic relations between the linked clauses can be manner, reason (T27), and, when *bV* is preceded by *tà*, purpose.

3.3.1.4 Noun phrase

3.3.1.4.1 NOUN COORDINATION

Nominal conjunction is achieved by the comitative marker *ǂ'á* which cross-references the following noun (T1), or by placing the invariable *'àhn* after both conjuncts as in (654).

(654) *ǀû.m* *'àhn* *ǀa̰.lu-tê* *'àhn*
springbok.32 both wildebeest.14-PL and
'springbok and wildebeest' (T94.197)

To convey 'or' the two constituents are linked by *kùn* followed by the copulative *kV*, on which the second nominal is cross-referenced (T33).

3.3.1.4.2 HEAD–MODIFIER CONSTRUCTIONS

The majority of modifiers like adjectives, deictics, and relative clauses follow the nominal head and show anaphoric agreement. A noun can also be followed by what appears to be a plain pronoun; this might be a device to mark definiteness. Genitive constructions, however, have the modifier before the head. Traill (1994: 25f.) describes two genitive structures: juxtaposition of modifier and head is reserved for inalienable possession; the other structure is characterized by the medial attributor *ǀV*, which agrees with the possessee noun phrase and expresses alienable possession. Compare the following contrastive examples.

(655) a. *n̄* *a̰a*
1SG father
'my father'

b. *n̄* *ǀè* *!na̰a*
1SG GEN:3> money.3
'my money' (T94.26)

The juxtapositional structure also underlies adpositional phrases where a relational noun is the head of the construction. If the verb valence does not provide for an object slot, the MPO marker must be used, yielding a circumposition as in (656) below.

There is a third construction for expressing attributive possession which will be called the "possessor–pro-form" strategy here (T34, T38, T40, T43, T46, T51). In this, the nominal possessor is repeated before the possessee in the form of a co-referential pronominal – the "pro-form" giving the structure its name. This element could be viewed as a definite marker of the possessor. However, it can also be argued that it forms a constituent of genitive juxtaposition with the possessee, which in turn is extended by the initial noun specifying the possessor lexically. The data are insufficient to determine conclusively the strategy's function; all available examples involve inalienable relations.

3.3.1.5 Pronominal enclitics and agreement

Above, I have given many cases where a pronominal enclitic, called "concord" by Traill, obligatorily attaches to a gram or a lexical stem, called the "clitic host" here. Simple postnominal modifiers like adjectives etc. as well as the final relative marker *kV* hold a special position regarding this phenomenon in that they are the only hosts which take a concord referring to the *preceding* noun.

In all other cases, the co-reference trigger of the incorporated clitic *follows* the host. Here, the basic factor for the enclitic's category of person, gender, and number is unusual from a typological perspective. It is predominantly determined by adjacency~proximity in that the co-reference trigger is the nominal referent which, in terms of pure linear order, comes *first* in the following phrase or clause.

The function of a particular clitic host and the word order in the following phrase or clause determine the type of syntactic function the co-reference trigger is found to perform. Three trigger types can be distinguished:

(a) subjects after grams of sentence type and subordination (e.g. of question *|á*; term focus *kV*, *tV*; MPO *kâ*, *tâ*; manner–reason–purpose *bV*; relative *tV*; intention *tV*);
(b) complements of predicates (verbs; copulative *kV*, *tV*; similative *bV*) and relational grams (e.g. MPO *kâ*, *tâ*; dative *|nàa*; comitative *ǂ'á*; genetive *|V*);
(c) possessors, which can occur after all grams under (a) and (b).

It is important to recognize that, according to the above proximity principle, co-reference triggers need not be direct syntactic dependants of the clitic host. This is exemplified again in (656) by two genitive constructions which are in the scope of the MPO marker as clitic host; *kâ* does not agree in class, as could be expected, with the possessee as *head* of the genitive construction, but with the initial possessor *satellite* 'tree', which is class 3 in the singular and class 2 in the plural (the only apparent exception to this general rule in the available data seems to be in (T2) and (T40) which contrast with canonical examples like (T44)).

(656) *ké* *'Θnà.je* *|nà.n* *ką́* *'Θnà.ã* *|nà.ã*
MPO:3> tree.32 head.22 MPO:2> tree.32 head.22
'on top of the tree' 'on top of the trees' (Dickens and Traill 1977: 136)

Simple postnominal modifiers and the final relative marker aside, agreement in the conventional sense is therefore only found if (a) the clitic host has direct syntactic scope over the co-reference trigger and (b) this trigger follows immediately as a separate nominal. These two conditions do often not apply simultaneously to contexts involving pronoun cliticization. The different status of a third person pronominal enclitic as an agreement index of a separately expressed nominal vs. as a true pro-form is reflected in the present interlinearization according to the explanation given in Chapter 6: while in the first case the glossed agreement class of the clitic host is accompanied by an arrow pointing towards the trigger, in the second case the enclitic is glossed as an anaphoric pronoun.

Sample text (Traill, in prep.)

1. *!ù.m* *ǂ'í* *!nų̀.ũ*
eland.3 COM:1> scrub.hare.14
'Eland and Scrub hare.'

2. *!ù.m* *à* *ǁ'à-be* *!nų̀.ũ* *Θaa*
eland.3 PAST take.SG-3> hare.14 child.34
'Eland took the child of Hare.'

3. *!nų̀.ũ* *ǁ'à-be* *!ù.m* *Θàa*
hare.14 take.SG-3> eland.3 child.34
'Hare took the child of Eland.'

4. *ǂnûm* *khàla*
two separate
'The two parted.'

5. *!ù.m 'ée ǀgâã*
eland.3 3PRO spend.day
'As for Eland, she spent the day.'

6. *!nų̀.ũ ì à ǁ'à-be !ù.m Θàa sâa*
hare.14 1PRO PAST take.SG-3> eland.3 child.34 thither
'As for Hare, she took Eland's child away

7. *sí dts'āã ǂ'é'e sâa ǂ'é'ee*
CONN hide COM:3PRO go COM:3PRO
and hid with it, went away with it.'

8. *!ù.m 'ée ǀgâã !àã ké*
eland.3 3PRO spend.day wait MPO:3PRO
'As for Eland, she waited the whole day for it,

9. *kè Θàa*
MPO:3PRO child.34
for her child,

10. *sí ǀgâã !àã ké ǀgâã !àã ké*
CONN spend.day wait MPO:3PRO spend.day wait MPO:3PRO
and waited for it and waited for it,

11. *sí kū tẽ́*
CONN indeed QUOT
and finally said,

12. *ǀē tâa āh'ã sâa ǂ'ā-n Θàa*
Q:3> person.3 be.somewhere go COM-1SG child.34
"Where did the person go with my child?

13. *ǀē ǀqhúa bà sîi ǁ'à-be Θàa*
Q:3PRO NEG IMPF come take-3PRO child.34
Doesn't she come and take her child

14. *sí ǀū-n Θàa ǀnā-n*
CONN take.SG-1SG child.34 DAT-1SG
and give my child (back) to me?"'

15. *èh ǀgâã ń bà tá-n ǀgâã ń bà tá-n*
3PRO spend.day ? IMPF speak-5PRO spend.day ? IMPF speak-5PRO
'She is saying it and saying it all the time.'

16. *ùh ǀų́-n*
4PRO refuse-5PRO
'They (other people) disapproved of this

17. *sí tẽ́*
CONN QUOT
and said,

18. *'ĩ'ĩ īh bà ǀnā.e*
no 1PL IMPF sing
"No! Let us all be singing

19. *èh sí ǹh sîi ǂ'é'e*
3PRO CONN FUT come COM:3PRO
so that she will bring it (back)!'"

20. *ǀîi tê ùh sí ǁnā.e*
so 4PRO CONN sing
'So they sing

21. *sí ǁnā.e*
CONN sing
and sing.'

22. *kùma 'áã ń ǁâo ǀîi*
curing.dance.2 2PRO ? hot STAT
'The song is intense

23. *!úlu ǀèhe-sè kx'ùa*
fork.tailed.drongo.33-SG descend
for Fork-tailed-drongo to come down.'

24. *ùh ǂháni mà ǁnā.e*
4PRO be.up IMPF sing
'They raise the singing.'

25. *ùh ǀáli-sà bà ǁnā.e*
4PRO big-NOM IMPF sing
'They sing intensively.'

26. *ùh !núm ǀîi ǂ'é !úlu ǀèhe-sè*
4PRO stay STAT COM:3> drongo.33-SG
'They stay with Drongo,

27. *bé !ù.m 'ée ǂkx'ân 'ée ńnà*
CAUS:3> eland.3 3PRO young.sibling.34 DEI.3 ID.COP
because it is Eland's younger brother.'

28. *!úlu ǀèhe-sè kâ bà tá̰-ã kùma*
drongo.33-SG BG IMPF sense-2> song.2
'When Drongo hears the song,

29. *èh ń bà ǀxâã*
3PRO ? IMPF dance
he is dancing,

30. *'áu tám*
thus be.like
this way.'

31. *!úlu ǀèhe-sè kx'ùa ǂ'í gǀqhúu*
drongo.33-SG descend COM:1> flywhisk.14
'Drongo descends with a flywhisk.'

32. *sí kâ bà kx'ùa ǂ'í gǀqhúu tíi'i*
CONN BG IMPF descend COM:1> flywhisk.14 DEI.1
'And when coming down with this flywhisk,

33. *|ạ.li* *|à.ũ* *kùn* *kí* *ǂxà.m* *|à.ũ*
wildebeest.14 tail.22 or be:1> gemsbok.14 tail.22
it is a wildebeest tail or a gemsbok tail.'

34. *hàkírí* *g|qhúu* *ke* *sîi* *bà* *ǁ'à-be* *!ù.m* *'ée* *Ɵàa* *'ée*
'isn't it' flywhisk.14 be:3PRO come IMPF take-3> eland.3 3PRO child.34 DEI.3
'You see, it's a *flywhisk* with which he comes fetching this child of Eland.'

35. *|îi tê* *!úlu |èhe-sè* *kâ* *bà* *kx'ùa* *ǂ'í* *g|qhúu* *tíi'i*
so drongo.33-SG BG IMPF descend COM:1> flywhisk.14 DEI.1
'So Drongo when descending with this flywhisk

36. *sí* *dtshọhũ ká* *kùma* *táa'ã* *ǂ'í* *g|qhúu* *tíi'i*
CONN stamp.2> dance.2 DEI.2 COM:1> flywhisk.14 DEI.1
and stamping this dance with this flywhisk,

37. *'|neh'ẽ* *tûu* *dtshọhũ ká* *sâa*
right.then be.involved.in stamp:2PRO go
right then was stamping and went away.'

38. *èh* *|àa* *tshxûa tâ* *'ǂnạ-le* *!ù.m* *'é* *Ɵàa* *kì* *g|qhúu* *tíi'i*
3PRO go.off snatch take.out-3> eland.3 3PRO child.34 MPO:1> flywhisk.14 DEI.1
'He went off to snatch away Eland's child with this flywhisk.'

39. *hàkírí* *!nụ.ũ* *kí* *gǁkx'ó-e* *|îi*
'isn't it' hare.14 be:1PRO carry-3PRO STAT
'You see, it's *hare* carrying it (Eland's child).'

40. *|îi* *!ù.m* *'é* *sí* *gǁkx'ó-e* *!nụ.ũ* *'í* *Ɵàa* *|îi*
so eland.3 3PRO CONN carry-3> hare.14 1PRO child.34 STAT
'So Eland, she is carrying Hare's child

41. *ùh* *sí* *bà* *|xâã*
4PRO CONN IMPF dance
and they are dancing.'

42. *!ù.m* *'ée* *à* *bà* *tshûu*
eland.3 3PRO PAST IMPF sit.SG
'As for Eland, she was sitting.'

43. *ǁq'ái tâ* *kx'âba*
straight.up.suddenly get.up.SG
'Suddenly (she) jumped up

44. *sí* *bà* *'ǂnạ-li* *!nụ.ũ* *'í* *Ɵàa*
CONN IMPF remove-1> hare.14 1PRO child.34
and was taking out Hare's child (from the skin she was carrying it in)

45. *sí* *bà* *|ú-e* *|ná-i* *!nụ.ũ* *'íi*
CONN IMPF take.SG-3 DAT-1> hare.14 DEI.1
and giving it to Hare.'

46. *è* *à* *bà* *ǁ'à-be* *Ɵàa*
3PRO PAST IMPF take-3PRO child.34
'She was taking her child.'

47. *!úlu ǀèhe-sè kâ 'ǂną́-le !ù.m 'ée Θàa kí !nų̀.ũ*
drongo.33-SG BG remove-3> eland.3 3PRO child.34 MPO:1> hare.14
'When Drongo had taken Eland's child from Hare,

48. *!ù.m 'ée ǁnâe kx'âba*
eland.3 3PRO CONS get.up.SG
(only) then Eland got up

49. *í ǁnâe kx'âba 'ǂną́-li !nų̀.ũ 'íi Θàa*
CONN CONS get.up.SG remove-1> hare.14 1PRO child.34
and surrendered Hare's child

50. *î ǁnae ǀù-e ǀná-e*
CONN CONS take.SG-3PRO DAT-3PRO
and gave it to her.'

51. *è à ǁnâe sâa ǁ'à-be Θàa ké !úlu ǀèhe-sè 'ée*
3PRO PAST CONS go take-3> child.34 MPO:3> drongo.33-SG DEI.3
'Then she went to take the child from Drongo

52. *sí ǀùa 'ǂną́-le Θàa ké !ù.m 'ée ǂ'úm tshô.e*
CONN take remove-3> child.34 MPO:3> eland.3 3PRO palm.22
and took out the child from Eland's (apparently: Drongo's) palm

53. *sí ǁnâe bà gǁkx'ó-e*
CONN CONS IMPF carry-3PRO
and then was carrying it.'

3.3.2 ǀXam

3.3.2.1 Structure of unmarked clause[13]

Unmarked clauses have the order Subject–Predicate–Object–Adjunct. Most verbs have a valence for maximally one non-subject nominal so that additional nominals usually go in the final adjunct position introduced by the multi-purpose oblique (MPO) marker *au*; accordingly, sequences of MPO adjuncts occur as in (657). Since this position can host all non-subject roles, it is best viewed as a *structural* slot defined by linear order and the term "oblique" here means a post-verbal valence-external nominal.

(657) *!k'waa nǀa-ng ǀam u'i !hãu au !k'waa ts'axau.*
hartebeest head-PSE take.up rise thong MPO hartebeest eye
'The hartebeest's head removed the thong from its eye.' (Bleek and Lloyd 1911: 6f.)

(658) *hi-ng ǀũeng-ki ǁ'ee ǁxauken au ǀǫ'a au hĩ ǀx'aa.*
2PRO-PSE be.thus-? enter blood MPO stomach MPO 2PRO hand
'They put the blood in the stomach by hand like this.' (Bleek and Lloyd 1911: 278f.)

Only one basic verb has so far been found which can be followed by two post-verbal nominals without any relational gram, namely *a* 'give', as in (659).

(659) *hĩ* *n|e* *|'a-ng* *a* *!u-koo* *hĩ.*
2PRO IMPF go-? give person-other 2PRO
'They go to give them to the other man.' (Bleek and Lloyd 1911: 280f.)

Other predicates with such a pattern have their valence increased by means of the transitive-benefactive suffix *-a*, which in fact is likely to originate from *a* 'give'. Possible examples are (T27) and (T31), although the pronouns after the verbs there could also be analysed as referring to the possessor.

Nominals higher on the animacy hierarchy are regularly closer to the verb. This leads to a structure where the patient is not adjacent to the verb. If an MPO marker appears, the patient is marked more than the recipient (see T25, T29, T32, T34 where the patient nouns are clearly preceded by a possessor pronoun). In naming constructions, however, the human participant occurs at the end; such constructions are not normal transitive clauses but pertain to the domain of reported discourse.

(660) *hĩ* *n|e* *ta* *|g̹o* *ãa.*
2PRO IMPF QUOT 'youth' MPO:1PRO
'They call him *|g̹o*.' (Bleek and Lloyd 1911: 378f.)

Like East !Xoon of Taa, |Xam is a verb-serializing language. It has an even stronger preference for keeping verbs in one uninterrupted chain followed by all post-verbal nominals (the only clear exception found so far is when this entire verb phrase is repeated to express pluractionality (T6)). This phenomenon also leads to *non-causative* sentences in which the subject of an intransitive verb is raised to be the higher clause object. This is regular with matrix verbs of perception but may also occur with other verbs.

(661) *si* *tang* *|'a-ng* *dǫ'a* *n|ĩi* *tẽe* *!k'waa* *aa* *|uuk-a.*
1PL.EX ?PF go-? ?can see lie hartebeest.1 1REL die-STAT
'We did see a dead hartebeest lying there!' (Bleek and Lloyd 1911: 10f.)

(662) . . . *he* *hã* *|ii* *s'oo* *ĩi*
2REL 1PRO have sit.on MPO:2RES
'. . . which (flesh.2) he has on (his body)' (Bleek and Lloyd 1911: 4f.)

The order of predicate elements between subject and object is comparable to that in East !Xoon and most remarks made above also hold for |Xam. The above schema is repeated here.

I	II	III	IV
absolute deixis (spatial/temporal)	manner or concomitant event	main event	relative deixis (path/location/aspect)

The verb encoding the central state of affairs is framed by elements which convey supplementary information. Since this verb is directly preceded by the supposed imperfective marker *n|e*, it can be identified more easily in such contexts. The first semantic slot contains deictic stems like *|ee* and *kang*, or the altrilocal-future marker *|'aa* derived from 'go' (T27, T38). The second position encoding manner and concomitant activity is *inter alia* established by *|xam(ki)* 'again' (T26), *|ũeng(ki)* 'thus' (2), *tamΘwa* 'a little' (T20), and by reduplicated verb stems, which are possibly nominalized forms. Some manner adverbials also appear after the main verb, for example, *aken* 'be good > well' or *|wẽ'i* 'strongly, very' (T14). The final slot for relative deixis contains such motion and postural verbs as *s'aa* 'come' > 'hither', *//'aa* 'go' > 'thither', *uu* 'go away', *u'i* 'rise', */hing* 'go out', */'ee* 'enter', *!khee* 'stand', etc. Motion verbs, when employed to express a static position, are followed by an additional postural verb in order to remove its dynamic notion of path, for example, */'ee taa* 'enter'+'lie' > 'in'.

Sometimes, elements like *kV* and *ng* follow auxiliary verbs and particles (cf., e.g., *kx'au-ki* negation, *‡xam-ki* 'again', *//'a-ng* 'go and') as well as lexical verbs, and then can interrupt a sequence of bare verb stems. They are mostly written as suffixes on the preceding element but also occur as separate orthographic words; their functional significance remains unclear.

3.3.2.2 Special clause types

3.3.2.2.1 DECLARATIVES

One group of declarative sentences is unmarked in lacking formal features which characterize such sentence types as imperatives or interrogatives. However, this is not the case for the majority of declaratives. There is an enclitic element occurring after the subject noun phrase. It has a number of allomorphs: the basic form *-ken* changes to *-gen*, *-ten*, *-ng*, and *-(y)ang* after long, front, nasal vowels and nasal consonants, respectively. Bleek (1928–30: 87f.) treats it under "case" and calls the relevant noun forms "emphatic nominatives", without making clear what this means; an analysis of such clauses across the surveyed texts reveals that this *-ken* marks neither case nor focus. It shows, however, a strong tendency to be absent in the following contexts: complement and relative clauses, clauses with predication focus or marked modality features, and clauses introduced by the conjunctive elements *taa*, *he (ee)*, *he ti hing ee*, *he tiken ee*. (These elements introduce either background clauses or what underlyingly are relative clauses; see below.) In other words, *-ken* is largely restricted to assertive contexts suggesting that it is a marker of declarative sentences. There are sentences with an apparent *ken*-allomorph, albeit rare vis-à-vis the general picture, which are not declarative in the conventional sense as, for example, the interrogative in (664) below. Such cases do not necessarily preclude the declarative hypothesis, for two reasons. First, an apparent instance of *-ken* may turn out to be another gram with the same surface form. Second, if such a clause indeed contains the *-ken* in question, this could still be reconciled with the proposed analysis, because cases of declarative markers in interrogatives exist (see Sadock and Zwicky 1985: 166f.). An alternative approach is to analyse the marker as indicating entity-central theticity in terms of Sasse (1987). Since identifying markers of sentence type, attitude, and information structure is a generally difficult issue and the surveyed data are still relatively limited, I will provisionally gloss the post-subject enclitic *-ken* neutrally as PSE.

3.3.2.2.2 QUESTIONS

The particles *ba*, *xa*, *n/u* (or */nũ*) in post-subject position give to a clause a general irrealis meaning of doubt and are also used to mark polar questions as in (673) below. It is not clear whether there are functional differences between the three markers in the interrogative domain except that only *n/u* seems to occur in contexts of indirect questions, as in (663).

(663) . . . *au* *hã* *ǀ'aa* *ǀx'o'en* *gǃau'e* *!k'e* *ti* *ee*
CONN 1PRO go look.at seek people matter.2REL 2REL

!k'e *nǀu* *ǀ'aa* *ǀ'en-a* *ha* *!khoa*
people Q go dwell-?TR 1DEI water.1
'. . . he goes looking for the people, whether they went to dwell at that water' (Bleek and Lloyd 1911: 380f.)

Content questions also employ the above markers but display, in addition, interrogative pro-forms in place of the questioned constituents. Most of them are transparently composed of an abstract noun denoting the onomasiological category of the questioned term and the final element *de*, conveniently translated as 'which'. Such forms are *!ude* 'who' (< 'which person', additional form *!udi*), *tsade* 'what, why' (< 'which thing', additional form *tsara*), and *tide* 'where' (< 'which place'). Compare (664) and (665).

(664) *nǃein-yang* *nǀu* *nǃa* *ti-de?*
house-PSE Q be.at place-which
'Where is the house?' (Bleek 1928–30: 168)

(665) *!u-di* *xa* *aa* *nǀaa* *!utau?*
person.1-which Q 1TF see sirius
'Who was it who saw Sirius?' (Bleek and Lloyd 1911: 338f.)

Like East !Xoon *āh'ã*, the element *de* also conveys 'where', as in (666), so that it seems to be an indefinite existential predicate to be translated as 'be somewhere'. Therefore, it is likely that the adnominal notion 'which' is also triggered in ǀXam by the co-occurrence of the non-referential locative *de* and a general interrogative marker.

(666) *a* *xa* *de?*
2SG Q be.somewhere
'Where art thou?' (Bleek 1928–30: 168)

3.3.2.2.3 IMPERATIVES

Imperative clauses generally lack a subject and have the plain stem of the verb in sentence-initial position. However, if the addressee is expressed, subject inversion takes place: the second person pronouns (*a* singular, *u* plural) follow the verb phrase, as in (667); they are mostly written as suffixes on the verb.

(667) *!ann* *ǀwẽ'i-yu* *au* *!õ'ing!*
hold strongly-2PL MPO old.man
'Grasp you the old man firmly!' (Bleek and Lloyd 1911: 48f.)

3.3.2.3 Biclausal periphrases

There is a set of auxiliary verbs which require a bisected predicative expression in that both the initial auxiliary and the following propositional main verb display a subject nominal referring to the same referent. Those found in the surveyed texts are: *mą'i* 'do first' (T10, T11), *ǀ'ẽi* 'do oneself'; *ka*, *ta* 'intend, do soon'; *!ãna* 'do repeatedly'; *ǀxã* 'do again, also'; *ǀũe da* 'do thus' (669). (Slightly different forms of the last two items, i.e. *ǀxam(ki)* and *ǀũeng(ki)*, have been discussed above in connection with the manner-slot II not requiring subject copy.)

Matrix and dependent clause need not agree regarding the occurrence of the post-subject enclitic. This can have different reasons. In example (668), the matrix does and the second predicate does not have the enclitic. The construction with the auxiliary *ta* is a declarative utterance, but derives from a configuration in which a predicative encoding intention controls an irrealis clause. The fact that irrealis clauses are not declarative seems to motivate the lack of *-ken*.

(668) *!u-koo-ken* *kx'auki* *n|e* *ta* *hã* *!u'iten.*
person.1-other-PSE NEG IMPF do.soon 1PRO return
'The other is not going to return soon.' (Bleek and Lloyd 1911: 380f.)

There are also cases where the subject enclitic occurs only in the second predicate, as in (669). Here, the higher clause is in the scope of a relative marker – a syntactic environment imposing restrictions on the occurrence of *-ken*, but the declarative sentence type is semantically relevant for the entire periphrasis, which possibly triggers the appearance of *-ken* in the lower predicate.

(669) *ti* *ee* *n|u-tara* *|ũe* *da* *hã-ng* *ǂaken* *ĩĩ*
matter.2 2REL elder-female.1 thus do 1PRO-PSE speak MPO:2RES
'the same manner in which the old woman spoke.' (Bleek and Lloyd 1911: 46f.)

3.3.2.3.1 NOMINAL PREDICATES AND COPULATIVES

Bleek (1956: 1, 35) gives both *a* and *e* as copulative elements. While on account of their forms it is tempting to associate them with the two agreement classes, there are counter-examples. The general picture remains inconclusive and is complicated by two factors: there exists the formally similar verbal deictic *a* 'be here' and it remains unclear whether equational and identificational clauses are formally distinct. The available data only allow the secure identification of the copula *e*, as shown in (670) and (671).

(670) *au* *!oo-wa-ken* *n|e* *e* *!oo*
CONN milky.way.2-DEF-PSE IMPF COP milky.way.2

au *hĩ* *sing* *e* *!u'i.*
CONN 2PRO PAST.HAB COP ashes
'The milky way is becoming what it is, while it used to be ashes.' (Bleek and Lloyd 1911: 72f.)

(671) *!k'waa* *kx'auki* *e.*
hartebeest.1 NEG COP
'It's not a hartebeest.' (Bleek and Lloyd 1911: 4f.)

3.3.2.3.2 CLAUSES WITH MARKED INFORMATION STRUCTURE

The clauses treated so far were mostly categorical statements where some state of affairs, the predicate, is attributed to some nominal entity, the subject or predication base. This information structure is not universal. |Xam seems to distinguish more configurations of information structure inside the clause by means of several morphosyntactic devices.

A construction of the cleft type can be used if a nominal constituent is the most salient information: this nominal is fronted and set off from the rest of the clause by the agreeing relative~term focus marker, as in (T35), (T37), and (672).

(672) *g!wa̱xu-ken* *|u* *taa.*
sky-PSE PAST lie
'The sky lay (still).

|u̱a-|u̱at-a-ken *|u* *ee* *ta̱i* *||'aa.*
PL-star-?DEF-PSE PAST 2TF walk thither
The stars travelled along.' (Bleek and Lloyd 1911: 74f.)

The relative~term focus marker, which might be a contraction of a copula and the deictic pronouns *hã* (class 1) and *he* (class 2), serves as a syntactic pivot in the bisected structure and also occurs in content questions, as in (665) above, and in relative clauses (see below). It is important to note that this construction not only occurs with contrastive focus, but seems to serve generally for the creation of an initial clause position whose nominal filler is in some way pragmatically sensitive (cf. Güldemann 2010).

Predication focus seems to be expressed by *kang* (*tang* after front vowels), placed in the same position as the subject enclitic. The sentence pair below is instructive: children report to their parents their adventure with the trickster. Trying to make sense of the story, the parents first express a conjecture (673); having heard the whole story they confirm what they had suspected from the very beginning (674).

(673)	*u*	*ba*	*sing*	*se*	*ǀu*	*ǁ'aa*	*ǀ'ãa*	*hoo*	*!õ'ing*	*ǀagen?*
	2PL	Q	IRR	SUBJ	PAST	go	carve.up	take.up	old.man	trickster

'Have you perhaps gone to carve up the old man ǀAgen?' (Bleek and Lloyd 1911: 12f.)

(674)	*u*	*kang*	*ǀu*	*ee*	*ǁ'a-ng*	*ǀ'ãa*	*ǀi-ǀii*	*!õ'ing*	*ǁangdoro!'*
	2PL	PF	PAST	2TF	go-?	carve.up	?-get	old.man	tinderbox.owner

'You **did** go and carve up the old man ǁAngdoro!' (Bleek and Lloyd 1911: 12f.)

There is also a kind of presentational clause marked by an element *ǀǫang* occurring after the subject enclitic as in (T1). Sentences marked by it frequently start a discourse or introduce a new discourse topic. While they are often akin to so-called thetic statements, the precise function of this particle must be clarified on the basis of more extensive data.

3.3.2.4 Clause linkage

3.3.2.4.1 COORDINATE CLAUSES

The particle *au* is a functionally versatile element. Apart from being indistinguishable from the MPO marker it is a kind of default connector of sentences. The clause relation can but need not be sequential. (Con)sequential linkage is overtly conveyed by the complex conjunctives *he ti hing ee*, *he tiken ee*, *he (ee)* 'therefore, so, then'. Their surface forms betray the fact that they are copulatives which contain or notionally refer to the class 2 noun *ti* 'place, matter, way'. Syntactically speaking, the entire complex sentence is a cleft construction with a non-subject relative clause (see below) based on the antecedent noun *ti*, literally something like 'this is (the matter) why . . . , when . . .'. That the construction is underlyingly a relative structure is also clear from the fact that the class 2 resumptive pronoun *ĩi* usually closes the sentence, especially with the two long forms with overt *ti* (T12, T40).

These complex expressions have a high text frequency, although their appearance is that of paragraph markers rather than mere conjunctives. It can be conjectured that this is an artifact of Bleek and Lloyd's method of text elicitation which must have resulted in an unnatural communicative setting for the speaker. By necessity, they had these long texts dictated sentence by sentence, in many interrupted working sessions, sometimes taking several weeks. It is likely, then, that the high frequency of these marked linkers betrays the impeded flow of speech on the part of the narrators who could only take up the thread of discourse after the previous phrase had been written down.

3.3.2.4.2 COMPLEMENT CLAUSES AND RELATED CONSTRUCTIONS

In combinations of two clauses where the second clause can be conceived of as the notional object of the verb in the first clause, there are no clear signs that the second clause is a syntactic argument of the initial matrix, so the relation between the two clauses should not be viewed as proper subordination. This linkage type can be achieved by mere juxtaposition; this seems to be frequent when the second clause is irrealis (T24+25, T33+34). Also some of the biclausal periphrases discussed above can be viewed as grammaticalized cases of this type of juxtaposition.

There is also a syndetic linkage type exemplified in (663) above and again in (675), which seems to be restricted to factive clauses after verbs of locution, cognition, perception, etc.; the marker *ti ee* is literally 'matter which' (cf. the coordinators discussed above).

(675)	*hã*	*!x'wgin-ya*	*hã*	*xo'a*	*ti*	*ee*	*hã*	*xo'a*
	1PRO	be.angry-TR	1PRO	mother	matter.2	2REL	1PRO	mother

	kx'auki	*a*	*hã*	*!huing*	*eng-eng*	*ee*	*|x'wai-ya.*
	NEG	give	1PRO	plant.name	PL-root	2REL	be.abundant-STAT

'She was angry with her mother that she had not given her enough *!huing* roots.' (Bleek and Lloyd 1911: 76f.)

Reported discourse directly follows the intransitive speech verb *ǂaken* or semantically less transparent elements like *ka* or *ku'i*. In particular, *ku'i* is a quite versatile predicative which generally marks mimetic expressions (Bleek 1928–30: 171).

3.3.2.4.3 RELATIVE CLAUSES

A relative clause is introduced by the class-sensitive relative focus markers *aa*, *ee*, if it immediately follows the head noun, e.g. (661) and (669) above, and by the deictic pronouns *hã*, *he* if separated from its antecedent, as in (676).

(676)	*kum-ang*	*aa*	*a*	*ha*	*ng*	*ǂak-a*	*haa*	*ha.*
	matter.1-PSE	1TF	be.here	1REL	1SG	speak-TR	2SG.OBL	1RES

'This is what I tell you.' (Bleek and Lloyd 1911: 46f.)

Subject relative clauses as in (661) lack a subject constituent; it is recoverable from the co-referential head noun. Object relatives are more complex in that they have a separate subject, and are closed by a second pronoun referring back to the antecedent, indicating the right margin of the embedded structure. This pronoun can occur with (662, 669) and without (676) the MPO marker. Since this seems to depend on the valence of the verb, this pronoun appears to be treated syntactically according to the function of the head noun in the relative clause, hence the gloss "resumptive pronoun".

In certain contexts, however, it does not occur. In (677), for example, the relative clause depends on the conjunctive *he ti hing ee* and is itself followed by a complex constituent, namely a string of reported discourse (indicated by [. . .]).

(677)	*he*	*ti*	*hi-ng*	*ee*	*ha-ng*	*n|e*	*ǂaken*	*[. . .]*
	2DEI	matter.2	2PRO-PSE	2REL	1PRO-PSE	IMPF	speak	

'so he says, . . .' (Bleek and Lloyd 1911: 50f.)

3.3.2.4.4 ADVERBIAL CLAUSES

The information on how the different relations in adverbial hypotaxis are expressed is largely incomplete. In general, simple and complex conjunctives can be identified. The default linker *au* possibly conveys temporal clauses; it is often translated by Bleek and

Lloyd as 'while'. Reason clauses and semantically similar background clauses are introduced by the element *taa* (T26, T35, T37), cf. (681). Notions like 'usually when', 'whenever', 'if', which focus on the (regular) temporal coincidence of two states of affairs, can be expressed by the verb *n!au* followed itself by a complex sentence. The first clause after the auxiliary would contain the background information and often be introduced by the default linker *au*. Example (678) illustrates the alternative without this *au*.

(678) *hã-ng* *n!au* *hã* *kook-a* *!u-koo* *hã-ng* *ka* */eng.*
1PRO-PSE do.this 1PRO love-?STAT person.1-other 1PRO-PSE QUOT mate
'If one likes somebody, one says '*/eng*'.' (Bleek and Lloyd 1911: 8f.)

Another type of reason clause is marked by the conjunctive [*au* S *ta ti (ee)*]: *au* is the default connective, *ta* is a predicative expressing an experience (either some internal awareness of its subject or some sensation emanating from it), and the final *ti (ee)* is the complementizer treated above. The whole expression could be translated as something like 'realizing, having the idea that' or 'giving the sensation that'. The co-reference relation of its subject vis-à-vis the relevant nominals in main and dependent clause depends largely on the particular sense in which *ta* is used. The subject of *ta-* in (T22+23), for example, is co-referential with both the main and the dependent clause subject so that the pattern is 'they leave they thinking they return'. In (T16+17), the subject of *ta* is only co-referential with the dependent clause subject resulting in 'it is abundant they doing they anoint'. The subordinate clause after the *ta*-predicate encodes the reason for the state of affairs in the matrix and is factive.

Non-factivity is the major characteristic of the formally related conjunctive of purpose [*au* S *ta*]. It lacks the complementizer *ti (ee)* and is followed by an irrealis subjunctive clause (cf. T14+15 and T17+18).

Purpose clauses can also be achieved by the plain sequence of a matrix and a following irrealis clause; this can also yield the related reading 'until', as in (679).

(679) *u* *ko̯a-ng* *s'a̯ng* *!e-!e* *ǁõ'ing* *ǁõ'ing* *se* *Θoin* *tẽe.*
2PL OBL-? CONT PL-wait sun sun SUBJ sleep lie.down
'You must wait for Sun until he lies down to sleep.' (Bleek and Lloyd 1911: 44f.)

3.3.2.5 Noun phrase

3.3.2.5.1 NOUN COORDINATION

Nouns are coordinated by the comitative marker *hing* (T34, T41) or the more complex *hing ko'a* (T26). Devices for expressing 'or' have not been identified so far.

3.3.2.5.2 HEAD–MODIFIER CONSTRUCTIONS

With the exception of genitives, noun phrases are head-initial in that modifying attributes follow the nucleus. Apart from the fact that relative clauses come last, nothing definitive can be said about the relative order of the different modifiers, because there are only a few tokens in the available data where they co-occur.

There are three types of genitive constructions which are all head-final. The most simple one is when modifier and head are merely juxtaposed. This strategy is used first of all, though not exclusively, to encode inalienable possession. It is also employed in locative expressions where a relational noun is used as the head of a complex nominal.

(680) *au* *hã-ng* *!aten-!aten* *ba̧'-ya* *!uiri* *||ai'e.*
CONN 1PRO-PSE PL-trot race-TR riverbed inside
'And he ran with all his might into the river bed.' (Bleek and Lloyd 1911: 12f.)

Another type of noun attribution encoding alienable relations inserts a gram *ka* (*ga* after long and *ta* after front vowels, respectively) between modifier and head, as in (T23).

Finally, there is the construction introduced above for East !Xoon of Taa as the possessor–pro-form strategy. It does not correlate with an alienable–inalienable distinction. It seems to be often, though not invariably, triggered by a syntactically complex possessor satellite. In (681), for example, the possessor 'her father' is modified by a subject relative clause.

(681) *taa* *hã* *|u* *hĩ* *hã* *o'a* *aa* *n|u-kx'o* *hã* *!khwai.*
BG 1PRO PAST eat 1PRO father.1 1REL elder-male 1PRO game
'For, she ate the game of her father, who was an old man.'
(Bleek and Lloyd 1911: 76f.)

3.3.2.5.3 REFERENCE TRACKING

An intricate task, often unresolved in Bleek and Lloyd's translations of the |Xam texts, is to determine what referent is referred to by a third person pronoun or a generic noun. This is *inter alia* caused by the fact that there are only two agreement classes which do not encode consistently such disambiguating features as number and gender, and by the absence of a genuine reflexive pronoun. Apparently, speakers relied on other strategies of reference tracking, which are not yet understood completely.

One interesting device can, however, be discerned from the second half of the sample text (T21 onwards). Note that in this text there are two central referents, namely the two exchange partners (indexed here as X, the one who provides the specularite and ochre, and Y, the one who provides the bags). If these and other singular human referents had to be referred to by the only possible pronoun *ha* of class 1, there would be considerable potential for confusion. The solution in the text is that a reference change is encoded by the consistent alternation between *hã*$_y$ 'he', referring to Y, which is the person primarily talked about, and *!ukoo*$_x$ 'other', which is introduced in this form in (T22). Only when X occurs for a second time in a clause, for example, as a reflexive possessor, is (s)he referred to by an unmarked class 1 pronoun (T25, T29, T34, T39).

While reference tracking as a whole is not yet fully understood, the pattern described above seems to be functionally similar to a so-called "obviation" system. That is, the speaker introduces the referents in the discourse but chooses at any one time only one referent as the central character talked about; this is encoded by a normal anaphoric pronoun (in the text Y). Provided there is no change in the speaker's vantage point, all other referents (in the text X and the wife of Y) are referred to by fuller lexical forms.

This principle may even be applied to contexts where most languages would use a pronoun. This can be seen in (657) above: since the hartebeest is not the main story character, a lexical copy, rather than an anaphoric pronoun, can even show up in the role of a reflexive possessor.

Sample text

1. *ǁhara ǁo̰ang ee ǀee ǀho'ak-a*
specularite.2 PRES 2TF DEI.1 be.black-STAT
'Specularite is black.' [perhaps *nǀe* instead of *ǀee*, cf. (T3)]

2. *!k'e-ten tam ĩi hĩ nǀa-ng ĩi*
people.2-PSE anoint ? 2PRO head.2-? MPO:2PRO
'People anoint their heads with it.'

3. *au too-gen nǀe !ii-ya*
CONN red.ochre.2-PSE IMPF be.red-STAT
'But ochre is red.'

4. *he !k'e !x'au'i hĩ eng-eng ĩi*
2DEI people.2 rub 2PRO PL-body.part MPO:2PRO
'Those people rub their body with it.'

5. *au hĩ !ãu hĩ*
CONN 2PRO pound 2PRO
'They pound it.'

6. *hĩ nǀe !ãu hĩ !ãu hĩ !ãu hĩ*
2PRO IMPF pound 2PRO pound 2PRO pound 2PRO
'They pound it, and pound it, and pound it.'

7. *hĩ nǀe !x'au'i hĩ eng-eng ĩi*
2PRO IMPF rub 2PRO PL-body.part MPO:2PRO
'They rub their body with it.'

8. *hĩ nǀe !ãu ǁhara*
2PRO IMPF pound specularite.2
'They pound specularite.'

9. *hĩ nǀe tam hĩ nǀaa*
2PRO IMPF anoint 2PRO head
'They anoint their heads.'

10. *au hĩ ma̰'i hĩ !ãu too*
CONN 2PRO do.first 2PRO pound ochre.2
'But they first pound ochre.'

11. *hĩ nǀe ma̰'i hĩ !x'au'i hĩ eng-eng au too*
2PRO IMPF do.first 2PRO rub 2PRO PL-body.part MPO ochre.2
'They first rub their body with ochre.'

12. *he hĩ nǀe !ãu ǁhara ĩi*
then 2PRO IMPF pound specularite.2 MPO:2PRO
'Then they pound specularite.'

13. *hĩ nǀe tam hĩ nǀaa*
2PRO IMPF anoint 2PRO head
'They anoint their heads.'

14. *hĩ n|e tam ku'i aken ǁwẽ'i hĩ n|aa*
2PRO IMPF anoint MIM be.good very 2PRO head
'They anoint their heads very carefully

15. *au hĩ ta hĩ n|aa |khu-wa se ǁkho'e*
CONN 2PRO EXP 2PRO head hair.2-?DEF SUBJ ?go.down
so that their head's hair grows downwards.'

16. *he hĩ n|e !u'i ĩi*
then 2PRO IMPF be.abundant MPO:2PRO
'So it becomes abundant,

17. *au hĩ ta ti hĩ tam ĩi hĩ n|aa*
CONN 2PRO EXP matter 2PRO anoint MPO:2PRO 2PRO head
because they anoint their heads

18. *au hĩ ta |khu-k-a se !u ǁkho'e*
CONN 2PRO EXP hair-?PL-?DEF SUBJ grow ?go.down
so that the hair may grow downwards.'

19. *hĩ n|aa se di ku ǁkho kx'ueriten au |ho'aken-|ho'aken*
2PRO head SUBJ become ? ?become darken MPO NOM-be.black
'Their heads are to become dark because of the blackness.'

20. *au hĩ n|aa kx'au tamΘua |ho'ak-a*
CONN 2PRO head NEG a.little be.black-STAT
'Their heads are really black.'

21. *he hĩ n|e !u'iten*
then 2PRO IMPF return
'Then they return.'

22. *au hĩ n|e |hing !u-koo*
CONN 2PRO IMPF leave person.1-other
'They leave the other person$_x$

23. *au hĩ ta ti hĩ n|e !u'iten hĩ ta n|ei-ng*
CONN 2PRO EXP matter 2PRO IMPF return 2PRO GEN house-?
because they return to their hut.'

24. *au hĩ ǂak-a !u-koo ãa*
CONN 2PRO speak-TR person.1-other MPO:1PRO
'They inform the other$_x$ about it (< *kum* 'matter.1')

25. *!u-koo se d-a hĩ ãa ǁhara hing ko'a too*
person.1-other SUBJ make-BEN 2PRO MPO:1PRO specularite.2 COM also ochre.2
that he$_x$ should prepare for them (more of) his$_x$ specularite as well as ochre,

26. *taa hã ǁxam-ki ǁ'aa*
BG 1PRO do.again-? go
as he$_y$ also goes [to say]

27. *|'aiti se ǁ'aa |uak-a hã ǁho-ǁho*
female SUBJ go make.soft-BEN 1PRO PL-bag
that the wife is to prepare bags for him$_y$

28. *‖ho-‖ho ee hã se ‖xam-ki |ii s'aa !u-koo hĩ*
PL-bag 2REL 1PRO SUBJ do.again-? take hither person.1-other 2PRO
bags which he$_{y}$ is to offer in exchange to the other$_{x}$

29. *au !u-koo aa se ‖xam-ki |u-wa hã ãa ‖hara*
CONN person.1-other 1TF SUBJ do.also-? put-BEN 1PRO MPO:1PRO specularite.2
the other one$_{x}$ should in turn put aside for him$_{y}$ his$_{x}$ specularite.'

30. *au !u-koo-wa !xõ'a ‖hara*
CONN person.1-other-?DEF collect specularite.2
'This person$_{x}$ collects specularite

31. *he !u-koo n|e s'aa |u-wa hã ‖hara*
then person.1-other IMPF come put-BEN 1PRO specularite.2
and stores the specularite for him$_{y}$.'

32. *au hã ‖xam-ki |uaken |u |ii-ya !u-koo*
CONN 1PRO do.also-? make.soft put get-BEN person.1-other

ãa ‖ho-‖ho
MPO:1PRO PL-bag
'He$_{y}$ in turn prepares his$_{y}$ bags for the other$_{x}$ (or probably passive: he$_{y}$ in turn having his$_{y}$ bags prepared for the other one$_{x}$).'

33. *au hã ǂak-a !u-koo ãa*
CONN 1PRO speak-TR person.1-other MPO:1PRO
'He$_{y}$ tells him$_{x}$ about it

34. *!u-koo kọaa s'ang ‖xam-ki |ii s'aa hã*
person.1-other OBL CONT do.also-? take hither 1PRO

ãa ‖hara hing too
MPO:1PRO specularite.2 COM ochre.2
that he$_{x}$ must bring him$_{y}$ in exchange his$_{x}$ specularite and ochre.'

35. *taa hã aa sing ‖'aa !u-koo*
BG 1PRO 1TF PAST.HAB go person.1-other
'After all, **he**$_{y}$ used to go to the **other**$_{x}$.'

36. *he hã kx'auki s'ang n|e s'e !u-koo*
then 1PRO NEG CONT IMPF come person.1-other
'So he$_{y}$ would not be coming to him$_{x}$,

37. *taa !u-koo aa s'ang n|e ‖'e hã*
BG person.1-other 1TF CONT IMPF go 1PRO
because **the other**$_{x}$ would be going to **him**$_{y}$.'

38. *!u-koo se ‖'aa |ã ‖ho-‖ho*
person.1-other SUBJ go take PL-bag
'He$_{x}$ is to go and fetch (?'from him$_{y}$', *|ã* < *|ii-hã* 'take+1PRO') the bags

39. *au !u-koo-wa |ii ‖'aa hã too*
CONN person.1-other-?DEF take thither 1PRO ochre.2
while he$_{x}$ brings his$_{x}$ ochre there.'

40. *he* *ti-ken* *ee* *!u-koo* *ka-g* *n|e* *ǂxam-ki* *ĩi*
2DEI matter.2-PSE 2REL person.1-other ?-? IMPF do.also-? MPO:2PRO
'So the other one$_x$ is going to (?pay a visit) in return.'

41. *hã* *n|e* *|ii* *‖'aa* *!u-koo* *too* *hing* *‖hara*
1PRO IMPF take thither person.1-other ochre.2 COM specularite.2
'He$_y$ takes from him$_x$ the ochre and specularite.'

3.4 Eastern ǂHoan

Henry Honken†

For details regarding ǂHoan syntax, see section 3.4.11 in Chapter 6.

3.5 Kwadi[14]

Tom Güldemann

3.5.1 Clause structure

Kwadi seems to be a consistent SOV language. Sometimes an element occurs between object and verb, which could represent a relational gram.

(682) *Ta* *sa-le* *kwaditʃi'e* *laŋa.*
1SG 2SG-? Kwadi teach
'I (?am to) teach you Kwadi.'

(683) *Ala* *kɔ-la* *'ɲu.*
1PL meat-? eat
'We eat meat.'

Negation is expressed by *tçala*, *tçela*, *tçele*, *kçele*, occurring after the subject, and a verbal suffix on the simple stem.

(684) *Ta* *tçala* *ka* *kx'a-la.*
1SG NEG FUT drink-?NEG
'I shall not drink.'

Very little can be said about questions. In polar questions, no segmental change seems to be required, as in (685); the question whether *tçala* in (686) is the above negative gram or an interrogative sentence type marker cannot be answered.

(685) *Sa* *ũnda-t'-ɲũ?*
2SG EXT-?-eat
'Have you eaten?'

(686) *Hamu* *tçala* *kõ?* *Ee* *hamu* *kõ!*
1DU ? go yes 1DU go
'Shall/may we two go?' 'Yes, let's go!'

Copulative and possessive predicates are also poorly represented in the data. Equational and locative copulatives cannot be identified clearly. The element *ya* before a number of nominals could be an identificational copula 'it is'. Predicative possession is encoded in a clause-final string, which possibly co-varies with subject features and tense and which mostly displays an element *ka*. The most frequent forms are *kalena* as in (687) and, seemingly in negative contexts, *kanani*.

(687) *Ta tʃi ǀã mupa-wa kalena.*
1SG 1SG.POSS two friend-DU have
'I have (my) two friends.'

3.5.2 Noun phrase structure

The encountered constructions involving a noun and a modifier are all head-final and without a special form of linkage. The only types of modifier found in the data are possessor pronouns, deictics, quantifiers, and attributive adjectives. It is not clear whether the frequent examples with number and sex encoded by both a modifier and a gender–number suffix as in (688) are a characteristic of the language or an artifact of data elicitation. Some adjectives seem to index number as in (689) and possibly also gender.

(688) *ǀã tyena ya-wa* — *kx'o kho-de*
two big thing-DU — male person-M.SG
'two big things' — 'male person'

(689) *nǀwiʃi kie tçe* — *nǀwina tala kwa'e*
small woman — small women
'small woman' — 'small women'

Associative constructions do not seem to distinguish alienable and inalienable relations.

(690) *tʃi hanyu* vs. *tʃi ǀamo*
1SG.POSS father's.brother — 1SG.POSS knife
'my father's brother' — 'my knife'

Locative phrases display suffixes and/or postpositions; some postpositions are possibly derived from relational nouns (cf. *tshõ* 'front' in (691) with *tshũ-* 'head').

(691) *phɛlɛ tshõ.m-ba* — *Tshõ kha.βa pɛ!*
house front-LOC — front LOC put
'in front of the house' — 'Put in front!'

NOTES

1 From a conversation about an old woman who had senile dementia and would go to the bush and sleep there.
2 We wish to thank Tom Güldemann for many valuable suggestions made on an earlier version of this chapter. Our thanks are also due to the !Xun people who assisted us during our field research in Namibia, and to the *Deutsche Forschungsgemeinschaft* (German Research Society) for having sponsored the work on which this chapter is based.
3 W2 "ǁ" is a retroflex, alveo-palatal, forward-released click corresponding regularly to palatal clicks in other dialects.
4 For (453a–b) the proper translation should be: 'They are Khwe having killed a kudu.'
5 The singular forms end in *-e* instead of *-i*.
6 *Idem*.
7 Note that the subordinate sentence contains the main verb ('he refuses').
8 It seems as if the PGN marker *zi* is repeated, but in the main sentence *zi* is a PGN-7 marker, while in the dependent sentence it is a PGN-1 marker. It marks the object in the main sentence and the subject in the dependent sentence.

9 *á* has the allomorphs [á ~ já ~ wá] which are phonologically conditioned: [já] occurs after /*i*, *ĩ*/, [wá] after /*u*, *ũ*/, and [á] elsewhere.
10 *ìĩχò* is etymologically analysed as *ìĩ* and *χò*; the original meaning of *ìĩ* is unclear, but *χò* means 'thing, matter, place'.
11 The word *máã* is related to the interrogative clitic *má*, which is used for the identification construction outlined in 3.2.6.8.1.
12 Acknowledgements and sources as in Chapter 6, section 3.3.1. Numbers in parentheses refer to examples, if preceded by T these are found in the sample text.
13 If preceded by T, examples are from the sample text taken from L. Lloyd's research notes which are deposited in the "Manuscripts and Archives Department (University of Cape Town)" (Bleek and Lloyd 1911: 374–77; cross-checked with Lloyd, notebook A2.1.89: 7273'-6').
14 Sources as in section 3.5 of Chapter 4.

REFERENCES

Bala 1998; Berger 1943; D.F. Bleek 1928–30, 1956; Bleek and Lloyd 1911; Dickens 1991, 1994, 1997, 2005; Dickens and Traill 1977; Eaton 2002, 2005; Frawley 1992; Güldemann 2000b; Güldemann and Vossen 2000; Haacke 1977, 1979, 1985, 1986, 1992a, 1992b; Hagman 1977; Heikkinen 1986, 1987, n.d.; Heine 1975c, 1986, 1997; Heine and König 2012; Jelinek 1984; Kießling 2002; Kilian-Hatz and Naude 1999; Köhler 1962, 1971a, 1973, 1981, 1989, 1991; Maingard 1962; Meinhof 1930; Miller-Ockhuizen and Sands 1999; Moritz 1963; Rust 1965; Sadock and Zwicky 1985; Sasse 1987; Silberbauer 1981; Snyman 1970, 1997; Traill 1994; Vedder 1910/11; Vossen 1997a; Widlok 1997.

CHAPTER EIGHT

LANGUAGE CONTACT AND SOCIOLINGUISTICS

Since time immemorial the southern African subcontinent was inhabited by speakers of mainly two – genetically unrelated – linguistic groupings: Khoesan and Bantu. While the former have traditionally been divided into herders (Khoekhoe) on the one hand, and hunter-gatherers (San) on the other, the latter are generally referred to as agro-pastoralists or mixed farmers. To the best of our knowledge, Khoesan speakers had long been distributed over much, if not all, of southern Africa when, probably more than 2,000 years ago, the first Bantu-speaking immigrants from the north arrived there.

Three of the ten sections of this chapter deal with some major aspects of the Khoesan–Bantu encounters and the traces that these have left behind in modern languages. While J.A. Louw (section 1) discusses earlier periods of the history of contacts with particular reference to Khoe and Nguni (Southeast Bantu) in what is South Africa today, Gabriele Sommer (section 2) and Wilhelm J.G. Möhlig (section 3) focus on most probably more recent Khoe–Bantu interactions in the larger Kavango area (Southwest Bantu) of Namibia and Botswana.

Not long after the advent of the first Europeans in the coastal areas of South Africa, i.e. roughly from the seventeenth century onwards, a third language component became part and parcel of the overall history of contacts in southern Africa: Dutch and, later on, Dutch-based Afrikaans. In section 4 Hans den Besten highlights major issues of South African Khoekhoe in contact with Dutch/Afrikaans, whereas Wilfrid H.G. Haacke (Nama/Damara, section 5) and Thomas Widlok (Hai‖om, section 7) outline the essentials of Namibian Khoekhoe in contact with Afrikaans. Of a very recent origin are the Afrikaans-based, contact-induced changes as described in Amanda Miller's contribution on Northern Khoesan Ju|'hoan (section 6).

At no time in history, one may assume, were language contact situations in southern Africa confined to Khoesan–Bantu or Khoesan–Dutch/Afrikaans interactions. Given the long-term presence of Khoesan speakers in this part of Africa, it would come as a real surprise if there had been no linguistic impact whatsoever among the Khoesan languages themselves. However, this is almost impossible to demonstrate for the pre-Bantu era, and is still difficult enough with respect to later periods. Tom Güldemann's contribution (section 8) is an interesting attempt, though, to point to the lines along which future research on Khoesan-internal contacts could be carried out.

Against the background of a current Khoesan presence in East Africa (Sandawe, Hadza), an investigation of Khoesan impact in that part of the continent suggests itself. In section 9 Christopher Ehret deals with interactions between extinct Khoesan-speaking communities on the one hand, and early Southern Cushitic, Kuliak ("Rub") and Yaaku (Eastern Cushitic) speech communities on the other. In view of the great time-depth involved, the author's conclusions are drawn largely from linguistic reconstruction.

The final section, 10, begins with a summary of features of the current sociolinguistic situation of Khoesan-speaking communities in southern Africa (Gabriele Sommer). It is followed by the presentation of the Hai‖om case as a specific situation (Thomas Widlok).

1 THE IMPACT OF KHOESAN ON SOUTHERN BANTU

J.A. Louw

1.1 Introduction

Since the earliest contacts with the Cape Nguni (Xhosa) most travellers, missionaries and linguists became aware of the influence of Khoe on the Southern Bantu dialects. The influence of San, the "Bush people", was not so apparent to the first observers. This name, San, which the Khoe applied to them, is considered by them to be a derogatory term, emphasising their lowly status as collectors of the bounties of nature. However, one of the oldest place names from the seventeenth century near Cape Town is *Sonkwasdrif*, i.e. 'the ford of the San people'.

One of the first linguistic observations of the impact of Khoe on a Bantu language was made in a Xhosa grammar by the missionary Boyce (1844: xi):

> Thus the Kaffir, as spoken on the colonial border, has adopted the Hottentot click, which is unknown in the Sechuana dialects, except the Sitlokwe . . .

A very early observer of the influence of Khoe was Colonel Gordon, a commander of the Dutch garrison at the Cape from 1780 till 1795. He spoke Khoe and was a great traveller into the interior of the Cape. He says in his published diaries translated into English by Raper and Boucher (1988-I: 114f.):

> Today, and also [before] in Cafferland, I saw a number of old Hottentot graves. In addition the rivers in Cafferland, as far as I have heard, have Hottentot names. Just as we have, I think that the Kaffirs have advanced [their territory] further, since the Kaffirs say that they and all of their cattle come from the direction of the Mtamboenas.

Here we have the first evidence that the Late Iron Age Africans who entered South Africa came with their own cattle. There were some doubts expressed about this because the Nguni, Sotho, Tsonga and Venda adopted a Khoe word for cattle. As Louw (1958a) pointed out, the cattle strains of the Nguni and Sotho differ from those of the Khoe.

Mtamboenas is the river *Mthamvuna* on the border between Natal and the Eastern Cape. Many of the river names are easily recognisable as Khoe borrowings because of the clicks. The terminating feminine gender *s* in Gordon's *Mtamboenas* indicates that he must have made use of Khoe interpreters as he was fluent in their language. Many Xhosa were indeed bilingual as indicated by Gordon (1988-I: 142): "Tsaka who spoke Hottentot, asked for a gift . . ." It is not surprising with the close contact between the Xhosa and Khoe that there was a marked degree of assimilation as noticed by Gordon (1988-I: 145):

> These Gounacas or Gounaqua Hottentots are larger than the other Hottentots; they have also been absorbed by the Kaffirs and have intermingled with them.

Appleyard (1850: 49) says in his important Xhosa grammar on which so many others were based that one of the great differences between Nguni and Sotho is that Nguni has

> adopted *clicks*, as it is generally supposed, from the Hottentots, and in some instances words. In these respects, the kafir branch has apparently suffered more than others.

> It would be wrong to suppose, however, that every word which contains a click sound is of Hottentot derivation. The fact appears to be, that the Kafirs have substituted the Hottentot clicks for other characters.

He made here an observation which has, since then, had among linguists many supporters, but also opponents. We cannot accept many of the examples he gave on the same page. Most of the examples are variations between palatal plosives or other post-alveolars and clicks. This is a variation which is also common in Nguni as we shall see. Traill (1980, 1986a) and, more recently, Traill and Vossen (1997) made several studies of the replacements in Khoe of clicks by non-clicks and we shall return to their remarks.

It seems as if San had a lesser impact on Southern Bantu. Very few words can be ascribed to them. Kropf (1889: 32) says about Rarabe after he crossed the Kei River and settled with the permission of the Khoe chieftainness Hoho in present-day Eastern Cape with his father Phalo:

> Die Buschleute schaffte er aus dem Wege und vertilgte sie in ihren Höhlen und Felsenlöchern, bis er nach Kobonqaba kam. (He got the Bush people out of his way and destroyed them in their caves and caverns until he reached Kobonqaba.)

This persecution of the "Bush people" is immortalised in the praises of Rarabe and his grandson Ngqika. The lack of intimate contact between the Nguni and the "Bush people" may explain the little influence they had on one another. Doke (1926: 305) was more or less of the same opinion:

> Evidently the Hottentots were strongest along the fertile south-east coast, so that it was the Zulus who came most into contact with them in the vanguard of the Bantu migration southwards, and acquired three types of click as part of this influence. It is possible also that the Zulus acquired a certain amount of this influence direct from the Bushmen, as they were to be found in close touch with them until comparatively recent times. No doubt the Sutos borrowed to a certain extent from the Zulus, but their having a retroflex nasal click points to direct contact with Bushmen influence as well.

The "Suto" is the Southern Sotho of Lesotho and the adjoining areas in the Free State, Natal and Eastern Cape. Sotho as the southernmost of the three Sotho languages shows the most Khoe and "Bush" influences, but most of it derives from later contact with Nguni. Sotho has, like Xhosa and Zulu, a special speech to express respect, used by women. It shows a marked influence of Nguni.

Sotho and Nguni are the two most southern groups of languages of Southern Bantu. Louw and Finlayson (1990) gave their attention to the time and routes of the entrance of Nguni and Sotho into South Africa. According to archaeological data, the Nguni were the first to cross the northern border of Natal. The Sotho entered further north, just south of the Limpopo River and made for the Highveld of the former Transvaal and the Free State. The Nguni came about 1000 AD and the Sotho about 1200 AD. As representatives of the Late Iron Age, they had as precursors members of the Early Iron Age who must have arrived before 300 AD. Who they were is very difficult to say, but they were probably related to early members of the present-day Shona of Zimbabwe. The Sotho is basically the people of the high plateau of South Africa and the Nguni is below the escarpment of the plateau along the regions of the south-eastern coast.

In their progress down to the Fish River, the Nguni had to cross very rough and sometimes mountainous terrain and in summer a number of not easily fordable rivers. Certain areas close to the coast were also densely forested. This country lent itself well as a terrain where the Khoe and "Bush peoples" could defend themselves with great tenacity over a long time against any invaders.

The Nguni dialects have two main sub-divisions, the *zunda* and *tekela*, i.e. those who use a /z/ where the other would have a /t/. Southern Nguni and Zulu as *zunda* show the most marked indications of contact with Khoe and the "Bush people". The *tekela* makes use of only the dental click /c/ and its variations; cf. Swati, the Lala dialects of Natal and Ntlangwini in the Eastern Cape.

Msimang (1989) in his thorough study of the *tekela* dialects showed that they have marked influences of Tsonga which has undergone at various times the influence of Nguni (cf. Louw and Marivate 1992: 282):

> Note that not all breathy-voiced nasal compounds can be related to an underlying **mp* in Tsonga. Nouns borrowed from Nguni have *mbh* for the breathy-voiced Nguni *mb* [mb̤].

Tsonga has like *tekela*, but only to a minor extent, the dental click /c/ with its variations. It has taken over from the neighbouring Zulu certain words of Khoe origin, a language with which Tsonga had no direct contact in historic times.

Venda is the connecting link with those languages north of the Limpopo River. For that matter many Venda live beyond the Limpopo River in Zimbabwe. As indicated by Finlayson (1972) Venda is a language which developed from the influence of Sotho on Shona-like dialects. The only traces of Khoe which one can find in Venda are those derived from a Sotho source.

It is by now clear that Southern Nguni, of which the peak dialect is Xhosa, showed the most influence of Khoe and "Bush". The closely related Zulu is the other Southern Nguni language. The different Sotho languages did adopt to a lesser degree Khoe words, but with the exception of Southern Sotho they did not take over the clicks. Our study will therefore concentrate mainly on Xhosa.

1.2 The influence of the Khoe and "Bush" sound systems

1.2.1 Preliminary remarks

The clicks which occur in Khoe and "Bush" are the most obvious speech sounds which one can find in lexical items adopted from these languages. The *zunda* Nguni dialects have taken over three basic clicks with their aspirated, nasalised, prenasalised, and breathy-voiced forms. These clicks are:

c [|']: ejected dental click
q [!']: ejected alveo-palatal click
x [‖']: ejected lateral click

Only the dental click occurs in the *tekela* dialects which are not contaminated by *zunda*. Xhosa, which has the longest history of an intimate association with the Khoe, has the highest percentage of lexical items from this foreign source. Zulu has less. It must be pointed out that the more northern Zulu speech forms lack in most cases the lateral click. This is also the case for the Nzundza-Manala Ndebele dialects in Gauteng and

Mpumalanga. They probably left Northern Kwazulu-Natal before the end of the seventeenth century.

It is important to remember that Khoe and "Bush" also have non-click consonants. Moreover, the Bantu languages were associated with the Khoe and "Bush" for a long time in their prehistory. One must be careful not to find Khoe influence because of certain correspondences. Only one word can be given here which shows a remarkable similarity with a starred Bantu form and its reflex in Nguni:

Nama *bous* 'veld mouse'; cf. Guthrie (CS 194) *búgí/búgé* 'squirrel':
Xhosa *îbûzi* (cl. 5) 'rat'

We shall be very careful not to force correspondence, but only take examples where the similarities are quite evident.

1.2.2 The transfer of syllable peaks

Khoe and "Bush" show marked phonetic differences in the syllable peaks from the relatively simple vowel system of Southern Bantu where the usual situation is that only single vowels can act as peaks with the exception of certain sonorant consonants (liquids, nasals, trills).

The single syllabics in Khoe syllables give no problems, but the juxtaposed vowels of Khoe are usually simplified to one vowel or separated by a glide:

Nama *!arab* 'throat; gullet'	Xhosa *um̃qala* (cl. 3) 'throat' Zulu *um̃qala* (cl. 3) 'neck'
Nama *ǂaub* 'peak, top'	Xhosa *íncophó* (cl. 9) 'peak, pinnacle'
"Bush" *ǂnaˈidú* 'make, do' (Snyman 1975a)	Xhosa *ukúnceda* 'help' Zulu taken from Xhosa.
Nama */aiseni* 'sickness'	Xhosa *icesina* (cl. 9a) 'sickness'
Nama */hao* 'come together; cf. congregation'	Xhosa *íCáwa* (cl. 9a) 'Sunday'; *ícáwé* (cl. 9a) 'church'

The time when certain Khoe words were adopted can in certain cases be dated. The word for 'church' is one. The missionaries became active among the Xhosa during the first decade of the nineteenth century. They used Khoe interpreters, who took over Khoe words when there was not a Xhosa word. The class 9a prefix *í-* on nouns indicates that they are foreign adaptations.

The vowel cluster /ai/ becomes /e/ according to the rule of vowel coalescence in Nguni. The same rule applies when Khoe /au/ becomes /o/. Much more can be said, but the above examples ought to give an idea of how the Khoe vowels were adapted to Xhosa.

Khoe has the syllabic bilabial nasal *m* [m̩] which influenced the phonology of Xhosa very strongly. Nearly all examples of *mu* become a syllabic bilabial nasal in Xhosa. In many adaptations this syllabic nasal was taken over, except when it is transposed to an intervocalic position in the Xhosa adoption:

Nama *khom* 'speak'	Xhosa *úkhum̃sha* 'interpret' Zulu *úkuhumúsha/úkukhumúsha* 'interpret'
Nama */am* 'void urine'	Xhosa *ukúchama* 'void urine' Zulu *ukúchama* 'void urine'

1.2.3 The transposing of non-click consonants

There are many lexical items in Khoe without clicks. Quite a number of these were adapted in Xhosa. They caused very few problems:

Nama *xoro* 'make/dig a hole'	Xhosa *úkurholósha* 'thrust hand or stick into a hole, ferret out'
Nama *has* 'mare'	Xhosa *îháshe* (cl. 5) 'horse'
	Zulu *îhháshi* (cl. 5) 'horse'
Nama *khowob* 'bondsman'	Xhosa *ikhóboka* (cl. 5) 'slave'
	Zulu *ikhóboka* (cl. 5) 'vanquished person, slave'

Tsonga has *hánci* (cl. 5) for 'horse'. The nasal gives it a slightly different form from Zulu, which must have as its source Xhosa. It was always a custom for Dutch governors and colonists to give to the Xhosa horses as gifts and from there these animals spread. The grooved alveo-palatal fricative *sh* [ʃ] is a typical variant for Khoe [s].

-sha is a verbalising extension suffixed to foreign adaptations in Nguni. The *-ka* in *îkhóboka* is a fossilised case suffix. Appleyard (1850: 18) gives the plural suffix for the masculine gender as *-ku*, while in the *Nama/Damara Orthography* (1977: 73) it is *-gu*, cf. *goragu* 'crows'. Nama [g] can, therefore, be in Eastern Cape Khoi [k]. Moreover, the dative suffix is *-ga* in Nama, cf. *Nama/Damara Orthography* (1977: 70) *guure-aoga* 'for the shepherds'. The dative *-ga* in Nama must have been *-ka* in Eastern Cape Khoi and this was the origin of the last syllable in *ikhóboka*.

The most important word without clicks taken over from Khoe is the one for 'cattle', cf. Nama *gomab/gomas*, which is found in Nguni (Zulu and Xhosa) *ínkomó* (cl. 9), Sotho (Tswana) *kgomó* (cl. 9), Venda *kholomó* (cl. 9), and Tsonga *homú* (cl. 9). The Khoe word *gomab* shows remarkable correspondence with Guthrie's CS 849 **-gòmbè* 9. It is possible that the word for 'cattle' might have come for the Khoe and the Bantu from the same foreign source. We shall return to this word again when tone is discussed.

1.2.4 The adapted clicks

At the most, three basic clicks are used in Nguni (cf. Louw 1975). These sounds had been adapted to fit more or less into the sound system of the specific Nguni dialects. In my opinion there is no specific explicit velar release as given for Xhosa by Ladefoged and Maddieson (1996: 26):

> These clicks may be accompanied by a voiceless, or an aspirated, or what we call a breathy voice velar plosive k, kʰ, g̤.

Nowhere do they give a specific indication of how such an explicit velar release was established. All Xhosa speakers whom I approached failed in their pronunciation to enunciate clearly a voiceless and an aspirated velar release. The velar suction of clicks implies a velar breath control and it is completely redundant to indicate it in a phonetic transcription. What is said here about the velar release is in agreement with Snyman (1999: 115f.):

> The release of the post-dorsal contact is therefore incidental to the production of the rarefied airstream and is not relevant for the click articulation.

The voiceless clicks in Xhosa are usually accompanied with ejection in careful speech: *c* [|'], *q* [!'], *x* [ǁ']. This ejection is also characteristic of other voiceless stops, cf. the plosives *k* [k'], *t* [t'], *p* [p'].

As indicated the palatal click [ǂ] does not occur in Nguni. In adaptations it is usually subsumed under the dental *c*, but sometimes it is under the alveo-palatal *q*. Examples for the adaptation of voiceless clicks are:

Nama *|awe* 'devise, plan, scheme' Xhosa *úkucêba* 'plan, devise, advise, conspire'
Zulu *úkucéba* (same as in Xhosa)
Nama *!awa* 'climb up, mount' Xhosa *úkuqabéla* 'climb up, mount'
Nama *ǁama* 'buy' Xhosa *ukúxhama* 'gaining bride by paying too much'

Some examples for the aspirated and breathy-voiced clicks are:

Nama *!hoo* 'mock' Xhosa *ukúqhula* 'tease'
Nama *ǁhaa* 'chop' Xhosa *ukúxhaxha* 'chop'
Nama *ǁgarab* 'shoulder' Xhosa *îgxalába* (cl. 5) 'shoulder (blade)'
Nama *|gum* 'grove, thicket' Xhosa *îgcúme* (cl. 5) 'grove, thicket'

Not all the transpositions are so regular. One example given is that of *ìCáwa* (cl. 9a) 'Sunday', of which the Khoe original had an aspirated click. One must also remember that Nama was not exactly the same as Eastern Cape Khoe. Many of the breathy-voiced clicks in Nama are rendered as voiceless in Xhosa so one can only accept that these clicks might not have been pronounced the same in Eastern Cape Khoe:

Nama *!gae* 'hire' Xhosa *úkuqésha* 'hire'

Breathy-voiced Nama clicks can also be rendered as aspirated in Xhosa:

Nama *!gowi* 'thick and round' Xhosa *îqhubu* (cl. 5) 'protuberance, a swelling'

Breathy-voiced clicks in Xhosa and Zulu are all pronounced with delayed breathy voice phonation, the same as all the other egressive breathy voice stops (cf. Doke 1926). The phonetic transcription of the delayed breathy voiced clicks is my own. The superscript [^{g}] indicates delayed breathy-voiced phonation and does not imply an explicit egressive velar plosive release. As usual vowels following on the breathy phonation receive the delayed breathy voice of the consonants:

Nama *|gara* 'disturb' Xhosa *ukúgcala* [ukú|^{g}a̤la] 'disturb'
Nama *ǁgaa* 'hang around shoulders' Xhosa *amágxa* (cl. 6) 'shoulders'

The rendering of the different clicks in a nasal enunciation is not an easy matter. One must be really well acquainted with the language to express an opinion here. Basically we have:

modal voiced nasalised click: *nc*
prenasalised ejected click: *nkc*
nasalised breathy-voiced click: *ngc*
prenasalised breathy-voiced click: *ngc*

The Xhosa lateral and the alveo-palatal clicks occur in the same manner as the dental. The Xhosa clicks with a nasal enunciation as given by Ladefoged and Maddieson (1996:

260) are, as one can see, not complete. The above list of clicks in a nasal context is based on the Rarabe speech which is more common in the former Ciskei than across the Kei River towards the east.

The distinction between the modal voiced nasalised and the prenasalised ejected click has more or less disappeared in Zulu, but this difference is still very much a feature of Xhosa:

Nama *ǁga* 'be thirsty'	Xhosa *úkunxâna* 'be thirsty'
Nama *!neib* 'kidney'	Xhosa *ísinqé* (cl. 7) 'small of back'
	Zulu *ísinqé* (cl. 7) 'buttock'
Nama *ǂaub* 'peak, top'	Xhosa *íncophó* (cl. 9a) 'peak, top'
Nama *|â|âs* 'irrigation'	Xhosa *úkunkcenkcéshela* 'irrigate'
Nama *ǁhoro* 'cut a hole'	Xhosa *ukúxhola* 'carve, stab, peck'; cf. *ínkxola* (cl. 9) 'chisel'

The verb 'irrigate' in Xhosa can also be used with a nasalised click as a variant: *úkuncencéshela*. However, the prenasalisation of the ejective click is still very much a productive rule when nouns of class 9 are formed in Xhosa, cf. *ínkxola*. The word for 'irrigate' in Xhosa must have been adopted during the last quarter of the eighteenth century, because by then the colonists were settling down near the Fish River and building dams for irrigation. The word for 'irrigation' in Khoe must have been known to the Khoe early in the eighteenth century, because on the Elsenburg estate at Stellenbosch near Cape Town, irrigation was already used at that time. All aspirated initial stem consonants, whether egressive or ingressive, become ejective when prenasalised in the formation of nouns of class 9.

Most Xhosa no longer make a distinction between the nasalised breathy-voiced click and the prenasalised breathy-voiced one (cf. Pahl 1989-III: xlix). Written Xhosa is based on the speech of those Xhosa who made this distinction, and it is still very common. In Zulu this distinction has been dropped, but it still occurs among some Zulu speakers.

The prenasalised breathy-voiced click occurs when the ejected click as the initial stem consonant is prenasalised in the formation of class 9 and 10 nouns:

Nama *(xue) |ee* 'ask for something'	Xhosa *úkucêla* 'ask for something'; cf. (cl. 9) *íngcêlo* 'a request'
Nama *!gao* 'cut'; *!gao-ǂui* 'cut out'	Xhosa *ukúqoqa* 'notch'; cf. *úqoqo* (cl. 11) 'a notch'; see *íingqoqo* (cl. 10) 'notches'
Nama *ǁan* 'settle, live at'	Xhosa *úxandé* (cl. 11) 'rectangular European styled house'; *íingxandé* (cl. 10) 'rectangular houses'

The nasalised breathy-voiced clicks do not occur in Rarabe type Xhosa, according to a productive phonological rule. They are just adaptations of clicks of a Khoe or "Bush" origin, cf.

Nama *ǂnao-ǂnao* 'make dirty'	Xhosa *ukúngcola* 'be dirty'
Nama *!hû* 'pound, stamp'	Xhosa *úkungqúsha* 'pound, stamp'
Nama *ǁnora* 'annoy, pester, bother'	Xhosa *úkungxôla* 'quarrel, be noisy'

The *-la* and the *-sha* extensions in the Xhosa adaptations are verbalisers. The Nama examples show that it is Khoe words with a click followed by a nasal or by a nasalised vowel which can give rise to the nasalised breathy-voiced clicks in Xhosa. There is also another possibility when the {N} of class 9 is prefixed directly to an initial Khoe click forming a class 9 noun without being derived from a verb stem:

Nama *ǀhowas* 'grave' Xhosa *íngcwaba* (cl. 9) 'grave'

1.2.5 The replacement of clicks by palatal stops

Traill (1980: 188) makes the following important observation for "Tshukhoe" (i.e. Kalahari Khoe), which has important implications for Xhosa:

> What is interesting is that there seems to be some sort of structural pressure in these languages to have non-click palatal series of consonants. In one case this is satisfied by replacing the palatal click /ǂ/ with a non-click palatal stop and in another by replacing the dental stops with palatal or palatalized ones in all environments.

If one makes an in-depth study of the phonology of Xhosa one will find that there is also a structural pressure to replace certain phonemes by post-alveolar or palatal obstruents (Louw 1976b). Xhosa differs from the other *zunda* language Zulu insofar as it has a full set of palatal stops, viz. *ty* [c'], *tyh* [cʰ] and *dy* [ɟ]. As in "Tshukhoe" they can be used to replace clicks and it must be accepted that these palatals were taken over from Khoe and/or "Bush" dialects; cf.

Nama *ǂob* 'salt'	Xhosa *ítyuwa* (cl. 9a) 'salt'
Nama *ǀhawo* 'get an eye infection'	Xhosa *ukutyháphaka* 'become blind'

1.2.6 The replacement of clicks in Sotho

Sesotho (Southern Sotho) is the only Sotho language with clicks, but they are mostly derived in a secondary manner from Nguni. We do not have up to now a decent study of the influence of Khoe and "Bush" on Sotho. It seems that the clicks were replaced in Sotho by egressive consonants. This one can see from Tswana:

amáXhosa	Tswana *Mathosa*
ukúxoxa 'discuss'	Tswana *go tlotla* 'converse'
Nama *ǀkamab* 'hartebeest'	Tswana *kgáma* (cl. 9) 'hartebeest'
	Xhosa *íxhama* (cl. 5) 'red hartebeest'

In the first example the lateral click was replaced by an aspirated alveolar plosive and in the second example by a lateral plosive. In the last example attention was given to the velar release of the click in the Tswana adaptation. One can see from these examples that there must not have been any close linguistic contact between Sotho and Khoesan.

1.2.7 Tone

The Nguni and Sotho languages are all tone languages like Khoe and "Bush". Several different interpretations have been made about tone in Khoesan, which shows in any case widely different tonal structures. However, there seems to have been an attempt to keep as far as possible to the original tone patterns in Khoe when it comes to adaptations in Xhosa.

The initial syllable in *ǀgarab* 'shoulder' in Nama is low while the final one has a tone which is high. Several interpretations of the tone in Nama have been made and three to four tonemes are given by different linguists (for a recent analysis, see Haacke 1999). We cannot go into any detail here, but the Xhosa transposition of *îgxalába* comes close to a reasonable interpretation of the original tone pattern.

The adaptation of the word 'head of cattle' from Khoe is interesting when one looks at Nguni. This word must have been taken over by Nguni at a very early date, because the kind of delayed voice phonation in Nama is given as voiceless as in many other stops in Eastern Cape Khoe.

Nama *gomab/gomas* 'head of cattle' Xhosa and Zulu *ínkomó* (cl. 9)

However, the tone pattern on the stem in Nguni is a close approximation to that of Khoe, viz. LH as given in the example for Zulu and Xhosa.

1.3 Influence on the morphology

Louw (1986: 152f.) points out that quite a number of Khoe morphemes are found as fossilised parts of word stems in Xhosa. The actual productive morphemes in Xhosa are limited. The most common one is the adjectival suffix *-rha*, which is derived from an adjective suffix in Khoe; cf. Nama *-rha*:

Xhosa *-mhlóphe* 'white' *-mhlópherha* 'somewhat white'

Xhosa is an agglutinating language in which morphemes are usually affixed round a root. Sotho and Nguni do not have the noun class prefixes 12 **ka-* and 13 **-tu*. These are the so-called diminutive classes. Guthrie (1967-I: 95) says that "it is highly likely they arose late". It is very likely that Sotho and Nguni had broken away before these classes became common. It was therefore possible to indicate diminutives in a different manner in these languages. One must be careful not to be over-eager to ascribe the influence of Khoe to certain morphological innovations, like the use of the diminutive *-(y)ana* and feminine suffix *-(k)azi*, which can also be used as augmentative and in a derogatory manner. After all, these suffixes can be traced back as reflexes of starred Bantu noun stems. Rather, a wide comparative study should be made within Southern Bantu.

Indications of the gradual grammaticalisation of these stems can be found in the Shona dialects. Hannan's revised Shona dictionary (1984) gives some interesting examples:

munhukadzi (cl. 1) 'female person';	*munhurume* 'a male person';
cf. *mukádzí* (cl. 1) 'married woman'	cf. *murúmé* (cl. 1) 'man, husband'
mukómáná (cl. 1) 'boy'	cf. *mukóma* (cl. 1) 'older brother/sister' *mwaná* (cl. 1) 'young animal, young human or small unripe fruit'

In the first two examples, the noun stems had been downgraded to suffixes as they had lost their original high tones. A similar observation can be made in the case of 'boy'. This shows that even in Shona the transformation of old Bantu noun stems to a new distinctive function is under way. Shona is certainly not a language where one would look for Khoe influence, except for those well-attested examples of recent Ndebele contact.

1.4 Conclusion

A thorough investigation of the influence of Khoe and "Bush" on the Southern Bantu languages is certainly of major importance in a comparative diachronic study of these languages. Much of the prehistory of these languages can be explained in this manner. It will certainly show that Khoe and "Bush" did not disappear into thin air, but were an important part in the structuring of these languages.

The influence of Khoe and "Bush" on Sotho is not so obvious as for Nguni, but as shown in this section, it is there. This merits a much more thorough investigation and ought to give us some worthwhile insights into the impact of these languages on Sotho.

Only a very preliminary reference is made here to the influence of Khoe tone in the adaptations into Nguni. Standard written Xhosa is based on the men's language, which was influenced the most by Khoe. There is also the language of the *ábákhwêtha* 'young initiates undergoing circumcision', the court language of the king and the avoidance in speech of the names of people of a certain standing. The language use of the Xhosa was always of a sophisticated nature.

2 BANTU–KHOESAN LANGUAGE CONTACTS IN NORTHERN BOTSWANA

Gabriele Sommer

Outside Botswana, the linguistic consequences of historical contact between Khoesan speakers and members of the Nguni group (e.g. Xhosa, Zulu) have long been recognized (see Louw, this chapter, section 1). In contrast to this, the investigation of contacts between Khoesan and south-western Bantu languages has hardly begun (for examples, see Donnelly 1990 on Caprivi Yeyi; Sommer and Vossen 1992 on Ngamiland Yeyi; Baumbach 1997 on Caprivi Bantu; Legère 1998 on Kavango Bantu). From a historical perspective Bantu–Khoesan contacts must have taken place in several regions of south-western Africa – including early migration routes of Bantu speakers along the Okavango, Linyanti and Zambezi river systems. The most likely extension of these contact zones stretches from areas in present-day Angola, Namibia (including the Caprivi) and Zambia to the Chobe, Ngamiland and Central districts of Botswana.

Among the Bantu languages with traces of Khoesan influence in phonology and the lexicon are Kavango languages such as Mbukushu, Kwangali and Manyo (see Möhlig, this chapter, section 3) as well as some Caprivi Bantu languages, viz. Fwe, Mbalangwe and Yeyi. The Yeyi language is also spoken in the Okavango Delta and along the Botletle River in Botswana. In most cases the exact circumstances of early Bantu–Khoesan interactions can no longer be reconstructed on the basis of synchronic evidence. Nevertheless, the assumption still prevails that for several millennia southern Africa including Botswana was inhabited by scattered groups of Khoesan-speaking hunter-gatherers, whereas Bantu-speaking agro-pastoralists arrived much later from areas in the north (Legère 1998, Janson 2000). Archaeological evidence, however, strongly implies that in some Kalahari regions and in the Okavango Delta area of north-western Botswana socio-economic differentiation may have characterized the early subsistence patterns of Bantu and Khoesan groups alike (Wilmsen 1989).

While the external setting of early and current Bantu–Khoesan contacts – or more precisely the socio-economic relationship between Bantu and Khoesan populations – is often conceived of as involving Bantu dominance over Khoesan, past and present linguistic transfers appear to have followed the opposite direction. Khoesan influence varies between and within languages of the Kavango group as well as among Bantu languages of the Caprivi and Ngamiland areas. Differences also exist between regional varieties of individual Bantu languages such as Caprivi and Ngamiland Yeyi (see Table 8.1).

TABLE 8.1 PHONOLOGY – CLICK CONSONANTS IN THE NGAMILAND AND CAPRIVI VARIETIES OF YEYI

	dental		alveolar		palatal		lateral	
	Ng	C	Ng	C	Ng	C	Ng	C
voiceless	|	|	!	!	ǂ	ǂ		‖
voiced	|g	g|	!g				‖g	
prenasalised-voiced	n|g	n|g*		n!g*	nǂg			
nasalised emphatic	n|n		n!n		nǂn		n‖n	
vl uvular fricative	|x				ǂx			
ejective-uvular	|x'				ǂx'			
aspirated	|h	|h	!h	!h	ǂh		‖h	‖h
glottalised	|'	|'	!'	!'	ǂ'	ǂ'		‖'
prenasalised ejective	n|'		n!'		nǂ'		n‖'	

Notes: Ng = Ngamiland Yeyi, C = Caprivi Yeyi.
Sources: Ng = Sommer and Vossen (1992: 6), C = Gowlett (1997: 257).
* Gowlett further differentiates between prenasalised /nx, nq/, nasalised /xn, qn/, and nasalised voiced /ŋx, ŋq/ dental and alveolar clicks in the Caprivi Yeyi variety.

Moreover, Khoesan influence on south-western Bantu can in a few cases only be traced back to a specific "living" Khoesan source. Among those Khoesan languages that have so far been identified as possible donor languages for lexical borrowings into Bantu are Central Khoesan ‖Ani, Buga and Khwe on the one hand, and Northern Khoesan dialects on the other (see Table 8.2; Sommer and Vossen 1992: 24–7; Legère 1998: 201–5).

Khoesan influence has led, *inter alia*, to the adoption of a variety of click consonants in some of the south-western Bantu languages. Kavango languages in general have only a single (dental) click influx combined with several effluxes (see Möhlig, this chapter, section 3). Lexical evidence for click consonants in most of the Caprivi Bantu languages is also rather rare. Subiya and Totela do not seem to possess click phonemes at all while Fwe and Mbalangwe have incorporated a few lexemes with either alveolar or dental places of articulation (see Mbalangwe *-!imbila* 'herd fish together', Fwe *mu-ng|ulya* 'monitor lizard', cf. Baumbach 1997: 346, 398). Caprivi Yeyi, on the other hand, exhibits a more complex inventory of eighteen clicks with dental, alveolar, palatal and lateral influxes occurring in a larger number of lexemes. Most of these click words still have equivalents in the neighbouring Ngamiland variety of Yeyi where the number of click phonemes amounts to twenty-seven (see Table 8.1).

Borrowings from Khoesan differ not only with respect to the complexity and symmetry of click consonant inventories, also the overall percentage of click-containing words in the respective language's vocabulary varies considerably. Click word borrowings from Khoesan are mostly not confined to particular semantic areas and in some cases even include core vocabulary (see Table 8.2; rarely are click words [re]borrowed into Khoesan, e.g. Mbukushu *mu-|iŋgɔ* 'trap' which occurs as *mú-cìngo* and, thus, with a Bantu noun class 3 prefix *mu-* in Khwe; cf. Legère 1998: 202). Although the actual source of Khoesan elements in Bantu is often no longer identifiable, some linguistic features appear to indicate long-term and intense contact relations between speakers of Bantu and Khoesan languages in different regions of south-western Africa (e.g. retention of clicks in Bantu vis-à-vis their egressive substitutes in Khoesan, or degree of morphological integration into Bantu grammar).

TABLE 8.2 LEXICON – SOME CLICK WORDS IN BANTU LANGUAGES OF NORTH-WESTERN BOTSWANA

Gloss	Evidence from Bantu languages	Evidence from Khoesan
The Kavango group and Yeyi		
(1) ‘basket’	*θi-ǀuma* ‘basket made of reeds’ Mb *si-ǀukuma* ‘basket made of bark’ Kw *shì-ǀháò* ‘basket, bag’ Ng (SV 31) < Khwe into Kavango (L 202)	*ǀèúma* ‘basket’ Kh ?
(2) ‘papyrus’	*rù-!ómà, shì-!óámà* Ng < ǁAni into Ngamiland Yeyi, early loan (SV 26)	*kòmá* ǁA, alveolar influx → vl velar
(3) ‘thick, narrow’	*-ǀɔ* ‘very thick’ Mb (L 213) *βù-ǂ’ó* ‘thick, narrow’ Ng (SV 32), also *wù-nkǀó* ‘smallness’$_{1}$ C (Do 87) < ǁAni into Ngamiland Yeyi (SV 27)	? *ǂ’ǒ* ‘narrow’ ǁA ?
Both Yeyi varieties		
(4) ‘leaf, thicket’	*shì-ǀgá* ‘area covered with small plants’ Ng (SV 30) *shì-gǀá* ‘thicket’ C (Do 15) < Khoe language into Yeyi (SV 25)	ǀgã ‘leaf’ Kx
(5) ‘(part of) leg’	*mù-nǀnú* ‘leg’ Ng (SV 31) *mù-ngǀú* ‘lower leg’ C (Do 22) < ǁAni or closely related language (SV 25)	*nǀnù* ‘lower leg’ ǁA
(6) ‘chameleon’	*ú-nǂgòàrà* Ng (SV 34) *ú-gǀwàrá* C (Do 23) < unknown source	?
Ngamiland Yeyi only		
(7) ‘woman’	*mú-ǁg̀ɛ-kwá* ‘woman, female person’, *mù-!gú* ‘barren woman’ Ng ǁ → ! *mù-kázì* ‘woman’ C (Do 49) < some Central Khoesan languages (SV 27)	*ǁgɛ-khoe* ‘woman’, *nǁnó-ǁgɛ̂-khoè* ‘barren woman’ Kx
(8) ‘millet sp.’	*mà-nǂnú-khòá* Ng < ǁAni (SV 27)	ǁAni: *nǂnú-kho(a)ba* ‘millet’
(9) ‘red’	*βù-ǀóá* Ng < Buga or a member of the Shua group (SV 25)	ǀóá ‘red, brown’ Bu ǀoa ‘red’ Shua group

Notes: ǁA = ǁAni; Bu = Buga; C = Caprivi Yeyi; Do = Donnelly (1990); Kh = Khwe language; Kw = Kwangali; Kx = Kxoe group; L = Legère (1998); Mb = Mbukushu; Ng = Ngamiland Yeyi; SV = Sommer and Vossen (1992).

3 TRACES OF BANTU–KHOESAN INTERACTION IN MANYO (KAVANGO BANTU, NAMIBIA)

Wilhelm J.G. Möhlig

3.1 Introduction

The Manyo people are some 60,000 individuals living east of the district capital Rundu, in the middle section of the Kavango valley, which forms the national boundary between Namibia and Angola. Their economy is based on agriculture and cattle-keeping. There has been a strong component of fishing and, in former times, of hunting. The social structure of the people is matrilineal and they live under a traditional chief. Nowadays they have their elected deputies in the regional and central parliaments.

The Manyo speak a Bantu language which they call *ruManyo*. Their country is called *uManyo* and the people are named *waManyo*. According to their tradition, the Manyo originally came from the Upper Mashi in Zambia. Their forefathers took a south-western route and reached the Lower Kwito, whose course they followed up to its confluence with the Kavango River. They first settled along the Lower Kwito and the northern shores of the Kavango. This area was the original uManyo. Later the name spread over the whole area that is now settled by the Manyo. Their language forms a cluster of two dialects, *ruGcîriku* in the east and *ruShámbyu* in the west. With the language still further to the west, Kwángali, the Manyo dialect cluster has close genetic relations. However, with Mbúkushu, the language spoken to the east, genetic relationship is rather remote. As far back as they can remember the Manyo recruited dependants from the San community. From oral sources we know that the Kavango area was previously inhabited by Khoesan people called *waTjáube*. The Tjáube king was killed by the Bantu invaders, whilst most of his subjects were enslaved (Hartmann 1985–87; Fleisch and Möhlig 2002: 29–55). Yet some survived and were integrated into the Manyo community. Thus, historical tradition offers at least two possibilities of how Khoesan loans could have entered the Manyo language. In this section we shall deal with the most conspicuous Khoesan traces in the language, the lexical items that are marked by a click sound. There are certainly further Khoesan loans, but they are difficult to ascertain.

3.2 The click sounds

Manyo has forty-one phonemes and two distinctive prosodemes marked by either an acute [á] or a circumflex [â]. The phonemes can be divided into five oral vowels and thirty-six consonants. Five of them are click sounds. (A comprehensive description of the Manyo sound system can be found in Möhlig 2005.) Their phonological status cannot be attested by minimal pairs due to the rare occurrence of click words on the whole. In our lexical database of over 10,000 items only 128 words have a click. There is, however, a list of about forty place-names in the area south of the Kavango River which also contain a click sound.

If we follow the Khoesanist usage in distinguishing the two phases of influx and efflux in the production of clicks, the influxes of the Manyo clicks are mostly dental. However, in front of back vowels the place of articulation is rather alveo-palatal. There appears to exist a large individual variety as to the point of articulation. The influx can be voiceless [ǀ] (written as *c*) or voiced [ǀg] (*gc*). It can be prenasalised voiceless [nǀ] (*nc*) or prenasalised voiced [nǀg] (*ngc*). In all cases the efflux can be "direct" (*c* or *gc* + vowel) or nasal (*cn* or *gcn*). There is only one click sound where the efflux is distinct. It is a prenasalised voiceless click with a strongly aspirated efflux [nǀh] (*nch*), as in the word *nchunú* 'quiver'.

3.3 Lexical material

Our list of 128 click words contains 77 nouns and 51 verb stems. If we count only the roots with a click sound, Manyo has 65 independent nominal roots and 39 verbal roots of this kind. It is conspicuous that almost 90 per cent of the click words fall under only six conceptual categories. These are: aquatic concepts (20.5 per cent), sensations and feelings (18.9 per cent), parts of the body and bodily activities (17.3 per cent), concepts of non-aquatic nature (11.8 per cent), objects (11 per cent), social concepts and behaviour (9.4 per cent).

All click nouns are integrated into the nominal class system of Manyo. However, not all of them are also preceded by a class prefix. Nouns without a prefix are, for instance:

cégca (cl. 9/10) 'bed' (trad.)
cókwe (cl. 9) 'tinder'
cumáte (cl. 7/2) 'tomato'
gcára (cl. 1/2) 'peer'
gcérembe (cl. 9/2) 'hippopotamus bull'

The majority of the click nouns do have class prefixes, e.g.:

ka-cána (cl. 12/13) 'wooden plate'
li-gcûli (cl. 5/6) 'horse-fly'
ma-câva (cl. 6/2+) 'crocodile'
Mu-cù (cl. 1/2) '!Kung, San'
ngcéve (cl. 9/10) 'pipe'
ngcnogcnokádi (cl. 9/2+) 'matron'
shi-cámakáku (cl. 7/8) 'sandal' (trad.)
u-gcûli (cl. 14) 'underbelly of a hippopotamus'

Some of the click nouns are derived from verbal stems which are also used as such:

mu-ncôkoncoko (cl. 3/10+) 'addiction' < *-ncôkoka* v.intr. 'be addicted'
mu-ncâkuro (cl. 3/10+) 'click sound' (phon.) < *-ncâkura* v.intr. 'click'

Many click verbs form part of the verbal derivation system in Manyo, e.g.:

-gcúmp-uk-a v.intr. 'go/climb down, descend'
-gcúmp-uk-ir-a v.tr. 'climb down to' [applied form]
-gcúmp-ut-a v.tr. 'bring/take down' [agentive]
-gcúmpw-it-a v.tr. 'cause to unload' [causative agentive]

Other click verbs can clearly be identified as derived forms, but the simplex stems are absent or lost, e.g. *-gcáp-ek-a* v.tr. 'put aside (e.g. some food)' [causative resultative]. The double suffix *-ek-a* marks a causative which aims at a particular result. The simplex verb would be **-gcápa*; however, it is not present in the actual lexicon.

There are a few disyllabic verbal stems which look like simplex forms; to our knowledge, however, they fall outside the system of verbal derivation. In other words, they cannot trigger derived forms. Examples are:

-gcára v.intr. 'be satisfied'
-gcígca v.intr. 'shiver with cold or fear'
-ncánta v.tr. 'pinch'

3.4 Hypothetical conclusions

On the whole we can say that because of the articulatory uncertainty of the click sounds and their low occurrence in the lexicon, click words are a comparatively young component of the Bantu lexicon. Yet, it is our basic assumption that even the short list of 128 click words reflects at least two different strata of Khoesan contacts: one of probably Northern, the other of Central Khoesan origin. Most, if not all, of the items which are marked by class prefixes or verbal derivative suffixes belong to the Northern Khoesan stock. From the fact that they are integrated into the grammatical system we draw two conclusions: first, they must be due to a long-enduring contact situation; second, the contact must be more ancient than in the case of the non-inflected and non-derived forms. To this day some of the Manyo families, particularly those of the royal clan, use San servants. From oral tradition we know that in former times "semi-dependent" San (*Mu-cù*) played a much greater role in the daily life of the Manyo than is the case today. Until recently, the San living among the Manyo belonged to the !Kung people. However, since the comparison with Snyman's extensive wordlist of the !Kung dialect cluster (Snyman 1997) did not reveal any similarities with our Manyo list – although many glosses are comparable –, we conclude that "the old stratum" of click words came into the language at a much earlier stage of history when the forefathers of the Manyo still lived in the Upper Mashi area. Unfortunately, no living testimony of the San with whom the Manyo ancestors were associated is available. The only conclusion that can be drawn with some certainty is that they were genetically different from the present-day !Kung.

A small portion of click words might have entered Manyo after the extermination of the Tjáube, who probably spoke an ǁAni-like language. Whereas in most cases the donors of the click words in Manyo cannot be identified, we have at least some potential correspondences as to the latter group of loans, e.g.:

có n. (cl. 9) 'thicket' < ǁAni *ǂ'òó* 'narrow' (Vossen 1997a: 431)
-ncûmita v.tr. 'kiss' < Proto-East Kalahari Khoe **n/númá* (Vossen 1997a: 461)
ṇncwà n. (cl. 9/10) 'stick' < ǁAni *nǂúà* (Heine 1999: 117)

4 SOUTH AFRICAN KHOEKHOE IN CONTACT WITH DUTCH/AFRIKAANS

Hans den Besten†

4.1 Before 1652

In 1510 over fifty Portuguese men, including Francisco d'Almeida, viceroy of the Portuguese East Indies, died in a "skirmish" near Table Bay, then called Saldanha Bay. The Portuguese seem to have shunned the Cape ever since. Whether the Portuguese period left any traces in Cape Khoekhoe is questionable. Nienaber's collection of early (mainly Cape) Khoekhoe only mentions two Portuguese Creole etyma, which points at the Dutch era as the period of borrowing (Nienaber 1963 sub a) *ramkie*, b) *kommandeur*, *meneer II*.)

In the 1590s the English and the Dutch arrived at the South African coast. They were soon followed by the French and the Danes. On the basis of Raven-Hart (1967) and Nienaber (1963: Ch. 1–3) we can more or less reconstruct the history of contact before 1652 – a period of barter and rudimentary L2 acquisition during short stopovers.

In the early years signs and onomatopoeia were essential for communication. Dutch *boe* 'moo' soon became a word for 'bovine animal', which was succeeded by *boeba* 'ox, cow' in the early colonial period (< *boe* + Khoekhoe *-b* '3SG.M' + *-a* 'dependent case'); cf. Nienaber (1963) sub *koei I*, *melk II*, and *os I*, *II*, and *III*.

The acquisition of such words was part of a more general process of lexical learning, through which the Khoekhoen could create two trade jargons. These trade jargons, one English-based, one Dutch-based, were more or less kept apart, although there were "shifters", such as Dutch *boe(ba)*, English *bras* 'copper' and *broqua/bruqua* 'bread, ship's biscuits' (< Dutch *brood* 'bread' or *brok* 'piece, chunk' + Khoekhoe *-gu* '3PL.M' + *-a* 'dependent case'), while *breba/bree* etc. 'bread' (< English *bread*) became part of Khoekhoe (cf. Nienaber 1963 sub *koper I*, *brood I* and *II*.)

At the end of this period the Dutch coined the ethnonym "(H)ottento", soon followed by "Hottentot", which are slightly "Dutchified" versions of a dancing ditty that the Frenchman Augustin de Beaulieu (1620) heard as "hautitou" (Raven-Hart 1967: 101; for the etymology, see Nienaber 1963: Ch. 3–6; 1989: 514–48).

The two trade jargons mentioned above are relevant for the early colonial period. But there may have been another, French-based one, witness data in Bosman and Thom (1952–57-I: 84) and ten Rhyne (1686 [1933]: 110). Note that a speaker of a trade jargon often had to resort to signs to support his rudimentary lexicon; cf. two cases in van Riebeeck's diary (1652; Bosman and Thom 1952–57-I: 24, 27).

In order to improve communication the English and the Dutch educated interpreters but most probably the quality of their English and Dutch was low. We know this only with certainty for Coree, an early interpreter, whose broken English foreshadows properties of the Dutch pidgin of the colonial period: SOV word order and empty *have* (Raven-Hart 1967: 63f.):

(1) Coree home go, Souldania go, home go (1613)
[Souldania: the Table Bay region]

(2) England God, great God, Souldania no God (1616)
[*no* 'negation']

Empty *have* may reflect the expression of possessive predication by means of *be* plus direct object in Cape Khoekhoe – if my interpretation of the Cape Khoekhoe version of the Lord's Prayer in Leibnitz (1717: 375f.) is correct.

The level of the Khoekhoen's knowledge of Dutch and English was directly related to the shortness of the periods of communication – the sole exception being the one year stay at the Cape of the crew of the shipwrecked *Haerlem* (1647/48). Four years later day-to-day contact with Dutch became the rule, when Jan van Riebeeck started a refreshment station at the Cape in 1652, which soon turned into a rapidly expanding colony. This colony was to give rise to a new language, Afrikaans (i.e. African (Dutch)). Part of this process was the replacement of most of South African Khoekhoe by Cape Dutch/Afrikaans (cf. Raidt 1983, 1991; van Rensburg 1989; Roberge 1994; Ponelis 1993).

4.2 The early Cape Colony

The first sixty years of Cape Colonial Dutch–Khoekhoe language contact were characterized by mutual borrowing and by the use of Cape Dutch Pidgin (henceforth CDP). For Dutch loans in Cape Khoekhoe, see Nienaber (1963, 1964). However, his main source, de Flacourt's glossary of 1655 (Saldanha Bay) contains unlikely loanwords such as *ouata* 'water', but they may tell us something about the pronunciation of CDP.

Our CDP corpus spans a period from 1652 through 1825. However, the bulk of it stems from the period up until 1724 with ten Rhyne (1686) and Kolb (1719, Dutch translation 1727) as our main sources. In 1831 there is a fictitious letter by an *Ingesete van Stellebos* ('Resident of Stellenbosch', Nienaber 1971: 54; henceforth 'the pidgin letter'), which probably mimics Masbieker-Afrikaans (a new SVO pidgin), but which also evidences syntactic features of CDP.

The following overview is based upon den Besten (1986, 1987, 1999, 2001, 2002, 2007) and ongoing research.

4.2.1 The syntax of CDP

CDP may be characterized as a relexified version of Cape Khoekhoe stripped of all its functional elements, clitics included. This explains its SOV word order, empty *have* and *be* and optional pro drop under inversion:

(3) *'tZa lustigh, duijtsman een woordt Calm, ons V kelum*
tza quiet, Dutch-man-[PL] one word say, we you cut-throat
(1672; Franken 1953: 113)

(4) *Namaqua boeba kros mos coqua* [= mosco qua]
Namaqua-[PL] ox hide-[PL] very angry
(1661; Bosman and Thom 1952–57-III: 484)

(5) *wat maakum zoo?*
what [3/2SG] do FUT?
(Kolb 1727-I: 502; II: 163; cf. the pidgin letter)

Note that SOV is easy to access for speakers of Dutch. Dutch is SOV + verb2 and can be purely SOV in infinitival speech or foreigner-talk.

The loss of functional elements was remedied by the introduction of tense/aspect adverbs like *strack* 'future' (< Dutch *strak(s)* 'presently') as well as the Dutch negative adverb *niet* 'not' in sentence-medial position.

Only seldom do Khoekhoe functional elements show up:

(6) *Was makom?* =
Wat-ts makom?
what-2SG.M do?
(ten Rhyne 1686 [1933]: 140)
(For the analysis of -*om*/-*um* as a pgn marker, see 4.2.3.)

Originally noun phrases were not marked for plural or definiteness. However, soon an optional definite article *die* (predecessor of Afrikaans *die* 'the') developed out of the distal demonstrative *die*: e.g. *die oud volk* 'the old people [= our forebears]' (Kolb 1727-I: 520). Dutch Pidgin-internal word order was a compromise between Khoekhoe and Dutch in that the Khoekhoe postnominal attributives (*ao-b gei-b* 'man-M.SG big-M.SG') were shunned in CDP.

Unlike Khoekhoe CDP was prepositional. However, there is evidence for unmarked locatives and in the pidgin letter we find a postposition *sa(a)m* 'with' (< Dutch *(met) . . . samen* '(with) . . . together'):

(7) *nie bemoei ander mense sam*
[I] not interfere other people with

For other attestations, see Trigardt (1836–38 [1977]: 61) and Engelbrecht (1936: 207, 209). *Saam* 'with', which can still be heard among some speakers (J. Oosthuizen, p.c.), survives as a suffix in Khoekhoe Afrikaans *handsaam* 'with the hand(s)' (cf. van Jaarsveld *et al.* 2001: 153).

4.2.2 Lexicological matters, the phonology of CDP, etc.

CDP was used by the Khoekhoen, the slaves and the colonists. As example (4) shows, certain lexical skills were required. Furthermore phonetics may have been a complicating factor, witness complaints by a visiting Dutch East Indian Company official, H.A. van Reede (1685 [1941]: 36, 202, 220).

To start with the latter, if we combine the scarce unedited pidgin data with the Dutch and English words in de Flacourt's Khoekhoe glossary and with data on early twentieth-century Khoekhoe Afrikaans, we find (a) *r* < *l* but also *l* < *r*, (b) apocope of [r] and [d]/[t], (c) strengthening of non-coronal fricatives, (d) raising of mid-vowels, (e) unrounding of front vowels, (f) palatalization of velars, and (g) change of place of articulation with stops. Cf. Raven-Hart (1971-II: 405), examples (3) and (4) above; Nienaber (1963) sub *skaap II* and *God I*; Rademeyer (1938: 45, 53f.); Links (1989: 8, 14f., 23f.), and ten Rhyne (1686 [1933]: 140).

As for the lexicon, we have come across a couple of non-Dutch pidgin words already, such as *bras* (English), *k(a)ros* (Khoekhoe), and new formations such as *boeba, broqua.* There are more of such etyma in CDP but all in all our phrasal and sentential data seem to be completely "Dutch" in lexis, which might mean that Khoekhoe is grossly underrepresented, but this may be due to context, witness the list of *Mere Hottentottonica quae obiter occurrunt* 'purely Hottentot words which occasionally show up', with which ten Rhyne (1686 [1933]: 154) illustrates the limited contribution of Khoekhoe words to the language [= pidgin] of the Khoekhoen near the fortress.

This list is thematically organized and no doubt can be expanded with more words and categories, but only *Onkey* 'Dutchman' could have been used in the sentences and phrases of my database, and only by accident do we find *kros* 'hide' as in (4) above or *gisje/gisie* 'ten' as in *5 gisjes schapen . . . dewelke 50 in 't getal zoude zijn* '5 *gisies* of sheep . . . which would be 50 in number' (Rhenius 1724 [1947]: 134).

4.2.3 CDP morphology and ***-um/-me***

CDP morphology is not particularly interesting: there is (a) compounding, (b) adjectival *-s* '-ic/-ish', (c) semantic bleaching of *-man* in compounds as in *Teeckemans* 'steal-men' [= 'thieves'] (1660; Nienaber 1989: 873), which is comparable to the bleached use of *-ao-* 'man' in Nama.

Intriguing, however, is the verbal ending *-um/-om/-(e)m* with its postvocalic allomorph *-me*. It also attaches to one or two adjectives and it sporadically alternates with Dutch infinitival *-en*. The verbs in the contemporaneous English pidgin are bare stems (cf. Bosman and Thom 1952–57-I: 417).

There are also three nouns that take this ending: *tabaqkom, Tubaccum* 'tobacco' (< Dutch *tabak/toebak*), and the nominalization *kortom* 'small piece, the chief's rightful share in case of bartering' (< Dutch *kort* 'short' or *korten* 'to cut back').

In nouns *-Vm/-me* may be the Cape Khoekhoe pgn marker 3SG.M, which had many allomorphs, including *-m* and *-mi*, and which was also used as a nominalizer (cf. Nienaber 1963, e.g. sub *oog* 'eye'). Therefore, the nouns ending in *-Vm* may very well – like *boeba* and *broqua* – go back to a very early period.

It seems nonsensical to derive V + *-um* verbs from nominalizations. But this may be due to the colonists, who may have perceived the Khoekhoe nominalizations of their own verbs as the Khoekhoe equivalents of infinitives, which they needed for infinitival (SOV) speech.

In view of our sources verbal *-Vm/-me* must have disappeared somewhere between 1745 and 1825. During that period there is only one attestation of a word with *-Vm*: the noun *kortom* (Wikar 1779 [1935]: 26). However, in quite a few cases *-um/-om/-me* can also be analysed as a Khoekhoe subject or object clitic 3SG.M. Since in one instance it can be shown beyond doubt that Kolb (1719, 1727) has added *-um* to an element which he mistook for a verb (*hottentot* interpreted as 'to give'), more cases of "suffixal" *-um* may be artificial (cf. den Besten 2007).

4.2.4 An aside on Cape Khoekhoe sources

Most probably ten Rhyne could not distinguish between Khoekhoe and pidgin words. Nor could others, I fear. His own list of Khoekhoe words contains three pidginisms: *boeba* 'ox, cow', *debitja* 'steers' and *acqua* 'horse'.

As Nienaber (1963) shows sub *os III*, more authors assign *boeba* to Khoekhoe. Similarly for *debitja*, whose <tj> is a transcription mistake, witness *Tibbesa-* and *dwiessa* 'ox' (Nienaber 1963 sub *os V*), and which – in view of Khoekhoe phonetics – may derive from L2 Dutch *die bees* 'the/that bovine animal' + Khoekhoe *-a* (standard Dutch *dat beest*).

The most telling case is *acqua* 'horse', usually spelt *hacqua*. Ten Rhyne and nine sources after him (up until 1805) treat this frozen masculine plural (*ha-gu-a*) as a singular. It also appears as a word for 'ass, donkey' in the Cape Khoekhoe translation of the Tenth Commandment (Leibnitz 1717: 381). This pidginism can be dated back to the van Riebeeck period, when a certain type of zebras (*haqua*) were identified as 'wild horses' (cf. Bosman and Thom 1952–57-III: 308).

In view of the above there may be more pidginisms in the Khoekhoe glossaries of the seventeenth and eighteenth centuries, similarly for the texts in Leibnitz (1717).

4.3 After 1700: Khoekhoe and Cape Dutch/Afrikaans

Around 1700 groups of Khoekhoen as well as colonists started to move out of the Cape Colony. Consequently the area of language contact was expanded, although the smallpox epidemic of 1713 broke off Dutch–Khoekhoe language contact in the original colony.

In the east and in the interior the subjugation and incorporation of the Khoekhoen (and the San) led to rapid language loss. Nevertheless, there must have been a long period of bilingualism among certain groups such as the Griquas. The Griquas belonged to the so-called *oorlamse*, i.e. acculturated, Khoekhoen who founded their own communities outside the Cape Colony – alongside groups of so-called Basters, who stressed their mixed descent. (For the history of the South African Khoesan until 1840, see Elphick 1977 and Elphick and Giliomee 1989.)

Due to the Oorlamse Khoekhoen and the Basters, Dutch/Afrikaans spread among free Khoekhoen outside the Cape Colony (roughly the present North Cape and southern Namibia and some adjacent areas). Due to special circumstances a Khoekhoe variety of Cape Dutch/Afrikaans could survive in these areas. Khoekhoe Afrikaans (henceforth KhA) owes its existence to a combination of L2 acquisition and further adaptation of CDP. Afrikaans itself resulted from language contact between Dutch and various languages: Malay, Creole Portuguese, Khoekhoe, etc. Continuing migration exported the Asian influences to the north and the east, while the influx of "detribalized" Khoekhoen brought some Khoekhoe influences to the southwest.

Nowadays Southern Khoekhoe (including varieties such as Griqua and Korana) seems to be extinct, similarly for Southern Khoesan to the south of the Gariep (Orange River).

However, Nama still survives – in tandem with Afrikaans – in the Richtersveld to the south, and in villages like De Mier to the north of the Gariep, similarly for southern Namibia.

Due to extensive bilingualism during the nineteenth century a new variety of relexified Khoekhoe arose, as we know through a letter by Theophilus Hahn to Hugo Schuchardt (1882; den Besten 1986: 216, 226). Hahn mentions imperatives like *Loop-tse* 'go-2SG.M' (< *!gun-tse*) and the case of an interpreter during a sermon, who rendered Cape Dutch "Van Natuur geheelenall [*sic*] bedorven" ('completely depraved by nature') as:

(8)	*Heeltemal-se*	*Natuur-a-xu*	*bedorven-he*	[relexified Khoekhoe]
	completely-ADV	nature-OBJ-from	depraved-PASS	
	←			
	Hoaraga-se	*ǂũb-a xu*	*ǁgau-ǁgau-he*	[Khoekhoe]

Relexified Khoekhoe may be due to heavy borrowing or to the wish to overcome dialectal differences between Southern Khoekhoe and Nama.

The following subsections will deal with lexical borrowings and the like and with structural influences from Khoekhoe in Afrikaans – the latter mainly on the basis of den Besten (1986, 1999, 2002, 2007) and ongoing research.

4.3.1 Borrowings and onomastics

Lexical borrowings from Dutch/Afrikaans into Southern Khoekhoe mainly concern artefacts and institutions, witness the Korana glossaries in Engelbrecht (1928) and Meinhof (1930). A special case is Korana *kukuru-b*/*kukuru-s* 'rooster, hen', which derives from CDP *Courcour* 'bird', a Dutch onomatopoeia.

Khoekhoe borrowings in Afrikaans concern artefacts, plant and animal names, toponyms, interjections and everyday words like *ou* 'to give' (rare) and maybe *ou* 'chap'. Clicks are not retained; cf. Nienaber (1953: 269–72), Boshoff and Nienaber (1967), Scholtz (1974) and Nienaber (1964).

Not surprisingly Links (1989: 61–66) found more loans for the KhA of Namaqualand, among which were many everyday words. Clicks are retained but their use is unstable, so Links decided to use only [!] for his phonetic transcriptions.

Note that many Dutch/Afrikaans toponyms such as *Vaal-rivier* 'grey river' are translations which we owe to the Khoekhoen themselves (cf. Nienaber and Raper 1977–80: 1983).

Similarly, several (often historical) Afrikaans names for Khoekhoe groups are translations, while others are free inventions, e.g. CDP *Kaepmans* 'Cape men', or are based upon surnames of tribal leaders, such as *Afrikaners* and *Witboois* (cf. Nienaber 1989).

4.3.2 Khoekhoe and CDP substrate in Afrikaans and Khoekhoe Afrikaans

One of the main contributions of Khoekhoe and CDP to Afrikaans syntax is invisible: they have helped to preserve the Dutch SOV word order. On the other hand, the absolute position 2 structure of Khoekhoe could not uproot the asymmetric verb2 + verb1 patterning of Dutch, although Afrikaans has become V2/V1-like in embedded interrogatives (wh-phrase finite verb; optional) and in *of*-clauses (*of* finite verb 'whether finite verb'; rare).

In KhA we find the following possessive paradigm (Links 1989: 81ff.):

(9)

SG		PL		REV	
1	*my*	1	*ons* (*se*)		
2	*jou*	2	*julle* (*se*)	2	*u* (*se*)
3F	*haar*/*hy se*, *sy se*	3	*hulle* (*se*)		
M	*sy*/*hy se*				
	[*hy* 'he, she' – *sy* 'a) she, b) his']				

Also compare Rademeyer (1938: 66f.). Contrary to what both authors – misled by le Roux (1923: 88), who was misled by his sources – believe, *se* in (9) does pattern like *di* in Khoekhoe. 1SG and 2SG are the sole possessive pronouns of Khoekhoe and they, therefore, hardly combine with *di* if at all. Note that the other pronominal expressions in the Khoekhoe possessive construction are in the nominative, which is mimicked by *sy se* and *hy se*.

Other potential Khoekhoeisms at the phrasal level in KhA are shared with (other varieties of) Afrikaans. Thus, circumlocutions like Afrikaans *hy*/*sy wat Piet*/*Anna is*, in 'he/she that Pete/Anne is', in KhA also *hy wat lou is* 'he that lion is', i.e. 'the lion' (Rademeyer 1938: 83f.), are reminiscent of the structure of noun phrases in Khoekhoe (e.g. Nama *xam-i* 'lion-3SG.M').

Less obvious is the connection between the Khoekhoe associative structure X-*hãã*-3PL and Afrikaans associatives like *Pa-hulle* 'Dad-3PL', in KhA also *Pa-goed* 'Dad-stuff/things' (Rademeyer 1938: 67f.; Links 1989: 31ff.). Yet, *-goed* may be a substitute for Khoekhoe *-gu* '3PL.M' and in a transitional dialect area we find the associative *Paandoe(n)* 'dad-and(?)-*doe(n)*', which may derive from the Khoekhoe construction with Cape Khoekhoe change of place of articulation (Nienaber 1994). Therefore, Khoekhoe may be one of the sources for the Afrikaans associative construction.

Note that *-goed* may also have been a plural marker in early KhA, witness a word like (Khoekhoe) Afrikaans *kleingoed* 'children' (< *klein* 'small') and KhA data in Jacobs (1942: *inter alia* 10, 26, 31, 47, 87, 115) and van Zyl (1947: 5, 110, 131). On the other hand, unmarked plurals in KhA such as *skaap* 'sheep' and *perd* 'horses' (Rademeyer 1938: 62; Links 1989: 34) may go back to the unmarked plurals of CDP.

Probably due to reanalysis of V–AUX and AUX–V sequences as single verbs in CDP – prior to the acquisition of V2 – KhA developed a "double" V2 pattern which was taken over in general Afrikaans. Compare:

(10) *Daar bly staan hy*
there keep stand he

Similarly, reanalysis of Dutch particle verbs in CDP created preposition + verb compounds in KhA, as in (11), which was not borrowed into other varieties of Afrikaans (cf. Rademeyer 1938: 63):

(11) *Aan-ja vir my die skaap*
on-drive for me the sheep

Both types of reanalysis may be due to interference from Khoekhoe, where V + V and verb + postposition compounds are quite normal.

Finally: negation. It has been suggested that the SOV–NEG pattern of Khoekhoe may have been the source for *nie*-2, the sentence-final negative marker of Afrikaans (Nienaber 1955, den Besten 1986). However, *nie*-2 is absent in CDP. Furthermore, *nie*-2 can follow extraposed material, which is impossible for the Khoekhoe negative marker (den

Besten 1986). Therefore, *nie*-2 may rather derive from a reinterpretation of the Dutch colloquial negative tag *nee* 'no' (Roberge 2000). Most probably this reinterpretation is due to SOV–NEG speakers such as the Khoekhoen.

5 CONTACT-INDUCED CHANGE BETWEEN KHOEKHOE AND AFRIKAANS

Wilfrid H.G. Haacke

The mutual changes induced by Khoekhoe and Dutch have been considerable, though of a disparate nature, because of the different socio-political status of the respective languages and their speakers. The influence of Khoekhoe (and also Malay) on Dutch amounted mainly to simplificatory substratum interference: these communities were shifting from their own language to Dutch without having mastered all the intricacies of the language, thus leading to the eventual emergence of the simplified language, Afrikaans. The influence of modern Afrikaans on contemporary Khoekhoe, though, amounts mainly to lexical interference through borrowing of vocabulary by the Khoekhoe. Since the combined substratum interference by these typologically very diverse languages (Khoekhoe and Malayo-Polynesian languages) allowed for the introduction of neither vocabulary nor any marked grammatical structures into the prestige language Dutch, the influence of these communities on modern Afrikaans tends to be somewhat overlooked, even though the communities were instrumental in bringing about the actual emergence of Afrikaans as a separate language (cf. Luijks 2000). Thomason and Kaufman (1988: 38f.) summarise this typical situation:

> Substratum interference is a subtype of interference that results from imperfect group learning during a process of language shift. That is, in this kind of interference a group of speakers shifting to a target language fails to learn the target language (TL) perfectly. The errors made by members of the shifting group in speaking the TL then spread to the TL as a whole when they are imitated by original speakers of that language.
> . . . interference through imperfect learning does *not* begin with vocabulary: it begins instead with sounds and syntax.

These authors (1988: 251–56) justifiably argue that Afrikaans is probably not a Creole language as occasionally claimed, but indeed Dutch-based and simplified through the imperfect mastery of second-language speakers that then passed on the simplified "bad Dutch" to the children of their white masters that they had to rear – a claim corroborated by a diary entry from 1685 (van Reede). The kind of Cape Dutch spoken by *inter alia* the shifting Cape Khoe led to variants of Afrikaans that were accepted among academics only more recently as not just non-standard (non-white) but legitimate varieties of Afrikaans, notably "Orange River Afrikaans". Those errors that were then imitated by the "original speakers" of Dutch – mainly by their children – led to the emergence of "standard" Afrikaans as spoken primarily by Whites. As said, the errors made did not lead so much to the introduction of marked grammatical structures, but mainly to a simplification of the inflectional system of Dutch and modification of the phonological system.

The reader is reminded that early Afrikaans was introduced to present-day Namibia not by white Afrikaners but by Africans, viz. by the Orlam Nama from South Africa who migrated over the Orange River in the early eighteenth century.

Superstratum interference of Dutch in Khoekhoe typically manifested itself most through lexical interference, i.e. through borrowing of terms for cultural or technological innovations obtained from the immigrant Whites. In the *Khoekhoegowab Dictionary* (Haacke and Eiseb 2002) over 85 per cent of the entries that are marked as loans from Afrikaans are nouns; the remainder consists almost exclusively of verbs. The dominance of nouns is to be expected as items from the foreign material culture are more readily acquired than habits or actions as reflected in verbs.

Borrowings can be grouped mainly into adoptions (direct borrowings with more or less phonological adaptation), calques and hybrids (see also Haacke 1989: 420ff. for the creation of terminology as part of corpus planning). Adoptions form by far the majority:

ábël-s 'apple' < Afrikaans *appel*
báìgì-b/*báìgì-s* 'jacket' < Afrikaans *baadjie*
spőók, *sőpók* 'be haunted' < Afrikaans *spook*

Calques are quite rare. This is not surprising, as direct adoption by way of language mixing requires less intellectual effort than translation of concepts.

ǀàẽ̋ǁgàù-b 'rocket' < Afrikaans *vuurpyl*; cf. *ǀàẽ̋-b* 'fire': Afrikaans *vuur*
ǁgàű-b 'arrow': Afrikaans *pyl*
ǁnäáǂgàãǁáè-b 'time to fall in line' < Afrikaans *invaltyd*;
cf. *ǁnäá* 'fall': Afrikaans *val*
ǂgàã 'enter': Afrikaans preposition *in*
ǁãé-b 'time': Afrikaans *tyd*

Calques pose an interesting question, namely which language borrowed (and translated) from which. The following Afrikaans words do not seem to have their roots in Dutch. Hence, the alternative possibility that Afrikaans adopted them from Khoekhoe cannot be ruled out. (I am grateful to Hans den Besten, who verified the possible existence of Dutch equivalents for me.)

sêgoed	***mĩxū-i***	'repartee, witty sayings'	cf.	***mĩ***	*sê*	'say'
				xū-'i	*goed*	'thing'
optelgoed	***hōkhãixū-n***	'things picked up/found'	cf.	***hōkhãi***	*optel*	'find, pick up'
				xū-n	*goed*	'things'
rybyl	***!nari!ō-b***	'adze'	cf.	***!nari***	*ry*	'drive'
				!ō-b	*byl*	'axe, chopper'

The Afrikaans word *draadtrek* (vulgar for 'masturbate (said of male)'; lit.: 'pull wire') is peculiar in its origin in that it is a calque not of the obvious Khoekhoe denotation 'stimulate to erection' of the causative verb *ǁnãiǁnãi* (from *ǁnãi* 'become erect' (v.intr.) (physiol.)), but is a pseudo-euphemistic calque of its meaning 'pull taut (e.g. wire)'. The overall meaning of the causative verb *ǁnãiǁnãi* is 'stiffen' (v.tr.).

The compilers of the *Khoekhoegowab Dictionary* frequently were led to observe that a ready equivalent for the Khoekhoe word is easier to find in Afrikaans than in English. This may be due to typological reasons, as Khoekhoe compound verbs are more readily rendered like Afrikaans phrasal verbs than like English phrasal verbs. Afrikaans (and German, for that matter) particles are more likely to be semantically equivalent to those of Khoekhoe than particles of English are. Ample instance is provided by verbs with Afrikaans *uit-* (lit.: 'out') and Khoekhoe *-ǂui*. Whether such words are calques borrowed into Khoekhoe or simply parallel manifestations of similar compounds cannot be said.

The following Afrikaans examples have cognates in Dutch and usually also German, so Khoekhoe has either borrowed them or has had them independently.

uitlag	***ãi‡ui***	'laugh at someone, to scorn'	cf.	***ãi*** ***‡ui***	*lag* *uit*	'laugh' 'out'
uitvra	***dĩ‡ui***	'question closely'	cf.	***dĩ*** ***‡ui***	*vra* *uit*	'ask, question' 'out'
(drank) wegslaan	***(ãxū-e) ra ‡naubē***	'down/quaff (drink)'	cf.	***‡nau*** ***bē***	*slaan* *weg (-gaan)*	'hit, beat' '(go) away'
afneem	***!khō//nā***	'photograph'	cf.	***!khō*** ***-//nā***	*neem*	'grasp' (in verbs: 'down')

The following instances of object incorporation in Afrikaans gerunds are paralleled in Khoekhoe verbs. In predicates, however, Afrikaans manifests incorporation as little as English, both being SVO languages.

skoolgaan	***skol!gū***	'go(ing) to school'	cf.	***skol-i*** ***!gū***	*skool* *gaan*	'school' 'go'
toutrek	***tsūri‡gae***	'play(ing) tug-of-war'	cf.	***tsūri-b*** ***‡gae***	*tou* *trek*	'rope' 'pull'

Hybrid borrowings are almost exclusively from Afrikaans into Khoekhoe:

*smokel**xū-n***	'contraband'	cf.	Afrikaans Khoekhoe	*smokkel (goed)* ***xū-n***	'smuggle' 'things'
*rōs**!khā-s***	'rose'	cf.	Afrikaans Khoekhoe	*roos* ***!khā-s***	'rose' 'flower'
*spul**//gam-mi***	'rinsing-water'	cf.	Afrikaans Khoekhoe	*spoel* ***//gam-mi***	'rinse' 'water'

Grammatical borrowing from Afrikaans is evident in Khoekhoe, though to a limited extent. Borrowing is to be expected, considering that the Khoekhoe as the shifting people have been bilingual for several centuries. On the other hand, it may have been constrained by the fact that the two languages are typologically fairly divergent.

An instance of grammatical borrowing in informal speech is that of the Afrikaans superlative suffix *-ste*, though not the comparative *-er*, e.g.:

*kai**ste** ao-b* 'big**gest** man'; cf. *kai* 'big', *ao-b* 'man'

Khoekhoe has to resort to periphrastic constructions for the comparative and superlative:

hoa-n xa a kai ao-b 'a man big from all, i.e. biggest man'

The opposite derivational process has also been observed: the Khoekhoe adverbial derivative suffix *-se* is appended to an Afrikaans root perceived as adjectival, to form an adverb in Khoekhoe:

*lāt**se***	'late' (adv.)	cf. Afrikaans *laat* 'late' (adj./adv.)
*frux**se***	'early' (adv.)	cf. Afrikaans *vroeg* 'early' (adj./adv.)

A few instances of phrasal calques that follow Afrikaans syntax irrespective of Khoekhoe syntax are on record, e.g.:

emers *!oa* *//gam-mi*
('n) emmer vol water
'a bucket full of water'

//hō-s *!oa* *!gãn*
('n) sak vol gras
'a bag full of grass'

A case of grammatical loan with wider-reaching consequences is attested in Khoekhoe. What makes the case extraordinary is that it is not an instance of *structural* change, but rather one of different *reading* of an existing pattern. The structure in question is the so-called "(co-referential) copulative" sentence with the alleged reading "NP_1 be NP_2", e.g.:

[*!Hõakaō*]-*b* *ge* [*Petrū*]-*b* + *a*
crook-PGN IND Peter-PGN + OBL

The question is whether such a sentence should be read as 'The crook is Peter' or as 'Peter is the/a crook'. In practically all grammars on Khoekhoe this kind of sentence is read in a left to right sequence "$NP_{subject}$ be $NP_{complement}$", with NP_1 taken to be the subject of a "copulative" reading. This is the typical reading as encountered in Bantu copulative sentences.

Textual analysis, however, reveals that speakers of Khoekhoe fluctuate between the two readings, depending on the context. While the first reading, the "copulative" reading, is the one *claimed* by the grammars to be the typical (if not only) reading, the original Khoekhoe reading is rather one that in function is similar to a (pseudo-)cleft sentence, in which the predicate head has been topicalised into the initial slot, and the subject specification has been deposed to the end of the sentence:

*Petru+**b ge a*** *!hõakao* > *!Hõakao* ***a~b ge*** *Petru+ba* >
!Hõakao~b ge *Petru+ba*
Peter IND PRES.STAT crook
'Peter is (a) crook.' > '**He** – that is Peter – **is a crook**.'

The lexical specification of the subject-NP (*Petru*) is demoted to a deposed subject, which as such takes the oblique case ending *-a*, which is the grammaticalised (present) stative marker *a* (cf. Haacke 1979). It is contended here that, as the second reading with the topicalised predicate (*!hõakao a*) consistently fits into the underlying syntax of Khoekhoe, the first, so-called "copular", reading is based on a misinterpretation of Khoekhoe syntax by analogy to Bantu. As such it has been unwittingly imposed on Khoekhoe by (mostly German) missionaries and linguists. The "copulative" reading is indeed now also offered by mother tongue speakers, but it appears as a result of some indoctrination from the European side.

It may be assumed that a considerable amount of contact-induced change has as yet gone unnoticed especially in the lexicon of both, Khoekhoe and Afrikaans, as the topic has not been seriously investigated yet by linguists conversant in both languages.

6 NAMIBIAN JU|'HOANSI IN CONTACT WITH SPEAKERS OF AFRIKAANS

Amanda L. Miller

6.1 Ju|'hoan–Afrikaans contact

Namibian Ju|'hoansi have had prolonged contact with Afrikaans speakers most notably through their participation in the South West African Army. The geographic conditions of Bushmanland (the Bushman homeland under apartheid consisting of a portion of traditional Ju|'hoansi lands), as well as the enforced segregation of Namibia through apartheid, lessened contact between Khoesan and Bantu groups. Thus, Namibian Ju|'hoan loanwords illustrate direct contact between Afrikaans and Khoesan languages. Afrikaans loanwords are usually obvious, as there are so many structural dissimilarities between the languages. Yet, interesting assimilation patterns are also found.

6.2 Syllable structure repairs

Epenthesis repairs illicit consonant clusters, often resulting in trisyllabic roots that disobey the disyllabic root maximum. An epenthetic vowel, identical to the initial underlying vowel, is inserted between initial obstruent + liquid, and fricative + stop clusters:

(1) Epenthesis into obstruent + liquid clusters

dö̀rö̀mä̀ 'drum, garbage container' *fə̀rúrù* 'floor'
pəlakisi 'flip flops' *búrúkhè* 'trousers'

Epenthesis into fricative + stop clusters

sikore 'school' *sitora* 'store'

The epenthetic vowel is prosodically weaker than the underlying vowels, resulting in more centralized vowels, when it creates a third syllable. Many loanwords are found in Dickens (1994) without epenthesis, due to the fact that bilingual Ju|'hoan speakers often pronounce the words in correct Afrikaans pronunciation. Monolingual speakers always epenthesize.

Illicit final consonants (all consonants except [m]), are also repaired through epenthesis:

(2) Epenthesis following final consonants

ə̀pə̀rə̀ 'apple' *búrù* 'ball' *k*^{h}*ání* 'milk can'*
kë̀tàngà 'chain' *rä̀dä̀* 'councillor' *píní* 'pen'

*Note that there is no height harmony in this root, presumably because the [i] is not underlying.

It is interesting to note that even final [ŋ] gains a final epenthetic vowel, which is evidence that final [ŋ] in roots like *n!àŋ* [n!ŋ̀] 'eland' is an allophone of [n] due to assimilation to the preceding click.

6.3 Illicit vowel sequences

Some Afrikaans words are borrowed into Ju|'hoan with epiglottalization on the vowels:

(3) Modal Afrikaans vowels are epiglottalized

rok 'dress' *hò*^{q}*'órók*^{h}*òè*
baaidjie 'jacket' *bä̀*^{q}*ìkì*
pyp 'hose' *pä̀*^{q}*ì*, *pä̀*^{q}*ìpà*

In the word 'dress', the presence of epiglottalization probably derives from the uvular Afrikaans [ʀ]. The epenthesis of the initial syllable is due to the fact that [ɾ] only occurs medially in Ju|'hoan. In the word meaning 'jacket' [ai] is illicit. As shown by Miller-Ockhuizen (1999a: 316–19), co-articulation results in the diphthong [əi]. Additionally, the diphthong [əi] never occurs after a labial consonant. In the word 'hose', the [aˤi] sequence arises through the assimilation of the Afrikaans front rounded vowel *y* [ø].

6.4 Direct contact

Visser (1998: 119f.) has claimed that many of the epenthesized words in Naro are first assimilated into Tswana, and then later borrowed into the Khoesan languages in their epenthesized forms. If this were always the case, then epenthesized forms in Khoesan languages would not tell us anything about the structure of the Khoesan languages themselves. In (4) below, I give a few illustrative forms of Afrikaans loanwords in Ju|'hoan that have native vocabulary forms in the neighbouring Bantu languages, or as with the case of the word 'chain', occur in very different assimilated forms in most other languages.

(4) Epenthesized forms in Ju|'hoan which correspond to native words in neighbouring Bantu languages[1]

Afrikaans	English	Ju|'hoan	Tswana	Herero	Kwangali	Mbukushu
vloer	'floor'	*fərúrù*	*bodílô*		*rugorongwa*	*thiramba*
ketang	'chain'	*këtàngà*	*kéétāne*	*ouketanga*	*elyenge*	*dyenge*
pampoen	'pumpkin'	*pàβú*	*lephutshé*	*otjimbakuna*	*etanga*	*dingadi*

Epenthesis in words such as 'pumpkin' is due to direct contact between Afrikaans and Ju|'hoan, and indicates the disallowance of consonant clusters in the language. Of course, this does not rule out the possibility that some words, such as 'chain', may have entered through neighbouring Bantu languages, such as Herero.

7 HAI||OM LANGUAGE CONTACT

Thomas Widlok

The Hai||om language has not been subject to the same efforts of standardization and canonization as Nama/Damara has been. This may partly be due to the low public status of Hai||om as a "Bushman" language but also due to a low academic status of Hai||om as a "dialect" of Nama or even a "bowdlerized" version of Nama. Present-day Hai||om speech includes borrowings from very different neighbouring languages. Borrowing from !Xũũ seems to occur less than one may expect, given the frequent interaction in some northern areas of Namibia. Important exceptions are the "words" used in the Elephant Medicine Dance of the ǂAkhoe which is practised frequently today and which is said to originate from the !Xũũ. The term for 'being in trance' itself is a compound verb, *!gai||o*, which is clearly related to the !Xũũ lexeme *!aia* 'to fall into trance' (Dickens 1994: 309).

Even though the following analysis is restricted to processes of borrowing from non-Khoesan languages this should not suggest that Afrikaans or Oshiwambo are, or have always been, more important sources of innovation to the Hai||om language than Khoesan languages. The Hai||om/ǂAkhoe lexicon shares many items with other Khoesan languages, in particular with Nama/Damara, so the line between shared origins and genuine borrowing may not always be drawn easily. Borrowings from non-Khoesan languages are usually easier to trace although words may be borrowed from a language that has only recently borrowed these items itself (see below). In a historically long line of borrowing Afrikaans was in many cases the most recent link in the chain and, therefore, features prominently in the following examples.

Borrowings are most evident for nouns, which are often also recognized as "foreign words" even though they are inflected like Khoekhoe nouns. Examples are:

bongi-e	'beans'	(< Afrikaans *boontjie*)
oroso-s	'watch'	(< Afrikaans *horlosie*)
stor-s	'shop'	(< English *store*)
stul-s	'chair'	(< Afrikaans/German *stoel/Stuhl*)
swesta-s	'nurse'	(< German *Schwester*)

With regard to borrowing of Afrikaans nouns Haiǁom shares some incorporation practices that have been noted for Nama (see Hagman 1977: 30). In compound nouns a nuclear noun root from Khoekhoe may be complemented with a word borrowed from Afrikaans. Well-known examples are the days of the week: *sontatses* (consisting of *sontag*, Afrikaans for 'Sunday' and *tses*), and similarly *freitatses*, *sataratses*. Note that this borrowing is very selective in Haiǁom since other days of the week are not borrowed from Afrikaans, e.g. *ǀgamitses* 'Tuesday' (lit. 'second day'). Similarly, the borrowing of numbers is selective. While numbers up to a hundred largely follow the Khoekhoe decimal system, the terms for 'hundred', *kai disi*, and 'thousand', *ǀoa kai disi*, are usually replaced by *honnorsa* and *taisensa*, respectively.

Note with regard to the weekdays that the Afrikaans words are borrowed as units without breaking them down into their constituent parts. The *sonda* part already includes 'day' but is still compounded with Khoekhoe *tses*.

A complementary strategy also occurs insofar as a unit is added where in the original word there is none. This happens with borrowed Afrikaans words ending with a final released *k*-sound (see Hagman 1977: 30 for the same strategy in Nama), which are lengthened in the following manner:

rok	'dress'	is turned into	*rokwes* (or *rokhoes*)
broek	'trousers'	is turned into	*burukwes*
tronk	'jail'	is turned into	*toronkwes*

As the preceding examples show, borrowed words may also be lengthened to allow easier pronunciation. It also facilitates the adding of the obligatory pgn endings. For instance, in everyday Haiǁom speech the Afrikaans word *trekker* 'tractor' is lengthened and shortened to facilitate its regular inflection according to the Haiǁom rules. The following phrases were elicited from a life history of a Haiǁom man:

terekeri ǀkha	'with a tractor'
axagua terekegua mãhe	'young men were given tractors'
gu ge na terekerka gere !gãri	'they (the men) drove these tractors'

In other instances Afrikaans adjectives such as *arm* 'poor' are borrowed and then used either in the adjectival form (*aram*) or in compound nouns in combination with a Khoesan word (*aramkhoen* 'poor people').

Afrikaans terms denoting objects or concepts that have been introduced by Europeans are frequently borrowed even though the manifold derivational morphemes of Haiǁom provide the means to create precise Khoekhoe correspondences. The linguistic potential notwithstanding, many Afrikaans nouns are now used so frequently that they are no longer considered foreign words. Examples are: *skoli* 'school' (< Afrikaans/English), *dorom* 'container' (< Afrikaans/English *trom/drum*), *keteb* 'chain' (< Afrikaans/German *ketting/Kette*). In some instances Khoesan words and borrowed words coexist. Examples:

'garden': *!hanas* (as in Nama/Damara) and *tuins* (Afrikaans)
'teacher': *//kha//khaobwa* (as in Nama/Damara) and *Mister* (also used as a general term for male Whites)

These examples show that there is a likelihood of imported borrowing, i.e. borrowings from a language into which the term was borrowed fairly recently, e.g. *Mister* from English into Afrikaans.

The reason for these borrowings from Afrikaans in cases where original Khoesan words readily exist may be found in the low status of Khoesan languages and the fact that many of these words are frequently used in dealings with outsiders. Another reason is the tolerance of Hai‖om speakers with regard to synonyms of apparently different linguistic roots. There are a considerable number of synonymous pairs being used in everyday Hai‖om speech which are clearly both of Khoesan origin but which seem completely unrelated in their lexical form. Examples are:

taub and *xaib*	'kudu'
tamb and *kovab*	'language'
ǂama and *!aroma*	'because'

In some cases the borrowed term retains some distinctive semantic features which separate it from the Khoesan lexeme. Examples:

nondas (< Ndonga *ondunda* or Kwanyama *onduda*) for 'house', *oms*, to designate a house built in Owambo style (that is with a thatched roof and wooden poles)

xeb (< Afrikaans *gif*) for synthetically produced poison, in contrast to plant poison (*!khore*)

This is also true with regard to more complex phrases (or elements thereof) that have been borrowed from Afrikaans and Oshiwambo. The use of Oshiwambo and Afrikaans in greeting phrases has also been noted. In these greetings ǂAkhoe speakers not only incorporate borrowed lexemes (*ombili* 'peace' and *tokela* 'evening' from Oshiwambo; *meda* and *xunda* from Afrikaans), but the pragmatic rules are selectively imported and transformed as well (see Widlok 1997: 119). This raises the question of correspondences between linguistic and social shifts. The example of the introduction of the Oshiwambo lexeme *olupale* and of the Owambo institutions of spatial behaviour associated with the *olupale* (the visitor's fire) shows that there is no deterministic relation between linguistic and social shifts but that, nevertheless, there are instructive parallels between these two processes that are often intertwined (see Widlok 1999b: 135).

8 KHOESAN-INTERNAL CONTACTS[2]

Tom Güldemann

8.1 Introduction

Despite the vastness of South African territory once populated by Khoesan peoples, the attested languages belong to only two lineages, each correlating fairly consistently with a particular mode of life of their speakers. The languages of hunter-gatherers alias San are from the Tuu family, predominantly from its !Ui subgroup. The pastoralists spoke varieties of Khoekhoe. Due to differences in the contact patterns and the structural divergence between the interacting languages, a distinction can be made between (a) pastoralist-internal contacts, (b) San-internal, and (c) San–pastoralist contacts. Only the last two will be dealt with here.

8.2 San-internal contacts

The misconception that speech varieties of San peoples are merely dialects of one language pervades the early literature, reinforced by the inappropriate use of the label "Bushman languages" in a genealogical sense. Even judgements by authorities like Wilhelm Bleek must be taken with reservation in this respect. One wonders, for example, what can be concluded from his report (1873: 2) that "the different Bushman dialects spoken within this Colony [roughly the Cape south of the Orange River] vary very little from each other, and that one language, quite different from Hottentot, is spoken by all these Bushmen". This statement may only have had a general typological significance for him, because he usually contrasted the then known San languages from !Ui against Khoe and Bantu (cf. Bleek 1869), rather than among one another. In any case, Bleek's data at the time were restricted to very little and predominantly lexical material from half a dozen distant localities. Pace Traill (1996: 177f.), these would not allow one to draw firm conclusions about the actual closeness/distance between varieties of a generally close-knit genealogical unit like !Ui, so Bleek's generalization over the vast area of the Cape is potentially misleading. Especially in the South African context, where language "documentation" sometimes means nothing more than a short list of poorly transcribed words, the assessment of such a variety vis-à-vis another in terms of language versus dialect remains a notorious problem.

Since it is unclear what kind of linguistic varieties were actually in contact with each other, any evaluation of the pre-colonial sociolinguistic situation among South African San can only give a very rough picture; moreover, this can only be reconstructed by largely extrapolating from patterns observed among San of other areas, which remained relatively undisturbed until recently.

A clearly discernible pattern is the existence of extensive dialect clusters, for example, |Xam in the Karoo and the group of varieties called by Dorothea Bleek ǁŋ (= Nǁng), which spread over a large area north of the Orange River (including ǂKhomani and N|huki, see Güldemann 2000a). The degree of their internal diversity remains unclear due to insufficient documentation. Generally, however, such dialect clusters can display considerable linguistic diversity so that non-adjacent varieties need not be mutually intelligible (cf. Traill 1974: 29f. on differences between West and East !Xoon with the Taa complex). At the same time speakers are usually able, if need be, to adapt their speech habits easily towards those of a related variety.

This is not the case across more pronounced linguistic boundaries which are also attested for South Africa. Speaker judgements to this effect, however problematic these may be, come from the Upper Orange River regarding !Ui varieties from different sides of the river (Traill 1996: 177f.) or from around Upington regarding a Nǁng variety vis-à-vis |Xam (D. Bleek, notebook A3.9: 302f.). Although the Lower Nosop area seems to be messy at first glance (see Güldemann 2000a), it provides an even clearer case of a language boundary on account of the available sociolinguistic and linguistic information (D. Bleek, notebooks A3.29+30), namely the distinctness of ǂKhomani from |'Auni and |Haasi. This case also demonstrates another important aspect, viz. the possible results of intensive social contacts between different speech communities in the form of bilingualism and mutual linguistic interference. Regarding the consequences of this type of language contact, it can safely be assumed that Traill and Nakagawa's (2000) conclusion is also valid for South Africa, namely that the contacts observed within and across genealogical units can account to a considerable extent for the existence of areal and sub-areal features in pre-Bantu southern Africa.

However, if the integrity of the different social units is retained, a possible linguistic boundary would be stable. Thus, the present entanglement of the ǂKhomani–ǀ'Auni complex cannot be interpreted as reflecting inherent fluctuation and fuzziness of San linguistic identities. It should rather be evaluated in the light of loss of access to traditional territories on the part of these groups and their subsequent disintegration.

8.3 San–Pastoralist contacts

For the colonial period, we are well informed that contacts between Khoekhoe speakers (especially !Ora, Xiri, and Basters) and San could be characterized by a fair amount of conflict (cf., e.g., Engelbrecht 1936). However, this will not have been the pattern throughout history, but rather seems to be associated with a particular historical situation: during the expansion of the Cape Colony in the nineteenth century, indigenous pastoralist and hunter-gatherer groups were societies under hard territorial, social, and economic pressure instigating a struggle for continuously dwindling resources.

One can also discern patterns of peaceful cohabitation of these different groups, which favoured mutual bilingualism and linguistic interference. That this was especially relevant in the early contact history is suggested by important structural isoglosses shared by !Ui and Khoekhoe (Güldemann 2002, 2006b). Despite the strong tendency in the previous literature to ascribe such similarities to the borrowing of Khoekhoe features on the part of San speakers, it is often far from clear which language is actually the source. In fact, substantial data clearly point in the opposite direction and justify to conjecture a Tuu substrate that pervades Khoekhoe in general and involves features defining this branch against Kalahari Khoe.

Later periods, too, give evidence for the fact that bilingualism was often not unilateral; for example, Krönlein's !Ui data on Nǀuusaan from beyond the Lower Orange River was furnished to him by a Nama-speaking Orlam (Güldemann 2006a). A similar situation can be assumed for linguistic contacts between !Ui and !Ora along the Middle Orange River. However, the recent history more often gives evidence for the knowledge of more prestigious Khoekhoe varieties on the part of the San. During their large-scale acculturation in the nineteenth and twentieth centuries, this pattern sometimes culminated in a complete language shift towards Khoekhoe (cf., e.g., Traill 1995a, 1996).

9 THE EXTINCT KHOESAN LANGUAGES OF EASTERN AFRICA

Christopher Ehret

Just two languages, Sandawe and Hadza, of those that have been proposed for membership in the Khoesan language family are spoken today in East Africa. Both these speech communities inhabit areas not far from each other in north-central Tanzania. But indirect evidence exists that other languages of possible Khoesan relationship were formerly spoken in East Africa as far north as northern Kenya and north-eastern Uganda. What is the evidence for the existence of these now vanished communities? How do they fit into the earlier history of eastern Africa? These are the questions we will be considering here.

The crucial evidence for the existence of these former communities consists of sets of loanwords adopted from their languages into the languages that superseded them. These word borrowings give us clues as to the locations and cross-cultural interactions of the different communities involved in this history. The most numerous examples of this kind of word borrowing occur in the Southern Cushitic (SC) languages of East Africa, but additional cases of loanwords from extinct languages of possible Khoesan relationships appear in the Rub ("Kuliak") languages of the Nilo-Saharan phylum, spoken in recent centuries in north-eastern Uganda.

9.1 Loanwords in early SC

The Southern Cushites were livestock-raising peoples whose cultural origins go back to the far southern Ethiopian highlands in the fourth millennium BCE. Over the last 3,500 years BCE, Southern Cushitic communities spread across successively wider areas of East Africa. As a result of these expansions, the Southern Cushites successively diverged into a number of distinct speech communities, as depicted in the updated tree of relationships in Figure 8.1 (Ehret 2011). The dating estimates for this history derive from archaeological correlations first laid out in Ambrose (1982).

A number of apparently distinct sets of loanwords from the languages of the previous inhabitants of the land into which the early Southern Cushites moved can be discerned in the lexicons of SC languages. These reflect several eras of cross-cultural interaction. They include loanwords dating back to the Proto-SC period, to the Proto-Rift-Mbugu (PRM) era, and to the Proto-Rift period, as well as sets of words limited to particular SC languages.

What must be noted about the various sets of loanword data we will be considering here is that it is likely that they form only a portion of all the loanwords actually adopted in these early periods into SC from earlier-spoken East African languages. In addition,

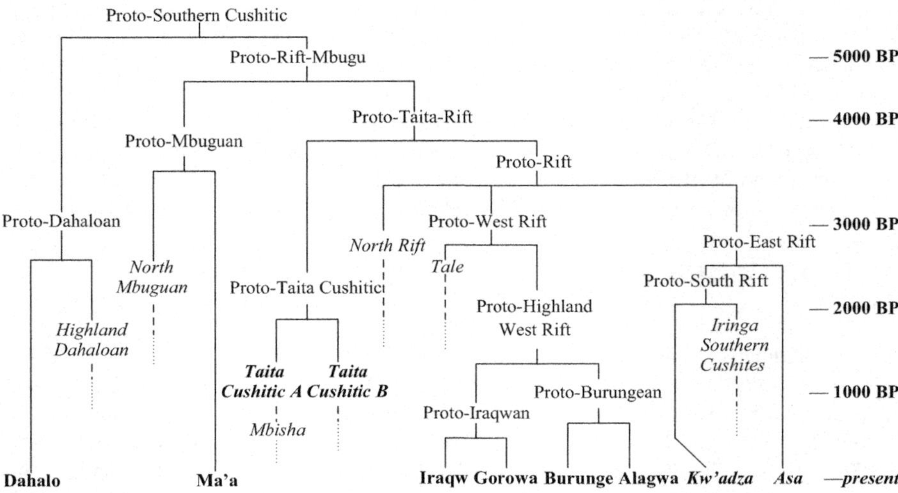

FIGURE 8.1 EXPANDED FAMILY TREE OF THE SOUTHERN CUSHITIC LANGUAGES (EHRET 2011)

the languages from which the borrowings into SC came, if these languages did indeed belong to a greater Khoesan phylum, would have been separated by thousands of years of differentiation from any of the still extant related tongues and so have had great differences in vocabulary from those existing languages, making the process of identifying loanwords all the harder.

On present evidence four words, and probably a fifth (for the *siafu* ant), of borrowed origin and with prototypes in Khoesan and proposed Khoesan languages (cf. List 1) can be tracked back to the Proto-SC language itself. The defining characteristic of these terms identifying them as probable loanwords are that they are not found anywhere else in the Cushitic branch of the Afroasiatic language phylum or in other branches of the phylum.

LIST 1 LOANWORDS OF PROPOSED KHOESAN ATTRIBUTION IN PROTO-SC

Proto-SC	"Khoesan" attestations
*(b)aab- 'carry child on back'	Southern African Khoesan (SAK): Khoe: Proto-Khoekhoe *aba
*ɗama '(young?) female animal' (Dahalo 'female lungfish'; West Rift 'heifer')	SAK: Ju: Proto-Ju (PJ) *dama 'child'; Sandawe *dámà* 'female (of large animals)' (proposed original meaning 'young female')
*keek- 'to pay attention to'	Sandawe *k*^{h}*é'é* 'to hear'; SAK: Proto-Khoe (PKh) *khe 'to hear' (cf. also Sandawe *kéké* 'ear')
*k'ad- 'arrow poison'	SAK: Ju *kx'aru*; Hadza *k'ade*
*k^w'atl'aaʕ- '*siafu* ant'	Sandawe *!wetl'áá* '*siafu* ant'

A notable feature of the set of words in List 1 is that their plausible source forms can occur either only in SAK (Khoe, Ju, and Tuu groups of southern Africa), Sandawe, or Hadza, or in Hadza and Sandawe, or in Hadza and/or Sandawe and in one or more SAK languages. This distribution pattern is one we will encounter repeatedly in the lexical sets considered here. It has implications for the hypothesis of a wider Khoesan phylum including Hadza and Sandawe that we will return to later.

A second set of such loans entered SC at least as early as the immediately subsequent PRM period.

LIST 2 LOANWORDS IN PRM FROM A SANDAWE-RELATED LANGUAGE

PRM	Attestations outside Rift-Mbugu
*haaka 'four'	Sandawe *haka-*; PKh *haka
*kǒ'an- 'five'	Sandawe *kwǎ'áná* 'five' (stem *kwa- plus Sandawe *-ana* nominal suffix); Hadza *'ukwa* 'arm; finger'
*kôr- 'year'	SAK: PKh *kuri; PJ *kúrí; Tuu: !Xõõ *kúli*
*saax- 'organ of chest'	Sandawe *sákà* 'chest'; also SAK: Tuu: !Xõõ *tshxàã̃* 'pith; mesophyll (of *Senseveria* sp.)': proposed semantics: earlier 'heart' > 'core of anything', hence 'pith'; for proposed pre-SAK *CVCV > CCV, hence !Xõõ *tshxàã̃* < earlier *tshaxa, see Ehret 1986)
*k'ǎr- 'lad, young man'	Sandawe *k'àré* 'youth'; SAK: PKh *kx'ado 'boy'; Ju *kx'arò* 'young male animal, young man'
*ɗiɗi 'ground hornbill'	Sandawe *didi*, *dudu* 'ground hornbill'

Unlike the loanwords in Proto-SC (List 1), the features of the set of borrowings in List 2 do suggest a particular relationship for its source language. The presence of all but one of the six loanwords in the Sandawe language, along with the fact that the word for 'five' appears to be a specifically Sandawean innovation, strongly imply that the source language of the loans, spoken on the order of 4,000 years ago, was an offshoot of the same line of linguistic descent as Sandawe. It is possible that one or more of the words of this set may actually go back to the Proto-SC period and might therefore once upon a time have been found in Dahalo. But the general attribution of these loanwords, unlike those in List 1, to a Sandawe-related language makes this possibility highly improbable for all except perhaps the one word, for 'year', not found in Sandawe today.

Moreover, in the case of the words for 'four' and 'five', we can specifically trace these terms to the PRM stage. The reason for this conclusion has two parts. First, the borrowing of numerals in language history does not normally occur individually, except for the adoption of a few higher nodal terms, namely 'ten', 'hundred', or 'thousand'. Instead, what tends to take place is the borrowing of a sequence of numbers, consisting of a nodal item and one or more of the numbers immediately preceding it in counting order. The speakers of Proto-Southern Nilotic, for instance, borrowed all the numerals from 'ten' down to 'six' (as well as the higher nodal items, 20, 30, 40, 50, 60, 70, 80, 90, and 100) from Eastern Cushitic, while they maintained older inherited words for 'one' to 'five'. So we would have to argue that the PRM terms for 'four' and 'five', which form a sequence topped off by the nodal item 'five', were most likely borrowed as a single historical development. The second part of the argument rests on the fact that, although Dahalo has innovated its own unique word for 'five', it has retained the old Cushitic root *soʕal- for 'four' (Dahalo *saʕala*), showing that the Khoesan word for 'four' was adopted into SC after the Dahaloan branch had begun to diverge from the Rift-Mbugu branch. Assuming, as seems most probable, that the numerals 'four' and 'five' were borrowed at the same time, then the borrowing of 'five' should also have been a development of the PRM language.

9.2 Historical implications of the early Khoesan loanwords in SC

The Proto-SC society and its immediate descendant people, the PRM, inhabited lands to the east of Lake Turkana in the second half of the fourth millennium BCE. We must therefore locate the communities with whom they interacted in the same broad region.

If in fact the East Turkana communities were simply gatherer-hunters in contact with expanding, food-producing Southern Cushites, the semantic reach of the influences from a Sandawe-related language into the PRM vocabulary in particular seems surprisingly deep. The adoption into PRM of the old term for 'year' found so widely in the SAK languages suggests that the Southern Cushites, in moving into the northern Kenya regions, may have taken on their predecessors' conceptions of the yearly cycle, despite presumed differences in their economic activities. The adoption of a term for a life stage already very old in Cushitic social history, that of a young man between circumcision and marriage, is even more surprising because it implies an outside cultural input affecting one of the core features of ancient custom in Cushitic societies.

Most surprising of all, however, was the Rift-Mbugu borrowing of their words for 'four' and 'five' from the Sandawe-related "East-Turkana" language. Gatherer-hunter communities in eastern African history have frequently adopted numerals from neighbouring, economically dominant food producers, but borrowing the other way around is virtually unknown. The normal pattern in numeral borrowing, as we have seen, is for the higher part of a particular subset of numbers to be borrowed. In the case of PRM this same pattern appears, with older Cushitic roots used for 'one' and 'two' and apparently 'three' (Ehret 1980), but with 'four' and 'five' coming from the East-Turkana source language.

What this all strongly indicates is that we are not dealing here with a historical situation of simple expansion of food producers into previously gatherer-hunter country. The East-Turkana communities seem likely, from the loanwords they have left behind in SC languages, to have been a relatively numerous grouping of people long able to hold their own against the advance of Southern Cushites into their lands. Two explanations for this history seem possible. One is that these particular people were themselves already in part food producers; the other is that they followed a kind of gathering and hunting that allowed them to support a denser population than is typical of most gatherer-hunters.

The archaeology of the Turkana basin of the fourth and earlier third millenniums BCE offers a third alternative that combines these two. On the east of Lake Turkana there lived people who combined the highly productive Aquatic way of life – brought into the basin several thousand years earlier – with the raising of livestock. The pottery of these particular peoples living on the east of Lake Turkana belongs to the styles of the Southern Cushites (Ambrose 1982). The utilization of fishing resources, on the other hand, clashes with the general Cushitic avoidance of fish eating. What we may have here, in other words, might be a mixture of sites – some inhabited by the proposed East-Turkana society, who fished but also kept livestock and used pottery they had adopted from their SC neighbours, and others inhabited by the PRM communities. If this kind of close interconnection held true, then the penetration of the East-Turkana loanwords into deep portions of Rift-Mbugu culture vocabulary would begin to make sense.

9.3 Loanwords in Proto-Rift SC

A third significant set of loanwords of proposed Khoesan attribution (List 3) can be traced at least as far back in time as the Proto-Rift SC language, spoken at around 3,000 years ago. Also a very few words are known at present from just the East Rift or the West Rift subgroup. These are too few as yet to justify setting up additional later loanword periods and so may be treated for now as Proto-Rift borrowings retained in just one or the other subgroup. Because only a single language of the Mbuguan branch, Ma'a, has survived in use down to the present, it is possible that one or two of these items may remain from the earlier set found in the PRM language, but happened to have been retained only in Rift languages. Against this possibility is the fact that the one borrowing that does have a prototype in Sandawe differs in its phonology from the borrowed shape, favouring the conclusion that these words entered Rift languages from a different source language or languages after the PRM period.

The proposed source forms of these lexemes in List 3, as in the case of the loanwords in Proto-SC (List 1), occur across a range of languages: in SAK (Khoe, Ju, and Tuu groups), in Sandawe, in Hadza, and, in one instance, in both Sandawe and SAK languages.

The Proto-Rift language was spoken most probably somewhere in the plains of southern Kenya and adjoining parts of Tanzania, considerably farther south than the Proto-SC and PRM languages that were ancestral to it. So the language or languages that were the sources of the influence on Proto-Rift must be placed somewhere in that expanse as

LIST 3 WORDS OF PROPOSED KHOESAN ATTRIBUTION IN RIFT SC

Proto-Rift	Attestations in SAK, Hadza, and Sandawe
*daʕ- 'to burn' (tr.)	SAK: PKh *dao 'to burn'; Ju *dà'á* 'fire'
*dabi 'salt' [corrects root in Ehret 1980: 19, 162]	SAK: PKh *dabi; Ju *díbí*; Tuu: Nǀuuki *dyiβe*, etc.
*tlan- 'arrows'	Hadza *ǀ'ànà* 'poisoned arrow'; Sandawe *ǀ'ani ~ dlaní* 'arrow'
*tanaʕ- 'brain'	SAK: Khoekhoe *tana- 'head'; Sandawe *tónó* 'crown of head' (also Sandawe *tíní* 'brain': loanword back from Rift SC, specifically < Alagwa *tiniʕo*)
*c'i'- 'aardwolf (?)'	SAK: !Xõõ *ǀâi* 'aardwolf'; Ju *ǀa̰i̯* 'red jackal'; PKh *ǀgi ~ *ǀi 'aardwolf'

Word known so far only from West Rift:

Proto-West Rift *dan- 'honey' [Ehret 1980 makes the no longer tenable postulation of this root as a Proto-SC item.]	SAK: PKh *dani-

Words known so far only from East Rift:

Proto-East Rift *'alala 'scorpion' (Kw'adza *aleleto*, Asa *'alala*)	Sandawe *'ilàálàà*; Hadza *hala*
Kw'adza *dundumayo* 'area below chin' (reduplicated stem plus Kw'adza nominal suffix *-ayo*)	SAK 'throat': PKh *dom; Ju *dọm*

well. Some of the loans, too, indicate a strong influence of the earlier peoples on SC culture history. They include words for parts of the body, notably for 'brain' and also, it appears, at least one very basic verb, for burning in a transitive sense. At the least, the speakers of one of the source languages of these borrowings may initially have been numerically preponderant over the earliest incoming Proto-Rift people. The borrowing of a term for 'arrows', when this was a weapon of ancient provenance among the Cushites and their Proto-Afroasiatic ancestors (see Ehret 1995 and Orel and Stolbova 1995 for reconstructed bow and arrow lexicon), would fit with the donor people of the loanword having been gatherer-hunters.

In all three sets of early loanwords in SC, the number of words so far proposed is not great. In the cases of PRM and Proto-Rift, the penetration of the loans into core areas of culture and even into basic vocabulary suggests, though, that these items are the remnants of once significantly larger bodies of loanwords, in which many of the less basic items dropped out of use over the long intervening time span or remain still to be discovered by future research.

The single West Rift item listed here is likely to be an isolated retention of a word actually borrowed earlier, possibly at the Proto-Rift period. But the words limited to East Rift may be part of a larger set of Khoesan loanwords yet to be properly identified because of the paucity of evidence from the two East Rift languages cited here. A closer investigation still needs to be done in this instance, and there may well be more such items to be discovered once that effort is undertaken. The remaining Asa speakers in the twentieth century were gatherer-hunters in economy, and the oral traditions of the Kw'adza claimed such a background for themselves in earlier times, thus enhancing the possibility that each community evolved out of a previously non-SC-speaking society that gave up their former language in favour of an SC one.

9.4 Loanwords in Dahalo

By far the largest and most striking set of loanwords attributable to a language of proposed Khoesan relationship occurs in Dahalo (List 4), the sole extant language of the Dahaloan branch. This language adopted not only numerous words but, most notably of all, a significant corpus of words containing that especially distinctive feature of Khoesan phonology, click consonants. A significant minority of the click-containing words in Dahalo can already be matched up with plausible source forms in Sandawe, Hadza, or SAK languages, but many more will probably be discovered in the future to have such prototypes. An interesting recent research discovery (author's unpublished field recordings, 1997 and 2007) is the presence in Dahalo of two less common click consonants, // and *n//*, additional to the more highly visible / and *n/* of that language.

Previous studies have argued that the Dahalo, who up till recently were gatherer-hunters in economy, were in fact direct descendants of an earlier Khoesan-related society, who at some point in the past, probably as early as the last millennium BCE, adopted the language of their SC food-producing neighbours. The evidence presented here gives renewed support for that conclusion. Borrowed words, with clicks, carried over from the earlier gatherer-hunter language, include such core vocabulary terms as for 'woman's breast', 'night', 'star' and 'yellow' (the latter two are not included in List 4), along with a large number of everyday verbs. This type of borrowing is a defining indicator that the majority component in Dahalo ancestry came from the society whose language contained these words (Ehret 2011: ch. 4). In addition, a variety of cultural terms, such as for a 'shell scraper' and for 'arrowshaft', reveal cultural knowledge passed along from that more ancient past despite the shift of language.

The overabundance of dental click consonants (/) in the Dahalo word-borrowings in comparison to the lateral clicks (//) – with 71 dental-click words versus seven lateral-click words in the combined published (Ehret *et al.* 1989, Tosco 1991) and unpublished data (writer's field collections, 1997 and 2007) – is striking. Superabundance of one consonant over its equivalent consonant at a second point of articulation typically in historical linguistics reflects an earlier history of consonant merger. The presence of the pattern in this instance makes it highly probable that all the clicks except for the lateral had merged either in the donor language of the loanwords or became the default click for non-laterals in Dahalo as part of the process of borrowing. This expectation is borne out by the consistent existence of plausible lateral-click correspondents for the lateral-click words in Dahalo, but the occurrence of dental, alveolar (!), and palatal (≠) click parallels for Dahalo's dental-click words. In keeping with the proposals in Ehret (1986), two examples from Hadza show merger of the dental and palatal clicks (/ and ≠) where the parallel terms in Southern African languages distinguish the two consonants. In addition, the click loanwords in Dahalo do not distinguish aspirated and glottalic clicks.

LIST 4 LOANWORDS OF PROPOSED KHOESAN ATTRIBUTION IN DAHALO

Dahalo	Sandawe	Hadza	SAK
ǀóóne 'breast'	[*ǀ'ine* 'breast' probably does not belong here]		!Xõõ *ǀò'na* 'pectoral muscle'
ǀa'- 'to dry out'			SAK *ǀa 'to become stiff': Khoekhoe *ǀkhàà* 'to stiffen'; Ju *ǀãǀáã* 'to be stiff'
ǀaaʕ- 'to wring'			Khoekhoe *ǀàá̃* 'to squeeze, press'; Khwe *ǀ'ạ́* 'to wring out'
ǀu'u 'excrement'			Khoekhoe *ǀùù-s* 'excrement', *ǀùù-b* 'urine' (*ǀ'u-)
ǀímbìrìk'-iṯṯe 'kind of lizard' (Dahalo sg. suffix *-iṯṯe*)	*ǀ'èmbê'là* 'kind of lizard' (proposed earlier *ǀ'èmbêk'elà* by metathesis < *ǀ'èmbêlek'*-)		
ǀwiɲi 'night' (ideoph.)	*ǀ'unǀ'uŋ* 'to deprive of light, block out light'		
ǀàβà 'nice smell (of oil)'			Khoekhoe *ǀàwà-p* 'taste of blood'
ǀénǀè 'sunbird'	*ts'ents'éna* 'sunbird': proposed example of occasional Sandawe *ts'* ~ *ǀ* alternance < original *ǀ		
ǀunyuu'ið- 'to kiss' (stem + Dahalo *-ið*- causative)			Khwe *nǀúnú* 'to inhale deeply'
ǀnuʕiṯe 'thing that hurts the body, pain; bitterness' (stem + Dahalo ṯ nom. suff.)		*ǀnu'u*- 'to feel ill'; *ǀnu'-ana* 'bitter' (Hadza *-ana* adj. suffix)	
ǀook- 'to fill' (stem + Dahalo *k verb extension)		*ǀ'o* 'to be full'	!Xõõ *ǂ'óo* 'to be stuffed, packed together'; PKh (Khoekhoe, Khwe, etc.) *ǂ'o 'confined, tight'

LIST 4 (*cont'd*)

Dahalo	Sandawe	Hadza	SAK
ǀúúṯu 'joint of tool; waist' (!Xõõ and Dahalo meanings both apply to longitudinal link point of tool; Dahalo 2nd meaning and Hadza meaning both relate to longitudinal link point on body)		*ǀʰútì* 'neck' (joint of head with torso)	!Xõõ *ǂqhúli* 'linkshaft of an arrow' (in SAK only *l ~ *r = PKh *d exists root-medially; hence, if earlier *t existed, then > *d ~ *r ~ *l)
ǀnaβa 'forest'			!Xõõ *ǂnāhbi* 'small clump of trees or bushes'
ǀap'- 'to plug' (i.e., stick stopper into)		*!'api* 'to sew' (i.e., stick needle into)	Ju *!'àbè* 'to cut open (animal)'; Khwe *!'ávé* 'to chop with axe' (i.e., stick blade into)
ǀoʕ- 'to pick fruit'		*!'o̤* 'to pull out, pluck'	
ǀook- 'to pierce'		*!ʰoko* 'to pierce'	
ǀweh- 'to strip back maize husks'	*!ʰwě* 'to crack' (e.g., potato skin when done) (semantics: peel away [intr.] of potato husk)		
ǀuʕ- 'to strip, peel' *ǀuʕuṯ*- 'to hatch (of egg)' (stem + Dahalo *ṯ* intr. extension)		*!ʰu'*- 'to split' (intr.)	SAK 'to split, crack apart': !Xõõ *!húu* 'to cut open, slit open'; Khoekhoe *!hùũ* 'to crack bones for marrow'; Khwe *!hú* 'to crack'
nǀap'ið- 'to smack someone' (stem + Dahalo *-ið-* caus.)			Ju **n!àbà* 'whip' (areal term, also in Khoekhoe)
nǀákwi 'deserted homestead' (i.e., fallen, collapsed residence) (regular Dahalo shift: *x > *k*)	*!naxi* 'fallen tree trunk, branch'		

LIST 4 (*cont'd*)

Dahalo	Sandawe	Hadza	SAK
ǀaʕ- 'to carry child on back'	*ǀ'aa* 'to hold/take in one's hands'		
ǀa'- 'to sew'		*ǀa* 'to tie'	!Xõõ *ǀa̰a* 'to tie up, tether'
ǀaaʕ- 'to tell'	*ǀ'à'mé* 'to mention' (stem + Sandawe *-me* v. extension)		
ǀnó'o 'sound of ripping or breaking'	*nǀwě* 'to break, break off a piece'		Khoekhoe *ǀnòë* 'to cut open abdomen (of animal)'
k'wai 'arrowshaft'		*hik'o* 'arrow' (common Hadza *hV-prefix + stem *-k'o)	SAK 'sharp stick, arrow': Khoekhoe *òã̋-s* 'arrow tip, point of arrow' (< PKh *kx'oa); Ju *kx'óá* 'stick (planted in grave)'
nuunu 'younger brother'	*nunu* 'younger sibling'		
sool- 'to catch after chasing'	*sóólà* 'to run to meet'		

In several cases the Dahalo language adds a seemingly unnecessary causative suffix to an already transitive verb. This reflects a tendency also noted in Dahalo's borrowed verbs from Swahili. It probably originated as a means of adjusting vowel-final verb stems to Dahalo's own consonant-final pattern.

The extant occurrences of the source forms of the loanwords of Khoesan attribution in Dahalo, at least those so far discovered, are distributed very similarly to the borrowings in Proto-SC (List 1). They appear in relatively equal proportions in Sandawe, Hadza, and SAK, and in Sandawe or Hadza and South African groups.

The data we have considered so far highlight an interesting point for general borrowing theory. Click-containing words are rare in the three early loanword sets of possible Khoesan source in SC, but it is not difficult to discover non-click loanwords. This pattern suggests a more general principle, namely, that languages without click consonants, when strongly influenced by speakers of click languages, borrow non-click words relatively easily but tend to resist adopting words containing clicks.

The corollary of this conclusion would be that when click words do begin to be borrowed in large numbers, as in Dahalo, an extraordinarily strong impact of click speakers is present. In the case of Dahalo, it seems probable that the ancestral speech community carried over a great deal of lexical material, and thus phonological material also, into their adopted SC language. For southern African Bantu speakers such as the Nguni and Yeyi, we can similarly argue, because of the extraordinary penetration of click loanwords into their lexicons, that very large proportions of the human ancestry of such societies would have been speakers of a non-Bantu language. The Yeyi, in particular, might be an example of a society that, like the Dahalo, shifted en masse to a new language, in this instance from Khoesan to Bantu.

9.5 Loanwords of proposed Khoesan origin in the Rub languages

A very few loanwords of apparently Khoesan connections have been identified so far from the Rub (Kuliak) language group (List 5), a member of the Nilo-Saharan phylum of languages spoken in former times in eastern Uganda and far western Kenya. Again, however, more such loans probably remain to be discovered by future research.

LIST 5 WORDS OF PROPOSED KHOESAN ATTRIBUTION IN THE RUB LANGUAGES

	Sandawe	Hadza
Proto-Rub *bosan 'blue-grey colour' (stem + Rub *-an adj. suffix)	*bus* 'wildebeest'	*biso* 'wildebeest' (also Proto-Kalenjin [Nilo-Saharan] *pus 'bluish grey' [wildebeest colour]; also in Takama [Bantu of western Tanzania] *-pusi 'wildebeest')
Ik *lok'ú* 'gourd for drinking'		*n‖ókw'à* 'gourd'
Ik *tıts'*- 'to cover up hole' (i.e., by stuffing something in it)	*tʰats'é* 'to shoot'	*tets'*- 'to stick (into)'
Soo *rɔti* 'sausage tree (*Kigelia africana*)'	*rata* 'sausage tree' (also Rub loan in Proto-Kalenjin *rɔːtin and Kalenjin loan to Thagiicu [Mt. Kenya Bantu] as *-raatina)	

The loanwords in Rub seem attributable in roughly equal proportions to Hadza and Sandawe prototypes, and in two cases to prototypes with reflexes in both languages. The vowel outcome in the Proto-Rub *bosan fits closer to the Sandawe than the Hadza pronunciation, but the Ik verb *tıts'*-, on the other hand, shows vowel fronting as does the Hadza, but not the Sandawe equivalent. So again, as in all but one of our previous cases, the putative Khoesan source language cannot be considered closer related to any existing language than to any other.

A few other words suggestive of old Hadza contacts with speakers of Rub languages have also been identified, but these are ones that can better be understood as Rub loanwords in Hadza. The most striking of these is Hadza *wela* 'morning', corresponding to Ik *wel*^{a} 'morning hours'. Here the Ik word can be shown to be a regular reflex of a Proto-Nilo-Saharan root (Ehret 2001, root 1395) and thus Hadza must in this case have been the borrower. Another example may be Hadza *kwic'i* 'centipede' and Proto-Rub *kw'ic' 'worm'. This term, however, has a third referent in Dahalo *k'utsi* 'bee larva', suggesting the additional possibility that the Hadza and Rub terms may have been separate borrowings from early SC. Hadza *kwitsili* 'worm' appears to be still a fourth example of this root, but with an additional consonant. A possible explanation is that it was borrowed from an extinct Rub language in which ejection was lost from the two stem consonants and the Rub noun suffix in *l was added to the stem, or alternatively from an SC language with these characteristics.

In addition, several plant names appear to be shared by Hadza and Ik (List 6). Some of these may be additional instances of Rub loanwords in Hadza; others may be old loans in Rub. The consonant *tl'* occurs in Ik only in loanwords; SC, Sandawe, and Hadza, which today have this consonant, are the possible candidates from which these terms could be borrowed. And because Elderkin's field collections, from which the Hadza terms come, do not identify the species of plant involved, some of the comparisons may, of course, be chance resemblances.

LIST 6 APPARENT SHARED PLANT NAMES IN HADZA AND IK

Ik	Hadza
tl'ɔt '*Adenium obesum*'	*tl'atana* 'a fruit tree' (*-ana* ending is a common SC suffix, so an intermediate SC transmission may be involved here)
táb '*Lannea triphylla*' (its fruits and young roots are eaten)	*tafa* 'a fruit tree'
móz '*Grewia villosa*'	*modzema* 'a bush sp.' (*-ema* ending has the shape of a common SC noun suffix, probably therefore indicating an intermediate SC source for this item)
tl'ao '*Grewia bicolor*' (it is used for spearshafts and hoe handles; Proto-Rub *h > Ik Ø/V_)	*tl'eha* 'a tree (used for arrows)'

The presence of demonstrable Rub loanwords in Hadza – *wela* 'morning' is the clearest example – does not require that the Hadza have ever lived anywhere else than their current territories near Lake Eyasi. Several sets of Rub loanwords in Bantu languages indicate that erstwhile Rub-speaking societies formerly inhabited a number of areas extending from the eastern and southern sides of Lake Nyanza (Victoria) as far as the Kondoa area east of Lake Eyasi. These consist of Rub loanword sets in the Bantu languages of each of these regions (Ehret 1998). And if the writer's identification of Oltome ware as the pottery of early Rub peoples (Ehret 1998) is correct, then the fact that this kind of pottery appears at Late Stone Age locations near Lake Eyasi further supports the indications of the word evidence that Rub communities did at one time live as neighbours of the Hadza.

In contrast, the loanwords in Rub cannot be attributed to a history that took place in north-central Tanzania. The examples so far identified either go back to the Proto-Rub language, which most certainly was spoken in north-eastern Uganda, or are known from the Ik and Soo languages, each of which evolved as a distinct Rub tongue in the same broad region. These considerations require that lands of people with the putative Khoesan words in their languages, too, must once have extended into eastern Uganda.

In a previous work this writer suggested that Khoesan loanwords occurred as well in an East African Eastern Cushitic language, Yaaku (Mokogodo), spoken on the north side of Mt. Kenya (Ehret 1974). This case seems in hindsight not to be supported. At least two of the items proposed as loans, *muc'a* 'bone' and *dɛɛ'ɛw* 'thick, big', can now be shown to be Yaaku retentions of older Cushitic or Afroasiatic root words (in Ehret 1987 for 'bone' and Ehret 1995 for 'thick, big'). Another item, Yaaku *mɔqɔy* 'man', does bear a resemblance to Sandawe *máxà* 'young man'; but the question to be asked is why Yaaku, which has the consonant /x/ in its own phonology, should not have maintained that sound, if the word is indeed a borrowing. We must conclude that, after all, the Yaaku and Sandawe words in this instance are simply chance resemblances. A last item, Yaaku *damatú* 'woman' (Ehret 1974), does indeed appear to be ultimately of Khoesan origin, but most likely entered Yaaku indirectly, as a loan from an SC language (see List 1 above for this root).

9.6 Discussion

The majority of the proposed loanword sets presented here are not compelling by themselves. The members of the sets are few in number, and the proposed parallels for these words are scattered through several potential source languages. But two sets stand out as exceptions.

The first example is the set of reconstructed roots dating to the PRM stage in the evolution of the SC language group (List 2). Their number is relatively small, on current information comprising six items. On the other hand, the words in this set do have a consistent source: all but one of them is specifically attested in Sandawe, and the semantics of the comparisons are usually one-to-one. Most of the roots are demonstrable on phonological, distributional, or morphological grounds to have been loanwords in PRM. All but one of the root words in List 2 seem certainly to have come into PRM from a Sandawe-related language, and the most economical explanation of the one exception, the root word for 'year', is that it also came from the same ancient, long extinct Sandawe-related language as the rest of the set, but happened to have dropped from use at some point along the line of descent leading to modern-day Sandawe.

The second exception is the set of words, most of them with click consonants, cited from the Dahalo language (List 4). First off, the set is large. What is particularly striking for the hypothesis of a Khoesan source for the set is that 25, almost a third of the 78 words with click consonants recorded so far in Dahalo, match up with plausible source forms, both phonologically and semantically, in the lexicons of Sandawe and/or Hadza and/or SAK. This is a strikingly high proportion, considering the immense length of time separating the source language or languages of the proposed loanwords from any still spoken language, and the great amounts of lexical change that must have taken place over such long spans.

Second, although the plausible source items of these words appear today in a variety of click-possessing languages, a particular type of source consistency characterizes this set. What form does it take? The plausible parallels of the Dahalo word borrowings distribute in similar proportions across the various language groups that have been proposed to belong to a greater Khoesan language phylum. Ten of the Dahalo borrowed roots have counterparts in Sandawe, and ten in Hadza. The Dahalo parallels with lexemes in a third proposed deep division of Khoesan, comprising the Southern African groups Tuu, Ju, and Khoe, are somewhat more numerous, at fifteen, but that is only to be expected, considering that Sandawe and Hadza are single languages, while the Southern African data combines evidence from several languages. A better measure is the relatively even distribution of the proposed parallel terms amongst the SAK groups: nine are from the best-attested language of the Khoe group, Khoekhoe, and five from less-well-attested Khwe; four from Ju; and six from !Xõõ of the Tuu group. In several instances the plausible parallel terms occur in more than one of the Southern African languages or both in one or more of those languages and in Sandawe or Hadza.

Does this mean that three or more source languages need be posited for the loanwords in Dahalo? Not at all. Rather, this is exactly the pattern that would be expected if

(1) the words all indeed did come from one particular source language, and
(2) that source language had a similar distance of relationship, although at a very deep remove in time, to Sandawe, to Hadza, and to the SAK language groups.

In such a situation, the great length of the span of time since the common point of ancestry of the still-spoken languages would mean that great amounts of lexical change would have taken place in each remaining language. Each would retain roughly comparable portions of the lexicon from the common ancestor language, but only now and then would different languages have happened to retain the same particular words with the same or with a clearly relatable meaning. The terms parallel in phonological shape and in meaning to the loanwords in Dahalo have just the relatively even mix of distributions across Sandawe, Hadza, and the Southern African languages that this particular history would be expected to engender.

Because of the transitive logic of language relationship, this pattern has a further implication for the historical linguistics of the languages involved. It is probative evidence for the common membership of Sandawe, Hadza, Tuu, Khoe, Ju, and the extinct source language of the Dahalo word borrowings in one greater Khoesan phylum. The most parsimonious explanation of this kind of word distribution, in other words, is that Sandawe, Hadza, and the Southern African languages are related. Just one extinct language, formerly spoken in north-eastern Kenya and belonging to its own, fourth deep branch of the same "Khoesan" phylum, need be postulated to explain the Dahalo evidence.

At least one other now-extinct contact language in far northern East Africa, as already argued, belonged to the same deep line of descent as Sandawe. This "East-Turkana" loanword set in PRM (List 2) came from a language that would have been spoken around 4,000 years ago in northern Kenya. The possible sources of the very small set of loanwords so far identified in the Rub languages of north-eastern Uganda (List 5) remain unclear.

The two remaining sets of proposed loanwords, those in Proto-SC (List 1) and those limited to the Rift branch (List 3), present a pattern similar to that in Dahalo, in that the plausible source forms of the individual lexemes of the set occur either in only SAK (Khoe, Ju, and Tuu groups of southern Africa), Sandawe, or Hadza, or in Hadza and Sandawe, or in Hadza and/or Sandawe and in one or more SAK languages. The sets are small enough, if considered in isolation, to be considered suspect, as combining old *Wanderwörter* with a few chance resemblances. But the close distributional parallelism between the large Dahalo set and the two small sets favours applying the same interpretive stance as in the Proto-SC and the Proto-Rift cases – that the attested words reflect separate contact periods, although earlier in time, at 5,000-plus and 3,000-plus years ago respectively, with languages belonging, like the source language of the Dahalo word borrowings, to separate deep branches of a very deep-time Khoesan language phylum.

If these hypotheses turn out to be correct – and they are the most parsimonious explanations of the evidence as it currently stands – much of eastern Africa would have been inhabited, before the arrival of Southern Cushites in the later fouth millennium BCE, by peoples speaking languages of one very widespread phylum, Khoesan. The geographically parallel distribution of facies of one overall archaeological complex, the Eastern African Microlithic or "Wilton" tradition, across much of eastern and southern Africa during those same eras fits this proposal very well indeed (Ambrose 1982, Ehret 1998).

Note on sources

Without the work and data collections of many other scholars, this contribution would not have been possible. Because of the data formatting followed here, their contributions are not adequately cited in the body of the chapter. On the Rub languages, Bernd Heine's several published works (1974, 1975b, 1976), the thesis of Eithne Carlin (1993), field materials collected by John Weatherby, and my own field collections provide the evidence used here. For Hadza and Sandawe I have principally used the field materials of Edward Elderkin, although backed up by field collections of Bonnie Sands and Ian Maddieson and the field notes of Eric ten Raa. My use of SC materials takes advantage of a growing variety of new works by younger scholars on that group of languages, although again some of my own field collections and those of Derek Nurse have provided additional data. On the SAK languages, new dictionaries, in particular those of Anthony Traill for !Xõõ (1994), Christa Kilian-Hatz (2003) for Khwe, and Patrick Dickens for Ju|'hoan (1994), have given much valuable information (and are cited elsewhere in the volume), as has Rainer Vossen's ground-breaking Khoe reconstruction, *Die Khoe-Sprachen* (1997a). These writers are of course not to blame for any mistakes I may have made in using their materials.

10 THE SOCIOLINGUISTIC SITUATION OF KHOESAN LANGUAGES TODAY

Gabriele Sommer and *Thomas Widlok*

10.1 The situation in general

The sociolinguistic situation of Khoesan-speaking groups in southern Africa has for a long time been characterized by their status as minority language speakers (Traill 1995b, Batibo and Smieja 2000). One of the consequences of this situation as well as a reaction to it has been the tendency towards language shift among Khoesan speakers, i.e. the replacement of a Khoesan first language by some other Khoesan, Bantu or European language of wider communication (e.g. Nama, Tswana or Afrikaans).

In the past, language shift must have led to the extinction of a great number of Southern Khoesan languages. As Traill (1995b) has pointed out, very little is known about the actual process of increasing bilingualism, the gradual language replacement and final extinction of Southern Khoesan languages such as |Xam or ǁXegwi in South Africa. Among the few surviving Southern Khoesan languages are |'Auni, spoken by a small number of terminal speakers mostly trilingual in |'Auni, Nama and Afrikaans in the Cape region, as well as N|nuu of Gordonia District, South Africa (Crawhall 2004). !Xõõ, on the other hand, is still used by approximately 2,000 first language speakers in south-western Botswana and eastern Namibia. Most of these speakers also have a good proficiency in at least one other Khoesan language and in Kgalagadi, the language of their Bantu neighbours in the south-western Kalahari.

In some cases the vitality profile of Khoesan-speaking groups in southern Africa points to a common trend towards language shift. However, there are also a number of North and Central Khoesan languages which function as vital means of communication for a considerable number of bi- or multilingual speakers. Ju|'hoan in Botswana and Namibia as well as Naro in Botswana, for instance, are still used on a regular basis in intra-group communication. Both languages are also transmitted as first languages to the younger generations. In addition, both speech communities have meanwhile gained some official support. A variety of language planning activities are thus meant to strengthen or to revitalize the prestige of these minority languages in a multilingual environment and to support and enlarge language loyalty among its bi- or multilingual speakers (see Biesele and Hitchcock 2000; Visser 2000).

Central Khoesan-speaking groups in Botswana and Namibia, however, react quite differently to language shift and maintenance even under similar socio-economic conditions. Some of the East Kalahari Khoe languages such as Deti and Shua, currently spoken along the Botletle River and in the Makgadikgadi Salt Pans area of Botswana, are threatened by extinction. The minority status of their speakers as well as the impact of Tswana as the only officially recognized national language in Botswana have severely weakened the ethno-linguistic vitality of these Central Khoesan languages (Chebanne and Nthapelelang 2000). Nevertheless, speakers of Khwe in the Western Caprivi area, Namibia, appear to resist language shift under similarly unfavourable socio-economic conditions and without any official support. According to Brenzinger (1998), Western Caprivi Khwe still functions as a vital language. Parents continue to transmit Khwe as the first language to their children. Khwe is the dominant language in all intra-group contexts, it is used as the preferred medium of communication in mixed marriages and also functions as a *lingua franca* in the wider Western Caprivi context. There is thus some good reason to assume that in spite of official neglect and even under unfavourable socio-economic circumstances, at least some of the Khoesan languages of southern Africa will still be maintained in the future.

10.2 The case of Hai‖om

Hai‖om speakers have little difficulty in conversing with Nama/Damara speakers depending on the intensity of previous contacts and on their exposure to these other variants of Khoekhoe (Widlok 1997: 120f.). Therefore, code-switching in the strict sense occurs primarily between Hai‖om and Afrikaans. In specific speech situations Hai‖om speakers exploit the fact that there is a status difference between the two languages (Widlok 1999a: 139). In the particular instance referred to here a Hai‖om man with aspirations to local leadership switched to Afrikaans in what appeared to be an attempt to claim externally sanctioned authority.

Most Hai‖om speakers are bilingual, either in Afrikaans (for those living in the commercial farming districts) or in Oshiwambo (for those living in or near the settlement areas that were allocated to Owambo people). Multilingual Hai‖om are often mastering both these languages which are the *linguae francae* in their respective region. Many ǂAkhoe in particular also speak !Xũũ. Those who went into exile with SWAPO have some basic knowledge of Angolan languages; those who spent most of their lives on farms owned by German speakers sometimes speak and understand German. Recently the number of English speakers has been growing among young Hai‖om. Despite this multilingual competence in everyday life, the community of Hai‖om speakers is at a disadvantage in the national context. When dealing with outsiders, especially language policy makers, Hai‖om speakers have to cope with two kinds of discrimination. First, they suffer from the fact that their language is looked down upon as a language of "Bushmen" and second, their language is sometimes considered to be not a genuine language in its own right, but an imported dialect of the (once) dominant Nama. Leaving aside the arguments of historical linguistics, it needs to be pointed out that the assumption of a historical language shift towards Khoekhoegowab erroneously assigns an impoverished language competence to Hai‖om speakers. In contrast to this, it has been demonstrated in detail (Heikkinen n.d., Widlok 1999a) that the ǂAkhoe and Haiǁom that are currently in use are rich linguistic devices for complex social interaction as well as rich means for poetic creativity. Against this background the description and analysis of language in context seems an important corrective that may in the long run help to counter the prejudices against Haiǁom. However, the deplorable situation that Haiǁom is not a medium of school education anywhere in Namibia and that no mother-tongue teaching materials are being used with Haiǁom pupils is unlikely to change as long as the Haiǁom community remains underprivileged in other spheres of life, including land rights, political influence and a sufficient share in economic returns.

Apart from these policy-oriented considerations, there is also a more fundamental argument to be made about the role of pragmatics for a better understanding of languages such as Haiǁom. The argument (Widlok 1997) may be summarized as follows: instead of analysing any speech data firstly in terms of grammaticalized language, secondly in terms of a dialect within that language, thirdly in terms of a sociolect, and finally in terms of the pragmatic language use, there is an advantage in taking the inverse route. That is to say, the pragmatic strategies of the ways in which ǂAkhoe and Haiǁom are spoken can help to clarify the relation between languages and boundaries of a community of speakers which in turn sheds new light on the commonalities and diversities among Khoekhoe variants and between the Khoesan languages.

NOTES

1 Thanks to Beth Myre and Jouni Maho for their assistance with collecting the words from the neighbouring languages.
2 The unpublished material collected by the Bleek family is hosted by the "Manuscripts and Archives Department" (University of Cape Town).

REFERENCES

Ambrose 1982; Appleyard 1850; Batibo and Smieja 2000; Baumbach 1997; Biesele and Hitchcock 2000; W.H.I. Bleek 1869, 1873; Boshoff and Nienaber 1967; Bosman and Thom 1952–57; Boyce 1844; Brenzinger 1998; Carlin 1993; Chebanne and Nthapelelang 2000; Crawhall 2004; den Besten 1986, 1987, 1999, 2001, 2002, 2007; Dickens 1994; Doke 1926; Donnelly 1990; Ehret 1974, 1980, 1986, 1987, 1995, 1998, 2001, 2011; Ehret *et al.* 1989; Elphick 1977; Elphick and Giliomee 1989; Engelbrecht 1928, 1936; Finlayson 1972; Fleisch and Möhlig 2002; Franken 1953; Gowlett 1997; Güldemann 2000a, 2002, 2006a, 2006b; Guthrie 1967–71; Haacke 1979, 1989, 1999; Haacke and Eiseb 2002; Hagman 1977; Hannan 1984; Hartmann 1985–87; Heikkinen n.d.; Heine 1974, 1975b, 1976, 1999; Jacobs 1942; Janson 2000; Kilian-Hatz 2003; Kolb 1719, 1727; Kropf 1889; Ladefoged and Maddieson 1996; le Roux 1923; Legère 1998; Leibnitz 1717; Links 1989; Louw 1958a, 1975, 1976b, 1986; Louw and Finlayson 1990; Louw and Marivate 1992; Luijks 2000; Meinhof 1930; Miller-Ockhuizen 1999a; Möhlig 2005; Msimang 1989; Nama/Damara Language Committee 1977; Nienaber 1953, 1955, 1963, 1964, 1971, 1989, 1994; Nienaber and Raper 1977–80; Orel and Stolbova 1995; Pahl 1989; Ponelis 1993; Rademeyer 1938; Raidt 1983, 1991; Raper and Boucher 1988; Raven-Hart 1967, 1971; Rhenius 1724 [1947]; Roberge 1994, 2000; Scholtz 1974; Snyman 1975a, 1997, 1999; Sommer and Vossen 1992; ten Rhyne 1686 [1933]; Thomason and Kaufman 1988; Tosco 1991; Traill 1974, 1980, 1986a, 1994, 1995a, 1995b, 1996; Traill and Nakagawa 2000; Traill and Vossen 1997; Trigardt 1836–38 [1977]; van Jaarsveld *et al.* 2001; van Reede 1685 [1941]; van Rensburg 1989; van Zyl 1947; Visser 1998, 2000; Vossen 1997a; Widlok 1997, 1999a, 1999b; Wikar 1779 [1935]; Wilmsen 1989.

BIBLIOGRAPHY

ABBREVIATIONS

AAP	*Afrikanistische Arbeitspapiere*
AS	*African Studies*
ASIUW	African Studies Institute, University of the Witwatersrand
ASM	*African Study Monographs*
AuÜ	*Afrika und Übersee*
BS	*Bantu Studies*
CUP	Cambridge University Press
CWPL	*Cornell Working Papers in Linguistics*
EAPH	East African Publishing House
IfAUK	Institut für Afrikanistik, Universität zu Köln
IfAUL	Institut für Afrikanistik, Universität Leipzig
IU	Indiana University
JAAS	*Journal of Asian and African Studies*
JAL	*Journal of African Languages*
JALL	*Journal of African Languages and Linguistics*
KFWP	Khoisan Forum, Working Papers
LI	*Linguistic Inquiry*
SAJAL	*South African Journal of African Languages*
SAL	*Studies in African Linguistics*
SUGIA	*Sprache und Geschichte in Afrika*
SWJA	*Southwestern Journal of Anthropology*
UChP	University of Chicago Press
UCP	University of California Press
UCT	University of Capetown
WUP	Witwatersrand University Press
ZfES	*Zeitschrift für Eingeborenen-Sprachen*

Ambrose, S.H. (1982) Archaeological and linguistic reconstructions of history in East Africa, in C. Ehret and M. Posnansky (eds) *The Archaeological and Linguistic Reconstruction of African History*, Berkeley and Los Angeles: UCP. 104–57.

Appleyard, J.W. (1850) *The Kafir Language*, Graham's Town: Godlonton and White.

Argyle, W.J. (1994) Thinking the unthinkable: a possible genetic relationship between Khoisan and Niger-Congo, paper read at the International Symposium on Khoisan Studies: Multidisciplinary Perspectives, Tutzing/Lake Starnberg, 11–14 July, 1994.

Bala, G.G. (1998) *Hadza Stories and Songs* (coloured edition), ed. by B. Sands and W. Grundy, translated by B. Sands, Los Angeles: Friends of the Hadzabe.

Barnard, A.J. (1985) *A Nharo Wordlist, with Notes on Grammar*, Durban: Department of African Studies, University of Natal.

——(1992) *Hunters and Herders of Southern Africa: A Comparative Ethnography of the Khoisan Peoples*, Cambridge: CUP.

Batibo, H.M. and Smieja, B. (eds) (2000) *Botswana: The Future of the Minority Languages*, Frankfurt am Main: Peter Lang.

Batibo, H.M. and Tsonope, J. (eds) (2000) *The State of Khoesan Languages in Botswana*, Gaborone: University of Botswana, Basarwa Languages Project.

Baucom, K.L. (1974) Proto-Central Khoisan, in F.K.E. Voeltz (ed.) *Third Annual Conference on African Linguistics, 7–8 April, 1972*, Bloomington: IU. 3–37.

Baumbach, E.J.M. (1997) Bantu languages of the Eastern Caprivi, in Haacke and Elderkin (eds) 307–451.

Beach, D.M. (1938) *The Phonetics of the Hottentot Language*, Cambridge: W. Heffer & Sons.

Bell, A.J. and Collins, C. (2001) ǂHoan and the typology of click accompaniments in Khoisan, in A. Bell and P. Washburn (eds) *Khoisan: Syntax, Phonetics, Phonology, and Contact*, Ithaca, NY: Cornell University. 126–53.

Berger, P. (1943) Überlieferungen der Kindiga, *Afrika* 2: 97–122.

Berlin, B., Breedlove, D.E. and Raven, P.H. (1968) Covert categories and folk taxonomies, *American Anthropologist* 75: 214–35.

——(1974) *Principles of Tzeltal Plant Classification: An Introduction to the Botanical Ethnography of a Mayan-speaking People of Highland Chiapas*, New York: Academic Press.

Biesele, M.A. and Hitchcock, R.K. (2000) Juǀ'hoan-language education in Namibia and its relevance for minority-language education in Botswana, in Batibo and Smieja (eds) 237–65.

Bleek, D.F. (1928) *The Naron: A Bushman Tribe of the Central Kalahari*, Cambridge: CUP.

——(1928–30) Bushman grammar: a grammatical sketch of the language of the ǀxam-ka-!k'e, *ZfES* 19: 81–98; 20: 161–74.

——(1929) *Comparative Vocabularies of Bushman Languages*, Cambridge: CUP.

——(1931a) The Hadzapi or Watindega of Tanganyika Territory, *Africa* 4: 273–86.

——(1931b) Traces of former Bushman occupation in Tanganyika territory, *South African Journal of Science* 28: 423–29.

——(1936) Special speech of animals and the moon used by the ǀXam Bushmen. From material collected by Dr. W.H.I. Bleek and Miss L.C. Lloyd between 1870 and 1880, *BS* 10: 163–99.

——(1956) *A Bushman Dictionary*, ed. by Z.S. Harris, New Haven: American Oriental Society.

——(2000) *The ǁN !ke or Bushmen of Griqualand West: Notes on the Language of the ǁN !ke or Bushmen of Griqualand West*, ed. by T. Güldemann (KFWP 15), Cologne: IfAUK.

Bleek, W.H.I. (1869) The Bushman language, in R. Noble (ed.) *The Cape and Its People and Other Essays by South African Writers*, Cape Town: Trübner. 269–84.

——(1873) Report, concerning his researches into the Bushman language, presented to the House of Assembly, by command of His Excellency the Governor. Cape parliamentary papers. A. 17–1873.

——(1875) *A Brief Account of Bushman Folk-Lore and Other Texts*. Second report of Dr. Bleek concerning Bushman researches, by W.H.I. Bleek, Ph.D., Curator of the Grey Library, foreign member of the Royal Bavarian Academy of Sciences, &c., presented to both Houses of Parliament by command of His Excellency the Governor, Cape Town: Juta.

Bleek, W.H.I. and Lloyd, L.C. (1911) *Specimens of Bushman Folklore*, London: George Allen.

Boshoff, S.P.E. and Nienaber, G.S. (1967) *Afrikaanse etimologieë*, Pretoria: Suid-Afrikaanse Akademie vir Wetenskap en Kuns.

Bosman, D.B. and Thom, B. (eds) (1952–57) *Daghregister gehouden by den oppercoopman Jan Anthonis van Riebeeck*, 3 vols, Cape Town: A.A. Balkema.

Boyce, W.B. (1844) *A Grammar of the Kafir Language* (2nd edition), London: Wesleyan Missionary Society.

Brenzinger, M. (1998) Moving to survive: Kxoe communities in arid lands, in M. Schladt (ed.) 321–57.

Brenzinger, M. and König, C. (eds) (2010) *Khoisan Languages and Linguistics: Proceedings of the 1st International Symposium, January 4–8, 2003, Riezlern/Kleinwalsertal*, Cologne: Rüdiger Köppe.

Brown, C.H. (1984) *Language and Living Things*, New Brunswick: Rutgers University Press.

Carlin, E. (1993) *The So Language*, Cologne: IfAUK.

Chebanne, A.M. and Nthapelelang, M. (2000) The socio-linguistic survey of the Eastern Khoe in the Boteti and Makgadikgadi Pans areas of Botswana, in Batibo and Smieja (eds) 79–94.

Clements, G.N. (2000) Phonology, in Heine and Nurse (eds) 121–60.

Coates Palgrave, K. (1997) *Trees of Southern Africa*, Cape Town: C. Struik.

Collins, C. (1998) *Plurality in ǂHoan* (KFWP 9), Cologne: IfAUK.

——(2001) Aspects of plurality of ǂHoan, *Language* 77(3): 456–76.

——(2002) Multiple verb movement in ǂHoan, *LI* 33(1): 1–29.

——(2003) The internal structure of the verb phrase in Juǀ'hoan and ǂHoan, *Studia Linguistica* 57(1): 1–25.

Collins, C. and Namaseb, L. (2011) *A Grammatical Sketch of Nǀuuki with Stories*, Cologne: Rüdiger Köppe.

Copland, B.D. (1938) Notes on the phonetics of Sandawe, *Le maître phonetique* 16: 60–64.

Corbett, G.G. (1991) *Gender*, Cambridge: CUP.

Crawhall, N. (1997) *Taking Language into New Domains in the Feasibility of Technical Development in African Languages*, Pretoria: Department of Arts Culture Science and Technology.

——(1999) San and Khoe rights, identity and language survival in South Africa, in G. Maharaj (ed.) *Between Unity and Diversity: Essays on Nation Building in Post Apartheid South Africa*, Cape Town: IDASA.

——(2004) Too Good to Leave Behind. The Nǀuu Language and ǂKhomani People of Gordonia District, PhD thesis, UCT.

Dalgish, G.M. (1979) Subject identification strategies and free word order: the case of Sandawe, *SAL* 10(3): 273–310.

Dempwolff, O. (1916) *Die Sandawe: Linguistisches und ethnographisches Material aus Deutsch-Ostafrika*, Hamburg: L. Friedrichsen.

——(1934/35) Einführung in die Sprache der Nama-Hottentotten, *ZfES* 25: 30–66, 89–134, 188–229.

den Besten, H. (1986) Double negation and the genesis of Afrikaans, in P. Muysken and N. Smith (eds) *Substrata versus Universals in Creole Genesis*. Papers from the Amsterdam Creole Workshop, April 1985, Amsterdam and Philadelphia: John Benjamins. 185–230.

——(1987) Die niederländischen Pidgins der alten Kapkolonie, in N. Boretzky, W. Enninger and Th. Stolz (eds) *Beiträge zum 3. Essener Kolloquium über 'Sprachwandel und seine bestimmenden Faktoren' vom 30.9.-2.10.1986 an der Universität Essen*, Bochum: Brockmeyer. 9–40.

——(1999) Speculations on elision and intersonorantic [õ] in Afrikaans, in R.P. Botha (ed.) *Language Genesis* (Stellenbosch Papers in Linguistics 32), Stellenbosch: Stellenbosch University. 45–66.

——(2001) What became of the Cape Dutch pidgin(s)?, in B. Igla and Th. Stolz (eds) *'Was ich noch sagen wollte . . .' A multilingual festschrift for Norbert Boretzky on occasion of his 65th birthday*, Berlin: Akademie Verlag. 205–22.

——(2002) Khoekhoe syntax and its implications for L2 acquisition of Dutch and Afrikaans, in R. Mesthrie and P.T. Roberge (eds) *Focus on Afrikaans Sociohistorical Linguistics*, Part II, *Journal of Germanic Linguistics* 14(1): 3–56.

——(2007) Relexification and pidgin development: the case of Cape Dutch Pidgin, in U. Ansaldo, S. Matthews and L. Lim (eds) *Deconstructing Creole*, Amsterdam and Philadelphia: John Benjamins. 141–64.

Dickens, P. (1991) Ju|'hoan orthography in practice, *SAJAL* 11(3): 99–104.

——(1994) *English–Ju|'hoan, Ju|'hoan–English Dictionary*, Cologne: Rüdiger Köppe.

——(1996) The place of Lloyd's !Kun texts in the Ju dialects, in J. Deacon and Th.A. Dowson (eds) *Voices from the Past: |Xam Bushmen and the Bleek and Lloyd Collection*, Johannesburg: WUP. 161–211.

——(1997) Relative clauses in Ju|'hoan, in Haacke and Elderkin (eds) 107–16.

——(2005) *A Concise Grammar of Ju|'hoan, with a Ju|'hoan–English Glossary and a Subject Index*, ed. by R. Vossen and M. Biesele, Cologne: Rüdiger Köppe.

Dickens, P. and Traill, A.T. (1977) Collective and distributive in !Xõo, in Traill (ed.) 132–44.

Doke, C.M. (1925) An outline of the phonetics of the language of the Chu: Bushmen of the north-west Kalahari, *BS* 2(3): 129–65.

——(1926) *Phonetics of the Zulu Language*, Johannesburg: WUP (Special Number of *BS* 2; reprint: Nendeln, Kraus, 1969).

——(1936) An outline of ǂKhomani Bushman phonetics, *BS* 10(1): 433–60.

Donnelly, S.S. (1990) Phonology and Morphology of the Noun in Yeyi, B.A. dissertation, UCT.

Eaton, H. (2001) Word order and focus in the Sandawe irrealis, *Reading Working Papers in Linguistics* 5: 113–35.

——(2002) The Grammar of Focus in Sandawe, PhD thesis, University of Reading. Published online in 2010 as SIL e-Book 20.

——(2005) Focus as a key to the grammar of Sandawe, Languages of Tanzania [LOT] Project, University of Dar es Salaam, *Occasional Papers in Linguistics* 1: 9–37.

Ehret, C. (1974) *Ethiopians and East Africans: The Problem of Contacts*, Nairobi: EAPH.

——(1980) *The Historical Reconstruction of Southern Cushitic Phonology and Vocabulary*, Berlin: Dietrich Reimer.

——(1986) Proposals on Khoisan reconstruction, *SUGIA* 7(2): 105–30.

——(1987) Proto-Cushitic reconstruction, *SUGIA* 8: 7–180.

——(1995) *Reconstructing Proto-Afroasiatic (Proto-Afrasian): Consonants, Vowels, Tone, and Vocabulary*, Berkeley and Los Angeles: UCP.

——(1998) *An African Classical Age: Eastern and Southern Africa in World History, 1000 BC to AD 400*, Charlottesville: University Press of Virginia.

——(2001) *A Historical-Comparative Reconstruction of Nilo-Saharan*, Cologne: Rüdiger Köppe.

——(2011) *History and the Testimony of Language*, Berkeley: UCP.

Ehret, C. and Ehret, P. (eds) (2012) *A Dictionary of Sandawe*, from the field collections of E. ten Raa with the advice of E.D. Elderkin, Cologne: Rüdiger Köppe.

Ehret, C., Elderkin, E.D. and Nurse, D. (1989) Dahalo lexis, *AAP* 18: 5–49.

Elderkin, E.D. (1976) The Phonology of the Syllable and the Morphology of the Inflected Word in Dahalo, M.A. thesis, University of Nairobi.

——(1978) *Loans in Hadza: Internal Evidence from Consonants*. (Occasional Paper No. 3) Dar es Salaam: Department of Foreign Languages and Linguistics, University of Dar es Salaam.

——(1982) On the classification of Hadza, *SUGIA* 4: 67–82.

——(1986a) Diachronic inferences from basic sentence and noun structure in Central Khoisan and Sandawe, *SUGIA* 7(2): 131–56.

——(1986b) Kxoe tone and Kxoe 'jonctures', in Vossen and Keuthmann (eds) vol. 1: 225–35.

——(1988) Patterns of sound in northern Khoisan, *African Languages and Cultures* 1(2): 123–48.
——(1989) The Significance and Origin of the Use of Pitch in Sandawe, D. Phil. thesis, University of York.
——(1998) Sandawe stems, in Schladt (ed.) 15–33.
——(2008) Proto-Khoe tones in Western Kalahari, in Ermisch (ed.) 87–136.
Elphick, R. (1977) *Kraal and Castle: Khoikhoi and the Founding of White South Africa*, New Haven: Yale University Press.
Elphick, R. and Giliomee, H. (eds) (1989) *The Shaping of South African Society, 1652–1840*, Cape Town: Maskew Miller Longman.
Engelbrecht, J.A. (1928) *Studies oor Korannataal*, Stellenbosch: Universiteit van Stellenbosch (Annale van die Universiteit van Stellenbosch, Jaargang VI, Reeks B, Afl. 2: 1–45).
——(1936) *The Korana: An Account of their Customs and their History with Texts*, Cape Town: Maskew Miller.
Ermisch, S. (ed.) (2008) *Khoisan Languages and Linguistics: Proceedings of the 2nd International Symposium, January 8–12, 2006, Riezlern/Kleinwalsertal*, Cologne: Rüdiger Köppe.
Finlayson, R. (1972) Affinities between Venda and Other Southern Bantu Languages, PhD thesis, University of London, School of Oriental and African Studies.
Fleisch, A. and Möhlig, W.J.G. (2002) *The Kavango Peoples in the Past: Local Historiographies from Northern Namibia*, Cologne: Rüdiger Köppe.
Fleming, H.C. (1986) Hadza and Sandawe genetic relations, *SUGIA* 7(2): 157–87.
Foley, W. (1986) *The Papuan Languages of New Guinea*, Cambridge: CUP.
Franken, J.L.M. (1953) *Taalhistoriese bydraes*, Cape Town: A.A. Balkema.
Frawley, W. (1992) *Linguistic Semantics*, Hillsdale, NJ: Lawrence Erlbaum.
Gowlett, D. (ed.) (1992) *African Linguistic Contributions* (presented in honour of Ernst Westphal), Pretoria: Via Afrika.
——(1997) Aspects of Yeyi diachronic phonology, in Haacke and Elderkin (eds) 235–63.
Greenberg, J.H. (1949–54) Studies in African linguistic classification, part I-VIII, *SWJA* 5, 6 and 10.
——(1950) Studies in African linguistic classification: The click languages, *SWJA* 6(3): 223–37.
——(1959) Africa as a linguistic area, in W.R. Bascom and M.J. Herskovitz (eds) *Continuity and Change in African Cultures*, Chicago: UChP. 15–27.
——(1963a) Some universals of grammar with particular reference to the order of meaningful elements, in J.H. Greenberg (ed.) *Universals of Language*, Cambridge, MA: The M.I.T. Press. 58–90.
——(1963b) *The Languages of Africa* (2nd edition, 1966), Bloomington: IU.
Gruber, J.S. (1973) ǂHoã kinship terms, *LI* 4(4): 427–49.
——(1975) Plural predicates in ǂHoã, in Traill (ed.) 1–50.
Guenther, M.G. (1986) *The Nharo Bushmen of Botswana: Tradition and Change*, Hamburg: Helmut Buske.
Güldemann, T. (1998a) *San Languages for Education: A Linguistic Short Survey and Proposal*, Okahanja: NIED, Ministry of Basic Education and Culture.
——(1998b) The Kalahari basin as an object of areal typology – a first approach, in Schladt (ed.) 137–69.
——(1999) Head-initial meets head-final: nominal suffixes in eastern and southern Bantu from a historical perspective, *SAL* 28(1): 49–91.
——(2000a) Editor's introduction, in D.F. Bleek (ed. by T. Güldemann), *The //N !ke or Bushmen of Griqualand West: Notes on the Language of the //N !ke or Bushmen of Griqualand West* (KFWP 15: 7–13), Cologne: IfAUK.
——(2000b) Noun categorization systems in non-Khoe lineages of Khoisan, *AAP* 63: 5–33.

——(2001) *Phonological Regularities of Consonant Systems across Khoisan Lineages* (University of Leipzig Papers on Africa – Languages and Literatures 16), Leipzig: IfAUL.

——(2002) Die Entlehnung pronominaler Elemente des Khoekhoe aus dem !Ui-Taa, in T. Schumann, M. Reh, R. Kießling and L. Gerhardt (eds) *Aktuelle Forschungen zu afrikanischen Sprachen: Sprachwissenschaftliche Beiträge zum 14. Afrikanistentag, Hamburg, 11.–14. Oktober 2000*, Cologne: Rüdiger Köppe. 43–61.

——(2004a) Complex pronominals in Tuu and Ju, with special reference to their historical significance, *AuÜ* 87: 79–103.

——(2004b) Reconstruction through 'de-construction': the marking of person, gender, and number in the Khoe family and Kwadi, *Diachronica* 21(2): 251–306.

——(2005) Tuu as a language family, in T. Güldemann (ed.) *Studies in Tuu (Southern Khoisan)*, Leipzig: IfAUL. 11–30.

——(2006a) The San Languages of southern Namibia: linguistic appraisal with special reference to J.G. Krönlein's N|uusaa data *Anthropological Linguistics*, 48(4): 369–95.

——(2006b) Structural isoglosses between Khoekhoe and Tuu: the Cape as a linguistic area, in Y. Matras, A. McMahon and N. Vincent (eds) *Linguistic Areas: Convergence in Historical and Typological Perspective*, Hampshire: Palgrave Macmillan. 99–134.

——(2010) The relation between focus and theticity in the Tuu family, in I. Fiedler and A. Schwarz (eds) *The expression of information structure: a documentation of its diversity across Africa*, Amsterdam: John Benjamins. 69–93.

Güldemann, T. and Elderkin, E.D. (2010) On external genealogical relationships of the Khoe family, in Brenzinger and König (eds) 15–52.

Güldemann, T. and Vossen, R. (2000) Khoisan, in Heine and Nurse (eds) 99–122.

Guthrie, M. (1967–71) *Comparative Bantu: An Introduction to the Comparative Linguistics and Prehistory of the Bantu Languages*, 4 vols, Farnborough: Gregg Press.

Haacke, W.H.G. (1977) The so-called 'personal pronoun' in Nama, in Traill (ed.) 43–62.

——(1979) Nama 'coreferential copulative sentences' re-assessed, in Snyman (ed.) 80–106.

——(1985) Noun phrase accessibility to relativization in Herero and Nama, *SAJAL* 5(2): 43–48.

——(1986) Preliminary observations on a dialect of the Sesfontein Damara, in Vossen and Keuthmann (eds) vol. 1: 376–96.

——(1988) Nama/Damara I, Guide 2: Morphology and Syntax, mimeographed.

——(1989) Nama: survival through standardization, in I. Fodor and C. Hagège (eds) *Language Reform History and Future*, vol. 4, Hamburg: Helmut Buske. 397–429.

——(1992a) Dislocated noun phrases in Khoekhoe (Nama/Damara): further evidence for the sentential hypothesis, *AAP* 29: 149–62.

——(1992b) Compound noun phrases in Nama, in Gowlett (ed.) 189–94.

——(1995) Instances of incorporation and compounding in Khoekhoegowab (Nama/Damara), in Traill, Vossen and Biesele (eds) 339–61.

——(1998) *The Tonology of Khoekhoe (Nama/Damara)*, Cologne: Rüdiger Köppe.

——(1999) Tonogenesis in Khoekhoe (Nama/Damara), in Sh. Kaji (ed.) *Proceedings of the Symposium on Cross-Linguistic Studies of Tonal Phenomena: Tonogenesis, Typology, and Related Topics*, Tokyo: University of Foreign Studies. 69–85.

——(2003) Review of Rainer Vossen, *Die Khoe-Sprachen: Ein Beitrag zur Erforschung der Sprachgeschichte Afrikas*. Cologne: Rüdiger Köppe, *JALL* 24: 91–98.

Haacke, W.H.G. and Eiseb, E. (2002) *A Khoekhoegowab Dictionary, with an English–Khoekhoegowab Index*, Windhoek: Gamsberg Macmillan.

Haacke, W.H.G., Eiseb, E. and Namaseb, L. (1997) Internal and external relations of Khoekhoe dialects: a preliminary survey, in Haacke and Elderkin (eds) 125–209.

Haacke, W.H.G. and Elderkin, E.D. (eds) (1997) *Namibian Languages: Reports and Papers*. Cologne: Rüdiger Köppe.
Hagman, R.S. (1977) *Nama Hottentot Grammar*, Bloomington: IU.
Halle, M. (1995) Feature geometry and feature spreading, *LI* 26(1): 1–46.
Hannan, M.J. (1984) *Standard Shona Dictionary*, Harare: The College Press.
Hartmann, B. (1985–87) Die Tjaube, eine Vorbevölkerung im Kavangogebiet (nach einer Erzählung von R. Haushiku), Einführung, Karte und Photos von M. Fisch, *Journal of the SWA Scientific Society* XL/XLI: 75–96.
Hastings, R. (2001) Evidence for the genetic unity of Southern Khoesan, *CWPL* 18: 225–46.
Heikkinen, T. (1986) Phonology of the !Xũ dialect spoken in Ovamboland and western Kavango, *SAJAL* 6(1): 18–28.
——(1987) *An Outline of the Grammar of the !Xũ Language, Spoken in Ovamboland and West Kavango* (SAJAL, Supplement 1987.1), Pretoria: African Languages Association of Southern Africa.
——(n.d.) A Description of the Language of ǂ'Akhoen, unpublished manuscript.
Heine, B. (1974) Tepes und Nyang'i: zwei ostafrikanische Restsprachen, *AuÜ* 58: 263–300.
——(1975a) Ik: eine ostafrikanische Restsprache, *AuÜ* 59: 31–56.
——(1975b) Language typology and convergence areas in Africa, *Linguistics* 144: 27–47.
——(1975c) The study of word order in African languages, *Ohio State Working Papers in Linguistics* 20: 161–83.
——(1976) *The Kuliak Languages of Eastern Uganda*, Nairobi: EAPH.
——(1986) Bemerkungen zur Entwicklung der Verbaljunkturen im Kxoe und anderen Zentralkhoisan-Sprachen, in Vossen and Keuthmann (eds) vol. 2: 9–22.
——(1997) *Kxoe Texts* (KFWP 8), Cologne: IfAUK.
——(1999) *The ǀAni: Grammatical Notes and Texts* (KFWP 11), Cologne: IfAUK.
Heine, B. and Honken, H. (2010) The Kx'a family. A new Khoisan genealogy, *JAAS* 79: 5–36.
Heine, B. and König, C. (2001) *The Ekoka !Xun: A Demographic and Linguistic Report* (KFWP 17), Cologne: IfAUK.
——(2012) *The !Xun Language: A Dialect Grammar of Northern Khoisan*, Cologne: Rüdiger Köppe.
Heine, B. and Nurse, D. (eds) (2000) *African Languages: An Introduction*. Cambridge: CUP.
Heine, B., Schadeberg, Th.C. and Wolff, E. (eds) (1981) *Die Sprachen Afrikas*, Hamburg: Helmut Buske.
Heine, B. and Vossen, R. (1981) Sprachtypologie, in Heine, Schadeberg and Wolff (eds) 407–44.
HIPA (1999) *Handbook of the International Phonetic Association: A Guide to the Use of the International Phonetic Alphabet*, Cambridge: CUP.
Honken, H. (1977) Submerged features and Proto-Khoisan, in Traill (ed.) 145–69.
——(1988) Phonetic correspondences among Khoisan affricates, in R. Vossen (ed.) *New Perspectives on the Study of Khoisan*, Hamburg: Helmut Buske. 47–65.
——(1998) Types of sound correspondence patterns in Khoisan languages, in Schladt (ed.) 171–91.
——(2008) The split tones in Central Khoisan, in Ermisch (ed.) 185–224.
Hunziker, D.A., Hunziker, E. and Eaton, H. (2005) A Description of the Phonology of the Sandawe Language, unpublished manuscript.
Ito, J. and Mester, A. (1986) The phonology of voicing in Japanese: theoretical consequences for morphological accessibility, *LI* 17(1): 49–73.
Jacobs, J.F. (1942) *Die Grikwas en hul bure*, Bloemfontein: Nasionale Pers.
Janson, T. (2000) The history of the minority-language speakers in Botswana, in Batibo and Smieja (eds) 3–12.

Jelinek, E. (1984) Empty categories, case, and configurationality, *Natural Language and Linguistic Theory* 2: 39–76.
Kagaya, R. (1993) *A Classified Vocabulary of the Sandawe Language*, Tokyo: Institute for the Study of Languages and Cultures of Asia and Africa, Tokyo University of Foreign Studies.
Keuthmann, K. and Vossen, R. (1997) Von Schnalzen und anderen Zungenschlägen, *Forschung Frankfurt* 2/1997: 48–59.
Kießling, R. (2002) Verbal plurality in Sandawe, *Hamburger afrikanistische Arbeitspapiere* 1: 59–90.
Kilian-Hatz, C. (2003) *Khwe Dictionary*, Cologne: Rüdiger Köppe.
——(2008) *A Grammar of Modern Khwe (Central Khoisan)*, Cologne: Rüdiger Köppe.
Kilian-Hatz, C. and Naude, D. (1999) *Folktales of the Kxoe in the West Caprivi*, narrated by Dao Ngyengye, Cologne: Rüdiger Köppe.
Köhler, O. (1960) Sprachkritische Aspekte zur Hamitentheorie über die Herkunft der Hottentotten, *Sociologus* 10(1): 69–77.
——(1962) Studien zum Genussystem und Verbalbau der zentralen Khoisan-Sprachen, *Anthropos* 57: 529–46.
——(1963) Observations on the Central Khoisan language group, *JAL* 2(3): 227–34.
——(1971a) Noun classes and grammatical agreement in !Xũ (ʒu|hoà dialect), *Annales de l'Université d'Abidjan, Série H (Linguistique) 1971*, 489–522.
——(1971b) Die Khoe-sprachigen Buschmänner der Kalahari. Ihre Verbreitung und Gliederung (mit einer Karte), in *Forschungen zur allgemeinen und regionalen Geographie, Festschrift für Kurt Kayser* (Kölner Geographische Arbeiten, Sonderband), Wiesbaden: Franz Steiner. 373–411.
——(1973) Grundzüge der Grammatik der !Xũ-Sprache, typescript, Universität zu Köln.
——(1973/74) Neuere Ergebnisse und Hypothesen der Sprachforschung in ihrer Bedeutung für die Geschichte Afrikas, *Paideuma* 19/20: 162–99.
——(1975) Geschichte und Probleme der Gliederung der Sprachen Afrikas – Von den Anfängen bis zur Gegenwart, in H. Baumann (ed.) *Die Völker Afrikas und ihre traditionellen Kulturen*, part I: *Allgemeiner Teil und südliches Afrika*, Wiesbaden: Franz Steiner. 135–373.
——(1981) Les langues khoïsan, in J. Perrot (ed.) *Les langues dans le monde ancien et moderne*, part one: G. Manessy (ed.) *Les langues de l'Afrique subsaharienne*, Paris: Editions du Centre National de la Recherche Scientifique. 455–615 + map insert.
——(1989) *Die Welt der Kxoé-Buschleute im südlichen Afrika: Eine Selbstdarstellung in ihrer eigenen Sprache*, vol. 1: *Die Kxoé-Buschleute und ihre ethnische Umgebung*, Berlin: Dietrich Reimer.
——(1991) *Die Welt der Kxoé-Buschleute im südlichen Afrika. Eine Selbstdarstellung in ihrer eigenen Sprache*, vol. 2: *Grundlagen des Lebens: Wasser, Sammeln und Jagd, Bodenbau und Tierhaltung*, Berlin: Dietrich Reimer.
Kolb, P. (1719) *Caput Bonae Spei Hodiernum, das ist vollständige Beschreibung des Africanischen Vorgebürges*, Nürnberg: Peter Conrad Monath.
——(1727) *Naaukeurige en Uitvoerige Beschryving van De Kaap de Goede Hoop, waarby een beschryving van den oorsprong der Hottentotten*, beschreven door Peter Kolbe, 2 vols, Amsterdam: Balthasar Lakeman.
König, C. and Heine, B. (2008) *A Concise Dictionary of Northwestern !Xun*, Cologne: Rüdiger Köppe.
Kropf, A. (1889) *Das Volk der Xosa-Kaffern im östlichen Südafrika nach seiner Geschichte, Eigenart, Verfassung und Religion*, Berlin: Buchhandlung der Berliner Evangelischen Missions-Gesellschaft.
Ladefoged, P. and Maddieson, I. (1996) *The Sounds of the World's Languages*, Oxford: Blackwell.
Ladefoged, P. and Traill, A.T. (1994) Clicks and their accompaniments, *Journal of Phonetics* 22: 33–64.

Lakoff, G. (1987) *Women, Fire, and Dangerous Things: What Categories Reveal about the Mind*, Chicago: UChP.
Lanham, L.W. and Hallowes, D.P. (1956) An outline of the structure of Eastern Bushman, *AS* 15: 97–118.
le Roux, J.J. (1923) *Oor die Afrikaanse sintaksis*, part I: *Woordgroepe en volsin*, Amsterdam: Swets en Zeitlinger.
Legère, K. (1998) Khoisan traces in Kavango languages, in Schladt (ed.) 193–215.
Leibnitz, G.W. (1717) *Collectanea etymologica, etc*., Hannover: Nicolaus Förster.
Links, T. (1989) *So praat ons Namakwalanders*, Cape Town: Tafelberg.
Louw, J.A. (1958a) *The Nomenclature of Cattle in the South-Eastern Bantu Languages*, Pretoria: University of South Africa.
——(1958b) The early settlement of South Africa by the first Nguni tribes, *Journal of Geography (Stellenbosch)* 1(3): 24–33.
——(1974) The influence of Khoi on the Xhosa language, *Limi* 2(2): 45–62.
——(1975) The click loans in Xhosa, in Snyman (ed.) 82–100.
——(1976a) The influence of Khoi on Xhosa morphology, in W.J. De Klerk and F.J. Ponelis (eds) *Gedenkbundel H.J.J.M. van der Merwe*, Pretoria: J.L. van Schaik. 87–95.
——(1976b) Palatalization of bilabials in the passive, diminutive and locatives in Xhosa and Tsonga, *AuÜ* 59(4): 241–78.
——(1977a) The adaptation of non-click Khoi consonants in Xhosa, in Traill (ed.) 74–91.
——(1977b) The linguistic prehistory of the Xhosa, in W.J.G. Möhlig, F. Rottland and B. Heine (eds) *Zur Sprachgeschichte und Ethnohistorie in Afrika: Neue Beiträge afrikanistischer Forschungen*, Berlin: Dietrich Reimer. 127–51.
——(1979) A preliminary survey of Khoi and San influence in Zulu, in A.T. Traill (ed.) *Khoisan Linguistic Studies 5*, Johannesburg: Department of Linguistics, University of the Witwatersrand. 8–21.
——(1986) Some linguistic influence of Khoi and San in the prehistory of the Nguni, in Vossen and Keuthmann (eds) vol. 2: 141–65.
Louw, J.A. and Finlayson, R. (1990) Southern Bantu origins as represented by Xhosa and Tswana, *SAJAL* 10(4): 401–10.
Louw, J.A. and Marivate, C.T.D. (1992) Restraints on the formation of nasal compounds in Tsonga, in Gowlett (ed.) 272–310.
Luijks, C. (2000) The Realisation of Syntactic Principles in Non-Standard Afrikaans: The Correspondence of Jan Jonker Afrikaner (1820–1889), PhD thesis, UCT.
McCarthy, J.J. (1991) Semitic gutturals and distinctive feature theory, in B. Comrie and M. Eid (eds) *Perspectives on Arabic Linguistics III*, Amsterdam: John Benjamins. 63–91.
——(1994) The phonetics and phonology of Semitic pharyngeals, *Phonological Structure and Phonetic Form: Papers in Laboratory Phonology* III: 191–233.
Maingard, L.F. (1957) Three Bushman languages. Part II: The third Bushman language. *AS* 16(2): 100–15.
——(1961) The Central group of the Click languages of the Kalahari, *AS* 20(2): 114–22.
——(1962) *Korana Folktales: Grammar and Texts*, Johannesburg: WUP.
——(1963) A comparative study of Naron, Hietshware and Korana, *AS* 22(3): 97–108.
Meinhof, C. (1905/06) Hottentottische Laute und Lehnworte im Kafir. *Zeitschrift der Deutschen Morgenländischen Gesellschaft* 58: 727–69, 59: 36–89.
——(1930) *Der Koranadialekt des Hottentottischen*, Berlin: Dietrich Reimer.
Meriggi, P. (1928/29) Versuch einer Grammatik des |Xam-Buschmännischen, *ZfES* 19: 117–53, 188–205.
Miller, A.L. (2007) Guttural vowels and guttural co-articulation in Ju|'hoansi, *Journal of Phonetics* 35: 56–84.

——(2010) A prosodic account of Ju|'hoansi consonant distribution patterns, in Brenzinger and König (eds) 40–73.

——(2011) The representation of clicks, in M. van Oostendorp, C. Ewen, E. Hume and K. Rice (eds) The Blackwell Companion to Phonology, Oxford: Blackwell (in press).

Miller, A.L., Holliday, J., Howcroft, D.M., Phillips, S., Smith, B., Tsz-Him, T. and Scott, A. (eds) (2011) The Phonetics of the Modern-Day Reflexes of the Proto-Palatal Click in Juu Languages, paper presented at the 4th International Symposium on Khoisan Languages and Linguistics, 10–14 July 2011, Riezlern/Kleinwalsertal.

Miller-Ockhuizen, A.L. (1997) A decompositional analysis of Khoisan lexical tone, *Studies in the Linguistic Sciences* 27(1): 153–68.

——(1998) Towards a unified decompositional analysis of Khoisan lexical tone, in Schladt (ed.) 217–43.

——(1999a) C-V coarticulation and complex consonants: new evidence for the ordering of place gestures in click consonants, in O. Fujimura, B.D. Joseph and B. Palek (eds) *Proceedings of LP '98: Item Order in Language and Speech*, Prague: The Karolinum Press. 301–30.

——(1999b) Issues in Ju|'hoansi orthography and their implications for the development of orthographies for other Khoesan languages, in Batibo and Tsonope (eds) 108–24.

——(1999c) Reduplication in Ju|'hoansi: tone determines weight, in P. Tamanji, M. Hirotani and N. Hall (eds) *Proceedings of the North-East Linguistic Society* 29(1), Amhurst: Graduate Linguistics Student Association.

——(2000) A Field Database for the Multi-Faceted Investigation of Length Contrasts, poster presented at the 7th Laboratory Phonology Conference, Nijmegen, The Netherlands.

——(2001a) Contrastive vowel-length and variable weight: reduplicative templates in Ju|'hoansi. *CWPL* 18: 104–25.

——(2001b) Grounding Ju|'hoansi Root Phonotactics: The Phonetics of the Guttural OCP and other Acoustic Modulations, PhD thesis, Columbus, Ohio State University.

——(2003) The Phonetics and Phonology of Gutturals: A Case Study from Ju|'hoansi, New York: Routledge.

Miller-Ockhuizen, A.L. and Sands, B.E. (1999) !Kung as a linguistic construct, *Language and Communication: An interdisciplinary Journal* 19(4): 401–13.

——(2000) Contrastive lateral clicks and variation in click types, in *Proceedings of ICSLP 2000*, Bejing (China). 17–26.

Möhlig, W.J.G. (2005) *A Grammatical Sketch of Rugciriku (Rumanyo)*, Cologne: Rüdiger Köppe.

Moritz, W. (1963) *Einführung in die Namasprache*, Wupperthal (South Africa).

Msimang, C.Th. (1989) Some Phonological Aspects of the Tekela Nguni Dialects, PhD thesis, University of South Africa, Pretoria.

Müller, F. (1888) *Grundriß der Sprachwissenschaft 4,1: Nachträge zum Grundriß; aus den Jahren 1877–1887. Die Sprache der |Kham-Buschmänner (|kham-ga !e) im Norden der Cap-Colonie*, Vienna: Hölder. 1–18.

Nakagawa, H. (1996a) A first report on the click accompaniments of |Gui, *Journal of the International Phonetic Association* 26(1): 41–54.

——(1996b) An outline of |Gui phonology, *ASM, Supplementary Issue* 22: 101–24.

——(1998) Unnatural palatalization in |Gui and ‖Gana?, in Schladt (ed.) 245–63.

——(2006) Aspects of the Phonetic and Phonological Structure of the G|ui language, PhD thesis, Johannesburg, University of Witwatersrand.

Nama/Damara Language Committee (1977) *Nama/Damara Orthography*, Windhoek: Department of Education.

Nichols, J. (1992) *Linguistic Diversity in Space and Time*, Chicago: UChP.

Nienaber, G.S. (1953) *Oor Afrikaans*, vol. 2, Johannesburg: Afrikaanse-Pers-Boekhandel.

——(1955) Iets naders oor die ontkenning in Afrikaans, *Herzog-Annale*, reprinted in P.J. Nienaber (ed.) [1965] *Taalkundige Opstelle*, Cape Town: A.A. Balkema. 22–38.

——(1963) *Hottentots*, Pretoria: J.L. van Schaik.

——(1964) Raakpunte met Hottentots, in H.J.J.M. van der Merwe (ed.) *Studierigtings in die Taalkunde*, Pretoria: J.L. van Schaik. 192–207.

——(1971) *Afrikaans in die vroeër jare*, Johannesburg: Voortrekkerpers.

——(1989) *Khoekhoense stamname: 'n voorlopige verkenning*, Pretoria: Academica.

——(1994) *Pa-hulle* is kreools, in G.S. Nienaber, *Khoekhoe en Afrikaans in gesprek*, Linguistic Society of Southern Africa/Linguistevereniging van Suider-Afrika (South African Journal of Linguistics/Suid-Afrikaanse Tydskrif vir Taalkunde, Supplement 21: 14–67).

Nienaber, G.S. and Raper, P.E. (1977–80) *Toponymica Hottentotica. A*, 2 vols; *B*, 1 vol., Pretoria: S.A. Naamkundesentrum.

Obst, E. (1912) Von Mkalama ins Land der Wakindiga, *Mitteilungen der Geographischen Gesellschaft in Hamburg* 26(1): 1–45.

Odden, D. (1995) Tone: African languages, in J. Goldsmith (ed.) *The Handbook of Phonological Theory*, Cambridge: Blackwell. 444–75.

Orel, V.E. and Stolbova, O.V. (1995) *Hamito-Semitic Etymological Dictionary: Materials for a Reconstruction*, Leiden/New York/Cologne: E.J. Brill.

Pahl, H.W. (1989) *The Greater Dictionary of Xhosa*, vol. 3, Alice: University of Fort Hare.

Ponelis, F. (1993) *The Development of Afrikaans*, Frankfurt am Main: Peter Lang.

Rademeyer, J.H. (1938) *Kleurling-Afrikaans: die taal van die Griekwas en Rehoboth-Basters*, Amsterdam: Swets en Zeitlinger.

Raidt, E.H. (1983) *Einführung in Geschichte und Struktur des Afrikaans*, Darmstadt: Wissenschaftliche Buchgesellschaft.

——(1991) *Afrikaans en sy Europese Verlede*, Cape Town: Nasou.

Raper, P.E. and Boucher, M. (eds) (1988) *Robert Jacob Gordon, Cape Travels, 1777 to 1786*, vol. 1 and 2, Johannesburg: Brenthurst Press.

Raven-Hart, R. (1967) *Before Van Riebeeck. Callers at South Africa from 1488 to 1652*, Cape Town: C. Struik.

——(1971) *Cape Good Hope 1652–1702: The First Fifty Years of Dutch Colonization as Seen by Callers*, 2 vols, Cape Town: A.A. Balkema.

Rhenius, J.T. (1724) Dagh Register gehouden op de togt naar de Amaquas Hottentots . . . onder directie van den Vaandrijck J.T. Rhenius in den Jaare 1724, in E.E. Mossop (ed.) *The Journals of Brink and Rhenius*, Cape Town: Van Riebeeck Society. 122–53 [1947].

Roberge, P.T. (1994) *The Formation of Afrikaans* (Stellenbosch Papers in Linguistics PLUS 23), Stellenbosch: Stellenbosch University.

——(2000) Etymological opacity, hybridization, and the Afrikaans brace negation, *American Journal of Germanic Linguistics and Literatures* 12(1): 101–76.

Ruhlen, M. (1994) *On the Origin of Languages: Studies in Linguistic Taxonomy*, Stanford: Stanford University Press.

Rust, F. (1965) *Praktische Namagrammatik*, School of African Studies, UCT.

——(1969) *Nama Wörterbuch (Krönlein redivivus)*, J.G. Krönlein's Wortschatz der Khoikhoin (erschienen 1889 bei der Deutschen Kolonialgesellschaft Berlin), überarbeitet und ergänzt, Pietermaritzburg: University of Natal Press.

Sadock, J.M. and Zwicky, A.M. (1985) Sentence types, in T. Shopen (ed.) *Language Typology and Syntactic Description*, Cambridge: CUP. 155–99.

Sands, B.E. (1998a) *Eastern and Southern African Khoisan: Evaluating Claims of Distant Linguistic Relationships*, Cologne: Rüdiger Köppe.

——(1998b) The linguistic relationship between Hadza and Sandawe, in Schladt (ed.) 265–83.

——(2001) Borrowing and diffusion as a source of lexical similarities in Khoesan, *CWPL* 18: 200–24.

——(2010) Juu subgroups based on phonological patterns, in Brenzinger and König (eds) 85–114.

Sands, B.E., Maddieson, I. and Ladefoged, P. (1996) The phonetic structures of Hadza, *SAL* 25(2): 171–204.

Sands, B.E. and Miller-Ockhuizen, A.L. (1999) Changing Click Types: Evidence from Northern Khoisan, paper presented at the 30th Annual Conference on African Linguistics, University of Illinois at Urbana-Champaign.

——(2000) Comparative Evidence for New Click Types in Northern Khoisan, paper presented at the 74th Annual Meeting of the Linguistics Society of America.

Sasse, H.-J. (1987) The thetic/categorial distinction revisited, *Linguistics* 25: 511–80.

Schapera, I. (1930) *The Khoisan Peoples of South Africa: Bushmen and Hottentots*, London: Routledge and Kegan Paul.

Schladt, M. (1997) *Kognitive Strukturen von Körperteilvokabularien in kenianischen Sprachen*, Cologne: IfAUK.

—— (ed.) (1998) *Language, Identity, and Conceptualization among the Khoisan*, Cologne: Rüdiger Köppe.

——(2000) *A Preliminary List of Kxoe Wild Plants* (KFWP 14), Cologne: IfAUK.

Scholtz, J. du P. (1974) *Naamgewing aan Plante en Diere in Afrikaans: Bydrae tot 'n geskiedenis van die Afrikaanse woordeskat* (2nd revised edition), Elsiesrivier: Nasou.

Schultze, L. (1928) *Zur Kenntnis des Körpers der Hottentotten und Buschmänner*, Jena: G. Fischer.

Sebba, M.S. (1995) Some remarks on Ju|'hoan serial verbs, in Traill, Vossen and Biesele (eds) 363–70.

Silberbauer, G.B. (1981) *Hunter and Habitat in the Central Kalahari Desert*, London: CUP.

Snyman, J.W. (1970) *An Introduction to the !Xũ (!Kung) Language*, Cape Town: A.A. Balkema.

——(1975a) *Žu|'hõasi Fonologie & Woordeboek*, Cape Town and Rotterdam: A.A. Balkema.

——(1975b) Some phonetic and lexical aspects of Zu|'hõasi, in Traill (ed.) 61–76.

——(ed.) (1975c) *Bushman and Hottentot Linguistic Studies*, Pretoria: University of South Africa.

——(ed.) (1977) *Bushman and Hottentot Linguistic Studies*, Pretoria: University of South Africa.

——(ed.) (1979) *Bushman and Hottentot Linguistic Studies*, Pretoria: University of South Africa.

——(ed.) (1980) *Bushman and Hottentot Linguistic Studies*, Pretoria: University of South Africa.

——(1997) A preliminary classification of the !Xũũ and Žu|'hõasi dialects, in Haacke and Elderkin (eds) 21–106.

——(1999) The phonetic description of the Žu|'hõasi clicks: a confusion of sounds?, in R. Finlayson (ed.) *African Mosaic: Festschrift für J.A. Louw*, Pretoria: University of South Africa. 92–117.

Sommer, G. and Vossen, R. (1992) Schnalzwörter im Yei (R. 41), *AuÜ* 75: 1–42.

Starostin, G. (2003) A lexicostatistical approach towards reconstructing Proto-Khoisan, *Mother Tongue* 8: 81–126.

——(2008) From modern Khoisan languages to Proto-Khoisan: the value of intermediate reconstructions, *Aspects of Comparative Linguistics* 3: 337–470.

Steeman, S. (2011) *A Grammar of Sandawe: A Khoisan Language of Tanzania*, Utrecht: LOT.

Story, R. (1999) *K'u|ha:si Manuscript*, ed. by A.T. Traill (KFWP 13), Cologne: IfAUK.

Tanaka, J. (1978) *A San Vocabulary of the Central Kalahari: G||ana and G|wi Dialects*, Tokyo: Institute for the Study of Languages and Cultures of Asia and Africa, Tokyo University of Foreign Studies.

——(1996) The world of animals viewed by the San, *ASM, Supplementary Issue* 22: 11–28.

Taylor, J.R. (1989) *Linguistic Categorization: Prototypes in Linguistic Theory*, Oxford: Clarendon Press.

ten Rhyne, W. (1686) *Schediasma de Promontorio Bonae Spei; ejusve tractus incolis Hottentottis*, corrected and briefly annotated by Henr. Screta S. a Zavorziz, Schaffhausen: Joh. Mart. Oswald. With a translation and a foreword by B. Farrington, in I. Schapera (ed.) *Early Cape Hottentots, Described in the Writings of Olfert Dapper (1668), Willem ten Rhyne (1686) and Johannes Gulielmus de Grevenbroek (1695)*, Cape Town: Van Riebeeck Society. 78–153 [1933].

Thomason, S.G. and Kaufman, T. (1988) *Language Contact, Creolization, and Genetic Linguistics*, Berkeley: UCP.

Tosco, M. (1991) *A Grammatical Sketch of Dahalo*, Hamburg: Helmut Buske.

Traill, A.T. (1973) '4 or S7'?: another Bushman language, *AS* 32: 25–32.

——(1974) *The Compleat Guide to the Koon: A Research Report on Linguistic Fieldwork Undertaken in Botswana and South West Africa*, Johannesburg: ASIUW.

——(ed.) (1975) *Bushman and Hottentot Linguistic Studies*, Johannesburg: ASIUW.

——(ed.) (1977a) *Khoisan Linguistic Studies 3*, Johannesburg: ASIUW.

——(1977b) The phonological status of !Xõo clicks, in Traill (ed.) 107–31.

——(1980) Phonetic diversity in the Khoisan languages, in Snyman (ed.) 167–89.

——(1985) *Phonetic and Phonological Studies of !Xóõ Bushman*, Hamburg: Helmut Buske.

——(1986a) Click replacement in Khoe, in Vossen and Keuthmann (eds) vol. 2: 301–20.

——(1986b) Do the Khoi have a place in the San? New data on Khoisan linguistic relationships, *SUGIA* 7(1): 407–30.

——(1994) *A !Xóõ Dictionary*, Cologne: Rüdiger Köppe.

——(1995a) Interpreting |Xam phonology: the need for typological cleansing, in Traill, Vossen and Biesele (eds) 509–24.

——(1995b) The Khoesan languages of South Africa, in R. Mesthrie (ed.) *Language and Social History: Studies in South African Sociolinguistics*, Cape Town and Claremont: David Philip. 1–18.

——(1996) *!Khwa-Ka Hhouiten Hhouiten*, 'The Rush of the Storm': the linguistic death of |Xam, in P. Skotnes (ed.) *Miscast: Negotiating the Presence of the Bushmen*, Cape Town: University of Cape Town Press. 161–84.

——(1997) *Extinct: South African Khoisan Languages* (Compact disk and booklet), Johannesburg: Department of Linguistics, University of the Witwatersrand.

——(1999) Editor's introduction, in R. Story, *K'u|ha:si Manuscript*, ed. by A.T. Traill (KFWP 13), Cologne: IfAUK. 9–17.

——(2001) Structural typology and remote relationships between Zhu and !Xóõ, *SUGIA* 16/17: 437–54.

Traill, A.T. and Nakagawa, H. (2000) A historical !Xóõ-|Gui contact zone: linguistic and other relations, in Batibo and Tsonope (eds) 1–17.

Traill, A.T. and Vossen, R. (1997) Sound change in the Khoisan languages: new data on click loss and click replacement, *JALL* 18(1): 21–56.

Traill, A.T., Vossen, R. and Biesele, M. (eds) (1995) *The Complete Linguist: Papers in Memory of Patrick J Dickens*. Cologne: Rüdiger Köppe.

Treis, Y. (1998) Names of Khoisan languages and variants, in Schladt (ed.) 463–503.

Trigardt, L. (1836–38) [*Die dagboek van* –], in T.H. le Roux (ed.) *Die Dagboek van Louis Trigardt*, uitgegee met Inleiding, Aantekeninge en Glossarium (3rd edition), Pretoria: J.L. van Schaik [1977].

Tucker, A.N. (1967a) Fringe Cushitic: an experiment in typological comparison, *Bulletin of the School of Oriental and African Studies* 30: 655–80.

——(1967b) Erythraic elements and patternings: some East African findings, *African Language Review* 6: 17–25.

Tucker, A.N., Bryan, M.A. and Woodburn, J. (1977) The East African click languages: a phonetic comparison, in W.J.G. Möhlig, F. Rottland and B. Heine (eds) *Zur Sprachgeschichte und Ethnohistorie in Afrika: Neue Beiträge afrikanistischer Forschungen*, Berlin: Dietrich Reimer. 300–23.

Van de Kimmenade, M. (1954) *Essai de grammaire et vocabulaire de la langue Sandawe*, Fribourg (Switzerland): Posieux.

van Jaarsveld, G.J., Jenkinson, A.G., and de Wet, A.S. (2001) Die intertaalteorie en taalverskeidenheid, in A. Carstens and H. Grebe (eds) *Taallandskap*, Pretoria: J.L. van Schaik. 148–56.

van Reede, H.A. (1685) [1941] Aentekeningh van 't gene in den dienst van de Compagnie is voorgevallen aen de Cabo da Boa Esperance, in A.L. Hulshof (ed.) H.A. van Reede tot Drakenstein, Journaal van zijn verblijf aan de Kaap, *Bijdragen en mededeelingen van het Historisch Genootschap* 62: 1–245.

van Rensburg, M.C.J. (ed.) (1989) *n Verkenning van Afrikaans: Gister* (3rd edition), Bloemfontein: Patmos.

van Zyl, D.H. (1947) *n Griekwa-'Ietsigeit' (Iets oor die Griekwas)*, Cape Town: Nasionale Pers.

Vedder, H. (1910/11) Grundriß einer Grammatik der Buschmannsprache vom Stamm der !Kũ-Buschmänner, *Zeitschrift für Kolonialsprachen* 1: 5–24, 106–17.

Visser, H. (1998) The phonological system of Naro, in Schladt (ed.) 117–36.

——(2000) Language and cultural empowerment of the Khoesan people: the Naro experience, in Batibo and Smieja (eds) 193–216.

——(2001) *Naro Dictionary: Naro–English, English–Naro* (4th edition), Gantsi, Botswana: Naro Language Project.

Vossen, R. (1985) Encoding the object in the finite verb: the case of ǁAni (Central Khoisan), *AAP* 4: 75–84.

——(1986a) Preliminaries of Khoe comparative tonology, *ALASA Khoisan Special Interest Group Newsletter* 4 (June 1986): 15–21.

——(1986b) Zur Phonologie der ǁAni-Sprache, in Vossen and Keuthmann (eds) vol. 2: 321–45.

——(1986c) Some observations on nominal gender in Naro, in F. Rottland (ed.) *Festschrift zum 60. Geburtstag von Carl F. Hoffmann*, Hamburg: Helmut Buske. 373–90.

——(1991) What do we do with irregular correspondences? The case of the Khoe languages, *History in Africa* 18: 359–79.

——(1997a) *Die Khoe-Sprachen: Ein Beitrag zur Erforschung der Sprachgeschichte Afrikas*, Cologne: Rüdiger Köppe.

——(1997b) What click sounds got to do in Bantu. Reconstructing the history of language contacts in southern Africa, in B. Smieja and M. Tasch (eds) *Human Contact through Language and Linguistics*, Frankfurt am Main: Peter Lang. 353–66.

——(1998) Forms and functions of *!'o in some Khoe languages, in Schladt (ed.) 285–303.

——(2004) Verbal tone and stress in ǁAni (Central Khoisan), in R.-J. Anyanwu (ed.) *Stress and Tone: The African Experience*, Cologne: Rüdiger Köppe. 181–91.

——(2006) Verbal negation in Khoe (Central Khoisan), in K. Winkelmann and D. Ibriszimow (eds) *Zwischen Bantu und Burkina: Festschrift für Gudrun Miehe zum 65. Geburtstag*, Cologne: Rüdiger Köppe. 253–64.

——(2010) The verbal 'Linker' in Central Khoisan (Khoe) in the context of verbal derivation, *JAAS* 80: 47–60.

Vossen, R. and Keuthmann, K. (eds) (1986) *Contemporary Studies on Khoisan, in Honour of Oswin Köhler on the Occasion of his 75th birthday*, 2 vols, Hamburg: Helmut Buske.

Westphal, E.O.J. (1962a) On classifying Bushman and Hottentot languages, *African Language Studies* 3: 30–48.

——(1962b) A re-classification of Southern African Non-Bantu languages, *JAL* 1: 1–8.

——(1963) The linguistic prehistory of Southern Africa: Bush, Kwadi, Hottentot, and Bantu linguistic relationships, *Africa* 33(3): 237–65.

——(1971) The click languages of southern and eastern Africa, in T.A. Sebeok (ed.) *Current Trends in Linguistics 7: Linguistics in Sub-Saharan Africa*, The Hague: Mouton. 367–420.

——(1974) Notes on A. Traill 'N4 or S7'?, *AS* 33: 243–47.

Widlok, T. (1995) The 'irrealis' at work in Hai‖om, in Traill, Vossen and Biesele (eds) 371–82.

——(1997) ǂAkhoe pragmatics, Hai//om identity and the Khoekhoe language, in Haacke and Elderkin (eds) 117–24.

——(1999a) *Living on Mangetti: Hai‖om 'Bushmen' Autonomy and Namibian Independence*, Oxford: Oxford University Press.

——(1999b) A place to rest and to talk: spatial and linguistic shifts in northern Namibia, in S. Neumann (ed.) *Comparing African Spaces*, Cologne: Rüdiger Köppe. 125–44.

——(n.d.) A Hai‖om Sourcebook: The T. Heikkinen Papers, unpublished manuscript.

Wikar, H.J. (1779) *Berigt aan den Weleedelen Gestrenge Heer Mr. Joachim van Plettenburg*, in E.E. Mossop (ed.) *The Journal of Hendrik Jacob Wikar (1779)*, with an English translation by A.W. van der Horst, Cape Town: Van Riebeeck Society. 20–201 [1935].

Wilmsen, E.N. (1989) *Land Filled with Flies: A Political Economy of the Kalahari*, Chicago: UChP.

Winter, J.C. (1981a) Die Tonmuster des Gemein-Zentralkhoisan, in H. Jungraithmayr and G. Miehe (eds) *Berliner afrikanistische Vorträge (XXI. Deutscher Orientalistentag, Berlin 24.-29.3.1980)*, Berlin: Dietrich Reimer. 235–57.

——(1981b) Die Khoisan-Familie, in Heine, Schadeberg, and Wolff (eds) 329–74.

Wuras, C.F. (1920) *Vokabular der Korana-Sprache*, ed. and annotated by W. Bourquin, Berlin: Dietrich Reimer [Nendeln: Kraus Reprint, 1970].

INDEX

Printed in Great Britain
by Amazon

37740451R00295